W9-BGR-210

Two Revolutions in
Economic Policy

Two Revolutions in Economic Policy

The First Economic Reports
of Presidents Kennedy
and Reagan

edited by James Tobin and
Murray Weidenbaum

The MIT Press
Cambridge, Massachusetts
London, England

This book was set in Palatino by Compset, Inc., and printed and bound by Halliday Lithograph in the United States of America.

Library of Congress Cataloging-in-Publication Data

Two revolutions in economic policy.

   1. United States—Economic policy—1961–1971. 2. Kennedy, John F. (John Fitzgerald), 1917–1963. 3. United States—Economic policy—1981–. 4. Reagan, Ronald. 5. Council of Economic Advisers (U.S.) Annual report of the Council of Economic Advisers. I. Tobin, James, 1918–. II. Weidenbaum, Murray L. III. United States. President. Economic report of the President transmitted to the Congress.
HC106.6.T93 1988   338.973   87-35828
ISBN 0-262-20070-8
ISBN 0-262-70034-4 (pbk.)

Contents

Preface

At the start of each year the *Economic Report of the President* is transmitted to the Congress, together with *The Annual Report of the Council of Economic Advisers*. These two documents are published jointly and are commonly referred to as the Economic Report. The first annual Reports of Presidents Kennedy and Reagan came in January 1962 and February 1982, respectively. The Economic Reports of 1961 and 1981 were prepared by the outgoing Administrations. A new President and Council may wish to outline new economic policies soon after taking office. Kennedy and Reagan and their Councils did so in March 1961 and February 1981. This volume reprints those initial reports as well as the formal Economic Reports published a year later.

The early 1960s and the early 1980s were both watersheds in federal economic policy. The elections of 1960 and 1980 brought into power Administrations with economic ideas significantly different from their predecessors. In each case public dissatisfaction with economic performance in the previous decade, the 1950s or the 1970s, had been an important factor in the election outcome. In each case, the Council of Economic Advisers to the new President felt a special obligation at the outset to explain the new approach of his Administration to the Congress and the general public. As professional economists, each Council also wished to explain its stance convincingly to colleagues and students.

The 1961 and 1981 inaugurations were not, of course, the only ones since 1946 that changed the political party of the President. They were, however, the two that brought the most conscious and substantial shifts in the theory and practice of economic policy. Eisenhower's succession in 1953, after Republicans had suffered twenty years of frustration with the New Deal and Fair Deal, might have been a comparable revolution, or counterrevolution. But it did not generate economic manifestos like those of the Kennedy and Reagan Councils. One reason may have been that, because of doubts about the agency in the new Republican Congress and Administration, the Council was not fully reconstituted for most of the year 1953. Other postwar presidential successions, even when parties changed, maintained considerable continuity in economic analysis even though they somewhat altered policy priorities.

The revolutions of Kennedy and Reagan differ sharply in substance. The contrast is apparent in the Council reports. The 1961 Council's macroeconomics, which the popular media called "New Economics," was then the neo-Keynesian mainstream of the profession. The 1981 and 1982 reports reflect later intellectual counterrevolutions—supply-side, monetarist, and new classical—against that mainstream.

For these reasons, the publisher, the editors, and other participants in the original writings believe that joint republication of these reports will be of interest to teachers, scholars, students, and others interested in political economy. The 1962 Economic Report is out of print at the Government Printing Office, and the 1961 and 1981 "minireports" are not conveniently accessible.

The Employment Act of 1946 pledged the federal government to use its economic powers to promote "maximum employment, production, and purchasing power." The Act did not specify the means to this end, and limited them to those "calculated to foster and promote free competitive enterprise and the general welfare." The Act was an important bipartisan declaration of federal responsibility for the nation's economic performance. The electorate takes this responsibility for granted nowadays, but it was by no means generally acknowledged before World War II.

The Act did not and could not bind future Congresses, Presidents, and Federal Reserve governors to any specific measures of policy. It did establish mechanisms for reviewing economic conditions and policies in light of the objectives of the Act. The President is required to report to the Congress on these matters at least once a year.

To assist the President in preparing the required reports and in meeting his other responsibilities under the statute, the Act established the Council of Economic Advisers, a Chairman and two other Members appointed by the President subject to Senate confirmation, all serving at the pleasure of the President. Almost all appointees have been professional economists, usually university professors. The Act also established in the Congress the Joint Committee on the Economic Report (now called the Joint Economic Committee) to receive and appraise the President's reports and to make its own reports to the Congress on economic conditions and policies.

The Council is a purely advisory agency. It has no operating responsibilities or powers. Its staff is small, 15 to 20 professionals. It is dependent on other agencies for data. Its influence in the Executive branch and beyond depends almost wholly on how seriously the

President takes its advice. Consequently, the importance of the Council has varied from Administration to Administration. The President has many other sources of economic advice, among them his Cabinet Secretaries, members of Congress, outside consultants, personal friends and associates. His White House assistants are important in all policy decisions, and some Presidents, not Kennedy, have had an economist on their personal staffs. Presidential policies are bound to reflect considerations beyond the professional expertise of his economic advisers. With respect to the Council's central concerns under the Employment Act, the Office of Management and Budget (formerly Budget Bureau) and the Treasury are also heavily involved.

The volume is divided into two parts, the first containing the two Kennedy reports, the second the two Reagan reports. Each part begins with an introduction written for this publication by economists who participated in the preparations of the reports.

James Tobin
Murray Weidenbaum

October 1987

I

The Kennedy Economic Reports

Introduction

Robert M. Solow and
James Tobin

This introduction was planned to be the work of three veterans of the first year of the New Frontier. Walter Heller was taking the lead, as he did in 1961 as Chairman of the Council of Economic Advisers, the post he held throughout the first Kennedy-Johnson term. He was enthusiastic about this republication of the Council's work. Alas, Walter died suddenly on June 16, 1987. We had already lost two other comrades, Kermit Gordon, Council Member 1961–62 (Budget Director 1962–64), and Arthur Okun, staff member 1961–64 (later Council Member and Chairman). We miss all three, most acutely when a project like this recalls the happy excitement of our work together a quarter-century ago. To their memory we dedicate our part of this book.

The Preparation of the Reports

The first weeks after the January 20 inauguration of a new Administration are hectic. Not yet fully organized or staffed, Kennedy's new Council was immediately assigned major responsibility for drafting the President's first economic message to the Congress, transmitted on February 2, 1961. A message to Congress states the President's policies and legislative recommendations, reflecting advice from his own White House staff and from interested agencies throughout the Executive branch. Kennedy's second economic message to Congress appears over his signature as the first part of the 1962 *Economic Report of the President*.

The Council's March 6, 1961, statement, *The American Economy in 1961: Problems and Policies*, reprinted below, was its other immediate task—Heller, boasting that it was accomplished in 44 days, naturally counted Saturdays and Sundays. This statement was prepared for the regular hearings of the Joint Economic Committee on the annual Economic Report, which in 1961 had been submitted in January by the outgoing President and Council. In addition to receiving our statement, the Committee took extensive further testimony, oral and written, from the three Council members.[1]

A major purpose of the testimony was to explain and elaborate the program the President set forth in his February 2 message. More broadly, the Council's statement and testimony were its own analytical exposition of the Administration's general approach to economic policy and its application to the circumstances of the day. In this respect it is analogous to our *magnum opus,* the second part of the 1962 *Economic Report of the President,* the annual Economic Report of the Council.

In preparing the 1962 Economic Report, the Council saw the opportunity not only to meet the statutory requirements of the Employment Act as we interpreted them but also to offer a careful and thorough exposition of the theoretical and empirical foundations of macroeconomic policies. Like *The American Economy in 1961,* the 1962 Economic Report was a team effort. The Council attracted a staff remarkable for its talents and its enthusiastic dedication. Two staff members, Robert Solow and Arthur Okun, had become in all but name additional members of the Council. The Council decided the architecture of the report, and staff members submitted drafts in their fields of expertise. Gordon, Okun, Solow, and Tobin synthesized these materials and drafted the four chapters. After receiving comments from the staff, other federal agencies, and the White House, Walter Heller and the four principal authors of the draft chapters prepared the final version.

Besides Solow and Okun, staff economists contributing to the 1962 Economic Report were Richard Attiyeh, Barbara Berman (now Bergmann), Charles Cooper, Richard Cooper, Rashi Fein, Marshall Kaplan, David Lusher, Richard R. Nelson, George Perry, Lee Preston, Vernon Ruttan, Walter Stettner, Lloyd Ulman, Leroy Wehrle, and Sidney Winter. The Council also relied heavily on outside economists. Joseph Pechman and Paul Samuelson were constantly consulted. Others who gave help on the report included Kenneth Arrow (who later joined the staff), Otto Eckstein, Peter Kenen, Robert Lampman, Charles Schultze, and Robert Triffin. Knowledgeable readers will recognize many persons of professional distinction among these names; some were already distinguished in 1961, and others were young then but destined to become leaders in the profession.

Frances James was the conscience of the agency from its inception in 1946 to her retirement in 1977. She would not allow any factual

[1] *January 1961 Economic Report of the President and the Economic Situation and Outlook,* Hearings before the Joint Economic Committee, 87th Congress, First Session, Washington, DC: U.S. Government Printing Office, 1961, pp. 290–419, 563–614. The prepared statements reprinted in this book appear on pp. 310–392 and 564–574.

allegation or statistic to appear in print without assuring herself of its accuracy. She was invaluable to our Council. So was her assistant, Catherine Furlong, who succeeded Frances and continues her tradition to this day.

The Economics of Kennedy's Economists

The authors of these 1961 and 1962 reports were all, despite individual differences of interest and emphasis, exponents of the synthesis of Keynesian and neoclassical economics developed over the previous fifteen years. American economists, notably Samuelson, played leading roles in this intellectual development. By 1961 it was becoming the mainstream of macroeconomics. The Council sought to set forth its principles and to apply them to the United States of the 1960s, in language accessible not just to economists but to all earnest readers.

Journalists on the Washington economics beat dubbed our approach the "New Economics," but they exaggerated its novelty. The Council was following well-trodden Keynesian paths in its analyses of fiscal policies: the utility of the budget as an instrument, automatic or discretionary, of economic stabilization; the priority of macroeconomic performance over the traditional convention of annual budget balance; the distinction between deficits and surpluses resulting from business cycles and those resulting from budget programs and tax laws; the possibility of unintended "fiscal drag" on the economy. In these respects, the Kennedy Council was reviving, in its own way, themes of the Truman Council.

Commentators seeking simple labels called the "new" economists of the Council "fiscalists," conveniently contrasting them to the "monetarists" led by Milton Friedman, who stressed the central macroeconomic role of money and Federal Reserve policy. The dichotomy was quite inaccurate. Long before 1960 the neo-Keynesian neoclassical synthesis recognized monetary measures as coequal to fiscal measures in stabilization of aggregate demand. Council economists understood that the same short-run outcomes, aggregate employment and output, could be achieved by various combinations of fiscal and monetary policies. To choose among these "policy mixes," they suggested other criteria—in particular, the long-run growth of the economy.

Two of the authors of the 1962 Economic Report, Solow and Tobin, had contributed to neoclassical growth theory in the 1950s, and chapter 2 was devoted to long-run growth. Taming the business cycle and maintaining full employment were the first priorities of macroeconomic policy. But this should be done in ways that promote more rapid growth in the economy's capacity to produce. We were not one-eyed demand-siders. Demand calls the tune in the short run, but advances in supply determine long-run progress. For this reason, we saw the desirability of policy mixes that emphasized private and public investment for the future, relative to current consumption. These mixes would usually entail low interest rates and tight government budgets.

The principles are very relevant today; the Reagan Administration has ignored them, at considerable danger to the country.

Educating the President and Others

The Council's reports were educational documents, aimed at readers within the federal government as well as outside. The Congress needed to be persuaded, and so did the Federal Reserve, the Treasury, the Commerce and Labor departments, and other executive agencies. Our most important reader was the President himself.

John F. Kennedy, unlike Ronald Reagan, came to the White House without a settled economic agenda or ideology. As Senator and candidate, he sought advice from academics in his home state of Massachusetts, notably J. K. Galbraith and Paul Samuelson, who differed on many issues. His speeches during the campaign of 1960 did not present a coherent program. He attacked the Eisenhower Administration for the economy's sluggish performance under its stewardship and promised to "get the country moving again." The fact that he entered the White House without deep personal understanding of economic issues or firm convictions on policies suggested to us that he could be persuaded by cogent argument.

Kennedy's instincts and politics were generally liberal. But as he assumed the presidency, he was keenly aware that financial markets' suspicions of a liberal Democratic President could cause him trouble. Moreover, again unlike Reagan, Kennedy had just barely won the election. Although his party controlled both houses of Congress, conservatives senior to the former Massachusetts Senator held most of the positions of power.

Throughout Kennedy's presidency, Walter Heller taught him economics; we others helped, but no one could match Heller's knack of making points in concise readable colorful language. The President was an apt pupil, intrigued by the subject intellectually as well as pragmatically. His 1962 Yale Commencement Address showed that he had found his own political economy.

The caution and ambivalence of Kennedy and his close advisers were evident during the transition from election to inauguration. Samuelson chaired a Task Force on economic conditions. Among the members were Heller and Tobin, until their selection for the Council in December 1960. Early in the group's deliberations, the Florida "White House" passed the word that the President-elect was not prepared to take antirecession measures that would significantly increase the budget deficit.

Samuelson's report, January 6, 1961, made only modest proposals for immediate action. However, in his diagnosis of the state of the economy and his precepts for future fiscal and monetary policy, Samuelson anticipated most of the themes of the Council reports yet to come.

A parallel Task Force on economic policy chaired by Alan Sproul, retired president of the New York Federal Reserve Bank, paid special attention to the country's international financial problems and the constraints they placed on domestic expansion. One motivation in organizing the Sproul group was to reassure the financial community at home and abroad that liberal academics, Galbraith, Samuelson, et al., were not the only sources of economic advice to the new President. Robert Roosa of Sproul's bank was a key member of this Task Force and became an Undersecretary of the Treasury.

The new Secretary of the Treasury, Douglas Dillon, a Republican investment banker who had served as an Undersecretary of State under Eisenhower, was announced at the same time as the appointment of Heller. The Samuelson-Sproul differences were to become Heller-Dillon differences. They were not irreconcilable. Eventually the Administration's policies were a synthesis in which major elements of both approaches survived.

The Council's View of the U.S. Economy in 1961

In the perspective of recent experience the economy's overall performance in the eight Eisenhower years 1953–1960 looks better than it did to the Council in 1961. Real Gross National Product grew at an average annual rate of 2.35 percent, comparable to the 2.45 percent average growth during 1973–1986, even though the civilian labor force grew more rapidly in the second period, 2.2 percent per year instead of 1.4 percent. But the Council thought that the 1953–1960 performance fell far short of the standards of the Employment Act.

Three recessions occurred during Eisenhower's two terms, in 1953–54 following the end of the Korean War, in 1957–58, and in 1960. The unemployment rate drifted up from 3 percent in early 1953 to 5 percent at the peak of the 1958–59 recovery. Kennedy's economic advisers, before and after election and inauguration, were disturbed by the record and by the fatalistic complacency with which it was generally viewed.

In our view, business cycles of such frequency and amplitude could be prevented or at least significantly moderated by federal fiscal and monetary policies. Instead, deliberate Federal Reserve monetary policies had contributed to all three recessions, especially the second and third. Moreover, official anxiety over a $13 billion budget deficit in fiscal year 1959 had provoked contractionary fiscal measures that helped to bring on the 1960 recession. The anxiety was misplaced, because the deficit was largely a consequence of the depressed economic conditions of 1958.

In our view, the policies of the 1950s were cutting off recoveries before they were complete, at higher and higher rates of unemployment. We saw the recession conditions of early 1961 as stemming from inadequate aggregate demand, partly policy-induced and partly inadvertent. In either case, the appropriate short-run policy response was demand management: fiscal and monetary stimulus.

Interpreting the Rise in Unemployment

The Council's diagnosis of the rise in unemployment was not widely shared, even within the new Kennedy Administration. Most people, especially noneconomists, viewed business cycles fatalistically and complacently, as immutable natural phenomena that policy neither caused nor could ameliorate. Likewise, they saw the upward drift of unemployment as the result of structural and technological trends in the economy. This was the well-publicized view of the Federal Reserve Chairman, William McChesney Martin, and it was shared by Representative Thomas Curtis of Missouri, the ranking Republican member of the Joint Economic Committee. The moral was that demand stimulus could not reduce unemployment but would ignite wage and price inflation.

This view appealed to conservatives, presumably because it could be used as an argument against policy activism. But similar interpretations of the rise of unemployment came from left-wing critics of capitalism. The views of Robert Theobald and other latter-day Luddites were fashionable among intellectuals: the economic system was obsolete because automation was destroying jobs and producing goods without disbursing the wages to buy them. Within the new Administration itself, leaders of the Labor Department emphasized policies tailor-made to the diverse problems of individual unemployed workers and distrusted the Council's macroeconomic recipes for job creation.

To refute these interpretations of the rise in unemployment in the 1950s, the Council included in *The American Economy in 1961* a thorough statistical analysis finding that demographic and industrial breakdowns of unemployment showed no evidence that structural unemployment was increasing. What they showed was a general shortage of jobs of all kinds for workers of all kinds. Then and always, the Council recognized that much unemployment was structural, beyond the reach of macro remedies. We supported policies to help displaced workers and new jobseekers obtain the educations and skills required in the modern world, and to help them locate available jobs. We regarded macroeconomic and structural policies as complementary rather than competitive. We saw no reason that aggregate demand policies could not bring unemployment down to about 4 percent, and even further as structural policies succeeded.

We economists looked at unemployment statistics not just as measures of the personal deprivations and hardships of the millions unemployed, but also as barometers of the overall economic weather. Compared to the prosperity accompanying a 4 percent unemployment rate, a 7 percent rate signified bad news in many dimensions: among them production, incomes, profits, capital investment, capacity utilization, and government budgets. This point was not widely appreciated. For example, Kennedy and his closest adviser on domestic policy, Ted Sorenson, wondered why raising the employment score from 93 to 96 percent, "A minus to A," deserved high political priority.

The Council undertook to document quantitatively the large changes in general economic conditions and well-being associated with small changes in employment and unemployment rates. Similar research had been done at the Joint Economic Committee by James Knowles. Much of the Council's work on the subject was done by Arthur Okun, before and after he joined the staff in Washington, D.C. Thus was born "Okun's Law," which proved to be one of the most reliable and useful empirical regularities of economics.

Okun estimated that 3 extra percentage points in unemployment meant a 10 percent "gap" between actual and potential GNP. Okun, like Knowles, estimated at 3.5 percent per year the trend growth rate of potential GNP, that is, the real output associated with keeping unemployment constant at 4 percent. Thus the mere avoidance of recession, conventionally defined as absolute decline in national output, meant the unemployment rate would be increasing by more than a point a year. That is why the Council stressed that the objective of policy should be to achieve and maintain full employment and potential output, not just to avoid recessions.

Fiscal Policy

A gap between actual output and potential spelled also a shortfall in federal revenues and usually a budget deficit. But, as Keynesian fiscal analysis had long stressed, in these circumstances it is perverse policy to take austere measures to cut spending and raise taxes. This was a mistake made in the Great Depression and also in 1959, as previously remarked. The Council revived the full employment budget concepts of the Truman council and estimated them in the light of Okun's analysis.

In 1961 the continuing strength of the balanced-budget convention in political and financial circles foreclosed any major initiative of fiscal stimulus to promote recovery. The Council sought and exploited some small targets of opportunity—for example, starting sooner rather than later scheduled improvements in Social Security benefits, which were at the time "off-budget" (as they now are once again), liberalization of unemployment insurance benefits, and early release to the states of allocations from the Interstate Highway Trust Fund.

The Berlin crisis at midyear occasioned a modest increase in defense spending. The instincts of the President and all his advisers except the Council were to ask for an equal increase in taxes. Kennedy, after all, had called on the nation to sacrifice for the cause of freedom, and a tax increase would demonstrate the nation's resolve. The Council argued that a tax increase was the last thing needed in an economy just beginning to recover, and Heller carried the day.

In 1962 Kennedy requested authority to initiate temporary income tax cuts when specified statistical evidence signaled incipient recession. This was the first of several similar proposals originating with the Council designed to facilitate timely countercyclical fiscal policy. Presidents Kennedy and Johnson regularly recommended them to Congress, which ignored all of them except a proposal for statistically triggered temporary increases in unemployment compensation.

In 1962 the Administration proposed a tax reform intended to be revenue-neutral. The principal item was the Investment Tax Credit, favored by both Council and Treasury. As an incentive for business investment in equipment, it could enhance both short-run demand and long-run supply. At the same time the Treasury was liberalizing its tax rules on depreciation. The proposed revenue-increasing measures included both limits on deductibility of employees' expenses for meals, lodging, and entertainment and withholding of taxes on interest and dividends. These got nowhere in the Congress.

Heller eventually triumphed in his campaign to educate Kennedy, Dillon, and Congress on the need for fiscal stimulus to assure full recovery. The young recovery was faltering in 1962 and inflation was quiescent. The budget was not balanced despite the Administration's restraint. The business and financial communities were hostile to Kennedy in spite of his efforts to be fiscally "sound."

The President adopted the idea of an income tax cut in mid-1962 and proposed the legislation in January 1963. The Revenue Act of 1964 was passed and the cuts took effect only after his death. For the first time, fiscal stimulus was undertaken not to arrest a recession but to invigorate and prolong a recovery. Thus was accepted the Council's point that achieving and maintaining full employment, not just damping the business cycle, is the proper objective of policy under the Employment Act. Unfortunately, this triumph was not destined to be permanent.

At the time and since, the tax cut has drawn criticism from two sides. Some critics conceded the need for fiscal stimulus but preferred to obtain it by increasing federal nonmilitary spending. The Council was sympathetic to this alternative, but it was not politically feasible at the time. (Indeed even the tax cut made it through Congress only on the wave of sentiment that followed Kennedy's assassination in November 1963.) The Council did not agree with Galbraith, who preferred no stimulus to a tax cut. His motto, never give away tax revenues because you may need them later, looked good in 1966–68 when President Johnson escalated Vietnam War spending without raising taxes, against the advice of his own Council.

Other critics preferred monetary to fiscal stimulus, encouraging investment relative to consumption in the interest of long-run growth. But international balance of payments problems ruled out a monetary policy significantly more expansionary than it was already. Heller was probably never as convinced of the efficacy and desirability of substituting monetary for fiscal stimulus as Samuelson, Solow, and Tobin. The first priority of full employment was agreed by all.

Economic Growth

The Council wanted to expand demand enough to bring GNP back to its full employment potential. But that was not all.

From the beginning, the Council supported policies that would eventually increase the rate of growth of potential output itself. This meant a focus on investment activities, broadly construed. As early as *The American Economy in 1961* we urged the importance of investment in physical, human, and intellectual capital, and recommended policies to promote them. The 1962 Economic Report devoted one of its four chapters to making this case.

Two aspects of that chapter are worth emphasizing. First, its scope was very wide, ranging from natural resources (including timber and agricultural land) at one end of the spectrum, through plant and equipment, skill training, and research and development, all the way to health and education at the other. Thus the Council asserted unambiguously that business investment in plant and equipment, while central to progress in a market economy, is by no means the sole vehicle of capital formation for future well-being. Of course, the Administration's Investment Tax Credit was a major incentive for business—not at first welcomed by its beneficiaries, though appetite grew with eating. Second, we pointed out the multiple purposes served by some forms of investment. Plant and equipment spending helps close employment and output gaps, while also lifting the trend of potential. Investments in human resources improve productivity and also help equalize opportunity throughout society.

The International Balance of Payments

In the late 1950s a new element in the economic situation of the United States was our adverse balance in international payments. Foreign governments and central banks were accumulating dollars in liquid form, bank deposits and Treasury bills. Their holdings were potential claims on the U.S. gold stock. As some were exercised, U.S. gold reserves began to decline, after a long and massive buildup beginning in 1933. Financiers throughout the world were voicing suspicions that the United States might not always be able and willing to convert dollar claims into gold on demand. The influential head of the International Monetary Fund, Per Jacobsson, criticized the 1959 federal budget deficit from this standpoint.

As the Sproul Task Force urged, the balance of payments and confidence in the "dollar" became constraints on U.S. macroeconomic policies. Avoiding inflation, which would make U.S. goods less competitive in world trade, took on heightened importance. Moreover, if monetary policy were to push U.S. interest rates too low, funds would flow out to overseas markets where rates were higher. As a consequence, in 1960 the Federal Reserve held interest rates above their usual recession lows.

The Council's position can be summarized as follows:

1. The dollar problem was not a reason to abandon recovery and full employment as the major priorities of macroeconomic policies. The value of the dollar in gold and foreign currencies was not sacred writ. The Council was not proposing devaluation, even though the dollar appeared to be overvalued. But in our view devaluation would not be so cataclysmic that all other goals should be sacrificed to avert it.

Eventually, it took a Republican President to devalue the dollar (as it did, for similar reasons, to make friends with Red China.)

2. Greater emphasis would have to be placed on fiscal stimulus, and less on monetary stimulus, because of the dollar problem. The "easy money, tight budget" policy mix desirable to raise future potential output would have to give way, to some extent, to a mix that would limit balance of payments deficits. Investment incentives that could not be given by low interest rates could, however, be given by tax legislation, the Investment Tax Credit, and accelerated depreciation.

3. As economists committed to a liberal international trading system, we opposed protectionist measures, "buy American" regulations such as tying foreign aid to purchases of U.S. products, and other expedients for "saving gold."

4. National and international monetary measures could mitigate the imbalance in our external accounts and its consequences. We urged the Federal Reserve and the Treasury to shorten the maturities of outstanding federal securities, selling bills while purchasing bonds. Short interest rates seemed to be the more important for international flows of funds, while long rates were important for domestic investment, especially homebuilding. We wanted to twist the term structure, lowering long rates relative to shorts. Unfortunately the Federal Reserve, having committed itself to a "bills only" policy in 1953, could not bring itself to intervene significantly in long-term bond markets. The Treasury, while giving lip service to "Operation Twist," was lengthening the debt by large-scale advance refundings of securities close to maturity. In the international arena, the Council favored measures to take pressures off the dollar and gold by creation of alternative reserve assets through the International Monetary Fund. With gold scarce and the reserve status of the dollar questioned, the world faced a possible shortage of internationally accepted liquid assets.

Inflation

President Kennedy and his Council were the first and last to specify a numerical target for full employment. Our 4 percent unemployment target was cautiously chosen to be unlikely to set off excess-demand-pull inflation. For the Kennedy Administration, the silver lining of the two preceding Eisenhower-Martin recessions was that they had lowered the inflation rate from 4 percent in 1957 to 1.5 percent in 1961. Yet from the very beginning the Council was worried about the possibility of inflation's setting in before anything worth calling "full employment" had been achieved. This fear was an aftereffect of the "creeping inflation" of the mid-fifties. The CPI had risen by a total of 6 percent during two prosperous years 1955–57, and then by another 2.5 percent in one year of recession between 1957 and 1958. Between 1960 and 1961 prices rose another 1 percent; even that attracted attention in the press. Survivors of the 1970s may laugh, but the slightest inflation was unnerving then.

As a purely practical matter, the Council thought that there was so much slack in the economy that inflation was hardly a threat for the next few years. (That turned out to be right; when the unemployment rate finally fell to 4 percent at the end of 1965, the price level was still rising less than 2 percent per year with no serious acceleration.) We were worried, not because we thought that slow inflation was very damaging to the economy by itself, but because we could see that it could undermine the credibility of the expansionary policy that was the prime necessity.

Accordingly *The American Economy in 1961* pointed out that most of the cumulative inflation of the past 15 years had occurred in two bursts of genuine excess demand: 1946–48, when wartime controls were lifted, and again at the time of the Korean War. If similar shocks were to happen again, one knew what to do. As a defense against "premature inflation" we suggested active antitrust enforcement (to preserve competition), accelerated productivity growth (to take advantage of nominal wage inertia), training and education programs (to make for mobility of labor and to relieve localized skill shortages), and—even then!—voluntary wage and price restraint.

By the time of the 1962 Economic Report this passage had grown into a whole chapter, "Price Behavior in a Free and Growing Economy." It talked a lot, rather didactically, about the need to combine flexibility of relative prices with stability of the general price level. This could only happen if some prices were free to fall. By that time we had learned that the Labor-Management Advisory Committee the President had established was going to be a disappointment to us, because it would not be the vehicle for changing either the ideology or the practice of collective bargaining. We were reduced to urging, rather unspecifically, that while it was perfectly acceptable for workers and employers to bargain unstintingly over the division of real revenue, it was not acceptable for them to join forces to pass their conflict on to the economy at large in the form of rising prices. The parties themselves seemed inclined to "peace at any price level," and the fraternity of private and federal mediators and arbitrators acquiesced.

That chapter ended with the famous "Guideposts for Noninflationary Wage and Price Behavior." In form they were a description of the way wages and prices *would* behave in a well-functioning market economy free of market power and discretion in wage- and price-setting. The innocent hope was expressed that they would serve as a focus of public understanding and discussion, and thus help to bring about an atmosphere in which market power would be exercised "responsibly." Thanks largely to Kermit Gordon's foresight and initiative, the President and Secretary of Labor Arthur Goldberg began in 1961 to use their influence and good offices to preserve price stability, beginning with the bellwether steel industry. The Council tried to provide analytical underpinnings for this effort. We may even have guessed that the endemic problem of achieving full employment without inflation would prove intractable without organized "incomes policy." That still seems to be the case. We may not be able to do it with incomes policy; there is still little reason to believe that it can be done without incomes policy.

The intellectual framework that led the Council in this direction is clear in retrospect and was quite clear then. We believed we were trying to shift favorably the *level* of the Phillips curve, by talking it down in the first instance and by informal intervention if necessary. Phillips curves appeared on the backs of our envelopes. A. W. Phillips's original article had been published in 1958. The famous—some would say notorious—article by Samuelson and Solow, "Analytical Foundations of Anti-Inflationary Policy," appeared in 1960. George Perry's Ph.D. thesis was accepted in August 1961 and delayed in publication while he served on the Council staff.

Since then there has been much debate about the meaning and validity of a "trade-off between unemployment and inflation." The use made of this notion in the 1962 Economic Report has sometime been characterized as naive. We do not think it was; but we may have banked too heavily on the stability of the Phillips curve indicated by postwar data through 1961.

The Council's estimate in 1961 was that 4 percent unemployment was a reasonably safe "interim target." We meant to state our belief that expansion of aggregate demand could return the economy to an unemployment rate of 4 percent—last achieved in 1957—without much danger of wage-induced inflation. Since then, much research effort has gone into estimation of the "natural rate of unemployment," a closely related but much more theory-laden concept. Some of that research suggests that 4 percent was too low a target unemployment rate in 1961, and some suggests that it was close to being right. We observe that the unemployment rate did indeed get down to 4 percent at the very end of 1965 without signs of labor-market strain and with negligible acceleration of inflation. It took the clear wartime excess demand of 1966–68 to set off a wage-price-wage spiral.

Conclusion

No doubt we would write a somewhat different Economic Report if were we to be transported back to the circumstances of 1961 with our 1987 mental furniture intact. It would be a sad comment on macroeconomics were that not so. Nevertheless we look back at *The American Economy in 1961* and the 1962 Economic Report with affection, respect, and indeed defiant pride. We gladly reprint them now, not just because they may have historical interest but because we believe they contain much that is still valid and useful for macroeconomics and its relation to public policy.

The American Economy in 1961: Problems and Policies

Statement of the Council of Economic Advisers (Walter W. Heller, Chairman; Kermit Gordon; James Tobin) before the Joint Economic Committee Monday, March 6, 1961

Contents

Mr. Chairman and Members of the Committee:
We have looked forward with genuine pleasure to this first appearance before the Joint Economic Committee. The Committee's studies and reports are among the references most frequently used by the Council—and indeed by the economics profession and by business—as a source of economic information, analysis and wisdom. We sincerely hope that we can continue to benefit from and perhaps contribute to the high standards of research and investigation to which the Committee and its subcommittees have adhered.

The submission of a prepared statement by the Council to the Committee is, to the best of our knowledge, without precedent. Indeed, this is the first time since enactment of the Employment Act of 1946 that a Council has testified before the Joint Committee on the occasion of a change of administration. In all previous years—save 1953, when Council operations were temporarily suspended—the Council could, in effect, let the annual Economic Report serve as its statement on economic conditions and policy. We are not in this position.

We do not mean to suggest that our written statement can serve as a fully developed Economic Report; there have been, after all, only 44 working days since January 20—including Saturdays and Sundays. Nevertheless, a new President has taken office, and an Administration has been organized which looks at our economic problems in a new perspective. Accordingly, we have felt under obligation to present to this Committee a reasoned and fairly lengthy statement of the Council's views.

In our testimony today, we first examine briefly with you the role of the Council as we conceive of it. Second, we review the serious problems of recession, chronic slack, and inadequate growth rates in the American economy today. Because of the length of our analysis, we will ask that some of this material be handled by reference rather than by a full reading before the Committee. Third, we examine the broad lines of policy that are appropriate to the current problems of the economy, particularly in terms of the program which the President has announced in his State of the Union Message and his Message of February 2, "Program to Restore Momentum to the American Economy."

We shall discuss with candor the problems and prospects of the American economy, neither minimizing its difficulties nor underestimating its capacity to overcome them. Workers, consumers, and businessmen would surely not gain confidence in the future of the economy from official reassurances that plainly contradict or ignore their every-day experiences and observations. Economic confidence will be better sustained by evidence that the government assesses real problems soberly and attacks them resolutely. The public will in the long run have confidence in the government only if the government shows confidence in the public.

I. The Role of the Council of Economic Advisers

On the occasion of the first appearance of this Council before the Joint Economic Committee, we wish to express some general principles that we hope will guide our future relationships with the Committee. They have no special relevance to the particular subject matter of our first testimony, but are designed to set the stage for what we hope will be a period of mutual understanding and constructive cooperation between the Council and the Committee.

1. The Council has a responsibility to explain to the Congress and to the public the general economic strategy of the President's program,

especially as it relates to the objectives of the Employment Act. This is the same kind of responsibility that other Executive agencies assume in regard to programs in their jurisdictions.

2. It is not appropriate or necessary for the Council to go into the details of legislative proposals or of administrative actions which fall primarily in the domain of operating Executive departments or agencies, who can and do testify before the appropriate committees. Our concern is with the over-all pattern of economic policy.

3. The program of the President is, of course, the outcome of a decision process in which advice, recommendations, and considerations of many kinds, from many sources, inside and outside the Executive, play a part. The professional economic advice of the Council is one element; it is not and should not be the sole consideration in the formulation of Presidential economic policy, or of Congressional policy.

4. In Congressional testimony and in other public statements, the Council must protect its advisory relationship to the President. We assume that the Committee does not expect the Council to indicate in what respects its advice has or has not been taken by the President, nor to what extent particular proposals, or omissions of proposals, reflect the advice of the Council.

5. Subject to the limits mentioned, members of the Council are glad to discuss, to the best of their knowledge and ability as professional economists, the economic situation and problems of the country, and the possible alternative means of achieving the goals of the Employment Act and other commonly held economic objectives. In this undertaking, the Council wishes to cooperate as fully as possible with the Committee and the Congress in achieving a better understanding of our economic problems and approaches to their solutions.

6. The Council is composed of professional economists. But economic policy, as the Committee well knows, is not an exact science. The Council is, and necessarily must be, in harmony with the general aims and direction of the President and his Administration. A member of the Council who felt otherwise would resign. This general harmony is, of course, consistent with divergences of views on specific issues.

We should also note that the President has expressed his intention to "return to the spirit as well as the letter of the Employment Act of 1946," and to have the economic reports "deal not only with the state of the economy but with our goals for economic progress." (News conference, December 23, 1960) The Committee will find this desire reflected in today's testimony and in future Council reports as well.

Further, the President has stated that we should not "treat the economy in narrow terms but in terms appropriate to the optimum development of the human and natural resources of this country, of our productive capacity and that of the free world." To carry out these larger responsibilities, the President asked the Chairman of the Council, "to find ways and means of providing us with the best possible staff assistance and advice." We hope that it will be possible to restore the Council staff at least to its size of eight or ten years ago so that the Council will be in a position to meet its full responsibilities as envisioned by the President and the Congress.

II. State of the Economy

In spite of great inherent strength, the American economy today is beset not only with a recession of nearly 10 months' duration but with persistent slack in production and employment, a slowdown in our rate of growth, and pressure on our international balance of payments.

Recession and Current Outlook

The fourth postwar recession of economic activity in the United States began last spring. May 1960 is generally taken as the peak month, although some cyclical measures began to fall earlier and some later. Charts 1, 2, and 3 display the recession since last spring as evidenced by important economic series (all seasonally adjusted). Industrial production—the Federal Reserve index—in January 1961 was off 8 percent from January 1960. Nonagricultural employment showed a 1½ percent decline from May 1960 to January 1961. Retail sales in constant prices dropped by 7 percent from April to January. Unemployment was up from 5.1 percent of labor force in May 1960 to 6.6 percent in January of this year. Gross national product (GNP) corrected for price changes was down 1 percent from the second quarter of 1960 to the last quarter.

Charts 2 and 3 compare the four postwar recessions. The fourth recession has thus far been shallower than its predecessors. But the gentleness of the current decline is small consolation, because the descent began from relatively lower levels. The previous recovery was abortive, and the recession began with an unemployment rate which earlier recessions did not reach for 3 to 6 months.

In the current recession, as in earlier postwar cyclical fluctuations, business inventories have been the principal element of instability. In the upswing of an inventory cycle, business firms build up their stocks to adjust them to rising levels of output and sales. When out-

INDEX, MAY 1960 = 100 *

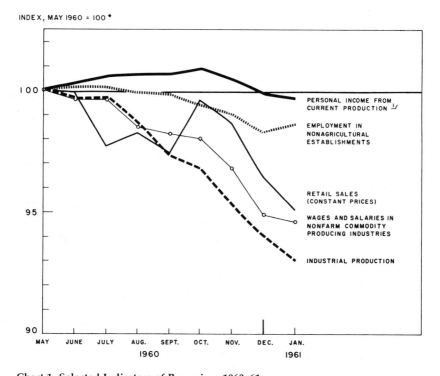

Chart 1. Selected Indicators of Recession, 1960–61
*Based on seasonally adjusted data.
[1]Personal income less transfer payments and net interest paid by Government.
Sources: Department of Commerce, Department of Labor, and Federal Reserve.

put and sales level off, inventory building slackens or ceases. Unless inventory expansion is promptly replaced by increased final demand, production falls. Downward adjustment of stocks then leads to further contraction. Once again inventories pursue output and sales, this time downhill. When inventories have caught up, the economy gets a lift just from the substitution of new production for inventory withdrawals.

In the present case, the reversal of business inventory change from plus $11.4 billion (annual rate) in the first quarter of 1960 to minus $3.0 billion in fourth quarter was a reduction of $14.4 billion in demand. Table 1 shows how this reduction was offset by changes in other components. In current prices the $14.4 billion was more than matched by a $16.6 billion increase in other sources of demand. But in constant (1960) prices, the offsets were only $10 billion. Increases in government purchases and net exports have been the principal reasons for the shallowness of the recession. Consumption rose in absolute terms, but it fell in proportion to disposable income. Disposable income grew at an annual rate of $8.9 billion more than GNP,

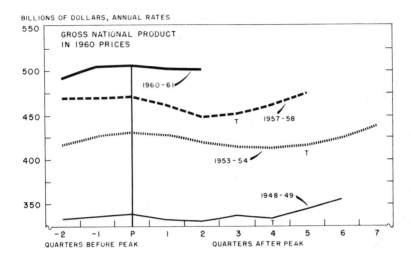

BILLIONS OF DOLLARS, ANNUAL RATES

GROSS NATIONAL PRODUCT
IN 1960 PRICES

1960-61

1957-58

1953-54

1948-49

QUARTERS BEFORE PEAK   QUARTERS AFTER PEAK

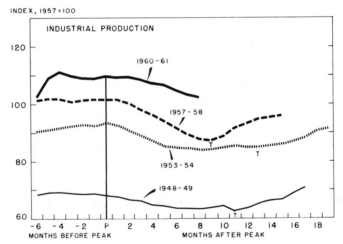

INDEX, 1957=100

INDUSTRIAL PRODUCTION

1960-61

1957-58

1953-54

1948-49

MONTHS BEFORE PEAK   MONTHS AFTER PEAK

Chart 2. Production in Four Postwar Recessions
P = cyclical peak.
T = cyclical trough.
Note: Data are seasonally adjusted and are plotted from 2 quarters (6 months)
before cyclical peak to 2 quarters (6 months) after cyclical trough.
Sources: Department of Commerce and Federal Reserve.

thanks mainly to increases in government transfer payments and decreases in government receipts.

It is always difficult to know when an inventory decline has run its
course and to judge where current inventories stand compared with
normal ratios to sales. At present, the short-run inventory cycle is
superimposed on a longer-run trend towards lower stocks growing
out of more efficient management. It would be surprising if inventory
liquidation in the fourth quarter of 1960 had been sufficient to adjust
stocks to current levels of output and sales. If the patterns of the three

MILLIONS OF PERSONS

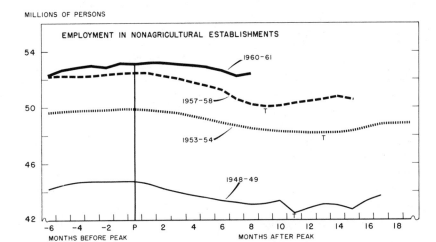

PERCENT OF CIVILIAN LABOR FORCE

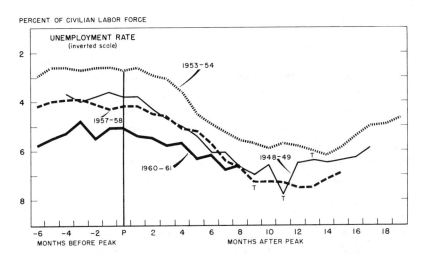

Chart 3. Employment and Unemployment in Four Postwar Recessions
P = cyclical peak.
T = cyclical trough.
Note: Data are seasonally adjusted and are plotted from 6 months before cyclical peak to 6 months after cyclical trough.
Source: Department of Labor.

previous recessions are repeated, further inventory liquidation would be expected unless GNP rises from other causes. The prospects of reversal of the recession in the first two quarters of this year depend, therefore, on modest advances in components of demand other than inventory change. A quickening of the pace of recovery following a reversal of the inventory-cycle mechanism does not appear likely until after midyear.

The principal prospects for early expansion of demand lie in the continued upward trend in government purchases—Federal, State,

Table 1
Changes in components of gross national product from first quarter to
fourth quarter 1960 (billions of dollars, seasonally adjusted annual rates)

Component	Current prices	1960 prices
Change in business inventories	− 14.4	− 14.4
Offsetting expenditure components		
Gross private fixed investment	1.1	1.1
Personal consumption expenditures	7.5	3.5
Government purchases	4.6	1.9
Federal	1.5	− .4
State and local	3.1	2.4
Net exports	3.4	3.5
Total offsetting components	16.6	10.0
Change in gross national product	2.2	− 4.4

Source: Department of Commerce.

and local—and in increases in consumer spending with the aid of
governmental income-maintenance programs. Net exports cannot be
expected to repeat the dramatic gains of 1960. In the absence of special measures of stimulus, business fixed investment is unlikely to
rise above 1960 levels before GNP itself increases significantly. The
same is true, in this recession in contrast to 1958, of residential construction. Once GNP rises from other causes, the upswing will be
reinforced by upward revision in business and residential
investment.

Developments which would weaken final demand cannot be excluded. These include the possibilities (a) that consumers will maintain or even increase the abnormally high personal saving ratio of the
last half of 1960, (b) that business firms will once again revise downward their plans for plant and equipment expenditure, and (c) that
the deteriorating financial position of State and local governments
might interrupt the strong and steady upward trend in their expenditures. If these weaknesses develop, the end of the recession may
have to await the rhythm of the inventory cycle.

Whenever it occurs, reversal of the recession is only the beginning,
not the end, of the task of restoring momentum to the American
economy. Even if GNP in the last quarter of this year were to achieve
an all-time record level 3.5 percent higher than the fourth quarter of
1960—a gain of $18 billion in constant (1960) prices—the unemploy-
ment problem would still be of roughly the same magnitude as today.
This sobering statistic dramatizes the challenge and the opportunity
presented to us by the continuous expansion of United States economic potential.

The Problem of Chronic Slack and Full Recovery

Economic recovery in 1961 is far more than a cyclical problem. It is also a problem of chronic slack in the economy—the growing gap between what we *can* produce and what we *do* produce. This is graphically illustrated in Charts 4 and 5. Especially since 1955, the gap has shown a distressing upward trend. As these charts make clear, the movement of the gap is roughly parallel to the unemployment ratio both within cycles and between cycles. However, the numerical level of the unemployment ratio greatly understates both the amount and the human cost of wasted economic potential.

The Gap between Actual and Potential Output. One symptom of increasing noncyclical slack is that successive upswings are shorter and weaker, as shown by several measures in Table 2. It is striking, for example, that unemployment was below 5 percent of the labor force in only one month at the top of the most recent cycle, but was below 3 percent in 11 months of the 1953 prosperity.

In the first year of the 1958–60 expansion, real GNP rose by 10 percent, but from the second quarter of 1959 to the second quarter of 1960 the rise was disappointing, amounting to only 2 percent. As a result of this incomplete recovery, the actual output of the American economy fell considerably short of its potential output even before the decline began last spring. A year ago, the 1960 *Joint Economic Report* stated, "An expected $510 billion gross national product for 1960 would be $20 billion to $30 billion below the economy's potential output, based upon a 4 percent rate of unemployment." In fact, 1960 GNP was $503 billion, or $7 billion short of expectations. The gap between actual and potential output for 1960 as a whole can thus be estimated at $30–35 billion, or 6 to 7 percent of total output.

This unused potential is equal to $500 per American household. It is two-thirds the amount we spend on national defense. It is almost twice the amount spent on public education. It is about one and a half times the amount spent on new homes last year. Even the world's most prosperous nation cannot afford to waste resources on this scale.

The problem of unused potential becomes continually more urgent. As the President stated in his economic message to the Congress on February 2, the potential of the American economy currently grows at about 3.5 percent a year. This growth in our economic capacity is made up of a rise in the labor force that follows a 1.5 percent per year upward trend and a secular increase in real gross national product per man averaging 2 percent per year. It is this 3.5 percent trend which is taken as the measure of growth of potential in Charts 4 and

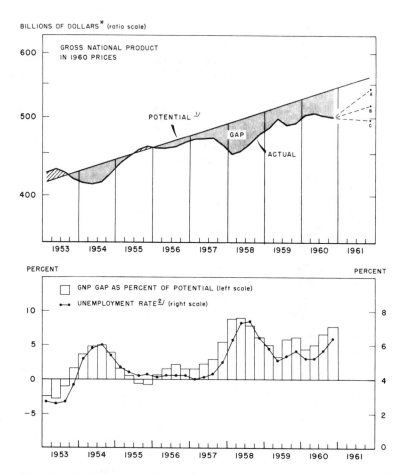

Chart 4. Gross National Product, Actual and Potential, and Unemployment Rate
*Seasonally adjusted annual rates.
[1]3½% trend line through middle of 1955.
[2]Unemployment as percent of civilian labor force; seasonally adjusted.
Note: A, B, and C represent GNP in 1961 IV assuming unemployment rate of 5%, 6½%, and 8%, respectively.
Sources: Department of Commerce, Department of Labor, and Council of Economic Advisers.

5. (See Supplement A for a discussion of the data and technical analysis underlying these figures.)

The 3.5 percent rate is an estimate of the economic growth available to the nation in the absence of either new forces in the private economy or new governmental policies designed to accelerate the expansion of national productive capacity. In other words, it represents the rate of advance of gross national product (corrected for price changes) that our economy now achieves when it operates at reasonably full employment. But, as the President made clear in his message, the 3.5

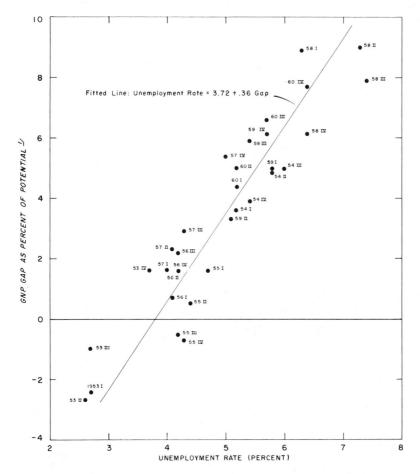

Chart 5. Relationship between Unused Potential Gross National Product and Unemployment Rate
[1]GNP gap (potential GNP less actual GNP) as percent of potential GNP (all in constant prices). Potential GNP is 3½% trend line through middle of 1955.
[2]Unemployment as percent of civilian labor force.
Note: All computations are based on seasonally adjusted data.

Source: Council of Economic Advisers (based on Department of Commerce and Department of Labor data).

percent growth rate is not high enough. It can and should be increased.

The level of the 3.5 percent trend of potential in Chart 4, from which the gap estimates of Charts 4 and 5 are derived, is fixed by a conservative estimate of the current capacity of the economy. An unemployment rate of 4.0 percent is taken as a reasonable target for full utilization of resources consistent with reasonable price stability. This target was achieved and surpassed during 1951–53 and was approached in late 1955 and early 1956. It is an attainable objective. If

Table 2
Measures of cyclical expansion and prosperity

Date of cyclical peak	Duration of previous upswing (months)	Unemployment rate				Industrial production: annual growth rate from previous cyclical peak (percent)
		Rate at cyclical peak (percent)	Number of months around cyclical peak with rate below (months)			
			5 percent	4 percent	3 percent	
1953: July	45[1]	2.7	42	35	11	7.1[1]
1957: July	35	4.2	34	3	0	2.0
1960: May	25	5.1	1	0	0	2.8

[1]Previous cyclical peak was November 1948.
Source: Council of Economic Advisers (based on Department of Labor and Federal Reserve data).

the target has seemed out of range in recent years, the fault lies in our poorer marksmanship.

We estimate that, if the seasonally adjusted unemployment ratio had been 4.0 percent rather than 6.4 percent in the last quarter of 1960, output would have been about 8 percent higher. Instead of just over $500 billion, output would have been $540 billion. This estimate is confirmed by several different methods of calculation.

First, a statistical relationship between real GNP and unemployment, based on quarterly data from 1947 to 1960, indicates that a fall of 2.4 percentage points in the unemployment ratio—from 6.4 to 4.0 percent—would yield an estimated rise in real GNP of about 8 percent. (See Supplement A.)

Second, according to calculations of potential output by James W. Knowles of the staff of the Joint Economic Committee in *The Potential Economic Growth in the United States*, the gap exceeded 8 percent by the end of 1960.

Third, the figure of 8 percent as the fourth-quarter 1960 gap is also arrived at by projecting the 3.5 percent trend from a base of actual economic performance in mid-1955. The year 1955 was one of prosperity and stable prices. The unemployment rate was slightly above 4.0 percent at midyear.

The underlying sources of the potential 8 percent expansion of output are spelled out in Table 3. The table reflects previous economic experience, which has demonstrated that a rise in output to its potential is accompanied not only by a decline in unemployment but by (a) an increase in the civilian labor force; (b) a rise in the average workweek; and (c) a marked increase in output per man-hour.

Table 3
Sources of estimated potential 8 percent increase of gross national product, fourth quarter 1960

Source	Associated increase of output
1. Reduction of unemployment to 4 percent	2.6
2. Increase of labor force in response to greater demand	.8
3. Increase of hours of work per man associated with higher utilization	1.1
4. Increase of productivity per manhour associated with higher utilization	3.3
5. Interactions of the above effects	.2
Total	8.0

[1]Detailed calculations underlying this table are shown in Supplement A.
Source: Council of Economic Advisers.

The size of the gap for the last quarter of 1960 illustrates a general point that is not widely enough appreciated in interpretation of the unemployment index. Unemployment runs parallel with the gap, as Charts 4 and 5 clearly show. But the rise in percentage unemployment rates greatly understates the waste of economic potential. The data analyzed in Supplement A shows that when the unemployment rate rises by 1 percentage point above the 4 percent level, the gap between actual and potential production typically widens by a little more than 3 percentage points. At an unemployment rate of 7 percent (seasonally adjusted), the production gap would normally be between 9 and 10 percent.

Our current gap, as noted earlier, is not far from these levels today. This gap of about $50 billion (1960 prices) defines the urgency of the economic problem facing the nation today and in the months ahead.

Composition of Unemployment. Some have attributed the growth of unemployment in recent years to changing characteristics of the labor force rather than to deficiencies in total demand. According to this view, the new unemployment is concentrated among workers who are intrinsically unemployable by reason of sex, age, location, occupation, or skill. Expansion of overall demand, it is argued, will not meet this problem; it can only be met by educating, retraining, and relocating unsuccessful job-seekers.

The facts (which are examined in Supplement B) clearly refute this explanation of the rise of unemployment over the last 8 years. Only an insignificant fraction of this rise can be traced to the shift in composition of the labor force. The growth of unemployment has been a pervasive one, hitting all segments of the labor force.

In a free economy as large as ours, a certain amount of frictional unemployment caused by changes in the structure of industry and manpower is unavoidable. In addition, a small fraction of the adult population is unemployable. Yet, there is no evidence that hard-core unemployment has been growing as a percent of the labor force. Measures to improve the mobility of labor to jobs and of jobs to labor, to better our educational facilities, to match future supplies of different skills and occupations to the probable pattern of future demand, and to improve the health of the population—these are and should be high on the agenda of national policy. But they are no substitute for fiscal, monetary, and credit policies for economic recovery. Adjustments that now seem difficult, and unemployment pockets that now seem intractable, will turn out to be manageable after all in an environment of full prosperity.

The Promise of Full Recovery. Restoring the economy to capacity operations, apart from abating the misery and human waste of unemployment, would make impressive contributions to our national economic objectives: (a) to the fiscal capacity of government at all levels; (b) to the flow of capital investment so urgently needed to maintain economic growth and improve the competitive position of American industry; and (c) to the welfare of all segments of our population.

Government revenues, particularly those of the Federal Government, are highly sensitive to economic activity. Chart 6 is illustrative of the dependence of Federal budget receipts on gross national product. Were the economy to operate at full employment levels in 1961, and at comparable rates in the first 6 months of 1962, it is estimated

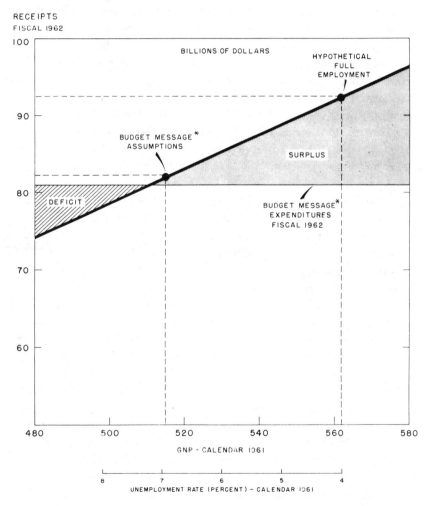

Chart 6. Dependence of Federal Budget Receipts on Gross National Product (Illustrative Estimate)
*Based on January 1961 budget message.
Source: Council of Economic Advisers.

that Federal revenues in fiscal 1962 would be $92 billion. This would exceed the expenditures estimated in the Budget Message of January 16, 1961, by $11 billion and the revenues by $9½ billion. Moreover, if the economy grows at 3½ percent per year, the present Federal tax structure will increase budget receipts by $3 to $3½ billion per year. The revenues of a fully operating economy would finance the Federal programs needed to accelerate the growth of productive capacity and meet national priorities at home and abroad, while leaving room for substantial retirements of Federal debt from budget surplus.

Economic recovery will also improve the financial position of hard-pressed State and local governments. The growth of population and of needs for facilities and services provided by these governments is straining their financial resources. During the last quarter of 1960, these governments were spending at a rate $4.2 billion above their receipts (on an accrual basis). With full recovery, their receipts would approximately cover their present outlays.

In 1960, business expenditures for new plant and equipment, corrected for price changes, were 9 percent below the levels achieved in 1956 and 1957. Investment in new productive facilities has been falling absolutely. It has fallen even more sharply in relation to actual GNP, let alone, to potential GNP. To increase the attainable rate of growth of the economy, we must increase the share of our current potential output that we devote to new investment. Full recovery can make two contributions to this objective. The first is to add the pressure of vigorous consumer demand and resulting profits to the incentives for expansion and modernization of productive facilities. The second is to provide additional saving to finance investment—direct personal saving, retained business earnings, and government surplus. Corporate profits were about $44 billion in 1960. In a fully operating economy in 1961 corporate profits would be about $58 billion, providing enhanced incentive to undertake investment and greater resources to finance it, as well as more revenue for the Federal Treasury.

Table 4 shows personal income and consumption in 1960, in comparison with the levels which would be generated by hypothetical full employment in 1961. Disposable income and consumption per capita—in constant prices—could be 5 percent higher. This increase in resources available for private households would permit an intensified attack on poverty, hunger, ill health, and financial insecurity, while allowing for gains in well-being by all segments of the population.

While full recovery would significantly increase total consumption, it would—as Table 4 shows—diminish the ratio of consumption to gross national product. The great sensitivity of government revenues

Table 4
Selected components of national output and income

Output component	1960 actual Amount (1960 prices, billions of dollars)	Percent of GNP	1961 potential (estimated) Amount (1960 prices, billions of dollars)	Percent of GNP
Gross national product	503.2	100.0	554	100.0
Disposable personal income	354.2	70.4	378	68.2
Personal consumption expenditures	327.8	65.1	350	63.2
Corporate profits before taxes	44	8.7	58	10.5
Government net receipts on income and product account[1]	99.9	19.9	117	21.1
Federal	55.5		68	
State and local	44.4		49	
Per capita				
Disposable personal income (dollars)	1,969		2,068	
Personal consumption expenditures (dollars)	1,822		1,915	

[1]Receipts less transfer payments, interest, and subsidies. Grants-in-aid are deducted from Federal receipts and included in State and local receipts.
Sources: Department of Commerce and Council of Economic Advisers.

and corporate profits to cyclical increases of GNP has been noted. As the economy approaches full employment, this sensitivity increases the share of national output available for private investment and government purchase—in relative proportions that depend on how increased government revenues are divided between expanded programs and budget surplus. This change in the composition of national expenditure is one of the several ways in which full recovery can contribute to acceleration of growth, at the same time that it provides a generous increase in total and per capita consumption.

The Problem of Accelerating Growth

As indicated above, the underlying changes in the supply of labor and productivity per man would have permitted real output to grow at roughly 3.5 percent a year since 1955. This potential has not vanished; it is still there. The questions we consider in this section are, first, whether it will continue to grow unchecked if we do not close the production gap; and, second, whether deliberate policy can increase the long-run growth of output.

Between the first quarter of 1947 and the fourth quarter of 1953, GNP grew from $316.5 billion to $419.6 billion (annual rates, 1960 prices), or nearly 4.5 percent per year. Calculations similar to those in Supplement A confirm that this is a reasonable approximation to the rate of growth of potential during the early postwar years. Of course, the fact that 4.5 percent growth of real output occurred then— and at occasional earlier periods in our history—is by itself no guarantee that 4 percent growth or better would be sustainable now. To some extent the years after 1948 were still affected by the aftermath of the war. To judge how much faster than 3.5 percent a year the economy could grow now, we must consider the sources of increase in potential output.

Between 1947 and 1953, the total labor force grew at approximately 1.5 percent per year. This is roughly the same rate that we estimate for the years just past and just ahead. The difference between the 4.5 percent potential growth rate then and the 3.5 percent now is accounted for by a more rapid increase of productivity per man.

The twin keys to an accelerated growth of productivity and output are two forms of investment: investment in education, health, natural resources, research and development for technical advance; and investment in the expansion and modernization of the Nation's stock of business plant and equipment. Capital expansion is especially hobbled and slowed by the continued presence of slack and unused capacity. One of the reasons for the recent slowdown in the rate of growth of productivity and output is a corresponding slowdown in the rate at which the stock of capital has been renewed and modernized. And even the less material kinds of investment—in research and in human resources—may be expected to respond to a quickening of the economic pulse.

Some of the elementary facts showing that there has been a slowdown in the renewal and expansion of our capital stock are as follows:

1. Investment in fixed capital (producers' durable equipment plus "other construction") stood at 12.5 percent of GNP in 1948. This ratio has declined more or less steadily since then (with a partial recovery to 11 percent in 1956), until in the last three years it has fallen below 10 percent and stood at 9.1 percent in 1959 and 9.6 percent in 1960. The relative fall in the "producers durable equipment" component has been even more dramatic, falling from 8.3 percent of GNP in 1948 to 5.6 percent in 1959–60. The sharper fall in the equipment rate is significant because equipment, more than plant, is *par excellence* the carrier of new processes, new commodities and technological progress.

2. In 1945 the average age of the stock of equipment was 10.6 years, and the average age of plant was 27.2 years. As a consequence of the high rates of investment in the immediate postwar years, the average age of equipment declined step by step to a minimum of 8.5 years in the period 1952–1955. Since then the average age of equipment has begun to creep upward again, reaching 9.0 years in 1959, the same as in 1948. Since 1945 the average age of the stock of plant has declined slightly—but steadily—to 24.2 years in 1959.

3. The fraction of the stock of business equipment which is 5 years old or less has been declining from a high of 50 percent in 1950, to something like 37 percent in 1959. Other estimates show that the annual rate of increase of the gross stock of privately-owned producers' durables fell from 8.2 percent in 1947 and 9.6 percent in 1948 to 3.9 percent in 1957 and 2.9 percent in 1958.

In brief, since 1955–1957 the increase in stock of plant and especially equipment per worker has been slowed. In the same period, the age distribution of the country's capital equipment has been shifting somewhat unfavorably. It seems likely that these developments are responsible for the observed slowdown in the rate of economic growth and, particularly, in the rate at which productivity per man-hour increased.

In recent years, economists have assigned a much larger role to improvements in human resources and increases in knowledge as a source of growth relative to increases in physical capital. This shift in emphasis and its implied consequences for policy toward education, training and research are overdue. Yet, as has been confirmed by more recent research, the great importance of capital investment lies in its interaction with improved skills and technological progress. New ideas lie fallow without the modern equipment to give them life. From this point of view the function of capital formation is as much in modernizing the equipment of the industrial worker as in simply adding to it. The relation runs both ways: investment gives effect to technical progress and technical progress stimulates and justifies investment.

A second causal factor tending to slow down the rate of growth since 1955 is the failure of market demand to expand adequately. This factor in part operates independently and in part underlies the retardation in investment. In the long run, productive potential will not grow faster than the demand for output for consumption and investment purposes, for public expenditures and for export. The best stimulus to capital expansion is pressure on present capacity, and that has been noticeably lacking in most industries since the mid-fifties.

In summary: The long-run rate of growth off the labor force has been about 1.5 percent per year. There have been periods of slower growth owing to declines in the birth rate, as in the 30's, and to slack in the demand for labor. Demographic factors indicate that for the near future we can count on a return to the historical 1.5 percent increase. Normal growth of productivity per man at the recent rate of 2 percent per year will permit a return to a growth line rising at 3.5 percent a year from the peak of 1957. As the gap between current and potential product narrows, as firmer markets for commodities and special programs create a more favorable climate for business investment, new possibilities for improvements in productivity will emerge. The cultivation of the country's human and natural resources, and the devotion of a larger fraction of current output to the modernization and expansion of the stock of capital will accelerate the process of improving skills and technology.

The question will then arise: is the "normal" growth rate enough? This question should be considered even before the Nation achieves full recovery. Among the alternative measures for meeting the short-term and intermediate goals of reversing the recession and achieving full recovery, some will strongly stimulate long-run growth more than others.

First, it is necessary to grasp the magnitudes involved. Starting from a 1960 potential GNP of $535 billion and assuming constant prices, growth at 3.5, 4, and 5 percent per year would lead to aggregate output levels of $755 billion, $792 billion, and $871 billion respectively in 1970. Even an increase from 3.5 to 4 percent in the rate of growth of potential output means an extra $38 billion of goods and services available for use in 1970. Population will have been increasing at about 1.5 percent so that a 4 percent growth in gross national product will mean an increase in output per person of 2.5 percent per year.

If we adopt policies to improve our human and natural resources and return to the rate of capital expansion and renewal experienced in the late 40's and early 50's, the Nation could achieve impressive gains of output in the present decade. Few Americans would wish to miss this opportunity. Despite the enviably high average standard of living the country already enjoys, the age of abundance is not yet with us, nor will it be with us in 1970. Averages conceal pockets of poverty and missed opportunity especially among the aged, the uneducated, nonwhites, and families broken by disease, death or divorce. An equitably distributed increase of private consumption has a strong claim on the extra output available from stepped-up growth.

There are also vital public uses for output. On the domestic scene, the President has pointed to the urgent needs for expanded resource use in education (for leisure as well as work), in health and medical research, in the renewal and beautification of our cities, in highways, water supply and the control of pollution, and in conservation. We can never be sure that requirements for the military security of the Nation and the free world will not increase in the future.

Finally, America's international obligations, especially economic aid to the underdeveloped countries of the world, offer an important opportunity which it will be easier to grasp if domestic output grows rapidly. It is to be expected and welcomed that living standards the world over will become more rather than less equal over the decades. But this is not to say that the fruits of economic growth of the advanced countries have a low order of priority. In this connection, a demonstration of the ability of a free economy to achieve high rates of growth is of incalculable value.

For all these reasons, opportunities to accelerate economic growth are important. Programs to reverse the recession and attain recovery should be followed and accompanied by policies designed to raise our growth in potential above the 3.5 percent rate which has become "normal" in the slack years since 1955. Short-run policies should, as far as possible, also serve long-run ends. Fortunately, the objectives are consistent and mutually reinforcing.

The Balance of Payments

During 1960 the United States ran a $3.8 billion balance-of-payments deficit. This was almost as large as in 1959, the previous high. The 1960 gold loss totaled $1.7 billion; the increase in our short-term liabilities to foreigners, $2.0 billion.

The 1960 payments deficit and the accompanying gold drain were greatly enlarged by short-term capital movements from the United States—money which moved abroad in search of high interest rates and in response to unfounded rumors that we would devalue the dollar. The total short-term outflow may have amounted to more than $2 billion.

Speculation against the dollar came to an end early this year, largely because of the President's firm commitment to defend the dollar. The outflows of short-term funds induced by interest-rate differences also seem to have tapered off, but capital flight due to speculation could resume if we were to go on running a deficit in our other transactions with the rest of the world. We now have a needed respite—time in which to reduce this deficit and to strengthen international financial arrangements.

"Deficit" in the remainder of this discussion of our international position refers to the difference between U.S. outlays for goods, services, long-term securities, and industrial assets, and the corresponding U.S. receipts. This deficit concept excludes short-term capital movements and unrecorded transactions and is consequently more appropriate in appraising our fundamental international economic position. It is estimated that this deficit totaled $1.6 billion for 1960. This is a considerable improvement over 1958 or 1959, but it would be imprudent to extrapolate this favorable trend.

While our exports increased sharply in 1960 we cannot reasonably expect a further increase this year. We must expect declines in some exports, such as cotton, which were unusually high in 1960. Further increases in exports can be foreseen because of recent reductions in discrimination against dollar goods. Moreover, if the European boom continues, and if recovery here raises the foreign exchange earnings of traditionally favorable markets in Canada and Latin America, we can expect a substantial improvement in our exports to those areas over the unusually low levels of the past two years. Altogether, we will do well to maintain our over-all 1961 export total at least year's level. On the other hand, we must anticipate some increase in our imports, as recovery gets under way in the United States. This could mean a decrease in our trade surplus. On the favorable side, we may see other changes—a decline in U.S. long-term private investment in other industrialized countries as our own business prospects improve, an increase in our earnings on past foreign investment, and the measures taken by the Government to economize on its overseas spending. These favorable changes will tend to offset any worsening in our trade balance.

Full recovery might increase the import bill by $1.5 to $2.0 billion over its 1960 level, as it would enlarge our demand for raw materials and finished goods. We could expect some offsetting benefits, as investment in the United States becomes relatively more attractive because of improved American profit opportunities. And a rise in imports from the raw materials producing countries will provide them the funds to import from this country. In the process of attaining full employment, we might enjoy a large reflux of short-term capital.

The increase in the United States deficit in recent years has produced widespread concern that we may have "priced ourselves out of world markets." The statistical evidence is not conclusive. Some measures of price change during the 1950's showed greater increases in Europe than in the United States, while others showed the opposite. Wage costs per unit of output have risen faster here than in Italy, Japan, or France, but no faster than in Germany, or Canada, and more slowly than in Britain, the Netherlands, or Sweden.

The prices of some key American export goods, notably steel and steel-intensive products, seem to have risen more rapidly than export prices abroad, and these price movements have damaged our trade balance. But some of our difficulties are not the result of any sudden deterioration in our position. They may be better explained as a consequence of foreign competitive advantages long latent but only recently exploited. Many American products have long been vulnerable to a competitive challenge here and in foreign markets. By the middle 1950's Europe and Japan, having finished repairing the damage done by World War II, began to seize opportunities here and in other markets.

Compounding our payments problem, some American manufacturers have been slow to respond to the challenge of foreign competition and to redesign their products to meet changing needs and tastes here and abroad. The final response of these industries has usually been powerful enough, but too slow to prevent doubts about the competitiveness of American industry. Other American products, notably coal and oil, have been afflicted by global shifts in supply and demand and by trade policies abroad.

New direct foreign investments of American firms (including profits reinvested) have run near $3 billion a year for several years. American firms have been going abroad to save on labor and transport costs, to claim sizable tax benefits, to participate more fully in the rapid growth of other industrial countries and, most recently, to vault over Europe's new common tariff. The expansion of U.S. production in other countries has probably pre-empted a part of our export market and swelled our import bill. It has also shortened our technological lead, because our skill and product design go abroad with our capital.

While pursuing vigorously our policies for domestic recovery, we must seek also to strengthen our international position. We must encourage business investment designed to reduce costs and to improve products as well as to expand capacity. We must advance the skill and efficiency of our workers. But efforts to increase productivity will be of little help to our balance of payments if wage and price advances gobble up the gains.

The United States still enjoys great competitive power and financial strength. Our exports far exceed our imports. Our gold reserves are still very large, nearly as large as our obligations as an international banker. Few banks or banking nations have ever been as liquid. There is growing realization abroad that the U.S. payments position is a world problem and that other governments have an obligation to cooperate in corrective policies and to defend and strengthen the international monetary system.

III. Economic Policy

In this section, we shall discuss major governmental policies to reverse the recession, achieve full recovery, and promote growth. By focusing on governmental policies, we do not intend to suggest that recovery and growth depend exclusively—or even primarily—on the government. The prosperity and progress of a free society depend principally on the enterprise and skill of private citizens. The government seeks to strengthen the forces of recovery and growth in the private economy.

Monetary Policy and Debt Management

In this recession, for the first time since 1931–32, expansionary monetary policy has been limited by the international financial position of the United States. Over the past six months our balance of payments deficit has been severely aggravated by the outflow of short-term capital attracted by higher short-term interest rates abroad. To stem the outflow, Federal Reserve authorities have had to limit expansion of money and credit, especially in recent months, to keep short-term interest rates from falling too far. Short-term rates have remained 1.5 to 2 percentage points above past recession levels. The Federal Reserve discount rate, which fell as low as 1.75 percent in the 1958 recession, is 3 percent today. The Treasury bill rate reached 0.6 percent in May 1958 but stands at 2.6 percent today, up from its recent low of 2.1 percent in November 1960.

The Federal Reserve has sought since October to expand bank reserves in ways that do not directly lower bill rates and other rates important in holding internationally mobile liquid funds. These efforts have met with some success. The money supply (defined conventionally as demand deposits and currency) has risen 1.4 percent since June 1960, and the money supply (defined to include also time deposits) has risen about 4 percent. However, interest rates have remained relatively high throughout all segments of the money and capital markets. Whether interest rates are regarded as a cause or as a symptom of borrowing and lending activity, substantial monetary and credit expansion can scarcely occur without significant easing of rates.

The "prime rate"—the rate New York banks charge their prime-risk customers for commercial loans—is 4.5 percent now, in comparison with 3.5 percent in 1958 and 3 percent in 1954. Corporate Aaa bonds yield 4.2 percent now, in comparison with 3.6 percent and 2.8 percent in the two preceding cyclical troughs. Table 5 compares interest rate levels today with those in previous recessions, and shows in the same

Table 5
Interest rates and bond and mortgage yields (percent per annum)

| | U.S. Government securities | | | | Corporate Aaa bonds (Moody's)[1] | | State and local Government Aaa bonds (Moody's)[2] | | FHA home mortgages | |
| | 3-month Treasury bills[1] | | U.S. Government long-term bonds[1] | | | | | | | |
Date	Rate	Period	Rate	Period	Rate	Period	Rate	Period	Rate	Period
1953–54										
High	2.416	6/6/53	3.19	6/6/53	3.42	6/20/53	2.73	6/25/53	4.87	9/53
Low	.616	6/12/54	2.45	8/7/54	2.85	3/20/54	1.90	9/2/54	4.56	12/5
1957–58										
High	3.660	10/19/57	3.76	10/18/57	4.14	9/28/57	3.45	8/31/57	5.63	9/57
Low	.635	5/31/58	3.07	4/26/58	3.55	5/3/58	2.64	4/26/58	5.35	7/58
1959–61										
High	4.670	12/26/59	4.42	1/9/60	4.61	12/31/59	3.65	9/26/59	6.24	1/60
Low	2.127	11/5/60	3.75	8/6/60	4.23	8/27/60	2.99	8/27/60	6.00	1/61

[1]Weekly averages of daily figures.
[2]Thursday figures.
Sources: Board of Governors of the Federal Reserve System, Treasury Department, Moody's Investors Service, and Federal Housing Administration.

comparative perspective how little long-term interest rates have fallen so far in this recession.

The Federal Reserve has recently announced that it is purchasing long-term U.S. Government securities on the open market. The new policy is an extension of its efforts to provide additional reserves by purchases that do not directly depress the short-term rate. The objective is to lower long-term interest rates, in order to increase business investment and residential construction, while maintaining the discount rate and related short-term rates at internationally competitive levels. Treasury public debt operations are also geared to this objective. Federal Reserve and Treasury operations may be expected to result in reduction of the stock of long-term bonds available to private investors, relative to the outstanding supplies of short securities. The extent to which the maturity structure of rates can be "twisted" by these operations remains to be seen. But the experiment must be tried. The domestic economy urgently needs the stimulus of lower effective long-term and commercial rates. At the same time, as confidence in the dollar is restored and as interest rates abroad continue to fall, the constraint on our short-term rate can safely be relaxed.

The economy needs the stimulus of low interest rates and greater credit availability, not merely for recovery of the ground lost in the recession but for the more difficult and important tasks of restoring full employment and promoting growth. As shown in Chart 6 and Table 4, the present Federal revenue system would produce a substantial surplus over current budget expenditure levels at full employment. The corresponding revenues would provide an excellent opportunity to promote economic growth both through government programs and through private investment. But the "latent surplus" may also make the attainment of full recovery more difficult. Full recovery requires that investment by business, and by State and local governments, be expanded significantly and maintained at high and increasing levels. Although some of the stimulus for investment can be provided by tax incentives, it is important to maintain monetary and credit conditions that are favorable to the necessary flow of funds. Monetary policy must at all times be flexible and interest rates must be higher in booms than in recessions. But the larger the share of the task of preventing inflationary excesses of demand that is assigned to fiscal policy, the smaller the burden that will fall on restrictive monetary policy.

The Western world has recently entered a new era of convertible currencies, in which short-term funds can move in large volume and at great speed from one country to another. Losses—or gains—of funds can restrict a country's freedom of action in domestic policy to an undesirable degree. The recent experience of the United States is an example; similar outflows may embarrass us again, or strike countries less well insulated by international reserves. The President noted in his message of February 6 two measures by which the United States could, if necessary, seek to hold foreign official dollar balances while lowering domestic short-term interest rates. The first, which requires Congressional approval, is to permit U.S. commercial banks to compete for official foreign time deposits by offering rates above the general ceiling set by the Federal Reserve. The second, which is already within the power of the Secretary of the Treasury, is to offer special securities for foreign central banks and governments. In the long run, however, reconciling the requirements of domestic economic stability with those of international currency convertibility will require multilateral understanding and accommodation. In this connection, the President said in his balance of payments message, "I have requested the Secretaries of State and Treasury to work for still closer cooperation between the monetary and financial authorities of the industrialized free nations with a view toward avoiding excessive short-term money flows which could be upsetting to the orderly development of international trade and payments."

Housing Credit

Credit policy affects many families directly through its impact on the mortgage market.

Private housing starts have been declining for nearly two years. Inventories of unsold new houses are significantly higher than in early 1959. In the three previous postwar recessions, revived strength in housing activity operated to sustain the economy; in the current recession, this has not been the case.

The present weakness in housing construction is in part a legacy of the high level of building activity in 1958–59. It is also, in part, a consequence of demographic factors; because of low birth rates in the 1930's, the number of persons reaching the average age of first marriage in the last few years has been temporarily low. Private housing starts reached an annual rate, seasonally adjusted, of 1.6 million in April 1959, then declined to 980,000 in December 1960. A recovery to 1.1 million occurred in January 1961.

This is not, however, the whole story. Residential construction has been further depressed by high interest rates on mortgages. It is difficult to accept the view that the housing market is so glutted that it would not respond to lower monthly financing costs. The possibilities for such reduction through lower interest rates are substantial, for example, a reduction of 1 percent in the rate of interest on a 30-

year mortgage could reduce monthly mortgage payments by more than 10 percent.

Mortgage interest rates are sticky prices. Though availability of mortgage funds improved in 1960, interest rates responded only sluggishly. The average decline was less than ¼ of 1 percent. In the face of a depressed level of home building activity, rising liquidity in many lending institutions, and a continuing decline in long-term interest rates generally, the cost of housing credit should have fallen more sharply. Mortgage interest rates of 6 to 7 percent are out of touch with the realities of 1961.

The Administration has taken a number of steps to hasten the decline in mortgage lending rates. The maximum permissible interest rate on FHA-insured loans has been reduced. The FNMA, in its secondary market operations, has increased both its selling prices and its buying prices for mortgages. At current FNMA selling prices, most lenders will find it more attractive to seek other investments than to buy existing mortgages from FNMA. The search for other investments will help, directly or indirectly, to push down interest rates on new mortgages.

The Federal Home Loan Bank Board has assisted the Administration's effort to stimulate housing construction and lower the cost of housing credit by a number of revisions in its policies and regulations. Also, the President has requested the Chairman designate of the FHLBB to meet with leaders in the savings and loan field and to urge them to reduce mortgage rates.

Further measures to stimulate housing demand will become possible as general monetary conditions are further eased.

Fiscal Policy

The Federal budget serves as an important stabilizing force in our economy. In part, this force is exerted through the rhythm of automatic changes in tax receipts and transfer payments as incomes rise and fall. In part, it is the result of conscious changes in tax and expenditure programs. For example, taxes were reduced several billion dollars in 1954 through scheduled expirations of certain taxes and new legislation; expenditures were increased several billion dollars in 1958 by expansion and acceleration of government programs. In recent years, revenues have risen and expenditures have fallen slightly as a percentage of gross national product. As a result, both the automatic cycle of the budget and the impact of legislative changes revolve around a higher ratio of revenues to expenditures than was formerly the case.

As demonstrated in Chart 7, the combination of automatic and dis-

BILLIONS OF DOLLARS

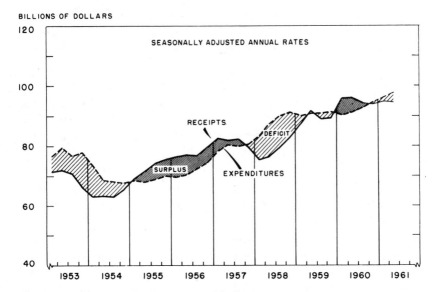

Chart 7. Federal Government Receipts and Expenditures (National Income Accounts Basis)
Sources: Department of Commerce and Council of Economic Advisers.

cretionary budget forces has generated substantial surpluses in prosperity and deficits in recession. There is wide consensus that the surpluses have been helpful in restraining inflation, and the deficits in cushioning recession and promoting recovery. This is not to say that either the size or the timing of budget changes have been perfectly fitted to the movement of the business cycle. But by and large, the fiscal system has served as an important stabilizing influence.

Three important characteristics of the automatic responses of the budget should be noted, especially as they bear on the current recession and the outlook for recovery. First, under present conditions and tax rates, the "built-in" flexibility of the Federal budget offsets between 25 and 30 percent of the drop (or increase) in GNP, with approximately one-half of the offset coming from corporate taxes, one-quarter from personal income taxes, and most of the rest from the various social security programs. As Chart 6 illustrates, Federal receipts alone decline $3.4 billion for every 1 percent increase in the rate of unemployment.

Second, welcome as the built-in stabilizers are when the economy contracts, they are a mixed blessing when it expands. As soon as business conditions take a turn for the better, we can expect the Federal tax system automatically to cut into the growth in private incomes. When the economy again reaches the boom phase, this drain on private incomes will serve as a desirable restraint on inflation. But up to that point, it tends to slow down the recovery process.

Third, because economic growth automatically broadens the tax base, the revenue-raising power of the Federal tax system has been rising relative to expenditures. Indeed, tax revenues—even at stable tax rates—rise more than proportionately to GNP. Table 6 drives home this point. At roughly comparable phases of business activity— 8.9 percent below potential in the first quarter of 1958 and 7.7 percent below potential in the fourth quarter of 1960, and in both cases prior to the impact of active anti-recession measures—the deficits were vastly different. In the first quarter of 1958, the deficit was running at an $8 billion annual rate. Last quarter it was less than $1 billion. In other words, the relative growth of revenues in recent years brings the budget into balance substantially below full employment at current levels of Federal expenditures and tax rates. In the absence of tax cuts, large expenditure increases, or a substantial worsening of the economic situation, only modest deficits are likely to develop.

Deficits as large as those experienced in the 1958 recession could materialize in the current recession only if unemployment and unused potential grew substantially larger than they were at the bottom of the 1958 recession, or if a very much greater expansion of government programs than now contemplated were undertaken. Indeed, recent fiscal trends make clear that full recovery with the present tax structure would generate substantially more revenue than is required by the President's proposed programs, thus leaving a generous margin for retirement of debt and restraint of inflation. Whether this margin is consistent with the achievement and maintenance of full employment cannot yet be determined.

In his "Program to Restore Momentum to the American Economy," President Kennedy announced executive action and recommended legislation to help reverse the decline and set the American economy on the road to recovery. Since that time, the President has also proposed programs in education, health, natural resources and highways, which, while fully justified on their own merits, promise additional benefit in the form of speedier recovery. The exact cost of all these programs, their timing, and their impact on the 1961 and 1962 Budget and on receipts from and payments to the public (the consolidated cash budget) are not yet known. A review will be undertaken by the Director of the Budget in his appearance before the Joint Economic Committee later this month.

However, the costs of the largest programs are already known. It may be useful to the Committee to appraise in general terms the economic impact of these programs as they relate to the problems of recession and recovery. For this purpose, we have estimated the overall magnitude of the programs. However, this estimate does not refer to Budget expenditures, for two reasons.

Table 6
Comparison of federal receipts, expenditures, and deficit in recessions of 1958 and 1960 (income and product accounts)

Item	First quarter 1958		Fourth quarter 1960		Calendar 1958		Calendar 1960	
	Billions of dollars[1]	Percent of GNP	Billions of dollars[1]	Percent of GNP	Billions of dollars[1]	Percent of GNP	Billions of dollars[1]	Percent of GNP
Federal receipts	75.4	17.5	94.0	18.7	78.6	17.7	95.3	18.9
Federal expenditures	83.5	19.3	94.6	18.8	87.9	19.8	92.3	18.3
Surplus (+) or deficit (−)	−8.1		−.6		−9.3		3.0	
Gross national product	432.0		503.5		444.2		503.2	
Gap as percent of								
Potential GNP[2]		8.9		7.7		8.0		6.0
Actual GNP[2]		9.8		8.3		8.7		6.3

[1]Seasonally adjusted annual rate.
[2]Based on GNP in constant prices.
Sources: Department of Commerce and Council of Economic Advisers.

First, it is an estimate of the impact of the programs in the income-and-product account. Unlike either the Budget or consolidated cash accounts, the income-and-product data are assimilated directly to the GNP accounts and are shown, to the extent possible, on a current (accrued) basis. These accounts diverge from the conventional and cash budget figures. Moreover, some of the President's recommendations, like the improvement in old age, survivors, and disability insurance, affect only the trust accounts and thus are reflected in the income-and-product account without any direct effect on the conventional Budget.

Second, the times of enactment of the various programs are uncertain. Some programs are likely to be enacted very quickly, e.g., temporary unemployment compensation, and will therefore still affect the fiscal 1961 budget, while others will not take effect until fiscal 1962. To simplify matters, we have put all the available calculations on the same basis by making the assumption—unrealistic but adequate to our present purpose—that all the recommended legislation is enacted at the same time.

This calculation shows that the President's program would generate an estimated flow of at least $3 billion to consumers and business during the first 12 months after enactment. This estimate includes only programs for which costs have already been made public: temporary unemployment compensation, aid to dependent children, OASDI changes, area redevelopment, aid to education, and several smaller programs. It omits such items as advanced procurement, speed-up in funded public works, and proposals that may be developed in the field of housing. Further, it does not include the impact of such additional defense expenditures as may prove to be necessary for national security.

Even if this estimate included all of the President's proposals, it would not measure the full stimulative effect of the Administration program. First, only the primary effects are measured, leaving out the further expansionary effects as funds are spent by the recipients. Second, acceleration of construction and contract letting may not be reflected in the Government's income accounts for a long time but may have immediate stimulative effects on the inventory, employment, and equipment needs of the contractors. Third, the nonbudgetary programs—notably, the move to reduce interest rates and increase credit availability—can have important stimulative effects.

The President said in his February 2 message, "If economic developments in the first quarter of this year indicate that additional measures are needed, I will promptly propose such measures." Any such measures will, of course, have substantial fiscal impacts. A further program for economic recovery might consider a speed-up in Government construction and related projects, an expansion of housing programs, and tax reduction.

If a new reading of the economic and fiscal situation indicates that additional measures are needed, a temporary income tax reduction offers one of the most important methods for further economic stimulus. It offers a method of stimulating the economy quickly and effectively, at the same time preserving the basic revenue-raising power of the tax system for later use in financing Government programs and stemming inflation. The beneficiaries of a personal income tax cut, especially in the lower brackets, would promptly spend a large part of the proceeds on goods and services, thereby stimulating production, employment, and income.

In appraisal of the usefulness of expanded Government expenditures in promoting recovery, the timing of their impact is often considered to be of decisive importance. This may be the case in a recovery which starts from a position not far below the economy's full potential. In such a recovery there is a danger that the impact of slow-starting Government projects comes too late to aid the recovery but instead aggravates an inflationary boom. The present situation is not of this kind. The decline began from a position of substantial unemployment and excess capacity. We face a stubborn problem of chronic slack, and the road to full recovery is a long one. The expansionary effects of Government programs will be welcome even if they occur well after the recession has been reversed.

In the spring and summer of 1958, the delayed impact of new expenditure programs may have appeared to be a real danger. Output was rebounding rapidly, and the outlook for housing was bright. As it turned out, fears of perverse timing were unnecessary, because the recovery was abortive. With that incomplete recovery behind us, the problem of chronic slack is more clearly evident today. Also, the outlook in housing—which played such an important role in recovery from the 1949, 1954, and 1958 recessions—is much less encouraging in 1961. Thus, the risk of bad timing of Government outlays is smaller in 1961 than it has appeared in any previous postwar recession. In our present circumstances we should not shrink from launching needed projects because of misplaced fears of bad timing.

The success of fiscal and budget policies cannot be measured only by whether the budget is in the black or in the red. The true test is whether the economy is in balance. Only an economy which is realizing its potential can produce the goods and create the jobs the country needs. If at the end of this year the unemployment ratio is still near 7 percent, our fiscal policies would have to be viewed with great concern, even if there is little or no deficit in the budget. On the other hand, if we have succeeded in reducing the unemployment ratio and expanding output significantly by year's end, we will be on our way to the goals of a stronger economy and the restoration of budgetary strength.

Policy for Growth

For the near future, economic policy justifiably places first emphasis on measures to expand aggregate demand to levels that will overcome the recession and, in time, close the gap between actual and potential production. Since demand pushing hard on existing capacity stimulates investment in plant and equipment, measures for economic recovery form an essential part of a balanced program for economic growth. But at high levels of activity, the major emphasis of growth policy is necessarily focussed on the uses of our output, i.e., on the channeling of a larger share of our resources to the expansion and improvement of both the human skills and the physical capital of the country.

A basic component of any program for accelerated economic growth must be investment in the extension of knowledge, the general education of the population, and the training of the labor force. The improvement of technology and the increase of skills go hand-in-hand with ordinary capital formation to increase productive capacity. Their interaction is far more powerful than the sum of their independent effects. Technical advance without modernization of facilities loses much of its potential effect on output, and it has been observed that mere increase of capital without technological progress also has weak effects on productivity. But together they are responsible for the long-term growth of American productive potential.

It is a deeply-held American belief that education is a good thing in itself, both as the foundation stone of equality of opportunity and as an enrichment of everyday life. Continuing education of the labor force also makes a contribution to economic productivity. Literacy has economic, as well as social, value. In a qualitative way, we can easily imagine how hard it would be to operate an advanced industrial economy with a labor force in which the ability to read and to add or divide was a scarce commodity. More quantitatively, one recent study attributes a quarter of the growth-rate of the real national income since 1929 to the increase in the educational level of the labor force. While the United States now educates an unprecedented fraction of its citizens, there is more to be done in improving the amount and the quality of education. There are few activities which contribute in so many ways to strengthening the fabric of American society.

In his special message of February 23 on natural resources, the President announced that the Council would report to him, the Congress, and the public on the status of resource programs in relation to national needs. At the same time he mentioned estimates that by 1980 the Nation's consumption of water would double and of electric power would triple. These, like forests, are renewable resources. But the consumption of metals and other minerals will also increase and the domestic supply of these resources is ultimately fixed. Here wise management must take the form of promoting rational use and developing access to leaner sources of supply. Research and the development of new technology will play a fundamental part in this important aspect of economic growth.

Effective translation of advances in knowledge and technology into advances in the quantity and quality of output requires additional business investment. As noted earlier, the fraction of our GNP devoted to investment in plant and equipment has been declining since 1948. If we choose as a Nation to accelerate our rate of economic growth and productivity increase, we must reverse the tendency of our capital stock to age. This will require an increase in the rate of investment relative to GNP, perhaps beyond the levels of early postwar years. Some of this investment will be for expansion of capacity and some to give effect to technical progress and potential increase in productivity.

The revenue-raising power of the existing Federal tax system can be an important asset in achieving the levels of investment needed for rapid advance in productive capacity. First, the potential high-employment surplus can be used, as discussed above, to finance the desirable Government programs which contribute to the build-up of human capital. Second, it can indirectly increase incentives for private investment by facilitating a policy of relative monetary ease, as noted in the preceding section. Third, it can be placed at the disposal of the economy for investment purposes by the process of debt retirement. When the Federal Government retires debt it, in effect, exchanges cash for an asset which had been a store of wealth for the owners of the debt. These owners then seek other assets to hold, primarily the debt and equity securities of business firms and the bonds of State and local governments. In other words, the debt retirement process channels savings into uses which facilitate investment for economic growth.

In addition, the tax system can be used to provide specific financial incentives for investment. In his Economic Message, the President announced that he would propose a modification of the income tax law to favor investment in plant and equipment. This can be done in such a way as to yield strong incentive effects per dollar of revenue loss. Accompanying measures would restore the revenue loss and improve the fairness of the tax system.

Measures to stimulate business investment directly will contribute to our recovery from the present recession, but that is not their main purpose. All who have confidence in the American economy must look ahead to the day when the slack will be taken up and high levels of output and employment will again be the rule. The full benefit of our decision to supplement increases in consumer demand now with a higher rate of capital expansion and modernization will then be realized.

As noted earlier, these efforts to step up the rate of productivity increases have important implications for our balance of payments position. It is not the rate of increase in hourly wages which is directly relevant to the competitive position of our export and import-competing industries, but rather the movement of unit costs and prices. Wage rates in some industrialized countries have risen further than U.S. wages, but a high rate of productivity increase has held down costs and prices in these countries, with consequent benefit to their foreign trade position. A speeding up of the rate of productivity improvement in the United States would, by the same logic, strengthen the position of American industry in the international economy.

Price Stability

In his Economic Message of February 2, the President said:

We must not as a nation come to accept the proposition that reasonable price stability can be achieved only by tolerating a slack economy, chronic unemployment, and a creeping rate of growth.

Neither will we seek to buy short-run economic gains by paying the price of excessive increases in the cost of living. Always a cruel tax upon the weak, inflation is now the certain road to a balance-of-payments crisis and the disruption of the international economy of the Western World.

The task of reconciling full recovery and accelerated growth with reasonable price stability carries an urgency which justifies the emphatic tone of the President's language. The work of the Joint Economic Committee has been of major importance in extending awareness that inflation in America is not one problem but many, and that there is no single easy formula for achieving the reconciliation we all seek.

As we look ahead to the price problems of the next few years, the following considerations will contribute to a clearer appreciation of the issues:

1. By far the greater part of the postwar inflation occurred in two periods of over-all excess demand—the years 1946–48 and the period of the Korean conflict. If the problem should recur in this form, the

powerful tools of fiscal and monetary policy are available, and will be used, to bring aggregate supply and demand into balance.

2. The inflation of the years 1955–58 cannot be characterized by any single label. Some price and wage increases in those years were delayed reactions to the earlier demand inflations. Others were compounded of temporary excess demand in some sectors, slow response of productive resources to secular shifts in demand, sluggish productivity gains in some industries, and the exertion of market power by some elements of labor and management.

3. The goal of reasonable price stability does not mean that no price should rise. It does mean that price increases for some goods and services, necessitated by smaller-than-average productivity gains or other causes, must be roughly balanced by price reductions of other goods or services, made possible by larger-than-average productivity gains or other factors. Moreover, price level stability is not the equivalent of absolute stability in the official price indexes; as noted in the Report of the Price Statistics Review Committee, which the Joint Economic Committee has just published, many experts believe that the price indexes, by failing to take full account of quality improvement, contain a systematic upward bias.

To create a climate which will reduce the likelihood of a repetition of the 1955–58 experience, public and private policy should focus on several objectives:

First, the forces of competition should be strengthened by the vigorous enforcement of the antitrust laws and by other appropriate means. Some excessive price increases in 1955–58 might not have occurred if market control had not been so strong.

Second, continuing efforts should be made to enlist the cooperation of labor and management in a voluntary program of price and wage restraint. In this connection, the President has appointed an Advisory Committee on Labor-Management Policy which will concern itself, among other things, with actions that may be taken by labor, management, and the public to promote sound wage and price policies.

Third, a higher rate of productivity increase should be sought, not only for the direct benefits which higher productivity will yield, but also because a highly progressive economy is able to absorb steadily rising wage rates into a stable price level. The President's Labor-Management Committee will also seek to achieve agreement on methods of raising productivity.

Fourth, efforts should be made to foresee emerging needs for skilled manpower, to aid in the adaptation of skills to present and prospective demands, and to promote geographical and occupational mobility. For example, because the supply of medical services has not responded adequately to a steady increase in demand, sharply rising costs of medical care have contributed to the increase in consumer prices. In this connection, the President has proposed legislation to support the expansion of medical and dental education facilities and, through a program of scholarships, to increase the number of new doctors and dentists graduated each year. Studies are also under way looking toward the modernization and redirection of the National Vocational Education Act. Programs of this sort, modest though they may be, can increase the resiliency and efficiency of the economic system and strengthen its resistance to price increases.

IV. Summary and Conclusion

As we review the state of the economy and the policies for recovery and growth, these points stand out:

1. The recession itself, while not as severe as the other three postwar recessions, has proceeded steadily since last spring. Current hopes for an economic upturn lie principally in a possible rise in consumer spending aided by the stimulus of the President's programs; the continued upward trend in local, state and Federal government purchases; and some prospect of an assist from inventories within several months.

2. An economic upturn would be only the beginning, not the end, of the solution to our economic problems. The recession followed an incomplete recovery in which the American economy fell substantially short of its potential levels of employment, production and income. Indeed, the gap between what we *are* producing and what we *can* produce reached 8 percent at the end of 1960. Today, it may be even closer to the 10 percent gap that developed at the worst stage of the 1958 recession. Taking up this slack of some $50 billion in economic activity, rather than merely reversing the economic decline, is the real challenge of economic policy in the months ahead.

3. In addition to the problems of recession and slack, we are confronted with a disturbing slowdown in the rate of growth of our national economic potential. The rate at which the stock of the country's capital has been expanded and modernized has slowed down in the face of unused capacity, with a consequent slackening of growth in productivity. Also, we have not made full use of possibilities for increased investment in human capital through education, training, and research.

4. The risk of bad timing of government outlays—in the sense that anti-recession projects may have a delayed impact which will aggravate an inflationary boom—is smaller in 1961 than it has appeared in

any previous postwar recession. Given the continued and stubborn problem of economic slack—and given the less encouraging outlook for the housing sector, which played such a major role in the early phase of the 1958 recovery—one can only conclude that we must not shrink from launching needed projects because of misplaced fears of bad timing.

5. Substantial opportunities exist in the field of monetary policy, debt management and housing credit to contribute to economic recovery and growth. The Federal Reserve and the Treasury are pursuing policies to reduce the cost and increase the flow of long-term credit while keeping short-term interest rates from falling to levels which would lead to further withdrawals of short-term capital. With the support of the general measures to lower the cost of long-term credit, specific steps are being taken to lower mortgage rates and increase the availability of funds to home-builders.

6. The President's programs, which promise substantial support to consumer income and demand, can be a major factor in strengthening the American economy in the months ahead. However, the President, in his February 2 message, stated: "If economic developments in the first quarter of this year indicate that additional measures are needed, I will promptly propose such measures." A further program for economic recovery might consider a speed-up in government construction and related projects, an expansion of housing programs, and tax reduction. Temporary income tax cuts, in particular, provide a fast method for enlarging the private income stream and speeding recovery. At the same time, the temporary nature of such a tax reduction would preserve the basic revenue-raising power of the tax system for later use in financing government programs, retiring debt, and stemming inflation. Whether such additional stimulative measures will be needed depends, as the President has indicated, on further economic developments.

7. In pursuing the expansionary policies required by the serious economic problems we face, we cannot lose sight of the possible impact of those policies on domestic price levels and our balance of payments. We do not accept the gloomy doctrine that economic expansion is inherently inconsistent with reasonable price stability and balance in our international accounts. For example, added investment to stimulate increases in productivity, with consequent reductions in cost, simultaneously serves all three objectives. In addition, the work of the President's Advisory Committee on Labor-Management Policy gives promise of improvement in public and private policy for maintaining price stability.

8. Together with policies to reverse the recession, close the employ-

ment and production gap, and maintain reasonable price stability, it is important to initiate further steps to promote faster economic growth. These would include tax incentives to stimulate business investment and expanded programs in education, training, and research to build up America's human capital.

The foregoing considerations underscore the importance of the economic goals placed before the Nation in the President's February 2 message to Congress:

Realistic aims for 1961 are to reverse the downtrend in our economy, to narrow the gap of unused potential, to abate the waste and misery of unemployment, and at the same time to maintain reasonable stability of the price level. For 1962 and 1963 our programs must aim at expanding American productive capacity at a rate that shows the world the vigor and vitality of a free economy. These are not merely fond hopes, they are realistic goals. We pledge and ask maximum effort for their attainment.

Supplement A: Relationships among Potential Output, Actual Output, and Employment

This Supplement gives a full description of the theoretical and statistical procedures underlying the estimates of potential output and degree of slack reported in the text. Calculations like this are at best hazardous and uncertain and ours do not pretend to be definitive. Work along these lines is proceeding at the Council and elsewhere, and further reports will describe the results.

Table 3 of the text shows the sources of the 8 percent potential increment in output during the last quarter of 1960. In addition to the reduction of unemployment, a rise in output would be accompanied by (a) an increase in the civilian labor force; (b) a rise in hours per man; and (c) a marked increase in output per man-hour.

(a) *Labor Force*—In his testimony to the Joint Economic Committee, February 9, 1961, Ewan Clague, Commissioner of Labor Statistics, showed that the actual labor force has fallen considerably below trend projections during the past 3 years. This shortfall is attributable to the disappointing performance of the economy; many people have stayed out of the labor market although they would take employment if jobs were available. Following Mr. Clague's calculations, we estimate that the labor force associated with capacity output at the end of 1960 would have been higher by 561,000 persons, or 0.8 percent as shown in Table 3.

(b) *Hours*—There has been a desirable secular decline in hours worked per man, as progress has made possible increased voluntary leisure. On the average, in the 1947–59 period, hours per man in the private sector fell by ⅓ of 1 percent per year, while GNP rose at a 3.6

percent annual rate. However, hours per man fell more rapidly when the growth of GNP was below its average. And increases in real output have been associated with relatively small declines, or even rises, in hours per man. The indicated 1.2 percent increment of GNP due to increased hours of work per man is based on the estimate that each one percent difference in output-growth is associated with a difference of 0.14 percent in hours per man, including both overtime and part-time work. The estimate is necessarily tentative and inexact because of the incomplete nature of the economy-wide data on man-hours.

The figure of 0.14 is obtained by fitting a least-squares regression line to annual data for 1947–59. The data are found in the Bureau of Labor Statistics Release (USDL-4155) of June 28, 1960. The variables are percent change in man-hours of work per person employed (Y) and percent change in private nonagricultural output (X), restricted to private nonagricultural output and employment; establishment figures are the source of the man-hour estimates. The fitted line is:

$$Y = -.843 + .142X \qquad (r = .85)$$

According to this relationship, annual hours per man remain constant from one year to the next when output rises by 6 percent. On the other hand, if output declines over a year by 1 percent, man-hours per man will also fall by 1 percent. When the equation is used to compare different possible outputs at the same point in time, it supports the estimate in Table 3.

(c) *Productivity*—The rate of productivity growth in the postwar period has shown a consistent and close relationship to the rate of expansion of output. The economy uses labor more efficiently as it utilizes its productive capacity fully. Recessions produce "on-the-job under-employment." In many firms, a substantial part of the work force is essentially a fixed cost in a period of recession. A manufacturing firm which cuts its production by 10 percent in a recession ordinarily finds it difficult or impossible to curtail significantly its clerical help, its managerial or supervisory personnel, or its sales force. It may also be reluctant to lay off production workers, both to maintain morale and to avoid the expense of hiring and training new labor when business activity recovers.

Just as productivity is retarded by economic slack, large gains in output per man occur with a return toward full utilization of resources. Table A-1 shows the increase in real GNP, employment, and output per employed person for the first year of each of the three postwar cyclical recoveries.

In each expansion, output per man grew by more than its postwar trend. The average gain in the three recovery years is nearly 7 per-

Table A-1
Increase of product per man in three postwar expansions (percent)

Item	1949-IV to 1950-IV	1954-III to 1955-III	1958-II to 1959-II
Rise in real gross national product	13.1	9.5	10.1
Rise in employment	3.6	4.7	3.3
Rise in real gross national product per person employed	9.1	4.5	6.5

Source: Council of Economic Advisers (based on Department of Commerce and Department of Labor data).

cent, while the trend growth in output per man for the entire postwar period is slightly over 2 percent. Reduction in unused capacity is responsible for the extra 5 percent gain in output per man. Translated into a gain of output per man-hour, the five percent increase in output per man is somewhat above the 3.3 percent increment in man-hour productivity shown in Table 3 of the text.

The data for the entire postwar period offer solid confirmation of the relationship between productivity gains and the growth of total production. One piece of evidence is supplied by a statistical estimate derived from quarterly data for real GNP and total civilian employment covering 1947–II to 1960–IV. The variables are percent change in output per person employed (Y), and percent change in real GNP (X). The 55 quarterly observations yield the following relationship:

1) $Y = .02 + .66X$ ($r = .86$)

According to this equation, a rise of 1 percent in output requires an increase in employment of only one-third of 1 percent.

Two further statistical relationships are derived from data on unemployment and real GNP. One of these is shown as Chart 5 of the text above. It relates the ratio of unemployed to the civilian labor force (Y) to the percentage gap in actual output (X), as measured from the 3.5 percent trend line through mid-1955, with quarterly data for 1953 to 1960. The resulting equation is:

2) $Y = 3.72 + .36X$ ($r = .93$)

Here, each extra 1 percent of output is associated with a decline of 0.36 percentage points in the unemployment ratio.

The third statistical relationship is based on data for the change in the percent of the labor force unemployed (Y) and the percentage change in real GNP (X). With 55 quarterly observations from 1947–II to the end of 1960, the estimated regression line is:

3) $Y = .30 - .30X$ ($r = .79$)

The estimated unemployment ratio is lower by 0.3 points for each one percent rise in output.

Equations 1) through 3) all have implications for the rise in man-hour productivity that could be expected to accompany an 8 percent increment in output. To compare these implications directly, certain adjustments are necessary. Equation 1) is given in terms of output per man, and must be amended for the rise in man-hours per man. Equations 2) and 3), which are based on the unemployment ratio, require adjustment for both increases in the labor force and rises in hours per man. With the adjustments, an increase of 8 percent in output would raise productivity as follows:

Equation	Expected percentage rise in output per man-hour
1)	4.2
2)	3.0
3)	3.3

These results differ somewhat but agree in showing a substantial gain in productivity. The 3.3 percent increase used in Table 3 of the text lies near the middle of the alternative estimates.

To summarize, the estimate of the ratio of potential GNP to actual is obtained as the product of the ratios of potential to actual labor force, employment, hours per man and output per man-hour.

Trend Projections of Recent Growth

Table A-2 shows the annual rate of growth of selected magnitudes from the first quarter of 1947 to the last quarter of 1960. It also divides

Table A-2
Annual rates of growth of output and employment (percent per annum)

Item	1947-I to 1960-IV	1947-I to 1953-IV	1953-IV to 1960-IV
Gross national product in constant dollars	3.4	4.3	2.5
Employment	1.1	1.1	1.2
Gross national product per person employed	2.2	3.2	1.3
Civilian labor force	1.3	1.1	1.6

Source: Council of Economic Advisers (based on Department of Commerce and Department of Labor data).

the period into halves, using the last quarter of 1953 as a dividing line. The growth in productivity and output decelerated in the last half of the period while the growth rate of the labor force increased for demographic reasons. The 1.5 percent growth rate of the labor force used in the text is consistent with experience of the last several years. The present trend rate of growth of output per person employed has been taken in the text as 2 percent. This is considerably above recent experience. The low rate of productivity growth in recent years is, in part, attributable to the increasing gap between actual and potential output; but it also, in part, reflects a lower rate of growth of potential output. The close relationship shown in Charts 4 and 5 between the calculated gap and unemployment ratios offers support for the estimate of a 3.5 percent rate of growth in potential output.

Real GNP per person employed rises at a lower rate than output per man-hour in the private sector. With annual data for 1947 to 1959, the annual growth of real GNP per man was 2.5 percent, while gross private product per man-hour rose at a 3.2 percent rate. About half of the difference between the two figures is attributable to the secular decline in hours of work per person employed; the other half is accounted for by output and employment in government. Definitions of government output are such that the productivity gain in the government sector is necessarily negligible.

Supplement B: Unemployment and the Structure of the Labor Force

The question sometimes arises whether the obstinate refusal of the unemployment rate to decline below 5 percent since the end of 1957 is a consequence of long-term "structural" changes in the age, sex, and other composition of the labor force, and not of weakness in aggregate demand. If this were so, it would mean that measures to stimulate the general level of economic activity might fail to get the overall unemployment rate down to tolerable levels. Indeed, as the cyclical component of unemployment vanished, leaving only the "hard core," the result might be inflationary wage increases.

But this argument can be shown to be false. There is little evidence that current unemployment is unusually concentrated in particular compartments of the labor force, whether age, sex, color, marital status, or education. Nor can the current level of unemployment be attributed to certain industry or occupation groups. There is little evidence that current unemployment is primarily a result of unfavorable changes in the labor force. The evidence is that our high over-all rate of unemployment comes from higher unemployment rates group by group, category by category, throughout the labor force.

We begin by looking at the age and sex composition of the unemployed in say, 1957 and 1960. If the "hard core" argument were true, women and older workers ought to be a larger fraction of the unemployed group in the later year. But, as Table B-1 shows, the age and sex distribution of the unemployed is essentially the same in the two years. Indeed, workers in the over-65 age group formed only 3.1 percent of the body of unemployed in 1960 as against 3.8 percent in 1957. There is an approximately compensating increase in the proportion of workers under 24 among the unemployed: 34.2 percent in 1957, 35.0 percent in 1960. As for the breakdown by sex, women were 35.3 percent of the unemployed in 1960 and 35.6 percent in 1957. Clearly there is little or no difference between the two years and what there is does not especially favor the "hard-core" hypothesis.

Another way of looking at the data is shown in Table B-2. The overall unemployment rate was 5.6 percent in 1960, 4.3 percent in 1957, an increase of about 30 percent. We can make a similar calculation for each age-sex category, and observe which ones show a substantially greater-than-30 percent increase in the incidence of unemployment. It turns out that the oldest age groups of both sexes had *below*-average increases in unemployment rate, and the largest increase in incidence was suffered by men in the 24–34 year age group.

When we turn to other labor-force categories, the statistical evidence has similar implications. We can compare unemployment rates by industry (Table B-3) and by occupation (Table B-4) in 1957 and 1960. We find that even in those industries and occupations which have been enjoying secular expansion the incidence of unemployment has increased as much or almost as much as for the whole labor force. In trade, in finance, insurance, and real estate, even in public administration; among professional and technical workers, among managers, officials and proprietors, among white-collar workers in general, unemployment rates have gone up at about the same rate as for other occupations.

To probe more deeply into the effect of labor force changes on unemployment, and to carry the analysis back to 1953, we can perform an experiment. For 1953, 1957 and 1960 we classify the labor force by important demographic or economic characteristics: age, color, marital status, educational attainment, occupation and industry, and in each case we cross-classify by sex. For each year we also have the unemployment rate within each category.

Suppose that in 1960, unemployment rates for each age-sex category had been the same as they were in 1957. The age-sex composition of the 1960 labor force was, however, different from 1957. If we hypothetically apply the 1957 unemployment rates to the actual 1960 labor force, we calculate what 1960 unemployment would have been with the 1957 age-specific unemployment rates. How much of the actual increase in unemployment for the second quarter of 1957 to the second quarter of 1960 is accounted for in this way? The answer is given in the first column of Table B-5. Actual unemployment increased by 933,000. With the 1957 rates and the 1960 labor force, unemployment would have increased by 185,000. This measures the increase in unemployment attributable purely to changes in the age-sex structure of the labor force. Fully 80 percent of the increase is a consequence of increased unemployment rates. Only 20 percent of the increase would have occurred had unemployment rates remained constant at 1957 levels.

The second column of Table B-5 shows what happens when 1960 unemployment rates are applied to the 1957 labor force. The results are broadly similar. About 22 percent of the observed increase in unemployment is attributable to changes in the age-sex composition of the labor force. By far the greater part is a consequence of higher unemployment rates, age-group by age-group.

The third and fourth columns of Table B-5 answer the same question in a comparison of the second quarter of 1953 with the second quarter of 1960. Only between 12 and 22 percent of the two-million increase in unemployment is structural. The rest is cyclical.

Table B-6 puts these answers in terms of unemployment rates. The rate of unemployment increased by 1.14 from 1957 to 1960. Between .09 and .14 of that increase is structural. The remaining increase of 1.00 or 1.05 is cyclical.

Together Tables B-5 and B-6 cover the effects of changes in the age, color, occupational and industrial composition of the labor force. In all cases, the labor force effects are weaker than those for age. The inescapable conclusion is that observed changes in unemployment and unemployment rates are overwhelmingly the result of increases in the category-by-category unemployment rates and only to a minor extent due to structural factors.

Tables B-7 and B-8 repeat the analysis for the factors marital status and educational attainment, and with the same results. Indeed, the observed changes in the educational attainment of members of the labor force would by themselves have reduced unemployment rates between 1953 and 1960, and again between 1957 and 1960.

It must be granted that some structural unemployment will not show up in the data, because older workers and possibly very young workers may leave the labor force in the absence of demand for their services. The 1960 labor force is indeed below trend in the male 14–19 and 65-and-over age classes. A rough calculation suggests that if the "missing" workers were put back in the 1960 labor force, the 1957 rates might account for only another 29,000 of the 1960 unemployed.

We stress that in a test like this the cards are stacked *in favor* of the theory of increasing hard-core unemployment, and still it fails. Any student of the workings of a free enterprise market economy will see this at once. Workers in one age group are after all fairly close substitutes for workers in neighboring age groups. The same is true for the other classifications studied. When supply conditions change, with one group increasing more rapidly than another, market forces will induce some offsetting wage changes. They need not restore the old over-all unemployment rate; the point is that some equilibration occurs in the market. The test we have performed leaves this out of account. It assumes that extra workers in any age-sex class, or occupational group, or other category cannot increase their chances of finding employment by accepting lower wages, or working inconvenient hours, or in any other way. Even so, it appears that changes in the demographic occupational and industrial make-up of the labor force are a minor source of increased unemployment.

What are we left with? We are left with the fact that in 1960, there was more long-term unemployment than in 1957, as shown in Table B-9. In 1960, 24.3 percent of the unemployed were unemployed 15 weeks or more, against 19.1 percent in 1957. Of these, 11.5 percent were unemployed for 27 weeks or more in 1960, against 8.1 percent in 1957. Does this entail that in 1960 more of the unemployed were in fact unemployable? Not at all. Even if spells of unemployment were distributed at random through the labor force, each member subject to the same risks, an increase in the over-all unemployment rate would inevitably show up in a higher average duration of unemployment and a larger number of longer spells of unemployment. The increase in long-term unemployment may simply signify that jobs were harder to get for everyone, not that there is a special class of people called "long-term unemployed" who are increasing in number.

Finally, we turn to a pressing aspect of the problem of cyclical and structural unemployment, the existence of chronically distressed labor markets, or what the Department of Labor calls areas of substantial and persistent labor surplus. These are labor market areas which at any time whose unemployment rates are above 6 percent for other than temporary reasons and have been 50 percent or more above the national average for an extended period of time. In November 1960, the areas in this category, large and small combined, had 7.3 percent of the national labor force and 12.2 percent of the unemployment.

It is noteworthy that over the years the labor force in the major labor surplus areas has been declining, counter to the movement of the national labor force. In the 17 major areas in this classification as of January 1961, the total labor force declined by 6.3 percent in the 7 years from May 1953 to May 1960, while the national civilian labor force was increasing by 11.1 percent. It is not known how much of the decline represents a movement to disguised unemployment in rural areas, or a withdrawal of persons from the labor force because of the lack of job opportunities.

Whatever the economic situation, there will always be areas with above average unemployment rates. And as industries decline because of technological change and shifts in demand, there will inevitably be some areas in which unemployment persists. The important question to answer is whether the magnitude of the distressed-area component of unemployment has been increasing over time, whether this structural aspect of the problem of unemployment is now a larger part of the whole than it once was.

This question is answered in Table B-10. The answer is that the major labor surplus areas always suffer relatively more than the country as a whole when the national unemployment rate rises, but the size of the differential does not appear to have increased since 1953.

The Table refers to the 17 major areas of substantial and persistent labor surplus as of 1961. It shows clearly the relatively greater fluctuation in unemployment rates to which they have been exposed since 1953. These fluctuations themselves show that there is large cyclical unemployment even within the labor surplus areas. For the 17 areas combined Table B-10 gives the percentage by which the unemployment rate in these areas exceeded the national average in each period. These percentages show no tendency to increase over time. The excess was especially high in May 1958, but in May 1960 it fell below what it had been at the previous business cycle peak in May 1957. The extraordinarily high excess in 1958 is largely due to the extremely severe unemployment rate—18.3 percent in the Detroit area in that year; passenger car production fell by about a third from 1957 to 1958. If Detroit is removed from the group of 17 areas, it is seen that the excess unemployment rate for the remaining areas behaves quite uniformly over the period. It was 72 percent, 68 percent and 67 percent in the three business cycle peak periods of May 1953, May 1957 and May 1960. It was 81 percent in May 1954, 89 percent in May 1958, and 81 percent in November 1960. There is no indication that this structural aspect accounts for more of the unemployment problem than it did in the two earlier business cycles.

At the end of this long argument it is worth saying that it is no part of our intention to cry down structural unemployment or explain it away. The problems of younger and older workers, of nonwhite members of the labor force, of the technologically displaced, and of the distressed need to be attacked at the source. But our concern for them ought not to divert our attention from the real cause of weakness in 1961's labor market—and that is inadequate demand.

Table B-1
Unemployment by age and sex, 1957 and 1960

Age and sex	1957		1960	
	Thousands of persons	Percent of total	Thousands of persons	Percent of total
Total unemployment	2,936	100.0	3,931	100.0
Young workers	1,003	34.2	1,373	35.0
14 to 19 years	573	19.5	790	20.1
Male	351	12.0	480	12.2
Female	222	7.6	310	7.9
20 to 24 years	429	14.6	583	14.8
Male	283	9.6	369	9.4
Female	147	5.0	214	5.4
Adult workers	1,931	65.8	2,553	64.9
26 to 64 years	1,820	62.0	2,432	61.9
Male	1,175	40.0	1,593	40.5
Female	645	22.0	839	21.3
65 years and over	111	3.8	121	3.1
Male	83	2.8	96	2.4
Female	28	1.0	25	.6

Detail will not necessarily add to totals because of rounding.
Source: Department of Labor.

Table B-2
Unemployment rates by age and sex, 1957 and 1960

Age and sex	Unemployment rate (percent)[1]		Percentage change
	1957	1960	
Total	4.3	5.6	30
Male	4.1	5.4	32
14 to 19 years	11.3	14.0	24
20 to 24 years	7.8	8.9	14
25 to 34 years	3.3	4.8	46
35 to 44 years	2.8	3.8	36
45 to 54 years	3.3	4.1	24
55 to 64 years	3.5	4.6	32
65 years and over	3.4	4.2	24
Female	4.7	5.9	26
14 to 19 years	10.1	12.9	28
20 to 24 years	6.0	8.3	38
25 to 34 years	5.3	6.3	19
35 to 44 years	3.8	4.8	26
45 to 54 years	3.2	4.2	31
55 to 64 years	3.0	3.4	13
65 years and over	3.4	2.8	− 18

[1]Percent of civilian labor force in each age group who were unemployed.
Source: Department of Labor.

Table B-3
Unemployment rates by industry, 1957 and 1960

Industry	Unemployment rate (percent)[1]		Percentage change
	1957	1960	
Total[2]	4.3	5.6	30
Experienced wage and salary workers	3.9	5.7	46
Agriculture	6.7	8.0	19
Nonagricultural industries	4.5	5.6	24
Mining, forestry, and fisheries	6.3	9.5	51
Construction	9.8	12.2	24
Manufacturing	5.0	6.2	24
Durable goods	4.9	6.3	29
Nondurable goods	5.3	6.0	13
Transportation and public utilities	3.1	4.3	39
Wholesale and retail trade	4.5	5.9	31
Finance, insurance, and real estate	1.8	2.4	33
Service industries	3.4	4.1	21
Public administration	2.0	2.6	30

[1]Percent of civilian labor force in each category who were unemployed.
[2]Includes self-employed, unpaid family workers, and persons without previous work experience not shown separately.
Source: Department of Labor.

Table B-4
Unemployment rates by occupation, 1957 and 1960

Occupation	Unemployment rate (percent)[1]		Percentage change
	1957	1960	
Total	4.3	5.6	30
Professional, technical, and kindred workers	1.2	1.7	42
Farmers and farm managers	.3	.3	0
Managers, officials, and proprietors, except farm	1.0	1.4	40
Clerical and kindred workers	2.8	3.8	36
Sales workers	2.6	3.7	42
Craftsmen, foremen, and kindred workers	3.8	5.3	40
Operatives and kindred workers	6.3	8.0	27
Private household workers	3.7	4.9	32
Service workers, except private household	5.1	6.0	18
Farm laborers and foremen	3.7	5.2	40
Laborers, except farm and mine	9.4	12.5	33

[1]Percent of civilian labor force in each category who were unemployed.
Source: Department of Labor.

Table B-5
Net change in unemployment by age, sex, color, occupation, and industry, selected periods, 1953–60 (thousands of persons)

Characteristic	Second quarter 1953 to second quarter 1960		Second quarter 1957 to second quarter 1960	
	Standardization method I	Standardization method II	Standardization method I	Standardization method II
Actual change (all workers)	2,119	2,119	933	933
Change resulting from change in labor force size and composition by				
Age and sex	249	473	183	221
Color and sex	201	409	124	156
Occupation and sex[1]	129	190	92	108
Industry and sex[2]	198	337	145	153

[1]Data relate to experienced workers in April. Actual changes were 1,577 for 1953–60 and 835 for 1957–60.
[2]Data relate to experienced workers. Actual changes were 1,628 for 1953–60 and 705 for 1957–60.
Source: Department of Labor.

Table B-6
Net change in unemployment rates by age, sex, color, occupation, and
industry, selected periods, 1953–60 (percent)

Characteristic	Second quarter 1953 to second quarter 1960		Second quarter 1957 to second quarter 1960	
	Standardization method I	Standardization method II	Standardization method I	Standardization method II
Actual change (all workers)	2.70	2.70	1.14	1.14
Change resulting from change in labor force size and composition by				
Age and sex	.07	.38	.09	.14
Color and sex	.00	.29	.00	.05
Occupation and sex[1]	− .06	.03	− .01	.01
Industry and sex[2]	.04	.24	.07	.08

[1]Data relate to experienced workers. Actual changes in the rate were 2.03
for 1953–60 and 1.06 for 1957–60.
[2]Data relate to experienced workers. Actual changes in the rate were 2.07
for 1953–60 and 0.86 for 1957–60.
Source: Department of Labor.

Table B-7
Net change in unemployment by marital status and education, selected
periods, 1953–60 (thousands of persons, 14 years of age and over)

Characteristic and change	April 1953 to March 1960		March 1957 to March 1960	
	Standardization method I	Standardization method II	Standardization method I	Standardization method II
Marital status and sex				
Actual change (all workers)	2,419	2,419	1,324	1,324
Change resulting from change in labor force size and composition by marital status and sex	170	331	154	139
	October 1952 to March 1959		March 1957 to March 1959	
Educational attainment and sex				
Actual change (workers 18 years old and over)	2,719	2,719	1,445	1,445
Change resulting from change in labor force size and composition by education attainment and sex	75	85	−13	6

Source: Department of Labor.

Table B-8
Net change in unemployment rates by marital status and education,
selected periods, 1953–60 (percent)

Characteristic and change	April 1953 to March 1960		March 1957 to March 1960	
	Standardization method I	Standardization method II	Standardization method I	Standardization method II
Marital status and sex				
Actual change (all workers)	3.24	3.24	1.77	1.77
Change resulting from change in labor force size and composition by marital status and sex	.01	.24	.09	.07
	October 1952 to March 1959		March 1957 to March 1959	
Educational attainment				
Actual change (workers 18 years old and over)	3.96	3.96	2.11	2.11
Change resulting from change in labor force size and composition by education attainment and sex	−.06	−.04	−.11	−.08

Source: Department of Labor.

Table B-9
Unemployment by color and sex, and duration of unemployment,
1957 and 1960

Duration of unemployment, and color and sex	1957		1960	
	Thousands of persons	Percent of total	Thousands of persons	Percent of total
Total unemployment	2,936	100.0	3,931	100.0
Color and sex				
White	2,350	80.0	3,127	79.5
Male	1,519	51.7	2,032	51.7
Female	832	28.3	1,095	27.9
Nonwhite	585	19.9	804	20.5
Male	374	12.7	508	12.9
Female	211	7.2	295	7.5
Duration				
Less than 5 weeks	1,485	50.6	1,799	45.8
5 to 14 weeks	890	30.3	1,176	29.9
15 weeks and over	560	19.1	956	24.3
15 to 26 weeks	321	10.9	502	12.8
27 weeks and over	239	8.1	454	11.5
Average duration (weeks)	10.4		12.8	

[1]Detail will not necessarily add to totals because of rounding.
Source: Department of Labor.

Table B-10
Cyclical fluctuations of unemployment in the national economy and in major areas of substantial and persistent labor surplus[1]

Labor force and unemployment by area	Unit	May 1953	May 1954	May 1957	May 1958	May 1960	Nov. 1960
National totals							
Civilian labor force	Thousands	63,285	64,425	67,893	68,965	70,667	71,213
Unemployment	Thousands	1,571	3,690	2,715	4,904	3,459	4,031
Unemployment rate	Percent	2.5	5.7	4.0	7.1	4.9	5.7
17 major areas of substantial and persistent labor surplus[2]							
Civilian labor	Thousands	4,138	4,082	4,108	4,156	3,879	3,848
Unemployment	Thousands	133	397	277	633	303	354
Unemployment rate	Percent	3.2	9.7	6.7	15.2	7.8	9.2
Percentage excess over national rate	Percent	28	70	68	114	45	61
Detroit							
Civilian labor force	Thousands	1,523	1,499	1,528	1,528	1,403	1,391
Unemployment	Thousands	20	132	104	280	99	102
Unemployment rate	Percent	1.3	8.8	6.8	18.3	7.1	7.3
Pittsburgh							
Civilian labor force	Thousands	962	935	924	973	948	943
Unemployment	Thousands	26	78	35	109	71	109
Unemployment rate	Percent	2.7	8.3	3.8	11.2	7.5	11.6
16 major areas without Detroit[1]							
Civilian labor force	Thousands	2,650	2,583	2,580	2,628	2,476	2,457
Unemployment	Thousands	113	265	173	353	204	252
Unemployment rate	Percent	4.3	10.2	6.7	13.4	8.2	10.3
Percentage excess over national rate	Percent	72	81	68	89	67	81

[1]There are also 83 smaller areas of substantial and persistent labor surplus having in November 1960 a total labor force of 2,393,000, total unemployment of 276,000 and rate of unemployment of 11.5 percent.
[2]January 1961 classification. Data are for major mainland areas; exclude 3 areas on Puerto Rico.
Source: Department of Labor.

January 1961 Economic Report of the President and the Economic Situation and Outlook

MONDAY, APRIL 10, 1961
CONGRESS OF THE UNITED STATES,
JOINT ECONOMIC COMMITTEE,
Washington, D.C.

REPLIES OF THE COUNCIL OF ECONOMIC ADVISERS (WALTER W. HELLER, CHAIRMAN; KERMIT GORDON, JAMES TOBIN) TO QUESTIONS SUBMITTED BY THE HONORABLE THOMAS B. CURTIS

Question 1: "On page 19, it is stated that the President has expressed his intention to 'return to the spirit as well as to the letter of the Employment Act of 1946,' and to have the economic reports 'deal not only with the state of the economy but with our goals for economic progress.' The use of the verb 'return' presupposes that there had been an abandonment of the spirit of the Employment Act.

"Will you clarify this point? Just what is your conception of the 'spirit' of the act; what is the basis for assuming that your conception is the 'spirit' of the act if it goes beyond the 'words' of the act? Wherein do you feel that this spirit had been abandoned in the past?"

The Employment Act of 1946 specifically requires that the President's Economic Report set forth "the levels of employment, production, and purchasing power obtaining the United States and such levels needed to carry out the policy declared in section 2 [which pledges the Federal Government to promote maximum employment, production and purchasing power]." Since 1953 the Economic Report has not set forth the "levels needed." Chairman Arthur F. Burns argued in a statement to this committee in January 1955 that the act requires no more than "as good a specification of objectives, whether in terms of numbers or otherwise, as can be made." Whether or not this is a proper interpretation of the letter of the act, we believe that the spirit of the act is better served by quantitative estimates of the capabilities of the economy. These estimates, although subject to inevitable imprecision, are yardsticks against which the administration, Congress, and the public can appraise the current performance of the economy and consider future policies and plans.

Question 2: "On pages 19–20, it is stated, 'Further, the President has stated that we should not "treat the economy in narrow terms but in terms appropriate to the optimum development of the human and natural resources of this country, of our productive capacity and that of the free world."' There is an implication in this statement that the past treatment has been 'narrow.' Will you clarify this point? Where in the past has the economy been treated in narrow terms and in what particular specific ways is the Council now broadening the treatment?"

The quoted statement was made by President-Elect Kennedy at his press conference of December 23, 1960. He went on to say that he would look to the Council for advice "in the major fields of economic and social policy with which the administration will be concerned." At a later point in the same statement President-Elect Kennedy indicated that he might ask the Council to undertake new responsibilities in such fields as natural resources, consumer problems, and manpower.

The President evidently envisaged the Council's advisory role to embrace new fields of interest, which lay outside the range of major concerns and assignments of previous Councils.

Question 3: "On page 20, it is stated, "The fourth recession has thus far been shallower than its predecessors. But the gentleness of the current decline is small consolation, because the descent began from relatively lower levels. The previous recovery was abortive, and the recession began with an unemployment rate which earlier recessions did not reach for 3 to 6 months.'

"What is meant by 'began from relatively lower levels,' relative to what? Lower levels of what? What is the basis for the use of the adjective 'abortive'? If these statements are based solely upon the model set forth later in the statement in respect to attainment of economic capacity, merely so state, but if there are other bases for the statement please set them forth."

The statements regarding the "abortive" character of the previous recovery and the "relatively lower levels" from which the recession of 1960 began are based on the evidence presented in table 2 regarding unemployment, and on the estimate—shown graphically in chart 4—that even in the peak quarter output was 4.4 percent below potential. Although recovery from the trough of April 1958 proceeded briskly for 1 year, it did not carry the economy to satisfactory levels after the steel strike of 1959.

Question 4: "On pages 21–22, it is stated that disposable income grew at an annual rate of $8.9 billion more than GNP and reference is made to inventory declines. Then it is stated that, "The prospects of reversal of the recession in the first two quarters of this year depend, therefore, on modest advances in components of demand other than inventory change.' How does this jibe with later proposals to increase disposable income at a faster rate as an anti-recession measure? Doesn't this suggest that disposable income is not a basic factor in the recent recession? Contrary to the suggestions in the next paragraph which refers to the need of 'increases in consumer spending?' Do you distinguish between the terms 'disposable income' and 'consumer spending?' Isn't it true that the present level of living of the bulk of our people has made these two terms no longer interchangeable, if indeed they ever were?"

The course of disposable income was not, the Council agrees, a basic factor in the recession of 1960–61. Indeed, as the cited passage of the Council's statement indicates, the maintenance of disposable income has moderated the recession. Even though the recession cannot be attributed to a decline of consumer spending, an increase in consumer spending—induced by a rise of disposable income—can contribute to recovery. Recovery does not require that each kind of spending rise as much, and only as much, as it fell in recession. One kind of spending can substitute for another. It is the aggregate that counts. In a growing economy aggregate spending must rise more in each upswing than it fell in the preceding downswing. There is no inconsistency in according to inventory decumulation a major role in the recession while advocating measures to increase consumer spending as an aid to recovery.

The terms disposable income and consumer spending are by definition not interchangeable. The difference between them is personal saving. Personal saving generally runs at a rate in the neighborhood of 7 percent of disposable income. The relationship of consumer spending and saving to disposable income is close but certainly not invariant. There is no surer way of inducing a rise in consumer spending than putting more income at the disposal of consumers, especially consumers whose spending has been limited by unemployment or other financial reverses.

Question 5: "On page 24 it is stated that the personal saving ratio of the last half of 1960 was 'abnormally high.' It was unquestionably high, relatively, but why do you regard this as 'abnormal'? This rate has occurred in the immediate past and is less than in some other industrial countries. If it is 'abnormal' for 1960, do you believe that that abnormality might become the norm? Do you believe that this rate of saving is economically bad or good? Would you encourage this high rate of saving through public monetary and fiscal policies, or would you discourage this rate?"

The term 'abnormally high' was used in regard to the personal saving ratio in the second half of 1960 to mean unusually high in U.S. postwar experience. The average for the years 1947–60 is 6.9 percent; in 1960, the ratio was 7.5 percent, and in the second half of the year 7.9 percent. Perhaps personal saving will return promptly to a more usual ratio to disposable income. Perhaps the personal saving ratio will remain high in 1961 or longer. No one can be sure at this time.

No value judgment about the personal saving ratio was intended by the use of the word "abnormally," and the Council offers none now. The personal saving ratio is the result of decisions freely made by the Nation's 53 million households. The personal saving ratio is—in the short run at any rate—a fact of life to which the Government's economic stabilization policy must adapt rather than a quantity than can be directly influenced.

Strength in consumer spending would be a welcome stimulus to our economy, which is suffering from inadequate demand. But a low saving ratio is not a sine qua non of recovery if investment or public expenditure expand sufficiently.

The higher the personal saving ratio, the more the burden of restoring and maintaining full employment falls on investment demand. If investment demand is to expand sufficiently, both the tax system and monetary policy must provide adequate incentives to investment. There are advantages to a sustained prosperity of this kind. A high-investment economy is likely to be a high-growth economy. High personal saving can contribute powerfully to economic growth, but only if the thrift of the population is translated into real capital formation and not into unemployment.

Question 6: "On page 24, it is stated that the financial position of the State and local governments is 'deteriorating.' What is the basis for this statement which is certainly contrary to the fact of the rapid development of State and local expenditures vis-a-vis Federal governmental expenditures in recent years? (It would be helpful if the hypotheses which become the basis for important conclusions were set forth straightforwardly as hypotheses instead of in the form of participle clauses as uncontroverted premises upon which other conclusions are based.)"

The main evidence for the deteriorating financial position of the State and local governments is the growth of their deficits and their debts. These deficits (calculated on national income and product account) rose from an annual average of $0.4 billion in the period 1948–50 to an average of $2 billion in 1958–60. The Commerce Department projects a deficit of $3 billion for 1961.

The total debt of States and localities rose from $18.5 billion in 1948 to $67 billion in 1960.

A State or local government is constrained in its ability to borrow by the market's evaluation of its debt-carrying capacity as based on its revenue-raising possibilities. Furthermore, many of these governmental units are subject to constitutional debt limitations. There is a serious danger that their increasingly difficult debt situation, together with their inability to increase their tax revenues sufficiently, will act to choke off some of the expenditure they urgently need to make.

The "rapid development of State and local expenditures," far from contradicting our assertion of growing financial weakness, is a prominent cause of that weakness. The States and localities have very properly responded to the need for better educational and hospital facilities, urban redevelopment, mass transportation, etc. They have not been able to afford to do enough in the past, and the needs will grow in the future.

At the same time, their revenues do not grow with GNP to the same degree as do Federal revenues. Moreover, a State or locality is inhibited from imposing a new or increased tax by the fear that economic activity will flee its borders, thus complicating its revenue problem.

Question 7: "The premise for much of the economic philosophy advanced in the testimony seems to be an alleged gap between actual and potential output of our economy. Is this a fair statement?"

The economic philosophy underlying the Council's testimony is independent of the gap. But the diagnosis of present economic difficulties advanced in the testimony is indeed based on our finding that actual output falls short of potential output.

Question 8: "(a) Do you recognize any limitations to the gross national product as a meaningful series of statistics in measuring economic potential? If so, please set forth what these limitations are and what we must guard against in relying upon GNP in obtaining a meaningful picture of our economy. (b) Specifically, do you believe that GNP is valuable primarily as a long-range measure of economic growth and economic capabilities? (c) If not, how do you take account of economic mistakes which become just as much a part of the GNP of a particular year as economic activities that prove to be fundamentally sound? (d) Do you recognize a difference in an economy based upon war and one based upon peace, particularly as measured in terms of GNP? (e) Do you recognize a difference between an economy that is becoming industrialized and one that has been industrialized for some time in using GNP as a method of measuring the further advancements of both economies? (f) Do you recognize a difference between an industrialized economy that has had its industrial plant largely destroyed by war and is rebuilding with an industrialized economy that has not had this experience in using GNP as a method of measuring the further advancements of the two different kinds of economy? (g) Do you believe that as an industrial economy develops and advances technologically that there is a shift from manufacturing to service and distribution? (h) If so, do you recognize a limitation in the use of GNP as a measurement of economic development to reflect this shift? (i) Do you believe that the U.S. economy is experiencing a noticeable shift in economic emphasis from manufacturing to service and distribution? (j) Do you believe that money spent in research and development and in education is measured with the same weighting that money spent on capital expansion such as more steel capacity by the GNP statistical series?"

(a) Gross national product, like any aggregative index of economic activity, is an imperfect measuring rod. Most of its limitations are inherent in trying to describe a complex economic system by a single number. Inevitably much that is important and interesting is left out. Other difficulties and limitations stem from:

1. The very concept of production (e.g., the omission of leisure), the exclusion of many nonmarket activities (e.g., the services of housewives), and the necessity of imputing values to other goods and services that do not pass through the market (e.g., the services of owner-occupied homes).

2 The often tenuous distinction between final and intermediate output (in particular the treatment of Government expenditures, the replacement of plant and equipment, and research and development expenditures).

3. Questions of valuation and price correction, and the related problems posed by product changes.

Despite these difficulties, we believe, in common with the overwhelming majority of economists, that GNP corrected for price change is the best over-all measure of economic activity that we possess.

(b) Each of the difficulties mentioned above becomes more substantial as the time scale of comparisons is lengthened. For this reason GNP, like any summary measure, is a safer guide to short-range comparisons than to very long range ones.

(c) A basic principle underlying GNP computations is that goods and services are valued at market prices. The economist does not presume to substitute his judgments about the relative worth of things for the market's judgments. Expenditures which, with the advantage of hindsight, may be seen to be misdirected are nevertheless included in the national product. So are expenditures which yield greater benefits than are foreseen on the market. This problem does not seem to us to be a serious one to the user of GNP data—first, because we do not believe "mistakes" of valuation to be quantitatively large, and second, because, unless their magnitude changes markedly from year to year, comparisons over time will not be affected.

(d) There are several differences between wartime and peacetime economies with respect to GNP measurement:

1. Military goods are not always priced on a free market, and price control and rationing may be introduced even for civilian goods. For this reason the problem of appropriate valuation may be especially severe in wartime.

2. Military commodities are essentially destructive or defensive and do not contribute to social welfare in the same way as ordinary peacetime goods and services. They should not therefore be omitted from GNP. After all, economic output is not all there is to social welfare, and GNP purports only to measure economic output. Moreover, even in peacetime we count regrettable necessities, like police departments, as contributions to national output.

3. In normal peacetime conditions a strong case can be made that net national product, which makes proper allowance for wear and tear of durable equipment, is a more appropriate measure of aggregate output than GNP. It is not often used because of the unreliability of estimates of capital consumption. But in wartime, when the short sprint is of prime importance, it may

be desirable to consume capital in order to maximize military potential. In this case GNP is the appropriate measure.

4. In the Second World War, one source of the rapid rise in GNP was the extraordinary increase in the labor force and in hours worked, in response to the national emergency.

(e) The two most important distinctions between industrializing and already industrialized economies with respect to the use of GNP are these:

1. The relation between NNP and GNP will differ. The larger and older capital stock of an industrialized country makes it necessary to charge a larger share of GNP to capital consumption.

2. A country becoming industrialized will normally experience a transfer of many productive activities from the nonmarket to the market sector of the economy, and this will distort GNP comparisons over time. For already advanced economies this source of difficulty does not seem to be very large.

(f) War destruction and reconstruction offer no fundamental problems to the user of GNP statistics. They have, of course, important economic effects, but these are reflected in the size, composition and rate of growth of GNP and could be analyzed in normal ways.

(g) and (i) It is often claimed that, as an industrial economy develops, there is a shift from manufacturing to service and distribution. The facts in the United States since 1929 are far from clear. It is certain that during that period the part of the population engaged in agriculture declined sharply and the part engaged in government and government enterprises increased sharply. Eliminating these two sectors from the total, one can roughly divide the remaining industries into a commodity-producing group and a distribution-and-service group. Between 1929 and 1953 the first group increased while the second decreased (in terms of fraction of persons engaged), and between 1953 and 1959 the reverse was true. Between 1929 and 1959 there is almost no difference in the distribution of the working population between the two groups. The shift to services since 1953 may represent a new long-run trend, or it may simply reflect the development of general slack in the economy.

(h) The great merit of GNP as a measure of overall economic activity is that it is not affected by a shift of final demand from one kind of output to another. Equal market values are counted equally in all sectors of the economy. This is not true of other production indicators, which emphasize particular sectors—e.g., the industrial production index. To the extent that there is a shift to services, the major problem with respect to GNP arises from the public sector, which is increasing in importance. Since the services of Government are not generally sold at a market price, the convention has been adopted of measuring their value by their cost. Any increase in the productivity of general government is thus underestimated. It follows that the rate of growth of an economy in which general government is growing relative to market output is somewhat understated by the rate of growth of GNP.

In addition, as already noted, it is sometimes argued that much of government expenditures on goods and services consist of intermediate rather than final uses. The standard examples are the commercial use of roads and the provision of police protection for business property. If it were true that the advance of productivity is inherently slower in service than in manufacturing, the shift to private services since 1953 might account in part for the indicated slowdown in growth.

The facts are difficult to disentangle. The staff of this committee has produced figures which show that between 1947 and 1953 productivity increased in the service sector at an average annual rate of 1.8 percent and in trade at 2.4 percent. Between 1953 and 1958 (1957 for trade) these rates fell to 1.5 percent and 1.4 percent; and between 1955 and 1958 to 0.8 percent and 0.1 percent respectively.

Before we leap to any interpretation of these facts we should note that there was a parallel reduction in the rate of productivity increase within manufacturing. Between 1947 and 1953 manufacturing productivity rose by 3.3 percent per year and from 1953 and 1957 the rate of improvement fell to 1.9 percent per year. Moreover, it is possible that the poor performance of the service and trade sectors after 1955 does not reflect an inherent sluggishness in productivity. Instead it may be that general weakness in the economy released workers from relatively high-productivity employment in all sectors and left them to be absorbed in low-productivity and low-wage employment in services and trade.

Since the shift in resources to services after 1953 was small, and since the productivity growth differential was also small in those years, this factor cannot account for more than a very small fraction of the slowdown in overall growth of GNP.

(j) There is indeed an anomaly in the treatment both of education and of research and development in the national accounts. Both types of expenditures are in large part a kind of capital formation, indeed an important kind of capital formation; yet both are treated as current expenditures. Public education, as noted, enters into the measured GNP simply at cost. Private research and development expenditures, except for buildings and equipment, are treated as current expenses by business firms. They enter into GNP only indirectly as they are reflected in the value of final goods and services, but do not themselves appear as final product. Since the volume of research and development expenditures is growing more rapidly than GNP, the result is to underestimate somewhat the rate of growth of national product. But since the absolute volume of such outlays is small relative to GNP, the amount of the underestimate cannot be great.

Question 9. "Do you agree that the CPI has an upward bias resulting from the difficulties in measuring increases in quality and choice of goods and services? If so, do you not believe that the adjustment of GNP in 1960 or the current year prices will reflect this bias and so not give us an accurate a picture of real GNP for the particular year as GNP unadjusted?"

The Council said in the March 6 statement: ". . . as noted in the report of the Price Statistics Review Committee, which the Joint Economic Committee has just published, many experts believe that the price indexes, by failing to take full account of quality improvement, contain a systematic upward bias." Unless the extent of the bias varies widely from year to year, it will not seriously distort comparisons of rates of growth. The Consumer Price Index is not used to "deflate" GNP for price change. This "deflation" is done by special price indexes with appropriate weights, one for each major GNP component. These indexes are subject to the same sources of upward bias as the CPI. But it is certain that this bias cannot be so large or so erratic that undeflated GNP would be a better measure of changes in real output. Genuine changes in the general price level are often very substantial and vary widely from year to year. In common with nearly all economists, we believe that deflated GNP gives a more accurate picture of real output and its changes than current-price GNP.

Question 10: "In the model to demonstrate potential output you refer to unemployment as 'wasted economic potential.' This seems to ignore completely the economic forces (capital formation, business organization, trained labor force, research and development, invention and discovery) that are necessary in order to give meaningful employment to workers. I would appreciate your comments upon this observation and I would ask that these observations be made in context with the manner in which you have built upon this model of so-called unused potential. Do you agree that in a growing economy there will always be an incident of unemployment? If so, why do you not adjust for this when you build upon unused potential in your model?"

Unemployment at any time on the scale that now exists in the United States is "wasted economic potential." In addition, at the present time there exists substantial unemployed capital in the form of excess capacity in many industries throughout the country. For example, in February 1961 overall metal production was running at only 55 percent of capacity, as against 72 percent in May at the peak of the current business cycle, and an average 99 percent in 1951. In textiles the comparable figures are 70 percent, 84 percent, and 96 percent, respectively, while in pulp, paper, and paperboard these figures are 82 percent, 87 percent, and 90 percent. Unemployment and excess capacity together constitute therefore a major economic problem. We have estimated that the current gap between actual production and potential is of the order of $50 billion. This estimate is based not only on the visible evidence of unemployment and excess capacity, but also on our confidence—reinforced by the experience of previous recoveries—that the necessary business organization and know-how would be forthcoming if aggregate demand were sufficient.

Question 11: "Do you believe that the faster an economy grows the greater is the incidence of unemployment?"

This hypothesis is not borne out by recent U.S. economic history. Years in which gross national product grows at a good rate tend to be years in which unemployment declines. Years of increasing unemployment tend to be years in which gross national product is stable or declining.

Rapid technological progress tends directly to increase employment in the production of new plant and equipment. At the same time, rapid technological progress which causes major shifts in the pattern of production will often generate temporary unemployment in particular industries, localities, or skills. This unemployment may become chronic if the economy is not growing rapidly enough to reap the full gains of technological advance. So long as overall demand for labor remains strong, the displaced workers will be absorbed into areas of expanding employment. Public programs to facilitate labor mobility can make an important contribution to the process by which the labor force adapts to dynamic growth.

Question 12: "Do you believe that as an economy grows technologically the need for unskilled and semiskilled workers becomes less? If so, why do you not relate the high rate of unemployment which exists among the unskilled and semiskilled, the new entrant and the old entrant to this rapid technological growth in our society?"

It is clear that the composition of employment and the labor force has been shifting against unskilled and semiskilled workers. But in our earlier pre-pared testimony, we were dealing with changes in the rate of unemployment in recent years, and we found evidence that recent increases in the incidence of unemployment among unskilled and semiskilled workers were not out of line with the experience of other occupational groups. During the whole postwar period (and in 1940 as well) unskilled and semiskilled workers have experienced relatively higher rates than other occupational groups. That is not a new phenomenon. Moreover, we believe that the pattern of labor sup-ply can in time, and in favorable economic environment, adapt to the pattern of demand. If the demand for skilled and white-collar labor were more active, more transfer into these groups would occur. In a thriving economy, struc-tural decreases in employment are not the same thing as increases in struc-tural unemployment.

Question 13: "I have suggested (speech, February 17, 1961, pp. 5–9) that the problems we experience in the area of unemployment, far from being those resulting from a tired, sluggish, or sick economy, are primarily the result of an economy that has been growing so fast we have growing pains. I am enclosing a copy of that speech. I would appreciate your observations on this aspect of the speech."

We certainly do not believe that the U.S. economy is tired, sluggish, or sick. Its potential is enormous, but we cannot be satisfied with our recent economic performance. It is impossible to accept current levels of unemploy-ment as simply the growing pains of a rapidly growing economy because there is no independent evidence that the economy is growing rapidly. Prog-ress in invention, science, and management skills do not themselves consti-tute rapid growth. They represent a great potential for growth, which it is the responsibility of private initiative and public policy to realize. Otherwise we will have growing pains without growth.

Rapid growth both creates, and helps to solve, problems of economic ad-justment and adaptation. Dynamic growth inevitably entails redundancy of some skills and specialized capital, while at the same time creating demands for new skills and new capital. The long-term growth record of the American economy is evidence that we have solved these problems in the past, and we are confident that we can continue to solve them in the future.

Question 14: "The Chairman of the Federal Reserve Board testified before the Joint Economic Committee and he gave a picture of the economics behind the relatively high incidence of unemployment that many people, including myself, thought was at variance with the one expressed in your testimony. Since then, Mr. Martin has submitted a further statement made after he had a chance of reviewing yours. He states, 'It seems to me that the apparent differences with my testimony (and yours) are mainly ones of definition and emphasis.' With this I agree and I think, far from reconciling the differences, Mr. Martin's further statement confirms the differences in both emphasis and definition to be fundamental differences. Your statement is very positive. On page 30 you state, 'Some have attributed the growth of unemployment in recent years to changing characteristics of the labor force rather than to de-ficiencies in total demand. . . . Expansion of overall demand, it is argued, will not meet this problem; it can only be met by educating, restraining, and relocating unsuccessful jobseekers.

"'The facts clearly refute this explanation of the rise of unemployment over the last 8 years.'

"We are primarily interested in examining into the problems of unemployment so that we can apply the proper remedies. Your analysis suggests expanding overall demand (which I believe you regard as being synonymous with disposable income, which I do not). Mr. Martin clearly does not recognize this as a method of attacking structural unemployment.

"I would be pleased to have your comments."

Our statement and our calculations demonstrated that recent increases in the unemployment rate at cyclical peaks could not correctly be attributed to increases in the extent of structural unemployment. We know of no evidence that contradicts this conclusion and the analysis that supports it.

The Council's statement recognized the importance of structural unemployment. We stated, as did Chairman Martin, that policy should move ahead simultaneously against structural unemployment and against unemployment stemming from weak aggregate demand. We pointed out, as did Chairman Martin, that expansionary fiscal and monetary policy would create an environment in which the pull of jobs in the growing sectors of the economy would attract workers from the declining sectors and areas. Thus, general prosperity contributes to the effectiveness of policies aimed specifically at structural unemployment. Our March 6 statement said:

"Measures to improve the mobility of labor to jobs and jobs to labor, to better our educational facilities, to match future supplies of different skills and occupations to the probable pattern of future demands, and to improve the health of the population—these are and should be high on the agenda of national policy. But they are no substitute for fiscal, monetary, and credit policies for economic recovery. Adjustments that now seem difficult, and unemployment pockets that now seem intractable, will turn out to be manageable in an environment of full prosperity."

The 4-percent unemployment rate we mentioned as a clearly attainable target allows plenty of room for the unemployment stemming from shifting demands and technical progress. The unemployment rate is close to 7 percent now. As recently as February 1960 it was 4.8 percent. A rise in the unemployment rate by 2 percent of the labor force in the short space of a year can scarcely be attributed to basic changes in the structure of the economy and of the labor force. It is the result of the recession, i.e., of weakness in overall demand. Nor can all of the 5 percent unemployment of early 1960 be accepted as hard-core structural unemployment; there is independent evidence that the economy was then operating short of reasonable capacity.

We certainly do not view 4 percent unemployment as a rockbottom minimum. As policies to improve the mobility and the skill composition of the labor force take effect, it will be possible in sustained prosperity to hold the rate of unemployment somewhere below that figure.

Finally, we do not regard overall demand as synonymous with disposable income. Overall demand is the aggregate of spending by government, business, and households. Consumer spending, which is related to disposable income in the manner explained in No. 4, is only one component, though the single largest component, of overall demand.

Question 15: "On page 42, it is stated, 'Monetary policy must at all times be flexible and interest rates must be higher in booms than in recessions.' I am puzzlied by the verb 'must be' in lieu of 'will be.' 'Must be' implies some force other than economic forces. Is it your opinion that the Federal Government can set interest rates and that political force is sufficiently powerful to control the economic forces here at play?"

Interest rates are determined by supplies and demands in a set of interconnected markets for loans and securities. The Federal Government— through the Treasury and the Federal Reserve—plays an important role in Government securities markets, determining through its public debt and open market operations the outstanding supplies of securities of various types and maturities. By these operations the Government, if it wishes, can within broad limits offset or reinforce changes in private supplies and demands in Government securities markets and thus affect the interest rates which these markets determine. Interest rates and asset prices in other money and capital markets are linked, some very closely and others quite indirectly, with interest rates on Government securities. The passage cited expresses our view that Government influence in the securities markets should not be carried to the point of eliminating the cyclical movement of interest rates that would follow from fluctuations of private supplies and demands.

Question 16: "On pages 43 and 44 two adjectives are used in relation to the homebuilding sector of our economy which suggest that it is the Council's opinion that the tapering off of homebuilding activity is not a reflection of our economy catching up with demand but something else (undefined). On page 43, it is stated, 'It is difficult to accept the view that the housing market is so glutted. * * *' On page 44 a sentence starts out, 'In the face of a depressed level of homebuilding activity * * *.' What are the Council's views of the homebuilding industry? Do we have less consumer demand? Is supply catching up with demand? It is dangerous to talk about a normal economic phenomenon as if it were 'depressed' simply because it has declined relatively, for valid reasons, unless this is so. It is unfair to refer to those who believe this to be the fact as having said, 'the market is so glutted.' The rate of home building is still high and will continue to be relatively high, though we may count upon it to continue to decline from this high point if consumer demand is indeed being met. What is the view of the Council?"

In referring to the depressed level of homebuilding activity, the Council had in mind the fact that the rate of new private housing starts at the end of 1960 was at a low level when measured against the record of the preceding decade.

Among the factors which help to account for the recent weakness in residential construction were the high level of building activity in 1958–59; the accumulation of inventories of unsold new houses in 1960; and a temporary decline in the expected rate of family formation. In addition, residential construction has been further depressed by high interest rates on mortgages. These factors were cited in the Council's March 6 statement, as explanations of the low level of residential construction at the turn of the year.

While the housing deficit of the 1930's and the war years has been largely filled by postwar construction, and while some traditional sectors of housing demand show signs of continuing weakness, we do not interpret these facts as decreeing a bleak prospect for residential construction. The urgent and clearly visible needs of millions of lower income families for improved housing can be translated into effective demand as the employment situation improves, as economic growth raises incomes, and as homebuilders adapt their production to newly emerging demands.

Lower interest rates can also make an important contribution to an improvement in housing activity. As we stated in our March 6 testimony, "It is difficult to accept the view that the housing market is so glutted that it would not respond to lower monthly financing costs."

Question 17: "On page 45, it is stated, 'welcome as the built-in stabilizers are when the economy contracts, they are a mixed blessing when it expands.' I would suggest that this phenomenon, with which I agree, has more to do with the nature of 'recoveries' than that suggested by the earlier language in this statement, which refers to the previous recovery as 'abortive.' Would you comment upon the built-in stabilizer effects on the present recovery and the past recoveries, in this light."

We agree that built-in stabilizers temper the pace of economic recovery just as they moderate recession. As chart 7 of our March 6 statement shows, the Federal Government fiscal position changed sharply from net deficit to surplus at the beginning of 1960. This change represented partly the effects of built-in stabilizers and partly deliberate policy decisions. This was one of the factors in the premature end of the recovery in early 1960.

Question 18: "On page 46 it is suggested that 'full recovery . . . would generate substantially more revenue than is required by the President's proposed programs, thus leaving a generous margin for retirement of debt and restraint of inflation.' Since this date, the President's budgets have been sent to the Congress. Mr. Bell, the Director of the Bureau of the Budget, has testified before this committee. Obviously, even with full recovery, we will have deficit financing for fiscal year 1961 and fiscal year 1962; without 'full' recovery (whatever that may be), both years will reach new highs of economic endeavor measured by the GNP indicator. Will you comment?"

In our testimony, the term "full recovery" was used specifically to mean a rise in GNP to its potential level, implying a reduction of unemployment to the 1955–56 rate of 4 percent of the labor force. We estimate potential GNP, thus defined, to be $562 billion for calendar 1961. With that level of economic activity, budget receipts for fiscal 1962 would be about $92 billion, far above the $81.4 billion of revenue now anticipated. There is a difference of about $50 billion between potential GNP for 1961 and the GNP underlying current revenue estimates. At potential GNP, corporate profits would be higher by about $13 billion and personal income would exceed the expected level by some $35 billion. As a result, corporate income taxes would yield an additional $6 billion and individual income taxes would be more than $4 billion higher. These are estimates, not precise figures; but even allowing for a large margin of error in our estimates of potential GNP, corporate profits, and personal income, the statement which you quote is correct. With a 4-percent unemployment rate, revenues would substantially exceed the $84.3 billion level of prospective expenditures for fiscal 1962.

The prospective deficit for fiscal 1962 is attributable to slackness in the economy. We estimate that a balanced budget would be achieved if GNP for calendar 1961 were $526 billion, with a prospective unemployment rate of nearly 6 percent. Even so incomplete a recovery is more than can now be reasonably foreseen in 1961. We agree with your expectation that GNP will reach record highs during fiscal years 1961 and 1962. But we call attention to the disturbing fact that the average unemployment rate during fiscal 1961 will be the highest of any postwar fiscal year. Because of the growth in labor force and productivity, output must grow for unemployment to stand still. A record output can be associated with record unemployment. For this reason, we have emphasized that the economic performance of the United States must be evaluated in relation to its capacity to produce. By this standard, fiscal year 1962 will start from a depressed base. Even with the stimulus provided by the administration's antirecessionary programs, it will take time to achieve full recovery.

Question 19: "In light of anticipated deficit financing and a requirement which indicates the need for the public marketing of $8 billion additional Federal bonds in the next 2 years, will this not create inflationary pressures that cannot be controlled under the present state of our economy? What will be the impact of 2 years of deficit financing in 2 prosperous years in respect to our balance of payments abroad and the psychological effect this fiscal policy will have on the nations abroad?"

Deficits do not, in and of themselves, cause inflationary pressures and balance-of-payments difficulties. A high and expanding level of economic activity may, in the absence of vigilant preventive measures, have these unwelcome by-products. But they are byproducts of the expansion itself, not of its sources. Budget deficits will give rise to these problems only to the extent that the budget contributes to general economic recovery. And, if the same degree of general recovery occurs from exuberant private demands, without help from budget deficits, the same pressures on prices and on the balance of payments will arise. In the present situation of the American economy, if one believes that expansion generated by budget deficits would result in unacceptable risks of inflation and external imbalance, he should logically favor measures to discourage forces of expansion in the private economy as well.

The administration is seeking a vigorous and complete recovery, and is taking steps aimed at preventing expansion of demand from wasting itself in inflationary pressure and deterioration of the balance of payments.

It is not the relation between Federal receipts and outlays, but the relation between total public and private spending and aggregate economic capacity, that determines the strength of inflationary pressures in the economy. Budget surpluses are no guarantee against inflation if, as in 1947 and 1950, private demands for goods and services rise excessively. And in a slack economy, budget deficits do not automatically spell inflation or even full recovery.

Deficit financing of increased public expenditure in the two fiscal years 1961 and 1962, on the scale contemplated, will not create uncontrollable inflationary pressures. Unless private demands are unexpectedly strong, the President's budget will not strain the productive capacity of the economy in fiscal year 1962. The economy is now suffering from unemployment and excess capacity. Increased spending, whether public or private, will result in increased production. Output and employment can expand without appreciable upward pressure on prices and wages. If and when recovery proceeds to the point where the economy is straining productive capacity, further increases in spending, public or private, would increase prices rather than production. Under such conditions, overall demand could be and should be restricted by fiscal and monetary measures.

Developments in our economy are watched keenly and critically by other nations. Our economic performance in recent years has elicited widespread concern. American prestige abroad would be raised by a successful program to restore momentum to the American economy. A budgetary deficit would be considered both a normal result of recession and a proper instrument of recovery. Western European nations have generally accepted the need for compensatory fiscal policy. Moreover, many European budgets distinguish, as the U.S. budget does not, between current and capital outlays.

Economic expansion, whether the result of deficit-financed public expenditures or of sharply rising private demands or of both, will increase U.S. imports. On the other hand, improvement in business prospects at home will reduce the net outflow of long-term capital. The President listed in his balance-of-payments message a number of steps to improve the U.S. payments position. One of the purposes of the investment-tax incentive which the administration will propose is to accelerate advances in productivity in order to maintain and improve the competitiveness of American products in world markets. We are determined to balance the international accounts of the United States, but we reject as a counsel of despair the view that only an economy depressed at home can be in balance abroad.

Question 20: "On page 53, it is stated, 'Some excessive price increases in 1955–58 might not have occurred if market control had not been so strong.' What do you mean by 'market control'? Is this another name for the discredited term 'administered prices'? If so, let me ask if the firms having this so-called market control aren't the very firms that spend the most amount of money on market research? And if that is essentially true, isn't it rather conclusive that the market does the controlling and the businesses merely try to estimate the market? During the same period (1955–58) we had one of our most vigorous enforcements of antitrust legislation. Does the Council suggest that the antitrust laws be further strengthened to get at the alleged 'market control' and, if so, in what area? To limit the bargaining power of national labor unions?"

We mean by "market control" the ability of sellers of goods or services to exercise discretion over prices and other terms of sale. The term "administered prices" is sometimes used in this sense.

The degree of market control—the extent of sellers' ability to exercise this discretion—varies widely among product and labor markets. This discretion is never absolute; it is always subject to impairment by the entry of new competitors, by the development of new products or processes, by alterations in the legal bases of market control, by disruption of understandings among competitors, and by a host of other contingencies.

Hence, although many firms which possess a significant degree of market control also spend large sums on market research, the latter fact does not negate the former. Rarely if ever is a firm's position so impregnable, or its sales so incapable of further expansion, that it is not concerned to improve its product, to heighten the effectiveness of its sales promotion efforts, or to find out what its rivals are doing.

The antitrust laws have been used effectively to reduce the degree of market control in particular markets, and they should continue to be so used. The Council is not advancing any proposals for amending the antitrust laws.

ECONOMIC REPORT
OF THE PRESIDENT

To the Congress of the United States:

I report to you under the provisions of the Employment Act of 1946 at a time when

—the economy has regained its momentum;

—the economy is responding to the Federal Government's efforts, under the Act, "to promote maximum employment, production, and purchasing power;"

—the economy is again moving toward the central objective of the Act—to afford "useful employment opportunities, including self-employment, for those able, willing, and seeking to work."

My first Economic Report is an appropriate occasion to re-emphasize my dedication to the principles of the Employment Act. As a declaration of national purpose and as a recognition of Federal responsibility, the Act has few parallels in the Nation's history. In passing the Act by heavy bipartisan majorities, the Congress registered the consensus of the American people that this Nation will not countenance the suffering, frustration, and injustice of unemployment, or let the vast potential of the world's leading economy run to waste in idle manpower, silent machinery, and empty plants.

The framers of the Employment Act were wise to choose the promotion of "maximum employment, production, and purchasing power" as the keystone of national economic policy. They were confident that these objectives can be effectively promoted "in a manner calculated to foster and promote free competitive enterprise and the general welfare." They knew that our pursuit of maximum employment and production would be tempered with compassion, with justice, and with a concern for the future. But they knew also that the other standards we set for our economy are easier to meet when it is operating at capacity. A full employment economy provides opportunities for useful and satisfying work. It rewards enterprise with profit. It generates saving for the future and transforms it into productive investment. It opens doors for the unskilled and underprivileged and closes them against want and frustration. The conquest of unemployment is not the sole end of economic policy, but it is surely an indispensable beginning.

The record of the economy since 1946 is a vast improvement over the prolonged mass unemployment of the 1930's. The Employment Act itself deserves no small part of the credit. Under the mandate and

3

procedures of the Act, both Congress and the Executive have kept the health of the national economy and the economic policies of the Government under constant review. And the national commitment to high employment has enabled business firms and consumers to act and to plan without fear of another great depression.

Though the postwar record is free of major depression, it is marred by four recessions. In the past fifteen years, the economy has spent a total of seven years regaining previous peaks of industrial production. In two months out of three, 4 percent or more of those able, willing, and seeking to work have been unable to find jobs. We must do better in the 1960's.

To combat future recessions—to keep them short and shallow if they occur—I urge adoption of a three-part program for sustained prosperity, which will (1) provide stand-by power, subject to congressional veto, for temporary income tax reductions, (2) set up a stand-by program of public capital improvements, and (3) strengthen the unemployment insurance system.

These three measures will enable the Government to counter swings in business activity more promptly and more powerfully than ever before. They will give new and concrete meaning to the declaration of policy made in the Employment Act. They will constitute the greatest step forward in public policy for economic stability since the Act itself.

As the Employment Act prescribes, I shall in this Report review "economic conditions" in the United States in 1961 and "current and foreseeable economic trends in the levels of employment, production, and purchasing power;" set forth "the levels of employment, production, and purchasing power obtaining in the United States and such levels needed to carry out the policy" of the Act; and present my economic program and legislative recommendations for 1962.

PROGRESS IN 1961

Last January the economy was in the grip of recession. Nearly 7 percent of the labor force was unemployed. Almost one-fifth of manufacturing capacity lay idle. Actual output was running $50 billion (annual rate) short of the economy's great potential. These figures reflected not only the setback of 1960–61 but the incomplete recovery from the recession of 1957–58. The task before us was to recover not from one but from two recessions.

4

At the same time, gold was leaving the country at a rate of more than $300 million a month. In the three previous years, the Nation had run a total deficit of $10 billion in its basic international accounts. These large and persistent deficits had weakened confidence in the dollar.

In my message to the Congress on February 2, I stated that this Administration's "realistic aims for 1961 are to reverse the downtrend in our economy, to narrow the gap of unused potential, to abate the waste and misery of unemployment, and at the same time to maintain reasonable stability of the price level." In a message on the balance of payments on February 6, I added a fifth aim, to restore confidence in the dollar and to reduce the deficit in international payments.

These five aims for 1961 have been achieved:

(1) The downtrend was reversed. Gross national product (GNP) grew from $501 billion (annual rate) in the first quarter to a record rate of $542 billion in the last quarter. In July, industrial production regained its previous peak, and by the end of the year it showed a total rise of 13 percent.

(2) These gains brought into productive use nearly half the plant capacity which was idle at the beginning of the year. The growth of GNP narrowed the over-all gap of unused potential from an estimated 10 percent to 5 percent.

(3) Unemployment dropped from 6.8 to 6.1 percent of the labor force. The number of areas of substantial labor surplus declined from 101 in March to 60 in December.

(4) Price stability has been maintained during the recovery. Since February, wholesale prices have fallen slightly, and consumer prices have risen only one-half of 1 percent.

(5) Confidence in the dollar has been restored. Our gold losses were cut from $1.7 billion in 1960 to less than $0.9 billion in 1961. The deficit in 1961 in our basic international transactions was about one-third as large as in 1960.

The "Program To Restore Momentum to the American Economy" which I proposed to the Congress on February 2 resulted in prompt legislation to

—extend unemployment insurance benefits on a temporary basis;
—make Federal aid available, through the States, to dependent children of the unemployed;
—liberalize social security benefits;
—promote homebuilding under the Housing Act of 1961;
—raise the minimum wage and extend it to more workers;

5

—provide Federal aid under the Area Redevelopment Act, to revitalize the economies of areas with large and persistent unemployment.

Prompt executive action was taken to accelerate Federal purchases and procurement, highway fund distributions, tax refunds, and veterans' life insurance dividends. The Administration raised farm price supports, expanded the food distribution program, and established eight pilot food stamp programs.

Monetary and credit policies responded to the dual demands of economic recovery and the balance of payments. On the one hand, the Federal Reserve System maintained general monetary ease; Federal Reserve open market operations, complemented by Treasury management of the public debt and of government investment accounts, assured an ample supply of credit which served to counter upward pressures on long-term interest rates; reduction of FHA ceiling rates, supported by FNMA mortgage purchases, eased mortgage credit and stimulated homebuilding; and the Small Business Administration made its credit more widely available at lower cost. On the other hand, both monetary and debt management policies countered downward pressures on short-term rates, with a view to checking the outflow of funds to money markets abroad.

The Federal Budget played its proper role as a powerful instrument for promoting economic recovery. The measures to relieve distress and restore economic momentum expanded purchasing power early in the year. Subsequently, major increases in expenditure for national security and space programs became necessary. In a fully employed economy, these increases would have required new tax revenues to match. But I did not recommend tax increases at this point because they would have cut into private purchasing power and retarded recovery.

The increase of GNP—$41 billion (annual rate) from the first to the fourth quarter—reflected increased purchases of goods and services by consumers, business, and governments:

—Consumers accounted for nearly half. As household incomes rose, consumer expenditure expanded by $18 billion.

—Residential construction and business expenditures for fixed investment responded promptly to the recovery and to favorable credit conditions. By the end of the year, they had risen by $8 billion.

—Business stopped liquidating inventories and started rebuilding them. This shift, which occurred early in the year and helped get recovery off to a flying start, added $8 billion to the demand for goods and services by the fourth quarter.

—Federal, State, and local government purchases rose by $8 billion.

—Although exports were somewhat higher in the fourth quarter than in the first, the rise in imports in response to recovery lowered net exports by $1 billion.

Labor, business, and farm incomes rose as the economy recovered. Wages and salaries increased by $19 billion (annual rate) from the first quarter to the fourth. Corporate profits after taxes recovered sharply, receiving about 15 percent of the gains in GNP. With the help of new programs, farm operators' net income from farming increased from $12 billion in 1960 to $13 billion in 1961, and net income per farm rose by $350. The after-tax incomes of American consumers increased by $21 billion, or $92 per capita, during the year. Since consumer prices rose by only one-half of 1 percent, these gains in income were almost entirely gains in real purchasing power.

One million jobs were added by nonagricultural establishments during the expansion. But employment did not keep pace with production and income. Productivity rose rapidly as capacity was more fully and efficiently utilized. And more workers on part-time jobs were able to work full time.

The record of 1961 demonstrated again the resiliency of the U.S. economy with well-timed support from government policy. Business responded to the expansion of purchasing power by producing more goods and services, not by raising prices. Indeed, the record of price stability in three quarters of expansion was better than in the three preceding quarters of recession. The rates of advance of production and income compared favorably with the two preceding periods of expansion. Production grew rapidly without straining capacity or encountering bottlenecks.

As 1961 ended, actual output was still $25 to $30 billion short of potential, and unemployment was far too high. But much of the industrial manpower, machinery, and plant that lay idle a year ago had been drawn back into productive use. And the momentum of the 1961 recovery should carry the economy further toward full employment and full production in 1962.

GOALS OF ECONOMIC POLICY

Though we may take satisfaction with our progress to date, we dare not rest content. The unfinished business of economic policy includes (1) the achievement of full employment and sustained prosperity without inflation, (2) the acceleration of economic growth, (3) the extension of equality of opportunity, and (4) the restoration of balance of pay-

7

ments equilibrium. Economic policy thus confronts a demanding assignment, but one which can and will be met within the framework of a free economy.

Our Goal of Full and Sustained Prosperity Without Inflation

Recovery has carried the economy only part of the way to the goal of "maximum production, employment, and purchasing power." The standing challenge of the Employment Act is not merely to do better, but to do our best—the "maximum." Attainment of that maximum in 1963 would mean a GNP of approximately $600 billion, wages and salaries of over $320 billion, and corporate profits of as much as $60 billion, all in 1961 prices. The material gains are themselves staggering, but they are less important than the new sense of purpose and the new opportunities for improvement of American life that could be realized by "maximum" use of the productive capacity now lying idle and the capacity yet to be created.

Involuntary unemployment is the most dramatic sign and disheartening consequence of underutilization of productive capacity. It translates into human terms what may otherwise seem merely an abstract statistic. We cannot afford to settle for any prescribed level of unemployment. But for working purposes we view a 4 percent unemployment rate as a temporary target. It can be achieved in 1963, if appropriate fiscal, monetary, and other policies are used. The achievable rate can be lowered still further by effective policies to help the labor force acquire the skills and mobility appropriate to a changing economy. We must also continue the cooperative effort, begun with the Area Redevelopment Act of 1961, to bring industry to depressed areas and jobs to displaced workers. Ultimately, we must reduce unemployment to the minimum compatible with the functioning of a free economy.

We must seek full recovery without endangering the price stability of the last 4 years. The experience of the past year has shown that expansion without inflation is possible. With cooperation from labor and management, I am confident that we can go on to write a record of full employment without inflation.

The task of economic stabilization does not end with the achievement of full recovery. There remains the problem of keeping the economy from straying too far above or below the path of steady high employment. One way lies inflation, and the other way lies recession. Flexible and vigilant fiscal and monetary policies will allow us to hold the narrow middle course.

Our Goal of Economic Growth

While we move toward full and sustained use of today's productive capacity, we must expand our potential for tomorrow. Our postwar economic growth—though a step ahead of our record for the last half-century—has been slowing down. We have not in recent years maintained the 4 to 4½ percent growth rate which characterized the early postwar period. We should not settle for less than the achievement of a long-term growth rate matching the early postwar record. Increasing our growth rate to 4½ percent a year lies within the range of our capabilities during the 1960's. It will lay the groundwork for meeting both our domestic needs and our world responsibilities.

In November of last year we joined with our 19 fellow members of the Organization for Economic Cooperation and Development in setting a common target for economic growth. Together we pledged ourselves to adopt national and international policies aimed at increasing the combined output of the Atlantic Community by 50 percent between 1960 and 1970. The nations of the West are encouraged and enlivened by America's determination to make its full contribution to this joint effort.

We can do our share. In the mid-1960's, the children born in 1943 and after will be arriving at working age. The resulting rapid growth in our labor force offers us an opportunity, not a burden—provided that we deliver not only the jobs but also the research, the training, and the capital investment to endow our new workers with high and rising productivity as they enter economic life.

Our Goal of Equal Opportunity

Increasingly in our lifetime, American prosperity has been widely shared and it must continue so. The spread of primary, secondary, and higher education, the wider availability of medical services, and the improved postwar performance of our economy have bettered the economic status of the poorest families and individuals.

But prosperity has not wiped out poverty. In 1960, 7 million families and individuals had personal incomes lower than $2,000. In part, our failure to overcome poverty is a consequence of our failure to operate the economy at potential. The incidence of unemployment is always uneven, and increases in unemployment tend to inflict the greatest income loss on those least able to afford it. But there is a claim on our conscience from others, whose poverty is barely touched by cyclical improvements in general economic activity. To an increasing extent,

9

the poorest families in America are those headed by women, the elderly, nonwhites, migratory workers, and the physically or mentally handicapped—people who are shortchanged even in time of prosperity.

Last year's increase in the minimum wage is evidence of our concern for the welfare of our low-income fellow citizens. Other legislative proposals now pending will be particularly effective in improving the lot of the least fortunate. These include (1) health insurance for the aged, financed through the social security system, (2) Federal aid for training and retraining our unemployed and underemployed workers, (3) the permanent strengthening of our unemployment compensation system, and (4) substantial revision in our public welfare and assistance program, stressing rehabilitation services which help to restore families to independence.

Public education has been the great bulwark of equality of opportunity in our democracy for more than a century. Our schools have been a major means of preventing early handicaps from hardening into permanent ignorance and poverty. There can be no better investment in equity and democracy—and no better instrument for economic growth. For this reason, I urge action by the Congress to provide Federal aid for more adequate public school facilities, higher teachers' salaries, and better quality in education. I urge early completion of congressional action on the bill to authorize loans for construction of college academic facilities and to provide scholarships for able students who need help. The talent of our youth is a resource which must not be wasted.

Finally, I shall soon propose to the Congress an intensive program to reduce adult illiteracy, a handicap which too many of our fellow citizens suffer because of inadequate educational opportunities in the past.

Our Goal of Basic Balance in International Payments

Persistent international payments deficits and gold outflows have made the balance of payments a critical problem of economic policy. We must attain a balance in our international transactions which permits us to meet heavy obligations abroad for the security and development of the free world, without continued depletion of our gold reserves or excessive accumulation of short-term dollar liabilities to foreigners. Simultaneously, we must continue to reduce barriers to international trade and to increase the flow of resources from developed to developing countries. To increase our exports is a task of highest priority, and one which gives heightened significance to the maintenance of price stability and the rapid increase of productivity at home.

Policies for 1962

Prospects for 1962

The Nation will make further economic progress in 1962. Broad advances are in prospect for the private economy. The gains already achieved have set the stage for further new records in output, employment, personal income, and profits. Rising household incomes brighten the outlook for further increases in consumer buying, particularly of durable goods. Business firms will need larger inventories to support higher sales, and improved profits and expanded markets will lead to rising capital outlays. The outlays of Federal, State, and local governments will continue to increase as we work for peace and progress.

In the first half of 1962, we may therefore expect vigorous expansion in production and incomes, with GNP increasing to a range of $565–570 billion in the second quarter, employment continuing to rise, and the unemployment rate falling further.

In the second half of 1962, business investment in plant and equipment should pick up speed and help maintain the momentum of progress toward full employment—and toward future economic growth. Rising output should push factory operating rates closer to capacity and raise profits still further above previous records. To these incentives for capital expenditures will be added Treasury liberalization of depreciation guidelines and, if the Congress acts favorably, the 8 percent tax credit for machinery and equipment outlays.

For 1962 as a whole, GNP is expected to rise approximately $50 billion above the $521 billion level of 1961. This would be another giant stride toward a fully employed economy. The record of past recoveries and of the U.S. economy's enormous and growing potential indicates that this is a gain we can achieve. In the perspective of our commitments both to our own expanding population and to the world, it is a gain we need to achieve.

Budgetary Policy

Prosperity shrinks budgetary deficits, as recessions create them. Budget revenues are expected to rise 13 percent between the fiscal years 1962 and 1963; revenues rose 14½ percent between 1959 and 1960 in the previous upswing. Such sensitivity of budget revenues to business activity is desirable because it moderates swings in private purchasing power.

I have submitted to the Congress a Budget which will balance in fiscal 1963 as prosperity generates sharply rising tax revenues. The Budget is appropriately paced to the expected rate of economic expansion. It will give less stimulus to business activity as private demand for goods and services grows stronger and shoulders more of the responsibility for continued gains. But the shift will be moderate and gradual. We have learned from the disappointing 1959–60 experience that an abrupt and excessively large swing in the Budget can drain the vigor from the private economy and halt its progress, especially if a restrictive monetary policy is followed simultaneously. This will not be repeated. Budget outlays will rise by $3½ billion from fiscal 1962 to fiscal 1963, whereas they fell by more than that amount from fiscal 1959 to fiscal 1960. The 1963 Budget starts from a much smaller deficit and will move to a moderate surplus as the recovery strengthens.

With support from increased government expenditures and other government policies, the momentum of the recovery is expected to raise GNP to $570 billion for 1962 as a whole. Prompt enactment of the proposed tax credit for investment would give the economy further strength. Economic expansion at the expected pace will yield $93.0 billion in Budget revenues in fiscal 1963 to cover $92.5 billion in Budget expenditures. If private demands for goods and services should prove to be weaker in 1962 than now anticipated, less private purchasing power will flow into taxes, and Budget revenues will fall short of the $93.0 billion figure. If private demands are stronger, tax receipts will rise further and Budget revenues will exceed expectations.

A surplus of $4.4 billion in fiscal 1963 is expected in the national income accounts budget—a budget constructed to measure the direct impact of Federal expenditures and receipts on the flow of total spending. The surplus would be several billion dollars higher if the economy were operating steadily at a level high enough to hold unemployment to 4 percent.

Either surplus—prospective or potential—is both a challenge and an opportunity. A government surplus is a form of saving—an excess of income over expenditure. Like any other form of saving, it releases labor and other productive resources which can be used to create new investment goods—plant, equipment, or houses. If investment demand is not strong enough to use the resources and labor, they will be wasted in unemployment and idle capacity, and the surplus itself will not be realized. But if the necessary investment demand is present, the surplus will make possible the acceleration of economic growth by enlarging the future productive power of the economy. The Government is seeking to help American industry to meet this challenge and seize this opportunity, through such measures as the 8 percent investment tax credit and revisions of depreciation guidelines.

We face 1962 with optimism but not complacency. If private demand shows unexpected strength, public policy must and will act to avert the dangers of rising prices. If demand falls short of current expectations, more expansionary policies will be pursued. In 1962, vigilance and flexibility must be the guardians of economic optimism.

Monetary and Credit Policies

Monetary, credit, and debt management policies can also help to assure that productive outlets exist for the funds that the American people save from prosperity incomes. The balance foreseen in the Budget for fiscal year 1963, and the surplus which would arise at full employment, both indicate that fiscal policy is assuming a large share of the burden of forestalling inflationary excesses of demand. With monetary and related policies relieved of a substantial part of this burden, they can more effectively be used to assure a flow of investment funds which will transform the economy's present capacity to save into future capacity to produce.

At the same time, monetary and debt management policies must continue to protect the balance of international payments against outflows of short-term capital. As in 1961, domestic expansion and the balance of payments confront these policies with a dual task, requiring continued ingenuity in technique and flexibility in emphasis.

Balance of Payments

The program launched last year to reduce our payments deficit and maintain confidence in the dollar will, I am sure, show further results in 1962. I am hopeful that the target of reasonable equilibrium in our international payments can be achieved within the next two years; but this will require a determined effort on the part of all of us— government, business and labor. This effort must proceed on a number of fronts.

Export expansion. An increase in the U.S. trade surplus is of the first importance. If we are to meet our international responsibilities, we must increase exports more rapidly than the increase in imports which accompanies our economic growth.

Our efforts to raise exports urgently require that we negotiate a reduction in the tariff of the European Common Market. I shall shortly transmit to the Congress a special message elaborating the details of the proposed Trade Expansion Act of 1962 and explaining why I believe that a new trade policy initiative is imperative this year.

To encourage American businessmen to become more export-minded, we have inaugurated a new export insurance program under the leadership of the Export-Import Bank, and we have stepped up our export promotion drive by improving the commercial services abroad of the U.S. Government, establishing trade centers abroad, planning trade fairs, improving the trade mission program, and working with business firms on export opportunities through field offices of the Department of Commerce and the Small Business Administration. Foreign travel to the United States, which returns dollars to our shores, is now being promoted through the first Federal agency ever created for this purpose.

Prices and productivity. Our export drive will founder if we cannot keep our prices competitive in world markets. Though our recent price performance has been excellent, the improving economic climate of 1962 will test anew the statesmanship of our business and labor leaders. I believe that they will pass the test; our Nation today possesses a new understanding of the vital link between our level of prices and our balance of payments.

In the long run, the competitive position of U.S. industry depends on a sustained and rapid advance in productivity. In this, the interests of economic recovery, long-run growth, and the strength of the dollar coincide. Modernization and expansion of our industrial plant will accelerate the advance of productivity.

Foreign investment. To place controls over the flow of private American capital abroad would be contrary to our traditions and our economic interests. But neither is there justification for special tax incentives which stimulate the flow of U.S. investment to countries now strong and economically developed, and I again urge the elimination of these special incentives.

The new foreign trade program which I am proposing to the Congress will help to reduce another artificial incentive to U.S. firms to invest abroad. The European Common Market has attracted American capital, partly because American businessmen fear that they will be unable to compete in the growing European market unless they build plants behind the common tariff wall. We must negotiate down the barriers to trade between the two great continental markets, so that the exports of our industry and agriculture can have full opportunity to compete in Europe.

Governmental expenditures abroad. Military expenditures form by far the greater part of our governmental outlays abroad. We are discussing with certain of our European allies the extent to which they can increase their own military procurement from the United States to offset our dollar expenditures there. As a result, the net cost to our balance of payments is expected to be reduced during the coming year, in spite of increased deployment of forces abroad because of the Berlin situation.

To curtail our foreign aid programs in order to strengthen our balance of payments would be to sacrifice more than we gain. But we can cut back on the foreign currency costs of our aid programs, and thus reduce the burden on our balance of payments. A large percentage of our foreign aid is already spent for procurement in the United States; this proportion will rise as our tightened procurement procedures become increasingly effective.

We have sought to induce other advanced countries to undertake a larger share of the foreign aid effort. We will continue our efforts through the Development Assistance Committee of the Organization for Economic Cooperation and Development to obtain a higher level of economic assistance by other industrial nations to the less developed countries.

Short-term capital movements. Outflows of volatile short-term funds added to the pressures on the dollar in 1960. Our policies in 1961 have diminished the dangers of disruptive movements of short-term capital. For the first time in a generation, the Treasury is helping to stabilize the dollar by operations in the international exchange markets. The Federal Reserve and the Treasury, in administering their monetary policy and debt management responsibilities, have sought to meet the needs of domestic recovery in ways which would not lead to outflows of short-term capital.

During the past year, we have consulted periodically with our principal financial partners, both bilaterally and within the framework of the OECD. These consultations have led to close cooperation among fiscal and monetary authorities in a common effort to prevent disruptive currency movements.

Strengthening the international monetary system. The International Monetary Fund is playing an increasingly important role in preserving international monetary stability. The reserve strength behind the dollar includes our drawing rights on the Fund, of which $1.7 billion is automatically available under current practices of the Fund. An additional $4.1 billion could become available under Fund policies, insofar as the Fund has available resources in gold and usable foreign currencies. Recently, the Fund has diversified its use of currencies in meeting drawings by member countries, relying less heavily on dollars and more heavily on the currencies of countries with payments surpluses. However, the Fund's regular holdings of the currencies of some important industrial countries are not adequate to meet potential demands for them.

In a message to the Congress last February, I said: "We must now, in cooperation with other lending countries, begin to consider ways in which international monetary institutions—especially the International Monetary Fund—can be strengthened and more effectively utilized, both in furnishing needed increases in reserves, and in providing the flexibility required to support a healthy and growing world economy."

We have now taken an important step in this direction. Agreement has been reached among ten of the major industrial countries to lend to the Fund specified amounts of their currencies when necessary to cope with or forestall pressures which may impair the international monetary system. These stand-by facilities of $6 billion will be a major defense against international monetary speculation and will powerfully reinforce the effectiveness of the Fund. They will provide resources to make our drawing rights in the Fund effective, should we need to use them. Moreover, the U.S. stand-by commitment of $2 billion will augment the resources potentially available through the Fund to other participants in the agreement, when our balance of payments and reserve positions are strong. I shall shortly submit a request to Congress for appropriate enabling legislation.

Prices and Wages

Prices and production need not travel together. A number of foreign countries have experienced both rapid growth and stable prices in recent years. We ourselves, in 1961, enjoyed a stable price level during a brisk economic recovery.

While rising prices will not necessarily accompany the expansion we expect in 1962, neither can we rely on chance to keep our price level stable. Creeping inflation in the years 1955–57 weakened our international competitive position. We cannot afford to allow a repetition of that experience.

We do not foresee in 1962 a level of demand for goods and services which will strain the economy's capacity to produce. Neither is it likely that many industries will find themselves pressing against their capacity ceilings. Inflationary pressures from these sources should not be a problem.

But in those sectors where both companies and unions possess substantial market power, the interplay of price and wage decisions could set off a movement toward a higher price level. If this were to occur, the whole Nation would be the victim.

I do not believe that American business or labor will allow this to happen. All of us have learned a great deal from the economic events of the past 15 years. Among both businessmen and workers, there is growing recognition that the road to higher real profits and higher real wages is the road of increased productivity. When better plant and equipment enable the labor force to produce more in the same number of hours, there is more to share among all the contributors to the productive process—and this can happen with no increase in prices. Gains achieved in this manner endure, while gains achieved in one turn of the price-wage spiral vanish on the next.

The Nation must rely on the good sense and public spirit of our business and labor leaders to hold the line on the price level in 1962. If labor leaders in our major industries will accept the productivity benchmark as a guide to wage objectives, and if management in these industries will practice equivalent restraint in their price decisions, the year ahead will be a brilliant chapter in the record of the responsible exercise of freedom.

Measures for a Stronger Economy

The final section of my Report is a summary of my recommendations for legislative action (1) to strengthen our defenses against recession, (2) to strengthen our financial system, (3) to strengthen our manpower base, and (4) to strengthen our tax system.

A Program for Sustained Prosperity

Recurrent recessions have thrown the postwar American economy off stride at a time when the economies of other major industrial countries have moved steadily ahead. To improve our future performance I urge the Congress to join with me in erecting a defense-in-depth against future recessions. The basic elements of this defense are (1) Presidential stand-by authority for prompt, temporary income tax reductions, (2) Presidential stand-by authority for capital improvements expenditures, and (3) a permanent strengthening of the unemployment compensation system. These three measures parallel important proposals of the Commission on Money and Credit, whose further recommendations are treated under the next heading.

In our free enterprise economy, fluctuations in business and consumer spending will, of course, always occur. But this need not doom us to an alternation of lean years and fat. The business cycle does not have the inevitability of the calendar. The Government can time its fiscal transactions to offset and to dampen fluctuations in the private economy.

Our fiscal system and budget policy already contribute to economic stability, to a much greater degree than before the war. But the time is ripe, and the need apparent, to equip the Government to act more promptly, more flexibly, and more forcefully to stabilize the economy—to carry out more effectively its charge under the Employment Act.

Stand-by tax reduction authority. First, I recommend the enactment of stand-by authority under which the President, subject to veto by the Congress, could make prompt temporary reductions in the rates of the individual income tax to combat recessions, as follows:

(1) Before proposing a temporary tax reduction, the President must make a finding that such action is required to meet the objectives of the Employment Act.

(2) Upon such finding, the President would submit to Congress a proposed temporary uniform reduction in all individual income tax rates. The proposed temporary rates may not be more than 5 percentage points lower than the rates permanently established by the Congress.

(3) This change would take effect 30 days after submission, unless rejected by a joint resolution of the Congress.

(4) It would remain in effect for 6 months, subject to revision or renewal by the same process or extension by a joint resolution of the Congress.

(5) If the Congress were not in session, a Presidentially proposed tax adjustment would automatically take effect but would terminate 30 days after the Congress reconvened. Extension would require a new proposal by the President, which would be subject to congressional veto.

A temporary reduction of individual income tax rates across the board can be a powerful safeguard against recession. It would reduce the annual rate of tax collections by $2 billion per percentage point, or a maximum of $10 billion—$1 billion per point, or a $5-billion maximum, for six months—at present levels of income. These figures should be measured against the costs they are designed to forestall:

—the tens of billions of potential output that run to waste in recession;

—the pain and frustration of the millions whom recessions throw out of work;

—the Budget deficits of $12.4 billion in fiscal 1959 or $7.0 billion this year.

The proposed partial tax suspension would launch a prompt counterattack on the cumulative forces of recession. It would be reflected immediately in lower withholding deductions and higher take-home pay for millions of Americans. Markets for consumer goods and services would promptly feel the stimulative influence of the tax suspension.

It would offer strong support to the economy for a timely interval, while preserving the revenue-raising powers of our tax system in prosperity and the wise traditional procedures of the Congress for making permanent revisions and reforms in the system. I am not asking the Congress to delegate its power to levy taxes, but to authorize a temporary and emergency suspension of taxes by the President—subject to the checkrein of Congressional veto—in situations where time is of the essence.

Stand-by capital improvements authority. Second, I recommend that the Congress provide stand-by authority to the President to accelerate and initiate up to $2 billion of appropriately timed capital improvements when unemployment is rising, as follows:

(1) The President would be authorized to initiate the program within two months after the seasonally adjusted unemployment rate

    (a) had risen in at least three out of four months (or in four out of six months) and

    (b) had risen to a level at least one percentage point higher than its level four months (or six months) earlier.

(2) Before invoking this authority, the President must make a finding that current and prospective economic developments require such action to achieve the objectives of the Employment Act.

(3) Upon such finding, the President would be authorized to commit

    (a) up to $750 million in the acceleration of direct Federal expenditures previously authorized by the Congress,

    (b) up to $750 million for grants-in-aid to State and local governments,

    (c) up to $250 million in loans to States and localities which would otherwise be unable to meet their share of project costs, and

    (d) up to $250 million additional to be distributed among the above three categories as he might deem appropriate.

(4) The authority to initiate new projects under the capital improvements program would terminate automatically within 12 months unless extended by the Congress—but the program could be terminated at any time by the President.

(5) Grants-in-aid would be made under rules prescribed by the President to assure that assisted projects (a) were of high priority, (b) represented a net addition to existing State and local expenditures, and (c) could be started and completed quickly.

(6) Expenditures on Federal projects previously authorized by the Congress would include resource conservation and various Federal public works, including construction, repair, and modernization of public buildings.

(7) After the program had terminated, the authority would not again be available to the President for six months.

The above criteria would have permitted Presidential authority to be invoked in the early stages of each of the four postwar recessions—within four months after the decline had begun. Furthermore, no false signals would have been given. Were a false signal to occur—for example, because of a strike—the authority, which is discretionary, need not be invoked.

The first impact of the accelerated orders, contracts, and outlays under the program would be felt within one to two months after the authority was invoked. The major force of the program would be spent well before private demand again pressed hard on the economy's capacity to produce. With the indicated safeguards, this program would make a major contribution to business activity, consumer purchasing power, and employment in a recession by utilizing for sound public investment resources that would otherwise have gone to waste.

Unemployment compensation. Third, I again urge the Congress to strengthen permanently our Federal-State system of unemployment insurance. My specific recommendations include

(1) Extension of the benefit period by as much as 13 weeks for workers with at least three years of experience in covered employment;

(2) Similar extension of the benefit period when unemployment is widespread for workers with less than three years of experience in covered employment. This provision could be put into effect by Presidential proclamation when insured unemployment reaches 5 percent, and the number of benefit exhaustions over a three-month period reaches 1 percent of covered employment;

(3) Incentives for the States to provide increased benefits, so that the great majority of covered workers will be eligible for weekly benefits equal to at least half of their average weekly wage;

(4) Extension of coverage to more than three million additional workers;

(5) Improved financing of the program by an increase in the wage base for the payroll tax from $3,000 to $4,800;

(6) Reinsurance grants to States experiencing high unemployment insurance costs;

(7) Provisions which permit claimants to attend approved training or retraining courses without adverse effect on eligibility for benefits.

Wider coverage, extended benefit periods, and increased benefit amounts will help society discharge its obligation to individual unemployed workers. And by maintaining more adequately their incomes and purchasing power, these measures will also buttress the economy's built-in defenses against recession. Temporary extensions of unemployment compensation benefits have been voted by the Congress during the last two recessions. It is time now for permanent legislation to bring this well-tested stabilizer more smoothly into operation when economic activity declines.

In combination, these three measures will enable Federal fiscal policy to respond firmly, flexibly, and swiftly to oncoming recessions. Working together on this bold program, the Congress and the Executive can make an unprecedented contribution to economic stability, one that will richly reward us in fuller employment and more sustained growth, and thus, in greater human well-being and greater national strength.

Strengthening the Financial System

Proposals of the Commission on Money and Credit. The Report of the Commission on Money and Credit, published last year, raises important issues of public policy relating to (1) the objectives and machinery of Government for economic stabilization and growth, (2) Federal direct lending and credit guarantee programs, and (3) the structure and regulation of private financial institutions and markets. The Commission's Report represents the results of thorough analysis and deliberation by a private group of leading citizens representative of business, labor, finance, agriculture, and the professions. The Commission's findings and recommendations deserve careful consideration by the Congress, the Executive, and the public—consideration which should result in legislative and executive actions to strengthen government policy under the Employment Act and to improve the financial system of the United States. The subjects covered by the Commission can—for the purposes of discussion and action in the Government—usefully be divided into four categories.

(1) To strengthen the instruments of policy for economic stabilization, the Commission recommends permanent improvement of unemployment compensation, flexibility in government capital expenditures, and flexibility in adjusting the basic Federal individual income tax rate. These key proposals are reflected in the three-part anti-recession program just described.

(2) In its comprehensive new look at existing financial legislation, the Commission concludes that the following financial restrictions no longer serve the purposes originally intended and unnecessarily complicate or obstruct other government policies: the ceiling on the public debt, the ceiling on permissible interest rates on U.S. Treasury bonds, and the required gold reserve against Federal Reserve notes and deposits. I am sure that the Congress will wish to examine carefully the Commission's recommendations on these points.

(3) The Commission re-examines the structure of the Federal Reserve System and its relationship to other arms of the Federal Government. The desirability of proposed changes in the structure which has evolved over the years can be determined only after extensive consideration by the Congress and by the public.

There are two reforms of clear merit on which there appears to be sufficiently general agreement to proceed at once, and which are of direct concern to the President in the exercise of his responsibility to appoint the members and officers of the Board of Governors of the Federal Reserve System.

The first is to give adequate recognition in the simple matter of salaries to the important responsibilities of the Board of ·Governors of the Federal Reserve System. The United States is behind other countries in the status accorded, by this concrete symbol, to the leadership of its "central bank," and I urge that the Congress take corrective action.

The second is to revise the terms of the officers and members of the Board so that a new President will be able to nominate a Chairman of his choice for a term of four years coterminous with his own. This change has the concurrence of the present Chairman of the Board of Governors. The current situation—under which the four-year term of the Chairman is not synchronized with the Presidential term—appears to be accidental and inadvertent.

Provision should be made now for smooth transition to new arrangements to take effect in 1965. I suggest that, on the expiration of the present term of the Chairman in April 1963, the next term expire on January 31, 1965. In order that, starting in 1965, the President may have a free choice when he begins his own term, it is also necessary to provide that the terms of members of the Board—which now begin and end on January 31 of even years—begin and end in odd years. This change can be accomplished very easily by extending the terms of present members by one year.

(4) Several of the Commission's recommendations require careful appraisal by the affected agencies in the Executive Branch as a basis for future legislative recommendations:

(a) *Banks and other private financial institutions:* The Commission proposes significant changes in the scope and nature of government regulations concerning reserves, portfolios, interest rates, and competition. I shall ask an interagency working group in the Executive Branch to examine the complex issues raised by these proposals. This interagency group will keep in close touch with the relevant committees of the Congress, which will no doubt wish to study these issues simultaneously.

(b) *Federal lending and loan guarantee programs:* It is clearly time for a thorough review of both their general impact on the economy and their effectiveness for the special purposes for which they were established. Again the Commission's Report has performed a valuable service in illuminating basic problems. One important question is the appropriate role—with account taken of both effectiveness and budgetary cost—of direct Federal lending, loan guarantees, and interest sharing. I shall ask a second interagency group in the Executive Branch to examine these programs.

(c) *Corporate pension funds and other private retirement programs:* It is time for a reappraisal of legislation governing these programs. They have become, in recent years, a major custodian of individual savings and an important source of funds for capital markets. The amendment to the Welfare and Pension Plans Disclosure Act which I recommend below will be an important step toward insuring fidelity in the administration of these Plans. But there is also need for a review of rules governing the investment policies of these funds and the effects on equity and efficiency of the tax privileges accorded them. I shall ask a third working group of relevant Departments and agencies to recommend needed actions in this field, taking into account the findings of the Commission as well as other studies and proposals.

A revision of silver policy. Silver—a sick metal in the 1930's—is today an important raw material for which industrial demand is expanding steadily. It is uneconomic for the U.S. Government to lock up large quantities of useful silver in the sterile form of currency reserves.

Neither is any constructive purpose served by requiring that the Treasury maintain a floor under the price of silver. Silver should eventually be demonetized, except for its use in coins.

(1) As a first step in freeing silver from government control, the Secretary of the Treasury at my direction suspended sales of silver on November 29. This order amounted to the withdrawal of a price ceiling on silver which had been maintained by Treasury sales at a fixed price.

(2) The next step should be the withdrawal of the Treasury's price floor under domestically produced silver. Accordingly, I recommend repeal of the Acts relating to silver of June 19, 1934, July 6, 1939, and July 31, 1946; this step will free the Treasury from any future obligation to support the price of silver.

(3) I also recommend the repeal of the special 50 percent tax on transfers of interest in silver; this step will foster orderly price movements by encouraging the development of a futures market in silver.

(4) Finally, I recommend that the Federal Reserve System be authorized to issue Federal Reserve notes in denominations of $1; this will make possible the gradual withdrawal from circulation of $1 and $2 silver certificates, and the use of the silver thus released for coinage purposes.

Strengthening Our Manpower Base

The labor force of the United States is its most valuable productive resource. Measures which enhance the skills and adaptability of the working population contribute to the over-all productivity of the economy. Several legislative proposals to serve these ends have already been put before the Congress.

(1) I urge speedy passage of the proposed Manpower Development and Training Act. A growing and changing economy demands a labor force whose skills adapt readily to the requirements of new technology. When adaptation is slow and occupational lines rigid, individuals and society alike are the losers. Individuals take their loss in the form of prolonged unemployment or sharply reduced earning power. Society's loss is measured in foregone output. These are losses we need not suffer. A few hundred dollars invested in training or retraining an unemployed or underemployed worker can increase his productivity to society by a multiple of that investment—quite apart from the immeasurable return to the worker in regaining a sense of purpose and hope. Both compassion and dollars-and-cents reasoning speak for this legislation.

(2) For the same reasons, I urge enactment of the Youth Employ-ment Opportunities Act. This bill provides three types of pilot programs to give young people employment opportunities which would enable them to acquire much-needed skills. These programs include training, employment in public service jobs with public and private nonprofit agen-cies, and the establishment of Youth Corps Conservation Camps. In the current decade, young men and women will be entering the labor force in rapidly growing numbers. They will expect, and they deserve, opportunities to acquire skills and to do useful work. The price of failure is frustration and disillusion among our youth. This price we are resolved not to pay.

(3) I have already made my recommendations for improvement of the Federal-State unemployment compensation system.

(4) I am asking the Congress for more funds to increase the effec-tiveness of the U.S. Employment Service. This important agency has already strengthened its operations, improving its staff and placement services particularly in the largest urban centers, and concentrating on labor market problems of nationwide significance—especially those con-nected with technological displacement of adult workers and the employ-ment of youth. But the matching of jobs and workers is especially difficult and especially important in a rapidly changing economy, and more can be done. When unfilled jobs and qualified unemployed workers coexist—but do not make contact because the flow of job in-formation is not sufficiently free—the employer, the worker, and the country lose. I urge the Congress to reduce that loss in the most effective way—by revitalizing further the agency charged with disseminating information about job opportunities and willing workers.

(5) I ask for enactment of the pending proposal to amend the Wel-fare and Pension Plans Disclosure Act so as (a) to provide adequate penalties for embezzlement and (b) to vest authority in a responsible Federal agency to enforce the statute by issuing binding regulations, prescribing uniform reporting forms, and investigating violations. Almost 90 million people rely on some welfare and pension plan for part or all of present or future income. These plans are a major support of the economic security of the American people. We are derelict if we do not provide adequate administrative and enforcement provisions to pro-tect the tremendous financial interest of participants in these funds.

Strengthening Our Tax System

The tax system of the United States has consequences far beyond the simple raising of revenue. The tax laws are a vital part of the economic environment; their effects may be equitable or inequitable; they create incentives which may help or handicap the national interest. We cannot safely ignore these important effects in the comforting illusion that what already exists is perfect. We must scrutinize our tax system carefully to insure that its provisions contribute to the broad goals of full employment, growth, and equity.

My legislative proposals in the tax field are directly related to these goals and the corollary need for improvement in the balance of payments. In particular, I urge the earliest possible enactment of the tax proposals now before the House Committee on Ways and Means. The centerpiece of these proposals is the 8 percent tax credit against tax for gross investment in depreciable machinery and equipment. The credit should be retroactive to January 1, 1962. The tax credit increases the profitability of productive investment by reducing the net cost of acquiring new equipment. It will stimulate investment in capacity expansion and modernization, contribute to the growth of our productivity and output, and increase the competitiveness of American exports in world markets.

The tax credit for investment is in part self-financing. The stimulus it provides to new investment will have favorable effects on the level of economic activity during the year, and this will in turn add to Federal revenues. My other proposals for tax reform are designed to improve the equity and efficiency of the tax system and will offset the remaining net revenue loss:

(1) Extension of the withholding principle to dividend and interest income;

(2) Repeal of the $50 dividend exclusion and the 4 percent dividend credit;

(3) Revision of the tax treatment of business deductions for entertainment, gifts, and other expenses, to stop abuses of "expense-account living";

(4) Elimination of the special tax preference for capital gains from the sale of depreciable property, real and personal;

(5) Removal of unwarranted preferences (a) to cooperatives, (b) to mutual fire and casualty insurance companies, and (c) to mutual savings banks and savings and loan associations; and

(6) Revision of the tax treatment of foreign income, to remove defects and inequities in the law. Removal of the unwarranted incentive to the export of capital will be consistent with the efficient distribution of capital resources in the world

and will aid our balance of payments position. Tax deferral privileges should be limited to profits earned in less developed countries, and opportunities for "tax haven" operations should be eliminated.

In addition, I recommend that the corporate income tax and certain excise taxes again be extended at present levels for another year beyond June 30, 1962, except that the structure of taxes and user charges in the transportation field be altered as proposed in my Budget Message.

In considering tax revision in the United States, we must not limit ourselves simply to Federal taxation. Our States, counties, and municipalities collect nearly half as much tax revenue as the Federal Government. There is great potential for equity or inequity, for incentive or disincentive, in their highly diverse tax systems. In addition, the effectiveness of Federal tax policies can be enhanced by harmonious coordination with State and local fiscal systems. There is wide latitude for improvements in the coordination of tax systems and in operations with intergovernmental implications. In this effort, the Advisory Commission on Intergovernmental Relations is performing a valuable service. I urge careful study of its recommendations at all levels of government.

Later this year, I shall present to the Congress a major program of tax reform. This broad program will re-examine tax rates and the definition of the income tax base. It will be aimed at the simplification of our tax structure, the equal treatment of equally situated persons, and the strengthening of incentives for individual effort and for productive investment.

The momentum of our economy has been restored. This momentum must be maintained, if the full potential of our free economy is to be released in the service of the Nation and the world. In this Report I have proposed a program to sustain our prosperity and accelerate our growth—in short, to realize our economic potential. In this undertaking, I ask the support of the Congress and the American people.

THE ANNUAL REPORT
OF THE
COUNCIL OF ECONOMIC ADVISERS

LETTER OF TRANSMITTAL

Council of Economic Advisers,
Washington, D.C., January 12, 1962.

The President:

Sir: The Council of Economic Advisers herewith submits its Annual Report, January 1962, in accordance with Section 4(c) (2) of the Employment Act of 1946.

Respectfully,

Walter W. Heller,
Chairman.

Kermit Gordon

James Tobin

CONTENTS

The contents are reprinted in entirety (original page numbers); however, only the body of the text is reprinted.

LIST OF TABLES AND CHARTS

INTRODUCTION

The Report of the Council of Economic Advisers is a document directed toward economic problems and national economic policy. It is written in keen awareness that the ultimate goals of the Nation are human goals, and that economics is merely instrumental to the making of a better life for all Americans. Involuntary unemployment is a sign of economic waste, but the fundamental evil of unemployment is that it is an affront to human dignity. Expenditures on better education and better health are investments in future capacity to produce; but even if they were not, they would be intrinsically desirable because ignorance and illness bar the way to happiness and security for many of our citizens. Social security and welfare benefits help to limit the depth of recessions, but their more important function is to protect human beings from hunger and despair. Statistical tables are to the economist what test tube and microscope are to the scientist—the tools of the trade; but for the one as for the other, the ultimate dedication is to the quality of human life.

The Employment Act of 1946 is a historic affirmation of the responsibility of the Federal Government "to promote maximum employment, production, and purchasing power." The Act commits the Federal Government to seek to create and to maintain an economic environment in which "there will be afforded useful employment opportunities, including self-employment, for those able, willing, and seeking to work." These goals, as the Act recognizes, must be sought within the broad framework of U.S. political and economic institutions—free competitive enterprise and the Federal system of government. And they must be sought by means consistent with other national needs, obligations, and objectives.

The people of this Nation—aided by an immense and fertile land, by rich stores of minerals and other gifts of nature, and by technologies and tools which lighten the work of man and multiply its fruits—can produce vast quantities of the goods and services human beings want. The Employment Act's broad goal of maximum employment, production, and purchasing power implies, first of all, that the vast productive capacity of the Nation should be used and not permitted to lie idle or run to waste. And, second, it implies that this capacity itself should be raised to enable each new generation to advance to higher standards of well-being.

The first of these objectives—maximum use of our existing productive resources—is the topic of Chapter 1. One requirement is to maintain aggregate demand for goods and services at, but not above, levels sufficient to buy the goods and services the economy is capable of producing. Since inadequate demand has in recent years been a major cause of unemployment and excess capacity, expansion of demand has been and remains a principal task of government policy. But expansion of demand is not the whole answer. The functioning of markets for labor and for its products can be improved in ways which will bring into effective use a greater proportion of the Nation's productive resources. Government policy can play a role here too. These two aspects of the current economic situation, and the relevance of current and proposed policies, are discussed in Chapter 1.

The second objective—to accelerate the growth of the productive powers of the United States—is the subject of Chapter 2. The United States has joined its partners in the Organization for Economic Cooperation and Development (OECD) in setting "as a collective target the attainment during the decade from 1960 to 1970 of a growth in real gross national product of 50 percent for the 20 Member countries taken together." This growth in production in Europe and North America is intended to lead both to an increase in standards of living in the industrial countries and to "a significant increase in aid to less developed countries."

The OECD declaration underscores the fact that free nations must pursue their economic objectives in concert. U.S. policy under the Employment Act must take full account of our international economic transactions. Chapter 3, therefore, examines the U.S. balance of payments and the external position of the dollar, particularly as they are related to domestic economic developments and policies.

The necessity of moving toward balance in U.S. international accounts has given price stability new and compelling importance as a requirement of economic policy for recovery and growth. An appropriate and responsive structure of relative prices is equally important, to bring resources into full and efficient use and to guide the growing productive capacity of the economy to serve the Nation's changing needs. Competition and mobility of resources, by contributing to the efficiency and flexibility of the price structure, will at the same time weaken upward pressures on the price level which sometimes accompany and endanger high employment. Chapter 4 is a discussion of recent, current, and prospective developments and policies affecting the course of prices in the United States.

Full utilization of manpower and other productive resources, faster growth in capacity to produce, balance of payments equilibrium, and price stability—these are necessarily the tasks of U.S. economic policy today. Significant progress has been made toward achieving all of them in 1961. In many important respects they are complementary; especially in the long run, measures which advance one task advance the others. But in other respects they are difficult to reconcile; measures useful for one purpose may be harmful for another. As perhaps never before, the complexity and importance of the tasks facing the U.S. economy in this decade challenge the wisdom and vision of Government and of all sectors of the private economy.

Chapter 1

Toward Full Recovery

PART I: OBJECTIVES, PROGRESS, AND PROSPECTS

THE U.S. ECONOMY made substantial advances in 1961 toward the goals of the Employment Act: "maximum employment, production, and purchasing power." Total production rose to a record rate of $542 billion a year in the fourth quarter, $41 billion above the level at the beginning of the year. Unemployment, which had been close to 7 percent of the labor force ever since December 1960, fell sharply toward the end of 1961; the rate was 6.1 percent in December. The annual rate of income, after taxes, of the American people rose from $1,940 per capita in the first quarter to $2,032 per capita in the last quarter of 1961. These gains in disposable income were almost entirely real gains in purchasing power. Prices were virtually stable during the year; the consumer index rose only 0.6 percent between December 1960 and November 1961. As the year ended, the economy was advancing vigorously.

Government fiscal and monetary policies contributed strongly to the favorable economic developments of the past year. Although the downswing probably would have ended early in 1961 in any case, the impressive pace of the economic expansion must be attributed in large measure to government actions. A summary of the Administration's program in 1961 to promote economic recovery is given in the Appendix to this chapter.

In spite of the significant gains of 1961, the economy at the turn of the year still fell short of the standards set forth in the Employment Act. Too many persons "able, willing, and seeking to work" were unable to find "useful employment opportunities." Even at record levels, national production had not yet reached its potential at full employment; and the purchasing power of the American people—the command over goods and services represented by their incomes—was still too low.

The prospect for 1962 is a continuation of the favorable trend of 1961. Whether the current expansion is sufficiently strong and durable to carry the economy to "maximum employment, production, and purchasing power", no one can now foretell with certainty. Current and proposed government actions will continue to give strong support to economic expansion. If these are coupled with continued strength in the private economy, the current expansion would reduce unemployment to 4 percent of the labor force by mid-1963. But, given the inevitable uncertainties, government policy must be alert and flexible, ready to promote the achievement of full recovery within the coming fiscal year and to counteract developments which might threaten its attainment. The President has made important proposals to increase the effectiveness and flexibility of government fiscal policy; these are discussed at length in Part II of this chapter.

Part I of this chapter discusses, first, the current implications of the objectives of the Employment Act: "maximum employment" as a guide to the fiscal and monetary policies of Government and to other public and private policies of equal ultimate importance; and the potential production and purchasing power of the American economy at levels of employment which full recovery can achieve. Next, it describes the progress of the economy in 1961 toward these objectives and the outlook for continued advance in 1962. Part II of the chapter discusses government policies for full recovery and maximum employment, with special emphasis on the Administration's policies in 1961 and its programs under way or proposed for the coming year.

THE OBJECTIVE OF MAXIMUM EMPLOYMENT

Reasons for Concern over Unemployment

The great depression led this Nation, and most other nations of the free world, to assume national responsibility for the human tragedy and economic waste of involuntary unemployment. Unemployment had previously been regarded as almost solely the personal responsibility of the individual; now it came to be acknowledged as a charge on the conscience of the Nation. The mass unemployment of the 1930's led to new understanding: that to be unemployed is not to be unemployable; that job opportunities for individual workers depend on national economic circumstances beyond their control.

There are three principal reasons why involuntary unemployment is a national concern: (1) the human obligation to prevent and to relieve economic distress, (2) the basic principle of a free economy that an individual should be able to choose freely how to use his time, whether to work for pay or not, and (3) the economic waste of leaving productive resources idle.

Preventing economic distress. First, a wealthy nation cannot in good conscience permit its citizens to be inadequately nourished, clothed, or housed; its sick to be denied medical care; or its young to be deprived of schooling. Unemployment insurance and public assistance are recognitions of this social obligation. But they are not substitutes for the opportunity to earn income from useful employment. For the breadwinner and his family, unemployment means a reduction in living standards. Only about three-fifths of the unemployed in 1961 were receiving unemployment insurance benefits. Even those who were insured generally found weekly benefits a pale shadow of their lost wages. When the unemployment insurance program was inaugurated in the late 1930's, the goal was to provide benefits equal to about half of previous earnings. As Table 1 indicates, benefits now do not meet this standard. The Administration has proposed permanent legislation to strengthen the unemployment insurance system in this and other respects.

TABLE 1.—*Weekly earnings in selected industries, and unemployment insurance benefits, 1961*

Item	Weekly average, 1961
Unemployment insurance benefits, all industries [1]	$33.80
Weekly earnings, selected industries: [2]	
Retail trade	64.01
Manufacturing	92.34
Telephone communication	92.75
Wholesale trade	93.32
Bituminous coal mining	112.10
Class I railroads	112.41
Contract construction	117.66

[1] For State programs only; see Table B-23.
[2] Gross earnings for production workers or nonsupervisory employees; see Table B-27.

Source: Department of Labor.

For all too many, unemployment has not been simply an uncomfortable interlude between jobs but a catastrophe of long duration; almost one-third of those unemployed in December 1961 had been out of work for 15 or more weeks and one-sixth had been unemployed for at least 27 weeks. Family savings vanish when unemployment is prolonged.

Unemployment is not a perfect measure of the incidence of economic distress. Failure to find work does not entail poverty for some unemployed persons: women whose husbands have good jobs, young people who can fall back on well-to-do parents, older people who have assured livelihoods from property incomes or annuities, people who earn an adequate annual income from work at a seasonal occupation during part of a year. On the other hand, there are many causes of economic distress other than unemployment. Some persons, though employed, suffer from reduced and inadequate incomes resulting from failure to obtain more than part-time or occasional work, or to earn decent returns from long hours of self-employment on the farm or in the shop. Other individuals are not regarded as unemployed simply because, discouraged by a lack of suitable opportunities, they have abandoned the search for jobs. Included in this group are individuals with personal disabilities who can find jobs only when labor markets are tight.

Nevertheless, changes in unemployment are indicative of changes in the over-all magnitude of economic distress. The same conditions of general prosperity which lead to lower unemployment figures also lead to lower rates of involuntary part-time idleness, to better rewards from self-employment, and to more job opportunities for persons on the fringes of the labor force. While effective measures to provide adequate job opportunities will not solve all problems of economic distress, they will solve a substantial share of them. And without successful policy against general unemployment, other attacks on poverty and insecurity stand little chance of success.

Assuring free choice. The second reason for national concern over unemployment is the basic principle of a free economy, embodied in the Employment Act, that "useful employment opportunities" be afforded "for those able, willing, and seeking to work." A free society abhors forced idleness as well as forced labor. This principle does not apply a means or needs test for job-seekers. It acknowledges that mature individuals should be able to choose for themselves how they spend their time, as between gainful employment, housework, leisure, and education. Involuntary unemployment can destroy morale and freedom of choice whether or not the individual is in economic need. Americans want to work. Neither welfare programs nor personal means can erase the frustration of the individual who is forced to conclude that society does not need or want his contribution. The general preference for gainful work over unemployment, however well compensated, is demonstrated by the low levels of unemployment in areas with buoyant labor markets, in occupations with ample job opportunities, and in the population at large during years of prosperity.

Avoiding economic waste. Finally, excessive unemployment is a waste of productive resources. When these resources are left idle, the useful goods and services they could have produced are forever lost to the Nation. These losses would be enormously wasteful at any time. They are dangerous in a decade when the economy must not only meet compelling domestic needs but underwrite the defense of freedom throughout the world. In coupling maximum production and purchasing power with maximum employment, the Employment Act recognizes the losses of national output and real income associated with unemployment. An estimate of these losses in present circumstances is attempted below. Changes in the unemployment rate are roughly indicative of changes in the "gap" between realized and potential production. The same measures of policy which will lower unemployment will also raise national output closer to capacity to produce. The national economic losses associated with unemployment are, of course, quite independent of the individual circumstances of the unemployed. If housewives, elderly persons, and teen-agers on vacation from school are eager and able to produce useful goods and services, it is foolish and wasteful for the Nation to forego their contributions.

Measures of unemployment. The global measure of unemployment as a percentage of the civilian labor force, provided monthly by the Current Population Survey and published by the Bureau of Labor Statistics, is the best single measure of the economic distress, the frustration of free choice, and the economic waste associated with unemployment. But there are other measures of independent interest. Four of these measures, along with the global rate, are shown in Chart 1:

(1) The unemployment rate among *experienced wage and salary workers*—those who have already held at least one job. This measure

excludes the self-employed and new entrants to the labor force. (2) The unemployment rate among *married men living with their wives*. This measure relates to individuals whose commitment to the labor force is permanent and necessary to the support of their families. It does not cover all individuals with such a commitment, and conceptually it is inappropriate both as a measure of economic waste and as an indicator of involuntary unemployment among persons "able, willing, and seeking to work." (3) A *full-time equivalent* measure which (a) adds to the wholly unemployed the full-time equivalent of work lost by involuntary part-time employment and (b) subtracts the self-employed from both the labor force and civilian employment on the grounds that they are not subject to the risk of unemployment. This concept has merit as a measure of econo.nic waste and of imbalance in markets for hired labor. (4) The number of

CHART 1

Measures of Unemployment

PERCENT UNEMPLOYED

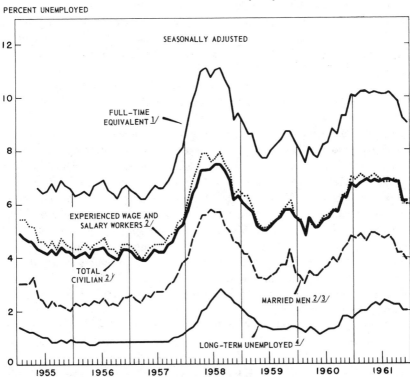

1/UNEMPLOYED PLUS|FULL-TIME EQUIVALENT OF PART-TIME EMPLOYED AS PERCENT OF CIVILIAN LABOR FORCE.EXCLUDES SELF-EMPLOYED AND UNPAID FAMILY WORKERS.

2/PERCENT OF CIVILIAN LABOR FORCE IN GROUP.

3/MARRIED MEN LIVING WITH THEIR WIVES.

4/PERSONS UNEMPLOYED 15 WEEKS OR MORE AS PERCENT OF CIVILIAN LABOR FORCE.

SOURCES: DEPARTMENT OF LABOR AND COUNCIL OF ECONOMIC ADVISERS.

long-term unemployed, those who have been jobless for more than 15 weeks, as a percentage of the labor force.   This rate is an important measure of the financial and social distress caused by the concentration of prolonged unemployment on a small fraction of the labor force.

The differences among these measures reveal more clearly than any single measure the anatomy of unemployment.   But they show no systematic tendency to widen or narrow.   If due allowance is made for volatility in month-to-month movements all five measures tell the same story about changes in economic conditions.

Full Employment as the Objective of Stabilization Policy

The goal of the Employment Act is "maximum employment," or—to put it the other way round—minimum unemployment.   Ideally, all persons able, willing, and seeking to work should be continuously employed.   Involuntary unemployment is an individual and social evil.   No one would prefer for its own sake a higher rate of unemployment to a lower one.   But zero unemployment is unattainable.   A more meaningful figure is needed to give content to the realistic and forceful declaration of policy in the Employment Act.   A feasible interim goal must reflect a balancing of employment and production objectives with other considerations of national policy, within the limits set by the existing characteristics of the economy.   Such a goal is set forth in the discussion which follows.   We must not forget, however, that any practical unemployment goal is only a temporary compromise, and its attainment must never be an occasion for relaxation, but rather an incentive to search out ways to achieve a still lower rate.

The partial conflict which exists between minimum unemployment and certain other national objectives—and which imposes the necessity of striking a balance between them—results mainly from the fact that these other objectives are served by stability of the general price level.   Given the existing structure of the economy and the nature of the processes by which prices and wages are determined, a serious attempt to push unemployment close to zero would produce a high rate of price inflation.   The result would be a weakening of the competitive position of U.S. products in world markets, an arbitrary redistribution of real income and wealth, and a threat of even more serious consequences if expectations of further inflation should become dominant.

Happily, however, the conflict between the goals served by price stability and the goal of minimum unemployment is only partial.   Stabilization policy—policy to influence the level of aggregate demand—can strike a balance between them which largely avoids the consequences of a failure in either direction.   Furthermore, the degree of conflict can be diminished by private and public policies which improve the functioning of labor and product markets.

There are various possible causes of unemployment, on the one hand, and of inflationary pressure, on the other.   These causes may be grouped

44

into (1) those related to aggregate demand and (2) those related to the structure and functioning of markets. It is necessary to distinguish carefully between these two groups of causes in setting an appropriate target for stabilization policy.

The relation of aggregate demand and of structural causes to unemployment may be briefly described as follows:

(1) The total effective demand for goods and services—by consumers, businesses, and governments—may be insufficient to employ all the persons seeking work at existing wage rates.

(2) Workers may be idle while vacancies are unfilled. This may arise because the workers live too far away from the available jobs, are not qualified for them, or simply are unaware of their existence. In a dynamic economy, there will always be workers between jobs, some seeking new positions out of preference, some displaced by economic and technological change. New entrants to the labor force will similarly be unemployed while locating jobs suitable to their qualifications and preferences. The length of "frictional" unemployment for any one worker, and the size of the pool of frictionally unemployed, depend on how smoothly the labor market functions, how well the skills, experience, and qualifications of workers match the specifications of available jobs, how ready workers are to change residence and occupation, how adequate are facilities for training and retraining, and how rapidly displacements resulting from economic change are occurring. Structural unemployment may be regarded as an extreme form of frictional unemployment. It occurs when inability or failure to make the necessary adjustments concentrates unemployment of long duration on displaced workers in particular areas and occupations, while elsewhere jobs are seeking workers of quite different qualifications.

Similarly, aggregate demand and the structure of markets are related to the price level, as follows:

(1) Inflation may result from excessive aggregate demand. Demands for goods and services by consumers, businesses, and governments may add to a total which exceeds the amount that the economy can supply. Prices will be bid up in all markets, and, as business firms try to expand output in order to seize the profit opportunities presented, increases in wages and in costs of materials will follow. The resulting rise in incomes will reinforce and renew the process. In less extreme circumstances, aggregate demand may press hard upon, but not exceed, the economy's productive capacity. Increases in prices and wages may occur nevertheless, reflecting the need to obtain additional output by using labor and capital more intensively—by making greater use of overtime labor, by attracting workers from great distances, by making employment attractive to persons formerly not in the labor force, and by making use of obsolescent capacity and inefficient production techniques.

(2) Upward pressure on prices may originate in those sectors of the economy where competitive forces are weak and large corporations and

unions have a considerable degree of discretion in setting prices and wages. (This discretion, and the public interest in its responsible exercise, are discussed in Chapter 4.) There are two ways in which wage and price decisions in these sectors may put upward pressure on the general price level. First, prices may be increased when demand is not strong in the aggregate or even in the specific industries involved. Because the prices of these industries affect costs elsewhere, increases in their prices tend to spread throughout the economy. Second, prices in these sectors may remain constant in the face of declining demand, although they rise in times of increasing demand. The result in the long run is an upward drift in prices in these industries, which again tends to be transmitted to the whole economy.

Expansion of aggregate demand is clearly the specific remedy for unemployment caused by a deficiency of aggregate demand. Excessive aggregate demand, however, is a source of inflationary pressure. Consequently, the target for stabilization policy is to eliminate the unemployment which results from inadequate aggregate demand without creating a demand-induced inflation. A situation in which this is achieved can appropriately be described as one of "full employment," in the sense that further expansion of expenditure for goods and services, and for labor to produce them, would be met by only minor increases in employment and output, and by major increases in prices and wages. Correspondingly, expansion of demand beyond full employment levels would involve a major sacrifice of the objectives served by price stability, and only a minor gain with respect to the goal of maximum employment.

The selection of a particular target for stabilization policy does not commit policy to an unchangeable definition of the rate of unemployment corresponding to full employment. Circumstances may alter the responsiveness of the unemployment rate and the price level to the volume of aggregate demand. Current experience must therefore be the guide.

In the existing economic circumstances, an unemployment rate of about 4 percent is a reasonable and prudent full employment target for stabilization policy. If we move firmly to reduce the impact of structural unemployment, we will be able to move the unemployment target steadily from 4 percent to successively lower rates.

The recent history of the U.S. economy contains no evidence that labor and commodity markets are in general excessively "tight" at 4 percent unemployment. Neither does it suggest that stabilization policy alone could press unemployment significantly below 4 percent without creating substantial upward pressure on prices.

When unemployment was about 5 percent, as in 1959 before the steel strike and in the first half of 1960, the economy showed many independent symptoms of slack, notably the substantial underutilization of plant and equipment capacity. The wholesale price index fell at a rate of 0.2 percent a year in the 15 months April 1959–July 1960; and at the consumer level, prices of commodities other than food rose at a rate of only 0.6 percent.

The economy last experienced 4 percent unemployment in the period May 1955–August 1957, when the unemployment rate fluctuated between 3.9 percent and 4.4 percent (seasonally adjusted). During this period, prices and wages rose at a rate which impaired the competitiveness of some U.S. products in world markets. However, there is good reason to believe that upward pressures of this magnitude are not a permanent and systematic feature of our economy when it is operating in the neighborhood of 4 percent unemployment. The 1955–57 boom was concentrated in durable manufactured goods—notably automobiles (in 1955), machinery and equipment, and primary metals. The uneven nature of the expansion undoubtedly accentuated the wage and price pressures of those years. Moreover, the review of the present price outlook in Chapter 4 points to a recent strengthening in the forces making for price stability. The experience of 1955–57 is nevertheless sobering, and experience at higher levels of activity will be needed to indicate whether stabilization policy can now undertake a more ambitious assignment than 4 percent unemployment.

There is no precise unemployment rate at which expansion of aggregate demand suddenly ceases to affect employment and begins to affect solely the general price level. The distinction between aggregate demand effects and structural effects is a matter of degree, both for employment and for the general price level. Sufficiently high levels of aggregate demand can, and have in the past, cut deeply into frictional and structural unemployment. When vacancies are numerous, the time required to find an attractive job is reduced. When there are vacancies everywhere, no one needs to travel far to find a job. And when no applicant for a job meets its exact specifications, the specifications may well be adjusted. Similarly, the degree of inflationary pressure arising from discretionary price and wage setting is not independent of the general strength of demand. Presumably, this pressure could be entirely eliminated by sufficient weakness in aggregate demand if that were the sole objective of stabilization policy.

But while stabilization policy would not be an ineffective cure for either one or the other of these economic ailments, it would be an extremely expensive cure. On the one hand, attempting to reduce frictional and structural unemployment by a highly inflationary expansion of demand would court disaster in our balance of payments position. On the other hand, an attempt to restrict aggregate demand so severely as to eliminate all risk of an increase in the general price level might well involve keeping the economy far below full employment. This would mean sacrifice rather than achievement of both of the major goals that price stability serves: Equity would be sacrificed because the economy as a whole, and the unemployed in particular, would suffer as a result of the manner in which a few individuals and groups exercise their economic power. Eventually, the balance of payments would also be weakened: under conditions of prolonged unemployment and excess capacity, the investment needed to keep our exports competitive in quality and cost would be unlikely to occur.

The 4 percent interim goal refers to the global measure of unemployment as a percentage of the civilian labor force. An objective stated in terms of any of the other measures of unemployment discussed above would have the same implications for stabilization policy, for the various measures tell the same story with respect to the degree of over-all tightness in the economy. The particular numerical statement of the goal must, of course, change with the unemployment concept used. For example, 4 percent in terms of the global measure is roughly equivalent to a rate of $2\frac{1}{4}$ percent among married men living with their wives; the latter figure, though lower, is at least as serious as the former in its implications for the human consequences of unemployment. Corresponding figures for the other measures of unemployment are $4\frac{1}{4}$ percent among experienced wage and salary workers, $6\frac{1}{4}$ percent for the full-time equivalent concept, and, if the 4 percent global rate is long sustained, a two-thirds of one percent rate of long-term unemployment.

Unemployment of 4 percent is a modest goal, but it must be emphasized that it is a goal which should be achievable by stabilization policy alone. Other policy measures, referred to in the next section and discussed in detail in Part II of this chapter, will help to reduce the goal attainable in the future below the 4 percent figure. Meanwhile, the policies of business and labor, no less than those of Government, will in large measure determine whether the 4 percent figure can be achieved and perhaps bettered in the current recovery, without unacceptable inflationary pressures.

Full Employment and Structural Unemployment

One way to raise the attainable level of full employment is to reduce frictional and structural unemployment by improving the mobility of labor and the efficiency of labor markets. The amount of frictional and structural unemployment varies from country to country and from time to time within any one country. It has sometimes been suggested that, though a 4-percent unemployment rate was once achievable in the United States with adequate levels of demand, it is no longer a feasible goal because of increasing technological displacement of workers, rapid obsolescence of skills, intractable pockets of depression, and greater numbers of young people swelling the labor force. Careful analyses at the Council and elsewhere—notably in a recent report by the staff of the Joint Economic Committee of the Congress—lend no support to the view that frictional and structural unemployment is a rising proportion of the labor force. It would be wholly wrong, however, to conclude that improvement in the structure of the labor market is not both possible and of high importance.

The displacement of labor through changes in technology, consumer tastes, and the geographic distribution of industry is an inevitable part of the growth of a free and progressive economy.   But the level of unemployment corresponding to any given pace of progress depends on the smoothness with which markets function.   The size of the pool of unemployed workers, like the size of a pool of water, is determined jointly by the flow into it and the flow out of it.   The flow into it depends on the rate at which workers leave jobs or are displaced and on the rate at which new workers enter the labor force without jobs.   The flow out depends on the speed with which the unemployed can transfer to jobs vacated by retirement, and to other skills, other industries, and other areas where jobs are available in expanding sectors of the economy.

Economic policy can reduce the size of the pool by providing opportunities for vocational training and retraining, by improving the flow of information about job opportunities, by facilitating the relocation of displaced workers, by acting to reduce and eliminate discriminatory hiring practices, and by assisting in the rehabilitation of depressed areas through the renovation of public facilities and the attraction of viable industry.   Administration policies and proposals to attain these ends are discussed in Part II of the present chapter.

The benefits to the United States from the pursuit of such policies are great.   In their absence, many of our citizens become, in a real sense, victims of progress; they are condemned to prolonged periods of unemployment which benefit no one and inflict an unjust penalty on an arbitrarily selected few.   In their absence, we can expect resistance to technological progress from those who would be harmed by it without prospect of reward.

The returns from such policies do not come instantaneously.   For that reason, we should undertake them now, even while unemployment and excess capacity are widespread.   There is still time to reap the benefits of the reduction of structural unemployment during the current recovery.   But these policies are no substitute for an adequate level of demand.   Experience tells us that the pull of expanding job opportunities is a vitally necessary condition for the success of policies to assure a better functioning labor market.

FULL PRODUCTION

Productive Potential

The Economic Report is required by the Employment Act to set forth "the levels of employment, production, and purchasing power obtaining in the United States and such levels needed to carry out the policy" of the Act.   In accordance with the obligation to set forth the levels of production needed to carry out the objectives of the Act, the Council has made the following estimates: (1) In the first quarter of 1961, a gap of $51 billion (1961 prices, annual rate) existed between actual gross national product (GNP) and the output obtainable at full employment.   (2) By the last quarter of the year, recovery had narrowed this gap to about $28 billion.

(3) For 1961 as a whole, production averaged $40 billion below potential.
(4) The production potential for the year 1962 is estimated at $580 billion
(in 1961 prices).

Estimates of this kind cannot, of course, be precise. But they are essential
in order to specify, within reasonable margins of error, a current measure of
"maximum production" linked to "maximum employment." They indicate
clearly that this Nation can achieve a huge bonus of output and income by
making full use of its resources.

The level of unemployment is a barometer of economic waste. Each
percentage point of progress toward 4 percent in the unemployment
rate has meant a gain of roughly 3 percent in total output in postwar periods
of expansion.

The sources of potential gains in output accompanying full employment
are given in Table 2, which shows the gain in output that each source could

TABLE 2.—*Allocation of estimated $40 billion gap between potential and actual gross nationa
product, 1961*

[Billions of dollars]

Source	Associated Increment of output
Total	40
Lower unemployment	15
Larger labor force in response to greater demand	4
Longer hours of work per man associated with higher utilization	5
Greater productivity per man-hour associated with higher utilization	16

Source: Council of Economic Advisers.

have contributed if aggregate demand in 1961 had been sufficient to reduce
unemployment to 4 percent of the labor force. The figures incorporate evidence from postwar relationships among labor input, productivity, and output. An unemployment rate of 4.0 percent instead of 6.7 percent for 1961
would in itself have increased the number of jobs by 3 percent of actual
employment. But it would have raised production by much more, about 8
percent. The reason that improved employment conditions yield magnified
gains in output is that, in addition to putting the jobless back to work, they
have a number of other favorable effects on output.

Higher output would have accompanied lower unemployment in the
following manner:

(1) Actual unemployment in 1961 was 4.8 million persons. Given the
actual 1961 labor force of 71.6 million persons, 2 million of the unemployed
would have been at work at an unemployment rate of 4 percent.

(2) At full employment, the labor force would probably have been considerably higher in 1961 and production would have been correspondingly
increased. Participation in the labor force is encouraged by greater availability of job opportunities. In recent years of slack activity, the actual

labor force has been abnormally low relative to the number of persons of working age.

(3) Furthermore, a brisker pace of economic activity is accompanied by a higher average number of hours a week worked by those employed. Part-time jobs are converted into full-time employment, and overtime work increases in private nonfarm industry.

(4) Because of these three factors—less unemployment, larger labor force, and longer hours of work—labor input at full employment in 1961 would have exceeded actual labor input by more than 4½ percent, the equivalent of 7 billion man-hours. The added man-hours could have increased production by $24 billion, at existing rates of productivity.

(5) The higher productivity that accompanies fuller use of resources would have meant still more output. In recessions, business firms cannot cut back their labor force as fast as their output falls. Clerical help and sales and supervisory personnel are essentially "overhead." Moreover, while firms can and do lay off production workers, they do so only with reluctance, preferring both to maintain morale and to avoid the expense of hiring and training new labor when business activity recovers. Recessions thus produce on-the-job underemployment, which is reflected in depressed levels of productivity. In movements toward full employment, recession losses in productivity are regained. At full employment, productivity in 1961 would, according to past evidence, have been 2 to 4 percent higher than it actually was. This gain is equivalent to a $10 to $20 billion increment of GNP. The table shows a $16 billion figure, near the middle of the range, bringing the total estimated gain from all sources to $40 billion.

These calculations receive further support from an alternative approach. Evidence on the relationship between output and unemployment suggests that actual GNP in mid-1955, when the unemployment rate was close to 4 percent, was equal to potential output. The trend rate of growth of GNP, adjusted for changes in unemployment levels, has averaged about 3½ percent in the post-Korean period. Thus the path of potential GNP can be represented by a 3½ percent trend from actual GNP in mid-1955 (Chart 2). The 1961 value of the trend exceeds actual output by $40 billion, which is equal to the sum of the components described above.

The distance between potential and actual GNP was narrowed by $23 billion from the first to last quarter of 1961, as output increased by $37 billion (1961 prices). Among the four factors listed above, the first two, reduction in unemployment and increase in the labor force, contributed less to the gain in production than past experience would have suggested. Of the other two factors, hours of work in nonfarm industries expanded roughly in accord with past behavior; but man-hour productivity achieved an exceptional gain, probably above 6 percent in the three quarters of expansion. As a result, the 7½ percent increase in total production was achieved with a very small increase in employment: nonfarm employment increased by about 1½ percent, but this rise was partially offset by a decline

CHART 2

Gross National Product, Actual and Potential, and Unemployment Rate

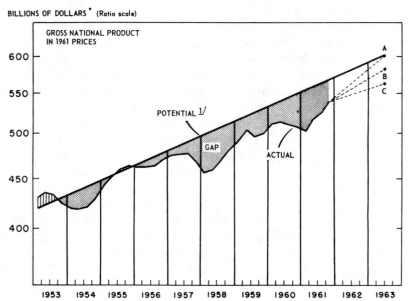

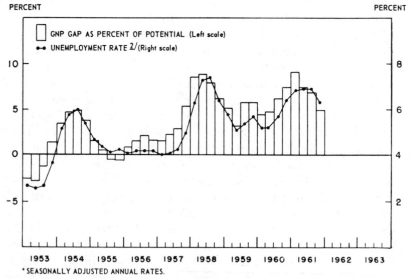

* SEASONALLY ADJUSTED ANNUAL RATES.

1/ 3½% TREND LINE THROUGH MIDDLE OF 1955.

2/ UNEMPLOYMENT AS PERCENT OF CIVILIAN LABOR FORCE; SEASONALLY ADJUSTED.

NOTE: A, B, AND C REPRESENT GNP IN MIDDLE OF 1963 ASSUMING UNEMPLOYMENT RATE OF 4%, 5%, AND 6%, RESPECTIVELY.

SOURCES: DEPARTMENT OF COMMERCE, DEPARTMENT OF LABOR, AND COUNCIL OF ECONOMIC ADVISERS.

in agricultural employment. It is primarily because latent productivity was exploited so effectively that unemployment remained high.

The estimated gap of $28 billion, or 5 percent, between potential and actual output in the fourth quarter of 1961 reflected principally a shortfall in persons employed. At the end of the year, there was room for a slight further rise in average weekly hours worked. The impressive gains in productivity during the year brought output per man-hour at the year-end close to the full employment level indicated by past experience. Nevertheless, further gains in productivity as a result of fuller utilization of existing capacity may still be ahead. In any case, further additions to output during the coming year are expected to require larger increases in employment than in 1961.

The unemployment rate will fall in the coming year if, and only if, production continues to rise in relation to the economy's potential. The prospects for 1962 are discussed later in this chapter.

A full-utilization economy in 1963 would provide nearly 72 million civilian jobs and generate an estimated $600 billion GNP (1961 prices). These figures—5 million more jobs and nearly $80 billion more output than 1961 levels—suggest the magnitude of the opportunity and challenge we face. To help visualize this challenge more concretely, Table 3 presents an illustrative pattern of employment, productivity, and output for the full year 1963 consistent with 4 percent unemployment.

TABLE 3.—*Employment, output, and productivity, 1961 actual and 1963 illustrative*

Sector	Employment (millions of persons)		Output (billions of dollars, 1961 prices)		Output per employed person (dollars)	
	1961 actual	1963 illustra-tive [1]	1961 actual [2]	1963 illustra-tive [1]	1961 actual [2]	1963 illustra-tive [1]
Total economy [3]	69.4	74.3	521.2	600	7,500	8,100
Agricultural	5.5	5.2	21.0	21	3,800	4,000
Private nonagricultural	54.2	58.8	449.4	525	8,300	8,900
General government [3]	9.7	10.3	50.8	54		
Addendum:						
Civilian employment	66.8	71.6				
Unemployment	4.8	3.0				

[1] Illustrative pattern projected at 4 percent unemployment; by Council of Economic Advisers.
[2] Estimates by Council of Economic Advisers.
[3] Includes military.

Sources: Department of Commerce and Department of Labor (except as noted).

Plant and Equipment Capacity

Periods of slack and recession in economic activity lead to idle machines as well as idle men. Only once since 1949, at the trough of the 1958 recession, was there more excess plant and equipment capacity in U.S. industry than at the start of 1961. While increases in output during the past year have led to fuller use of capital facilities, 1962 begins with considerable room for expanded output from existing plant and equipment, enough room to permit achievement of the full employment goal. This excess capacity is available to be tapped on demand. It is easier to expand employment at stable prices when tools are already available for new job-holders. Otherwise, capital might act as a bottleneck, obstructing the flow of increased demand for goods into improved employment opportunities for labor.

While unused capital is a reserve source of supply, it dampens the vigor of demand. Although much of investment is undertaken primarily for replacement and modernization, investment for expansion of capacity is important to aggregate demand as well as to economic growth. Induce-ments to expand plant and equipment are stronger when present facilities are fully utilized. The rate at which existing capacity is utilized also influences the ability of firms to finance investment out of retained earnings. Unused tools are a drag on profits. They yield no return and they impose overhead costs for maintenance and depreciation.

The reliability of measures of productive capacity and capital stock is severely limited by both conceptual and statistical difficulties. But an increasing amount of quantitative evidence is becoming available. Care-fully used, it can be very helpful in arriving at the needed qualitative judgments about productive capacity. Two series of data on capital utilization from 1953 to date are presented in Chart 3. One measures the ratio of actual output to capacity output for all manufacturing industry. The other shows the output-capital ratio: the ratio of the value of total ouput to the value of the stock of plant and equipment, both expressed in 1954 prices, covering all private domestic business except residential housing. Although the two measures are derived by substantially different methods, they move together very closely, offering encouraging evidence of their general validity as measures of capital utilization.

A number of significant points are evident from the chart:

(1) Measures of capital utilization, like unemployment rates, indicate the persistence of slack in the economy over the past five years. Even dur-ing the expansion of 1959–60, operating rates and the ratios of output to the stock of capital remained considerably below their 1955–56 levels.

(2) Recessions are clearly marked by excess capacity in plant and equip-ment. Capital was most underutilized at the 1958 trough; the low point of early 1961 lies about midway between the 1958 rates and those of the 1954 recession. Because capacity grew slowly in 1958–61, excess capacity in early 1961 was smaller than in 1958 even though unemployment was just as large.

(3) Output gains must match the growth of plant and equipment capacity in order to maintain rates of capital utilization. Periods of slow advance in production, like 1956–57 and 1959–60, lead to declining rates of utilization.

CHART 3

Capacity Utilization and Corporate Profits

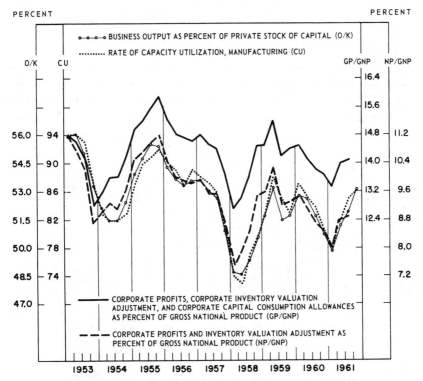

SOURCE: COUNCIL OF ECONOMIC ADVISERS (BASED ON DATA OF DEPARTMENT OF COMMERCE
AND BOARD OF GOVERNORS OF THE FEDERAL RESERVE SYSTEM).

(4) Considerable excess capacity remains in the economy despite the rapid rise of utilization rates during 1961. While there is no clear benchmark of full utilization of capital, the operating rates and output-capital ratios attained in late 1955 can serve as a reasonable indication. If GNP had been at its estimated potential level in the last quarter of 1961, capital utilization rates would have been approximately at the levels attained in late 1955. Existing excess capacity in plant and equipment is thus compatible with full employment of the labor force.

(5) Levels of capital utilization have a potent influence on corporate profits. The share of corporate profits in GNP moves closely with the measures of capital utilization, although it swings somewhat earlier. Corporate depreciation allowances have increased rapidly and "gross profits"— net profits and inventory valuation adjustment plus capital consumption allowances—have been maintained during the 1953–61 period. But net profits have declined as a fraction of GNP in recent years; the combination of unrelenting overheads and depressed levels of output can fully account

for this "squeeze." As corporate capacity is put to fuller use, profits benefit from larger margins as well as expanded sales.

PROGRESS IN 1961

The Situation at the Beginning of the Year

As 1961 began, economic activity was far below its full employment level, and production and income continued to contract through February. By most measures of the decline in economic activity, the 1960–61 recession was the mildest in the postwar period. But the peak reached in May 1960 had followed a year of very slow advance in output and ended the shortest expansion in the postwar period. At the 1960 peak, unemployment and excess capacity were higher than at any prior postwar peak. Unemployment rates were higher during the 1960–61 recession than during the slumps of 1948–49 and 1953–54; in this respect, the recession was almost as severe as that of 1957–58.

The rate of use of existing facilities in late 1959 and early 1960 was not conducive to substantial further increases in business fixed investment, nor were monetary conditions encouraging. Although there was a brief interlude in the first quarter of 1960 when investment demand rose sharply, this buoyancy was to a large extent a temporary aftermath of the steel strike of 1959. As orders, sales, and profits proved disappointing, investment in both fixed capital and inventories was cut back.

During this period, government fiscal programs gave little support to aggregate demand. Total Federal expenditures, on income-and-product account, showed little change between mid-1959 and mid-1960 as Federal purchases of goods and services actually declined. In January 1960, Federal social insurance taxes were increased by about $2 billion a year. Indeed, the sharp change in the relationship between Federal Government receipts and expenditures was perhaps the most important factor in choking off the recovery.

The recession followed the same pattern as previous postwar downswings. With activity weakening, purchases of goods were cut back throughout the private economy. Inventory investment, as usual, displayed the largest decline among major components of GNP (Table 4). The decline of inventories, as well as of other major categories of expenditure, was concentrated in durable goods. Correspondingly, a decline of 12 percent in durable goods manufacturing accounted for most of the fall in industrial production from May 1960 to February 1961. Unemployment, which had been 5.1 percent (seasonally adjusted) of the civilian labor force in May, rose to 6.8 percent in February.

Once the contraction began, it was certainly moderated, and perhaps shortened, by a rise in outlays at all levels of government. The automatic stabilizers in the Federal fiscal system contributed to the stability of personal consumption expenditure during the recession, as transfer payments rose

TABLE 4.—*Changes in output, income, and employment over the three quarters of the 1960–61 recession*

[Seasonally adjusted]

Item	Cyclical peak: Second quarter 1960	Cyclical trough: First quarter 1961	Change, peak to trough
	Billions of dollars, annual rates		
Output (1961 prices):			
Gross national product	514.2	502.9	−11.3
Personal consumption expenditures	333.9	331.7	−2.2
Gross private domestic investment:			
Fixed investment	69.5	64.2	−5.3
Residential nonfarm construction	21.2	19.4	−1.8
Other construction	19.9	20.6	.7
Producers' durable equipment	28.4	24.2	−4.2
Change in business inventories	5.4	−4.0	−9.4
Net exports of goods and services	3.0	5.3	2.3
Government purchases of goods and services	102.3	105.7	3.4
Federal	54.4	54.9	.5
State and local	47.9	50.8	2.9
Income (current prices):			
Disposable personal income	352.7	354.3	1.6
Corporate profits after taxes	23.3	20.0	−3.3
	Millions of persons		
Employment:			
Total civilian employment	67.0	66.8	−0.2
Employment in nonagricultural establishments	54.6	53.5	−1.1
Private	46.1	44.9	−1.2

NOTE.—Detail will not necessarily add to totals because of rounding.
See Tables B–2, B–11, B–15, B–19, and B–24.

Sources: Department of Commerce and Department of Labor.

by $3.0 billion and personal taxes fell by $0.7 billion (annual rates) to offset much of the fall in private wages and salaries resulting from lower employment.

Recovery During the Year

By the end of 1961, production and income had improved markedly, and most economic indicators had surpassed their 1960 peaks. In the final quarter of 1961, GNP, measured in constant prices, was 7½ percent higher than in the first quarter, and about 5 percent above the peak attained in the second quarter of 1960 (Tables 4 and 5). The only major category of expenditure that was lower than in the second quarter of 1960 was expenditure for producers' durable equipment. Industrial production in December exceeded its low point of February by 13 percent, and was 4 percent above the previous peak attained in January 1960.

The increase of $41 billion (current prices, annual rate) in GNP from the first to last quarters of 1961 distributed substantial gains in income widely through the economy. Personal income grew by $24 billion. Wage and salary disbursements expanded by $19 billion and accounted for

TABLE 5.—*Changes in output, income, and employment over three quarters of expansion, 1961*

[Seasonally adjusted]

Item	1961		Change, trough to fourth quarter
	First quarter (cyclical trough)	Fourth quarter [1]	
	Billions of dollars, annual rates		
Output (1961 prices):			
Gross national product	502.9	540.2	37.3
Personal consumption expenditures	331.7	347.8	16.1
Gross private domestic investment:			
Fixed investment	64.2	71.4	7.2
Residential nonfarm construction	19.4	23.2	3.8
Other construction	20.6	20.2	−.4
Producers' durable equipment	24.2	28.0	3.8
Change in business inventories	−4.0	4.5	8.5
Net exports of goods and services	5.3	4.0	−1.3
Government purchases of goods and services	105.7	112.5	6.8
Federal	54.9	59.9	5.0
State and local	50.8	52.7	1.9
Income (current prices):			
Disposable personal income	354.3	375.6	21.3
Corporate profits after taxes	20.0	[2] 23.8	[2] 3.8
	Millions of persons		
Employment:			
Total civilian employment	66.8	66.9	0.1
Employment in nonagricultural establishments	53.5	54.5	1.0
Private	44.9	45.5	.6

[1] Preliminary estimates of output and income by Council of Economic Advisers.
[2] Third quarter data and change from first to third quarter.

NOTE.—Detail will not necessarily add to totals because of rounding.
Sources: Department of Commerce and Department of Labor (except as noted).

most of the gain in personal income. Incomes from dividends and business ownership also rose. Farm operators' net income from farming increased from $12.0 billion in 1960 to $13.1 billion in 1961, and net income per farm rose by nearly $350. Disposable personal income (after taxes) grew by $21 billion over the three quarters of expansion, adding $92 to average per capita spendable income.

The effect of rising output is strikingly shown in the $3.8 billion increase—nearly 20 percent—in the annual rate of corporate profits after taxes from the first to the third quarter. By all indications, corporate profits rose further in the fourth quarter and probably exceeded $50 billion before taxes and $25 billion after taxes.

Higher private incomes meant larger tax liabilities: Federal receipts in the income-and-product budget rose by about $10 billion (annual rate) in the three quarters of expansion, and the yield of State and local taxes grew by $3 billion.

The recovery was paced by a prompt and sharp reversal in inventory investment, the volatile inventories of manufacturers of durable goods accounting for a major share of the movement. During recessions, output falls below final sales as some orders are filled out of excessive stocks. The end of inventory liquidation in itself raises production to the level of sales. And rising sales and orders in a period of economic recovery encourage the accumulation of stocks, creating further gains in production. In 1961, this characteristic switch from liquidation to accumulation occurred very promptly, only one month after the trough in over-all activity, and was a major factor in the $15 billion expansion of GNP in the second quarter. Incentives for restocking did not arise wholly independently; they were provided in large part by evidence of a strengthening in final purchases, i.e., expenditures for GNP other than for inventory accumulation.

A key element in the rise of final demand was the increase in expenditures at all levels of government. The upward trend of State and local government purchases continued unabated. The promotion of economic recovery was a major aim of Federal budget policy in 1961. Scheduled obligations and expenditures were speeded up in the numerous ways listed in Part II and the Appendix to this chapter. Additional outlays came from new Administration programs—some to assist individuals and areas hit by economic recession and others to meet national needs of high priority. Furthermore, in the spring and summer of 1961 when overriding national security requirements led to increased expenditures for defense and space activities, the existence of unutilized manpower and capital ruled against an increase in tax rates. A careful appraisal of the direct and indirect effects of increased Federal activity indicates that it was a major force—probably the principal driving force—of the recovery of 1961.

Investment in nonresidential construction and producers' durable equipment, taken together, rose at an annual rate of $3.4 billion (1961 prices) from the first to the last quarter of 1961, both responding to and contributing to the expansion (Table 5). With improving rates of utilization of capacity, larger corporate profits, and readily available credit, business fixed investment began to rise in the second quarter of 1961. In contrast, business capital outlays had continued to decline during two quarters of rising total output in both 1954 and 1958.

Residential nonfarm construction, which had fallen since mid-1959, picked up in the early months of 1961 and continued to rise through the year. Although the rate of new family formation has been relatively low, and vacancy rates have continued to rise steadily, increasing disposable incomes and favorable financial and liquidity conditions have stimulated home building. Through much of 1960 and well into 1961, individuals continued to increase their volume of liquid assets. Funds for conventional, FHA, and VA mortgages were readily available; mortgage yields declined moderately throughout the recession and into the summer of 1961 and remained fairly stable the rest of the year.

The favorable financial environment for business investment and residential construction reflected the monetary and credit policies of the

Government. These policies have facilitated the flow of funds into investment and have contributed to a stability of interest rates unusual for a year of recovery.

Exports in the fourth quarter were $0.8 billion (annual rate) higher than in the first quarter. But outlays on imports, partly to rebuild inventories, rose by $2.1 billion, reducing net exports by $1.3 billion. Net exports is the one component of GNP which tends to fall as business activity improves cyclically.

Consumer outlays accounted for somewhat less than half the increase in GNP from the first to the fourth quarter. Until the closing months of the year, consumer spending did not quite keep pace with disposable income. The ratio of personal saving to personal disposable income rose from 6.7 percent in the first quarter to 7.3 percent in the third. In the fourth quarter, however, consumption did keep pace with income and expanded by $8.0 billion (current prices, annual rate). Demand for new automobiles sparked a rise in the fourth quarter of $3.2 billion (annual rate) in outlays for consumer durable goods, which finally surpassed the peak that had been reached in the second quarter of 1960.

The gains in production, income, and employment during 1961, in comparison with previous expansions, are shown in Charts 4 and 5. Chart 4 displays the rise of GNP from its lowest quarter in each recession. In

ÇHART 4

Real Gross National Product
in Four Postwar Recoveries

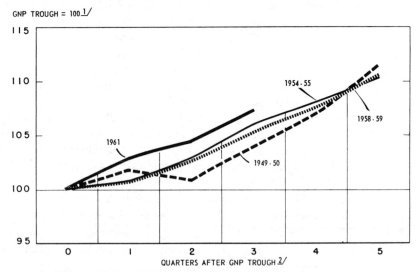

GNP TROUGH = 100.1/

1/BASED ON SEASONALLY ADJUSTED DATA.

2/TROUGH QUARTERS FOR GNP WERE 1949 II, 1954 II, 1958 I, AND 1961 I.

SOURCES: DEPARTMENT OF COMMERCE AND COUNCIL OF ECONOMIC ADVISERS.

CHART 5

Employment, Production, and Income
in Four Postwar Recoveries

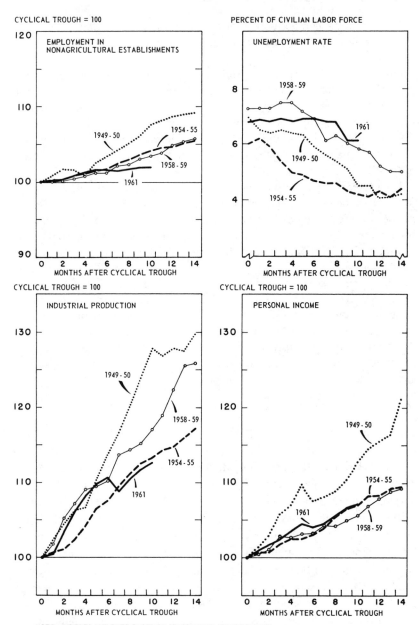

NOTE: INDEXES AND RATE BASED ON SEASONALLY ADJUSTED DATA.

SOURCES: DEPARTMENT OF LABOR, BOARD OF GOVERNORS OF THE FEDERAL RESERVE SYSTEM, AND
DEPARTMENT OF COMMERCE.

the three previous cycles, the trough quarter for GNP came before the month of the cyclical trough. In 1961 the cyclical trough, in February, was in the middle of the quarter of lowest GNP. In Chart 5 the reference point for all series is the cyclical trough month. These differences in timing must be taken into account in comparisons of recoveries. There are also differences in the composition of output: for example, the 1958–59 upswing was more heavily concentrated in industrial production than the current recovery.

On the whole, increases in production and income during the present expansion of economic activity compare favorably with the two preceding periods of expansion. However, these gains were not matched by equal improvements in employment and unemployment. As noted above, one of the principal reasons was that productivity gains during 1961 exceeded those of earlier expansions. The year ended with unemployment at 6.1 percent of the civilian labor force (seasonally adjusted).

In summary, real output rose during the 1961 recovery at an annual rate of 10 percent. The gap between actual output and estimated potential has been narrowed by $23 billion in three quarters; labor and capital have been more efficiently utilized; and widespread gains in income have been secured. The Nation has adjusted smoothly and easily to the marked change of pace: no evidence of strain can be found, no bottlenecks have developed, no excessive backlogs of orders have appeared. And prices have been exceptionally stable, as Chapter 4 makes clear. Although the economy at the end of 1961 was still short of full employment, the experience during the/year was gratifying and reassuring on many counts. And it demonstrated the ability of the economy to advance efficiently at a rapid pace when the underlying strength of private demand is reinforced by appropriate Federal fiscal and monetary policies.

Outlook for 1962

The Employment Act of 1946 requires an estimate of "current and foreseeable trends in the levels of employment, production, and purchasing power." Although the difficulties and risks of economic forecasting are well known, neither government nor private enterprise can conduct its affairs, develop its policies, and make its decisions without economic projections— without making the best estimates that economic and statistical tools permit of the economic framework within which it will have to operate in the future   For example, it would be impossible to formulate either Federal or State budgets without projections of future levels of income and business activity and the tax revenues they will produce. In the Budget Message, GNP for 1962 is projected at $570 billion (current prices), a rise of nearly $50 billion, or almost 9½ percent, over 1961. A somewhat higher figure is likely if the Congress enacts promptly the Administration's proposed tax credit for investment. This section presents, with full recognition of the margins of error inherent in economic projections, the appraisal of the economic outlook underlying the budget.

The momentum of the current recovery will carry the economy to new records in production, income, and employment during 1962. In the closing months of 1961, private demand was rising briskly. The resulting gains in consumer incomes, profits, business inventory requirements, and orders for durable goods will generate further increases in spending and business activity in the coming months. Broad advances in the private economy will be reinforced by a continued upward trend in Federal, State and local government outlays.

The favorable prospects for private demand, together with current economic programs and proposals of the Administration, point to a strong and sustained expansion. The percentage gain in GNP (current prices) in 1962 over the 1961 level can realistically be expected to match the increases of $8\frac{1}{2}$–$9\frac{1}{2}$ percent in 1955 and 1959. Those two years, like 1962, were the first full years of recovery from recession.

Expansion in GNP in 1962 is expected to be somewhat more moderate than the annual rate of 11 percent (current prices) attained over the past three quarters. But it is anticipated that output will continue to catch up with potential, reducing slack and unemployment. Substantial increases are expected in all major categories of expenditure. The expected total increase is made up, very roughly, of the following parts: one-half, consumer outlays; one-fifth each, government purchases and private fixed investment; and one-tenth, additions to inventories.

Survey of Major Categories of Expenditure

The rationale for this appraisal of the outlook may be indicated by a brief survey of the key components of GNP.

Consumption. The ratio of total consumer expenditure to personal disposable income, 93.0 percent in 1961, is expected to rise slightly in 1962. The proportion of income spent on nondurable goods and services typically declines during expansion and, this year, will probably fall below the 81.3 percent recorded in 1961. In prosperous periods, consumers devote a larger share of their incomes to increasing their wealth. But at the same time they show a preference for accumulating wealth in the form of consumer durable goods. The current strong liquid position of households is likely to moderate their desire for additional liquidity and to reinforce demands for durable goods this year. The brisk sales of automobiles in the fourth quarter of 1961 also point in this direction. An increase in expenditures for durables from 11.6 percent of disposable income in 1961 to some $12\frac{1}{2}$ percent, approaching the proportions recorded in 1959 and 1960, will probably outweigh the slight decline to be expected in the fraction devoted to nondurables and services.

Measured absolutely, rather than as shares of disposable income, all components of consumer expenditure seem headed upward in 1962. Personal disposable income is likely to grow substantially. It will probably advance at a somewhat slower rate than GNP for the following reasons: (1) Corporate profits rise sharply in cyclical upswings, and dividend payments lag behind. (2) Government transfer payments to individuals are held down when unemployment declines. (3) Collections from progressive personal income taxes rise somewhat faster than personal incomes. But disposable income will still absorb more than half of the dollar gains in GNP, and consumer expenditure will account for about half of the total increment in expenditure. Consumption is now about 65 percent of GNP; no economic expansion can go far without support from consumers, and every expansion provides substantial income gains for households. A rise of $50 billion in GNP for 1962 would be accompanied by an increase of about $100 in consumption per capita, permitting significant advances in standards of living.

Government. State and local governments can be expected to add about $1 billion a quarter to their purchases of goods and services, continuing their steady upward trend. Federal purchases of goods and services will rise during 1962 but more slowly than over the past year. The average increase during the course of 1962 seems likely to be $1 billion a quarter, compared with $1.7 billion in 1961. New Federal obligations, which have some effect on business activity before the outlays they foreshadow, are expected to rise by $5 billion in the year starting next July 1—after a rise of $12½ billion in the current fiscal year.

Inventories. Inventory-sales ratios have declined markedly during this expansion, as is usual in the first year of an upswing. The ratio of inventories to GNP fell by about 5 percent over the last three quarters of 1961. More rapid accumulation is to be expected—and welcomed—in the near future. Analysis supported by prior cyclical experience suggests that inventories will soon begin catching up with total output. If they were to rise at a quarterly rate of 2 percent, inventory investment would attain an annual rate of more than $8 billion some time in 1962.

The threat of a midyear steel strike may produce added stockpiling this spring. In the absence of a prolonged strike, the main effect would be on the pattern of activity during the year, with the second quarter stronger and the third quarter correspondingly weaker. Although the year-end levels and the full year totals might not be seriously affected, this abnormal factor in inventory behavior would increase the difficulties of appraising the real strength of the economy. A long strike, of course, could seriously imperil the prospects for continued vigorous expansion.

Quite apart from the steel situation, inventory investment is likely to reach its peak before the end of 1962 and cannot be expected to be a significant expansionary factor in the latter half of this year.

Residential construction. With the aid of continued credit ease and increased household incomes, residential construction ended 1961 with a rate of activity $2 billion above the average for the year. Further moderate gains are likely, in part from additions and alterations and in part from new housing starts. Industry and government specialists have predicted housing starts of 1.4 million in 1962. Mortgage availability will influence housing demand considerably. If funds remain readily available, gains in household incomes are likely to strengthen the demand for new homes.

Business fixed investment. As Chart 3 shows, rates of capital utilization have been more favorable to investment demand in the last year than in 1958. Business outlays for durable equipment and nonresidential construction have risen more promptly and more vigorously to date than in the comparable stage of the preceding expansion. Incentives to invest for modernization and replacement purposes are also favorable. Furthermore, business fixed investment is volatile; in peacetime expansions, it usually rises as a fraction of GNP. Even the weak expansion of 1958–60 produced a 22 percent increase in capital outlays from their low in the third quarter of 1958 to their peak in the second quarter of 1960. The same performance in the current expansion would mean a rise of $6 billion from the last quarter of 1961 to the last quarter of 1962. And the major determinants of investment—corporate liquidity and profit rates, capacity measures, conditions in financial markets—point to more strength than in the last expansion. It seems probable that capital outlays in 1962 will surpass their 1958–60 performance.

Prospects for plant and equipment investment are difficult to assess quantitatively. Recent surveys suggest that businessmen have not yet planned any major expansion of productive facilities. But improved economic conditions have consistently led to substantial upward revisions of plans. Whether business fixed investment as a share of GNP, 8.9 percent in 1961, will approach the 1956 and 1957 figure of 10.7 percent or even substantially surpass the 1960 figure of 9.3 percent cannot be foretold. Much depends on the extent to which excess capacity declines over the next few quarters and on the willingness of businessmen to count on continued prosperity. Capital outlays will also be significantly influenced by the state of financial markets. The financing of investment will be facilitated by the rising flow of internal funds from retained earnings and depreciation allowances. But corporate investment is almost certain to exceed corporate saving in 1962. Corporations as a whole have strengthened their liquidity position, in part by long-term financing ahead of investment needs in 1961. Nevertheless, they will probably require substantial net external financing this year, involving an increase in the security holdings of households and financial institutions. Monetary policy can facilitate this external financing.

An important stimulus to capital outlays would be provided by enactment of the proposed tax credit of 8 percent on expenditures for new durable equipment. This measure would raise significantly the after-tax return on new investment. Enactment of the tax credit will help assure sufficient strength in this central component of demand at the crucial stage of the recovery.

Another favorable factor for the later stage of recovery is the planned revision by the Treasury of guideline schedules of depreciation on plant and equipment. The revision will incorporate available current information about the economic lives of capital goods and the effects of technological change on obsolescence.

In 1955–57, capital outlays amounting to more than 10 percent of potential and actual GNP led to an annual rate of growth of slightly less than 4 percent in the business capital stock. Because total output did not grow at an equal pace after 1955, excess capacity developed and capital outlays were sharply reduced in the 1957–58 recession. The excess capacity that emerged is more accurately attributed to underbuying than to overbuilding. If purchases by consumers and government had been sufficient to keep the economy fully employed, rates of capital utilization would not have fallen. Business firms would have had sustained incentives to enlarge their productive facilities at the rate of nearly 4 percent a year. Better performance in maintaining full use of resources could justify business fixed investment amounting to 10 percent or more of the Nation's output.

Prospects for Full Employment

This appraisal of the prospects for production and income implies an unemployment rate of 5 percent or somewhat lower at the end of 1962, but not as low as 4 percent.

The achievement of 4 percent unemployment by mid-1963 requires a gain of about 11 percent in GNP (in constant prices) over the coming year and a half. This pace of advance would permit smooth and efficient adjustments, avoiding bottlenecks that might generate serious upward pressures on prices. It would also allow a gradual transition toward the rates of expansion that must be expected when full utilization is restored and output can no longer rise more rapidly than productive potential. A continued upward movement for more than two years with an over-all gain of 20 percent in real GNP would represent a very strong expansion. But a less ambitious rate of recovery to full employment would prolong the waste of unused resources without gaining appreciably greater assurance of stable prices.

While this rate of expansion seems feasible in the light of the prospects for private demand and Administration policies designed to promote expansion at a desirable pace, any appraisal of the economic outlook must take into account a wide range of possible outcomes. Weakening of consumer demand or lack of investment enthusiasm by business firms could endanger the prospective gains of 1962 and slow down the expansion. Because of the growth in the labor force and productivity, 1962 could achieve new highs in output and even in employment without any reduction in the currently excessive rate of unemployment. Large and continuing gains are needed to bring output up to the economy's potential and to reduce unemployment to 4 percent of the labor force for the first time since 1957.

An expansion that slows down prematurely is less likely to be lasting. A slowdown, or even an expected slowdown, in the growth of sales can diminish incentives to enlarge productive capacity and inventories. A decline in capital spending and inventory accumulation can convert a slowdown into a downturn. For this reason, prospects for a lasting expansion rest heavily on the vigor of the upswing over the next few quarters.

The buildup of inventories that is expected in the near future will contribute substantially to household incomes and to the strength of consumer demand. But by late 1962, continued advance will depend heavily on the ability of fixed investment outlays to replace inventories as a key expansionary force. If the expansion is vigorous earlier in the year, utilization rates will be favorable to investment demand in late 1962, and, therefore, to the continuation of the expansion itself.

On the other hand, private demand can rise too fast or too far. Too rapid an expansion may strain the adjustment mechanisms of the economy. In a dynamic economy, patterns of output and employment change from one cycle to the next. It takes time to re-employ the jobless and to return efficiently to full utilization of capacity. Hence, a very rapid expansion of demand might involve price increases, bottlenecks, and inefficiencies that could be avoided in a more gradual rise to the same levels. The current expansion has an enviable record to date: with a 10 percent annual rate of increase of real output, it has substantially narrowed the gap between actual and potential output; at the same time, the movements of prices, inventories, and orders show none of the symptoms of strain that would be associated with excessive speed. If demand for consumer durable goods and business capital formation were quickly to attain the same strength relative to incomes as in 1955, reasonable speed limits might be violated. In that event, full employment might be achieved sooner but policy might have to contend with excess demands and inflationary pressures.

Still another challenge to policy might come from unexpected behavior of unemployment relative to output. Given continued growth of potential output along the $3\frac{1}{2}$ percent trend discussed earlier, the achievement of full employment in mid-1963 would be associated with GNP of $600 billion in 1961 prices. Deviations from historical trends in the size of the labor force, average hours of work, and man-hour productivity can alter the relationship between output and unemployment. Full utilization of resources may correspond to a somewhat higher or somewhat lower GNP. In particular, the effects of measures (discussed in Chapter 2) to increase the rate of growth of productivity, while adding to investment demand during the expansion, may raise the productive potential output of the economy above its current trend as early as 1963.

Stabilization policy has contributed significantly to the gratifying progress of 1961 and to the favorable prospects for 1962. Policy will continue to promote progress toward full employment, remaining alert to unforeseen developments which might throw the economy off course. The flexibility in existing policy instruments can be used to good advantage, as it was in 1961. Furthermore, Administration proposals now before the Congress would greatly enhance the ability of stabilization policy to counter threats of oncoming recession with speed and vigor. The record of stabilization policy in 1961 and its tasks for 1962 are discussed in the remaining part of this chapter.

PART II: POLICIES FOR MAXIMUM EMPLOYMENT AND PRODUCTION

In Part I of this chapter, the progress of the economy in 1961 and the prospect for further progress in 1962 were reviewed in terms of the objectives of maximum employment, production, and purchasing power. Part II describes more fully and specifically how government policy can, does, and will promote progress toward these goals. Two major kinds of government policy are involved: measures for economic stabilization, which influence the total volume of spending; and measures to reduce structural unemployment and underemployment by better mutual adaptation between available jobs and available workers.

ECONOMIC STABILIZATION

Insufficient demand means unemployment, idle capacity, and lost production. Excessive demand means inflation—general increases in prices and money incomes, bringing forth little or no gains in output and real income. The objective of stabilization policies is to minimize these deviations, i.e., to keep over-all demand in step with the basic production potential of the economy.

Stabilization does not mean a mere leveling off of peaks and troughs in production and employment. It does not mean trying to hold over-all demand for goods and services stable. It means minimizing deviations from a rising trend, not from an unchanging average. In a growing economy, demand must grow in order to maintain full employment of labor and full utilization of capacity at stable prices. The economy is not performing satisfactorily unless it is almost continuously setting new records of production, income, and employment. Indeed, unless production grows as fast as its potential, unemployment and idle capacity will also grow. And when the economy starts from a position well below potential, output must for a time grow even faster than potential to achieve full utilization.

The Postwar Record

Despite the recessions of recent years and the inflationary excesses of the early postwar years, the postwar record of economic stabilization is incomparably better than the prewar. The economy fluctuated violently in 1919–21 and operated disastrously far below potential from 1930 to 1942. The 1929 level of GNP, in constant prices, was not exceeded, except briefly in 1937, until 1939. The difference between the 17 percent unemployment of 1939 and the 3 percent rate 10 years earlier is a dramatic measure of the growth of the labor force and productivity even during depression. Since the war, the economy's detours from the path of full employment growth have been shorter in both time and distance. There have been four recessions, but none of them has gotten out of hand, as did the decline of 1929–33. All of the declines have been reversed within 13 months, before unemployment reached 8 percent of the labor force. For this improved performance there are several reasons.

First, the war and preceding depression left business firms and households starved for goods. Further, wartime earnings coupled with scarcities of civilian goods, rationing, and price control, saturated business firms and consumers with liquid assets. For these legacies of depression and war, the economy paid a price in the inflations of 1946–48 and 1950, with delayed effects throughout the past decade.

Second, the structure of the economy was reformed after 1933 in ways which substantially increased its resistance to economic fluctuations. The manner in which government tax revenues and income maintenance programs serve as automatic or "built-in" economic stabilizers is described below. The New Deal strengthened and reformed the Nation's banking and financial system with the help of new governmental credit institutions, deposit insurance, and loan and guarantee programs. These have virtually eliminated the possibility that economic declines will be aggravated by bank failures, foreclosures, and epidemic illiquidity.

Third, there is a significantly improved understanding of the manner in which government fiscal and monetary tools can be used to promote economic stability. Under the Employment Act and the climate of opinion which it symbolizes, the Government has been expected to assume, and has assumed, greater responsibility for economic stabilization.

Finally, businessmen and consumers no longer regard prolonged and deep depression as a serious possibility. They generally expect recessions to end quickly; they anticipate a long-term upward trend in the economy; and they spend and invest accordingly. This stability of expectations is in part the result of stability achieved in fact, and reflects general understanding of the structural changes which have contributed to it. But expectations of stability are also a cause of stability—nothing succeeds like success.

Achieving Greater Stability

While our postwar performance is a great advance over that of prewar years, it is still far from satisfactory. We have had no great depression, but we have had four recessions. Even the relatively short and mild recessions of the postwar period have been costly. In the last decade, the Nation has lost an estimated $175 billion of GNP (in 1961 prices) by operating the economy below potential. Industrial production has been below its previous peak nearly half the time since 1946.

There is general agreement that economic fluctuations in the United States are intensified by—if not always caused by—a rhythm in inventory investment, alternating between periods in which stocks are accumulating at an excessively high rate and periods in which they are being liquidated. But it is not beyond hope that stabilization measures, both automatic and discretionary, can be strengthened in force and improved in timing so as to compensate for inventory swings better than has been true in the past. If this is done the swings themselves will be dampened.

The possible gains from improved economic stabilization are impressive. Losses of production, employment, and consumption will be cut. More saving and investment will be realized, contributing steadily to the long-run growth of production potential. Business, consumer, and labor decisions will allocate resources more efficiently when they respond less to cyclical prospects and more to long-run developments. There will be less need and less justification for restrictive practices which are now designed to provide sheltered positions in markets periodically hit by recession.

It is true that an economy operating steadily at a high level of employment, with only limited excess plant capacity, is more subject to the risks of price increases than an economy with heavy unemployment and large unused capacity. However, the dampening of economic fluctuations may itself help to counter this tendency. Cyclical fluctuations have been exerting a "ratchet effect" on prices; costs and prices have been relatively inflexible downward in recessions but have been responsive to increases in demand during recoveries. Cyclical swings in total spending also tend to be accompanied by sharp and transitory shifts in the composition of spending. Because prices and costs respond more readily to upswings than to downswings, these rapid changes in the composition of demand impart an upward bias to the whole price level. These sources of upward price bias will tend to be reduced as a more even pace of advance is achieved.

To capitalize on the potential gains of stabilization requires skillful use of all economic policy, particularly budgetary and monetary policy.

THE FEDERAL BUDGET AND ECONOMIC STABILITY

Federal expenditures and taxes affect total employment and production by influencing the total volume of spending for goods and services. Direct Federal purchases of goods and services are themselves part of total demand for national output. In addition, the Federal Government makes "transfer payments" to individuals, for which no current services are rendered in return. Examples are social security and unemployment insurance benefits, and veterans compensation and pension benefits. Both purchases of goods and services and transfer payments add to private incomes and thereby stimulate consumption and investment. Federal taxes, on the other hand, reduce disposable personal and business incomes, and restrain private spending.

By increasing the flow of spending, additional Federal outlays—with tax rates unchanged—have expansionary effects on the economy. Whether an expansion in spending—government or private—leads mainly to more output or mainly to higher prices depends on the degree of slack in the economy. Under conditions of widespread unemployment and excess capacity, businessmen respond to higher demand by increasing production; under conditions of full employment, prices rise instead. In the slack economy of 1961, for example, additional demand from both private and public sources was readily converted into increased production.

Built into the Federal fiscal system are several automatic defenses against recession and inflation. Given the tax rates, tax revenues move up and down with economic activity, since most taxes are levied on private incomes or sales. Indeed, tax revenues change proportionally more than GNP. Furthermore, certain Federal expenditures, such as unemployment compensation payments, are automatically affected by the state of the economy. Economic fluctuations, therefore, result in substantial changes in Federal expenditures and revenues, even when basic expenditure programs and tax rates remain unchanged. With the present system of tax rates and unemployment compensation payments, a one-dollar reduction in GNP means a reduction in Federal tax receipts and an increase in transfer payments totaling about 30 cents. Therefore, private incomes after Federal taxes fall by only 70 cents for each reduction of one dollar in GNP. For this reason, any initial decline in spending and output is transmitted with diminished force to other sectors of the economy.

These automatic or built-in stabilizers moderate the severity of cyclical swings in the economy. If the forces causing a downturn in economic activity are weak and transient, the automatic stabilizers cushion the severity of the decline and give the basic recuperative powers in the private economy a better opportunity to produce a prompt and full recovery.

But if the forces causing the downturn are strong and persistent, the built-in stabilizers may not suffice to prevent a large and prolonged recession. Furthermore, they are blindly symmetrical in their effects. When economic activity quickens after a slump, the rise in Federal revenues begins immediately and slows the recovery in employment and incomes. For these reasons, the task of economic stabilization cannot be left entirely to built-in stabilizers. Discretionary budget policy, e.g., changes in tax rates or expenditure programs, is indispensable—sometimes to reinforce, sometimes to offset, the effects of the stabilizers.

To be effective, discretionary budget policy should be flexible. In order to promote economic stability, the Government should be able to change quickly tax rates or expenditure programs, and equally able to reverse its actions as circumstances change. Failure to arrest quickly a downturn in income, production, and employment may shake the faith of firms and households in prompt recovery and thereby lead to a cumulative decline. Delay in countering inflationary pressures may permit the development of a self-propelling speculative boom, with disruptive consequences to the domestic economy and the balance of payments. If moderate fiscal action can be taken quickly and can be speedily reversed when circumstances warrant, the dangers of overstimulating or overrestricting the economy are much smaller than if fiscal responses are sluggish and difficult to reverse.

Fiscal policy can be made a more flexible and more powerful tool of economic stabilization by means that do not change the basic structure and level of taxation or the long-run size and composition of Federal expenditure programs. Changes in the basic structure and level of taxation should be made by the Congress with full deliberation in the light of the many relevant considerations, including the long-run revenue needs of the Government, equity among individuals and groups, and the effects of various taxes on economic efficiency and growth. Similarly, changes in the magnitude and content of government expenditures should represent the considered judgment of the people and the Congress on national priorities. For purposes of economic stabilization all that is needed of tax policy is temporary variation in the general level of tax rates within the existing structure, and all that is required of government outlays is timing of certain expenditures so that they bolster employment and purchasing power when the economy needs stimulus and taper off as it approaches full employment. In both cases, the form of action required for purposes of stabilization and the procedure for taking timely action can be agreed upon in advance.

The President's Recommendations

The President has recommended a three-part program for economic stabilization. Its enactment would be the most significant step forward in policy for economic stabilization since the Employment Act itself. These three measures parallel recommendations of the Commission on Money and Credit, a private group of leading citizens representing diverse economic interests and viewpoints.

Stand-by capital improvements authority. Under the first measure, the Congress would give the President stand-by authority to initiate at a time of rising unemployment up to $2 billion of public investments. More specifically, the program of accelerated capital improvements could be initiated by the President within two months after the seasonally adjusted unemployment rate (a) had risen in at least three out of four months (or in four out of six months) and (b) had risen to a level at least one percentage point higher than its level four months (or six months) earlier. Before invoking this authority, the President would be required to make a finding that current and prospective economic developments require such action to achieve the objectives of the Employment Act.

Under the program, the President would be authorized to commit up to (1) $750 million for direct Federal expenditures, (2) $750 million for grants-in-aid to State and local governments, (3) $250 million in loans to such States and localities as would otherwise be unable to meet their share of project costs, and (4) a further $250 million to be distributed among the above three categories as he might deem appropriate. Once initiated, the program could be terminated at any time by the President.

The program is designed to permit the timely initiation and execution of capital improvement projects which are desirable in their own right. To insure that the projects are appropriately timed, several important safeguards are incorporated in the proposal. An expanded capital improvements program initiated by the President under this authority would automatically be terminated within 12 months after initiation, unless extended by the Congress. Once a program had been terminated, a new program under this authorization could not be initiated by the President for 6 months. With respect to grant-in-aid expenditures, the President would be required to prescribe rules to assure that assisted projects were of high priority, were a net addition to existing State and local expenditures, and were of the type which could be started quickly and carried speedily to conclusion. Under existing legislation, Federal advances are provided to aid State and local governments to plan projects which would meet these specifications.

To insure that the projects are desirable on their own merits, the proposal would limit direct Federal expenditures to projects and programs previously authorized by the Congress. Appropriate projects would include resource conservation (e.g., reforestation, reseeding of range lands, timber stand improvement) and various Federal public works, including construction, repair, or modernization of Federal buildings. Examples of projects for which State and local governments could receive grants are hospitals, airports, schools, waste treatment facilities, street repairs and improvements, water and sewer systems, and deferred maintenance and improvement of public buildings.

The unemployment criteria for triggering the accelerated capital expenditures program are rigorous enough to prevent untimely or premature activation, but not so restrictive as to delay the effects of the program until late in the recovery period. The criteria for initiation of the program would have been met in the early stages of each of the four postwar recessions. Furthermore, no false signals would have been given. Even if the criteria were to give a false signal in the future—for example if unemployment were to rise because of a major strike—the President simply need not invoke the authority.

Table 6 shows the dates at which the unemployment criteria would first have been met in each recession of the past decade, the date of the previous peak, the date of the low point of the recession, and the date at which the economy subsequently returned to full employment. In every case, Presidential authority could have been invoked within four months after the previous cyclical peak and well before the trough of the recession. The first impact of orders, contracts, and expenditures under the program would have been felt within one or two months after the authority was invoked.

TABLE 6.—*Hypothetical timing of proposed capital improvements program in four postwar business cycles*

Business cycle peak	Unemployment criteria met [1]	Business cycle trough	Subsequent achievement of full employment [2]
November 1948	March 1949	October 1949	October 1950
July 1953	November 1953	August 1954	July 1955
July 1957	November 1957	April 1958	[3]
May 1960	August 1960	February 1961	[3]

[1] Criteria are met in any month in which the seasonally adjusted unemployment rate (a) had risen in at least three out of four months (or in four out of six months) and (b) had risen to a level at least one percentage point higher than its level four months (or six months) earlier. Program could be initiated within two months after criteria are met.
[2] The date at which the economy returned to the neighborhood of a 4 percent unemployment rate.
[3] Full employment has not been achieved since the beginning of the 1957 recession.

Source: Council of Economic Advisers.

The major impact of the program would occur when a stimulus is needed to arrest economic decline or support recovery. It would not be delayed until private demands are already pressing hard on the economy's capacity to produce. Table 6 indicates that a quick-starting, fast-moving capital expenditures program begun in the early stages of recession could have been terminated before the economy returned to full employment.

Stand-by tax reduction authority. The second recommendation is to establish a procedure for making quickly a temporary across-the-board reduction in the individual income tax rate. Such a reduction would be a speedy and powerful method of augmenting purchasing power throughout the Nation.

Specifically, the President would be given stand-by authority, subject to congressional veto, to reduce temporarily all individual income tax rates, in accordance with the following procedure:

(1) Before proposing a temporary tax reduction, the President must make a finding that such action is required to meet the stabilization objectives of the Employment Act.

(2) Upon such finding, the President would submit to Congress a proposed temporary uniform reduction in all individual income

tax rates. The proposed temporary rates may not be more than 5 percentage points lower than the rates permanently established by the Congress.

(3) This change would take effect 30 days after submission, unless rejected by a joint resolution of the Congress.

(4) It would remain in effect for 6 months unless revised or renewed by the same process or extended by a joint resolution of the Congress.

(5) If the Congress were not in session, a Presidentially proposed tax adjustment would automatically take effect but would terminate 30 days after the Congress reconvened. Extension would require a new proposal to the Congress, which would be subject to congressional veto.

An across-the-board variation in the basic individual income tax rate can be a potent stabilization measure. At the current level of taxable income, a reduction of 1 percentage point in the tax schedule would add about $2 billion, at annual rates, to disposable personal income, and a full 5 point reduction would increase disposable income by $10 billion. Since nearly three-quarters of the individual income tax is collected through payroll deductions, the rate reduction would have an immediate effect upon incomes available to consumers. Payments of taxes on estimated declarations would also be reduced, raising still further the current flow of consumer incomes. Higher consumer incomes mean higher consumer spending. The resultant expansion in output and employment by the consumer goods industries and their suppliers would increase the incomes of those already employed and create jobs for many of the unemployed.

Policy to reverse recession or speed recovery often calls for a temporary boost in private purchasing power. Permanent reduction in tax rates could give the economy as strong, or stronger, a stimulus but at the possible sacrifice of tax revenues which would be most desirable after the economy returned to full employment. Private demands are weak in periods of recession and slack, but a large part of their weakness results from recession and slack themselves. Once full employment has been restored, with the help of the temporary tax reduction as well as other measures, private demands will be stronger simply because capacity operation is itself a powerful stimulus. At that time, the private economy no longer needs the fiscal stimulus which is appropriate to reverse a decline or support a recovery. In that case a return to permanent tax rates may be desirable in order to provide room in a non-inflationary full employment economy for defense outlays and other continuing government programs of high priority. Indeed, a Federal surplus, normally to be expected at full employment, will provide saving to finance private investments stimulated by capacity operations and prosperity profits. Under the proposal, a tax adjustment can be speedily invoked to meet the temporary requirements of economic stabilization, without permanently sacrificing revenues needed at a later date.

Improvement of the unemployment compensation system. The third major recommendation is to strengthen the Federal-State unemployment compensation system. The proposed legislation will make the unemployment insurance system more effective in meeting its two objectives. Individual workers will be more secure against the risks of unemployment. The economy will be more secure against the risks of sharp declines in purchasing power.

As pointed out in Part I of this chapter, unemployment benefits are now generally smaller, relative to earnings, than the 50 percent envisaged when the system was first inaugurated a generation ago. Furthermore, it has been necessary during the last two recessions to enact temporary legislation to extend the period of unemployment compensation for the large numbers of workers who had exhausted their benefit rights. To insure that experienced workers who suffer long-term unemployment during periods of prosperity will receive the same benefits as during recessions, the Administration has proposed a permanent Federal program under which the period of unemployment compensation would be extended by as much as 13 weeks for workers who have had at least three years' experience in insured work. The proposal also provides, when unemployment is widespread, a Federal program extending the period of benefits for all insured workers, including those who do not qualify for the permanent program of extended benefits because they have had less than three years of experience in insured work. This extension could be put into effect upon proclamation by the President when insured unemployment has reached 5 percent and the number of benefit exhaustions in a three-month period has reached 1 percent of insured employment. In these periods, regular benefits are exhausted by large numbers of workers and particularly by workers who have only limited experience in insured employment.

To raise the percentage of wages compensated by unemployment insurance and to accomplish other needed reforms, the following recommendations are made: (1) an additional three million workers should be covered; (2) States should be required to meet higher standards with respect to the amount of weekly benefits; (3) States which have experienced heavy insured unemployment should receive reinsurance grants; (4) a State may not deny compensation to claimants undergoing approved training.

Since the unemployment compensation system is an insurance program designed to be self-financing, increased benefits must be matched by increased contributions. The proposal would increase the taxable wage base from $3,000 a year to $4,800 and make permanent the temporary increase adopted in 1961, which raised the net Federal unemployment tax from 0.4 percent to 0.8 percent.

These three recommendations together constitute a far-reaching innovation in discretionary fiscal policy. At the same time, they are moderate proposals, carefully defining and limiting the authority which they confer. They will go a long way toward providing the flexibility in fiscal policy which is essential if the Nation is to make prosperity the rule and not the exception in its economic life. In the past 7 years the Nation has undergone three recessions. In the $4\frac{1}{2}$ years since 1957, full employment has not once been attained. While some fluctuations in business and consumer spending will always occur, nothing in our free enterprise economy condemns us to repeat this recent experience. Prudent innovations in the tools of fiscal policy, and careful use of both new and old tools, can greatly improve the stability of our economy in the years ahead.

BUDGET POLICY, 1958–63

The Federal budget has influenced economic activity in recent years in two ways: through the workings of the built-in stabilizers, and through discretionary changes in the budget program. It is not easy to separate these two influences. In order to do so, it is necessary, first, to view Federal fiscal transactions in the same accounting framework used to describe the whole economy. The *national income accounts budget* is a way of measuring and classifying Federal transactions which accords with the national income and product accounts for the economy. Second, it is convenient to have a numerical measure of the expansionary or restrictive impact of a budget program on the economy. The *full employment surplus* is such a measure. This section discusses these two somewhat unfamiliar but highly useful tools and then applies them in an analysis of recent and prospective budget policies.

The National Income Accounts Budget

The effects of Federal receipts and expenditures on the income stream are most accurately represented when the budget is viewed in the framework of the national income accounts. These accounts present a consistent record and classification of the major flows of output and income for the entire economy, including the transactions of the Federal Government. There are three major differences between the Federal budget as it is conventionally presented (the so-called "administrative budget") and the accounts of the Federal sector as they appear in the national income. The major differences between these two budgets, and between both of them and the consolidated cash budget, are schematically summarized in Table 7. There are other, less significant differences among the budgets, such as the treatment of intragovernmental transactions.

First, the national income accounts budget, like the consolidated cash budget, includes the transactions of the trust funds, which amount currently to about $25 billion per year and have a significant impact on the economy. Highway grants-in-aid, unemployment compensation payments, and social security benefits are examples of trust fund transactions. Because

TABLE 7.—*Major differences among three concepts of the Federal budget*

Item	Budget concept		
	Administra-tive	Consolidated cash	National in-come accounts
Timing of receipts_____	Collections____	Collections____	Accruals_____
Treatment of net loans and other credit transactions____	Included_____	Included_____	Excluded_____
Treatment of trust fund transactions_____	Excluded_____	Included_____	Included_____

Source: Council of Economic Advisers.

the traditional budget—or administrative budget—is primarily an instrument of management and control of those Federal activities which operate through regular congressional appropriations, it excludes the trust funds, which have their own legal sources of revenue.

Second, transactions between government and business are, so far as possible, recorded in the national income accounts budget when liabilities are incurred rather than when cash changes hands. This adjustment in timing affects both government purchases and taxes, shifting them to the point in time at which they are likely to have their principal impact on private spending decisions. The choice of an accrual, rather than a cash, basis for timing is particularly important for the highly volatile corporate income tax. Since these taxes are normally paid more than six months after the liabilities are incurred, payments of corporate income taxes, as recorded in the administrative budget, run substantially below accruals in a period of rising economic activity. For fiscal year 1962, this difference is estimated at about $3 billion.

Finally, unlike the administrative budget, the national income accounts budget omits government transactions in financial assets and already existing assets. The largest omission is the volume of loans extended by the Federal Government. This volume is estimated at $4 billion net of repayments in fiscal year 1962. While these loans have important effects on economic activity, they are properly viewed as an aspect, not of fiscal policy, but of monetary and credit policy, and are so discussed later in this chapter. Borrowers from the Federal Government, like borrowers from private financial institutions, acquire cash by incurring debts. They add thereby to their liquidity, but not directly to their incomes.

The Full Employment Surplus

As pointed out earlier in this chapter, the magnitude of the surplus or deficit in the budget depends both on the budget program and on the state of the economy. The budget program fixes both tax rates and expenditure programs. The revenues actually yielded by most taxes, and the actual expenditures under certain programs like unemployment compensation, vary automatically with economic activity. To interpret the economic significance of a given budget it is, therefore, essential to distinguish the *automatic* changes in revenues and expenditures from the *discretionary* changes which occur when the Government varies tax rates or changes expenditure programs. The discussion that follows runs in terms of the national income accounts budget.

In Chart 6 this twofold aspect of fiscal policy is portrayed for the fiscal years 1960 and 1962. Since tax revenues and some expenditures depend on the level of economic activity, there is a whole range of possible surpluses and deficits associated with a given budget program. The particular surplus or deficit in fact realized will depend on the level of economic activity. On the horizontal scale, Chart 6 shows the ratio of actual GNP to the economy's potential, labeled the "utilization rate." On the vertical scale, the chart shows the Federal budget surplus or deficit as a percentage of potential GNP.

CHART 6

Effect of Level of Economic Activity
on Federal Surplus or Deficit

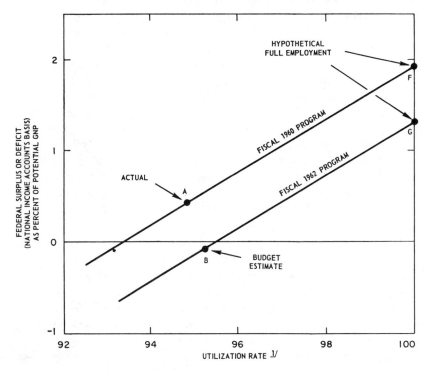

1/ACTUAL GNP AS PERCENT OF POTENTIAL GNP.
SOURCE: COUNCIL OF ECONOMIC ADVISERS.

The line labeled "fiscal 1960 program" represents a calculation of the budget surplus or deficit which would have occurred at various levels of economic activity, given the Federal expenditure programs and the tax rates of that year. For the reasons explained earlier, the same budget program may yield a high surplus at full employment and a low surplus or a deficit at low levels of economic activity. The actual budget position in fiscal year 1960, a surplus of $2.2 billion or 0.4 percent of potential GNP, is shown at point A; this accompanied a level of GNP 5 percent below potential. Had full employment been achieved that year, however, the same basic budget program would have yielded a surplus of about $10 billion, or nearly 2 percent of gross national product (point F in the chart). The line labeled "1962 program" similarly shows the relationship between economic activity and the surplus or deficit, for the budget program of 1962; the expected deficit is shown at point B, and the full employment surplus at point G.

It is the height of the line in Chart 6 which reflects the basic budget program; the actual surplus or deficit depends both on the height of the program line and the level of economic activity. In other words, discretionary fiscal policy, by changing the level of Government expenditures or tax rates shifts the whole program line up or down. The automatic stabilizing effects of a given budget program are reflected in the chart by movements along a given line, accompanying changes in economic activity. One convenient method of comparing alternative budget programs, which separates automatic from discretionary changes in surplus and deficits, is to calculate the surplus or deficit of each alternative program at a fixed level of economic activity. As a convention, this calculation is made on the assumption of full employment. In Chart 6, the points F and G mark the full employment surplus in the budget programs of fiscal years 1960 and 1962, respectively. The statement, "the fiscal 1960 budget had a larger full employment surplus, as a fraction of potential GNP, than the 1962 budget" is a convenient shorthand summary of the fact that the 1962 budget line was below the 1960 line, yielding smaller surpluses or larger deficits at any comparable level of activity.

The full employment surplus rises through time if tax rates and expenditure programs remain unchanged. Because potential GNP grows, the volume of tax revenues yielded by a fully employed economy rises, when tax rates remain unchanged. Full employment revenues under existing tax laws are growing by about $6 billion a year. With unchanged discretionary expenditures, a budget line drawn on Chart 6 would shift upward each year by about 1 percent of potential GNP.

The full employment surplus is a measure of the restrictive or expansionary impact of a budget program on over-all demand. Generally speaking, one budget program is more expansionary than another if it has a smaller full employment surplus. One budget program might have the smaller full employment surplus because it embodies greater Federal purchases of goods and services, in relation to potential GNP. By the same token, it leaves a smaller share of full employment output for private purchase. This means that full employment is easier to maintain under the budget program with the smaller surplus, because less private demand is required. It also means that inflation is more difficult to avoid, because there are fewer goods and services to meet private demand should it prove strong. Alternatively, one budget program might have a smaller full employment surplus than a second because it involves either lower tax rates or larger transfer payment programs. In that event, private after-tax incomes are larger at full employment for the first budget program than for the second. As a result, private demand would be stronger under the first program.

If the full employment surplus is too large, relative to the strength of private demand, economic activity falls short of potential. Correspondingly, the budget surplus actually realized falls short of the full employment surplus; indeed, a deficit may occur. If the full employment surplus is too small, total demand exceeds the capacity of economy and causes inflation.

But whether a given full employment surplus is too large or too small depends on other government policies, as well as on economic circumstances affecting the general strength of private demand. If the full employment surplus is too large, more expansionary monetary and credit policies may strengthen private demand sufficiently to permit full employment to be realized. Changes in tax structure, stimulating demand while leaving the yield of the tax system unchanged, might have the same effect. Similarly, restrictive changes in other government policies can offset the expansionary influence of a low full employment surplus.

A mixture of policies involving (1) a budget program with a relatively high full employment surplus and (2) monetary ease and tax incentives stimulating enough private investment to maintain full employment, has favorable consequences for economic growth, discussed in Chapter 2.

The Budget in 1958–60

The analysis of the budget program in terms of the full employment surplus points to a probable major cause of the incomplete and short-lived nature of the 1958–60 expansion. The most restrictive fiscal program of recent years was the program of 1960. Its full employment surplus exceeded any from 1956 to date. Estimates of the full employment surplus by half years are shown in Chart 7. The full employment surplus declined sharply as a result of higher expenditures during the 1957–58 recession until it reached an estimated $3 billion in the second half of 1958. Thereafter, it rose gradually through most of 1959 but then increased sharply to about $12½ billion in 1960. Thus, whereas the Federal budget contributed to stability during the contraction phase of the cycle and during the first year of the expansion, it was altered abruptly in the direction of restraint late in 1959 at a time when high employment had not yet been achieved.

CHART 7

Federal Surplus or Deficit:
Actual and Full Employment Estimate

(National Income Accounts Basis)

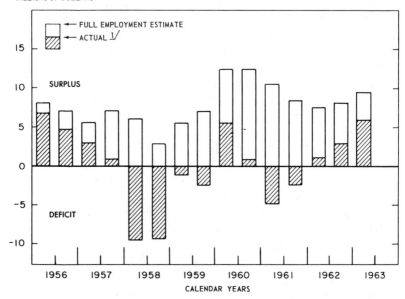

BILLIONS OF DOLLARS*

*SEASONALLY ADJUSTED ANNUAL RATES; DATA ARE FOR HALF-YEARS.
1/ESTIMATED BEGINNING SECOND HALF 1961.
SOURCES: DEPARTMENT OF COMMERCE, BUREAU OF THE BUDGET, AND COUNCIL OF ECONOMIC ADVISERS.

Federal Fiscal Activity in 1961–62

Immediately upon taking office, the new Administration moved vigorously to use the fiscal powers of the Federal Government to help bring about economic recovery. Federal procurement was accelerated by Presidential directive early in February, and tax refunds were also expedited. A listing of Administration stabilization policies during 1961 is provided in the Appendix to this chapter. Changes in transfer programs added about $2 billion to the combined total of transfer payments for fiscal years 1961 and 1962. The Veterans Administration advanced the payment of $150 million of veterans' life insurance dividends into the first quarter of calendar year 1961, and then made an extra dividend payment of $218 million at midyear. The Congress promptly adopted a number of measures requested by the President. A Temporary Extended Unemployment Compensation Act was adopted, providing for extension of exhausted benefits and giving the Administration time to develop a comprehensive program for permanent improvement in unemployment compensation. Social security benefits were increased effective in August, and aid was extended to children dependent on unemployed persons. Transfer payments represent a major element of flexibility in Federal expenditures. While transfer programs— like any Federal outlays—ought to stand on their merits, the precise timing of worthwhile new programs properly depends on economic conditions. The objectives of economic stabilization in 1961 argued strongly for speeding the introduction of programs like improvements in social security, scheduled to be adopted later.

Other Federal outlays increased in 1961 to meet specific national needs. Federal grants to States and localities for urban renewal, area redevelopment, highways, and public assistance increased. Direct payments to farmers were increased as a result of participation in the feed grains program. The largest increases in expenditures came in the areas of defense and space exploration. These programs were expanded for reasons of national security, not for economic stabilization. However, stabilization objectives ruled against any increases in tax rates to finance these new expenditures.

During 1961, the estimated full employment surplus declined significantly, from an annual rate of $12½ billion in the second half of 1960 to $8½ billion in the second half of 1961. As shown in Chart 7, the actual surplus or deficit has been substantially different from its full employment counterpart. Since private incomes declined during late 1960 and into 1961, the actual budget position shifted from a surplus of $1 billion in the second half of 1960 to a deficit of $5 billion in the first half of 1961. Then as the economy began to recover, the deficit, in the national income accounts, shrank to $2 billion in the second half of the year. The rising deficit in the early part of 1961 was due both to a shift downward in its budget program line (as discretionary budget outlays were increased) and to a movement to the left along the new line (as private incomes and Federal tax receipts declined).

The Federal national income accounts budget appropriately showed its largest deficit early in 1961, when the economy was near the trough of recession. Since then, the deficit has been steadily declining in spite of rising expenditures, and a surplus is expected in the first half of 1962. The administrative and cash deficits show a different time pattern, with deficits rising in the 1962 fiscal year, primarily because tax collections lag behind tax liabilities.

The fiscal actions taken during the past year reflect the Administration's philosophy that the budget is a positive instrument for economic stabilization. According to the original January 1961 budget estimates, expenditures on national income-and-product account were expected to reach a level of $98 billion in fiscal year 1962. Present estimates, which incorporate all of the changes made by executive and legislative action, indicate that these expenditures will amount to more than $106 billion. This increase in expenditures is itself responsible for a rise in the gross national product that can be estimated conservatively at $15 billion.

Budget Policy for Fiscal 1963

The balanced administrative budget proposed for fiscal year 1963 projects an increase over the current fiscal year of nearly $6 billion in Federal outlays on income-and-product account. Because of the $2 billion a year increase in social insurance taxes effective January 1, 1963, the full employment surplus rises in the first half of 1963. But it remains considerably below the level of 1960 (Chart 7). Fiscal policy will be less restrictive than it was in the late stages of the last recovery. The budgetary program, yielding a surplus on income-and-product account of $4.4 billion reflects the reasonable expectation that 4 percent unemployment will be reached by the end of the 1963 fiscal year. The feasibility of this objective and the outlook for the economy have been appraised in detail in Part I above. Obviously, the strength of private demand over the next 18 months cannot now be assessed with precision. Any plans covering the uncertain future are necessarily risky. A less expansionary budget with a larger full employment surplus would provide added assurance of price stability but only at the cost of increased dangers of an incomplete recovery. A more expansionary budget would, on the other hand, improve the outlook for maximum production and employment but increase the risks of rising prices.

The risks of an incomplete recovery, on the one hand, or of rising prices on the other, are fortunately reduced by the automatic stabilizing characteristics of the budget. If private demand proves excessively bouyant, the added revenues can be expected to enlarge the surplus in the budget, thereby moderating inflationary pressures. Conversely, any shortfall in private demand will likewise be partially countered by a shortfall in tax revenues. In addition, discretionary policy will remain flexible. First, monetary policy can be used flexibly. The Federal Reserve can attune its policies to the pattern of output, employment, and prices as it unfolds during the months ahead. Second, as the experience of 1961 demonstrated, the budget itself is a flexible tool which can be adjusted during the course of a fiscal year by varying the timing of outlays and by legislative action. Finally, the President's stabilization proposals described earlier in this chapter, would, if adopted, significantly strengthen the government's ability to act swiftly and energetically in meeting unforeseen economic developments.

MONETARY AND CREDIT POLICIES AND ECONOMIC STABILITY

The second major instrument of the Government for economic stabilization is monetary and credit policy, interpreted in the broadest sense to encompass all governmental actions affecting the liquidity of the economy and the availability and cost of credit. Here the Federal Government has broad and inescapable responsibilities, stemming basically from the sovereign right of Congress "to coin money, regulate the value thereof. . . ." The

Government's influence is exercised in several ways—principally through Federal Reserve control of the total volume of bank reserves, but also through Treasury management of the public debt and through the administration of a variety of government lending and credit guarantee programs. These powers can significantly affect the flow of funds into business investment, capital expenditures of State and local governments, residential construction, and purchases of consumer durable goods. Monetary and credit policies can be flexible, responding at short notice to changes in economic circumstances and prospects.

In an important sense, the private economy of the United States contains automatic or "built-in" monetary stabilizers. Unless the Government acts to make compensating changes in the monetary base, expansion of general economic activity, accompanied by increased demands for liquid balances and for investment funds, will tend to tighten interest rates and restrict the availability of credit. Similarly, a recession of business activity will normally lead to lower rates, easier terms, and less stringent rationing by lenders. Like fiscal stabilizers, the monetary stabilizers are often useful built-in defenses against recessions or against inflationary excesses of demand. But these defenses may not be strong enough. Being automatic stabilizers, they can only moderate unfavorable developments; they cannot prevent or reverse them. And at other times, unless the monetary authorities offset their effects, they can operate counter to basic policy objectives, braking expansions short of full employment. Discretionary policy is essential, sometimes to reinforce, sometimes to mitigate or overcome, the monetary consequences of short-run fluctuations of economic activity. In addition, discretionary policy must provide the base for expanding liquidity and credit in line with the growing production potential of the economy. For these reasons, the Federal Reserve System is continuously making and executing discretionary monetary policy.

The proper degree of general "tightness" or "easiness" of monetary policy, and the techniques by which the various governmental authorities can appropriately seek to achieve it, depend on the state of the domestic economy, on the fiscal policies of the Government, and on the international economic position. When the economy is in recession or beset by high unemployment and excess capacity, monetary policy should clearly be expansionary. How expansionary it should be depends very much upon the extent of the stimulus that the government budget is, and will be, giving to over-all demand. When demand is threatening to outrun the economy's production potential, monetary policy should be restrictive. How restrictive it should be depends, again, upon how much of the job of containing inflation is assumed by fiscal policy. There is, in principle, a variety of mixtures of fiscal and monetary policies which can accomplish a given stabilization objective. Choice among them depends upon other objectives and constraints. The relation of this choice to economic growth was noted above; the stabilization of demand at full employment levels by a budget surplus compensated by an expansionary monetary policy is favorable to growth. On the other hand, monetary policy may in some circumstances be constrained by the balance of payments. If low interest rates encourage foreign borrowing in the United States and a large outflow of funds seeking higher yields abroad, monetary policy may have to be more restrictive than domestic economic objectives alone would dictate. The first line of defense is to try to adapt the techniques of monetary control, so that policy can serve both masters at once. Even so, difficult decisions of balance between conflicting objectives may sometimes be unavoidable.

Monetary Policy and Debt Management

At the beginning of 1960, monetary policy was restrictive and interest rates were generally at postwar peaks. Despite bullish expectations about the economy, interest rates soon began a slow decline that lasted seven or eight months, aided by a gradual reversal of Federal Reserve policy (Table 8) beginning in March and furthered by the recession starting in May.

However, the Federal Reserve's anti-recession policy, for the first time since the early 1930's, was constrained by a serious balance of payments situation. Through its choice of expansionary monetary techniques, the Federal Reserve sought to avoid adding to the already large outflow of short-term capital. The 3-month Treasury bill rate did not fall below 2 percent. Long-term interest rates declined from their peaks but remained considerably above their previous cyclical troughs (Chart 8). This was a matter of serious concern because of the importance of long-term interest rates for business capital investment, residential construction, and State and local governmental spending on public facilities. And neither the money supply nor long-term private financing responded as promptly as in previous periods of monetary ease.

The new Administration faced in January 1961 both economic recession and a crisis of confidence in the dollar that threatened to limit sharply the use of expansionary monetary policy for economic recovery and growth. The Administration's forthright attack on the balance of payments problem restored confidence in the dollar. The resulting reduction in the discount on the dollar in the forward markets for foreign exchange eliminated any significant advantage in sending short-term funds abroad and helped to make it possible for monetary policy to support domestic expansion.

The ability of monetary policy to support economic expansion at home without stimulating outflows of short-term funds was simultaneously enhanced by new Federal Reserve open market techniques and by Treasurey debt management policies. In his Economic Message of February 2, the President had emphasized the importance of "increasing the flow of credit into the capital markets at declining long-term rates of interest to promote domestic recovery," while "checking declines in the short-term rates that directly affect the balance of payments." The Federal Reserve sold short-

CHART 8

Interest Rates in Three Business Cycles

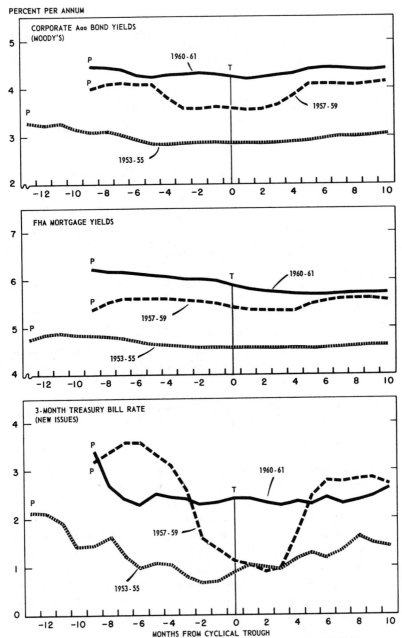

PERCENT PER ANNUM

NOTE: DATA ARE PLOTTED FROM CYCLICAL PEAK (P) TO 10 MONTHS AFTER CYCLICAL TROUGH (T).

SOURCES: MOODY'S INVESTORS SERVICE, FEDERAL HOUSING ADMINISTRATION, AND BOARD OF GOVERNORS OF THE FEDERAL RESERVE SYSTEM.

TABLE 8.—*Principal Federal Reserve monetary actions, 1960–61*

Date	Action
1960: March_____	Federal Reserve open market operations modified so as to exert moderately less restraint on bank reserve positions than in earlier months. Effect was to allow reduction in net borrowed reserves.
May_____	Open market operations modified to provide reserves for moderate expansion of bank credit and money supply.
June_____	Discount rates reduced from 4 percent to 3½ percent.
July_____	Margin requirements reduced from 90 percent to 70 percent.
August_____	Authorized member banks to count about $500 million of vault cash as required reserves. Reduced reserve requirements against demand deposits at central reserve city banks from 18 percent to 17½ percent, effective September 1, releasing about $125 million of reserves.
August–September_____	Discount rates reduced from 3½ percent to 3 percent. Open market operations modified to suggest a positive attitude toward increasing the availability of reserves.
October_____	Purchased short-term U.S. Government securities other than Treasury bills for first time since 1958 to minimize downward pressure on 3-month bill rate, thus keeping bill rate more competitive internationally.
November–December_____	Authorized member banks to count all vault cash in meeting reserve requirements, reduced reserve requirements against demand deposits at central reserve city banks from 17½ percent to 16½ percent, raised requirements for country banks from 11 percent to 12 percent. Net effect of actions was to release about $1.3 billion of reserves.
1961: January–early February_____	Open market operations aimed at maintaining ease in member bank reserve positions, with seasonal increases in reserve funds about offset by gold outflow and other factors draining reserves.
February–December_____	On February 20, began providing reserves through purchases of longer-term U.S. Government securities, while selling short-term Government securities at times.[1] Expansion in money supply became more rapid later in the year, with monetary ease being maintained throughout the year.
December_____	Board of Governors announced increase in maximum rates payable on savings and other time deposits, effective January 1, 1962. The action was taken to promote competition for savings and to encourage retention of foreign funds by member banks and thus moderate pressures on this country's balance of payments.

[1] Treasury also purchased very long-term U.S. Government securities for Government investment accounts. In his Economic Message of February 2, President Kennedy had announced that the Federal Reserve and Treasury were developing techniques to help keep long-term rates down while holding short-term rates at internationally competitive levels.

Source: Council of Economic Advisers.

term securities, while the Treasury further increased the outstanding supply through new cash offerings. On February 20, the Federal Reserve announced a new policy of providing bank reserves through purchases of U.S. Government securities of longer maturities, particularly in the 3- to 6-year range. Its purchases of U.S. Government securities of maturity of more than 1 year amounted to $2.6 billion in 1961. The Treasury, in administering the investment portfolios of various government investment and trust accounts, made substantial purchases of securities of maturities of more than 10 years. Aided by these actions, long-term bond rates declined until May and rose only moderately thereafter in the face of an economic recovery that had begun in February.

Through substantial net purchases of U.S. Government securities, the Federal Reserve increased member bank reserves in 1961 by about $1 billion. As a result banks steadily expanded their loans and investments; the increase during the year was considerably more than in 1960 and about the same as in the peacetime record year, 1958. Persistently expecting an up-trend in market interest rates, banks maintained lending rates in the face of generally weak demands for short-term loans, and added $6 billion to their holdings of U.S. Government securities. However, the expansion of bank holdings of Government securities made more funds available on the open market. And the high level of bank holdings of short-term government securities, combined with abundant free reserves, put pressure on banks to expand business loans and to lend directly in the capital markets. As mone-tary ease persisted and expectations of rising interest rates subsided, banks stepped up purchases of State and local securities and expanded mortgage lending. The 7 percent increase in total bank deposits and currency during 1961 fell just short of the peacetime record, although public preference for time deposits held the increase in the money supply (demand deposits and currency) to about 3 percent.

The liquidity of the economy was also increased by changes in the composition and level of the Federal debt held outside the Federal Reserve and the Treasury. Open market and debt management operations added substantially to the supply of U.S. Government securities maturing within 1 year. The volume of less liquid securities, maturing within 1 to 5 years, declined. The volume of outstanding securities greater than 5 years in maturity remained the same. The average maturity of that part of the debt held outside the Federal Reserve and U.S. Government investment accounts declined from 58 months to 56 months. The average maturity of the total marketable public debt changed little in 1961. Two advance refundings, designed to have a minimal impact on over-all liquidity, helped to offset shortening as a result of mere passage of time.

Federal Reserve and Treasury debt operations provided the basic liquidity necessary for economic expansion. Individuals, in addition to increasing their deposits in commercial banks, stepped up their accumulation of claims on such financial intermediaries as savings and loan associa-tions, mutual savings banks, and life insurance companies, while cutting down their purchases of securities on the open market. This behavior was in part a response to the high level of interest and dividend rates paid by financial intermediaries relative to yields of high-grade open market securi-ties. Liquid assets held by the public—defined to include the money supply, savings deposits and shares, U.S. Savings bonds, and short-term U.S. Government securities—grew by 7 percent in 1961, paralleling the rise in GNP. Financial intermediaries used the funds which flowed into them from the public to extend credit by acquiring mortgages, bonds, and other loans and securities. In this way, their operations both increased the liquidity of individuals and made more long-term credit available.

The total volume of mortgage, corporate, and State and local long-term financing rose sharply to what appears to be a new record (Table 9).

TABLE 9.—*Funds raised in money and capital markets, by type of instrument, 1957–61*

[Billions of dollars]

Type of instrument	1957	1958	1959	1960	1961 [1]
Total	36. 6	46. 2	61. 2	39. 5	50. 1
Federal obligations [2]	1. 1	9. 0	11. 3	−2. 2	6. 6
Short-term [3]	5. 5	−1. 2	5. 5	−5. 1	10. 5
Long-term [4]	−4. 4	10. 2	5. 8	2. 9	−3. 9
Private	35. 6	37. 3	49. 9	41. 6	43. 5
Short-term	7. 4	5. 3	16. 9	13. 4	9. 8
Business bank loans	2. 3	1. 3	7. 5	3. 2	2. 0
Consumer credit	2. 8	. 3	6. 4	3. 9	1. 1
Other	2. 3	3. 7	3. 0	6. 3	6. 7
Long-term	28. 2	32. 0	33. 0	28. 1	33. 7
State and local securities	4. 6	5. 7	4. 9	3. 6	5. 3
Corporate securities	9. 8	8. 2	6. 5	6. 9	7. 9
Other securities [5]	1. 7	2. 8	2. 5	2. 2	2. 4
Mortgages	12. 1	15. 3	19. 2	15. 4	18. 1

[1] Preliminary estimates by Council of Economic Advisers.
[2] Excludes consumer-held savings bonds and notes issued to international organizations; includes non-guaranteed securities issued by Federal agencies.
[3] Direct marketable issues maturing in one year or less.
[4] Includes direct Treasury issues maturing after one year and all nonguaranteed securities.
[5] Investment company share issues and foreign security issues.

NOTE.—Detail will not necessarily add to totals because of rounding.

Source: Board of Governors of the Federal Reserve System (except as noted).

Corporations borrowed unusually heavily in long-term capital markets but added in the aggregate almost as much to their financial assets, of a generally liquid character, as to their financial liabilities. Monetary ease, in facilitating this financing, laid the financial groundwork for expanded corporate capital spending in the future.

Because of the expansion in liquidity and in the supply of credit through financial institutions, interest rates were relatively stable during 1961, in sharp contrast to the previous upswing (Chart 8). The rate of 3-month Treasury bills fluctuated within the narrow range of 2¼ and 2½ percent during most of the year, rising somewhat above this range toward the close. Most long-term rates declined through May and thereafter increased by only a small amount. Rates on home mortgages, which are more sticky than most other rates, continued to fall until midyear, and then remained fairly stable. Thus, 1961 has demonstrated that interest rates do not have to rise sharply in cyclical recoveries. Their movement is not governed by immutable natural law. It depends upon all economic circumstances and governmental policies affecting the supply of funds and the demand for them.

The behavior of interest rates during the year may also have signaled the ending of the upward trend in rates from the low levels at which they were pegged prior to the Treasury-Federal Reserve Accord of 1951. While this trend was in part an adjustment to the profitability of investment in capital goods, it also reflected the spread of inflationary expectations. Recent stability in industrial and consumer prices may, however, diminish inflationary psychology, so that inflation premiums would gradually be shaken out of the interest rate structure.

The climate for equity financing was also favorable during 1961. Common stock prices rose by about 25 percent, anticipating in part a recovery of corporate profits, and the average dividend yield on stocks fell below 3 percent.

Federal Credit Programs

The Administration sought to make credit readily available at liberal terms through programs of Federal lending and Federal insurance and guarantee of private lending. Important steps were taken to stimulate housing construction. Early in the year, the Federal Housing Administration (FHA) reduced the maximum permissible rate on insured mortgages in two steps, from 5¾ to 5¼ percent. The Federal National Mortgage Association (FNMA) supported these reductions by its secondary market operations in mortgages, raising both its purchase and selling prices repeatedly. Up to midyear, sales of mortgages by FNMA exceeded purchases, but after midyear its operations added to the supply of funds available for mortgages. The Federal Home Loan Bank Board and the regional Banks liberalized regulations and reduced interest rates on advances in order to stimulate mortgage lending by savings and loan associations.

For the longer run, the Housing Act of 1961 expanded or liberalized many existing credit programs and initiated new ones. A new FHA insurance program was set up for middle-income housing, with FNMA also prepared to purchase these mortgages under its special assistance programs. Maturities up to 35 years, in some cases up to 40 years, were authorized for FHA-insured mortgages and insurable loan-to-value ratios were increased. A new FHA program for insurance of long-term home improvement loans was instituted. FNMA made the new home improvement loans eligible for purchase under its secondary market operations, and, when used to finance rehabilitation of homes in urban renewal areas, the new loans are eligible for purchase by FNMA under its special assistance program. FNMA also was authorized to make short-term loans secured by federally underwritten mortgages. Funds were provided for loans for public facilities, college housing, farm housing, housing for the elderly, and FNMA special assistance. The capital grant authority for urban renewal was increased by $2 billion.

Other Federal credit programs contributed to making credit more generally available at liberal terms in 1961. In particular, the Small Business Administration reduced the interest rate on loans made in areas of substantial unemployment and instituted a simplified program to expand bank participation in small business loans.

Federal credit programs will support economic expansion during the coming fiscal year. New commitments are expected to rise to record levels. Direct loans and mortgage purchases (including trust fund purchases) will approach $9 billion, $3 billion more than anticipated collections on out-standing loans. New commitments to guarantee or insure private loans will for the first time reach $20 billion.

Monetary Expansion and Recovery

As the economy advances toward full employment, it will need more liquidity. Throughout the postwar period, and particularly in the three previous economic recoveries, the growth in liquidity has fallen considerably short of the growth in GNP. The economy had to work off the excess liquidity inherited from the war, interest rates were generally rising, and expectations of higher prices were spreading. These factors worked to reduce the liquidity requirements of the economy relative to GNP. And the growth in nonmonetary liquid assets diminished even more the needed growth in the money supply (bank deposits and currency). Business firms, government units, and individuals learned, to their advantage, how to minimize holdings of cash.

For each 1 percent rise in GNP in the three past economic recoveries, commercial bank deposits and currency increased by only about one-third of 1 percent, while liquid assets, more broadly measured, increased by about two-fifths to three-fifths of 1 percent. If these relationships should hold in the current economic recovery, and if gross national product rises to full employment levels by the middle of 1963—an increase of more than 20 percent from the trough in the first quarter of 1961—commercial bank deposits and currency would grow over the same period by 7–8 percent and liquid assets by 11–12 percent.

In the current recovery, however, the factors that served to limit liquidity requirements in the earlier recoveries may well be less important. In particular, interest rates may appropriately be more stable, for reasons already explained. Thus, these estimates of needed liquidity are probably conservative. The appropriate expansion of liquidity will depend upon the strength of private demands, on the tightness of fiscal policy, and on the balance of payments position.

IMPROVING THE MOBILITY OF RESOURCES

Maximum employment and production depend not only on the success of stabilization policy in maintaining demand at appropriate levels but also on the mobility of labor and other productive resources in response to changes in demand and cost. If frictional and structural unemployment can be diminished, demand can be pressed further before encountering bottlenecks and price increases. Thus, measures to improve the mobility of resources enable stabilization policy to aim at, and to attain, higher levels of employment and production. Such measures are a basic part of the Administration's economic program.

Labor Market Policies

Changes in technology and tastes are constantly altering the pattern of demand for labor in our economy. New industries appear and expand while old ones decline; job opportunities multiply in one region and disappear in another; new skills are required as old ones become obsolete. The more rapidly an economy grows and changes, the greater the flux in its labor markets.

A high level of over-all demand is a prerequisite for the efficient allocation of labor resources in a dynamic economy. It furnishes the most important single incentive for economically desirable labor mobility—the magnetic attraction of available job openings. However, a high level of demand will not by itself ensure the best possible degree of occupational, industrial, and geographic labor mobility, for it will not eliminate some important impediments to the desirable response of labor to job opportunities. Certain features of seniority, pension, and other benefit rights may serve to hold labor in industries and areas experiencing declining demand. Lack of knowledge of job openings and lack of the skills required to fill them constitute important barriers to labor mobility, and the high cost of moving is an insurmountable obstacle to the migration of many low-income families to areas of expanding employment. It is in the best interest of the economy, as well as of the individuals involved, that these impediments be reduced and that every wage earner be in a position to select the most favorable alternative from the widest possible range of employment opportunities.

Employment exchange. Letting employers know about available workers and telling workers about available jobs are difficult administrative and technical problems in a labor market as complex as ours. Yet doing this well can significantly reduce the number and size of labor shortages and help eliminate pockets of unemployment and underemployment.

A major effort has begun to improve the United States Employment Service so that it can do a better job in matching job vacancies with people. The staff has been substantially expanded, particularly in the metropolitan areas where most workers and jobs are concentrated. This staff will need, most importantly, to emphasize improvement in the quality of its counseling and placement work. The flow of information about jobs should be made nationwide through more extensive exchanges of job information among the State agencies. Also, since the performance of the important labor exchange function should not suffer from the tremendous administrative problems of administering unemployment compensation, these two activities should be separated where the volume of work permits.

As the United States Employment Service succeeds in improving its services, more people will use it. The larger the number of employers and workers using the Employment Service, the more complete will be the knowledge of the labor market available to each of them. A greatly strengthened United States Employment Service will facilitate an expanded rate of economic growth and contribute to the effectiveness of such specific government programs as Area Redevelopment, Rural Redevelopment, and the proposed programs for Trade Assistance and Manpower Development and Training.

Training. The economic need for facilitating labor mobility through education and training programs is evidenced by the simultaneous existence of very low unemployment rates in various skilled, technical and professional occupations and relatively high unemployment among the less skilled groups. Programs for education and training should be directed particularly toward new entrants into the labor force and the training of adults for positions of increased productivity and income. Racial discrimination in training, as well as in hiring, must be eliminated. It is wrong—that is reason enough—and it is also an enormous waste of human talent.

The Administration is proposing a program to provide useful employment and training for young people through three pilot programs financed in whole or in part by the Federal Government. These programs provide for on-the-job training, public service employment and training, and employment, training, and educational opportunities through service in a Youth Conservation Corps. Special training programs for young people are contemplated; such programs are urgently needed in urban slum areas. Some of these programs for the training of youth should help, directly and indirectly, to stimulate and guide the flow of migration from the farm; in April 1960, 43.8 percent of the entire farm population and 59.0 percent of the nonwhite farm population were under age 20.

Lack of education certainly does not imply lack of aptitude, and widened educational opportunities enable individuals to improve their employment opportunities as well as the quality of their lives. The Administration's program for aid to States and educational institutions in extending and improving adult literacy programs is an important step toward reducing structural unemployment.

The Administration's key proposal for manpower development and training provides for the establishment of programs for selection, placement, and on-the-job training, and for improvement of State training facilities. Although intended primarily for the unemployed and underemployed, these programs would also be open to other qualified persons desiring to improve their skills or to acquire new skills.

Compensation for workers participating in a training program is essential. At present, many individuals are confronted with the hard choice between compensation without training and training without compensation; the necessity for this choice should be eliminated. Unemployed workers in most States are still disqualified from receiving unemployment insurance benefits if they participate in education and training programs.

Moreover, workers receiving benefits are required to be continuously available for job placement. Compensation for training would make it financially possible for an unemployed individual to complete a full course of training or retraining. Under the proposed program, allowances would be provided for certain trainees not receiving unemployment compensation benefits. Thus a large part of the cost of trainee compensation under the program would be offset by reductions in unemployment compensation payments and various other public assistance expenditures.

A major feature of the proposal is the provision for government studies on a national and local basis to determine the future requirements of the economy for various occupations and skills, to anticipate prospective manpower shortages, and to assure that workers are trained for occupations where opportunities will exist.

Resource Use in Agriculture

The agricultural population has long been a major source of manpower for U.S. industry. Many more children are born and raised on farms than will be needed to produce the Nation's food and fiber. They must be educated, trained, and guided to nonagricultural employment. Many adults now earn substandard incomes in farming. They are not in a technical sense structurally unemployed, but their distress is nevertheless a symptom of structural maladjustment. Programs of the kind just discussed—to facilitate labor mobility and training—can and should help many of these individuals to find new employment.

During the first two decades of this century, there was serious question whether agriculture could, with the closing of the land frontier, continue to meet the food and fiber demands of a growing national economy. The rate of growth in farm output was declining, and food and fiber prices were rising relative to other wholesale prices. The resulting public concern led to (1) increased emphasis on conservation and resource investment and (2) increased allocation of public funds for research and education designed to speed progress in agricultural technology.

By the mid-1920's, agricultural productivity was rising and farm employment declining. The full implications of rapid technological progress in agriculture were, however, obscured by the depression and by the Second World War and the Korean conflict. During the depression, the catastrophic decline in demand for farm products was the compelling problem, and policy was directed to protecting farm prices and incomes from its consequences. During the war and the Korean conflict, government programs were designed to encourage increases in output and to protect farmers from the effects of price reductions when emergency demands disappeared.

During the 1950's, the full effects of the programs set in motion early in the century began to be felt. The demand for farm output rose only slightly faster than the population. Rapid gains in productivity put farm prices and incomes under increasing downward pressure. Farm programs designed for depression and war were continued, in order to hold at least part of the social gains from increasing agricultural productivity within the agricultural sector. Farmers also responded by leaving agriculture at the most rapid rate in history. Use of labor declined by almost one-third while output increased by more than one-fourth between 1950 and 1961.

By 1960, it was clear that agriculture's relationship to the general economy had undergone a fundamental change in several respects. Agriculture can, without question, meet any foreseeable demands for food and fiber placed upon it. In 1910, it required 13.6 million farm workers to feed a Nation of 92.4 million people. By 1960, the population had increased to 180.7 million and farm employment had fallen to 7.1 million. The effects of fluctuations in national economic activity on the demand for farm output have been damped by built-in floors under consumer spending and by continuation of the emergency farm programs. Nevertheless, the stability and growth of the national economy are still of great importance to the farm population. Failure to maintain full employment limits the ability of industry to absorb farm workers displaced by advancing technology. During periods of peak economic activity, migration has been above 5 percent of the farm population. During recessions in the last decade, the migration rate out of agriculture has fallen considerably. Thus the problem of agricultural labor mobility is very largely a question of the availability of nonagricultural job opportunities. If job opportunities are available, the general manpower policies discussed above can facilitate the necessary migration and ease the human problems of adjustment.

Caught between the pressures of a slowly rising demand for farm products, rising productivity in agriculture, and limitations on nonfarm employment opportunities, total farm income and farm income per capita or per farm family have lagged behind incomes in the rest of the economy. The commodity programs have protected farm incomes from even greater declines, but at considerable budgetary expense and at some cost in delaying adjustment of patterns of resource use in agriculture. In 1961, farm incomes were increased and a significant start was made toward reduction of costs of surplus accumulation, storage, and disposal.

Objectives of agricultural policy as it develops in the future should encompass both (1) continuation of agriculture's historic role as a major contributor to national economic growth and (2) equitable distribution of gains in agricultural productivity between farmers and consumers. Achievement of these two objectives will require continued rapid transfers of labor from the farm to the nonfarm sector and reduction in resources devoted to the production, storage, and disposition of surplus production.

Appendix

PROGRAM FOR ECONOMIC RECOVERY AND GROWTH

When the new Administration took office on January 20, 1961, it moved with speed and vigor to deal with the recession that had begun in May 1960. At his press conference of February 1, the President announced a series of administrative actions. He followed this with a comprehensive "Program to Restore Momentum to the American Economy," delivered before the Congress on February 2. Legislative requests, some of them directed toward the immediate situation, others toward future recovery and growth, were laid before the Congress in this speech and in a series of messages during the year.

The following is a list of the actions taken during 1961 to foster economic recovery and growth. Included also are measures (other than defense and foreign aid) which, though primarily directed to other purposes, contributed significantly to growth.

A. EXECUTIVE AND ADMINISTRATIVE ACTIONS

1. *Accelerated Procurement and Construction*

The President directed Federal agencies to accelerate procurement and construction planned for the rest of fiscal year 1961 under existing funds.

2. *Post Office Construction*

It was announced that post office construction, originally scheduled for implementation over 18 months, would be compressed into 10 months (March to the end of the calendar year). Although changes were made in this directive before the end of the calendar year, there was a substantial acceleration during the first half of 1961 in the provision of new offices. Projects for post offices were concentrated in areas of high unemployment.

3. *Federal-Aid Highways, School and Other Construction*

On February 2, the President made available $718 million of Federal-aid highway. funds scheduled for release in the fourth quarter of fiscal 1961. Quarterly apportionments for the first and second quarters of fiscal 1962 were also released ahead of schedule, in May and August. On February 16, the President urged State Governors to speed the spending of $1.1 billion in Federal aid for highways, schools, hospitals, and waste treatment facilities.

4. *Accelerated Tax Refunds*

Taxpayers who were eligible for refunds were requested to file returns early to speed refund payments. In the first three months of 1961, individual income tax refunds totaled about $2.1 billion, 31 percent more than in 1960.

5. *Veterans Life Insurance Dividends*

On February 1, the President announced that he had directed the Veterans Administration to advance the payment of veterans life insurance dividends. The total payable, $258 million, over the entire calendar year was made available in the first quarter. In addition, a special dividend payment of $218 million was made in late June and in July.

6. *Price Supports and Farm Storage Payments*

Price supports were raised on corn, cotton, butterfat and milk, soybeans, and most other price-supported commodities for the 1961 crop year.

On February 8, the President directed the Department of Agriculture to speed payments to farmers for storage of crops under price support loans. The payments, advanced to early March, amounted to about $25 million.

7. *Food Distribution*

In his first executive order, the President, on January 21, directed the Secretary of Agriculture to expand the free food distribution program for needy families in areas of chronic unemployment. On January 24, the Secretary of Agriculture announced that, through additional purchases of protein foods, the Government would increase the variety of surplus foods being distributed. As a result of these actions, the annual rate of distribution was raised from about $60 million to more than $200 million.

8. *Food Stamp Program*

On February 2, the President announced the establishment of six area projects for operation of a pilot "food stamp" distribution program. This was subsequently expanded to eight areas.

9. *Farm Loans*

On February 8, the Department of Agriculture announced that, pursuant to a White House directive, it was making available an additional $50 million for housing loans to low-income farmers. On February 13, the Department announced that the Farmers Home Administration would release an additional $35 million for operating loans for farmers. Lending activity of the Farmers Home Administration for rural area development was accelerated.

10. *Rural Electrification Administration*

During the year, the Rural Electrification Administration intensified its activity in the field of rural area development.

11. *Monetary Policy and Debt Management*

As the President announced in his February 2 message, the Federal Reserve and the Treasury Department worked "to further the complementary effectiveness of debt management and monetary policy." During the year, their policies were directed toward fostering domestic economic recovery by providing the base for needed bank credit and monetary expansion and by encouraging the flow of savings and credit into long-term investment channels. The Federal Reserve provided bank reserves through purchases of securities of more than 1 year. The Treasury Department has been buying long-term U.S. Government securities for the trust fund accounts. At the same time, both monetary and debt management policies countered downward pressure on short-term rates, with a view to checking the outflow of funds from this country to money markets abroad.

12. *Housing Actions*

On February 1, the President announced a speeding up of the initiation of projects already approved (including the commitment of available college housing funds ahead of schedule).

On February 2, the maximum permissible interest rate on insured home loans of the Federal Housing Administration (FHA) was reduced from 5¾ percent to 5½ percent, and on May 29 to 5¼ percent.

The Community Facilities Administration reduced rates on new loans and broadened the program to include certain communities and projects previously excluded.

Purchase and sales prices for federally underwritten mortgages under Federal National Mortgage Association (FNMA) secondary market operations were raised in a series of steps. After the middle of 1961, purchases of mortgages by FNMA under secondary market operations exceeded sales.

The Federal Home Loan Bank Board liberalized terms under which Federal savings and loan associations can make mortgage loans; broadened the powers of insured associations to engage in participation loans; allowed member associations to borrow an amount up to 17½ percent of withdrawable accounts from Federal Home Loan Banks, in contrast to the former 12½ percent (this action was taken in two steps); caused Federal Home Loan Banks to reduce interest rates on advances to members; and instituted a new program of intermediate advances by Federal Home Loan Banks.

On February 2, the Urban Renewal Administration requested local public agencies to accelerate urban renewal activities.

On July 17, FHA eliminated the continuing service charge formerly permitted for home mortgages of $9,000 or less.

13. *Small Business Administration Loans*

On April 5, the Small Business Administration (SBA) announced a decrease from 5½ percent to 4 percent in the interest rate on loans to small businesses in areas of substantial unemployment, and a liberalization of size standards. The Agency also reduced from 5–5½ percent to 4 percent the interest rate on loans to State and local development companies in such areas. In August, it instituted a simplified bank loan participation plan designed to achieve expanded commercial bank participation in small business loans.

14. Government Procurement in Areas of Substantial Unemployment

On February 2, the President announced that he was directing the Secretary of Defense, Secretary of Labor, and the General Services Administration to take steps to improve the mechanism for channeling Federal contracts to firms both in areas of substantial unemployment and in areas of substantial and persistent unemployment. Accordingly, the Federal Procurement Regulations have been amended (1) to provide procedures for the setting aside of appropriate procurements for award to firms which will perform a substantial proportion of the contracts in areas of substantial unemployment and areas of substantial and persistent unemployment, (2) to assure that concerns in such areas are afforded an equitable opportunity to compete for subcontracts under government prime contracts, and (3) to clarify and strengthen the preference for firms in such areas in procurements where equal low bids are received. Similar instructions have been issued in the Armed Services Procurement Regulation.

15. United States Employment Service (USES)

On February 2, the President directed the Secretary of Labor to expand and improve services to jobless applicants registered with the USES. Placement services, especially in metropolitan areas, have been realigned to meet the needs of workers and employers in all occupations. The Bureau of Employment Security and affiliated State agencies have increased program emphasis on job development for the unemployed, and testing, counseling, and placement activities for young people out of school and out of work.

16. Manpower Retraining

In anticipation of passage of the proposed manpower development and training act, the Secretary of Labor on November 27 requested all States to develop plans for immediate implementation of the law. In addition, the Department of Labor and the Department of Health, Education, and Welfare have coordinated plans for effectively carrying out their responsibilities under the act.

17. Export-Import Bank

The Export-Import Bank announced two new programs which make available export credit guarantees, insurance and financing for semifinished and consumer durable goods, and export credit insurance for consumer goods. The first of these makes available export credit insurance, covering both political and credit risks on short-term and medium-term credit sales, which will be issued through a private association of insurance companies. The second program consists of guarantees issued to financial institutions and Bank participation with financial institutions which finance exporters' medium-term credit sales on a nonrecourse basis. Both programs are designed to enable the exporter to apply for assistance directly to his local commercial bank or insurance broker.

B. Legislative Recommendations and Actions

1. *Temporary Extended Unemployment Compensation*

The President requested the Congress to increase temporarily the period during which unemployment insurance benefits might be paid. The Congress enacted this proposal. The legislation establishes, on a self-supporting basis, a temporary program of extended unemployment compensation to persons who have exhausted their benefits under State and Federal laws. It provides for agreements with States to pay temporary extended unemployment benefits, for any worker who exhausts his State benefits between June 30, 1960 and March 31, 1962, equal to 50 percent of the amount received in State unemployment benefits or 13 times his weekly benefit amount. The increases in benefits are being financed by an increase of 0.4 percent in the unemployment tax rate for the calendar years 1962 and 1963.

In addition, the Congress authorized a temporary self-supporting program of extended railroad unemployment insurance to workers who have exhausted normal benefits under the Railroad Unemployment Insurance Act.

2. *Unemployment Compensation*

The President, on June 13, proposed major changes in the Federal-State unemployment compensation system. The Administration bill, introduced in the First Session of the 87th Congress, would extend the scope of the system by increasing coverage to include over three million more workers; increase benefits so that a great majority of eligible claimants would receive a weekly benefit equal to at least one-half of their average weekly wage; establish a permanent Federal program of additional compensation for unemployed workers who have exhausted their regular benefits; and improve the financing of the program by increasing the wage base on which the unemployment tax is based from $3,000 to $4,800.

In addition, the measure includes equalization grants to States with high unemployment costs, and a provision precluding denial of unemployment compensation to claimants who are attending approved training or retraining courses.

The Congress took no action on the Administration bill in 1961.

3. *Aid to Dependent Children*

The Congress was requested to extend the program of aid to dependent children by providing benefits to children who are needy because of the unemployment of their parents. A bill was passed by the Congress and signed by the President on May 8. It is estimated that expenditures of about $100 million in fiscal 1962 are being made under this program.

4. *Social Security Liberalization*

The President proposed legislation to improve the old age, survivors, and disability insurance and public assistance programs. Such legislation was passed by the Congress and approved by the President on June 30 to provide, among other things, increased minimum social security benefits, an earlier retirement age for men, and increased benefits for widows. To meet the increased benefit costs the Federal Insurance Contribution Act taxes were increased, effective January 1, 1962, by one-eighth of 1 percent each on employers and employees.

5. *Manpower Retraining*

The President proposed a manpower development and training program, providing for counseling, training, relocation assistance, and vocational education. The Administration's bill provides for retraining unemployed persons who cannot reasonably be expected to secure full-time employment without retraining and for upgrading the skills of other members of the work force. It also provides for continuing review and assessment of the Nation's manpower requirements, for appropriate methods of testing, counseling, and selecting workers for training, for determining the skills in which they should be trained, for referral of workers for training, for placement services after completion of training, and for financial assistance during the training period for those unemployed workers who cannot undertake a training program without it.

The Senate approved a manpower retraining bill, and a bill was reported out by the House Education and Labor Committee. The House Rules Committee postponed giving a rule for debate on the bill until 1962.

6. *Youth Employment Opportunities*

The President recommended the enactment of a Youth Employment Opportunities bill. The proposal includes on-the-job training programs conducted in cooperation with both private and public groups, public service employment programs established in cooperation with State and local public and nonprofit agencies, and a Youth Conservation Corps which would perform conservation and related work pursuant to agreements with State and Federal conservation agencies.

Both Senate and House Committees reported out bills on the subject in 1961, but no further action was taken.

7. *Minimum Wage*

The President signed the Fair Labor Standards Act Amendments on May 5, extending coverage to approximately 3.6 million additional workers and increasing the minimum wage to $1.25 an hour over a period of time. The amendments represent the first Congressional action on extension of coverage since the Act was passed in 1938.

8. *Area Redevelopment*

The Administration proposal to aid areas with substantial and persistent unemployment was enacted and signed by the President on May 1. The

Area Redevelopment Act provides loans to commercial and industrial enterprises, loans and grants for community facilities and urban renewal, all designed to increase employment opportunities in these areas. In addition, the Act provides for the training and retraining of unemployed and underemployed residents of these areas and for the payment of retraining subsistence benefits while in training.

In 1961, 359 redevelopment areas and 9 Indian Reservations prepared and submitted plans for their over-all economic development. Of these, plans covering 247 redevelopment areas and 9 Indian Reservations had been given provisional approval by the end of the year. Eleven projects involving industrial loans, grants and loans for public facilities, and technical assistance contracts were approved. Sixty-six more were under active consideration at the end of the year.

Occupational training programs for unemployed and underemployed persons were initiated in October 1961, under the provisions of the Area Redevelopment Act. As of January 5, 1962, training projects in 17 redevelopment areas located in 7 different States had been approved. These projects provided for the training of 3,500 workers in 45 courses of instruction. Fifty training proposals from as many areas are under active consideration, and an additional 50 are in various stages of preparation in local communities.

9. *Housing*

A Presidential message sent to the Congress on March 9 included the following proposals: a 4-year commitment of $2.5 billion for urban renewal; long-term, low-interest loans for nonprofit limited dividend rental and cooperative housing for moderate income families financed by special assistance from FNMA; expanded public housing and housing for the elderly; authority for FHA to insure long-term home improvement loans; additional aid for urban planning, community facilities, and housing research; an extension of the FHA insurance program for middle-income families to permit in certain cases a 40-year maximum mortgage period, to remove the downpayment requirement, and to make other changes to ease housing credit.

The Housing Act of 1961, incorporating the substance of these proposals, was approved on June 30.

The veterans home loan program was extended by legislation approved on July 6.

10. *Feed Grains Program*

The President signed an emergency feed grains bill on March 22. It authorized the Secretary of Agriculture to make payments to growers on 1961 crops to reduce acreage and output, and to increase support prices for feed grains. Advance payments were begun shortly after the bill was signed.

11. *Agriculture*

The President sent to the Congress an omnibus farm bill on March 16. A bill signed into law on August 8 extended and liberalized lending programs of the Farmers Home Administration, extended the emergency feed grains program to 1962 crops, authorized a program of payments to producers for reducing wheat acreage in 1962, extended the special milk program and the National Wool Act for 4 years, extended the program for the sale of surplus commodities for foreign currency for 3 years, and authorized marketing orders for additional commodities.

12. *Federal-Aid Highways*

The President, in a message sent to the Congress on February 28, recommended increased taxes and a schedule of authorizations which would permit completion of the Interstate System in 1972 and an expansion of other Federal-aid highway programs. The Federal-Aid Highway Act of 1961, approved on June 29, provides increased authorization and revenues required to permit completion of the Interstate System by 1972, while maintaining the pay-as-you-build principle.

13. *Natural Resources*

A Presidential message sent to the Congress on February 23 included a program calling for increased aid for waste treatment facilities and air pollution, expansion of the saline water program, accelerated forest planting, access roads to public forests, purchase of shoreline areas for park sites, and a 10-year program of grants to the States for planning comprehensive water development projects. On July 20, the President signed a bill almost doubling grants for water pollution control and strengthening federal authority to seek abatement of pollution. On September 22, an extension of the saline water program for 6 years was approved, with an authorization of $75 million. To carry out the President's forestry program, appropriations for the Forest Service were substantially increased with particular emphasis on the expanded reforestation program, acceleration of recreational facility development, and strengthening protection against forest fires. Authorization for the Cape Cod National Seashore was signed into law on August 7. In the Housing Act of 1961, approved on June 30, partial grants to localities in an aggregate amount of $50 million were authorized for the acquisition of land for permanent open space in or near urban areas.

14. *Airport Aid*

Administration bills authorizing construction grants of $75 million a year for 5 years were introduced in both the Senate and the House. A bill signed on September 20 authorized the extension of Federal construction grants to airports for 3 years. A 2-year grant of $150 million was included in the final money bill approved on September 27.

15. *Aid to Education*

The President sent a special message on education to the Congress on February 20. It included recommendations concerning elementary and secondary schools and higher education.

Elementary and secondary schools: The President recommended that the Congress authorize a 3-year program for school construction and teachers' salaries. The total cost would be $2.3 billion. The Senate passed a school aid program, but the House Rules Committee tabled the proposal.

Higher education: Legislation was proposed to provide more than $3 billion in assistance to higher education. The proposals included the extension and expansion of the low-interest loan program for college housing facilities; authorization of a new 5-year program under which $300 million would be loaned each year for the construction of academic facilities; authorization of a program of 4-year undergraduate scholarships; expanded student loans and fellowships through the National Defense Education Act.

The Administration supported legislation to provide matching grants for establishment of educational television stations and for State surveys of the need for such stations. The Senate passed a bill to authorize aid for establishment of such stations and the House reported a bill out of Committee which was substantially the same as the program submitted.

As part of the Housing Bill signed on June 30, the college housing fund was increased from $1.7 billion to $2.9 billion in four steps by July 1, 1964.

The National Defense Education Act was extended for two years on October 5, continuing the previous $90 million annual authorization for student loans.

16. *Health Programs*

A Presidential message sent to the Congress on February 9 included the following proposals:

(1) Increased grants for the construction of nursing homes; grants to States for community health programs, and project grants to develop new methods of out-of-hospital care; increased project grants for research into uses of medical facilities, including grants for the construction of experimental and demonstration facilities;

(2) A 10-year program of matching grants for the construction, expansion, and restoration of medical and dental schools with an authorization of $75 million a year and an anticipated first-year appropriation of $25 million;

(3) Authorization of Federal grants to schools for scholarships for medical and dental students;

(4) Increased appropriations for existing maternal and child welfare programs;

(5) Increased vocational rehabilitation grants;

(6) An extended and expanded program of matching grants for the construction of research facilities and increased appropriations for the

medical research and training programs of the National Institutes of Health.

The community health services and facilities bill, approved on September 20, increased from $30 million to $50 million the annual authorization for grants to States for public health services (with particular attention to community health service programs); authorized an additional $10 million a year for project grants to develop new methods of out-of-hospital care; raised from $10 million to $20 million the annual authorization for grants to build public or nonprofit nursing homes; and increased from $1.2 million to $10 million the authorization for research into uses of medical facilities (including construction of experimental facilities).

17. *Medical Care for the Aged*

The President recommended a health insurance program for those of age 65 or over who are eligible for Social Security benefits. The insurance would be financed by an increase in Social Security payroll taxes. Hospital and home health service benefits would begin October 1, 1962. Nursing home service benefits would begin July 1, 1963. Action by the Congress was postponed.

18. *Tax Recommendations*

Among his tax recommendations, the President asked for the enactment of an investment tax credit as an incentive for the modernization and expansion of private plant and equipment. He also recommended withholding taxes on interest and dividends and a series of measures to eliminate defects and inequities. This tax program would involve no net loss in revenue. On August 23, the House Ways and Means Committee announced that it was postponing further action until 1962.

19. *Special Insurance Dividend for Korean Conflict Veterans*

On September 13, the President approved a measure authorizing a one-time special dividend on the otherwise nonparticipating insurance issued to veterans of the Korean conflict. The dividend declaration amounted to $56 million of which approximately $30 million was disbursed to eligible policyholders by the end of calendar year 1961.

20. *Small Business Administration (SBA)*

Legislative action during 1961 liberalized the Small Business Investment Program and expanded and strengthened the activities of the Small Business Administration. Additional private capital was attracted into small business investment corporations by amendment of the Small Business Investment Act, which increased the maximum amount of Government participation in a single corporation from the previous limit of $150,000 to $400,000. The ability of the SBA to lend to State and local development corporations was also increased. Amendment of the Small Business Act provided for the development of a program to assure small business participation in subcontracts relating to government procurement, and broadened the authority for research and counseling services for small business.

Chapter 2

Economic Growth

FASTER ECONOMIC GROWTH in the United States requires, above all, an expansion of demand, to take up existing slack and to match future increases in capacity. Unless demand is adequate to buy potential output, accelerating the growth of potential is neither an urgent problem nor a promising possibility. Full utilization will itself contribute to growth of capacity. Saving and investment to increase capacity and improve productivity flourish in prosperity and wane when the economy is slack. Reduction of economic fluctuations lessens the risks associated with innovation and investment and diminishes the resistance to technological change. A full employment economy can achieve more rapid growth than an economy alternating between boom and recession; for that reason, effective stabilization policy is the first step toward a policy for economic growth. But stabilization policy is not enough. A sustained improvement in the growth rate requires also a concerted effort, private and public, to speed the increase of potential output. Chapter 1 has analyzed the current problem of underutilization. In this chapter the emphasis is on the growth of potential output.

The growth of the U.S. economy results primarily from decisions taken by individuals, families, and firms. However, all levels of government—Federal, State and local—have a role in the promotion of economic growth. It is no part of that role to force on unwilling households and business firms any particular rate of growth in their own individual activities. But if, as a Nation, we desire a higher rate of growth, there are two consequences for government policy. First, in those areas of economic activity traditionally allotted to some level of government, public expenditures must provide services which contribute to the growth of potential output and which satisfy the needs that accompany increasing income and wealth. Second, public policy—notably in the fields of taxation, education, training, welfare, and the control of money and credit—inevitably stimulates or retards the growth potential of the private economy, even if no such result is consciously intended. Accelerated economic growth requires coordinated policy at all levels of government to facilitate the increase of productivity and the expansion of capacity. No change is implied in the historic division of responsibility between public bodies and private citizens.

GROWTH: PROBLEM OR OPPORTUNITY

The sources of growth of potential output often present themselves as "problems." A rapidly expanding labor force provides new workers to man factories and perform services, and opens new opportunities for investment to equip them. But it accentuates simultaneously the "problem" of assuring useful jobs at satisfactory wages for an ever-growing number of job seekers. Rapid technological progress increases productivity, releasing labor and other resources for new uses. But it creates simultaneously the "problem" of displaced workers, declining industries, and depressed areas. The problems and the opportunities are opposite sides of the same coin. A commitment to accelerated growth is at the same time a commitment to solve even more such problems. The challenge is to find solutions which do not limit the economy's capacity to grow.

This is what is meant by saying that there are "growing pains" associated with economic progress. They are not new. Nor are they insoluble if the expansion of demand creates new opportunities for labor and capital as old ones disappear. An adequate level of demand, though not itself the solution to structural problems, is a necessary precondition to the solution.

The most pressing of the social problems resulting from rapid industrial progress is the creation of islands of obsolete capacity and unwanted skills. It is inequitable to inflict the costs of progress on an arbitrarily selected few, when the benefits are widely shared. It is more than inequitable—it is self-defeating—to invite resistance to progress, pools of idleness, low productivity, and poverty. The need for specific policies to restore the earning power of displaced workers and the vitality of depressed regions has already been emphasized in connection with the objectives of the Employment Act itself. That need is intensified with the acceptance of accelerated economic growth as a goal of national policy.

Faster economic growth incurs costs and imposes responsibilities. It must—if it is worth undertaking—confer even larger benefits. Potential output has been growing, on the average, at 2.9 percent annually since the turn of the century and at about 4 percent since the end of the second World War, though since 1954 the rate has slowed to 3.5 percent. Yet there are sound reasons for wanting even faster growth in the future—(1) unsatisfied needs at home and (2) threats to freedom abroad.

(1) Per capita disposable personal income, measured in 1961 dollars, has been increasing since 1947 at about 2 percent a year; it surpassed $2,000 a year in the last quarter of 1961. Nevertheless, about 30 percent of all families and unrelated persons have less than $1,000 of money income per person, and are now below the level that the average American achieved a quarter-century ago.

A high rate of economic growth today will enable increasing millions to enjoy better lives tomorrow. Only a limited imagination can fail to see opportunities for providing more fully both such basic needs as food, clothing and shelter and the amenities of civilized life—education, medical care, travel and recreation.

In many, though not all, contexts growth in per capita production will reduce the number of persons with low incomes. Poverty in the United States is disproportionately concentrated among the aged, the nonwhite, the poorly educated, marginal farmers, and families without a male bread-winner. The disadvantaged fare better in a buoyantly growing economy. But for some, the remedy lies in welfare or insurance payments coupled with substantially improved services and retraining to restore them to self-sufficiency. In the longer run, the provision of good education and adequate health services for the children of these families is essential to break the degrading cycle of dependency.

Other unfilled needs lie in the field of public or mixed public and private expenditures. The renewal of cities, the reconstruction of transportation facilities, the improvement of education at all levels, the provision of new facilities for the arts, the expansion of medical care facilities, the con-servation and expansion of our national parks and forests, all these things need more resources than we now devote to them. Economic growth will help create those resources.

(2) The leadership of the free world imposes heavy economic burdens on the United States. The primary responsibility for maintaining the mili-tary security of the free world falls on us. Although we hope that world tensions will slacken, we must be prepared if they do not. If the threat rises in intensity, we must increase our defense capabilities to meet that threat. The future needs of defense are uncertain but imperative; the larger and more efficient our economy, the more readily will we be able to shoulder larger military burdens, if we must.

Our responsibility is no less in the global battle against poverty, ignorance, and disease. The less developed nations need our capital and technique. They also need a further demonstration of the ability of a free economy to grow, to prosper, and to use its enhanced resources wisely.

The foreign trade policy of the United States should be formulated with regard for the obvious fact that a more satisfactory rate of economic growth can be achieved here and abroad if producers are stimulated to efficiency by active participation in international trade. A liberal trade policy works to this end by providing increased market opportunities abroad for U.S. products while promoting the efficient utilization of resources through the invigorating effects of foreign competition, whether encoun-tered in our home markets or in the markets of other countries.

GOALS FOR THE CURRENT DECADE

Goals, if they are to be useful, should be neither too easy nor too difficult. To set a goal that would have been achieved anyway serves no useful pur-pose. To set a goal that is obviously impossible of achievement invites a loss of confidence and perhaps failure to achieve what is possible. A good target is one that can be met, but not without effort.

This general limitation sets only a range of growth targets for the United States in the 1960's. It is no easy matter to say exactly how fast an economy can grow, or to obtain consensus on how fast it should grow. Some of the benefits of growth have already been discussed. The costs of growth are the diversion of resources from the satisfaction of current needs to those uses which will yield increased output in the future, and the strain on our institutions and social fabric which this diversion might entail. Ultimately, a democratic society achieves one rate of growth rather than another through the freely made economic and political decisions of its citizens. The task of economic analysis is to show what the choices are, what alternative choices will cost, and what benefits they may yield.

The basic determinants of a society's productive capacity in any year are as follows:

(1) The number of people available for employment, the number of hours they wish to work, their incentives and motivations, and their health, general education, occupational desires, and vocational skills;

(2) The stock of new and old plant and equipment, and its composition by age, type, and location;

(3) The terms on which the economy has access to natural resources, whether through domestic production or imports;

(4) The level of technology, covering the range from managerial and organizational competence to scientific, engineering, and mechanical understanding;

(5) The efficiency with which resources, domestic and foreign, are allocated to different economic ends, and the extent of monopolistic or other barriers to the movement of labor and capital from low-productivity to high-productivity uses.

These basic determinants interact in complex ways. For example, advanced machinery is of little use without skilled labor to operate it; advanced technology often requires capital equipment to embody it.

Next year's productive capacity will exceed this year's to the extent that the basic determinants can be expanded and improved. Success in achieving a higher rate of growth in the future depends on our willingness to spend current resources to expand our production potential and by our skill and luck in spending them effectively.

The record of economic growth in the United States does not suggest that the average growth rate realized in the past is an immutable natural constant, leaving no scope for growth-stimulating policies. The rate of growth of output has varied from one span of years to another, depending on specific economic circumstances (Chart 9). There was one prolonged period of stagnation—the decade of the 1930's—when potential output grew at less than the average long-term rate, and realized output grew more slowly still. Again, there have been periods when poten-

CHART 9

Output, Employment, and Productivity

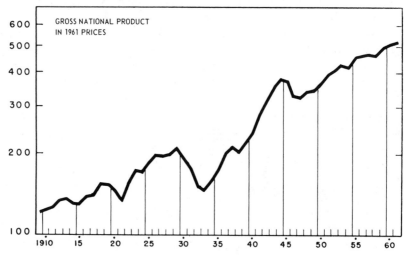

BILLIONS OF DOLLARS (Ratio scale)

GROSS NATIONAL PRODUCT
IN 1961 PRICES

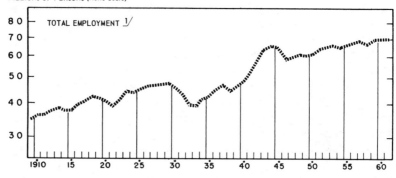

MILLIONS OF PERSONS (Ratio scale)

TOTAL EMPLOYMENT 1/

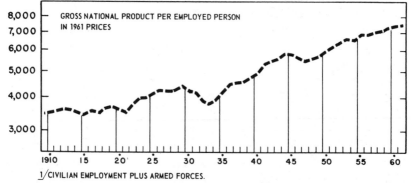

DOLLARS (Ratio scale)

GROSS NATIONAL PRODUCT PER EMPLOYED PERSON
IN 1961 PRICES

1/CIVILIAN EMPLOYMENT PLUS ARMED FORCES.
SOURCES: DEPARTMENT OF COMMERCE, DEPARTMENT OF LABOR, AND COUNCIL OF ECONOMIC ADVISERS.

tial output expanded more rapidly than the past average.   The postwar years have been such a period of accelerated growth.   Even including the years since 1954, during which growth was sluggish, real gross national product (GNP) in this postwar period has increased at an average annual rate of 3.5 percent.   Had potential output been realized in 1960, as it was in 1947, the realized growth rate would have been 4.0 percent a year.

Table 10 shows, for the 1947–60 period, the increases in realized and potential GNP, population, labor force, employment, man-hours, GNP per person, and productivity.   Approximately four-fifths of the annual increase in potential GNP during the period is explained by increases in output per man-hour and one-fifth by increases in total man-hours worked.   The increase in output per man-hour is, of course, the resultant of improvements in the quality of the labor force, the quantity and quality of capital, the level of technology, and still other factors.

TABLE 10.—*Output, population, labor input, and productivity, 1947–60*

Item	Unit	1947	1954	1960 [1]	Percentage change per year		
					1947 to 1954	1954 to 1960	1947 to 1960
Output:							
Gross national product.	Billions of dollars, 1961 prices.	324.9	422.0	511.1	3.8	3.2	3.5
Potential gross national product [2]	..do..	324.9	440.5	541.8	4.4	3.5	4.0
Population	Millions of persons.	144.1	162.4	180.7	1.7	1.8	1.8
Labor input:							
Labor force [3]	Millions of persons.	61.8	67.8	73.1	1.3	1.3	1.3
Employment [3]	..do..	59.4	64.2	69.2	1.1	1.3	1.2
Potential employment [4]	..do..	59.4	65.1	70.2	1.3	1.3	1.3
Man-hours	Billions of man-hours..	129.6	132.9	139.7	.4	.8	.6
Potential man-hours [5]	..do..	129.6	135.4	143.1	.6	.9	.8
GNP per capita	Dollars, 1961 prices.	2,255	2,599	2,828	2.0	1.4	1.8
Productivity:							
GNP per worker.	Dollars, 1961 prices.	5,470	6,573	7,386	2.7	2.0	2.3
Potential GNP per worker.	..do..	5,470	6,768	7,718	3.1	2.2	2.7
GNP per man-hour.	..do..	2.51	3.18	3.66	3.4	2.4	2.9
Potential GNP per man-hour.	..do..	2.51	3.25	3.79	3.8	2.6	3.2

[1] Data include Alaska and Hawaii.
[2] Same as actual in 1947; in 1954 and 1960, calculated from 3.5 percent trend line through mid-1955.
[3] Includes armed forces.
[4] Assumes 4 percent unemployment rate for all periods, with no adjustment for cyclical movement of the labor force.
[5] Same as actual in 1947; in 1954 and 1960, assumes 4 percent unemployment rate and corrects for decline in hours induced by recession.

Sources: Department of Commerce, Department of Labor, and Council of Economic Advisers.

But consideration of the years 1947–60 as a unit masks significant differences within the period.   There was a substantial slowing down in ,the growth of potential output between the first and the second part of this period.   From 1947 to 1954, potential GNP grew at a rate of 4.4 percent a year, and from 1954 to 1960 at a rate of 3.5 percent.   Since the labor force grew at a rate of 1.3 percent a year in both periods and average hours worked fell somewhat more slowly after 1954 than before, the slower rate of growth that has taken place since 1954 is explained by a decline in the rate of increase of productivity. This decline resulted in part from a more slowly rising trend of productivity within nonmanufacturing industry, and in part from a shift—usual in slack periods—from manufacturing to nonmanufacturing in the composition of economic activity.

Further evidence that modern industrial economies are not helpless prisoners of past long-term trends is to be found in Table 11, which shows that the major countries of Western Europe, and Japan as well, have recently exceeded their own long-term performances.

TABLE 11.—*Growth of gross national product per man-year, selected countries, 1913–59*

[Percent per year]

Country	1913–59	1950–59
Japan	2.6	6.1
Italy	1.7	4.7
Germany	1.4	4.5
France	1.5	3.6
Netherlands	1.3	3.4
Norway	1.9	3.1
Sweden	1.7	2.8
United States	1.8	2.2
Canada	1.5	2.0
Denmark	1.2	1.8
United Kingdom	.8	1.7

NOTE.—Gross national product at constant prices was used wherever available. See *National Institute Economic Review*, No. 16, July 1961, pp. 36 and 46–47, for data and description of sources of materials used.

Source: National Institute of Economic and Social Research.

On June 28, President Kennedy stated that a growth rate of 4.5 percent yearly is "well within our capability." On November 17, the United States joined with the other 19 member nations of the Organization for Economic Cooperation and Development in setting as a target the attainment of a 50 percent (4.1 percent a year) increase in their combined national product during the decade from 1960 to 1970. The ability of the United States to meet, and even to exceed, this target is the best guarantee of success for the OECD. A high rate of growth of potential output will not be reached immediately. The policies to achieve it, even if adopted now, will not bear fruit at once, and it will not be achieved without effort. But in the second half of the decade, with the help of a rapidly growing labor force, it should be possible to exceed a growth rate of 4.5 percent annually and to achieve an average rate of growth of potential output of 4.3 percent between 1960 and 1970.

If this growth is achieved and if, in addition, 1970 is a year of 4 percent unemployment, actual GNP will grow at an average annual rate of 4.9 percent (Table 12). The difference between this figure and 4.3 percent reflects the current shortfall of actual output from potential output. Such a rate of growth of total GNP would mean an annual increase of GNP per person in the population of 3.2 percent, nearly double the rate achieved during

TABLE 12.—*Output, population, labor input, and productivity, 1960 actual and 1970 illustrative*

Item	Unit	1960 [1]	1970 illustra- tive [2]	Percent- age change per year 1960–70
Output:				
Gross national product	Billions of dollars, 1961 prices	511.1	825	4.9
Potential gross national product	do	541.8	825	4.3
Population	Millions of persons	180.7	213.8	1.7
Labor input:				
Labor force [3]	do	73.1	87.1	1.8
Employment [3]	do	69.2	83.7	1.9
Potential employment	do	70.2	83.7	1.8
Man-hours	Billions of man-hours	139.7	162	1.5
Potential man-hours	do	143.1	162	1.2
GNP per capita	Dollars, 1961 prices	2,828	3,858	3.2
Productivity:				
GNP per worker	do	7,386	9,868	2.9
Potential GNP per worker	do	7,718	9,868	2.5
GNP per man-hour	do	3.66	5.09	3.4
Potential GNP per man-hour	do	3.79	5.09	3.0

[1] Potential series for 1960 based on the following assumptions: *GNP*, calculated from 3.5 percent trend line through mid-1955; *employment*, 4 percent unemployment rate; *man-hours*, 4 percent unemployment rate and correction for decline in hours induced by recession.
[2] Illustrative figures for 1970 based on the following assumptions: *Potential GNP growth* rate of 4.3 percent per year from 1960 to 1970, with actual and potential being the same in 1970; *population*, 1955–57 fertility levels continue to 1980; *labor force*, participation rate of 57.8 percent of noninstitutional population 14 years of age and over; *employment*, 4 percent unemployment rate; *man-hours*, continuation of previous trend.
[3] Includes armed forces.

NOTE.—Data includes Alaska and Hawaii.

Sources: Department of Commerce, Department of Labor, and Council of Economic Advisers.

the 1947–60 period. It is this figure which most nearly measures the gain to society from accelerated economic growth. If, by 1970, we succeed in achieving an unemployment rate below 4 percent, even further increases in output will become possible. To a first approximation, each 1 point decline in the 1970 unemployment rate would add about $8 billion to 1970 GNP and about 0.1 to the annual rate of growth.

Table 12 is in no sense a prediction of what will actually occur. It shows what would be required to move up to and beyond a 4.5 percent growth rate, giving us a rate of growth of potential for the full decade averaging 4.3 percent a year. Demographic factors lay the foundation for a significant acceleration of potential output. If labor force projections are realized and if past trends in hours worked per man year continue, available labor input will increase during the 1960's at more than one and one-half times its rate of growth during the 1947–60 period. With this increase in labor input, it is a matter of arithmetic that a 3 percent yearly increase in man-hour productivity would be needed if the annual rate of growth of potential GNP is to average 4.3 percent over the decade.

The required growth of output per man-hour was surpassed in the 1947–54 period, but since 1954 performance has fallen below what is required. The vigorous growth of the early postwar period benefited from the possibility of renewing a capital stock which had aged during the depression and war years of low investment. Making good this backlog of investment demand brought with it the quick realization of latent technological progress. Simple continuation of recent trends will not be sufficient to repeat that performance. The rest of this chapter suggests the kind of effort in education, technological development, capital formation, and other areas that may be required to do so. In particular, unless technical progress brings an unexpected increase in the productivity of capital, a major rise in capital investment will be needed.

The population upsurge which began in the 1940's, together with the expected decline in death rates, will give us a rapid increase in the population of working age. Adult women are expected to enter the labor force in increasing proportions; but because a larger fraction of our youth will remain in school and because the trend toward earlier retirement among male workers is likely to continue, over-all labor force participation rates are expected to remain steady. The resultant of these factors should be a labor force in 1970 of a little more than 87 million, an annual rate of increase of 1.8 percent in this decade, compared with the distinctly lower rate of 1.3 percent from 1947 to 1960. If 4 percent of the labor force is unemployed in 1970, total employment will come to 83.7 million. A reduction in the unemployment rate to 3 percent would add over 800,000 to employment.

The calculations of Table 12 assume that the average number of hours worked a year will continue to decline at the same rate as in the past. This reduction in the intensity of work has been going on for a long time. It will continue, both because our citizens choose to enjoy some part of their increased productivity in the form of longer vacations and perhaps a shorter workweek, and because much of the increase in the labor force will consist of part-time workers by preference, notably young people still in school and women with family responsibilities. Full employment will, however, eliminate one possible cause of a decline in average hours; when unemployment rates are high, as they are at present, pressure builds up for a reduction in the workweek. This pressure, motivated by a desire to share the limited volume of employment, is to be sharply distinguished from the desire for increased leisure reflected in the long-run decline in average annual hours. The second of these is to be honored; the first should be met by expanded employment opportunities. Variations in the number of hours worked, like variations in participation rates, also respond to economic forces in other ways. The lure of job opportunities in a growing and prospering economy may attract even more than the expected number of people into the labor force, and may induce some to abandon part-time for full-time work. On the other hand, it is also possible that full employment at the rising wage and salary levels permitted by rising productivity will lead some secondary wage earners to withdraw from the labor force, and others to retire at an earlier age.

The beneficial effects of labor force growth do not occur automatically. Productivity is preserved and increased primarily through acts of investment: investment in the improvement of human resources, in the creation of new technical and managerial knowledge, in the development of natural resources, and in the formation of physical capital. In the case of investment in human capital and in research and development, the link between expenditure and yield is difficult to measure, but there can be little doubt that the return is substantial. In regard to investment in plant and equipment and the development of natural resources, there is more statistical evidence available. No one of these investments can make its full contribution to the objective of accelerated growth without the others. Each of them is necessary; there is good reason to believe that together they can be sufficient, if vigorously pursued.

INVESTMENT IN HUMAN RESOURCES

Increased production is not an end in itself but only a means of providing increased real income for all to share. As indicated earlier, this is one of the reasons that more rapid growth is a desirable social goal. High levels of education and health, equality of opportunity—these are among the valid measures of a society's performance. They are desirable in their own right. In addition, they have an economic dimension. They are among the foundations of growth as well as among its benefits.

Americans have long spoken of foregoing consumption today in order to invest in their children's education and thus in a better tomorrow. For an economy, just as for an individual, the use of the word *invest* in this connection is clearly justified, since it is precisely the sacrifice of consumption in the present to make possible a more abundant future that constitutes the common characteristic of all forms of investment. That devoting resources to education and health is, in part, an act of investment in human capital explains why programs in the area of education and health are economic growth programs. This kind of investment has a long and remarkable history. Rough estimates, which take into account differences in the length of the school year and in school attendance, suggest that the stock of equivalent school years in the labor force rose more than sixfold between 1900 and 1957. The annual rate of growth of the stock of education was more than 3 percent, or about twice the rate of growth of the labor force itself.

Failure to pursue vigorous educational and health policies and programs leads to smaller increases in output in the long run; it is also associated with higher expenditures in the short run. If we fail to invest sufficiently in medical research, we lose not only what stricken individuals might have produced had they been well, but also the use of the resources and funds currently devoted to their care. Failure to invest sufficiently in education means that we will lose the additional output that would be possible with a better educated labor force; it may also mean the perpetuation of social problems necessitating public expenditures. Recognition of the costs of inadequate investment in social welfare is one of the reasons for the Administration's concern to strengthen family services in the public welfare field.

It is a waste of resources to restrict health and education to those who can afford them. Moreover, in addition to each person's interest in his own health and education, there is a public interest in everybody's health and education. The well-being of each citizen contributes to the well-being of others. As a result, we have organized programs to help the population to obtain a quality education, to require attendance in schools, to help ourselves and others to obtain needed medical care, to require that certain medical precautions, such as vaccinations, be taken by everyone.

Education

Estimates made by private scholars suggest that about one-half of the growth in output in the United States in the last 50 years has resulted from factors other than increases in physical capital and man-hours worked. Education is one of the "other factors." Even without allowance for the impact of education on invention and innovation, its contribution appears to account for between one-fourth and one-half of that part of the increase of output between 1929 and 1956 not accounted for by the increased inputs of capital and labor. Education is of vital importance in preparing the skilled labor force demanded by new investment and new technology.

Education's contribution to output is reflected by the well-documented fact that income—a measure of each individual's contribution to production—tends to rise with educational attainment. Of course, not all differences in money income are the result of education. Differences in native ability as well as parental economic and social status are also reflected. Nevertheless, a substantial proportion of the increase in income at increasing levels of education may be attributed to that education.

In 1930, $3.2 billion (3.3 percent of GNP in current prices) was spent for all schools at all levels of education. In 1960, expenditures had risen to about $24.6 billion (5.0 percent of GNP). In turn, in 1930, 29.0 percent of the population 17 years old graduated from high school. By 1958 this was true for 64.8 percent. Similarly, in higher education the number of earned degrees conferred rose from 140,000 in 1930 to 490,000 in 1960.

Though significant progress has been made, substantial opportunities and needs for investment in education still exist. There is a pressing need to improve curricula and teaching methods, make education more readily available to students of merit by reduction of financial barriers, expand facilities and staff to meet rising enrollments, improve the quality and productivity of our teaching staffs and increase their salaries, and narrow the gap in opportunities available to students in different parts of our country. These problems must be met—and met quickly—at all levels of government and at all levels of education if our standards of education are to keep abreast of our needs.

The program of the Administration includes specific proposals designed to meet urgent needs in the field of education: increased funds for scholarships; assistance to institutions of higher education for the construction of facilities; aid to the States for assistance to public elementary and secondary schools; and a program to improve the quality of elementary and secondary education through curriculum research, demonstration projects, teacher training institutes, and special project grants.

Work of this last kind has been begun, with the support of the National Science Foundation, in supplementary training of teachers of science and mathematics, especially in high schools, and in the development of new courses in physics, mathematics, chemistry, and biology. Similar support has been given by the U.S. Office of Education for improvement in courses in English and modern foreign languages; it should be extended to the other major academic fields.

Student opportunities. Of each 1,000 pupils who entered the fifth grade in 1952, 900 entered high school in 1956, 600 graduated from high school in 1960, and 300 entered college in the fall of 1960. Thus 40 percent of the original 1,000 students did not graduate from high school and half of those graduating from high school did not enter college. Many of these withdrawals are by children of better than average intelligence. It is generally agreed that improvement of teaching and expansion of guidance and counseling services will help to reduce the drop-out rate. Efforts to eliminate this waste of human resources have already begun, but more are needed.

Financial barriers to secondary education come chiefly from a pressing need for immediate income for the family. At the college level, the financial problem arises both from the direct costs of attending college and the income foregone. The Office of Education estimates that in the 1961–62 school year the average direct costs of attending public colleges are about $1,700 a year, and of attending private colleges, $2,300. These costs have risen rapidly in recent years, and they are expected to continue to rise. They are significant obstacles for large parts of our population. The Administration proposal for assistance to higher education would authorize 4-year scholarship aid for 212,500 capable students in need of financial assistance.

Personnel and facilities. Enrollments in elementary and secondary schools rose from 28.2 million pupils in 1950 to 42.5 million in 1960. Enrollment in 1970 is expected to be 53.0 million. In 1950, 2.3 million students were enrolled in institutions of higher education, and by 1960 the figure had risen to 3.6 million. The projected 1970 enrollment is 7.0 million. Rising enrollments have necessitated substantial expansion of personnel and facilities. Further expansion is required if quality is not to deteriorate.

Our educational system thus confronts unprecedented challenges. To accommodate doubled enrollments by 1970, outlays for college facilities must be more than doubled; total expenditures must rise two-to-threefold.

Needs at the below-college level, about the same in dollar terms, must also be met, lest the foundations of the educational system be eroded. The price of failure will be the irrevocable loss of valuable talent.

However urgent the need for additional facilities and for the rehabilitation and replacement of existing facilities, the personnel problem is especially acute, because of the time required to train teachers. Among beginning teachers in public elementary and secondary schools in 1956–57, 27 percent lacked a standard certificate, a bachelor's degree, or both. Demand for new teachers and for replacement of those leaving the profession will be very high. It can be met only by the training of new teachers, accompanied by programs to increase the productivity and quality of experienced teachers. Teachers' salaries at all levels must continue their recent rise if good teachers are to be attracted into and retained in the profession of educating the Nation's youth. Other programs for expansion of the educational system cannot succeed unless the rewards to teaching are increased.

State differences. In a highly mobile and interdependent society, the lack of educational opportunities is not simply a matter of concern to some States; it is of concern to the Nation. The support that the different States (and different areas within States) give to education varies substantially. Such support depends not only on the commitment that the population has to education, but also on the resources of the State and the number of children seeking a public education. As a consequence, some States with low per student expenditures for education have educational budgets that, as a percentage of personal income, are far above the national average. Increased Federal support for education, as outlined in the President's proposals, is essential to eliminate these imbalances as well as provide for programs to meet the national responsibilities that transcend State and local boundaries. Ultimately, the effectiveness of our democracy rests on an educated and informed citizenry.

Health

U.S. economic growth in the twentieth century has been associated with better health of the population as a whole as well as an increase in per capita expenditures on health and medical care. Public and private expenditures on health care increased from $3.6 billion, or 3.5 percent of GNP, in 1929 to $26.5 billion, or 5.4 percent of GNP, in 1960. This has been accompanied by a sharp increase in life expectancy and a reduction in death rates from communicable diseases.

At the same time that economic growth has contributed to an improvement in the health of our people, better health has contributed to economic growth. Better health makes possible an increase in the size of the labor force and in the effectiveness of effort on the job.

Further improvements in health would yield significant economic, as well as human, benefits. On an average day in 1960, 1.3 million employed persons—2 percent of civilian employment—were absent from work because of illness or accident. The days of work lost because of illness far exceeded the days of work lost because of industrial disputes; in fiscal year 1960, "currently employed" persons lost a total of 371 million days from work as a result of illness or injury, while the loss from industrial disputes in 1960 totaled 19 million days.

The costs of ill health have traditionally been calculated as the money spent for the prevention and treatment of accident and disease. The waste of human resources and the consequent loss of production is an important additional cost about which not enough is known. Where facts are available, as in the related area of vocational rehabilitation, the relationship between costs and benefits is impressive. In 1960, at an average cost of $900 per rehabilitant under Federal-State programs, median wages of rehabilitated persons were raised from $450 a year at acceptance to $2,350 at closure, a difference of $1,900 in the first year after rehabilitation.

Public support for medical research, the most basic of investments in better health, has been growing. In fiscal year 1962, total expenditures will exceed a billion dollars, of which 60 percent is supported by the Federal Government. Further expansion of research activities, where funds can be wisely spent and where qualified research personnel exist, is desirable both for humanitarian and economic reasons. Much of the necessary research is carried on by doctors of medicine. More rapid expansion of the number of physicians is required to insure that patient care needs, teaching needs, and research needs can all be met. This will be true even if needed improvements are made in the organization and financing of medical care.

Increased demands for medical services, stemming in part from new discoveries and in part from growth in population and changes in age and income structure, already mean unfilled internships and residencies in hospitals. The full medical needs of the country are not being met in many fields, including public health and preventive medicine. The Administration has presented a program to authorize Federal grants for the construction of medical, dental, osteopathic, and public health teaching facilities, project grants to plan for new facilities and improved educational programs, and scholarship aid to students. The importance of maintaining and improving the health of the Nation makes the enactment of this program a matter of great urgency.

Eliminating Racial Discrimination

Racial discrimination is a national disgrace. In this respect, above all others, practice in the United States is a standing affront to professions of democratic principle. Discrimination inflicts immeasurable human and social costs on a large number of our citizens. In addition—and this is why it deserves particular mention in this Report—it inflicts an economic loss on the country.

Discriminatory practices in education, training, employment and union membership impede the development and utilization of human resources.

They reduce the efficiency and slow the growth of the economy, at the same time that they alter—and alter inequitably—the distribution of the fruits of economic progress.

Although significant reductions in discriminatory barriers have been accomplished in recent years, important problems remain. Many nonwhite families are trapped in a vicious circle: Job discrimination and lack of education limit their employment opportunities and result in low and unstable incomes; low incomes, combined with direct discriminations, reduce attainable levels of health and skill and thus limit occupational choice and income in the future; limited job opportunities result in limited availability of vocational education and apprenticeship training. Unless action is taken, today's training practices, affecting tomorrow's employment possibilities, will help to perpetuate inequitable employment patterns.

Our economy loses when individuals who are capable of acquiring skills are denied opportunities for training and are forced into the ranks of the unskilled, and when individuals with education, skill, and training face discriminatory hiring practices that result in their employment in low productivity jobs.

Discrimination is reflected in the distribution of income and in disparities in the levels of education attained by white and nonwhite groups. Nonwhite families had a median money income of $3,233 in 1960. Although this represents a remarkable advance over the figure of $2,099 for 1947 (in 1960 prices), the magnitude of the problem still remaining is indicated by the fact that in 1960 the median income for white families was $5,835. In 1960, 11.0 percent of white but 31.7 percent of nonwhite families had money incomes of less than $2,000, while 36.6 percent of white but only 13.6 percent of nonwhite families had money incomes of $7,000 and over.

In 1947, 11 percent of the nonwhite population 14 years of age and over was illiterate; by 1959, this percentage had dropped to 7.5, with declines registered in every age group. The figure was, however, considerably higher than the 1.6 percent illiterate in the white population. Equally disturbing is the fact that in the nonwhite population the percentage of illiterates was higher for each age and sex group than the comparable percentage for the white population. While the median school years completed for the nonwhite population 25 years of age and over had risen from 5.8 in 1940 to 8.1 in 1959, the median for the total population was 11.0 in 1959.

The unemployment rate in December 1961 was 5.2 percent for white males and 4.7 percent for white females, but 12.4 percent for nonwhite males and 10.7 percent for nonwhite females. Nonwhite workers made up less than 12 percent of the labor force, but accounted for 22 percent of the total unemployed and 24 percent of those unemployed 15 weeks or more.

Economic growth will be furthered by the adoption of nondiscriminatory policies and practices to insure that all Americans may develop their abilities to the fullest extent and that these abilities will be used. The Department of Justice, the President's Committee on Equal Employment Opportunities, and the U.S. Commission on Civil Rights are already acting vigorously. They should be joined in the campaign by all parts of our population and all units of government, business, and labor.

INVESTMENT IN TECHNOLOGICAL PROGRESS

Technological knowledge sets limits on the productivity of labor and capital. As the frontiers of technology are pushed ahead, industrial practice and productivity follow, sometimes pressing close on the best that is known, sometimes lagging behind, with the gap varying from industry to industry and from firm to firm. A stimulus to economic growth can come either from increasing the rate at which the frontiers are advancing or from bringing the technology actually in use closer to the frontiers.

Research and Development

The advance of technological knowledge depends on the amount and effectiveness of the human and material resources devoted to research and development. The limited data available suggest that within industries and between industries there is a positive correlation between research effort and productivity growth. However, some of the most important developments affecting the productivity of a firm or industry may originate from research done by equipment and material suppliers, or from basic research done by government and the universities. The benefits of research activity are often widely shared.

Expenditures on research and development in 1960 totaled about $14 billion, as shown in Table 13. In 1961 the total was probably in the neighborhood of $15 billion, nearly three times the expenditures in 1953, and almost a third as large as business expenditures on fixed capital. After rough allowance for rising costs, the volume of research and development performed has approximately doubled since 1953. Between 1953

TABLE 13.—*Research and development expenditures, 1953 and 1957–60*

[Billions of dollars]

Type of research, financing, and performance	1953	1957	1958	1959	1960
Total expenditures	5.15	10.03	11.07	12.62	14.04
By type of research:					
Basic research	.43	.83	1.02	1.15	1.30
Applied research and development	4.72	9.20	10.05	11.47	12.74
By source of funds: [1]					
Federal Government	2.74	6.38	7.17	8.29	9.22
Industry	2.24	3.39	3.62	4.03	4.49
Universities and other nonprofit institutions	.17	.26	.28	.30	.33
By performer:					
Federal Government	.97	1.44	1.73	1.83	2.06
Industry [2]	3.63	7.66	8.30	9.55	10.50
Universities and other nonprofit institutions [2]	.55	.93	1.04	1.24	1.48

[1] Based on reports by performers.
[2] Includes research centers administered by organizations in this sector under contract with Federal agencies.

Source: National Science Foundation.

and 1960, research and development as a percentage of GNP in current prices doubled from 1.4 percent to 2.8 percent.

Research and development cover a wide range of activities aimed at increasing the stock of scientific and technical knowledge. As we move from basic research to applied research and to development, the goals become more closely defined in terms of specific practical objectives, the predictability of the results increases, and the benefits become less diffuse. More than 90 percent of research and development spending is for applied research and development—most of it for development. Slightly less than 10 percent is for basic research.

Approximately three-fourths of the Nation's total research and development effort is performed by industry, and over half of this is financed by the Federal Government. Profit considerations naturally lead private firms to concentrate on developing and improving marketable products. Even here, supplementary government support can pay off handsomely. Estimates suggest that hybrid corn research, of which perhaps one-third was publicly supported, yielded a substantial return to society over and above the returns to farmers and seed producers.

Less than one-third of all basic research is done by industry. Government, the universities, and other nonprofit institutions, although doing only one-fourth of total research, do most of the Nation's basic research. Such research seldom results directly or immediately in new products and processes. But in the long run, basic research is the key to important advances in technology. Fundamental inventions like the transistor—an outgrowth of basic research in solid-state physics—may revolutionize large sectors of industry and have a tremendous ultimate effect on productivity.

Although research and development spending is increasing rapidly in most industries, more than 55 percent of industrial research is performed by two industry groups, the aircraft and parts industry, and the electrical equipment and communications industry, as shown in Table 14. This heavy concentration of industrial research reflects primarily the concentration of defense contracts.

Industrial research is also heavily concentrated in large firms. In 1958, firms employing more than 5,000 persons accounted for 84 percent of total industrial research spending, significantly more than the share of these firms in manufacturing employment.

The Federal Government plays a much larger role in financing than in performing research. It is estimated that in 1961 the Government paid for about two-thirds of the total national research effort including, in addition to work done in government laboratories, almost 60 percent of the research undertaken in industry-run laboratories and over 70 percent of the research done by universities. About 70 percent of government research and development spending is accounted for by the Department of Defense. The Atomic Energy Commission and National Aeronautics and Space Administration together account for nearly 20 percent.

TABLE 14.—*Funds for industrial research and development, by source and industry, 1960*

Industry	Funds for research and development, 1960						Research and development funds as percent of net sales, 1959 [1]
	Amount (millions of dollars)			Percentage change from 1959			
	Total	Federal Government	Company	Total	Federal Government	Company	
Total	10,497	6,125	4,372	10	9	11	4.2
Food and kindred products	106	9	97	19	([2])	15	.3
Paper and allied products	66	1	65	12	([2])	12	.8
Chemicals and allied products	1,047	303	744	10	7	12	4.3
Petroleum refining and extraction	289	25	264	6	4	6	1.0
Rubber products	115	35	80	4	−5	8	2.0
Stone, clay, and glass products	82	4	78	14	([2])	11	1.4
Primary metals	164	18	146	19	20	19	.7
Fabricated metal products	126	54	72	2	−7	9	1.7
Machinery	993	384	609	5	−5	12	4.2
Electrical equipment and communication	2,405	1,634	771	7	4	16	11.3
Motor vehicles and other transportation equipment	849	216	633	−2	−13	3	3.4
Aircraft and parts	3,482	3,027	455	15	16	9	20.8
Professional and scientific instruments	416	211	205	18	21	15	8.3
Other industries	358	205	153	18	19	17	([3])

[1] Data apply to all manufacturing industries and to the communication and crude petroleum and extraction nonmanufacturing industries.

[2] Percent change not computed for an industry where the amount in the base period was less than $15 million.

[3] Not available.

NOTE.—Detail will not necessarily add to totals because of rounding.

Source: National Science Foundation.

In addition to its direct contributions to research and development spending, the Federal Government has stimulated private research and development activity. The science information services of the National Science Foundation, the Atomic Energy Commission, the Office of Technical Services of the Department of Commerce, and other government agencies contribute to the over-all efficiency of national research and development. Federal tax law encourages research and development by making such costs fully deductible in the year they are incurred. The Small Business Act encourages spending on research and development, including cooperative research, by small companies. Moreover, the Federal Government makes an important contribution to the training of future research scientists and engineers through its support of education and basic research in the universities.

Strengthening research and development. During the 1950's, the number of professional scientists and engineers in the United States increased at an annual rate of approximately 6 percent. Total resources allocated to research and development grew at an even faster rate because a rising proportion of all scientists and engineers were engaged in research, and because supporting personnel, equipment, and material per research scientist increased. During the 1960's, these trends will continue, but one limit to growth will be the supply of scientists and engineers in certain fields. Future investment in research will be limited largely by the quantity and quality of earlier investment in education.

Overemphasis on current research and development activity should not be permitted to erode the underlying educational base. Just as research is investment for the economy, education is investment for research. The needs for educational expansion stressed earlier in this chapter include urgent requirements for laboratories, laboratory equipment, and other science teaching facilities.

A greater share of research and development resources and talent should be devoted to basic research and to prototype development and experimentation in fields which promise major advances in civilian technology. Military research helped to create such important discoveries as isotope medicine, the computer, and the jet engine. The important impact on civilian technology of these offspring of military research suggests that high returns might be achieved if sights were set higher in nonmilitary research. Since the risks of basic research and experimental development are very great, and since the rewards for success are not confined to single firms or even industries, there is a case for public support to attract additional resources into this work.

In a number of industries, firms which are highly efficient in production and marketing may be too small to undertake an efficient research and development program. In others, a research tradition is lacking, or research is discouraged because the benefits tend to diffuse beyond the market grasp of individual firms. In agriculture, all these conditions are present, and the high returns to society from government support of research suggest that comparable programs to increase research in certain manufacturing industries might be highly desirable.

An Administration bill to create an Assistant Secretary of Commerce for Science and Technology has passed the Senate and is now pending before the House. Its enactment would be an important step in fulfilling the Government's responsibilities in this area. The competence and experience of the National Bureau of Standards could well be used in support of a program to fill the gaps in the national industrial research effort.

More Effective Use of Existing Technology

(1) In some industries there are legal obstacles to technical change. The housing construction codes of many localities provide a prominent example. In principle, these codes protect the public from shoddy construction; in practice, they often prevent the use of new materials, designs, and techniques which are superior to the old, and a lack of uniformity among codes in different localities discourages mass production of certain prefabricated housing components. With respect to construction codes in particular, the Housing and Home Finance Agency should continue to encourage the adoption of performance standards for codes and should strengthen its programs of testing and evaluation.

(2) American labor has a remarkable record of acceptance of new technology; but understandable resistance to the displacement of labor by new equipment has occasionally developed when opportunities for retraining and re-employment were not clearly visible. The Federal Government can help considerably, first, by pursuing effective policies to maintain full employment, and second, by expanding and improving its programs in job training and retraining.

(3) The process of technological change would be smoother if society knew better how to reap the rewards and reduce the costs. Research in the social, behavioral, and managerial sciences can lead to more efficient use of resources and to quicker grasp of the opportunities afforded by technological progress. Improved understanding may, in time, yield ways to ease the burdens of adjustment. Strengthening of research in these auxiliary fields is needed to gain maximum benefit from research which creates new technology.

(4) Innovation is facilitated by a flow of information about new technical developments. Since many firms, especially small ones, are not in a position to follow new technological developments closely, the Government can play a useful role by providing business with relevant information and analysis. These service functions of the Department of Commerce and the Small Business Administration should be substantially strengthened. The success of the Federal-State Extension Service in speeding the diffusion of agricultural technology serves to illustrate how effective such programs can be.

(5) The Panel on Civilian Technology, composed of a group of distinguished scientists, engineers, businessmen, and economists, has been brought together under the joint auspices of the office of the President's Special Assistant for Science and Technology, the Department of Commerce, and the Council of Economic Advisers. The panel is examining opportunities for stimulating civilian research and development as well as for more effective use of existing technology. It has begun to address itself particularly to those sectors of our economy where major social and economic benefits could be expected to accrue from technological advances.

(6) By eliminating monopolistic and collusive barriers to the entry of new business and by maintaining the spur of competition to innovation and the utilization of technology, antitrust enforcement tends to create conditions which encourage economic growth. (See Chapter 4.)

INVESTMENT IN PLANT AND EQUIPMENT

Between the resourcefulness of the labor force and the ideas of the laboratory on one side and the satisfaction of consumption needs on the other, the indissoluble link is the economy's stock of plant and machinery. Our own history and the experience of other industrial countries alike demonstrate the connection between physical investment and growth of productive capacity. Without investment in new and renewed plant and equipment, skills and inventions remain preconditions of growth; with it, they become ingredients.

Investment as a Source of Growth

Investment in fixed capital leads to increased capacity both by equipping new members of the labor force with capital up to existing standards and by providing greater amounts for all workers. Since 1929, the stock of privately owned plant and equipment (in constant prices) has grown relative to private man-hours worked by nearly 80 percent (Chart 10) and by nearly 50 percent relative to the private labor force. Nearly all of the latter increase has taken place during the postwar period. Between 1929 and 1947, the rate of investment was sufficient only to provide enough capital—although more modern capital—to keep pace with a growing labor supply. No increase in capital per worker occurred. Since 1947, the rate of growth in the ratio of capital stock to labor supply has been approximately 2.7 percent a year, but there is a perceptible difference between the growth records of the first and second halves of the postwar period. From 1947 to 1954, the amount of capital per worker increased by 3.5 percent a year; in contrast, the annual increase from 1954 to 1960 averaged only 1.9 percent.

CHART 10

Indexes of Business Output, Capital Stock, and Man-Hours

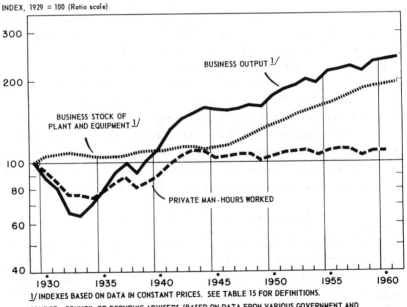

INDEX, 1929 = 100 (Ratio scale)

1/ INDEXES BASED ON DATA IN CONSTANT PRICES. SEE TABLE 15 FOR DEFINITIONS.

SOURCE: COUNCIL OF ECONOMIC ADVISERS (BASED ON DATA FROM VARIOUS GOVERNMENT AND PRIVATE SOURCES).

The importance of investment in the growth process is suggested by the parallel movement of the growth of potential output per man and the growth of capital per man (Table 15). Both ratios grew more rapidly after 1947 than before, and more rapidly between 1947 and 1954 than subsequently. In general, the experience since 1929 supports the belief that the more rapidly the capital stock grows relative to the labor force, the greater will be the growth in potential output per worker, provided that other necessary conditions are met.

TABLE 15.—*Growth in business potential capital-labor and output-labor ratios, 1929–60*

[Percent per year]

Item	1929 to 1947	1947 to 1960	1947 to 1954	1954 to 1960
Capital stock per worker [1]_____	0.0	2.7	3.5	1.9
Output per worker [2]_____	1.5	2.8	3.3	2.1

[1] Business capital stock is built up from private purchases of plant and equipment, with allowance for retirements; excludes religious, educational, hospital, other institutional, and farm residential construction.
[2] Business output is gross national product minus product originating in general government, government enterprises, households and institutions, the rest of the world, and services of existing houses.

NOTE.—Details of series are available upon request.

Source: Council of Economic Advisers.

Though there was no increase in capital per worker between 1929 and 1947, there was a slow increase in productivity which must be attributed to technical progress and to improvement in the quality of both labor and capital. When, as in subsequent years, investment was more rapid, there was an accompanying acceleration of productivity gains. These gains were not simply the result of the separate contributions of the advance of knowledge, the improved skills of the working population, and the rise in capital per worker, but came in large part from the interaction of all three.

Investment in new equipment serves as a vehicle for technological improvements and is perhaps the most important way in which laboratory discoveries become incorporated in the production process. Without their embodiment in new equipment, many new ideas would lie fallow. Conversely, the impact of a dollar's investment on the quality of the capital stock depends on how rapidly increases in knowledge have taken place. This interaction between investment and technological change permits each worker to have not only more tools, but better tools as well.

The slower rate of growth of the capital stock in recent years provides one explanation for the accompanying slower growth of labor productivity and potential output. The proportion of output devoted to investment, and the rate of growth of the capital stock itself, are measures of the diversion of current resources to the creation of future capacity. During the period 1947–54, expenditures on business fixed investment averaged 11.0 percent of GNP and the stock grew at an annual rate of 4.2 percent (valued in 1961 prices). In the period 1955–60, 9.8 percent of GNP was invested and the capital stock grew at an annual rate of 3.2 percent. The ratio of investment to potential GNP is even more relevant; in this case, the ratios are 10.9 percent and 9.4 percent for the two periods. This difference of 1.5 percent in the fraction of potential GNP invested represents nearly $45 billion of additional capital.

Policies to Encourage Investment

(1) *Adequate levels of demand.* The single most important stimulant to investment is the maintenance of full utilization of capacity. The historical record shows that when output falls below its potential the rate of growth of the capital stock declines. Expected profit from investment is strongly influenced by the expected demand for the output that the new capital will help produce, even if the investment is meant largely for cost reduction rather than capacity expansion. Estimates of future demand are colored by the experience of the present and the recent past. During periods of economic slack, estimates of future demand are relatively pessimistic, and many projects are foregone which would appear profitable under conditions of high demand.

There is a tendency to think of profitable investment opportunities for the whole economy as exhaustible: the more of them that are used up in any one year, the fewer remain. There may be some validity to this view for a single industry, which can mistakenly expand its capacity beyond the possibilities of future market demand. But for the entire economy, what appears as unavoidable excess capacity is in fact avoidable deficiency of demand. There are, and always will be, unsatisfied wants for a higher standard of living, though the demand for any particular product may perhaps be satiated. The investment boom of 1955–57 did not make inevitable the excess capacity that has ruled since then. Instead, it created an opportunity for higher levels of production in later years, had the demand been forthcoming. The opportunity was lost; even before the cyclical peak in the third quarter of 1957, the growth of demand slowed down and excess capacity began to emerge.

It is true that, with any given level of technology, a higher rate of investment can occur only through the acceptance of investment opportunities of lower profitability. But appropriate tax and monetary measures can make even these investments sufficiently attractive. And technical progress can have the same effect. To equip a more rapidly growing labor force also demands a larger volume of investment relative to potential GNP. Fortunately, if actual output is held close to a rising potential output, faster labor force growth will open opportunities for additions to plant and equipment which would be economically unattractive if the labor supply situation were tighter. Thus a higher ratio of investment to output can be more easily maintained. When excess capacity already exists, however, profitability is low for that reason alone, and the growing labor force appears as a threat, instead of the stimulus to investment it really is.

In addition to serving as an indicator of future profits, the level of aggregate demand, through its impact on current profits, plays an important role in providing finance for investment. The importance of the level of economic activity in determining profits is indicated in Chart 3, which shows that net and gross profits as a percentage of GNP fluctuate very closely with the rate of capacity utilization. A policy that sustains near-capacity operations goes beyond strengthening the profitability of investment; it insures an ample supply of low-cost internal funds, which itself encourages investment.

(2) *Monetary and credit policy.* The open market operations of the Federal Reserve and the debt-management operations of the Treasury exert a powerful influence on supply conditions in credit markets. If economic growth were the only end to be served, the sole object of monetary and credit policy would be to assure an adequate flow of funds to finance the needed capital formation at interest rates appropriate to the basic profitability of investment. This was pointed out by the Chairman of the Board of Governors of the Federal Reserve System in March 1961, in a statement to the Joint Economic Committee: "As I have said many times in the past, before this Committee and others, I am in favor of interest rates being as low as possible without stimulating inflation, because low rates can help to foster capital expenditures that, in turn, promote economic growth."

Use of monetary techniques for growth purposes must, of course, be limited by the demands placed on them by other national objectives. In the present situation, for example, monetary policy has a role to play in the attainment of recovery from recession and in the restoration of balance of payments equilibrium. Policies for growth and recovery are complementary, since any policy that stimulates investment will simultaneously stimulate aggregate demand. This situation, however, will not always prevail. When excessive demand threatens inflation, stability and growth goals will tend to push monetary policy in opposite directions. At such times, the importance of economic growth would suggest the major use of other measures—principally budgetary surpluses—to achieve stability. For when demand is strong enough to generate pressure on existing capacity, and only then, rapid growth requires that enough resources be withheld from other uses to make a sustained high rate of investment possible without inflation. Under these circumstances, a surplus in the Federal budget plays the constructive role of adding to national saving and making resources available for investment. The role of a policy of monetary ease at full employment is then to insure that the resources freed by a tight fiscal policy are indeed used for investment and not wasted in unemployment.

The current balance of payments problem puts additional constraints on the use of monetary policy to promote recovery and growth. The techniques developed by the Federal Reserve to meet the new situation have already been discussed in Chapter 1, Part II.

(3) *Tax policy.* Every tax system is the product of particular needs and economic conditions; no tax system can be neutral in its effects on the ways in which households and business firms earn and spend their incomes. If faster economic growth is desired, revision of the tax structure is called for, to permit a higher rate of investment once full use of resources is achieved.

The Administration's program encompasses two complementary approaches to this objective. The first is an investment tax credit equal to 8 percent of investment in eligible machinery and equipment; the second is revision of the guidelines for the tax lives of properties subject to depreciation.

The investment credit will stimulate investment by reducing the net cost of acquiring depreciable assets, thus increasing expected profitability. The increase will vary inversely with the expected life of the asset. For an asset with a service life of 10 years and an after-tax yield of 10 percent before the credit, the investment credit will increase the expected rate of return by about one-third. The increase in net yield will be greater for less durable equipment and smaller for more durable equipment.

Investment decisions are also influenced by the availability of funds. The investment tax credit will increase by some $1.5 billion the flow of cash available for investment under conditions anticipated for 1962.

Since the credit applies only to newly acquired assets, the entire incentive effect is concentrated on the profitability of new capital and no revenue is lost in raising the profitability of assets already held by business firms. It is an efficient way of encouraging re-equipment and modernization of productive facilities, as well as the expansion of capacity. The credit will thus help to accelerate economic growth and improve our competitive position. It will also increase the attractiveness of investment at home relative to direct investment abroad. In both ways the credit will help to ease our balance of payments problem.

Revision of tax lives for depreciable property is desirable as a matter of equity to reflect more accurately the influence of obsolescence on economic lives of capital assets. Present guidelines were established 20 years ago on the basis of replacement practices of the depressed prewar years. Depreciation, designed to reflect the loss in value of plant and equipment over time, is a function not alone of "wear and tear," but also of technological progress, changes in the relative costs of economic inputs, competitive conditions, and consumer tastes and demand. Through its favorable effects on cash flows, expected rates of return, and risk, liberalized depreciation will tend to stimulate investment.

The investment tax credit, coupled with liberalized depreciation, will provide a strong and lasting stimulus to the high rate of investment that is a major requirement for accelerated economic growth. Together, they will provide incentives to invest comparable to those available in the rapidly growing industrial nations of the free world.

Attention to Federal income tax adjustments to stimulate investment must not be allowed to obscure the role of State and local tax policies and practices in economic growth. The tax collections of these governments are nearly half as large as Federal collections. In fiscal year 1960, they increased by more than 10 percent, or $3.7 billion.

The power to tax under this governmental system is shared by thousands of separate jurisdictions. Improved coordination among them will improve economic efficiency. Identical tax sources are frequently utilized by two, three, and even four layers of government without appropriate cooperation. Taxing authorities occasionally use their powers in ways that capriciously affect decisions concerning the location of plants and disrupt normal competition. The result may be a misallocation of resources and economic loss.

The Congress has recognized the need for better intergovernmental coordination. It has provided for the creation of the Advisory Commission on Intergovernmental Relations to foster "the fullest cooperation and coordination of activities between the levels of government." The Advisory Commission, composed of representatives of the executive and legislative branches of all levels of government, has already made important recommendations for the coordination of local taxes by the States and for improved tax coordination and cooperation between Federal and State governments.

INVESTMENT IN NATURAL RESOURCES

Economic growth is not simply a matter of growth in the size and skills of the labor force, in the quantity and quality of capital goods, and in the productivity of the processes by which these inputs are combined. It is equally a matter of turning more and more of the earth's endowment of natural wealth—soil, sunlight, air, water, minerals, plant and animal life— to the purposes of man. America's position has generally been one of natural plenty, but we cannot complacently assume that the abundance of the past will also characterize the future.

But neither is there any reason to suppose that resource limitations will in the foreseeable future place serious limits on the growth of the economy. Technological change, substitution of abundant and cheap raw materials for scarce and expensive ones, investment in improved resource management and conservation, and increased reliance on imports all provide important offsets to the effects of increasing scarcity on the real cost of obtaining resource inputs. Taken together, these factors tend to keep the economy growing along the path of least resistance so far as its resource requirements are concerned. If the various offsets to increasing scarcity are not fully effective, resources can be obtained by digging and drilling deeper, utilizing lower grade deposits, constructing dams and better waste treatment facilities, and other measures involving higher costs. But the necessity to devote more labor and capital to these tasks would constitute a drag on the economy, tending to cancel some of the efforts we make to stimulate growth. Indeed, taking the economy as a whole, it is equivalent to a decline in productivity.

The Historical Record

A rough judgment as to the probable consequences of continued depletion of resources in the future can be derived by examining the record of the past. The long-term trend of raw materials prices relative to the prices of finished products is a useful, though by no means ideal, indicator of the effectiveness of the offsets to natural scarcity.

TABLE 16.—*Ratios of indexes of raw materials prices to index of finished products prices, 1900–57*

[1920–24 = 100]

Period	All raw materials [1] [2]	Agricultural products	Forest products	Minerals				
				Total [2]	Metals [2]	Fuels	Construction materials	Other non-metallic minerals
Annual average:								
1900–04	94	97	70	90	130	78	92	146
1905–09	96	103	77	81	139	68	79	127
1910–14	103	118	74	77	124	67	73	124
1915–19	108	121	74	87	130	76	72	124
1920–24	100	100	100	100	100	100	100	100
1925–29	112	122	94	94	112	89	103	103
1930–34	88	89	93	84	103	78	107	84
1935–39	102	104	109	94	131	88	100	77
1940–44	111	120	127	88	118	81	91	86
1945–49	125	134	158	93	109	92	82	93
1950–54	128	128	187	105	133	103	82	105
1955–57	118	108	184	111	147	107	85	130
1957	116	105	174	111	136	110	84	123

[1] Excludes fishery and wildlife products, for which adequate price data are not available.
[2] Excludes gold.

NOTE.—Figures for earlier years, especially prior to 1915, are less reliable than those for later years. Annual index for each group has been divided by the over-all finished products index.

Source: Department of Commerce (based on data, including finished products price index, to be published by the Bureau of the Census in the forthcoming report, *Raw Materials in the United States Economy, 1900–57*, Working Paper No. 6).

Table 16 shows the movements of price indexes for all raw materials and for broad subgroups, relative to an index of prices of finished products. From 1900–04 to 1955–57—the last period for which data are available—the over-all index increased by 25½ percent, an average rate of increase just over 0.4 percent per year. The most striking feature of the table, however, is not this slow but visible trend toward increasing costs as our resource endowment has been exploited more intensively but the varying patterns of price movement shown by different commodities and by the same commodity at different times. The outstanding example of a strong upward price trend is forest products. Even in forestry, however, there are preliminary indications that productivity gains are beginning to offset the effects of scarcity on prices. The index for all minerals has risen slightly less than that for all raw materials, and the subgroups of the minerals index show divergent movements. A considerably larger increase in the minerals index would undoubtedly have occurred if the opportunities of international trade had not been available. This is particularly true of the metals subgroup where net imports accounted for 44.8 percent of apparent consumption of metallic ores in 1957.

The index for agricultural products shows the effects of the great depression, the second World War and its aftermath, and the accelerated improvement of agricultural productivity in the 1950's. The last is largely responsible for the decline of the over-all index from its 1950–54 peak. It is reasonable to expect that improvements in agricultural productivity will continue to exert a substantial downward pressure on the over-all index in the future.

Implications for Public Policy

The lessons to be drawn from this review of past trends are these: First, it is likely that increasing resource scarcity has had only a negligible retarding effect on economic growth during the present century. Rising real costs of obtaining some resources have been largely compensated by declining costs of obtaining others. Second, the historical record does not indicate that more rapid economic growth will simply result in our "running out of resources" more quickly. On the contrary, past investments have permitted resources to be extracted more efficiently and used more efficiently.

Public policy has contributed to this success by limitation of economic waste, the development and adoption of improved methods in agriculture, forestry, and other fields, the unified development of river valleys, and a variety of other measures. Finally, the opportunity to obtain raw materials from abroad has been important in the past and will be increasingly important in the future.

Preventing resource scarcity from being a drag on economic growth is by no means the only objective of policy in this field. Particularly for water, forest, and scenic resources, an important objective is the provision of aesthetic and recreational benefits which are not reflected in aggregate measures of economic activity because they do not pass through the market place. The difficulty of determining objective standards by which such benefits can be weighed is obviously not a valid reason for neglecting them.

Water Resources

There is wide agreement that one of the most serious resource problems facing the United States at present and in the immediate future is the development of water resources. The use of water has been increasing rapidly as a result of population growth, higher living standards, increasing urbanization, rapid growth of industries that are heavy users of water, increases in the amount of land under irrigation, and other factors. In the Eastern United States and the Pacific Northwest, the problem presented by these trends can be met for the next few decades by an adequate and appropriately timed program of investment in (1) multiple purpose water resource development which, in addition to other benefits, permits the collection and storage of water for use as needed and (2) facilities for treatment of industrial and municipal wastes. In some of the dry regions of the West, however, the opportunities for further development of water resources will be exhausted within the next two decades. Barring major scientific breakthroughs, the continued economic development of these regions will soon come to depend upon how effectively an almost fixed supply of water is used to satisfy the most important of the various industrial, agricultural, and municipal needs for water.

It is certain that additional investment to increase the quantity and to improve the quality of the supplies of water will be a major part of any solution to the problem. Pollution control, in particular, will require major investment expenditures in the coming decades. The enactment last year of the Administration's proposal for an expanded program of grants under the Federal Water Pollution Control Act and extension of Federal authority to seek abatement of pollution of navigable waters were important steps forward. But the fact that water resources in some regions of the country will soon be close to fully developed calls attention to a consideration that is relevant to water resources policy for the country as a whole: investment in development of existing water supplies is not a complete solution to the problem of water scarcity, nor is it necessarily the economically desirable solution under every particular set of circumstances. A variety of offsets to increasing scarcity are available and each has a role to play. In particular, additional research and development in methods of conserving and augmenting water supplies, including desalinization, weather modification, reduction of evaporation losses, cheaper and more effective waste treatment and more efficient use of water in industry and agriculture may produce high returns.

Since expensive investments must be undertaken to increase the quantity and quality of water supplies, it is appropriate that the costs be reflected in prices charged industrial and agricultural users. To treat a costly commodity as if it were free only encourages excessive use. There is evidence that significant reductions in water withdrawals could be achieved in many important water using activities and that they can be expected to occur if proper deterrents are provided. The burdens of scarcity on the economy cannot be entirely eliminated by using scarce capital to augment the supply of scarce water. But the burden can be minimized by a proper balance between investments in increased supply on the one hand, and price increases to eliminate inefficient use on the other.

Agricultural Land

The problem of agricultural land stands in sharp contrast to the problem of water resources. Whereas in the latter the problems requiring attention are those posed by increasing scarcity, in the former they are problems of adjusting to abundance.

Agriculture is the major source of downward pressure on the price index for all raw materials, and land is in ample supply. There are approximately 640 million acres of land suitable for cultivation in the United States at present, but only about 450 million are actually used for crops or pasture. Present indications are that only slightly more than 400 million acres of cropland (including cropland pastured and idle) will be in use by 1980 to produce agricultural products.

The major land resource investments required during the next several decades will, therefore, involve the conservation and protection of remaining farmland and the transfer of land to nonagricultural use rather than bringing more land into agricultural production. There are currently close to 70 million acres of land used for cropland which are subject to severe erosion hazard or otherwise not suitable for cultivation over the long run. Much of this land could be transferred to provide products or services, such as forestry and recreation, for which the demand is rising. At the same time, about 17 million of the 240 million acres of good land now in pasture or forest could be converted to cropland.

The Department of Agriculture currently has plans for a long-range land use adjustment program. This program has three major facets: transfer of cropland to grass; transfer of cropland to forest; and greater emphasis on wildlife and recreational development in the small watershed programs. As the program develops, it will be possible for supply management to place less emphasis on temporary diversion of acreage from the production of specific crops.

The present problems of U.S. agriculture, which reflect in part the fact that the pace of technological progress in agriculture exceeds the rate of growth in demand for farm products, should not blind us to the important lessons to be drawn from the record. When strong policy measures are taken well in advance, technological progress affords an escape from increasing scarcity. Indeed, it is technology that largely determines which portions of the environment are regarded as resources and which are not. Research not only makes possible the more effective use of existing resources, as in the case of agriculture, but may create important new ones. The record of agriculture also illustrates, however, the long lag between the decision to act and the appearance of the benefits. Careful and continuing analysis of present and future resource needs, coupled with readiness to act when the indications of potential difficulties become persuasive, is the best hope for success in meeting the resource requirements of rapid economic growth.

INVESTMENT IN PUBLIC SERVICES

Accelerated economic growth will require increased public investment, just as it will require increased private investment. Without additional plant and equipment, governments at all levels will be unable to meet the increased demands for public services that arise both as a consequence of measures taken to stimulate growth and as a consequence of growth itself. If a high and rising educational level of the labor force is sought as a means to speed economic growth, additional investment in school and college buildings, furnishings, and laboratory equipment will be required. Demands for transportation of both people and goods will increase as a result of economic growth; meeting these demands will require additional investment in urban public transportation systems, airports, roads and highways.

Failure to make adequate investments in the physical basis of public services inevitably retards economic growth. In some cases, the connection is fairly easy to trace; inadequate investment in highways will bring an increase in congestion, with consequent declines in the productivity of trucks and truck drivers, and rising transportation costs. In other cases, the process by which a shortage of basic public services tends to retard the growth of output is less obvious, but no less real; education is an important example. As has been noted above, an inadequate effort to solve the water pollution problem will be paid for in higher costs of obtaining water of adequate quality—unless it is paid for by a decline in the health of the population and decreased productivity in water-using industrial processes. Inadequacy of public services also has effects on economic welfare that are not reflected in aggregate economic statistics. Commuters are well aware of the sacrifice of time that results from inadequate urban transportation systems. The sacrifice of recreational opportunities resulting from failure to make sufficient provisions for public parks as cities expand is another example.

The task of meeting the transportation, recreation, education, housing, and other needs of growing metropolitan areas poses a major challenge to our existing forms of political organization at the State and local level. Public facilities serving the needs of individual political jurisdictions within an urban area are often less efficient than they would be if they had been designed for all, or a large part, of the area. For example, lack of effective and well coordinated land use planning and zoning regulation has resulted in locational patterns of residential, commercial, and industrial developments that intensify transportation problems. Improved planning and coordination can increase the efficiency of public services and make cities better places in which to live. Progress can be achieved through continued Federal assistance to States and local bodies for the planning of urban area development, comprehensive urban renewal programs within cities, public improvement programs, and specific public improvements.

Although the Federal Government is making an important contribution to the solution of problems whose significance extends beyond the boundaries of political units at lower levels, it must be remembered that civil government is basically a State and local responsibility. About 80 percent of spending for civil government in 1960—for education, highways, water supply, sanitation, public health, police and fire protection, etc.—actually took place at the State and local level, with only about 15 percent of these local expenditures financed by Federal aid. State and local governments account for more than 70 percent of public civilian employment and for two-thirds of nonmilitary government payrolls. Their activities are a major factor in the economy.

As a Nation, we have surely not erred on the side of excessive public investment in recent years. Major sources of demand for public services have expanded sharply: for example, the number of automobiles and trucks has grown more rapidly than GNP, and the extent of urbanization has increased. Nevertheless, new nondefense public construction as a fraction of GNP was essentially unchanged in the 1950's from its level in the 1920's. It must also be noted that a substantial backlog of unsatisfied needs for schools, highways, and other public facilities was carried over into the decade of the 1950's from the second World War—probably a much greater backlog than was carried into the 1920's from the first.

Although these historical comparisons throw an interesting light on the changing role of the public sector in the U.S. economy, they do not provide firm standards for the future division of responsibility between the public and private sectors. That issue cannot be settled by the invocation of historical ratios any more than it should be settled by abstract argument. If our economy is to use its productive resources in reasonable accordance with a consensus as to national priorities, we must face the question of public versus private expenditures pragmatically, in terms of intrinsic merits and costs, not in terms of fixed preconceptions.

INVESTMENT IN HOUSING

The higher standard of living made possible by economic growth results from increased output of a wide variety of goods and services. Among these is one item which, by virtue of its economic importance, its great influence on the general quality of life, and the unique character of the capital investment required to expand its supply, deserves special attention in a discussion of economic growth. This item is housing.

The value of the current services supplied by the Nation's residential structures—the total of rents paid plus the imputed rental value of owner-occupied dwellings—accounted for 13.1 percent of personal consumption expenditures in 1961, or 8.5 percent of GNP. Another 4.1 percent of GNP was accounted for by residential nonfarm construction—the total expenditures on replacing, improving, and adding to the nonfarm portion of the stock of residential structures. That stock itself represents roughly one-fourth of our national wealth, about twice the share accounted for by producers' durable equipment.

These figures are, in part, a statistical image of the importance of the basic human need for shelter. To a greater extent, however, they reflect the fact that better housing is among the most important benefits that economic progress can confer. A dwelling that provides adequate protection against the elements may nevertheless be a serious hazard to the mental and physical health of its occupants, if it is overcrowded, lacking in hot and cold running water or plumbing facilities, or structurally unsound. A better home provides a healthier, safer, and more comfortable living environment; it affords greater opportunities for recreation, aesthetic enjoyment, and peace and quiet.

Few, if any, Americans actually lack a roof over their heads. But about one-fifth of the Nation's housing units are classified as "dilapidated" or else lack one or more of the basic plumbing facilities. Like the poverty that it reflects, substandard housing is a burden borne to a disproportionate extent by a few groups in the society; the aged, the nonwhite, the poorly educated, and families without a male breadwinner. The burden is perhaps most regrettable when it renders ineffective the measures society takes to promote equality of opportunity. The child who has no decent place in which to study can hardly take full advantage of the free education that is provided to him.

The elimination of substandard housing and the provision of a decent home in a suitable environment for all American families is an important objective of public policy in the housing field. The public interest has been deemed to extend also to the promotion of home ownership. Through the mortgage insurance and mortgage guaranty operations of the Federal Housing Administration (FHA) and the Veterans Administration (VA) and the secondary market operations of the Federal National Mortgage Association (FNMA), the Government facilitates homebuilding and the flow of private capital into home loans by providing insurance against the risk of default and making mortgage loans a more liquid investment for financial institutions.   In addition, FNMA assists in the financing of certain special types of home mortgages, as authorized by the Congress and directed by the President. Public housing amounted to just over 3 percent of all nonfarm housing starts between 1947 and 1960.

These various activities played a major role in the substantial progress toward better housing for the Nation that was made during the 1950's. Whereas in 1950, 55.0 percent of occupied housing units were owner-occupied, 61.9 percent were owner-occupied in 1960. Nonfarm housing starts exceeded the increase in the number of nonfarm households by roughly 25 percent for the decade, providing a margin for replacement of housing units demolished by public and private improvement programs, for improvement of average quality, and to accommodate housing needs arising from migration and mobility of the American people. In recent years, about

30 percent of sales of new nonfarm housing units have been under the FHA or VA programs.

A sharp rise in the rate of household formation will occur in the latter part of this decade, reflecting the high birth rates of the middle and late 1940's. It is all the more important, therefore, that substantial progress in improving the average quality of the Nation's housing be made in the early part of the decade, when the need to increase its quantity will be less urgent. The enactment in the last session of Congress of the Administration-sponsored Housing Act of 1961 was a major step toward meeting the Nation's housing needs. In addition to extending and expanding existing programs for public housing, housing for the elderly, college housing, and farm housing, the Act provides for major new programs of FHA-insured loans to finance construction and rehabilitation of housing for moderate income families, and long-term FHA-insured home repair loans. These new types of loans are eligible for purchase by FNMA. Other important provisions make Federal assistance available to States and localities for various measures in the field of urban affairs, including planning, loans, and demonstration grants for mass transportation projects, and acquisition of land for permanent open-space uses, such as parks. Additional funds were authorized to finance the construction of community facilities. Finally, a series of provisions make additional assistance available for households and businesses displaced by urban renewal programs or other government actions.

Rapid economic growth should bring the national goal of decent housing and a suitable living environment for every American family well within reach during the present decade. Estimates prepared for the Council of Economic Advisers by the Housing and Home Finance Agency indicate that no American households need occupy a dilapidated structure by 1970. This could be achieved with about the present ratio of residential construction expenditures to GNP—provided that GNP itself grows at approximately the rate discussed earlier in this chapter. This estimate includes an allowance for expenditures on additions and alterations based on extrapolation of the 1950–60 trend, but this allowance is probably not adequate to make possible the elimination of housing that is deficient for reasons other than dilapidation. It is clear, however, that the virtually complete elimination of deficient housing is by no means an unrealistic objective in a context of rapid economic growth.

Construction costs have risen more rapidly than broad price indexes in recent years. For example, while the all-inclusive price index for GNP rose by 40 percent between 1947 and 1961, the subindex for nonfarm residential construction rose by 50 percent. If this were to continue, it would mean that the share of current-price GNP devoted to the building of houses must rise if the proportion of real output going into housing investment is not to fall. There is a need to identify artificial barriers to technological progress and to efficient allocation of resources in the construction industry. Their reduction or removal can make a significant contribution to growth in this important sector of the economy.

CONCLUSION

This Chapter began with the observation that sustained long-run growth of potential supply is both difficult to achieve and pointless of achievement unless the growth of demand keeps pace. Capacity to produce is not an end in itself, but an instrument for the satisfaction of needs and the discharge of responsibilities. The needs will go unfilled and the responsibilities unmet to the extent that growing productive power runs to waste in idle machines and unemployed men.

Here the objectives of stabilization policy and growth policy coalesce. The mandate of the Employment Act renews itself perpetually as maximum levels of production, employment and purchasing power rise through time. The weapons of stabilization policy—the budget, the tax system, control of the supply of money and credit—must be aimed anew, for their target is moving. In particular, as Part II of Chapter 1 explains, with given expenditures and given tax rates, the Federal budget surplus at full employment grows with the economy. If it grows too rapidly, it can become an obstacle to full employment, to healthy economic growth, indeed to its own realization. If it grows too slowly, it can contribute to inflationary pressure.

Some surplus at full employment may be desirable, to help to finance the formation of capital. How large it should be depends on the size of the investment program required by the economy, on the freely made saving decisions of families and business firms, and on the level of government expenditures. It is the function of monetary policy, the tax system, and transfer payments to help to generate demand for the investment needed for economic growth. It is the function of over-all fiscal policy to insure that investment demand is matched, at full employment, by an equivalent volume of private and public saving.

The course of the budget surplus at full employment depends on the growth of the national income, the responsiveness of tax revenues to a rising tax base, and the changing level of Federal outlays. Even if Federal expenditures remain a constant proportion of GNP, as they have in recent years, the surplus at full employment will grow slightly because the progressive character of the tax system causes revenues to rise relative to GNP. If expenditures remain constant, or nearly so, the full employment surplus will grow much more rapidly.

As the economy returns to the full employment track, the full employment surplus will need to be kept from growing indefinitely, and perhaps to be reduced. The choice—or rather the division, for it is unlikely to be an "either-or" matter—is between reductions in tax receipts and increases in government expenditures, whether Federal, State or local. A pragmatic decision will almost certainly involve both. It is unlikely that the most urgent unmet needs of the population will lie all in the area of private consumption or all in the areas traditionally allotted to public consumption and investment. Undoubtedly much of the reduction in the full employment surplus should be channeled directly to private purchasing power, just as most, by far, of present consumption spending is in private hands. The choice of a balance between public and private expenditures is an important choice for society. It should be made consciously through the normal democratic processes. And it should be made by weighing the urgency of alternative uses of resources, rather than by appeal to simple slogans on one side or the other.

The concern of this chapter has been the source of rising productive potential and the policies that can strengthen them. Granted continued prosperity, we can have slower growth or faster growth. There is substitution between the composition of output in the present and the level of output in the future. Just as a single individual can increase his consumption possibilities in the future by present saving, so can a whole society provide more fully for its future by using present resources for acts of investment in the broadest sense. No absolute reduction in current consumption need occur; it is only necessary that consumption grow less rapidly than total output for a time. Indeed, future levels of consumption will be higher than they could otherwise be—the cost is primarily in postponement. Happily, for an advanced society like ours, much of what is described from this point of view as investment can also be seen as present enjoyment of some of the delights of civilization: widespread education, good health, and the search for knowledge.

Chapter 3

The Balance of International Payments

THE RECOVERY AND GROWTH of the U.S. economy are not important for the United States alone. On the vigor of our economy depend in large measure the strength and stamina of the free world and the standing of freedom in the minds of men everywhere. Leadership in the world requires the support of a growing and dynamic domestic economy, using to the full its vast productive capacity. The other nations of the free world rely heavily on the United States as a market for their products and as a source of capital and technology for their economic growth. The United States has taken the lead in meeting the responsibilities of the advanced countries to foster the economic development of the low-income nations. The less developed countries need both public and private investment capital; they need full opportunity to sell their products in world markets in order to earn the industrial imports that their development programs require; and they need a democratic alternative to the communist prescription for economic development.

The U.S. balance of international payments is the outcome of countless separate transactions by governments, private businesses, and individuals. The obligations of world leadership entail large government outlays abroad. U.S. business firms and consumers pay out billions of dollars for foreign goods and services. U.S. corporations, financial institutions, and individuals acquire properties, buy securities, and lend money abroad. The United States is one of a very few countries with a long standing policy permitting residents and foreigners complete freedom to make payments abroad in its currency. For many years, the United States had little reason to be concerned whether all these payments were covered by corresponding receipts from abroad. Foreign demands for U.S. goods and services were large; the dollar was, and still is, a ticket of entry to the world's largest and most diversified market. In some periods, the surplus of receipts was so large that the United States took actions to moderate its effects both at home and abroad. And if international payments happened to exceed receipts in any year, foreigners were willing to hold most of the dollars they acquired; only a small part of the deficit had to be met from our large gold reserves.

Recently, persistent payments deficits and gold losses have made it necessary for the U.S. Government to give greater attention to the net financial outcome of its transactions, and those of its citizens, with the rest of the world. Payments need not and should not be directly controlled, but the balance must be under control.   Many private international transactions depend in large part on economic circumstances at home.   Consequently, domestic economic policy must be framed with an eye to the balance of payments.   Action to safeguard the international position of the dollar is today an essential part of policy for full employment and growth.

The policies adopted in 1961 to strengthen the balance of payments are already beginning to take effect.   The deficit in the international payments of the United States, which had averaged $3.7 billion annually in each of the three preceding years, was less than $2.5 billion in 1961, according to preliminary estimates.   Gold reserves declined by less than $0.9 billion in 1961, compared with $1.7 billion in 1960.   The full effects of measures under way and proposed will in time restore a sustainable balance in U.S. transactions with the rest of the world.

This chapter examines first the background for policies to improve the balance of payments and safeguard the position of the dollar: the general objectives which guide U.S. international economic and financial policies; the trading, investing, and international banking functions of the United States and their interrelations; and recent changes in the world economy affecting the U.S. balance of payments.   In the final sections of the chapter, policies that are under way and proposed are discussed: measures to balance the basic international accounts; measures to limit disruptive flows of short-term capital; and measures to strengthen the international monetary system.

THE UNITED STATES IN THE WORLD ECONOMY

Objectives of U.S. Foreign Economic Policy

A basic objective of U.S. policy is to provide an economic environment in which the people of the United States and of all nations can steadily raise their standards of living.   Economic growth at home will support, and will be supported by, progress and development abroad, provided that international cooperation and commerce distribute equitably and efficiently the fruits of productive specialization among all free nations.   International financial arrangements and policies are means to this fundamental end.   A stable and efficient system of international payments is essential to facilitate desirable international flows of goods, services, and capital.   The dollar has become the principal international currency, and the stability of the dollar is the foundation of the international payments system which has evolved since the war.   For this reason, the President has declared that the present gold value of the dollar will be maintained.   To safeguard the stability of the dollar, the United States is determined to improve its balance of international payments.

Postwar progress.   U.S. foreign economic policy since the war has sought to build an international economic environment in which goods, services, and capital flow freely across national boundaries.   This policy has been based on the conviction that a free exchange of products and capital in world-wide markets will raise standards of living both in the United States and in the rest of the world. The example of the vast continental market of the United States attests to the economic gains afforded by geographical specialization and exchange and by the mobilization of savings in one region to finance productive investment opportunities in another. Without this huge internal market, unhampered by trade restrictions between States, American standards of living could not have risen to their present heights. Throughout the world, similarly dramatic gains can be achieved by international specialization and trade.

The framework of international economic cooperation in the free world today, especially among the industrial countries, represents a notable achievement. The great depression and the war left a legacy of national restrictions on movements of goods and capital—exchange controls, quantitative restrictions on imports, bilateral clearing and trading arrangements, discrimination against dollar goods. Since the war, the countries of the free world have been engaged in clearing away this restrictive legacy. Even before the war ended, the foundations were laid for the International Monetary Fund, the International Bank for Reconstruction and Development, and the General Agreement on Tariffs and Trade. The United States provided aid and leadership in European economic reconstruction and trade liberalization through the Marshall Plan and through association with the Organization for European Economic Cooperation. Substantial progress has been made toward a world of currencies convertible at fixed exchange rates and toward freedom from direct and discriminatory controls over trade and payments. Progress has also been made, though less rapidly, toward a world of lower tariff barriers; here is an opportunity for a major step forward.

Expanding trade: a new program. Foreign trade is not so vital to the United States as it is to most other countries. But the contributions of trade to our domestic welfare are nonetheless real and important. Net foreign purchases of our products contribute to output, employment, and economic growth in the United States. More significant, the opportunity to sell our products abroad in exchange for foreign goods enables us to specialize the structure of our production and to diversify the patterns of our consumption. By specializing in the production and export of goods in which the United States is unexcelled, Americans are enabled to import goods which would be impossible or costly to produce at home. Foreign trade raises living standards by widening the choice of goods available to the American consumer and by providing him with some goods and services at lower prices.

As other countries have recovered from the devastation of war and have rebuilt and modernized their productive capacity, they have become increasingly vigorous competitors of the United States in world markets. The most notable new source of competition is the European Economic Community, or Common Market, which now includes France, Germany, Italy,

Belgium, Holland, and Luxembourg, and which shortly may include the United Kingdom and several other European countries. Members of the Common Market are committed to the rapid elimination of tariffs among themselves and the establishment of a common external tariff on imports from the rest of the world.

Still in its formative years, the Common Market has imparted amazing vitality to the economies of its members. U.S. exports to Western Europe have risen sharply in response to the rapid economic growth within the Common Market countries. We cannot be sure that this rise in exports will continue unless we can negotiate substantial reductions of the Common Market's external tariff. The evolution and enlargement of the Common Market inevitably increases tariff discrimination against U.S. exports; we must compete over this tariff barrier while members of the Common Market have steadily freer access to each other's markets.

The Administration is therefore proposing to the Congress a major revision in foreign trade policy. The President's current authority to negotiate tariff reductions has been virtually exhausted. For the first time since the original Trade Agreements Act was passed in 1934, Congress is being asked to equip the President with new kinds of bargaining instruments for negotiating with the Common Market. We must assure access of the products of our farms and factories to the world's largest market outside our own. Successful negotiations will make possible increasing specialization of production in both Atlantic markets. It will also make it possible to offer the free nations of other continents greater access to markets on both sides of the Atlantic.

Safeguarding the dollar. A stable and efficient system of international payments is an integral part of the liberal international economic environment toward which the free world has been moving. Uncertainties about the value and convertibility of the proceeds of international transactions disrupt movements of goods, services, and capital between nations. Convertible currencies and stable exchange rates as envisaged in the Bretton Woods agreements provide assurance of the value of international claims acquired by trade or investment.

The United States performs a special world banking function in the present international payments system. The dollar, alone with the pound sterling among national currencies, has come to be used as a major international currency by the free world. Private traders, banks, and governments have chosen to use dollars both as a means of payment and as a store of value. Foreign countries hold liquid dollar balances, acquired in international transactions, in much the same way that individual depositors hold balances in commercial banks. Foreign governments and central banks accept dollars as a partial substitute for gold in their international reserves because the dollar is an international currency and because the policy of the U.S. Treasury is to sell gold on demand to foreign governments and monetary authorities at a fixed price. The dollar became a "reserve currency" without any conscious international decision to establish a payments system based on key national currencies. Use of the dollar as a reserve currency has met growing needs for international reserves and economized the limited and slowly growing supply of gold.

Foreign central banks and governments hold as part of their international reserves $11 billion of short-term dollar obligations, which can be used to purchase gold from the United States. In addition, foreign private short-term dollar holdings amount to $8 billion. Whenever dollars held by foreign private banks or individuals, or dollars held by U.S. residents themselves, are sold to foreign central banks for other currencies, they become potential claims on our gold stock.

Because of the strategic role of the dollar, maintenance of its established gold value is essential to the stability and efficiency of the present system of international payments. Accordingly, when the President pledged that the gold value of the dollar would be maintained, he stated that "the full strength of our total gold stock and other international reserves stands behind the value of the dollar for use if needed." This reserve strength comprises $17 billion in gold (two-fifths of the monetary gold stock of the free world), small amounts of convertible foreign currencies, and drawing rights on the International Monetary Fund (IMF), of which $1.7 billion is automatically available under current practices of the Fund. An additional $4.1 billion could become available in accordance with Fund policies, insofar as the Fund has available resources in gold and usable foreign currencies. The recent agreement to strengthen the IMF (discussed at the end of this chapter) should do much to assure the availability of such resources.

Reducing the deficit. Deficits in the U.S. balance of payments are financed either by drawing down our gold reserves or by increasing the potential foreign claims against them in the form of liquid dollar liabilities to foreigners, official and private. Large and continuing deficits cannot be financed indefinitely. U.S. reserves, although very large, are not inexhaustible. Foreigners have accumulated large liquid dollar balances, but they will not be willing to let these balances grow without limit.

Therefore, the policy of the U.S. Government, as stated by the President in his message to Congress of February 6, 1961, is to "gain control of our balance of payments position so that we can achieve over-all equilibrium in our international payments. This means that any sustained future outflow of dollars into the monetary reserves of other countries should come about only as a result of considered judgments as to the appropriate needs for dollar reserves."

Maintaining basic objectives. These related tasks—maintaining the external value of the dollar and bringing our international accounts into balance—must be accomplished by means which promote the basic national objectives from which the tasks derive. To balance our accounts by restrictions on trade and capital movements, for example, would confuse means and ends. Such restrictions would violate the fundamental principles of international economic relations for which our policy has striven for many years with so much success.   Similarly, the foreign policy of the United States calls for large loans and grants to foreign countries for development and for defense; and the maintenance of our military establishment abroad entails substantial overseas expenditures.   To curtail the substance of these programs would provide no solution to the "dollar problem." Rather, the task of balance of payments policy is to find the foreign exchange resources necessary to finance them.   Finally, full recovery and economic growth, primary national goals in themselves, are also essential elements in the long-run capacity of the United States to meet its international commitments and responsibilities.   Measures to rectify the balance of payments must be consistent with expansion of the U.S. economy.

The United States as Trader, Investor, and Banker

The accounts.   The U.S. balance of international payments over the last decade is shown in Table 17.   In the table, international transactions are classified into four accounts: (1) *current account and unilateral transfers,* encompassing merchandise trade, earnings on U.S. foreign investments less foreign earnings on investments in the United States, services including tourism and ocean freight, private remittances, and government military expenditures and development grants; (2) *long-term capital account,* cover-

TABLE 17.—*United States balance of international payments, 1951–61*

[Billions of dollars]

Type of transaction	1951–55 average	1956–60 average	1958	1959	1960	1961 [1]
Current account and unilateral transfers.............	−0.6	0.8	−0.1	−2.3	1.5	2.4
Merchandise trade balance......................	2.4	3.9	3.3	1.0	4.7	5.5
Exports..................................	13.4	17.7	16.3	16.3	19.4	19.7
Imports.................................	−11.0	−13.8	−13.0	−15.3	−14.7	−14.2
Military expenditures, net [2].................	−2.1	−2.8	−3.1	−2.8	−2.7	−2.5
Interest and dividends, net [3]..............	1.6	2.2	2.2	2.2	2.3	2.7
Other services, net.......................	.2	−.1	−.2	−.2	−.3	−.4
Government nonmilitary grants..............	−2.1	−1.6	−1.6	−1.6	−1.6	−1.9
Pensions and remittances..................	−.6	−.7	−.7	−.8	−.8	−.9
Long-term capital account......................	−.9	−3.0	−3.5	−2.1	−3.4	−2.5
U.S. direct investment [4]..................	−.7	−1.6	−1.1	−1.4	−1.7	−1.7
Other private U.S. investment.............	−.2	−.9	−1.4	−.9	−.9	−.6
Government loans (less repayments)..........	−.2	−.8	−1.0	−.4	−1.1	−.7
Foreign long-term investment [5]...........	.2	.4	....	.6	.3	.4
Balance on "basic" accounts (entries above).........	−1.4	−2.2	−3.6	−4.3	−1.9	−.1
U.S. short-term capital and foreign commercial credit..	−.2	−.5	−.4	.1	−1.4	−1.0
Errors and omissions................................	.4	.3	.4	.5	−.6	−.4
Over-all balance [deficit (−)]...................	−1.2	−2.3	−3.5	−3.7	−3.9	−1.5

[1] First 3 quarters at seasonally adjusted annual rate.
[2] Net of foreign military purchases in the United States.
[3] Excludes subsidiary earnings not repatriated.
[4] Excludes reinvested subsidiary earnings, amounting to $1.3 billion in 1960.
[5] Excludes reinvested subsidiary earnings, amounting to $0.2 billion in 1960.

NOTE.—Minus signs indicate payments to foreigners.
Detail will not necessarily add to totals because of rounding.

Source: Based on Department of Commerce data.

ing direct investments in business enterprise abroad, private purchases of foreign securities, U.S. Government loans, and long-term investments by foreigners in the United States; (3) *short-term capital account,* including commercial credits under one year and U.S. purchases of foreign short-term securities; (4) *over-all balance,* comprising net purchases of monetary gold and convertible currencies plus decreases in U.S. liquid liabilities to foreigners.

The accounts are, of course, far more interrelated than a simple classification of transactions suggests; foreign aid, private direct investment, and private remittances often consist in shipment abroad of U.S. goods. Even dollar outflows which are not so closely linked to the purchase of U.S. goods and services frequently result in reverse payments to the United States, either directly from the immediate recipient or indirectly through transactions involving third countries. The volume of our exports and indeed the size of the trade surplus are thus not independent of the size of our government outlays and private investments overseas.

The first account covers international transactions which relate to the earning and spending of national income. A surplus in this account means that the Nation as a whole is earning more than it is spending in its relations with the rest of the world, and this "saving" leads to an increase in the net assets of the country. Throughout the period covered by the table, the United States had a substantial merchandise trade surplus which, with other current receipts, was usually enough to pay for large overseas military expenditures and government grants for foreign reconstruction and development. In the first three quarters of 1961, the surplus on current account and unilateral transfers was at an annual rate of $2.4 billion.

The second account summarizes the transactions of the United States as an investing nation. In recent years the United States, as Table 17 shows, has invested in long-term foreign assets more than its surplus on current account and unilateral transfers. It has also lent to foreigners substantial amounts of short-term capital, as the third account in the table shows. The excess of our long-term investment and short-term lending over our surplus on current account and unilateral transfers—the over-all deficit—has been financed by increasing our liquid liabilities to foreigners and by selling gold.

The present payments problem of the United States is not one of solvency. The Nation is not "living beyond its means"; rather, its means are steadily increasing. At the end of 1960, the U.S. Government owned foreign assets totaling $21 billion, in addition to its gold holdings of $18 billion; and U.S. citizens owned another $50 billion in assets abroad (Table 18). In total, U.S. net claims on foreigners (including reinvested subsidiary earnings on investments abroad) rose by $4 billion in 1960, and the increase was perhaps as much in 1961. These increases substantially exceeded our losses of gold. Our foreign assets give basic long-run strength to the dollar; but because most of these assets are either privately owned or long-term investments or both, they cannot be quickly mobilized.

TABLE 18.—*International investment and gold position of the United States, 1949 and 1960*

[Billions of dollars, end of year]

Assets and liabilities	1949	1960 [1]
Assets	55. 2	89. 2
Gold, IMF subscription, and short-term	28. 6	26. 8
Monetary gold	24. 6	17. 8
International Monetary Fund subscription [2]	2. 8	4. 1
Short-term private	1. 3	4. 9
Long-term	26. 6	62. 4
Direct investment	10. 7	32. 7
Other private investment	4. 9	12. 6
U.S. Government claims [3]	11. 0	17. 0
Liabilities	16. 9	44. 7
Liquid	9. 8	26. 2
Short-term, by holders:		
Foreign official [4]	2. 9	10. 3
International Monetary Fund [5]	1. 3	2. 6
Other international organizations [4]	. 4	1. 4
Private [6]	4. 6	9. 6
Foreign and international holdings of U.S. Government bonds and notes	. 6	2. 3
Long-term	7. 1	18. 4
Direct investment	2. 9	6. 9
Other private investment	4. 2	11. 5
Excess of assets over liabilities	38. 3	44. 5

[1] Preliminary.
[2] Under current practices of IMF, the United States has a virtually automatic right to draw the amount of its subscription less the amount of U.S. liabilities to IMF as shown in the lower part of the table.
[3] Includes U.S. Government claims in inconvertible currencies.
[4] As reported by banks in the U.S.
[5] Noninterest-bearing notes (and, in 1949, deposits).
[6] Includes estimated foreign holding of U.S. currency and other liquid claims not accounted for elsewhere.

Note.—Detail will not necessarily add to totals because of rounding.

Sources: Department of Commerce and Board of Governors of the Federal Reserve System.

It is useful to distinguish net payments resulting from merchandise trade, services, unilateral transfers, and long-term investment—the so-called basic accounts—from net payments resulting from the more volatile, and sometimes substantial, flows of short-term capital. The balance on basic accounts and the over-all balance are shown in Table 17 and Chart 11. In 1959 the "basic" deficit was larger than the over-all deficit because of net inflows of short-term capital, while in 1960 and again in 1961 the over-all deficit exceeded the deficit on basic accounts as a result of net outflows of short-term capital.

The *over-all balance* exerts a significant influence on the liquidity position of the United States. The change in the U.S. position resulting from over-all deficits in the past decade can be seen from the reduction in the monetary gold stock and the increase in U.S. liquid liabilities to foreigners, shown in Table 18 and Chart 12.

Reserves and liquid liabilities. In 1949, the United States held 70 percent of the world monetary gold stock and half of the world total of official gold and foreign exchange reserves. Capital seeking haven from the political disruptions of the 1930's, followed by the import needs of war-torn Europe, produced this undue concentration of world reserves. In those

CHART 11

Balance of Trade and Payments

BILLIONS OF DOLLARS

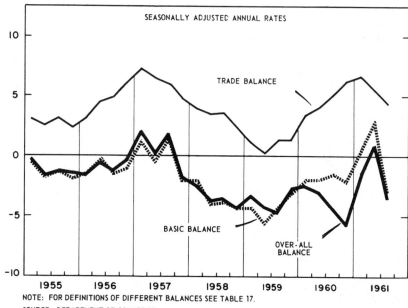

NOTE: FOR DEFINITIONS OF DIFFERENT BALANCES SEE TABLE 17.
SOURCE: DEPARTMENT OF COMMERCE.

circumstances, deficits in the U.S. balance of payments served the very useful function of rebuilding the depleted reserves of other countries.

Countries chose to replenish reserves largely by holding dollars rather than by purchasing gold. While cumulative deficits totaled $23 billion in the past 12 years (Chart 12), U.S. gold sales amounted to just $7 billion, of which $5 billion represented reacquisition of gold that the United States had obtained in the early postwar period. The rest of the deficit was settled by an increase in foreign dollar holdings.

Despite the continuous rise in foreign dollar holdings, the liquidity position of the United States is strong. The importance of the United States in international trade and international banking, the facilities offered by the New York money market, and the variety and quality of goods, services, and securities which dollars command within the United States make it advantageous for foreigners to hold large dollar balances. These working balances will not readily be withdrawn, although they are not entirely insensitive to yield opportunities abroad. Furthermore, as world trade expands, the size of these working balances is likely to rise.

The present position of the United States is satisfactory as long as foreign holders of dollars are confident that the gold value of the currency will be maintained. Loss of confidence can, however, result in a serious "run." Indeed—as the failures of basically sound and solvent commercial banks before the days of deposit insurance testify—there is no conceivable liquidity position which can withstand general loss of confidence.

Payments deficits and gold losses. As U.S. experience in the past 12 years indicates, there is only a loose link between external deficits and gold losses. Deficits occur when total payments to foreigners exceed total receipts from foreigners; a decline in gold reserves occurs when a foreign government or central bank converts dollars into gold at the U.S. Treasury. A deficit in the balance of payments need not, and usually does not, coincide with an equal decline in gold reserves. Foreigners may increase their dollar holdings by part or all of the deficit—or, as happened in 1956, even by more than the deficit (Chart 12). Similarly, this country may lose gold even when it has a balance of payments surplus, if foreign official institutions wish to convert dollars acquired in the past.

Payments deficits contribute indirectly to gold losses by adding to the supply of dollars in foreign hands, thus increasing the likelihood that they will be acquired by governments which may wish to convert them into gold. Moreover, the fact that there are persistent payments deficits may reduce foreigners' willingness to hold dollars.

Three years of large payments deficits contributed to a temporary decline in confidence in the dollar and to the large gold sales of late 1960. An outflow of short-term funds began in mid-1960 as a normal response to higher interest rates abroad, but it was augmented when doubts arose about the stability of the dollar, as evidenced by substantial private purchases of gold on the London market. These doubts reflected a number of factors: the large payments deficits of 1958 and 1959 and the loss of gold associated with them, the outflow of funds early in 1960 associated with differentials in interest rates, the initial rise in the London gold price, and fears that strong action to defend the dollar would not be taken. Confidence was restored when the new Administration declared and demonstrated its determination to defend the dollar, intensified measures taken by the previous Administration to reduce the payments deficit, and inaugurated new measures.

Recent Developments Affecting the U.S. Payments Position

Although the United States has been running deficits in its international accounts since 1950, these deficits were moderate in amount and did not cause concern until 1958. Concern has arisen since then, partly because of the unexpected persistence of large deficits and partly because the deficits could not be attributed to temporary developments likely to be soon reversed. Several significant new factors changed the U.S. position in the world economy: (1) The establishment of external currency convertibility by most of the European countries at the end of 1958 removed an important barrier to international capital flows. (2) The establishment of the European Economic Community promised a large, rapidly growing, tariff-free market in Europe, holding out much the same investment opportunities as the

CHART 12

Changes in U. S. Gold Stock
and Liquid Liabilities to Foreigners
(Annual and Cumulative)

BILLIONS OF DOLLARS

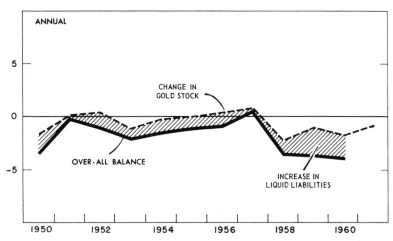

BILLIONS OF DOLLARS

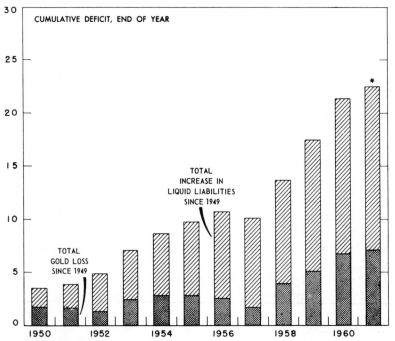

*FIRST 3 QUARTERS.

SOURCES: DEPARTMENT OF COMMERCE, TREASURY DEPARTMENT, AND BOARD OF GOVERNORS
OF THE FEDERAL RESERVE SYSTEM.

tariff-free internal market of the United States. (3) Intercontinental ballistic missiles and restoration of political stability in Western Europe reduced the special attractions of the United States as a haven for funds and as a location for capital investment. (4) The large overseas military expenditures and extensive foreign aid programs of the United States came to be clearly recognized as long-term commitments. (5) The decline of the U.S. trade surplus, from $6 billion in 1957 to a postwar low of $1 billion in 1959, focused attention on the long-run improvement in the competitive position of Western European countries and Japan relative to the United States—an improvement caused mainly by remarkable advances in output and productivity in those countries. (6) In addition, a sharp rise in certain key prices in the United States relative to those of major competitors weakened the competitiveness of some U.S. products in world markets. (This development is described in Chapter 4.) (7) By 1958, gold and foreign exchange reserves of many European countries had been rebuilt from their depleted postwar levels; U.S. payments deficits were no longer needed for this purpose.

These developments occurred within a short span of years and affected not only the U.S. payments position itself but attitudes and expectations about its future. The U.S. economy, which was geared to the entirely different environment of the years of "dollar shortage," suddenly had to adjust to a new situation. In brief, the required readjustment is that the United States must pay for overseas military commitments, grants, and investments to a greater extent by an export surplus earned in stiff world competition, and to a lesser extent by selling gold and accumulating liquid liabilities to foreigners. For the domestic economy, this implies changes in the structure of prices, wages, investment, and employment and a new orientation of American enterprise to world markets. A complete readjustment of this nature takes time.

POLICIES TO IMPROVE THE U.S. PAYMENTS POSITION

In the new environment of the 1960's, the United States cannot continue deficits of the size of the late 1950's. The balance of payments objective for the United States is to attain, at high employment levels, a balanced position in its basic international accounts during the next few years. We must move toward equilibrium at a pace which demonstrates clearly that the balance of payments is under control.

The objective of a balanced basic position does not mean that balance must be maintained continuously. In some years, a surplus in international payments will be appropriate; in other years, a deficit. But the average position over a period of years must be strong enough to maintain confidence in the parity of the dollar.

The primary task is to improve the position of the basic accounts. Progress toward balance in these accounts will itself diminish the likelihood of sustained short-term capital outflows. Therefore, in a discussion of prospects and policies for improving the balance of payments position, it is convenient to discuss, first, the basic accounts, and then the short-term capital account.

Basic Accounts

The underlying trend of the basic accounts position is not easy to discern from current quarterly and yearly statistics. It is difficult to disentangle movements of lasting significance from changes resulting from seasonal, cyclical, and random factors. When, in the first half of 1961, slack in the U.S. economy combined with boom conditions in Europe and Japan to bring our basic accounts into temporary surplus, it would have been clearly wrong to conclude that the problem was permanently solved. Conversely, subsequent reappearance of a deficit on basic accounts, which may even rise temporarily as recovery proceeds in the United States, reflects a reversal of cyclical influences rather than a deterioration in the underlying position. Long-run improvement resulting from competitive adjustments and government policies may be masked by temporary developments here and abroad.

The dimensions of the problem facing the United States may be indicated by the basic international accounts in the six-month period embracing the second and third quarters of 1961—the latest 6 months for which complete information is available—expressed in terms of annual rates (Table 19). Overseas military expenditures, less foreign military purchases in this country, were running at $2.4 billion in mid-1961. Government grants and loans amounted to $3.7 billion, but $2.5 billion of these resulted directly in the export of U.S. goods and services, leaving $1.2 billion to be otherwise financed. Long-term private investment abroad was running at about $2.0 billion, and pensions and remittances to foreigners cost nearly $900 million.

The overseas commitments and investments, resulting in payments of $6.4 billion (2.4 + 1.2 + 2.0 + 0.9, rounded), must somehow be financed by net receipts from other transactions. This requirement was partially met by debt repayments by foreign governments (excluding special prepayments in April) and net earnings on services (excluding military transactions and receipts associated with government aid) amounting to $2.2 billion at an annual rate. Full balance in the basic accounts would, therefore, have required a merchandise trade surplus (excluding exports financed directly by government grants and loans) of $4.2 billion. This contrasts with the trade surplus of $2.8 billion actually achieved. The resulting deficit of $1.4 billion had to be financed by a sale of gold and an increase in our liquid liabilities to foreigners.

Without temporary cyclical factors, the gap would probably somewhat exceed the deficit of $1.4 billion on basic accounts actually experienced during this period, since our gross national product (GNP) was still far below full employment levels. At full employment, imports can be expected to be higher than they were in mid-1961.

TABLE 19.—*United States balance of international payments, 1960–61*

[Millions of dollars, seasonally adjusted]

Type of transaction	1960, fourth quarter	1961			
		First quarter	Second quarter	Third quarter [1]	Second and third quarters (annual rates)
Current account and transfers, excluding major Government transactions	1,312	1,389	1,211	617	3,656
Merchandise trade balance [2]	999	1,080	911	488	2,798
Net balance on services [3]	543	519	521	340	1,722
Pensions and remittances	−230	−210	−221	−211	−864
Major Government transactions	−861	−870	[5] −713	−819	[5] −3,064
Military expenditures, net [4]	−642	−689	−611	−605	−2,432
Government grants and loans	−1,013	−1,000	−822	−1,014	−3,672
Exports of goods financed by Government grants and loans	563	580	452	605	2,114
Exports of services financed by Government grants and loans	86	107	87	115	404
Repayments of Government loans	145	132	[5] 181	80	[5] 522
Private long-term capital, net	−991	−356	−459	−542	−2,002
Balance on "basic" accounts (entries above)	−540	163	[5] 39	−744	[5] −1,410
U.S. short-term capital and foreign commercial credit	−567	−484	−31	−240	−542
Errors and omissions	−327	−25	−409	125	−568
Over-all balance [deficit (−)]	−1,434	−346	[5] −401	−859	[5] −2,520

[1] Preliminary.
[2] Excludes exports of goods financed by Government grants and loans.
[3] Excludes military expenditures, net, and exports of services financed by Government grants and loans.
[4] Includes private expenditures of foreign exchange by United States forces and their dependents; net of foreign military purchases in the United States.
[5] Excludes $649 million in receipts from foreign governments through extraordinary debt repayments.

Note.—Minus signs indicate payments to foreigners.

Source: Based on Department of Commerce data.

The payments position in the second and third quarters of 1961 reflects to only a small extent the impact of government balance of payments policies initiated during the year. The full effects of these measures, and of further measures planned or proposed, will take time. So will the full response of U.S. industry to the increased competitive challenge from abroad and to the improvement in the U.S. competitive position achieved in the past two years. But the gap to be narrowed and eventually closed is not large, less than 10 percent of our exports of goods and services and less than one-half of 1 percent of our GNP. Though it will take time to make the needed adjustments and for their effects to outweigh unfavorable cyclical factors, U.S. international reserves provide ample means to cover interim deficits on the basic accounts.

Improvement in the U.S. balance of payments is more than a U.S. problem. Our deficit is matched by corresponding surpluses elsewhere, especially in Europe. Unless the surplus countries allow their surpluses to decline, we cannot reduce our deficit without accentuating the payments problems of other deficit countries. Surplus and deficit countries bear joint responsibility for rectifying payments imbalances and for maintaining the stability of the international monetary system during the period of adjustment.

Reducing the basic deficit involves either diminishing the outflows on government and net capital account or increasing the current account surplus. Both these approaches are being taken. Measures to reduce the payments deficit must be consistent with the primary objectives of U.S. policy: to fulfill foreign economic and military obligations, to encourage the flow of goods, services, and capital among nations, and to expand the U.S. economy. There is no single dramatic cure-all for the payments problem. Accordingly, the Administration is pursuing a variety of measures on many fronts.

Military outlays. U.S. military outlays in foreign countries have averaged nearly $3 billion annually during the last six years even after foreign purchases of military equipment in the United States are deducted. These overseas expenditures by and for U.S. forces—for construction, logistical support, services, and personal purchases—are an integral part of the national defense effort. In addition, the United States provides substantial military grants in kind, valued at $1.8 billion in 1960, to the governments of friendly nations.

The Department of Defense has taken several measures to conserve foreign exchange, including increased procurement of its supplies from U.S. sources even at higher cost to the federal budget.

More than half of the military outlays are in Europe. The Berlin situation is causing an increase in these outlays. The United States is currently discussing with the Federal Republic of Germany and other NATO Allies measures which would have the effect of offsetting these dollar outlays for defense purposes. The Federal Republic of Germany is already making a substantial contribution in this regard. It is the objective of the Administration to work out arrangements which would offset as much of our overseas military expenditures as is feasible.

Government loans and grants. Government loans and grants have shifted markedly since the early 1950's from European countries and Japan to the less developed countries, and have risen from $2.5 billion annually in the mid-1950's to an annual rate of $3.8 billion during the first three quarters of 1961. Repayments on past government loans rose steadily during the 1950's, and in 1960 they exceeded $600 million.

The growing size of our aid expenditures reflects the pressing needs of the less developed countries for capital. The recent U.S. payments deficits, however, have necessitated policies to reduce the foreign exchange cost of these programs. The President has instructed the aid agencies to tie development aid directly to purchases of U.S. goods and services wherever possible. In the first nine months of 1961, before this policy had taken full effect, nearly 70 percent of government loans and grant disbursements resulted directly in the export of U.S. goods and services.

Though a policy of tied aid may be unavoidable under present conditions, it has the twofold disadvantage of reducing the efficiency of a given level of aid and of shielding some U.S. export industries from foreign competition. When the United States achieves over-all balance in its international accounts, it will be appropriate to discuss with European countries, Japan, and Canada the possibility of putting all the development aid of industrial countries on an untied basis.

The United States has encouraged other industrial countries to increase their aid efforts and to provide aid on an untied basis when their payments positions permit. Recent arrangements among several industrial countries to provide assistance for the development programs of India and Pakistan are examples of a new cooperative approach. Increased flows of development capital are of vital importance not only to the developing countries but also to the industrial countries, which will be able to sell to a vastly expanded market as the incomes and foreign exchange earnings of the less developed countries rise.

Private long-term investment. A highly developed economy like that of the United States today is quite naturally a source of capital for investment beyond, as well as within, its borders. This country is the world's largest source of savings. Since the United States is far ahead of many countries both in applied technology and in productive facilities per worker, there are bound to be attractive opportunities abroad for duplicating our advanced techniques of production.

Private long-term investment averaged $2.6 billion a year in the last five years, substantially higher than in the early 1950's. In addition, reinvested earnings of U.S. subsidiaries abroad averaged $1.1 billion annually. In 1961, U.S. private long-term investment abroad is estimated to have been about $2.3 billion.

While outflows of U.S. capital are adding to our national wealth foreign properties which may yield substantial return flows of earnings in the balance of payments over future years, these outflows increase the payments deficit in the short run.

Since 1958–59, the share of U.S. direct investment outflows going toward Europe has increased substantially. The promise of an expanding European Common Market has enhanced the attractiveness of Europe as a location for production. Flows of saving to develop productive opportunities abroad increase the efficiency of the world economy. However, capital is not allocated efficiently when it moves primarily in response to tax advantages or to restrictive or discriminatory trade barriers abroad. If the President's trade program is enacted and the new common external tariff in Europe is reduced through negotiations, artificial incentives to invest behind the European tariff wall will be reduced. This is one important way in which an expansionist trade policy will improve the U.S. payments position.

The Administration has also proposed changes in the tax treatment of foreign income which, in addition to achieving greater equity relative to tax treatment of domestic income, will ease our balance of payments deficit. Under the President's proposal, earnings on U.S. investments in other industrial countries would be taxed on the same basis as corporate earnings in the United States. This would be achieved by taxing U.S. corporations each year on their current share of the undistributed profits realized in that year by subsidiary corporations organized in economically advanced countries. Any decline in the outflow of U.S. capital resulting from a withdrawal of existing tax inducements would be consistent both with efficiency in the allocation of capital resources in the world and with equity between U.S. firms operating abroad and competing firms located in the United States. Legislation has also been proposed which would curtail tax haven privileges.

An additional proposal, discussed in earlier chapters, would provide a tax credit to spur domestic investment.

These measures, along with rising domestic activity, would increase the relative attractiveness of domestic, as opposed to foreign, investment. A higher rate of domestic economic expansion would increase the attractiveness of the United States for investment by foreigners.

The United States is urging countries in Western Europe to liberalize restrictions on the outflow of capital owned by their residents in order to permit more foreign capital issues to be offered in their markets and to permit more investment in the United States and in underdeveloped countries. Many European countries still limit foreign issues in their capital markets and control tightly purchases of foreign securities by their residents.

Services. Net exports of services, excluding military expenditures and sales, were at an annual rate of $2.3 billion during the first three quarters of 1961. These services include travel expenditures, transportation services, royalties, interest, and dividends. Repatriated earnings on U.S. investments abroad, which are counted as receipts for services in the balance of payments accounts, amounted to $3.2 billion in 1960. Our expenditures on foreign travel were $1.7 billion, and foreigners spent nearly $1.0 billion in this country.

During 1961, an Office of Tourism was established in the Department of Commerce to encourage foreign travel to the United States. In addition, the duty-free tourist allowance for returning U.S. travelers was reduced from $500 to $100 a person.

The proposed change in tax provisions regarding overseas investment should result in an increase in the repatriation of earnings from U.S. investments abroad.

Merchandise trade. Merchandise trade has earned large net receipts in every year since the war. The trade surplus has on average increased, but it has not increased sufficiently to cover the combined rise in overseas military, foreign aid, and investment outlays.

Restrictive commercial policies would be one way to try to check imports and increase the trade surplus. But raising tariffs and imposing quotas, while perhaps improving the trade position temporarily, would be inconsistent with the liberal trade objectives of the United States and would invite retaliatory action abroad, thus reversing any temporary gains.

Imports could also be checked by restraining domestic economic activity. But this would be an absurdly costly policy for the United States because imports comprise only a small part of each dollar of final demand. To obtain a $1 billion reduction in imports might require a $25–35 billion reduction of GNP. Even this decrease in imports would not result in an equivalent improvement in the trade balance, for, as the dollar earnings of other countries declined, some of our best customers would curtail their purchases in the United States. Moreover, the prospects for fundamental balance of payments improvement would be dim in a continuously slack economy beset by excess capacity and deficient in incentives to make investments at home which raise productivity and lower costs. Sacrificing recovery for a temporary gain in the balance of payments position would be shortsighted and would not inspire confidence in the dollar.

Clearly, our efforts to improve the trade position must be expansive rather than restrictive. A program has been established under the direction of the Department of Commerce to promote exports, both by increasing awareness among U.S. businessmen of sales opportunities abroad and by increasing foreign awareness of the wide array and high quality of U.S. products. The program includes regional conferences and a more active field service in the United States to provide information on foreign markets, trade exhibits and missions abroad, and an increased number of government commercial representatives to aid the U.S. businessman abroad.

In addition to improving the flow of information about export possibilities, steps have been taken to improve U.S. competitiveness in the important dimensions of credit availability and export insurance for commercial and political risks—steps designed to place the U.S. businessman on a par with foreign exporters. The Export-Import Bank has established, in cooperation with the commercial banks and a group of insurance companies, simplified and expanded opportunities for obtaining credit and export insurance. An exporter is now able to arrange for full credit and insurance advantages directly with his local bank.

A fundamental requirement for increasing our trade balance is a domestic environment of full recovery and growth without inflation. We must exploit the gains in productivity available from bringing into full use the excess capacity now prevalent in U.S. industry, and we must speed the advance of U.S. technology. The measures to accelerate the growth of productivity outlined in Chapter 2 are, for these reasons, essential elements of policy for long-run improvement in the balance of payments. In particular, the tax credit for investment proposed by the President and the revision of depreciation guidelines underway at the Treasury will promote investment at home and make American industry more competitive. It is true that economic growth, by raising incomes in the United States, will tend to increase the purchases of foreign goods by U.S. consumers and businesses. But economic growth achieved through advances in productivity and improvements in technology will also enable U.S. goods to compete more effectively with foreign products both in the United States and in foreign markets. The technological leadership and high productivity of the United States have proved in the past to be vital sources of our comparative advantage in world markets. And today, the most rapidly growing countries in the free world generally rank among those with the strongest international payments positions.

An accelerated advance in productivity will be of little help to the balance of payments, however, if the improvements are eroded away by increases in money costs and prices. The price increases of 1955–57 impaired the competitive position of several important U.S. industries in world markets. More recently, price and wage developments in the United States have been favorable relative to those in other countries. The stability of U.S. prices in the last three years, and the reasons for optimism concerning U.S. prices in the current economic recovery, are discussed in Chapter 4. Policies to avoid cost inflation at home can be reinforced by a liberal trade policy which expands the area of international competition to which U.S. producers are exposed.

The future course of exports will depend not only on U.S. policies but also on business activity, prices and wages, and commercial policy abroad. Successful international trade negotiations under the proposed Trade Expansion Act will provide increasing opportunities for U.S. exports. In addition, the United States continues to press for the elimination of open and concealed discrimination against U.S. goods—agricultural products provide outstanding examples—and against the products of third countries, many of which are good customers of the United States.

The continued expansion of the European economies is of great importance for the future of U.S. exports. And the rapid growth of all the industrial countries is of vital concern to the primary producing countries whose exports have been largely stagnant in recent years. As the exports of the primary producing countries increase, their purchases from the United States and other industrial countries will expand.

Short-Term Capital Account

Dollars are transferred to foreigners not only through deficits in the basic accounts of the United States, but also through short-term lending by Americans to foreigners. Much of this lending is commercially oriented and often provides financing for American exports. During the first half of 1961, for example, a large part of the short-term capital outflow from the United States was used to finance an increase in exports from the United States and other countries to Japan. An increase in such commercial credit will be a natural consequence of policies taken during 1961 to boost U.S. exports.

However, some flows of short-term capital are not linked directly to export financing. These flows of funds, both U.S. and foreign owned, have increased markedly since the establishment of external currency convertibility of the leading European countries in 1958, the relaxation of restrictions on capital transactions by their own nationals, and the re-establishment of confidence in the stability of European currencies.

Short-term capital movements are sensitive to differences in interest rates between major financial centers. In late 1960, for example, when yields on short-term securities were substantially higher in Canadian and European markets than in the United States, a significant volume of U.S. funds moved abroad. Again in the last few months of 1961 substantial amounts of capital moved abroad to benefit from higher yields.

Liquid funds also move in hope or fear of changes in exchange rates or regulations. For example, the revaluations of the German mark and the Dutch guilder in March 1961 led to expectations of further revaluations and resulted in large short-term capital flows. Movements of this kind often reflect objective factors related to basic balance of payments positions. But they sometimes respond to rumor and opinion unrelated to the basic situation.

A notable feature of the U.S. balance of payments in the past two years was the sharp swing in the balancing item, "errors and omissions," from a net inflow through 1959 of some $500 million a year to a net outflow of $650 million in 1960 and a further $400 million in the first half of 1961. Preliminary estimates for late 1961 also show a large unrecorded outflow. This change no doubt reflected a sizable transfer of U.S. capital abroad and a withdrawal of foreign private capital, both of which moved outside channels normally covered by our recording network.

Flows of short-term capital, although they frequently perform a useful function, can be seriously disruptive. They can be large, sudden, erratic, contagious, and self-reinforcing. Monetary authorities are gradually adjusting their policies and techniques to cope with these flows. During the past two years, several steps were taken to reduce the incentive to shift capital among financial centers. Foremost among these was increasing cooperation among central banks to avoid large differentials in short-term interest rates among countries. High interest rates in Europe were lowered in late 1960 and early 1961. U.S. monetary policy and technique have been adapted to the new international financial environment in the manner described in Chapter 1. Although the Federal Reserve has maintained generally easy money and credit conditions, U.S. short-term rates have been held above levels characteristic of previous recession and recovery periods.

In December 1961, the Board of Governors of the Federal Reserve System and the Federal Deposit Insurance Corporation raised permissible interest rates on commercial-bank time deposits. The ceiling rate for deposits exceeding 12 months was raised from 3 percent to 4 percent a year.   As banks move rates up to the new ceilings, they will increase the attractiveness of holding funds in the United States.

Finally, the U.S. Treasury has, for the first time since the mid-1930's, engaged in foreign exchange operations in cooperation with foreign central banks.   The Treasury this year undertook transactions in German marks and Swiss francs, both on a current basis and in the forward exchange market.   The aim was to increase the cost to traders and investors of exchange risk "cover" for movements out of dollars, diminishing the incentive to shift funds abroad and increasing the incentive to move funds here.

Although these policies will moderate the disruptive flows of short-term capital, they cannot eliminate them.   Further measures are therefore needed to neutralize or minimize the possible effects of such flows on the international monetary system.

MEASURES TO STRENGTHEN THE WORLD MONETARY SYSTEM

Stability of the present world monetary system depends upon confidence in the value of the dollar.   Therefore, a primary aim of the United States and of other countries must be to correct the underlying conditions which result in persistent U.S. deficits and persistent surpluses elsewhere.   This is fundamental, but it will take time.

While policies to achieve this fundamental adjustment are taking effect, full confidence must be maintained in the ability of the United States to meet foreign demands for gold.   There are a number of measures which can strengthen the "banking" or liquidity position of the United States while the fundamental adjustment of the payments position proceeds. Some of them apply to the dollar alone; others are general measures to strengthen the world monetary system.   All of them require a high degree of international consultation and cooperation.

One means of strengthening the U.S. liquidity position, as well as its payments position: at a given time, is to obtain advance repayment of long-term debts owed to the U.S. Government.   For example, in April the Federal Republic of Germany prepaid $587 million to the United States.   This translated a long-term U.S. asset partly into a reduction of short-term U.S. liabilities and partly into a rise in U.S. holdings of German marks.   The United States still has outstanding about $2 billion of long-term loans to countries that have strong payments positions.

The gross reserve position can also be strengthened by borrowing directly in foreign currencies from other governments or central banks.   This device was employed recently on a small scale when the United States borrowed from Switzerland $46 million in Swiss francs in order to support forward exchange operations of the Treasury.

Recently, there has been increasing recognition that, even when large movements of private short-term capital cannot be prevented, they can be offset by reverse movements of official capital. In March 1961, several central banks agreed through the so-called Basle arrangements to extend short-term credit to the United Kingdom to offset the flight of private funds from London.

Several countries now consider their drawing rights on the International Monetary Fund as an integral part of their foreign exchange reserves. In his Balance of Payments Message of February 6, 1961, President Kennedy stated that "access to the Fund's resources must be regarded as a part of our international reserves" and that, if appropriate, the United States would use its drawing rights. The drawing from the Fund of currencies equivalent to $1.5 billion by the United Kingdom in August, and the prompt repayment of $420 million as British reserves rose, indicate the flexibility with which drawing rights on the Fund can be used to supplement reserves. Furthermore, in accordance with recent IMF policy, member countries have increasingly made drawings in currencies other than the dollar, which the Fund formerly relied on heavily for most of its operations. This policy puts to effective use the Fund's holdings of the currencies of surplus countries. But the Fund's holdings of some of these currencies may not be fully adequate to meet the potential demands for them.

Improvement of the Fund's access to the currencies of the major industrial countries was discussed at the annual Fund meeting in Vienna in September. It was announced in early January that ten industrial countries have agreed to lend amounts of their currencies totaling $6 billion, to the Fund if these resources should be required to forestall or cope with an impairment of the international monetary system. Availability of these special resources should enable the Fund better to perform its function of financing temporary payments deficits in the interests of maintaining general exchange rate stability.

In his February Message the President said, "Increasing international monetary reserves will be required to support the ever-growing volume of trade, services and capital movements among the countries of the free world. Until now the free nations have relied upon increased gold production and continued growth in holdings of dollars and pounds sterling. In the future, it may not always be desirable or appropriate to rely entirely on these sources. We must now, in cooperation with other lending countries, begin to consider ways in which international monetary institutions— especially the International Monetary Fund—can be strengthened and more effectively utilized, both in furnishing needed increases in reserves, and in providing the flexibility required to support a healthy and growing world economy."

The agreement to supplement the resources of the Fund is an important step toward strengthening the international monetary system to meet the demands which the continuing economic progress of the free world will place upon it in the future.

Finally, the newly created Organization for Economic Cooperation and Development, comprising 18 European countries, the United States, and Canada, provides a continuing forum in which payments imbalances and internal or international monetary problems of concern to all members—as well as trade, development aid and other matters of common interest—can be discussed frankly and constructively. Still another forum for international cooperation is provided by the monthly meetings of central bankers at the Bank for International Settlements in Basle. Although the United States is not a member of the Bank for International Settlements, representatives of the Federal Reserve System participate informally in the discussions.

These measures of cooperation among nations, together with the large gold reserves of the United States, give this country the time to carry through the necessary adjustment in its balance of payments—and to carry it through in ways consistent with general economic expansion at home and abroad, with promotion of a world economy in which goods, services, and capital flow freely, and with the responsibilities of world leadership. They give us time, but not time to waste.

Chapter 4

Price Behavior in a Free and Growing Economy

The Objectives

PRICE BEHAVIOR embraces both changes in the over-all *level* of prices throughout the economy and changes in price *structure*—the relation of particular prices to each other. Changes in either the level or the structure of prices have far-reaching influences which can affect for better or worse the performance of a free economy. Both aspects of price behavior are closely related to major problems which confront the U.S. economy today.

Our success in solving the international payments problem (discussed in the previous chapter) will depend to a major extent on our ability to avoid inflation. To recognize this compelling reason for price stability is not to say that stable prices are desirable only for their contribution to the achievement of equilibrium in our balance of payments. Even creeping inflation has effects on the distribution of income which are always capricious and often cruel, and it may generate perverse changes in the structure of prices. Galloping inflation is profoundly disruptive of economic efficiency and growth. But to these persisting arguments for avoiding inflation is now added the pressing and immediate need to strengthen the competitiveness of U.S. industry in world markets.

International competitiveness is affected by many considerations, including quality, variety, service, credit facilities, and promptness in delivery. But after full weight is given to these considerations, price remains at the heart of the matter. The effect of price developments on our international competitive position will not, of course, be determined by the behavior of U.S. prices alone; what counts is the change in the ratio of U.S. prices to the prices of those countries with which we compete in world markets. There is independent reason to expect in the next few years a moderate upward price trend in some competitive countries, but a decline in the ratio of our prices to theirs is obviously more likely if our own prices remain stable than if they rise.

Large potential gains in national economic welfare are at stake in the course of price developments over the next year or two. Stable prices—together with the many other measures to strengthen our payments position discussed in Chapter 3—will move us toward equilibrium in our international payments.   This, in turn, will remove a possible impediment to the vigorous pursuit of full employment.

It is always possible to strengthen the balance of payments, at least for a time, by weakening the economy.   Checking and reversing the economic expansion would reduce our demand for imports by reducing our demand for all goods and services.   Raising interest rates sharply would probably attract some foreign capital to the United States, but it would raise the cost and reduce the volume of domestic expenditures for new business plant and equipment and residential construction.   This road to balance of payments equilibrium endangers the interests of the whole Nation and specifically the interests both of labor and of business; for the former it increases unemployment, while for the latter it lowers profits.   Both groups stand to gain from price level stability, which lays the foundation for the harmonious coexistence of balance of payments equilibrium with full employment and rapid economic growth.

Price level stability does not, of course, require stability of all prices. On the contrary, the structure of relative prices constitutes the central nervous system of a decentralized economy.   Changing relative prices are the signals and stimuli which foster the efficiency and guide the growth of such an economy.

Changing relative prices serve to ration scarce goods and services.   They encourage consumers and business firms to economize on the use of things which have grown scarcer, and to use more freely those things which have become more abundant.   They attract resources into the production of those things for which demand has increased, and encourage the outflow of resources from the production of things for which demand has declined. They provide generous rewards to innovators, and then assure that the benefits arising from innovation are widely diffused throughout the economy. They direct economic activity into the most productive channels.   A smoothly functioning price system, while it cannot solve all of the resource-use problems of our economy, is nevertheless an indispensable agent for reconciling decentralized private decision-making with national economic objectives.

In the context of current economic policy goals, flexible relative prices play an important role in encouraging maximum production and shaping the pattern of growth.   As the economy approaches full utilization of productive resources, premature and stubborn bottlenecks may arise in some sectors while labor and capital are underutilized elsewhere.   This danger is lessened if productive resources are sufficiently mobile to shift promptly into the sectors of the economy which are coming under pressure. Flexible price and wage relationships are not in themselves sufficient to assure that capital and labor will flow from relatively declining to relatively expanding sectors.   But flexible price and wage relationships can smooth the process, both by signaling the directions in which resource movements should occur, and by providing incentives to encourage such shifts. Prices must fall as well as rise, however, if changing relative prices are to play their role in guiding resource movements without forcing a steady rise in the over-all level of prices.

The Present Situation

Price Developments in Perspective

The frequent characterization of the postwar period as generally "inflationary" obscures two important facts. First, increases in wholesale prices were concentrated in three periods: 1946–48, 1950, and 1955–57. In the other 9 of the 16 postwar years taken together, the net movement of wholesale prices was downward. Second, since the middle of 1958, the wholesale price level in the United States has been stable, and there are signs that the inflationary impulses set off by the second World War and reinforced by the Korean conflict have been weakening.

War-induced inflation. By far the strongest burst of inflation occurred immediately after the end of the war, and for obvious reasons. The stock of consumers' and producers' durable goods had been depleted during the long years of depression and war. Private debt had been reduced, and the heavy reliance on public debt financing of the war had provided households and firms with large supplies of liquid assets.

The result was a demand for consumer goods and plant and equipment which far exceeded the capacity of the economy to produce them. Although the Federal Government ran a substantial cash surplus in the 1946–48 period, which had the effect of reducing total demand for goods and services, aggregate demand nevertheless outran supply until late in 1948. From the end of the war through September 1948, the consumer price index rose by 35.2 percent, and the wholesale price index by 54.4 percent. In the recession which followed, both consumer and wholesale prices fell, the former by 1.9 percent between November 1948 and October 1949, the latter by 6.5 percent.

A new burst of excess-demand inflation was set off by the Korean hostilities. Between June 1950 and February 1951, consumer prices rose by 8.0 percent and wholesale prices by 16.3 percent, as consumers and businesses, remembering the shortages of 1942–45, scrambled to build up stocks of goods.

These two inflationary episodes account for 70 percent of the increase in the level of consumer prices since the second World War, and more than account for the increase in the wholesale price level. Costs rose steeply in these periods, but the major force pulling prices upward was clearly pressure of excessive demand for a wide range of products.

Post-Korean price stability. The scare-buying of late 1950 and early 1951 drove prices to a level from which a mild reaction set in. From mid-1951 to mid-1955, except for construction costs and the index of services to consumers, most price indexes remained stable or fell. Consumer prices for food and other commodities, as well as wholesale price indexes of farm and nonfarm commodities, were lower in mid-1955 than they had been in mid-1951, despite the fact that large parts of the economy had operated at near capacity levels from the fall of 1952 to the fall of 1953.

Construction costs failed to stabilize in the post-Korean period; while the average of wholesale prices fell by 5.7 percent between February 1951 and May 1955, the Department of Commerce index of construction costs rose by 8.8 percent.

Another exception to this record of stability—consumer services—is highly important. Services have a weight of about one-third in the consumer price index. Prices of services, taken as a group, have risen in every year since the war, and have accounted for much of the rise in the consumer price index.

Because of the heterogeneous character of the services category, no single explanation can account for the behavior of the services index. Some tentative observations may be made, however, about the forces influencing the prices of particular services. *Residential occupancy* costs, with a weight of about 42 percent within the services category, include rents, mortgage payments and interest, real estate taxes, and property insurance. Rents and home prices tend to be influenced in the short run by the vacancy rate, and in the long run by changes in construction costs, interest rates, and property taxes. Movements in all these components tended to push the index upward in the postwar period. In addition, the retention of rent controls in some important areas well into the postwar period tended to delay the adjustment of rents to market forces. *Medical care service* prices, with a weight of about 14 percent, have been rising steeply. This is a sector, however, in which there has probably been a substantial improvement in the quality of services. If it were possible to take account of quality changes in the index, the rate of increase would have been less. *Regulated utility services* (telephone, gas, electricity, and water), with a combined weight of about 10 percent, are subject to substantial price lags. Depreciation costs recognized for rate-making purposes have tended to rise as the share of low-priced prewar capital goods in the rate base has diminished and the share of higher-priced postwar goods has increased. *Public transportation services* (transit fares and railroad fares), with a combined weight of about 4 percent, may have been influenced to a limited extent by the same forces mentioned in connection with regulated utility services, and to a further extent by the effects of declining demand on unit cost in industries where overhead costs are high. *Personal care services* (men's haircuts and certain beauty parlor services), with a weight of about 3 percent, are services not readily susceptible to improvements in labor productivity, though wages in this sector tend to move up in step with economy-wide trends.

Inflation, 1955–58. The relative price stability which began in 1951 gave way in 1955 to renewed inflationary pressure which persisted into early

1958. Although prices rose far less sharply than in 1946–48 or 1950–51, consumer prices rose by 8.0 percent from May 1955 to March 1958, and wholesale prices increased by 8.9 percent.

In contrast to the two earlier inflationary bursts, there is still considerable uncertainty as to the causes of rising prices during this period. A simple explanation running in terms of over-all excess demand is not satisfactory. If aggregate excess demand prevailed at all, it existed only briefly toward the end of 1955. After the end of 1955, capacity utilization slackened as investment created capacity more rapidly than final demands were increasing. Employment of production workers in manufacturing began to decline in the latter half of 1956 and was lower in 1957 than in 1955. The average work-week in manufacturing declined over this period—from 40.7 hours in 1955 to 40.4 in 1956 to 39.8 in 1957. Unemployment as a percent of the civilian labor force, seasonally adjusted, dipped below 4.0 percent in only three months during the entire period.

Any explanation of the 1955–58 price experience must give special weight to the fact that the 1955–57 boom was concentrated in durable manufactured goods. Demand strained production capacity in the machinery and equipment industries. Except for the third quarter of 1956, in which a strike occurred, the iron and steel industry operated at a rate above 90 percent of capacity from the second quarter of 1955 through the first quarter of 1957. Automobile production set an all-time record in 1955.

In this sector of the economy, prices and wages rose sharply. More than three-fourths of the 1955–58 rise in the index of wholesale industrial prices was directly attributable to price increases in metals and metal products and machinery and motive products (including motor vehicles). Substantial employment cost increases were negotiated in the automobile settlement of 1955 and the steel settlement of 1956. Both were three-year agreements, with the result that large wage commitments made in a boom environment became effective as the economy was slowing down. Price and wage behavior in this sector initiated impulses which spread to other parts of the economy, both via increases in materials and equipment cost and via imitative influences in wage settlements.

Elements of major importance in the 1955–58 episode were thus the existence of relatively high demand, principally in one sector of the economy; the use of market power by management to maintain profit margins despite rising costs; the exercise of market power by labor unions in an effort to capture a substantial share of rising profits for their membership; and the transmission of these developments to other sectors of the economy.

One of the striking and significant aspects of the 1955–58 inflation was the leading part played by industries which are important exporters. Metals, machinery, and transport equipment make up about two-thirds of U.S. exports of manufactures. What in this context is more important, these U.S. prices rose faster than the prices for similar goods in foreign countries. To take but one example, between 1956 and 1958 U.S. steel prices rose nearly 20 percent more than the average price rise in five other major steel exporting countries.

During this period the United States experienced a noteworthy decline in its share of world exports of manufactures—from 30 percent in 1956 to 27½ percent in 1958. The decline was even sharper for some product groups; the U.S. share of world exports of iron and steel products, for example, declined from 19 percent to 14 percent. The relative increase in U.S. prices probably contributed—along with the rapid postwar growth in capacity and output abroad—to the drop in American export shares.

Price behavior since 1958. Since mid-1958, there has been stability on the average in the prices of commodities at wholesale and retail, with a continuing upward trend in consumer service prices. This record of relative price stability is in part the result of widespread excess capacity in the last few years, but it may also reflect a weakening of lagged price responses to the sharply inflationary episodes of 1946–48 and 1950–51.

An important element in the cessation of inflationary pressure has been the stability shown in the prices of metals and machinery. The index of metal and metal products, which rose by 17 percent from the beginning of 1955 to the end of 1956, and drifted irregularly upward through late 1959, has since remained below its 1959 high. The index of machinery and motive products, which rose by 22 percent from January 1955 to September 1959, has also been stable since then. Steel prices were raised once a year in the period 1952–58, for a total increase of 50 percent, but have not been raised since 1958.

Movements in construction costs are in sharp contrast to this pattern of price stability. After increasing against the general price trend over 1951–55, they rose 10.5 percent from May 1955 through March 1958— an increase significantly greater than the 8.9 percent rise in the wholesale price level over the same period. From March 1958 through December 1961, the increase was 5.8 percent.

As Chart 13 shows, a period of stability in the wholesale price index tends to be a period of slow rise in the consumer price index and in the implicit price index for GNP. The reason for the divergent behavior of consumer prices is primarily the service component already discussed; the price index for GNP rises because of the methods of measurement used for the government sector (in which no allowance is made for productivity increase), and for plant and equipment spending (where only partial allowance is made for quality change).

The chart also calls attention to an important difference between price behavior in the 1961 recovery and in the recovery of 1958. In 1958, stability in the wholesale price index resulted from a significant reduction in the prices of farm products and processed foods, balanced by a rise in industrial prices. In the first 10 months of recovery in 1958–59, the index for industrial commodities rose by 1.8 percent. By contrast, in 1961, the index of industrial prices fell by 0.3 percent between February and

CHART 13

Price Developments

INDEX, 1961 = 100 (Ratio scale)

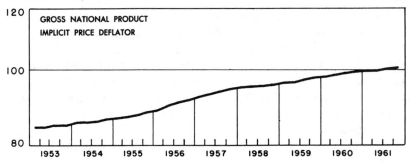

INDEX, 1947-49 = 100 (Ratio scale)

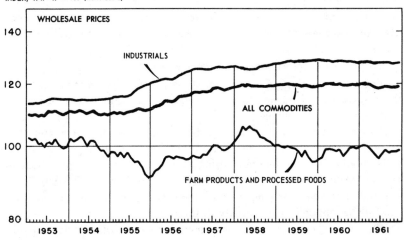

INDEX, 1947-49 = 100 (Ratio scale)

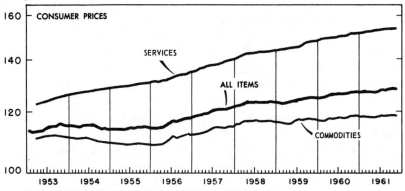

NOTE: TOP PANEL, QUARTERLY DATA; OTHER PANELS, MONTHLY DATA.

SOURCES: DEPARTMENT OF COMMERCE, DEPARTMENT OF LABOR, AND COUNCIL OF
           ECONOMIC ADVISERS.

December, reinforcing rather than offsetting a fall of 1.9 percent in farm and food prices. In all of the previous postwar recoveries, by contrast, the index of wholesale industrial prices rose over the first 10 months of recovery.

From the recession's turning point in February, through November, consumer prices rose by 0.6 percent. While this was a greater increase than the 0.2 percent by which the index rose in the first 9 months of recovery from the 1958 trough, the difference in performance is attributable to movements in the retail food index, which fell more sharply after the 1958 upturn than in 1961. The behavior of other major components was similar in the two recoveries, except for rents, which rose slightly more in 1958 than they did in 1961.

More than three-fourths of the rise in consumer prices during 1961 was attributable to higher service prices, particularly advances for health insurance and other health services, movie admissions, rent, and public transportation. Moderating the rise in the service price index were lower average mortgage interest rates and stable average prices for utilities.

Wage and Cost Developments in Perspective

Wages and salaries are at the same time the principal cost to employers, the main source of income to employees, and the major source of demand to the economy as a whole.

If living standards are to rise over time, real wages must increase. Stability in the general price level means, therefore, that average money wage rates should follow a generally rising path. As output per man-hour increases, rising money wage rates can be absorbed into stable labor costs per unit of output. So long as unit labor costs do not increase, rising wages are fully compatible with stability in the price level.

Whatever its cause, a rising price level is characteristically accompanied by a rate of wage increase in excess of the rate of increase in output per man-hour. It is quite true, of course, that when employment costs per man-hour rise more rapidly than output per man-hour, prices sooner or later will increase. But it is equally true that, when prices are pulled up by excess demand, competition for labor will tend to raise employment costs per man-hour faster than output per man-hour increases. Thus wage increases will tend to outstrip productivity increases *both* when the inflationary pressures arise from cost and when they arise from demand. The mere coexistence of rising prices and wages rising faster than productivity tells nothing about causation.

Postwar wage changes. While wages rose throughout the postwar period, they rose more rapidly in the first part of the period than in more recent years. The primary cause of the most rapid increases lies in the excess demand which was the legacy of the second World War and which arose again during the Korean mobilization. Hourly compensation in manufacturing increased at an average rate of nearly 7 percent a year between 1947 and 1953; the rate of increase fell to 5 percent between 1953 and 1957, and to less than 4 percent between 1957 and 1961 (Table 20). The period 1947–53, of course, included most of the two war-induced inflationary booms.

TABLE 20.—*Changes in compensation and productivity in all private nonagricultural industries and in manufacturing industries, 1947 to 1961*

Item	Percentage change per year			
	1947 to 1961 [1]	1947 to 1953	1953 to 1957	1957 to 1961 [1]
Private nonagricultural industries, all employees:				
Average hourly compensation [2]	5.1	6.2	4.6	4.0
Output per man-hour	2.5	2.7	2.3	2.5
Manufacturing industries, all employees:				
Average hourly compensation [2]	5.5	6.8	5.0	3.9
Output per man-hour	2.9	3.2	1.8	3.7
Manufacturing industries, production workers:				
Average gross hourly earnings	4.7	6.1	4.2	3.1
Average hourly earnings adjusted to exclude overtime and inter-industry shifts	4.7	5.9	4.2	3.4

[1] Preliminary.
[2] Wages and salaries of all employees and supplements to wages and salaries such as employer contributions for social insurance, for private pension, health, and welfare funds, for injuries, for pay of the military reserve, etc.
Sources: Department of Commerce and Department of Labor.

In the post-Korean years—a period which included three of the four postwar recessions—over-all demand conditions played a less decisive role in wage behavior. The movement of wages during this period reflected in part the power exercised in labor markets by strong unions and the power possessed by large companies to pass on higher wage costs in higher prices. Although the high demand of the 1955–57 period was concentrated in the area of durable manufactures, wages also rose by substantial increments in some less prosperous but highly organized industries.

The post-Korean years were marked by the coincidence of relatively large wage increases with declines in industry employment. Table 21 illustrates these developments as they are reflected in changes in average hourly earnings and the number of production workers for selected industries. Earnings in textiles and apparel, typically lower than the average for all manufacturing industries, fell further behind during the years 1954–61. Workers in retail trade received percentage wage increases equal to the average of those in manufacturing; the initial low wage level and the increase in employment in retailing suggest that this rise in wages reflects pressure of demand. Construction worker employment increased, and wages rose more than the average for manufacturing; indeed, over the entire postwar period, average hourly earnings in construction have risen more than 100 percent against a rise of 80 percent for production workers in manufacturing. In manufacturing and mining, unionization was undoubt-

TABLE 21.—*Changes in average hourly earnings and employment of production workers in selected industries, September 1954 to September 1961*

Industry	Average hourly earnings (dollars)		Employment (thousands)		Percentage change, September 1954 to September 1961	
	September 1954	September 1961 [1]	September 1954	September 1961 [1]	Average hourly earnings	Employment
Manufacturing [2]	1.78	2.33	12,821	12,407	31	−3
Blast furnaces and basic steel products	2.29	3.17	537	513	38	−4
Motor vehicles and equipment	2.24	2.84	479	470	27	−2
Flat glass	2.49	3.16	26	25	27	−4
Fabricated metals	1.89	2.48	835	839	31	(3)
Metal cans	1.98	2.91	55	54	47	−2
Petroleum refining	2.42	3.21	142	108	33	−24
Tires and inner tubes	2.25	3.13	84	75	39	−11
Textile-mill products	1.35	1.64	955	804	21	−16
Apparel and related products	1.38	1.65	1,065	1,082	20	2
Bituminous coal mining	2.41	3.15	201	128	31	−36
Contract construction	2.40	3.22	2,489	2,603	34	5
Class I railroads	1.94	2.69	[4] 1,064	[4] 723	39	−32
Retail trade [5]	1.30	1.70	5,589	6,096	31	9

[1] Includes data for Alaska and Hawaii.
[2] Also includes industries not shown separately.
[3] Increase of less than 0.5 percent.
[4] Data relate to all employees.
[5] Excludes eating and drinking places.
Note.—Data relate to production workers or nonsupervisory employees, except as noted.
Source: Department of Labor.

edly a factor in the increase in wages during a period of declining employment; the above-average increase in wages in construction reflects both unionization and the stimulus of strong demand.

The effect of unionization is also reflected in the contrast between earnings and employment of salaried workers in manufacturing and those of production workers in manufacturing over the period. Although aggregate salaries in manufacturing have risen twice as rapidly as aggregate wages, annual disbursements per worker for salaried workers increased at an average rate of only 3.8 percent a year during the period 1947–61, while disbursements per production worker increased at a rate of 4.9 percent. At the same time, the number of salaried workers was increasing at a rate of 3.7 percent a year, and the number of production workers declining at a rate of 0.5 percent.

Recent wage developments. Although wages and fringe benefits have continued to increase throughout the economy, the rate of increase in hourly earnings in manufacturing has declined steadily since 1957. The decline has been not only steady but large; as Table 22 demonstrates, the rate of increase in adjusted hourly earnings has fallen by one-half since 1955–56. These percentage movements are consistent with recent declines in median wage increases, measured in cents per hour, under major collective bargaining contracts. These are shown in Table 23.

TABLE 22.—*Changes in average hourly earnings and hourly compensation in manufacturing industries, 1955 to 1961*

Period	Percentage increase			
	Adjusted hourly earnings [1]		Average hourly compensation [2]	
	Current prices	Constant prices [3]	Current prices	Constant prices [3]
1955 to 1956	5.4	3.8	6.2	4.6
1956 to 1957	5.1	1.7	6.0	2.5
1957 to 1958	4.1	1.3	3.9	1.1
1958 to 1959	3.4	2.5	4.1	3.2
1959 to 1960	3.3	1.8	4.1	2.5
1960 to 1961 [3]	2.7	1.6	3.4	2.3

[1] Wages of production workers adjusted to exclude overtime and interindustry shifts.
[2] Wages and salaries of all employees and supplements to wages and salaries such as employer contributions for social insurance, for private pension, health, and welfare funds, for injuries, for pay of the military reserve, etc.
[3] Preliminary.

Sources: Department of Commerce and Department of Labor.

TABLE 23.—*Median hourly wage increases negotiated or effective in major collective bargaining situations, 1956–61*

Year	Median hourly wage increases (cents)	
	Negotiated during year	Negotiated or effective during year
1956	10.7	10.8
1957	10.6	12.7
1958	8.8	12.6
1959	8.8	8.8
1960	8.7	9.4
1961 [1]	7.0	8.0

[1] Preliminary.

NOTE.—Data are limited to major collective bargaining situations (generally those affecting 1,000 or more workers) in manufacturing and selected nonmanufacturing industries. The latter exclude construction, the service trades, finance, and government.

Source: Department of Labor.

Further evidence of this decline in the magnitude of wage increases is presented in Table 24. This table shows, for 1959–61, an increase in the number of workers affected by zero or negative wage changes and a decline in the number of workers receiving large percentage wage increases in major negotiations. The percentage of employees receiving wage increases of 3½ percent or more declined from 64 percent in 1959 to 35 percent in 1961.

Smaller percentage increases in hourly wages do not necessarily imply smaller percentage increases in real wages. In recent years, annual increases in consumer prices have tended to become smaller and thus have offset, to some extent, lower rates of increase in adjusted hourly earnings and total hourly compensation in manufacturing.

TABLE 24.—*Employees affected by major collective bargaining negotiations, by wage change, 1959–61*

Wage change	1959		1960		1961 [1]	
	Thousands of employees	Percent of total	Thousands of employees	Percent of total	Thousands of employees	Percent of total
Total employees affected_____	3,343	100	4,508	100	3,600	100
No wage change_____	111	3	191	4	234	7
Decrease in wages_____	4	(2)	2	(2)	17	(2)
Increase in wages_____	3,228	97	4,314	96	3,350	93
Under 2½ percent_____	254	8	994	22	1,095	30
2½ and under 3_____	198	6	414	9	625	17
3 and under 3½_____	597	18	1,131	25	385	11
3½ and over_____	2,144	64	1,763	39	1,245	35
Not specified or computed__	34	1	11	(2)		

[1] Preliminary.
[2] Less than 0.5 percent.

NOTE.—Data relate to changes negotiated during the year. They exclude changes negotiated in earlier years (i.e., deferred increases) and cost-of-living escalator adjustments.
  Data are limited to major collective bargaining situations (generally those affecting 1,000 or more workers) in manufacturing and selected nonmanufacturing industries. The latter exclude construction, the service trades, finance, and government.
  Detail will not necessarily add to totals because of rounding.

Source: Department of Labor.

For example, in 1956–57, a 5.1 percent rise in adjusted hourly earnings (as shown in Table 22) was translated into an increase of only 1.7 percent in real adjusted hourly earnings because consumer prices rose by 3.4 percent. In 1959–60, on the other hand, money earnings increased by only 3.3 percent, but real earnings rose by 1.8 percent because of a slower rise in consumer prices. Similarly, total hourly compensation in money terms increased by 6.0 percent in 1956–57 and by only 4.1 percent in 1958–59; however, as a result of differences in price movements, the percentage rise in real compensation was greater in the second period than in the first.

The recent slowing down in the rates of increase of money wages may signify a gradual weakening of some of the cost pressures in the economy. However, the continuation of this trend is by no means certain. With long-term contracts, the industries affected by negotiations vary considerably from year to year, and the behavior of average wage rates in any year may be fortuitously influenced by this consideration. Thus, in 1960, negotiations were concluded in basic steel; in 1961 new long-term agreements were negotiated in automobiles, automotive parts, meat-packing, farm equipment, and construction. In 1962 major contracts will expire in basic steel, aluminum, fabricated metals, construction, aircraft, airlines, and the maritime industry. It must also be remembered that the period 1957–61 was characterized by relatively high rates of unemployment; the test of wage behavior in a period characterized by stronger demand for labor is still ahead.

The shares of wages and profits. Employee compensation as a percent of corporate sales rose somewhat between the immediate postwar years and 1953–54, but since then the employee share has been below the 1953–54 high with no clear trend either up or down. This is shown in Table 25.

TABLE 25.—*Relation of employee compensation, profits, and capital consumption allowances to sales: All private corporations, 1947–61*

Period	Employee compensation	Profits			Capital consumption allowances	Profits after taxes plus capital consumption allowances
		Before taxes	Before taxes plus inventory valuation adjustment	After taxes		
			Percent of sales			
1947	23.3	8.3	6.6	5.0	1.8	6.9
1948	23.2	8.3	7.7	5.1	2.0	7.0
1949	23.7	6.9	7.4	4.1	2.3	6.4
1950	22.6	9.2	8.0	5.0	2.2	7.2
1951	23.2	8.4	8.1	3.8	2.3	6.0
1952	24.3	7.1	7.3	3.2	2.5	5.7
1953	25.3	7.1	6.9	3.2	2.7	5.9
1954	25.3	6.3	6.3	3.0	3.1	6.0
1955	23.7	7.2	6.9	3.6	3.1	6.7
1956	24.5	6.8	6.4	3.4	3.2	6.6
1957	24.2	6.1	5.9	3.0	3.2	6.3
1958	24.2	5.4	5.4	2.6	3.4	6.0
1959	24.2	6.3	6.2	3.0	3.3	6.4
1960	24.7	5.8	5.9	2.8	3.5	6.3
1961 [1]	24.5	5.8	5.9	2.8	3.6	6.4

[1] Preliminary estimates by Council of Economic Advisers.

NOTE.—The sum of compensation of employees, profits, and capital consumption allowances is a comparatively small percentage of sales because the latter includes all sales made by firms to other firms in successive stages of the production process, and, therefore, reflects a large amount of duplication. The comparative relations shown here would remain unaltered, however, if they were calculated on the basis of unduplicated sales.

Source: Department of Commerce (except as noted).

Corporate profits after taxes as a share of corporate sales were at their highest level in the 1947–50 period, when they were between 4.1 and 5.1 percent annually. Since 1951, the profit-after-tax share has been lower, fluctuating between 2.6 and 3.6 percent. Throughout the period, the profits share has shown a clear tendency to dip in periods of high unemployment and unutilized capacity.

A number of forces were involved in the behavior of profits. Unusually high inventory gains resulting from bursts of excess demand inflation swelled the profits share in 1947–48 and 1950; this can be seen in Table 25 by comparing corporate profits before taxes with profits before taxes plus inventory valuation adjustment. The rate of Federal corporate income taxation was increased in two steps from a level of 38 percent in 1947 to 52 percent in 1951, where it stands today; also, an excess profits tax was in effect from 1951 to 1953. Failure of the economy since the first half of 1957 to reach full employment has tended to depress the profits share in recent years.

Corporate capital consumption allowances (principally depreciation charges) have risen steadily throughout the postwar period as a share of corporate sales. One explanation of this trend is the fact that depreciation charges immediately after the war were based upon prewar prices of capital goods, and were thus further out of alignment with the replacement cost of business plant and equipment than they are today. In other words, as compared with recent years, corporate profits in the earlier postwar years were relatively overstated and depreciation charges relatively understated. Also, the rise in depreciation charges is related to the Korean accelerated tax amortization program, and to the more generous depreciation formula enacted in the Revenue Act of 1954.

Corporate profits after taxes plus capital consumption allowances—"cash flow"—have shown considerable stability in relation to sales, particularly if allowance is made for the large inventory gains of 1947–48 and 1950. This is shown in the last column of Table 25. Cash flow is of course not the same as net profits; only a part of it is return on investment, and the remainder is an element of cost. But cash flow is a significant measure as an indication of potential availability of internally generated funds for the financing of investment.

THE OUTLOOK FOR PRICES

Although over-all excess demand is unlikely to develop in 1962 and cost-price developments in the past year were favorable to continued price stability, the economic future can never be predicted with certainty. Unexpected inflationary pressures could emerge from any one of several sources: scare-buying induced by a national security crisis, the emergence of major bottlenecks caused by shifts in the pattern of demand, price increases for imported raw materials, exercise of market power by management or labor to increase their shares of the national income, or other causes which lie at least within the realm of possibility.

Nevertheless, a review of the relevant statistical and analytical evidence gives some grounds for optimism on the outlook for price behavior in the months ahead—though the evidence cannot, of course, be conclusive.

Changes in the wholesale price index are more closely related to our international competitiveness than are changes in the consumer price index or the GNP implicit price index. The consumer price index is heavily influenced by changes in the prices of consumer services and in wholesale and retail margins, which do not directly affect our international trade, and it does not encompass producers' durable equipment, which is a major component of our foreign trade. On the other hand, the all-inclusive GNP implicit price index includes major components which do not enter directly into international trade, such as consumer services and government services. As noted earlier in this chapter, stability in the wholesale price index is likely to be associated with a slow rise in the consumer price index and a slightly greater rise in the GNP implicit price index.

At the present time, we are on the plateau of a period of price stability. Wholesale prices have been stable for over 3½ years, and wholesale industrial prices (excluding farm and food prices) have been stable for more than 2½ years. Both the wholesale price index and wholesale industrial prices were lower in December 1961 than at the cyclical trough in February.

This was the first of the four postwar recoveries in which wholesale industrial prices fell during the first 10 months of recovery.

Recent wage changes have been consistent with these price developments. As indicated earlier, annual wage increases in manufacturing have been declining for several years. The index of wage and salary cost per unit of output in manufacturing changed little from the cyclical peak in July 1957 to the peak in May 1960; by contrast, there were substantial peak-to-peak increases from 1948 to 1953 and from 1953 to 1957.

Such encouragement as may be derived from these recent price and wage trends must be tempered by the realization that they do not provide full protection for fixed-income recipients, and relate mainly to a period characterized by excess unemployment and productive capacity. The U.S. economy last experienced full employment in the first half of 1957; the recovery of 1958–60 stopped well short of full employment. While some significance can be attached to the fact that adjusted hourly earnings in manufacturing increased slightly less in 1959, a year of recovery, than in 1958, a cyclical trough year, and from the further fact that wholesale industrial prices fell during the 1961 recovery, the behavior of wages and prices in a period of sustained slack is an insufficient basis for inferences about price-wage behavior when the economy is moving up toward full employment.

Other considerations provide somewhat firmer grounds for optimism. As indicated in the analysis of Chapter 1, the continued recovery of the economy in 1962 is not likely to create major supply bottlenecks or to reach a state of over-all excess demand. The supply outlook for major imported raw materials does not suggest that an inflationary stimulus will originate in this quarter.

Foreign competition in the last few years has injected a powerful price-restraining force into the U.S. economy. We are now faced with sharp competition from imports in our domestic markets and from the exports of other industrial countries in our traditional export markets. Competition of any kind, internal or external, provides strong discipline for prices; the effects of foreign competition are stronger than might be suggested by the absolute size of foreign trade in our economy. The response to import competition itself tends to limit imports, so that the volume of realized imports is not a full measure of the force exerted by foreign competition. Moreover, conventional views as to appropriate shares of markets have great weight in pricing and other decisions. The number of foreign automobiles imported never amounted to as much as 11 percent of sales in the United States, and yet they helped to bring about a radical change in the design and marketing policy of a great industry.

The commodities component of the consumer price index, which in the last few years has mirrored the stability in the wholesale price index, is likely to continue to follow the course of wholesale prices in the months ahead. The services component, which has risen steadily since the war will probably continue to do so. There are some favorable signs, however, which may indicate a slowing down in the rise of the prices of services. The great postwar expansion in the housing supply and higher vacancy rates seem to have slowed down the rise in rents. Also, movements in the rates charged by public utilities subject to rate regulation should reflect increasingly the narrowing of the gap between original cost and replacement cost of capital goods included in the rate base.

The slowing down since 1957 in the upward creep of consumer prices has reduced the effects on wages of cost of living escalator provisions in labor contracts, and may moderate somewhat the pressure of employees for large wage increases. It is also worthy of note that escalator provisions have been eliminated from, or modified in, a number of collective bargaining agreements.

Developments in the steel industry in 1961 were propitious for the continuation of price stability. Steel prices at the end of the year were slightly below the level of the end of 1958. This was a striking shift in trend for an industry in which prices had risen at the average rate of 5.8 percent a year from 1940 to 1958.

In early 1960, the steel industry, after a long strike, reached a wage settlement with the Steelworkers Union which provided for an estimated 3.7 percent annual increase in employment cost per worker. Though still somewhat above the over-all trend rate of productivity increase, this was a considerably smaller settlement than the 1956 contract, the cost of which was estimated at 8 percent a year.

Under the 1960 contract, a wage increase was scheduled to take effect on October 1, 1961. Confronted on one side with increasing foreign competition, stronger rivalry with substitutes, and intraindustry price shading, and on the other with an increase in wage rates, steel companies were reported in the press to be weighing the desirability of an October 1 price increase. In this setting, the President on September 6 addressed a letter to the heads of the 12 largest steel companies. Urging them to preserve price stability, the President stressed the damaging impact of a steel price increase on the balance of payments. "Steel is a bellwether," he said, "as well as a major element in industrial costs. A rise in steel prices would force price increases in many industries and invite price increases in others."

The President said:

> In emphasizing the vital importance of steel prices to the strength of our economy, I do not wish to minimize the urgency of preventing inflationary movements in steel wages. I recognize, too, that the steel industry, by absorbing increases in employment costs since 1958, has demonstrated a will to halt the price-wage spiral in steel. If the industry were now to forego a price increase, it would enter collective bargaining negotiations next spring with a record of three and a half years of price stability. It would clearly then be the turn of the labor representatives to limit wage demands to a level consistent with continued price stability. The moral position of the steel industry next spring—and its claim to the support of public opinion—will be strengthened by the exercise of price restraint now.

A week later, the President addressed a letter to the President of the United Steelworkers of America. Referring to the forthcoming collective bargaining negotiations, the President urged "a labor settlement within the limits of advances in productivity and price stability." The President expressed his confidence that "we can rely upon the leadership and members of the Steelworkers Union to act responsibly in the wage negotiations next year in the interests of all of the American people."

At the end of the year, steel prices had not been raised.

All of these considerations suggest that a resumption of inflation in the course of the economic expansion foreseen for 1962 is not inevitable. As the year opens, the atmosphere is favorable for reasonable price stability. Whether this atmosphere is preserved or dissipated will depend on the wisdom of Government, business, and labor, in evolving policies affecting prices and costs.

POLICIES AFFECTING PRICE BEHAVIOR

The Setting

The over-all stability of prices should be achieved in a manner consistent with the flexible response of individual prices and wage rates to changes in cost and demand within an environment of dynamic competition. Thus, government policies to promote price stability must work to maintain and increase the freedom of the private economy, not to limit it. In peacetime, attempts to stabilize prices through the imposition of direct wage and price controls or through interference with the rights of employees to organize and bargain collectively are unacceptable. Also unacceptable are policies which pursue price stability without regard for the effects on employment, production, and purchasing power. Prices might be stabilized in an underemployed economy; but to accept heavy unemployment and persistent slack as the necessary cost of price stability is to undermine the vitality and flexibility of the economy and to reduce American strength.

Competitive behavior throughout the economy involves more than rivalry among firms selling similar products in a single market; it also involves hard bargaining between firms buying and selling from each other and between firms and unions. Abridgement of competition may be evidenced as much in permissive wage increases which are simply passed along in higher prices as in agreements among firms to divide markets.

Public policies to encourage economy-wide competition not only contribute to the goal of price stability; they also promote efficiency and the advance of productivity. Hence, such policies serve both the goal of economic growth and the goal of balance of payments equilibrium. In addition, such policies have an independent justification in that they make the economy more responsive to the demands of consumers and thereby improve the qualitative nature of the output generated by the economy at rising levels of activity. Improving the range of consumer choices is an important facet of economic progress, and one that gives ultimate meaning to policies of full employment and economic growth.

Policies to Foster Market Competition

Competition in product markets is promoted by an increase in the number and diversity of market alternatives available and by the removal of anticompetitive restrictions on business behavior. Examples of the former are reduction of import barriers and encouragement of new and growing businesses. Examples of the latter are attempts to halt tendencies toward monopolization and to eliminate collusive agreements among firms through antitrust policy.

Reduction of import barriers widens and strengthens competition in domestic markets. The experience of the European Common Market has demonstrated clearly that a broadened scope for international competition tends to spur cost reduction and innovation and to stimulate economic vitality. Two factors have been of paramount importance in the success of this experiment. First, the terms of the Common Market agreement were such that producers understood well in advance the scope and timetable of coming tariff reductions and thus were able to prepare for them. Second, because free trade policies were pursued in an environment of rapid economic growth, increased foreign competition was not so much a threat to existing markets as an incentive to respond to new profit-making opportunities. Similar advantages can be reaped for the United States through the adoption of the new foreign trade expansion program proposed by the President. Although imports are now, and will remain, a much smaller proportion of sales in our market than in Europe, modest increases in imports can yield competitive benefits to the U.S. economy out of proportion to their size.

Public policy toward small business has as its purpose the strengthening of the small business sector of the economy and the removal of artificial and discriminatory barriers to the profitability and growth of small firms. Although some of the limitations upon small business participation in the economy arise from technological considerations and true cost economies associated with large size, important limitations arise from direct discrimination and from lack of access to capital, of widespread market contact, and of information. Programs which redress these imbalances of competitive advantage make possible the salutary competition of new and growing enterprises throughout the economy. Small firms are often particularly well-situated to perceive changing market needs and production possibilities, and to take the lead in adapting to them, thus contributing to the efficiency and growth of the economy.

Antitrust policies promote market competition by halting tendencies toward monopolization and by eliminating unfair methods of competition and illegal restraints upon trade. Antimerger actions are designed to prevent the disappearance of independent competitors and the consequent impairment of competition. Checking monopolistic price increases during periods of expanded demand is facilitated both by the continuing effort to prevent the increase of business concentration and by the detection and prosecution of market conspiracies. The dissolution of such conspiracies is especially important during periods of economic expansion, for it is during such periods that potential competitors find it easiest to reach agreement on market divisions and price increases. An important by-product of corrective antitrust action is the deterrent effect which successful prosecution has upon other potential offenders. To the extent that potential anticompetitive developments are deterred and existing competitive elements in the economy preserved and strengthened, antitrust policy contributes to the maintenance of competition and price stability far more than a simple list of prosecutions would indicate.

Guideposts for Noninflationary Wage and Price Behavior

There are important segments of the economy where firms are large or employees well-organized, or both. In these sectors, private parties may exercise considerable discretion over the terms of wage bargains and price decisions. Thus, at least in the short run, there is considerable room for the exercise of private power and a parallel need for the assumption of private responsibility.

Individual wage and price decisions assume national importance when they involve large numbers of workers and large amounts of output directly, or when they are regarded by large segments of the economy as setting a pattern. Because such decisions affect the progress of the whole economy, there is legitimate reason for public interest in their content and consequences. An informed public, aware of the significance of major wage bargains and price decisions, and equipped to judge for itself their compatibility with the national interest, can help to create an atmosphere in which the parties to such decisions will exercise their powers responsibly.

How is the public to judge whether a particular wage-price decision is in the national interest? No simple test exists, and it is not possible to set out systematically all of the many considerations which bear on such a judgment. However, since the question is of prime importance to the strength and progress of the American economy, it deserves widespread public discussion and clarification of the issues. What follows is intended as a contribution to such a discussion.

Mandatory controls in peacetime over the outcomes of wage negotiations and over individual price decisions are neither desirable in the American tradition nor practical in a diffuse and decentralized continental economy. Free collective bargaining is the vehicle for the achievement of contractual agreements on wages, fringes, and working conditions, as well as on the "web of rules" by which a large segment of industry governs the performance of work and the distribution of rewards. Similarly, final price decisions lie—and should continue to lie—in the hands of individual firms. It is, however, both desirable and practical that discretionary decisions on wages and prices recognize the national interest in the results. The guideposts suggested here as aids to public understanding are not concerned primarily with the relation of employers and employees to each other, but rather with their joint relation to the rest of the economy.

Wages, prices, and productivity. If all prices remain stable, all hourly labor costs may increase as fast as economy-wide productivity without, for that reason alone, changing the relative share of labor and nonlabor incomes in total output. At the same time, each kind of income increases steadily in absolute amount. If hourly labor costs increase at a slower rate than productivity, the share of nonlabor incomes will grow or prices will fall, or both. Conversely, if hourly labor costs increase more rapidly than productivity, the share of labor incomes in the total product will increase or prices will rise, or both. It is this relationship among long-run economy-wide productivity, wages, and prices which makes the rate of productivity change an important benchmark for noninflationary wage and price behavior.

Productivity is a *guide* rather than a *rule* for appraising wage and price behavior for several reasons. First, there are a number of problems involved in measuring productivity change, and a number of alternative measures are available. Second, there is nothing immutable in fact or in justice about the distribution of the total product between labor and nonlabor incomes. Third, the pattern of wages and prices among industries is and should be responsive to forces other than changes in productivity.

Alternative measures of productivity. If the rate of growth of productivity over time is to serve as a useful benchmark for wage and price behavior, there must be some meeting of minds about the appropriate methods of measuring the trend rate of increase in productivity, both for industry as a whole and for individual industries. This is a large and complex

TABLE 26.—*Annual rates of growth of output per man-hour, 1909 to 1960*

[Based on establishment series]

Industry series	Average annual percentage change [1]			
	1909 to 1960	1947 to 1960	1947 to 1954	1954 to 1960
Total private economy	2.4	3.0	3.5	2.6
Nonagriculture	2.1	2.4	2.7	2.2
Nonmanufacturing	([2])	2.2	2.6	1.9
Manufacturing	([2])	2.8	2.9	2.9
Manufacturing corrected for varying rates of capacity utilization	([2])	2.8	2.8	3.1

[1] Computed from least squares trend of the logarithms of the output per man-hour indexes. See Table B-31 for indexes for 1947-60.
[2] Not available.

Sources: Department of Labor and Council of Economic Advisers.

subject and there is much still to be learned.   The most that can be done at present is to give some indication of orders of magnitude, and of the range within which most plausible measures are likely to fall (Table 26).

There are a number of conceptual problems in connection with productivity measurement which can give rise to differences in estimates of its rate of growth.   Three important conceptual problems are the following:

(1) Over what time interval should productivity trends be measured? Very short intervals may give excessive weight to business-cycle movements in productivity, which are not the relevant standards for wage behavior. The erratic nature of year-to-year changes in productivity is shown in Chart 14.   Very long intervals may hide significant breaks in trends; indeed in the United States—and in other countries as well—productivity appears to have risen more rapidly since the end of the second World War than before.   It would be wholly inappropriate for wage behavior in the 1960's to be governed by events long in the past.   On the other hand, productivity in the total private economy appears to have advanced less rapidly in the second half of the postwar period than in the first.

CHART 14

Indexes of Output per Man-Hour

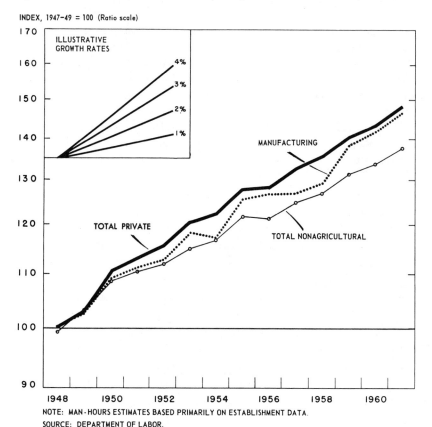

INDEX, 1947–49 = 100 (Ratio scale)

NOTE: MAN-HOURS ESTIMATES BASED PRIMARILY ON ESTABLISHMENT DATA.
SOURCE: DEPARTMENT OF LABOR.

(2) Even for periods of intermediate length, it is desirable to segregate the trend movements in productivity from those that reflect business-cycle forces. Where the basic statistical materials are available, this problem can be handled by an analytical separation of trend effects and the effects of changes in the rate of capacity utilization.

(3) Even apart from such difficulties, there often exist alternative statistical measures of output and labor input. The alternatives may differ conceptually or may simply be derived from different statistical sources. A difficult problem of choice may emerge, unless the alternative measures happen to give similar results.

Selected measures of the rate of growth of productivity in different sectors of the economy for different time periods are shown in Table 26. Several measures are given because none of the single figures is clearly superior for all purposes.

The share of labor income. The proportions in which labor and nonlabor incomes share the product of industry have not been immutable throughout American history, nor can they be expected to stand forever where they are today. It is desirable that labor and management should bargain explicitly about the distribution of the income of particular firms or industries. It is, however, undesirable that they should bargain implicitly about the general price level. Excessive wage settlements which are paid for through price increases in major industries put direct pressure on the general price level and produce spillover and imitative effects throughout the economy. Such settlements may fail to redistribute income within the industry involved; rather they redistribute income between that industry and other segments of the economy through the mechanism of inflation.

Prices and wages in individual industries. What are the guideposts which may be used in judging whether a particular price or wage decision may be inflationary? The desired objective is a stable price level, within which particular prices rise, fall, or remain stable in response to economic pressures. Hence, price stability within any particular industry is not necessarily a correct guide to price and wage decisions in that industry. It is possible, however, to describe in broad outline a set of guides which, if followed, would preserve over-all price stability while still allowing sufficient flexibility to accommodate objectives of efficiency and equity. These are not arbitrary guides. They describe—briefly and no doubt incompletely—how prices and wage rates would behave in a smoothly functioning competitive economy operating near full employment. Nor do they constitute a mechanical formula for determining whether a particular price or wage decision is inflationary. They will serve their purpose if they suggest to the interested public a useful way of approaching the appraisal of such a decision.

If, as a point of departure, we assume no change in the relative shares of labor and nonlabor incomes in a particular industry, then a general guide may be advanced for noninflationary wage behavior, and another for non-inflationary price behavior. Both guides, as will be seen, are only first approximations.

The general guide for noninflationary wage behavior is that the rate of increase in wage rates (including fringe benefits) in each industry be equal to the trend rate of over-all productivity increase. General acceptance of this guide would maintain stability of labor cost per unit of output for the economy as a whole—though not of course for individual industries.

The general guide for noninflationary price behavior calls for price reduction if the industry's rate of productivity increase exceeds the over-all rate—for this would mean declining unit labor costs; it calls for an appropriate increase in price if the opposite relationship prevails; and it calls for stable prices if the two rates of productivity increase are equal.

These are advanced as general guideposts. To reconcile them with objectives of equity and efficiency, specific modifications must be made to adapt them to the circumstances of particular industries. If all of these modifications are made, each in the specific circumstances to which it applies, they are consistent with stability of the general price level. Public judgments about the effects on the price level of particular wage or price decisions should take into account the modifications as well as the general guides. The most important modifications are the following:

(1) Wage rate increases would exceed the general guide rate in an industry which would otherwise be unable to attract sufficient labor; or in which wage rates are exceptionally low compared with the range of wages earned elsewhere by similar labor, because the bargaining position of workers has been weak in particular local labor markets.

(2) Wage rate increases would fall short of the general guide rate in an industry which could not provide jobs for its entire labor force even in times of generally full employment; or in which wage rates are exceptionally high compared with the range of wages earned elsewhere by similar labor, because the bargaining position of workers has been especially strong.

(3) Prices would rise more rapidly, or fall more slowly, than indicated by the general guide rate in an industry in which the level of profits was insufficient to attract the capital required to finance a needed expansion in capacity; or in which costs other than labor costs had risen.

(4) Prices would rise more slowly, or fall more rapidly, than indicated by the general guide in an industry in which the relation of productive capacity to full employment demand shows the desirability of an outflow of capital from the industry; or in which costs other than labor costs have fallen; or in which excessive market power has resulted in rates of profit substantially higher than those earned elsewhere on investments of comparable risk.

It is a measure of the difficulty of the problem that even these complex guideposts leave out of account several important considerations. Although output per man-hour rises mainly in response to improvements in the quantity and quality of capital goods with which employees are equipped, employees are often able to improve their performance by means within their own control. It is obviously in the public interest that incentives be preserved which would reward employees for such efforts.

Also, in connection with the use of measures of over-all productivity gain as benchmarks for wage increases, it must be borne in mind that average hourly labor costs often change through the process of up- or down-grading, shifts between wage and salaried employment, and other forces. Such changes may either add to or subtract from the increment which is available for wage increases under the over-all productivity guide.

Finally, it must be reiterated that collective bargaining within an industry over the division of the proceeds between labor and nonlabor income is not necessarily disruptive of over-all price stability. The relative shares can change within the bounds of noninflationary price behavior. But when a disagreement between management and labor is resolved by passing the bill to the rest of the economy, the bill is paid in depreciated currency to the ultimate advantage of no one.

It is no accident that productivity is the central guidepost for wage settlements. Ultimately, it is rising output per man hour which must yield the ingredients of a rising standard of living. Growth in productivity makes it possible for real wages and real profits to rise side by side.

Rising productivity is the foundation of the country's leadership of the free world, enabling it to earn in world competition the means to discharge its commitments overseas. Rapid advance of productivity is the key to stability of the price level as money incomes rise, to fundamental improvement in the balance of international payments, and to growth in the Nation's capacity to meet the challenges of the 1960's at home and abroad. That is why policy to accelerate economic growth stresses investments in science and technology, plant and equipment, education and training—the basic sources of future gains in productivity.

II

The Reagan Economic Reports

Introduction

William Niskanen,
William Poole, and
Murray Weidenbaum[1]

The 1982 Economic Report provided the first comprehensive statement of the perspectives on the government and the economy that led to the Reagan economic program. Although the initial *American's New Beginning: A Program for Economic Recovery* (released on February 18, 1981) and subsequent budget publications summarized the details, none of them presented a comprehensive exposition of the principles that guided the entire program. What was needed was a coherent rationale. That proved to be a difficult undertaking because the Reagan economic program, like the Reagan constituency, reflected a range of views on economic policy. In other words, there was broader agreement on the substance of this program than on the reasons for the major proposed changes in economic policy.

The Council of Economic Advisers, however, had a unique opportunity to provide a coherent rationale for Reaganomics based on shared political values and a common professional perspective. In preparing the 1982 Economic Report, the Council consciously approached this task with the hope of providing a set of principles that would sustain the Reagan program through the developing recession and the anticipated disputes among various groups on subsequent economic issues. The effort was not wholly successful, partly because even among the closest professional colleagues, there was disagreement on some issues. In retrospect, however, the 1982 Economic Report represents a remarkably coherent and comprehensive statement of the principles guiding the economic policies of a presidential administration. The professional staff of the Council participated ac-

[1]William Niskanen served as a member of the Council of Economic Advisers in 1981–85 and is currently Chairman of the Cato Institute. William Poole, who served as a member of the Council of Economic Advisers in 1982–85, is professor of economics at Brown University; he joined the CEA after the publication of the 1982 Economic Report. Murray Weidenbaum was Chairman of the Council of Economic Advisers in 1981–82 and is now Mallinckrodt Distinguished University Professor at Washington University. James Burnham, who served as special assistant to the CEA chairman in 1981–82, provided helpful comments and suggestions.

tively in the analysis contained in the report, which was prepared under the direction of Council members Jerry Jordan, William Niskanen, and Murray Weidenbaum.

Introduction

Chapter 1 of the 1982 Economic Report presents the basic legislative and administrative composition of President Reagan's economic program. The key elements of the proposed program were

• cutting the rate of growth in federal spending,

• reducing personal income tax rates and accelerating depreciation allowances for business investment in plant and equipment,

• instituting a far-reaching program of regulatory reform, and

• in cooperation with the Federal Reserve System, making a "new commitment" to a monetary policy designed to restore a stable currency and healthy financial markets.

As explained below, important parts of this ambitious program were carried out, notably the tax proposals and the reduction in inflation. But other key aspects, especially the budget cutting, remain largely unfulfilled.

Microeconomics

The three "microeconomic" chapters of the 1982 Economic Report each represented a different type of innovation.

The Role of Government

Chapter 2 of the report, "Government and the Economy," attempted to break the largest amount of new ground. It surely turned out to be the most controversial. This chapter presents a set of general principles for the role of government in a free society. These principles are based on three intellectual building blocks: welfare economics, federalism, and public choice. An aspect of welfare economics called the theory of market failures identifies the roles of government that may improve on the outcomes of market processes. Such activities may include the correction for marginal external costs or benefits of private activity, the provision of public goods, some types of social insurance, and the stabilization of the economy.

The theory of federalism, in turn, identifies the types of government activities likely to be performed best at different levels in a federal system. The allocation of functions is based primarily on two factors. The first is variations in preferences for governmental activities among people in different geographic areas. The second is the degree to which the costs and benefits of government activities are borne within each area.

The developing theory of public choice provides a cautionary note that the government is also subject to various types of failures, due to the nature of the political process and the reward structure in governmental institutions. The choice of the type and level of governmental activities, thus, involves a balancing of the costs of the different types of market and governmental failures.

Although this general framework is increasingly accepted by economists, there remain legitimate disputes about the appropriateness of many governmental activities. These disputes are based on different estimates of their costs and benefits and, sometimes, different political values. On the other hand, many current federal activities are clearly inconsistent with this framework. This chapter of the report concludes by interpreting the primary themes of the Reagan economic program within this framework.

Tax Policy

Chapter 5 of the report, "Tax Policy and Economic Growth," summarizes the effects of the tax code on the allocation of economic activity and, in turn, on economic growth. This chapter develops the important "supply-side" insight that the economic effects of fiscal policy depend importantly on the details of the budget and the tax code.

In the language of economics, this chapter focuses on the substitution effects of changes in marginal tax rates, rather than on the income and distribution effects that were the primary focus of fiscal policy analysis in prior reports. This approach is then applied to evaluate the expected effects of the Economic Recovery Tax Act (ERTA) of 1981. This analysis produced two surprises that led to some controversy.

Although ERTA reduced federal tax rates on nominal income by about 23 percent, the tax rates on real income were reduced only a few percent, since the individual income tax was not indexed for inflation until 1985. The primary effect of ERTA, thus, was to avoid what would otherwise have been a substantial increase in marginal tax rates on real income.

A second surprise was that the changes in business taxation, combined with declining inflation, led to a substantial net tax subsidy for investments in short-life business equipment. This analysis provided a basis for some of the subsequent changes contained in the tax legislation enacted in 1982 and 1986. Chapter 5 concludes with important discussions of the implicit tax effects of social security, the welfare system, and monetary policy. The chapter effectively summarized the theoretical and empirical basis for what has been described as "supply-side economics." It provided no basis for the irresponsible conjectures sometimes associated with this term, such as that a general reduction in tax rates would generate net increases in federal revenues.

Regulatory Reform

Chapter 6 of the report, "Reforming Government Regulation of Economic Activity," summarizes the Reagan administration's approach to federal regulation. The objectives of the administration were to improve the presidential review of current and proposed new regulations, to continue the substantial reduction of the older forms of price and entry regulation initiated during the Carter administration, and, initially, to reform some of the newer types of regulation of health, safety, and the environment.

This section of the report also lays out the rationale for using benefit/cost analysis in evaluating proposals for government regulation of economic activity. The motive is to achieve a more efficient allocation of resources by subjecting public sector actions to the same type of efficiency tests used in the private sector. In making an investment decision, for example, business executives compare the costs to be incurred with the expected revenues. The investment is likely to be pursued only if the anticipated revenues exceed the projected costs.

The government decisionmaker does not face the same array of economic incentives and constraints. If the costs of an agency action exceed the benefits, the result may not have an immediate adverse effect on the agency. Analytical information on economic costs in the past rarely existed in the public sector, so that, more often than not, the governmental decisionmaker has not been aware of approving a regulation that is economically inefficient. The aim of requiring agencies to perform benefit/cost analysis is to make the regulatory process more efficient and to eliminate regulatory actions that, on balance, generate more costs than benefits.

Chapter 6 suggests that analysis of federal regulatory activity should involve answering three types of questions. The first is whether some form of market failure has occurred that warrants the imposition of regulation. Observed differences in safety conditions among workplaces, for example, are not sufficient evidence of a market imperfection, because employer and employee knowledge of these conditions may lead to compensatory differences in wages and employment conditions.

The second question is whether federal regulation, in contrast to state and local rulemaking, is appropriate. Federal intervention is more likely to be appropriate where the externalities of an activity in one state have substantial effects in other states. Other possibilities include activities affecting basic constitutional rights or where interstate commerce would be significantly disrupted by varying local regulations.

The last question, assuming the response to the first two is positive, is whether a specific regulation will increase net benefits to society. When some federal regulation is clearly appropriate, an analysis of the benefits and costs can provide valuable information to help select the form and extent of the regulation.

In early 1981, the administration had centralized the regulatory review process in the Office of Management and Budget, established a benefit-cost test for review of current and proposed regulations, and had terminated the remaining regulation of oil prices.

This chapter identifies a large number of areas where the existing regulations should be reduced or eliminated and made the case for a substantial reform of the Clean Air Act and of the government programs, tax provisions, and regulations affecting the provision of medical care. Most of these desirable reforms, however, have yet to be achieved. The Reagan administration did not propose a general reform of environmental legislation, and only a few changes in regulatory legislation were approved by Congress.

In retrospect, the failure to maintain the considerable momentum for deregulation that developed in the late 1970s was a major missed opportunity in the execution of the Reagan economic program. This chapter, with a few changes, provides a valuable agenda of both deregulation and regulatory reform for the next administration. The brief analysis of the costs of protectionism in chapter 7, "The United States in the International Economic System," is an extension of the thrust of chapter 6.

Macroeconomics

Macroeconomic issues are conveniently divided into those involving the business cycle and those involving economic growth. The 1982 Economic Report deals mostly with growth. The orientation is neoclassical—"supply-side economics" as it came to be called in the political debates.

Sources of Economic Growth

Economic growth arises from increases in the quantity of productive resources and in their productivity. With regard to productivity, in the short run output per unit of factor input depends on the rate of utilization of labor and capital resources. There is only a modest role for traditional stabilization policy because the economy gravitates toward full employment when the government follows stable and predictable long-run policies. The focus of government policy ought to be to provide incentives to bring labor into gainful employment, to increase the rate of capital formation, and to improve the efficiency with which resources are used. Improving efficiency—productivity growth—rather than the utilization rate is the key to real GNP growth in the long run.

Chapter 5, "Tax Policy and Economic Growth," contains an analysis of the effect of marginal tax rates on the incentive to work. For married men the effect on labor supply of cutting marginal tax rates is probably small, but for married women the effect may be large. The 1981 Economic Recovery Tax Act (ERTA) scheduled substantial reductions in marginal tax rates, but the 1982 Economic Report makes clear that under ERTA marginal tax rates would for most individuals remain above those prevailing before 1975. The report calls for additional reforms to reduce the marginal tax rates of social security recipients and welfare recipients. Taking earnings tests into account, these taxpayers face effective marginal tax rates of 80 percent or more, and so it is not surprising that their labor force participation is low.

Increased saving and investment are required to increase the growth of the capital stock. ERTA increased the incentive to save in several ways. By lowering marginal tax rates and broadening eligibility for tax-sheltered saving through Individual Retirement Accounts (IRAs) and Keogh accounts (for unincorporated business proprietors), ERTA increased the posttax rate of return for any given pretax rate of return. The report anticipated that the higher posttax return would increase personal saving. ERTA's corporate investment incentives were expected to increase both corporate investment and corporate saving.

The report is, however, rather ambiguous on the politically sensitive issue of the effect of federal budget deficits. In part, this reflects the differences in views within the economics profession, some of which were mirrored in the Council's internal deliberations. Thus, the crowding-out proposition is stated clearly, but the report minimizes the likely magnitude of crowding out by suggesting that the deficit could be accommodated easily though private saving and saving from abroad. The report assumed policies to reduce federal spending to 19.7 percent of GNP and the federal budget deficit to 1.1 percent of GNP in fiscal 1987, but the administration and Congress took actions that increased the relative size of federal spending and that also enlarged the budget deficit.

The public debate over ERTA focused on the cuts in individual tax rates. However, the business tax cuts, which took the form of investment incentives, were proportionately larger. The report analyzes the investment incentives and showed that in many cases the combination of the investment tax credit and liberalized depreciation allowances provides an actual tax subsidy to new investment. One table in chapter 5 reports effective tax rates for 13 industries and shows that under ERTA three of the industries have negative effective tax rates. Because of the political sensitivity of the issue, other tables in this section of the report are more complicated, but nevertheless show the extraordinary size of investment incentives contained in the 1981 tax system.

The business investment incentives of ERTA were anticipated, naturally enough, to lead to an expansion of such investment. The report projects the capital stock to rise at an average rate of 3.5 percent a year over the period from 1979 to 1987, up modestly from the annual rate of 2.5 percent during 1973–79. The report makes clear that an implication of expansion of business investment is a less buoyant expansion of investment in consumer durables and housing.

Monetary Policy, Inflation, and Cyclical Stabilization

Inflation is discussed in a number of places in the 1982 Economic Report. The interaction of inflation and the tax system is examined in chapter 5. Chapter 4, "Federal Budget Issues," includes an analysis of the effects of inflation on the measured federal budget deficit. In short, the various impacts of inflation generate numerous costs, but these negative effects are not offset by sustained benefits.

Chapter 3, "Monetary Policy, Inflation, and Employment," states clearly that inflation comes from excessive money growth. To reduce inflation the administration assumed that the Federal Reserve would reduce the rate of money growth from 7.3 percent over the four quarters of 1980 to a rate half that by 1986. The reductions were to be gradual and predictable to reduce the transitional costs of bringing inflation down. Guideposts and price controls to reduce inflation are firmly rejected as ineffective.

The recession in progress at the time the 1982 Economic Report was written receives scant attention. The recession is mentioned, but no countercyclical policy actions are proposed to deal with it. Although the matter is not discussed explicitly, the view was that the recession would take care of itself if policies for the long run were pursued. The report contains a general discussion of past failures of fine-tuning of macroeconomic policy.

The importance of predictability of policy is discussed in numerous places throughout the report. More precise control of the money supply is expected to make monetary policy more predictable. Discretionary monetary and fiscal policies increase uncertainty and thereby encourage allocational mistakes and destabilize the macro economy.

The report encourages the government to increase policy predictability by eschewing fine-tuning and maintaining a long policy horizon. There is a fairly extensive discussion of monetary rules. Experience under the gold standard is reviewed, but that approach is rejected. Money growth and price level rules are discussed, but no specific rule is embraced. Fiscal policy rules involving limitation of federal revenues as a percent of GNP and the balanced budget are mentioned briefly.

Macroeconomic Conditions and Forecasts

When we look back on the first half of the decade of the 1980s, a half-dozen striking features of the economy come to the fore. The most visible are the rapid decline of the rate of inflation and the large federal budget deficits. Other factors of basic importance, although of a more technical nature, are the decline in the income velocity of the money, the high level of real interest rates, the appreciation of the dollar through early 1985, and the large international capital flows into the United States together with the accompanying current account deficits. Other key macroeconomic variables fell in an unsurprising and sometimes disappointing middle ground—real GNP growth, for example, averaged only 2.0 percent a year during 1979–86.

The 1982 Economic Report substantially underestimated the budget deficit for three reasons. First, real GNP growth over the five-year forecast horizon was substantially lower than projected. Second, inflation was substantially lower than forecast, which meant that real revenues yielded by the tax system were lower than expected because it turned out that there was less bracket creep than anticipated before indexation took effect in 1985. Third, federal expenditures grew more rapidly than had been planned, in good measure because the President and the Congress did not agree on large cuts in individual spending programs.

The report did not maintain a coherent view of the explanation of the high level of real interest rates, which is not surprising given that the economics profession is still arguing about the issue. The discussion of ERTA states that the Act would increase the posttax return on new business investment, but the implication of that increase for real returns on financial assets, which must bear returns competitive with real assets, is not explored. Chapter 8, "Review and Outlook," offers an explanation relying on a tendency for the posttax real rate of interest to be constant over time. The argument is that the pretax real rate of interest must be high when nominal interest rates are high, as in 1981, given that the tax system taxes nominal interest. In chapter 3 there is the suggestion that inflationary expectations may still be high, and so the expected real rate on long-term bonds may not be especially abnormal. The text also suggests that budget deficits and the market's fears of budget deficits may be responsible for high real rates.

The dollar appreciated substantially in 1981. The report attributed the appreciation to the more rapid adjustment of the exchange rate than of national price levels, to high real returns on U.S. securities, to the current account surplus, and to confidence in the economic recovery program. It was anticipated that the strong dollar would push the current account toward a deficit, and the report contains an analysis of the significance of external imbalances.

Retrospective

It is natural to look back on a document such as the 1982 Economic Report to ask what lessons flow from it. Political constraints, of course, color much of the language in every Economic Report and warp the forecasts. It is more interesting and more informative to reflect on the points that were made that are relatively free of politics. One guiding principle permeated all of the key policy positions in the report, as well as in other important administration statements: the desire to improve the performance of the American economy by reducing the scope, size, and burden of the public sector, especially the federal government.

The degree of success can be gauged by the fact that the presumption of "doing something" to solve every emerging issue has more often been replaced by the query, "Is this a federal problem?" In practice, the answer may still be "Yes" to a disappointingly large number of situations, but moving that question to the top of the agenda is a considerable achievement.

The authors of the 1982 Economic Report really believed in supply-side economics. Looking back, the problem was not with the economics but with the fact that the details of government policy did not shift as much as they had hoped. One key change was the investment incentives in ERTA, which reduced taxation of income from new business investment to the point of almost eliminating the corporate income tax. That single move was responsible for high real rates of interest, much of the appreciation of the dollar, and, through dollar appreciation, the rapid deceleration of inflation. Business investment held up better during the 1981–82 recession than might have been expected given the severity of the downturn. Once the recession was over, an investment boom occurred in 1983–84.

Much of the rest of the supply-side dream remains unfulfilled. Marginal tax rates for individuals remained above those prevailing before about 1975. By 1988 the Tax Reform Act of 1986 will return marginal rates applying to most taxpayers to the levels of the mid-1960s. But the cost of tax reform in 1986 was substantially increased taxation of business, wiping away ERTA's investment incentives and, as a consequence, derailing the investment boom. Because the government was not successful in cutting overall outlays to release resources for private use, it was not possible to cut tax rates for both individuals and businesses. Indeed, a large budget deficit remains, which will require in time either cuts in spending or increases in tax rates or a combination of the two.

Running along side the theme of supply-side economics in the 1982 Economic Report is the theme of constancy and predictability of policy. With regard to tax policy, recent years have seen major revisions in the law almost annually. Business tax relief may be necessary to obtain the investment the economy needs for sustained growth. In retrospect, the 1980s may be viewed as a transitional period for tax policy—a period of successful groping toward a sound and stable tax structure built on the principles of maintaining a broad tax base and the lowest possible marginal tax rates.

The problem of implementing a sound and predictable monetary policy might also be viewed in the same light. Once inflation and interest rates started to decline significantly, monetary velocity did also. The proposed policy of gradual reduction of money growth to a rate half that of 1980 turned out to be unwise, given the sharp decline in velocity. The monetarist principles enunciated in the 1982 Economic Report seem to have been overturned by events. That is unfortunate because the transition experience from high to low inflation does not bear directly on the issue of the appropriate monetary policy rule or principles for a long-run characterized by relatively low and relatively stable inflation.

The 1982 Economic Report was roundly criticized, and properly so, for excessively optimistic forecasts of GNP. But surely it is fair to crow a bit that the report was correct in contending that the Phillips tradeoff between inflation and unemployment does not exist. In fact, perhaps the clearest intellectual message of the report—subsequently confirmed—is its repeated statement that there is no long-run trade-off between unemployment and inflation. Experience in the 1980s shows clearly that reducing inflation requires at most a transitional recession. After the recession is over, inflation can fall as output rises. After the trough of the recession in late 1982, real GNP grew through 1986 with stable to declining inflation. This outcome cannot be dismissed as the result of a special disturbance such as the sharp appreciation of the dollar. Dollar appreciation, after all, served to depress output very substantially in agriculture and certain manufacturing industries.

Some Final Thoughts

The concluding points in the 1982 Economic Report, dealing with the limits to governmental economic power, remain pertinent today. Government efforts to intervene directly in wage and price decision-making in the private sector are usually ineffective or inefficient. Moreover, government cannot fully anticipate the future course of the economy. Neither can it direct economic outcomes with any degree of precision.

In retrospect, the initial Reagan economic program was the most ambitious attempt to change the direction of federal economic policy of any administration since the New Deal. The 1982 Economic Report summarized the principles that guided this program and reflected some of the enthusiasm and optimism that were the basis for its broad initial support. In the end, for various reasons, there was no "Reagan revolution"—but considerable evolution occurred in economic policy during the Reagan presidency. Citizens might well ask themselves, however, whether a future administration should also be guided by a coherent set of principles such as those presented in the 1982 Economic Report, principles that limit the role of government in the nation's economy.

America's New Beginning: A Program for Economic Recovery

I. A Program for Economic Recovery

Today the Administration is proposing a national recovery plan to reverse the debilitating combination of sustained inflation and economic distress which continues to face the American economy. Were we to stay with existing policies, the results would be readily predictable: a rising government presence in the economy, more inflation, stagnating productivity, and higher unemployment. Indeed, there is reason to fear that if we remain on this course, our economy may suffer even more calamitously.

The program we have developed will break that cycle of negative expectations. It will revitalize economic growth, renew optimism and confidence, and rekindle the Nation's entrepreneurial instincts and creativity.

The benefits to the average American will be striking. Inflation—which is now at double digit rates—will be cut in half by 1986. The American economy will produce 13 million new jobs by 1986, nearly 3 million more than if the status quo in government policy were to prevail. The economy itself should break out of its anemic growth patterns to a much more robust growth trend of 4 to 5 percent a year. These positive results will be accomplished simultaneously with reducing tax burdens, increasing private saving, and raising the living standard of the American family.

The plan is based on sound expenditure, tax, regulatory, and monetary policies. It seeks properly functioning markets, free play of wages and prices, reduced government spending and borrowing, a stable and reliable monetary framework, and reduced government barriers to risk-taking and enterprise. This agenda for the future recognizes that sensible policies which are consistently applied can re-

Issued by the White House 18 February 1981, Murray Weidenbaum the principal author.

lease the strength of the private sector, improve economic growth, and reduce inflation.

We have forgotten some important lessons in America. High taxes are not the remedy for inflation. Excessively rapid monetary growth cannot lower interest rates. Well-intentioned government regulations do not contribute to economic vitality. In fact, government spending has become so extensive that it contributes to the economic problems it was designed to cure. More government intervention in the economy cannot possibly be a solution to our economic problems.

We must remember a simple truth. The creativity and ambition of the American people are the vital forces of economic growth. The motivation and incentive of our people—to supply new goods and services and earn additional income for their families—are the most precious resources of our Nation's economy. The goal of this Administration is to nurture the strength and vitality of the American people by reducing the burdensome, intrusive role of the Federal Government; by lowering tax rates and cutting spending; and by providing incentives for individuals to work, to save, and to invest. It is our basic belief that only by reducing the growth of government can we increase the growth of the economy.

The U.S. economy faces no insurmountable barriers to sustained growth. It confronts no permanently disabling tradeoffs between inflation and unemployment, between high interest rates and high taxes, or between recession and hyperinflation. We can revive the incentives to work and save. We can restore the willingness to invest in the private capital required to achieve a steadily rising standard of living. Most important, we can regain our faith in the future.

The plan consists of four parts: (1) a substantial reduction in the growth of Federal expenditures; (2) a significant reduction in Federal tax rates; (3) prudent relief of Federal regulatory burdens; and (4) a monetary policy on the part of the independent Federal Reserve System which is consistent with those policies. These four complementary policies form an integrated and comprehensive program.

It should be clear from the most cursory examination of the economic program of this Administration that we have moved from merely talking about the economic difficulties facing the American people to taking the strong action necessary to turn the economy around.

The leading edge of our program is the comprehensive reduction in the rapid growth of Federal spending. As shown in detail below, our budget restraint is more than "cosmetic" changes in the estimates of Federal expenditures. But we have not adopted a simple-minded "meat ax" approach to budget reductions. Rather, a careful set of guidelines has been used to identify lower-priority programs in virtually every department and agency that can be eliminated, reduced, or postponed.

The second element of the program, which is equally important and urgent, is the reduction in Federal personal income tax rates by 10 percent a year for 3 years in a row. Closely related to this is an incentive to greater investment in production and job creation via faster tax write-offs of new factories and production equipment.

The third key element of our economic expansion program is an ambitious reform of regulations that will reduce the government-imposed barriers to investment, production, and employment. We have suspended for 2 months the unprecedented flood of last-minute rulemaking on the part of the previous Administration. We have eliminated the ineffective and counterproductive wage and price standards of the Council on Wage and Price Stability, and we have taken other steps to eliminate government interference in the marketplace.

The fourth aspect of this comprehensive economic program is a monetary policy to provide the financial environment consistent with a steady return to sustained growth and price stability. During the first week of this Administration its commitment to the historic independence of the Federal Reserve System was underscored. It is clear, of course, that monetary and fiscal policy are closely interrelated. Success in one area can be made more difficult—or can be reinforced—by the other. Thus, a predictable and steady growth in the money supply at more modest levels than often experienced in the past will be a vital contribution to the achievement of the economic goals described in this *Report*. The planned reduction and subsequent elimination of Federal deficit financing will help the Federal Reserve System perform its important role in achieving economic growth and stability.

The ultimate importance of this program for sustained economic growth will arise not only from the positive effects of the individual components, important as they are. Rather, it will be the dramatic improvement in the underlying economic environment and outlook that will set a new and more positive direction to economic decisions throughout the economy. Protection against inflation and high tax burdens will no longer be an overriding motivation. Once again economic choices—involving working, saving, and investment—will be based primarily on the prospect for real rewards for those productive activities which improve the true economic well-being of our citizens.

II. The Twin Problems of High Inflation and Stagnant Growth

The policies this Administration is putting forward for urgent consideration by the Congress are based on the fact that this Nation now faces its most serious set of economic problems since the 1930s. Inflation has grown from 1 to 1-½ percent a year in the early 1960s to about 13 percent in the past 2 years; not since World War I have we had 2 years of back-to-back double digit inflation. At the same time, the rate of economic growth has been slowing and the unemployment rate creeping upward. Productivity growth—the most important single measure of our ability to improve our standard of living—has been declining steadily for more than a decade. In the past 3 years our productivity actually fell.

The most important cause of our economic problems has been the government itself. The Federal Government, through tax, spending, regulatory, and monetary policies, has sacrificed long-term growth and price stability for ephemeral short-term goals. In particular, excessive government spending and overly accommodative monetary policies have combined to give us a climate of continuing inflation. That inflation itself has helped to sap our prospects for growth. In addition, the growing weight of haphazard and inefficient regulation has weakened our productivity growth. High marginal tax rates on business and individuals discourage work, innovation, and the investment necessary to improve productivity and long-run growth. Finally, the resulting stagnant growth contributes further to inflation in a vicious cycle that can only be broken with a plan that attacks broadly on all fronts.

The Role of the Government in Causing Inflation

Surges of inflation are not unusual in history; there were price explosions after both World Wars, as well as smaller outbursts in the 1920s and late 1930s. Therefore, in spite of the role played by food and energy prices in recent inflationary outbursts, it is misleading to concentrate on these transitory factors as fundamental causes of the inflationary bias in the American economy. Even when prices in these markets have been stable, inflation has continued with little relief.

What is unusual about our recent history is the *persistence of inflation*. Outbursts of high inflation in the last 15 years have not been followed by the customary price stability, but rather by long periods of continued high inflation. This persistence of inflation has crucially affected the way our economy works. People now believe inflation is "here to stay"; they plan accordingly, thereby giving further momentum to inflation. Since there are important long-term relationships between suppliers and customers and between workers and management, long-term contracts, sometimes unwritten, are often based on the view that inflation will persist. This robs the economy of flexibility which might otherwise contribute to reducing inflation.

The Federal Government has greatly contributed to the persistence of high inflation. Overly stimulative fiscal and monetary policies, on average, have financed excessive spending and thus pushed prices upward. Since government accommodation is widely expected to continue, inflation has become embedded in the economy.

When inflationary outbursts occur, policymakers all too often have made a quick turn toward restraint. Such turnabouts, however, have been short-lived and their temporary nature has increasingly been anticipated by savers, investors, and workers. Subsequent declines in employment and growth inevitably call forth stimulative policies before inflation can be brought under control. Such "stop-and-go" policies have only resulted in higher unemployment and lower real growth.

Finally, but equally important, government policies have increased inflation by reducing the potential of our economy to grow—directly through the increasing burdens of taxes and regulations, and indirectly through inflation itself. The result is a vicious circle. Its force can be measured by the statistics of our productivity slowdown, but it is seen more dramatically in the anxiety and concern of our people.

Government Contributes to the Productivity Slowdown

Productivity, popularly measured as output per worker-hour, is an indicator of the efficiency of the economy and consequently of our ability to maintain the rate of improvement in our standard of living. Over the past 15 years, the rate of productivity improvement has slowed, and now virtually halted.

Government policies have been a major contributor to the slowdown but they can be an even more important contributor to the cure. The weight of regulation and the discouragement that results from high marginal tax burdens are key factors, but inflation itself also plays an important role. Reduced capital formation is the most important and visible, but not the only, channel by which this occurs.

By increasing uncertainty about the future, inflation discourages investors from undertaking projects that they would have considered profitable but which, with today's inflationary environment, they consider too risky. Inflation also diverts funds from productive investments into hedging and speculation.

Although recent statistics show that the share of our economy's production devoted to investment is high by historic standards, the magnitude is illusory—an illusion fostered by inflation. Accelerating prices, and the high interest rates and shifting economic policy associated with them, have contributed to an unwillingness to make long-lived investments. As a result, our stock of productive plant and

Percent Annual Rate

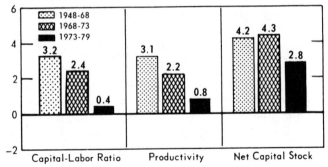

Rates of Growth in the Capital-Labor Ratio, Productivity, and Real Net Capital Stock

Capital-labor ratio is real net capital stock (gross stock less replacement requirements and pollution abatement expenditures) in the private business sector divided by employment; productivity is output per hour of all persons in the private business sector.

Source: Departments of Commerce and Labor and Council of Economic Advisers.

equipment depreciates faster, so that more investment is needed simply to stand still.

The regulatory requirements imposed by the government have likewise served to discourage investment by causing uncertainty in business decisionmaking. In addition, investments to meet regulatory requirements have diverted capital from expanding productive capacity. Some estimates have put regulation-related investment at more than 10 percent of the total level of business investment in recent years. The expanding intrusiveness of the government into the private sector also inhibits innovation and limits the ability of entrepreneurs to produce in the most efficient way.

Inflation, Growth, and the Tax System

The role of the tax system in reducing our past growth, and its potential for improving the prospects for future growth, deserve special attention. By reducing the incentives for investment and innovation, both by individuals and by businesses, the tax system has been a key cause of our stagnation. Restoring the proper incentives will make a major contribution to the long-run vitality of our economy.

The progressivity of the personal income tax system levies rising tax rates on additions to income that merely keep pace with inflation. Households therefore find that even if their gross incomes rise with inflation, their after-tax real income declines. Some households respond to these higher marginal tax burdens by reducing their work effort. "Bracket creep" also encourages taxpayers to seek out "tax

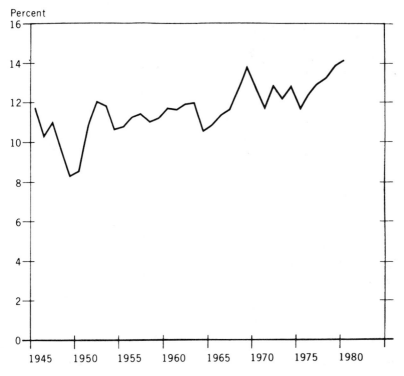

Effective Federal Personal Income Tax Rates
Federal personal taxes as a percent of taxable income.
Source: Department of Commerce and Council of Economic Advisers.

shelters," sources of income that offer higher after-tax returns but not necessarily higher before-tax returns than more productive sources, again contributing to economic inefficiency. In the last two decades the Congress has reduced personal income taxes seven times. Nevertheless, *average effective tax rates are now about 30 percent higher than their mid-1960's low.* (See Chart.) Marginal tax rates have climbed in tandem with average rates.

Due to inflation, the rate of return on corporate assets, after tax, and the level of corporate earnings have been seriously eroded over the past decade and a half. That was a major factor stunting capital spending from what it otherwise would have been. The tax treatment of depreciation has been an important contributor to this lowering of returns. We now allow write-offs at the cost of purchase, rather than at more realistic prices. This creates phantom profits upon which taxes are paid.

Finally, unless the Congress takes frequent actions to offset the revenue-generating effect of inflation on the progressive personal tax system, the Congress has available for spending unlegislated in-

Percent

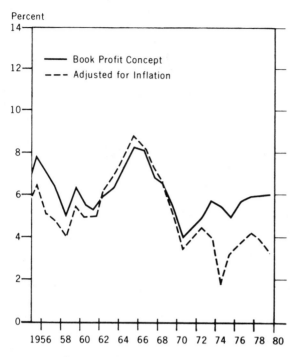

Rates of Return on Capital
Rates of return on net stocks of reproducible capital for non-financial corporations.
Source: Departments of Commerce and Treasury.

creases in funds. Inflation in tandem with the tax system thereby impairs the fiscal discipline of the budget process and facilitates higher levels of government spending than would result if the Congress were forced to vote on each tax increase. This offers further encouragement to inflation.

The Economy as a Whole Has Suffered

Because past policies have not reduced unemployment, even as they have encouraged rising inflation—the economy as a whole has suffered. Over the past two decades, we have seen the "misery index"—the sum of the inflation and unemployment rates—more than double, rising from 7.3 in 1960 to 17.2 in 1980. While unemployment rates have fluctuated over the business cycle, there has been no long-run tradeoff between unemployment and inflation. The upward movements in inflation have not brought us falling unemployment rates, nor has high unemployment brought lower inflation.

Thus, trends of the past are clearly disturbing in that they have sapped our Nation's economic vitality. Of greater significance, however, is the danger we face if the policies of the 1970s are continued.

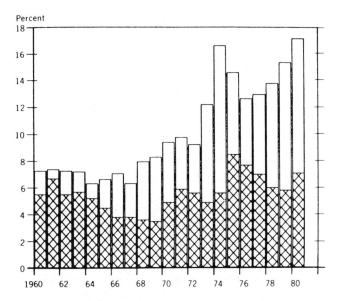

Misery Index (Unemployment Rate Plus Inflation)

Cross-hatching, unemployment rate; no cross-hatching, percentage change in the personal consumption expenditures deflator.

Source: Based on data from Departments of Commerce and Labor.

For the first time in American history financial markets reflect the belief that inflation will not retreat significantly from current high levels. The Nation's economy and financial system are on a dangerous course—one which, if not reversed, would lead to a prolonged stagnation of economic growth and employment, ever higher inflation and interest rates, and potentially a financial crisis. The solution to this growing economic threat calls for bold actions designed to reduce—dramatically and sharply—inflationary expectations. These policies must restore fiscal integrity; increase incentives for saving, investment, and production; attain monetary and financial stability; and enhance the role of the marketplace as the principal force in the allocation of resources.

III. Slowing the Growth of Government Spending

The uncontrolled growth of government spending has been a primary cause of the sustained high rate of inflation experienced by the American economy. Perhaps of greater importance, the continued and apparently inexorable expansion of government has contributed to the widespread expectation of persisting—and possibly higher—rates of inflation in the future.

Thus, a central goal of the economic program is to reduce the rate at which government spending increases. In view of the seriousness of the inflationary pressures facing us, the proposed reductions in the Federal budget for the coming fiscal year are the largest ever proposed.

Despite the tendency to refer to "cutting" the budget, it is clear that an expanding population, a growing economy, and a difficult international environment all lead to the need for year-to-year rises in the level of government spending. Thus, the badly needed effort to "cut" the budget really refers to reductions in the amount of increase in spending requested from one year to the next.

The magnitude of the fiscal problem facing the United States can be seen when we realize that, despite the $49.1 billion of savings including $5.7 billion in off-budget outlays that is being recommended for fiscal 1982, the total amount of Federal outlays for the year is likely to be $41 billion higher than the current year. (A separate document is being issued by the Office of Management and Budget that outlines the major spending reductions in considerable detail.)

It is essential to stress the fundamental principles that guided the development of that program.

First, and most importantly, all members of our society except the truly needy will be asked to contribute to the program for spending control.

Second, we will strengthen our national defense.

Finally, these fundamental principles led to nine specific guidelines that were applied in reducing the budget:

- Preserve "the social safety net."
- Revise entitlements to eliminate unintended benefits.
- Reduce subsidies to middle- and upper-income groups.
- Impose fiscal restraint on other national interest programs.
- Recover costs that can be clearly allocated to users.
- Stretch-out and retarget public sector capital investment programs.
- Reduce overhead and personnel costs of the Federal Government.
- Apply sound economic criteria to subsidy programs.
- Consolidate categorical grant programs into block grants.

The application of these guidelines has required great care, judgment, and sensitivity. However, we are putting forward over 80 proposals that will carry out these guidelines and affect virtually every segment of our economy except the truly needy. The Administration's insistence on this fundamental principle has meant that programs benefiting millions of truly needy beneficiaries have not been affected by the spending control effort. These programs include social insurance benefits for the elderly, basic unemployment benefits, cash benefits for the chronically poor, and society's obligations to veterans.

The selection of specific reductions has been a difficult task involving the entire Administration as well as much consolidation with representatives of business, labor, agriculture, minority groups, and State and local governments.

The spending reduction plan will shift Federal budget priorities so that Federal resources are spent for purposes that are truly the responsibility of the national government. As the table below indicates, our budget plans reflect the increased importance attached to national defense, maintain the Federal Government's support for the truly needy, and fulfill our responsibilities for interest payments on the national debt. The spending reductions will restrain Federal involvement in areas that are properly left to State and local governments or to the private sector.

Shift in budget priorities

Dollar amounts (in billions)	1962	1981	1984
DOD - military	46.8	157.9	249.8
Safety net programs	26.2	239.3	313.0
Net interest	6.9	64.3	66.8
All other	26.9	193.2	142.0
Total	106.8	654.7	771.6
Outlay shares (percent)			
DOD - military	43.8	24.1	32.4
Safety net programs	24.5	36.6	40.6
Net interest	6.4	9.8	8.6
All other	25.2	29.5	18.4
Total	100.0	100.0	100.0

Carrying out this program of budget restraint will also halt and begin to reverse the tendency of government to take an ever-larger share of our economic resources. From a high of 23 percent of the gross national product (GNP) in fiscal 1981, Federal outlays are now scheduled to decline to 21.8 percent in fiscal 1982 and to reach approximately 19 percent beginning in 1984.

The Federal budget and GNP

Fiscal year	Outlays as percent of GNP
1981	23.0
1982	21.8
1983	20.4
1984	19.3
1985	19.2
1986	19.0

In conjunction with the tax program that is being proposed, the present excessively high deficit in the budget will be reduced and, in a few years, eliminated. Because of the legacy of fiscal commitments that were inherited by this Administration, balancing the budget will require tough action over several years.

From a deficit of $59.6 billion in 1980—and of a similar deficit this year if past policies had continued—Federal expenditures are now estimated to exceed revenues by $45.0 billion in 1982, and $23.0 billion in 1983. By fiscal 1984—under the policy recommendations presented in this document—the Federal budget should be in balance. And that will not be a one-time occurrence. As shown in the table below, the Federal budget will actually generate a surplus in 1985 and 1986, for the first time since 1969.

Federal revenues and outlays

Fiscal year	Revenues[1]	Outlays[1]	Deficit (−) or surplus (+)[1]
1981	600.2	654.7	− 54.5
1982	650.5	695.5	− 45.0
1983	710.1	733.1	− 23.0
1984	772.1	771.6	+ 0.5
1985	851.0	844.0	+ 7.0
1986	942.1	912.1	+ 30.0

[1]In billions of dollars.

The Federal Budget and the Economy

The rewards that the economy will reap with enactment of the spending control plan are many and substantial. In the past, excessive deficit spending has been a major contributor to the initiation and persistence of inflation. Not only have Federal budget deficits at times of expanding private sector activity fueled inflationary pressures, but government's tendency to stop fighting inflation with the first signs of a slackening economy has persuaded firms and workers that they need not fear pricing themselves out of business with inflationary wage and price increases. With the plans for controlling government spending, the Federal budget will become a weapon against inflation, rather than one of its major causes.

During the decade of the 1970s, the Federal budget was in deficit every year. In 1970 the deficit was a relatively modest $2.8 billion; in 1980 it was nearly $60 billion. Outlays soared by almost 200 percent. When this Administration began, the prospect was for a continuation of these alarming trends.

Fiscal year	Receipts[1]	Outlays[1]	Deficit (−)[1]
1970	193.7	196.6	− 2.8
1971	188.4	211.4	− 23.0
1972	208.6	232.0	− 23.4
1973	232.2	247.1	− 14.8
1974	264.9	269.6	− 4.7
1975	281.0	326.2	− 45.2
1976	300.0	366.4	− 66.4
1977	357.8	402.7	− 44.9
1978	402.0	450.8	− 48.8
1979	465.9	493.6	− 27.7
1980	520.0	579.6	− 59.6

[1]In billions of dollars.

Many of the program reductions that are being proposed will contribute to a more efficient use of resources in the economy and thereby higher levels of production and income. No longer will the average American taxpayer be asked to contribute to programs that further narrow private interests rather than the general public interest. In many cases, such services are more appropriately paid for with user charges. By consolidating a variety of categorical grant programs into a few block grant programs, the resources spent will provide greater benefits because the levels of government closer to the people can better recognize their needs than can Washington. And by reducing Federal deficits and off-budget Federal financing we will ensure that Federal borrowing requirements do not crowd more productive private activities out of the market.

The budget that is being proposed will restore the Federal Government to its proper role in American society. It will contribute to the health of the economy, the strength of our military, and the protection of the less fortunate members of society who need the compassion of the government for their support. Many special interests who had found it easier to look to the Federal Government for support than to the competitive market will be disappointed by this budget, but the average worker and businessman, the backbone of our Nation, will find that their interests are better served.

IV. Reducing Tax Burdens

An integral part of the comprehensive economic program is a set of tax proposals to improve the after-tax, after-inflation rewards to work, saving, and investment. Inflation inevitably increases the burden of taxes on individuals by pushing them into higher and higher marginal rates. In businesses, inflation makes the purchase of new equipment progressively more difficult by reducing the amount of cash flow available for capital investment. The tax package addresses both of these problems.

Tax Relief for Individuals

Any increase in nominal income moves taxpayers into higher tax brackets, whether the increase is real or merely an adjustment for higher costs of living. As a consequence, taxes rise faster than inflation, raising average tax rates and tax burdens. In fact, every 10 percent increase in income—real or nominal—produces about a 15 percent increase in Federal personal income tax receipts. An average family requiring a $1,500 cost-of-living increase to maintain its standard of living must have $1,900 in wage increases to keep even after taxes.

Individual tax liabilities rose from 9.2 percent of personal income in 1965 to 11.6 percent last year. The average tax burden would have risen far more had not much of the inflation-related tax increases been offset by periodic tax cuts. Marginal tax rates, however, have been allowed to rise sharply for most taxpayers. In 1965, 6 percent of all taxpayers faced marginal rates of 25 percent or more. Today nearly one of every three taxpayers is in at least the 25 percent bracket.

As taxpayers move into higher brackets, incentives to work, save, and invest are reduced since each addition to income yields less after taxes than before. In the late 1960s and the early 1970s, Americans saved between 7 to 9 percent of personal disposable income. In 1979 and 1980, the saving rate was between 5 to 6 percent. The combination of inflation and higher marginal tax rates is undoubtedly a major factor in the lower personal saving rate.

To correct these problems and to improve the after-tax return from work and from saving, the President is asking the Congress to reduce the marginal tax rates for individuals across the board by 10 percent per year for the next 3 years starting July 1, 1981. This would reduce rates in stages from a range of 14 to 70 percent to a range of 10 to 50 percent effective January 1, 1984. These rate reductions will contribute materially above those which would be attained under present laws. At these higher income levels, the reductions in Federal tax revenues, compared with those which would be obtained under present law, are $6.4 billion in fiscal 1981, $44.2 billion in fiscal 1982, and rise to $162.4 billion in fiscal 1986.

The effect of these tax cuts on a 4-person family whose 1980 income is $25,000 would be a $153 tax reduction this year, and a $809 tax reduction for 1984, assuming no increase in income. If the family's nominal earnings rise to $30,300 in 1984, their tax reduction would be $1,112 in that year.

The Administration's proposals will bring down average individual tax receipts to 10.8 percent of personal income in 1984, still 1.6 percentage points above where it was in 1965. Without these marginal tax rate cuts, however, individual taxes would rise to 14.7 percent of personal income by 1984. Failure to enact these proposals is thus tantamount to imposing a tax increase on the average American taxpayer.

Tax Incentives for Investment

Since the late 1960s the rate of net capital formation (excluding spending mandated to meet environmental standards) has fallen substantially. For the 5 years ending in 1979, increases in real net business fixed capital averaged just over 2 percent of the Nation's real net national product, or one-half the rate for the latter part of the 1960s.

One of the major tasks facing the U.S. economy in the 1980s is to reverse these trends and to promote more capital investment. To combat the decline in productivity growth, to hasten the replacement of energy-efficient machines and equipment, to comply with government mandates that do not enhance production, we must increase the share of our Nation's resources going to investment. Both improvements in productivity and increases in productive jobs will come from expanded investment.

Inflation and an outdated capital equipment depreciation system have combined to lower the after-tax real rate of return on capital investments by business. High inflation causes a large discrepancy between the historic and the current replacement costs of physical assets of business. Thus, corporate financial records, utilizing historic costs and current dollar sales figures, significantly overstate nominal profits and understate true economic costs.

In 1980 alone, the replacement cost of inventories exceeded by over $43 billion the cost of the inventories claimed for tax purposes. Depreciation charges based on historical cost fell short of the replacement cost of capital assets consumed by another $17 billion. These arose from a failure to record inventory and capital assets at their true replacement cost.

On an inflation adjusted basis, many firms are now paying out more than their real income in the form of taxes and dividends. The result is that real investment in equipment, maintenance, modernization, and new technology is falling further behind the needs of our economy. Clearly, present incentives for business capital formation are inadequate.

As a consequence, the President is asking the Congress to provide for an accelerated cost recovery system for machinery and equipment and certain structures according to the following classes:

• Ten years on an accelerated write-off schedule for long-lived public utility property (with a 10 percent investment credit) and factories, stores, and warehouses used by their owners (no investment credit, consistent with present law).

• Five years on an accelerated write-off schedule (plus 10 percent investment credit) for all other machinery and equipment except long-lived utility property.

• Three years on an accelerated write-off schedule (plus 6 percent investment credit) for autos and light trucks and capital costs for research and development.

In addition, audit-proof recovery periods would be established for other depreciable real estate:

• Fifteen years straight line (and no investment credit) for other non-residential buildings and low-income housing.

• Eighteen years straight line (and no investment credit) for other rental residential structures.

A 5-year phase-in of the accelerated recovery rates for the 5-year and 10-year classes is proposed, but the effective date would be January 1, 1981, so that no pending investment plans are deferred in anticipation of the new system. These tax changes will make important contributions to raising economic activity above the levels of which would be attained under present laws. At this higher income, Federal tax revenues would be less than those which would be obtained under present law, by $2.5 billion in fiscal 1981, $9.7 billion in fiscal 1982, and $59.3 billion in fiscal 1986.

Direct revenue effects of proposed tax reductions (in billions of dollars)

	Fiscal years					
	1981	1982	1983	1984	1985	1986
Individual						
30 percent phased rate reduction	−6.4	−44.2	−81.4	−118.1	−141.5	−162.4
Business						
Accelerated cost recovery system after interaction with individual tax	−2.5	−9.7	−18.6	−30.0	−44.2	−59.3
Total	−8.8	−53.9	100.0	−148.1	−185.7	−221.7

These changes will simplify accounting procedures and raise after-tax profits of businesses. For example, a manufacturer of glass products that buys new machinery for $100,000 in 1982 will, as a result of these new cost recovery allowances, reduce its tax liability by $1,798 in that year, $2,517 in 1983, and additional amounts in later years.

The basic differences between the present accelerated depreciation law and proposed accelerated capital cost recovery system are shown in the following chart:

Present law depreciation and accelerated cost recovery system (comparison of major features)

Item	Present law depreciation	Accelerated cost recovery system
General applicability	Option of "facts and circumstances" or guidelines (ADR).	Mandatory.
Recovery periods		
Tangible personal property	Guidelines allow 2-½ to 50 years depending on asset type or activity, with optional 20 percent variance for each.	3 years (autos, light trucks, and machinery and equipment used for research and development), 5 years (most machinery and equipment), or 10 years (long-lived public utility property).
Real estate	Determined by facts and circumstances or by guidelines ranging from 25 to 60 years depending on the type of building.	10 years for owner-occupied factories, stores, and warehouses; 15 years for other nonresidential and for low-income housing; 18 years for other residential.
Recovery method		
Tangible personal property	Straight line; or for new property, taxpayer may elect declining balance up to 200 percent, or sum-of-years digits.	Accelerated write-off built into tables.
Real estate	Same for new residential; up to 150 percent declining balance for new, nonresidential; up to 125 percent declining balance for used residential; straight line for used nonresidential.	Same for 10-year property. Straight line for other.

Present law depreciation and accelerated cost recovery system (comparison of major features) (continued)

Item	Present law depreciation	Accelerated cost recovery system
Recapture provisions		
Tangible personal property	Ordinary income recapture up to prior allowances (section 1245).	Ordinary income recapture up to prior allowances (section 1245).
Real estate	Ordinary income recapture up to excess over straight line (section 1250).	Same for 10-year real property. No recapture for others.
Asset accounting		
General	Vintage accounting.	Vintage accounting.
First year	Ratably, or choice of conventions.	Half-year convention built into tables.
Investment tax credit	3-⅓ percent for machinery and equipment written-off or held for 3–5 years, 6-⅔ percent for 5–7 years, 10 percent if longer.	6 percent for 3-year class and 10 percent for 5-year and 10-year eligible property.
Carryovers	Choice of 20 percent shorter or longer lives; straight line or accelerated methods, where allowed. Deductions may add to net operating loss which can be carried over 7 years.	Extends net operating loss and investment credit carryover period from 7 to 10 years.
Timing of eligibility	When placed in service.	When placed in service, or for property with at least a 2 year construction period, as acquired.

V. Providing Regulatory Relief

The rapid growth in Federal regulation has retarded economic growth and contributed to inflationary pressures. While there is widespread agreement on the legitimate role of government in protecting the environment, promoting health and safety, safeguarding workers and consumers, and guaranteeing equal opportunity, there is also growing realization that excessive regulation is a very significant factor in our current economic difficulties.

The costs of regulation arise in several ways. First, there are the outlays for the Federal bureaucracy which administers and enforces the regulations. Second, there are the costs to business, nonprofit institutions, and State and local governments of complying with regulations. Finally, there are the longer run and indirect effects of regulation on economic growth and productivity.

The most readily identifiable of the costs are the administrative outlays of the regulatory agencies, since they appear in the Federal budget. These costs are passed on to individuals and businesses directly in the form of higher Federal taxes. Much larger than the administrative expenses are the costs of compliance, which add $100 billion per year to the costs of the goods and services we buy. The most important effects of regulation, however, are the adverse impacts on economic growth. These arise because regulations may discourage innovative research and development, reduce investment in new plant and equipment, raise unemployment by increasing labor costs, and reduce competition. Taken together, these longer run effects contribute significantly to our current economic dilemma of high unemployment and inflation.

In many cases the costs of regulation can be substantially reduced without significantly affecting worthwhile regulatory goals. Unnecessarily stringent rules, intrusive means of enforcement, extensive reporting and recordkeeping requirements, and other regulatory excesses are all too common.

During this Administration's first month in office, five major steps have been taken to address the problem of excessive and inefficient regulation. Specifically, we have:

• Established a Task Force on Regulatory Relief chaired by Vice President George Bush.

• Abolished the Council on Wage and Price Stability's ineffective program to control wage and price increases.

• Postponed the effective dates of pending regulations until the end of March.

• Issued an Executive order to strengthen Presidential oversight of the regulatory process.

• Accelerated the decontrol of domestic oil.

Presidential Task Force on Regulatory Relief

Previous efforts to manage the proliferation of Federal regulation failed to establish central regulatory oversight at the highest level. On January 22, the President announced the creation of a Task Force on

Regulatory Relief to be chaired by the Vice President. The membership is to include the Secretary of the Treasury, the Attorney General, the Secretary of Commerce, the Secretary of Labor, the Director of the Office of Management and Budget, the Assistant to the President for Policy Development, and the Chairman of the Council of Economic Advisers.

The Task Force's charter is to:

• Review major regulatory proposals by executive branch agencies, especially those that appear to have major policy significance or involve overlapping jurisdiction among agencies.

• Assess executive branch regulations already on the books, concentrating on those that are particularly burdensome to the national economy or to key industrial sectors.

• Oversee the development of legislative proposals designed to balance and coordinate the roles and objectives of regulatory agencies.

Termination of CWPS's Wage-Price Standards Program

The Council on Wage and Price Stability (CWPS) was created in 1974, and like many government agencies, rapidly grew in size and scope. But the CWPS program of wage-price standards proved to be totally ineffective in halting the rising rate of inflation.

On January 29, the President rescinded the CWPS's wage-price standards program. As a result, taxpayers will save about $1.5 million, employment in the Executive Office of the President will decline by about 135 people, and Federal requirements that businesses submit voluminous reports will end.

Postponing Pending Regulations

On January 29, the President also sent a memorandum to cabinet officers and the head of the Environmental Protection Agency (EPA), requesting that, to the extent permitted by law, they postpone the effective dates of those regulations that would have become effective before March 29 and that they refrain from issuing any new final regulations during this 60-day period.

This suspension of new regulations has three purposes: First, it allows the new Administration to review the "midnight" regulations issued during the last days of the previous Administration to assure that they are cost-effective. Second, the Administration's appointees now can become familiar with the details of the various programs for which they are responsible before the regulations become final. Lastly, the suspension allows time for the Administration, through the Presidential Task Force, to develop improved procedures for management and oversight of the regulatory process.

The Executive Order on Federal Regulation

The President has signed a new Executive order designed to improve management of the Federal regulatory process. It provides reassurance to the American people of the government's ability to control its regulatory activities. The Office of Management and Budget is charged with administering the new order, subject to the overall direction of the Presidential Task Force on Regulatory Relief.

The order emphasizes that regulatory decisions should be based on adequate information. Actions should not be undertaken unless the potential benefits to society outweigh the potential costs, and regulatory priorities should be set on the basis of net benefits to society. The order requires agencies to determine the most cost-effective approach for meeting any given regulatory objective, taking into account such factors as the economic condition of industry, the national economy, and other prospective regulations.

As part of the development of any important regulation, the order also requires that each agency prepare a Regulatory Impact Analysis to evaluate potential benefits and costs. The Task Force will oversee this process; OMB will make comments on regulatory analyses, help determine which new and existing regulations should be reviewed, and direct the publication of semiannual agendas of the regulations that agencies plan to issue or review.

Decontrolling Domestic Oil Prices

The President has also ordered the immediate decontrol of domestic oil prices, instead of waiting until October as originally scheduled. This has eliminated a large Federal bureauracy which administered a cumbersome and inefficient system of regulations that served to stifle domestic oil production, increase our dependence on foreign oil, and discourage conservation.

Integrating the Goals of Regulatory Relief with Paperwork Reduction

Our program to reduce regulatory burdens will dovetail with the efforts under the Paperwork Reduction Act of 1980. Lamentably, present regulations will require Americans to spend over 1.2 billion hours filling out government forms during 1981. This is equivalent to the annual labor input for the entire steel industry.

The Congress responded to the need for consistent management of Federal paperwork and regulatory issues by passing the Paperwork Reduction Act of 1980. The act creates an Office of Information and Regulatory Affairs within OMB with the power to review Federal regulations that contain a recordkeeping or reporting requirement and directs this agency to reduce the paperwork burden by 15 percent.

Future Targets for Regulatory Review

The program of regulatory relief is just getting under way. Future regulatory reform efforts will be directed not only at proposed regulations, but also at existing regulations and regulatory statutes that are particularly burdensome. This process has already begun: in the first month of the Administration several cabinet departments and agencies—on their own initiative and in coordination with the Task Force—have taken action on particularly controversial rules. For example, rules mandating extensive bilingual education programs, passive restraints in large cars, the labeling of chemicals in the workplace, controls on garbage truck noise, and increased overtime payments for executives have been withdrawn or postponed. The actions taken already are expected to save the American public and industry almost $1 billion annually. The Administration will be reviewing a host of other regulations in the near future.

Legislative Changes

Not all of our regulatory problems can be resolved satisfactorily through more effective regulatory management and decisionmaking. Existing regulatory statutes too often preclude effective regulatory decisions. Many of the statutes are conflicting, overlapping, or inconsistent. Some force agencies to promulgate regulations while giving them little discretion to take into account changing conditions or new information. Other statutes give agencies extremely broad discretion, which they have sometimes exercised unwisely.

The Administration will examine all legislation that serves as the foundation for major regulatory programs. This omnibus review, spearheaded by the Presidential Task Force on Regulatory Relief, will result in recommendations to reform these statutes. The Task Force will initially concentrate its efforts on those laws scheduled for Congressional oversight or reauthorization, such as the Clean Air Act.

VI. Controlling Money and Credit

Monetary policy is the responsibility of the Federal Reserve System, an independent agency within the structure of the government. The Administration will do nothing to undermine that independence. At the same time, the success in reducing inflation, increasing real income, and reducing unemployment will depend on effective interaction of monetary policy with other aspects of economic policy.

To achieve the goals of the Administration's economic program, consistent monetary policy must be applied. Thus, it is expected that the rate of money and credit growth will be brought down to levels consistent with noninflationary expansion of the economy.

If monetary policy is too expansive, then inflation during the years ahead will continue to accelerate and the Administration's economic program will be undermined. Inflationary psychology will intensify. Wages, prices, and interest rates will reflect the belief that inflation—will continue.

By contrast, if monetary policy is unduly restrictive, a different set of problems arises, unnecessarily aggravating recession and unemployment. At times in the past, abruptly restrictive policies have prompted excessive reactions toward short-term monetary ease. As a result, frequent policy changes can send confusing signals, and the additional uncertainty undermines long-term investment decisions and economic growth.

With money and credit growth undergoing steady, gradual reduction over a period of years, it will be possible to reduce inflation substantially and permanently. In this regard, the Administration supports the announced objective of the Federal Reserve to continue to seek gradual reduction in the growth of money and credit aggregates during the years ahead. Looking back, it seems clear that if a policy of this kind had been successfully followed in the past, inflation today would be substantially lower and would not appear to be so intractable.

Until recently, the Federal Reserve had attempted to control money growth by setting targets for interest rates, particularly the rate on Federal funds. Experience here and abroad has shown repeatedly that this interest rate management approach is not sufficient to achieve reliable control. Mistakes in predicting movements in economic activity or tendencies on the part of policymakers to avoid large interest rate fluctuations can lead to undesirable gyrations in the rate of money growth.

Under new procedures the Federal Reserve adopted in October 1979, the Federal Reserve sets targets for growth of reserves considered to be consistent with the desired expansion in the monetary aggregates. Interest rates are allowed to vary over a much wider range in response to changes in the demand for money and credit. A number of factors—such as the introduction of credit controls and their subsequent removal and frequent shifts in announced fiscal policies—have contributed to pronounced fluctuations in interest rates and monetary growth over the past year. At the same time, we need to learn from the experience with the new techniques and seek further improvements. The Federal Reserve has undertaken a study of last year's experience. We look forward to the results and encourage them to make the changes that appear warranted.

In that connection, success in meeting the targets that the Federal Reserve has set will itself increase confidence in the results of policy. Otherwise, observers are likely to pay excessive attention to short-run changes in money growth and revise anticipations upward or downward unnecessarily. Without confidence in the long-term direction of policy, such short-run changes may lead to unwarranted but disturbing gyrations in credit, interest rates, commodity prices, and other sensitive indicators of inflation and economic growth.

Better monetary control is not consistent with the management of interest rates in the short run. But, with monetary policy focusing on long-term objectives, the resultant restraint on money and credit growth would interact with the tax and expenditure proposals to lower inflation as well as interest rates.

The Administration will confer regularly with the Federal Reserve Board on all aspects of our economic program. The policies that are proposed in the program will help to advance the efforts of the independent Federal Reserve System. In particular, the substantial reductions of the Federal Government's deficit financing and the achievement of a balanced budget in 1984 and the years that follow should enable the Federal Reserve System to reduce dramatically the growth in the money supply.

To that end, the economic scenario assumes that the growth rates of money and credit are steadily reduced from the 1980 levels to one-half those levels by 1986.

With the Federal Reserve gradually but persistently reducing the growth of money, inflation should decline at least as fast as anticipated. Moreover, if monetary growth rates are restrained, then inflationary expectations will decline. And since interest rate movements are largely a mirror of price expectations, reduction in one will produce reduction in the other.

VII. A New Beginning for the Economy

This plan for national recovery represents a substantial break with past policy. The new policy is based on the premise that the people who make up the economy—workers, managers, savers, investors, buyers, and sellers—do not need the government to make reasoned and intelligent decisions about how best to organize and run their own lives. They continually adapt to best fit the current environment. The most appropriate role for government economic policy is to provide a stable and unfettered environment in which private individuals can confidently plan and make appropriate decisions. The new recovery plan is designed to bring to all aspects of government policy a greater sense of purpose and consistency.

Central to the new policy is the view that expectations play an important role in determining economic activity, inflation, and interest rates. Decisions to work, save, spend, and invest depend crucially on expectations regarding future government policies. Establishing an environment which ensures efficient and stable incentives for work, saving, and investment now and in the future is the cornerstone of the recovery plan.

Personal tax reductions will allow people to keep more of what they earn, providing increased incentives for work and saving. Business tax reductions will provide increased incentives for capital expansion, resulting in increased productivity for workers. Spending reductions and elimination of unneeded regulation will return control over resources to the private sector where incentives to economize are strongest. Stable monetary policy, combined with expanding productive capacity, will bring about a reduction of the inflation rate.

Inflation control is best achieved with a two-edged policy designed both to limit the rate of increase in the money stock and to increase the productive capacity of the economy. Neither policy can be expected to achieve adequate results alone.

A stable monetary policy, gradually slowing growth rates of money and credit along a preannounced and predictable path, will lead to reductions in inflation. At the same time, the effects of supply-oriented tax and regulatory changes on work incentives, expansion and improvement of the capital stock, and improved productivity will boost output and create a "buyers' market" for goods and services.

As a result of the policies set forth here, our economy's productive capacity is expected to grow significantly faster than could be achieved with a continuation of past policies. Specifically, real economic activity is projected to recover from the 1980–81 period of weakness and move to a 4 to 5 percent annual growth path through

1986, as shown in the table below. Concurrently, the general rate of inflation is expected to decline steadily to less than 5 percent annually by 1986 from the current 10 percent plus rate.

Economic assumptions

	Calendar years					
	1981	1982	1983	1984	1985	1986
Nominal gross national product (billions)	$2,920.0	$3,293.0	$3,700.0	$4,098.0	$4,500.0	$4,918.0
(Percent change)	11.1	12.8	12.4	10.8	9.8	9.3
Real gross national product (billions, 1972 dollars)	1,497.0	1,560.0	1,638.0	1,711.0	1,783.0	1,858.0
(Percent change)	1.1	4.2	5.0	4.5	4.2	4.2
Implicit price deflator	195.0	211.0	226.0	240.0	252.0	265.0
(Percent change)	9.9	8.3	7.0	6.0	5.4	4.9
Consumer price index[1] (1967 = 100)	274.0	297.0	315.0	333.0	348.0	363.0
(Percent change)	11.1	8.3	6.2	5.5	4.7	4.2
Unemployment rate (percent)	7.8	7.2	6.6	6.4	6.0	5.6

[1]CPI for urban wage earners and clerical workers (CPI-W).

In contrast to the inflationary demand-led booms of the 1970s, the most significant growth of economic activity will occur in the supply side of the economy. Not only will a steady expansion in business fixed investment allow our economy to grow without fear of capacity-induced inflation pressures, but it will also increase productivity and reduce the growth of production costs by incorporating new and more high-efficient plants, machinery, and technology into our manufacturing base. The result will be revitalized growth in the real incomes and standards of living of our citizens and significantly reduced inflationary pressures. As our economy responds to a new era of economic policy, unemployment will be significantly reduced.

The Administration's plan for national recovery will take a large step toward improving the international economic environment by repairing domestic conditions. Improving expectations and slowing inflation will enhance the dollar as an international store of value and contribute to greater stability in international financial markets. As interest rates come down and faster U.S. growth contributes to rising world trade, economic expansion in other countries will also accelerate. This Administration will work closely with the other major industrial countries to promote consistency in economic objectives and policies so as to speed a return to noninflationary growth in the world economy. Finally, rising U.S. productivity will enhance our ability to compete with other countries in world markets, easing protectionist pressures at home and thus strengthening our ability to press other countries to reduce their trade barriers and export subsidies.

The economic assumptions contained in this message may seem optimistic to some observers. Indeed they do represent a dramatic departure from the trends of recent years—but so do the proposed policies. In fact, if each portion of this comprehensive economic program is put in place—quickly and completely—the economic environment could improve even more rapidly than envisioned in these assumptions.

But, if the program is accepted piecemeal—if only those aspects that are politically palatable are adopted—then this economic policy will be no more than a repeat of what has been tried before. And we already know the results of the stop-and-go policies of the past.

Indeed, if we as a Nation do not take the bold new policy initiatives proposed in this program, we will face a continuation and a worsening of the trends that have developed in the last two decades. We have a rare opportunity to reverse these trends: to stimulate growth, productivity, and employment at the same time that we move toward the elimination of inflation.

ECONOMIC REPORT
OF THE PRESIDENT

ECONOMIC REPORT OF THE PRESIDENT

To the Congress of the United States:

In the year just ended, the first decisive steps were taken toward a fundamental reorientation of the role of the Federal Government in our economy—a reorientation that will mean more jobs, more opportunity, and more freedom for all Americans. This long overdue redirection is designed to foster the energy, creativity, and ambition of the American people so that they can create better lives for themselves, their families, and the communities in which they live. Equally important, this redirection puts the economy on the path of less inflationary but more rapid economic growth.

My economic program is based on the fundamental precept that government must respect, protect, and enhance the freedom and integrity of the individual. Economic policy must seek to create a climate that encourages the development of private institutions conducive to individual responsibility and initiative. People should be encouraged to go about their daily lives with the right and the responsibility for determining their own activities, status, and achievements.

This *Report* reviews the condition of the American economy as it was inherited by this Administration. It describes the policies which have been adopted to reverse the debilitating trends of the past, and which will lead to recovery in 1982 and sustained, noninflationary growth in the years to follow. And, finally, this *Report* explains the impact these policies will have on the economic well-being of all Americans in the years to come.

The Legacy of the Past

For several decades, an ever-larger role for the Federal Government and, more recently, inflation have sapped the economic vitality of the Nation.

In the 1960s Federal spending averaged 19.5 percent of the Nation's output. In the 1970s it rose to 20.9 percent, and in 1980 it reached 22.5 percent. The burden of tax revenues showed a similar pattern, with increasingly high tax rates stifling individual initiative and distorting the flow of saving and investment.

The substantially expanded role of the Federal Government has been far deeper and broader than even the growing burden of spending and taxing would suggest. Over the past decade the government has spun a vast web of regulations that intrude into almost every aspect of every American's working day. This regulatory web adversely affects the productivity of our Nation's businesses, farms, educational institutions, State and local governments, and the oper-ations of the Federal Government itself. That lessened productivity growth, in turn, increases the costs of the goods and services we buy from each other. And those regulations raise the cost of government at all levels and the taxes we pay to support it.

Consider also the tragic record of inflation—that unlegislated tax on everyone's income—which causes high interest rates and discour-ages saving and investment. During the 1960s, the average yearly in-crease in the consumer price index was 2.3 percent. In the 1970s the rate more than doubled to 7.1 percent; and in the first year of the 1980s it soared to 13.5 percent. We simply cannot blame crop fail-ures and oil price increases for our basic inflation problem. The con-tinuous, underlying cause was poor government policy.

The combination of these two factors—ever higher rates of infla-tion and ever greater intrusion by the Federal Government into the Nation's economic life—have played a major part in a fundamental deterioration in the performance of our economy. In the 1960s pro-ductivity in the American economy grew at an annual rate of 2.9 per-cent; in the 1970s productivity growth slowed by nearly one-half, to 1.5 percent. Real gross national product per capita grew at an annual rate of 2.8 percent in the 1960s compared to 2.1 percent in the 1970s. This deterioration in our economic performance has been accompanied by inadequate growth in employment opportunities for our Nation's growing work force.

Reversing the trends of the past is not an easy task. I never thought or stated it would be. The damage that has been inflicted on our economy was done by imprudent and inappropriate policies over a period of many years; we cannot realistically expect to undo it all in a few short months. But during the past year we have made a sub-stantial beginning.

Policies for the 1980s

Upon coming into office, my Administration set out to design and carry out a long-run economic program that would decisively reverse the trends of the past, and make growth and prosperity the norm, rather than the exception for the American economy. To that end, my first and foremost objective has been to improve the performance of the economy by reducing the role of the Federal Government in all its many dimensions. This involves a commitment to reduce Fed-eral spending and taxing as a share of gross national product. It means a commitment to reduce progressively the size of the Federal deficit. It involves a substantial reform of Federal regulation, eliminating it where possible and simplifying it where appropriate. It means eschewing the stop-and-go economic policies of the past which, with their short-term focus, only added to our long-run economic ills.

A reduced role for the Federal Government means an enhanced role for State and local governments. A wide range of Federal activities can be more appropriately and efficiently carried out by the States. I am proposing in my *Budget Message* a major shift in this direction. This shift will eliminate the "freight charge" imposed by the Federal Government on the taxpayers' money when it is sent to Washington and then doled out again. It will permit a substantial reduction in Federal employment involved in administering these programs. Transfers of programs will permit public sector activities to be more closely tailored to the needs and desires of the electorate, bringing taxing and spending decisions closer to the people. Furthermore, as a result of last year's Economic Recovery Tax Act, Federal taxation as a share of national income will be substantially reduced, providing States and localities with an expanded tax base so that they can finance those transferred programs they wish to continue. That tax base will be further increased later in this decade, as Federal excise taxes are phased out.

These initiatives follow some common sense approaches to making government more efficient and responsive:

- We should leave to private initiative all the functions that individuals can perform privately.
- We should use the level of government closest to the community involved for all the public functions it can handle. This principle includes encouraging intergovernmental arrangements among the State and local communities.
- Federal Government action should be reserved for those needed functions that only the national government can undertake.

The accompanying report from my Council of Economic Advisers develops the basis for these guidelines more fully.

To carry out these policies for the 1980s, my Administration has put into place a series of fundamental and far-reaching changes in Federal Government spending, taxing, and regulatory policy, and we have made clear our support for a monetary policy that will steadily bring down inflation.

Slowing the Growth of Government Spending

Last February I promised to bring a halt to the rapid growth of Federal spending. To that end, I made budget control the cutting edge of my program for economic recovery. Thanks to the cooperation of the Congress and the American people, we have taken a

major step forward in accomplishing this objective, although much
more remains to be done.

The Congress approved rescissions in the fiscal 1981 budget of
$12.1 billion, by far the largest amount ever cut from the budget
through this procedure. Spending for fiscal 1982 was subsequently
reduced by another $35 billion. The Omnibus Budget Recon-
ciliation Act of 1981 also cut $95 billion from the next 2 fiscal
years, measured against previous spending trends. Many of these cuts
in so-called "uncontrollable" programs were carried out by substan-
tive changes in authorizing legislation, demonstrating that we can
bring government spending under control—if only we have the will.
These spending cuts have been made without damaging the programs that many of our truly needy Americans depend upon. Indeed,
my program will continue to increase the funds, before and after allowing for inflation, that such programs receive in the future.

In this undertaking to bring spending under control, I have made a
conscious effort to ensure that the Federal Government fully dis-
charges its duty to provide all Americans with the needed services
and protections that only a national government can provide. Chief
among these is a strong national defense, a vital function which had
been allowed to deteriorate dangerously in previous years.

As a result of my program, Federal Government spending growth
has been cut drastically—from nearly 14 percent annually in the 3
fiscal years ending last September to an estimated 7 percent over the
next 3 years—at the same time that we are rebuilding our national
defense capabilities.

We must redouble our efforts to control the growth in spending.
We face high, continuing, and troublesome deficits. Although these
deficits are undesirably high, they will not jeopardize the economic
recovery. We must understand the reasons behind the deficits now
facing us: recession, lower inflation, and higher interest rates than
anticipated. Although my original timetable for a balanced budget is
no longer achievable, the factors which have postponed it do not
mean we are abandoning the goal of living within our means. The
appropriate ways to reducing the deficit will be working in
our favor in 1982 and beyond: economic growth, lower interest rates,
and spending control.

Reducing Tax Burdens

We often hear it said that we work the first few months of the year
for the government and then we start to work for ourselves. But that
is backwards. In fact, the first part of the year we work for ourselves.
We begin working for the government only when our income reaches
taxable levels. After that, the more we earn, the more we work for

the government, until rising tax rates on each dollar of extra income discourage many people from further work effort or from further saving and investment.

As a result of passage of the historic Economic Recovery Tax Act of 1981, we have set in place a fundamental reorientation of our tax laws. Rather than using the tax system to redistribute existing income, we have significantly restructured it to encourage people to work, save, and invest more. Across-the-board cuts in individual income tax rates phased-in over 3 years and the indexing of tax brackets in subsequent years will help put an end to making inflation profitable for the Federal Government. The reduction in marginal rates for all taxpayers, making Individual Retirement Accounts available to all workers, cutting the top tax bracket from 70 percent to 50 percent, and reduction of the "marriage penalty" will have a powerful impact on the incentives for all Americans to work, save, and invest.

These changes are moving us away from a tax system which has encouraged individuals to borrow and spend to one in which saving and investment will be more fully rewarded.

To spur further business investment and productivity growth, the new tax law provides faster write-offs for capital investment and a restructured investment tax credit. Research and development expenditures are encouraged with a new tax credit. Small business tax rates have been reduced.

Regulatory Reform

My commitment to regulatory reform was made clear in one of my very first acts in office, when I accelerated the decontrol of crude oil prices and eliminated the cumbersome crude oil entitlements system. Only skeptics of the free market system are surprised by the results. For the first time in 10 years, crude oil production in the continental United States has begun to rise. Prices and availability are now determined by the forces of the market, not dictated by Washington. And, helped by world supply and demand developments, oil and gasoline prices have been falling, rather than rising.

I have established, by Executive order, a process whereby all executive agency regulatory activity is subject to close and sensitive monitoring by the Executive Office of the President. During the first year of my Administration, 2,893 regulations have been subjected to Executive Office review. The number of pages in the *Federal Register,* the daily publication that contains a record of the Federal Government's official regulatory actions, has fallen by over one-quarter after increasing steadily for a decade.

But the full impact of this program cannot be found in easy-to-measure actions by the Federal Government. It is taking place outside of Washington, in large and small businesses, in State and local governments, and in our schools and hospitals where the full benefits of regulatory reform are being felt. The redirection of work and effort away from trying to cope with or anticipate Federal regulation toward more productive pursuits is how regulatory reform will make its greatest impact in raising productivity and reducing costs.

Controlling Money Growth

Monetary policy is carried out by the independent Federal Reserve System. I have made clear my support for a policy of gradual and less volatile reduction in the growth of the money supply. Such a policy will ensure that inflationary pressures will continue to decline without impairing the operation of our financial markets as they mobilize savings and direct them to their most productive uses. It will also ensure that high interest rates, with their large inflation premiums, will no longer pose a threat to the well-being of our housing and motor vehicle industries, to small business and farmers, and to all who rely upon the use of credit in their daily activities. In addition, reduced monetary volatility will strengthen confidence in monetary policy and help lower interest rates.

The International Aspects of the Program

The poor performance of the American economy over the past decade and more has had its impact on our position in the world economy. Concern about the dollar was evidenced by a prolonged period of decline in its value on foreign exchange markets. A decline in our competitiveness in many world markets reflected, in part, problems of productivity at home.

A strengthened domestic economy will mean a faster growing market for our trading partners and greater competitiveness for American exports abroad. At the same time it will mean that the dollar should increase in its attractiveness as the primary international trading currency, and thus provide more stability to world trade and finance.

I see an expansion of the international trading system as the chief instrument for economic growth in many of the less developed countries as well as an important factor in our own future and that of the world's other major industrial nations. To this end, I reaffirm my Administration's commitment to free trade. International cooperation is particularly vital, however, in confronting the challenge of increased protectionism both at home and abroad. My Administration will work closely with other nations toward reducing trade barriers on an even-handed basis.

I am sensitive to the fact that American domestic economic policies can have significant impacts on our trading partners and on the entire system of world trade and finance. But it is important for all concerned that the United States pursue economic policies that focus on our long-run problems, and lead to sustained and vigorous growth at home. In this way the United States will continue to be a constructive force in the world economy.

1981: Building for the Future

In 1981 not only were the far-reaching policies needed for the remainder of the 1980s developed and put into place, their first positive results also began to be felt.

The most significant result was the contribution these policies made to a substantial reduction in inflation, bringing badly needed relief from inflationary pressures to every American. For example, in 1980 the consumer price index rose 13.5 percent for the year as a whole; in 1981 that rate of increase was reduced substantially, to 10.4 percent. This moderation in the rate of price increases meant that inflation, "the cruelest tax," was taking less away from individual savings and taking less out of every working American's paycheck.

There are other, more indirect but equally important benefits that flow from a reduction in inflation. The historically high level of interest rates of recent years was a direct reflection of high rates of actual and expected inflation. As the events of this past year suggested, only a reduction in inflationary pressures will lead to substantial, lasting reductions in interest rates.

In the 6 months preceding this Administration's taking office, interest rates had risen rapidly, reflecting excessively fast monetary growth. Since late last summer, however, short- and long-term interest rates have, on average, moved down somewhat in response to anti-inflationary economic policies.

Unfortunately, the high and volatile money growth of the past, and the high inflation and high interest rates which accompanied it, were instrumental in bringing about the poor and highly uneven economic performance of 1980 and 1981, culminating in a sharp fall in output and a rise in unemployment in the latter months of 1981.

This Administration views the current recession with concern. I am convinced that our policies, now that they are in place, are the appropriate response to our current difficulties and will provide the basis for a vigorous economic recovery this year. It is of the greatest importance that we avoid a return to the stop-and-go policies of the past. The private sector works best when the Federal Government intervenes least. The Federal Government's task is to construct a sound, stable, long-term framework in which the private sector is the key engine to growth, employment, and rising living standards.

The policies of the past have failed. They failed because they did not provide the environment in which American energy, entrepreneurship, and talent can best be put to work. Instead of being a successful promoter of economic growth and individual freedom, government became the enemy of growth and an intruder on individual initiative and freedom. My program—a careful combination of reducing incentive-stifling taxes, slowing the growth of Federal spending and regulations, and a gradually slowing expansion of the money supply—seeks to create a new environment in which the strengths of America can be put to work for the benefit of us all. That environment will be an America in which honest work is no longer discouraged by ever-rising prices and tax rates, a country that looks forward to the future not with uncertainty but with the confidence that infused our forefathers.

Ronald Reagan

February 10, 1982

THE ANNUAL REPORT
OF THE
COUNCIL OF ECONOMIC ADVISERS

LETTER OF TRANSMITTAL

COUNCIL OF ECONOMIC ADVISERS,
Washington, D.C., February 6, 1982.

MR. PRESIDENT:

The Council of Economic Advisers herewith submits its 1982 Annual Report in accordance with the provisions of the Employment Act of 1946 as amended by the Full Employment and Balanced Growth Act of 1978.

Sincerely,

Murray L. Weidenbaum
CHAIRMAN

Jerry L. Jordan

William A. Niskanen

CONTENTS

The contents are reprinted in entirety (original page numbers); however, only the body of the text is reprinted.

List of Tables and Charts

List of Tables and Charts—Continued

List of Tables and Charts—Continued

CHAPTER 1

Economic Policy for the 1980s

THE YEAR JUST ENDED was an especially significant one for the economy and for economic policymaking. When future *Reports* are written, we hope that 1981 will be described as the watershed year in which the more than decade-old rising trend of inflation was finally arrested. This development should contribute to more rapidly rising standards of living, more productive patterns of investment and saving, and a strengthened U.S. position in the world economy.

At the same time that inflation was moderating, a far-reaching set of economic policies was being developed to provide a framework for growth and stability in the years ahead, reversing more than a decade of declining productivity growth and wide swings in economic activity.

The speed with which the economy adjusts to the Administration's policies will be largely determined by the extent to which individuals, at home and at work, believe the Administration will maintain, unchanged, its basic approach to personal and business taxation, Federal spending and regulation, and monetary policy. When public expectations fully adjust to this commitment, a necessary condition for both reduced inflation and higher growth will be fully established. In short, as this *Report* attempts to demonstrate, what some people have referred to as "monetarism" and "supply-side economics" should be seen as two sides of the same coin—compatible and necessary measures to both reduce inflation and increase economic growth.

THE LEGACY OF "STAGFLATION"

Over the last 15 years the U.S. economy has experienced progressively higher rates of inflation and unemployment, a combination of conditions commonly called "stagflation." This development was associated with a substantial increase in the Federal Government's role in the economy. Federal spending and tax revenues absorbed an increasing share of national output, Federal regulations were extended to a much broader scope of economic activity, and the rate of money growth increased substantially. Table 1–1 contrasts economic conditions during the 1960–65 period (the last business cycle prior to the

Vietnam war), the 1974–79 period (the most recent extended business cycle), and 1980.

TABLE 1–1.—*Major economic conditions and the Federal role, 1960–80*

[Percent; annual average, except as noted]

Item	1960–1965	1974–1979	1980
Economic conditions:			
Productivity increase	2.6	0.7	−0.2
Unemployment rate	5.5	6.8	7.1
Inflation	1.6	7.5	9.0
Interest rate	4.4	8.7	11.9
The Federal role:			
Spending share of GNP	18.8	21.7	22.9
Revenue share of GNP	18.6	19.7	20.6
Regulation increase	7.6	13.9	12.3
Money supply increase	3.0	6.6	7.3

Note.—For this table, the following are used:
Productivity—Output per hour, private nonfarm business, all employees.
Unemployment rate—unemployment as percent of civilian labor force, persons 16 years of age and over.
Inflation—Change in implicit price deflator for gross national product (GNP).
Interest rate—Corporate Aaa bond yield.
Spending share—Federal expenditures, national income and product accounts (NIPA), as percent of GNP.
Tax share—Federal receipts (NIPA) as percent of GNP.
Regulation—Number of pages in the *Federal Register.*
Money supply—M1 (fourth quarter to fourth quarter).

Sources: Department of Commerce (Bureau of Economic Analysis), Department of Labor (Bureau of Labor Statistics), Board of Governors of the Federal Reserve System, Office of the Federal Register, and Moody's Investors Service.

As this table illustrates, economic conditions worsened between the early 1960s and the late 1970s, and deteriorated sharply during the recession year 1980. Part of the decline in U.S. economic performance was clearly attributable to developments not affected by Federal economic policy, such as the oil price increases of the 1970s. Such developments, however, explain only a small part of the decline in overall U.S. economic performance.

A full explanation of stagflation in the United States and other countries has yet to be developed. An important lesson of this period, however, is that there is no long-term tradeoff between unemployment and inflation. The increasing role of the Federal Government in the economy—whether that role was to aid the poor and aged, to protect consumers and the environment, or to stabilize the economy—contributed to our declining economic performance. Most of the increase in Federal spending over the past 15 years has been in the form of transfer payments, which tend to reduce employment of the poor and of older workers. A combination of increases in some tax rates and inflation raised marginal tax rates on real wages and capital income. The rapid growth in regulatory activity—however measured—has significantly increased production costs. The Federal Government bears the most direct responsibility for the increases in inflation and interest rates, which were due to excessive expansion of the money supply. In short, Federal economic policies bear the major responsibility for the legacy of stagflation.

THE PRESIDENT'S PROGRAM FOR ECONOMIC RECOVERY

For the economy, the most important event of 1981 was the dramatic change in Federal policy. On February 18 the President announced a long-term program designed to increase economic growth and to reduce inflation. The key elements of the proposed program were:

- cutting the rate of growth in Federal spending;
- reducing personal income tax rates and creating jobs by accelerating depreciation for business investment in plant and equipment;
- instituting a far-reaching program of regulatory relief; and
- in cooperation with the Federal Reserve, making a new commitment to a monetary policy that will restore a stable currency and healthy financial markets.

Over the year, with the support of the Congress and the Federal Reserve System, most of this program was approved and implemented. The Federal Government's budget underwent its most significant reorientation since the mid-1960s. The rate of increase in total Federal outlays declined from 17.5 percent in fiscal 1980 to 14.0 percent in fiscal 1981 and to an anticipated 10.4 percent in fiscal 1982. The composition of Federal spending was also substantially changed. Real defense spending was accelerated, real spending for the major transfer programs for the poor and aged was maintained, and most of the spending reductions were made in other domestic programs.

The Congress approved the major features of the President's tax proposal while adding a number of other provisions. The long-term increase in Federal regulation was significantly slowed, as suggested by a 27 percent decline in the number of pages in the *Federal Register,* and the Federal Reserve reduced the rate of money growth to 4.9 percent during 1981. As finally implemented, the change in Federal economic policies was more substantial than during any recent Administration. The new policies comprise an innovative approach to reducing the rate of inflation while providing incentives to achieve sustained and vigorous economic growth. While such a development would be somewhat unusual in light of historical experience, we believe that a consistent policy of monetary restraint, combined with the Administration's spending and tax policies, and reinforced by continuing regulatory relief, will provide the policy framework for both reduced inflation and increased economic growth.

A SUMMARY OF ECONOMIC CONDITIONS

General economic conditions during 1981 reflected the transitory effects of the necessary changes in Federal economic policies. The major elements of the Administration's economic policy are designed to increase long-term economic growth and to reduce inflation. Uniformly favorable near-term effects were not expected.

The primary redirection of economic policy that affected economic conditions during the year was the reduction in the growth of the money supply relative to the record high rate of growth in late 1980. This monetary restraint reduced inflation and short-term interest rates but also influenced the decline in economic activity in late 1981.

Beginning in late 1979, substantial variability in money growth rates was associated with unusually large swings in interest rates. By the end of 1980, as a result of an unprecedented degree of monetary stimulus, interest rates had risen to new peaks. In December 1980 the Federal funds rate reached more than 20 percent, the prime rate was 21½ percent, and 3-month Treasury bills had doubled in yield from their midyear lows. Long-term interest rates had risen by as much as 3 full percentage points from their midyear lows.

The rise in interest rates that began in late 1979 gradually produced an ever-widening circle of weakness centering on the most interest-sensitive industries, notably homebuilding and motor vehicles. Falling demand for housing and autos gradually affected an increasing number of other sectors, ranging from forest products to steel and rubber to appliances and home furnishings. The high interest rates also contributed to a squeeze on farm incomes—already under pressure from weaker farm prices—and weakness in industries and services closely tied to the farm sector.

Excessive monetary expansion in the latter half of 1980 helped to drive interest rates to record highs. Rates were kept at those levels for the next 6 months or so by a variety of factors, including the transitory impact of the shift to monetary restraint. Rates then fell because of the monetary restraint that characterized Federal Reserve policy during most of 1981. The high interest rates were an important factor in precipitating the downturn in the final quarter of 1981, when real output fell at an annual rate of 5.2 percent.

In short, the conflict between continued expectations of rising inflation, based on the history of the last 15 years, and the more recent monetary restraint explains many recent problems. Continued monetary restraint and a reduction of the within-year variability of money growth, however, are necessary both to reduce inflation and provide the basis for sustained economic growth.

PROSPECTS FOR RECOVERY

The series of tax cuts enacted in 1981 provides the foundation for increased employment, spending, saving, and business investment. Inflation and short-term interest rates are now substantially lower than they were at the beginning of 1981. At the time this *Report* was prepared, it appeared that the recession which started in August—as determined by the National Bureau of Economic Research—will be over by the second quarter of 1982. This would make it about average in length for a post-World War II downturn. Output and employment are expected to increase slightly in the second quarter and at a brisk pace through the rest of the year, when growth in output is expected to be in excess of a 5 percent annual rate. Inflation is likely to continue to decline and to average about 7 percent for the year, with further reductions in 1983 and beyond.

The outlook for 1983 and subsequent years is based on continuation of the Administration's spending, tax, and regulatory policies, continued monetary restraint, and broader public recognition that the Administration is committed to each of these key elements of its program. Prospective budget deficits are a consequence of the difference in the timing of the spending and tax policy actions, and of the impact on nominal gross national product growth of continued monetary restraint. Although the prospective deficits are undesirably high, they are not expected to jeopardize the economic recovery program.

Concerns have been expressed that the Federal Reserve's targets for money growth are not compatible with the vigorous upturn in economic activity envisioned later in 1982. Any such upturn, it is feared, will lead to a renewed upswing in interest rates and thus choke off recovery. We believe that such fears, while understandable on the basis of recent history and policies, are unjustified in light of current policies and the Administration's determination to carry them through.

Interest rates, after more than a decade of rising inflation, contain sizable premiums to compensate lenders for the anticipated loss in value of future repayments of principal. It is our estimate, however, that such premiums will decline over the course of 1982 and beyond. Such a decline would occur while "real" (inflation-adjusted) interest rates remain high as a result of private and public sector credit demands even as private saving flows increase. In other words, the market rate of interest is likely to continue on a downward trend, even though short-run fluctuations around the trend can be expected.

A critical element in this outlook is the assumption that inflationary expectations will, in fact, continue to recede. If they recede at a relatively fast rate, market rates of interest will decline significantly, wage demands will continue to moderate, and the pro-inflationary biases that have developed throughout the economy over the past decade will quickly disappear. Thus, the greater the degree of cooperation between the Administration, the Congress, and the Federal Reserve in continuing to support a consistent, credible anti-inflation policy, as embodied in the Administration's program, the more rapidly will real growth and employment increase.

ORGANIZATION OF THIS REPORT

This *Report* presents the economic basis for the key elements of the President's economic program. Chapter 2 develops a general framework for the economic role of the Federal Government consistent with the principles of the President's program. Chapter 3 develops a framework for a stable, noninflationary monetary policy. Chapters 4 and 5 analyze the major effects of Administration policies on Federal spending, taxes, and deficits. Chapter 6 summarizes the major features of the program for regulatory reform, while Chapter 7 summarizes the international implications of the Administration's economic policies for monetary conditions, trade, and international organizations. Finally, Chapter 8 reviews economic conditions in 1981 and the outlook for the near future in somewhat more detail than in this opening chapter.

We hope that this *Report* will help both the public and our fellow economists to understand the basis, the importance, and the effects of the dramatic changes in Federal economic policy initiated by the President in 1981.

CHAPTER 2

Government and the Economy

POLITICAL FREEDOM AND ECONOMIC FREEDOM are closely related. Any comparison among contemporary nations or examination of the historical record demonstrates two important relationships between the nature of the political system and the nature of the economic system:

- All nations which have broad-based representative government and civil liberties have most of their economic activity organized by the market.

- Economic conditions in market economies are generally superior to those in nations (with a comparable culture and a comparable resource base) in which the government has the dominant economic role.

The evidence is striking. No nation in which the government has the dominant economic role (as measured by the proportion of gross national product originating in the government sector) has maintained broad political freedom; economic conditions in such countries are generally inferior to those in comparable nations with a predominantly market economy. Voluntary migration, sometimes at high personal cost, is uniformly to nations with both more political freedom and more economic freedom.

The reasons for these two relationships between political and economic systems are simple but not widely understood. Everyone would prefer higher prices for goods sold and lower prices for goods bought. Since the farmer's wheat is the consumer's bread, however, both parties cannot achieve all they want. The most fundamental difference among economic systems is how these conflicting preferences are resolved.

A market system resolves these conflicts by allowing the seller to get the highest price at which others will buy and the buyer to get the lowest price at which others will sell, by consensual exchanges that are expected to benefit both parties. Any attempt by one party to improve his outcome relative to the market outcome requires a coercive activity at the expense of some other party. The politicization of price decisions—whether of wages, commodities, or interest rates—tends to reduce both the breadth of popular support for the government and the efficiency of the economy. A rich nation can tolerate a good bit of such mischief, but not an unlimited amount. One should not be surprised that all nations in which the government has dominant control of the economy are run by a narrow oligarchy and in most economic conditions are relatively poor. In the absence of limits on the economic role of government, the erosion of economic freedom destroys both political freedom and economic performance.

Only a few dozen nations now guarantee their citizens both political and economic freedom. The economic role of government in these nations differs widely, without serious jeopardy to political freedom. Within the range of experience of the United States and the other free nations, the relation between the political system and the government's economic role is more subtle. Expansion of the economic role of the government tends to reduce both the level of agreement on government policies and the inclination to engage in political dissent. The link between political and economic freedom is important. Increasing economic freedom will also provide greater assurance of our political freedom.

A major objective of this Administration's economic program is to reduce the Federal Government's role in economic decisionmaking while strengthening the economic role of individuals, private organizations, and State and local governments. This shift will entail substantial reductions in the size and number of Federal spending programs, significant reductions in both personal and business Federal tax rates, major reforms of Federal regulatory activities, and a reduced rate of money growth. While an important element in this redefinition of the Federal Government's economic role is a political judgment about the appropriate relationship among individuals, the States, and the Federal Government, this redefinition also is supported by an extensive body of economic analysis.

This chapter discusses the extent to which government intervention in economic matters is appropriate, why concern over "too much government" appears to have emerged so strongly in recent decades, and why the Administration's program is an appropriate response.

In probing the role of government in the economy, economists usually start by analyzing the effects of a competitive economy on economic efficiency. In a rough sense, economic efficiency refers to the ability of an economy to satisfy each person as much as possible, consistent with the preferences of others. For such a competitive economy to be completely efficient, however, certain assumptions would have to be satisfied that are never fully satisfied in the real world. Therefore, it is often argued that government intervention is justified in order to correct the inefficiencies which occur when the desired conditions are not achieved.

However, failure to satisfy certain assumptions is not sufficient to justify government intervention. To show that a perfectly functioning government can correct some problem in a free economy is not enough, for government itself does not function perfectly. Moreover, many current interventions cannot be explained easily by arguments based on the alleged failure of the operation of free markets. Many current interventions, in other words, cannot be justified by any efficiency criterion.

The following section of this chapter discusses situations in which some types of government intervention in the economy may be justified. The section on The Division of Roles in a Federal System discusses the considerations involved in determining the appropriate level of government at which such intervention should take place. The section on Limits on the Exercise of the Federal Role discusses the political process and argues that government intervention will not always be consistent with the principles developed in the prior sections; that is, this section focuses on the possibility of "government failure" in intervening in the economy. The last section, Principles Guiding the President's Economic Program, discusses the Administration's economic program in light of the preceding analysis.

THE LIMITED CASE FOR GOVERNMENT INTERVENTION

Under certain assumptions discussed below, a competitive economy can be shown to lead to general economic efficiency. In standard economics, an economy is said to be "efficient" if it is impossible to make anyone better off without making someone else worse off. That is, there is no possible rearrangement of resources, in either production or consumption, which could improve anyone's position without simultaneously harming some other person. If there is a possibility of such a rearrangement occurring, then this means that someone could be made better off without harming anyone else. If such a possibility does exist, then the economy is not efficient.

Each person in such an economy is considered to be concerned primarily with his or her own welfare. Since there is no central authority directing the course of this economy, whatever results occur are the unintended consequences of millions of individual actions. Nonetheless, the outcome of this undirected but self-interested behavior is efficient in the sense mentioned above. Despite the absence of any central direction, it can be shown that an economic order is

generated which has the desirable characteristic of being economically efficient. Moreover, an efficient economic system is responsive to
individual wants; that is, efficiency is defined in terms of each person
achieving his or her own goals.

Such a system relies on the ability of people to trade freely with
each other, for a bargain entered into voluntarily by two individuals
is expected by both of them to make both of them better off. Two
conditions must be fulfilled for such trades to occur. First, individuals
must have the right to enter freely into whatever bargains they wish;
that is, there must be freedom of contract. Second, property rights
must be well defined in all cases except those where the cost of enforcing the right would be greater than the value of the right.

Certain additional characteristics must be present if the economy is
to be efficient. The most important of these characteristics are: the
absence of externalities, the absence of significant monopolies, and
the appropriate provision of public goods. Though such an economy
is efficient, "efficiency" says nothing about the distribution of income
which results from the process. By some criteria the market-generat-
ed distribution of income in an efficient economy may be unacceptable. Thus, government intervention may be justified to correct
market failures or to change the resulting distribution of income. It is
also possible that an efficient economy may be less stable than is
generally considered desirable.

EXTERNALITIES

An externality is said to exist where an economic agent (be it producer or consumer) either does not bear the full marginal costs of an
economic action or does not gain its full marginal benefits. Therefore, these agents may not undertake the activity at its optimal economic level. If there are external costs, the agent may undertake too
high a level of the activity. If there are external benefits, the agent
may not undertake enough of the activity.

An example of an activity with external benefits is education. Because some of the benefits of living in a nation of people with a
common language and culture are external, individuals considering
only their own benefit from education will most likely buy too little.
The standard example of an activity that imposes external costs is
manufacturing that results in pollution. Consider a factory which pol-
lutes the air. Those who live near the factory will suffer the costs of
the pollution, but the factory owner will probably not consider these
costs in deciding how much to produce. Since the factory owner does
not bear these costs, the product made in the factory will be under-
priced in relation to its true economic cost. Hence, too much of the
good, and too much pollution, will probably be produced. Govern-

ment intervention may therefore be justified where either marginal costs or benefits are external.

Private transactions between parties may sometimes be adequate to solve externality problems, but this requires that transaction costs be low. This requirement will not in general be satisfied when many parties are involved.

Since externality problems occur because decisionmakers either do not pay all the costs of their actions or do not reap all of the benefits, the most efficient way to correct the problem is to change the marginal costs and benefits. With respect to education the conventional solution has been to establish systems of public education paid for by taxes and offered below cost to students. This solution itself creates problems, since the creation of a tax-subsidized producer of education may lead to the producer having a monopoly over education. But monopoly is inefficient, whether it is public or private. An alternative would be to grant a "voucher," with the amount of this voucher equal to the difference between private benefit (the benefit to the student) and total benefit (the benefit which accrues to other members of society as well as to the student). This would avoid the problem of monopoly and might generate pressures for more efficient schools.

To deal with the external costs of pollution, the conventional solution has been regulation of pollution control technology by government agencies. Since this form of regulation often does not take account of differences in abatement costs for different polluters, it is often inefficient in that the public pays more than is necessary for a given amount of pollution reduction (or a smaller reduction in pollution is achieved for a given expenditure than would be possible with a more efficient scheme).

Two ways of reducing pollution more efficiently have been identified. One is to charge those who pollute a fee based on the cost imposed on others by the pollution. This method has been used in West German waterways and has been quite effective. Another alternative is for the government to create property rights in air or water. These rights would then be purchased by those who valued them most—that is, by those who would pay the highest cost to reduce their pollution. These two methods, if implemented correctly, would probably lead to the same outcome.

MONOPOLY

One of the conditions of market efficiency is that there must be enough buyers and sellers of a good so that each of them has little influence on its price. This condition is not always satisfied, however. Sometimes technical and cost conditions in an industry are such that

31

there will be room for only one or a few firms. Two approaches have been taken in the United States to this problem. In cases of natural monopoly, direct government regulation or ownership is common. In industries where only a few firms exist, the antitrust laws are more commonly used to avoid the costs of monopoly.

Most of the natural monopolies arise from the need to provide public utility services, such as electricity and water. Regulation of most of these natural monopolies occurs primarily at the State and local level and is not covered in this *Report*, but there are some monopolies regulated at the Federal level. In some cases of natural monopoly, however, newer technology may so change technical and cost considerations that additional firms would enter the market if permitted to do so by regulatory authorities.

In an industry with few firms it may be possible for the firms to act in collusion and thus behave as a monopoly. When this occurs, the profits of the firms are increased, but efficiency losses are imposed on the economy. Even though such collusions are unstable, losses of efficiency occur during their existence. The antitrust laws make such behavior illegal.

The effects of mergers on economic efficiency are more difficult to discern than the effects of illegal monopoly. Two firms in the same industry may merge for any of at least three reasons. First, a merger may be an attempt to obtain monopoly power. When this occurs the merger will be inefficient and should be stopped. But, firms may also decide to merge to take advantage of economies of scale or because one is better managed and can therefore increase efficiency in resource use. In these latter two cases a merger is likely to improve efficiency and should be allowed. The difficulty, of course, is that it is not always obvious whether monopoly or an increase in efficiency will be the dominant effect of any given merger.

Though there are difficult cases, this Administration has already made some changes in policy in the administration of Federal antitrust laws, changes based on economic analysis. First, a merger between two firms which have a relatively small share of the market should be allowed, for there is little danger of monopoly. Second, no significant economic problems are likely to arise from a merger of firms in unrelated industries (a conglomerate merger); such a merger will not create any significant monopoly power. Third, there is little danger of monopoly and therefore no reason for Federal intervention when a firm merges with another firm that is a customer or a supplier of the first (a vertical merger). Finally, a firm that obtains a large share of a market by being a more efficient competitor is acting in a desirable fashion and should not be punished by antitrust action on the part of the Federal Government. In recent years, those in charge of administering Federal antitrust laws sometimes have behaved as if they viewed their function as protecting existing firms from competition. From an economic viewpoint the purpose of the antitrust laws is to maintain competition, even if competition leads to the decline of firms which are less efficient.

PUBLIC GOODS

A public good has two distinctive characteristics. The first is that consumption of the good by one party does not reduce consumption of the good by others, and the second is that there is no effective way to restrict the benefits of such goods to those who directly pay for them. The standard example of a public good is national defense. If national defense deters a foreign aggressor, everyone in the country benefits. This means that no individual will have sufficient incentive to spend his own resources on national defense, since he will benefit from his neighbor's spending. Hence, such public goods as national defense are usually provided by some action of the national government. Government action is usually necessary for the optimal provision of many public goods, and this point does not arouse controversy among economists. Sometimes there are debates, however, about whether a particular good is sufficiently public in nature to justify its being provided by the government.

Another public good is information. If one person learns some valuable fact and tells someone else, the use of the information by one does not reduce the use of the same information by the other. If a consumer organization spends resources to find out which products are best and sells a publication that provides this information to subscribers, these subscribers may then pass the information on to others who did not pay for it. This can be shown as a market failure, in the sense that the private market did not generate enough information; if the organization could capture all of the returns, it would provide additional information. Patents and copyrights are designed to reduce this problem by giving inventors and writers property rights in their product, thus providing incentives for production, but there are still cases where the private market does not generate sufficient information. This provides the rationale for government financing of certain kinds of research.

INCOME REDISTRIBUTION

In a market economy, individual income depends upon what one has to sell and on the amount which others are willing to pay for it. What most people sell on the market is their labor. About 75 percent of national income is in the form of wages and salaries and other forms of labor remuneration. Others have capital or land to rent, and their return is interest and dividends, or rent income. Most people earn income from both capital and labor over their lifetimes. But some persons may have few or no valuable things to sell, and these persons will have low incomes. A decision may then be made to transfer income to such people directly through government. Two justifications can be presented for such transfers of income, one based on the social value of providing certain forms of income insurance, the other based on benevolence. We consider each.

Anyone may lose his ability to earn income. A worker may become physically disabled or find that technological progress has made his or her skills obsolete. Or an investor may find that changing market conditions have eroded the return on capital. Since individuals generally do not like the risk of losing their ability to earn income, they often seek to insure themselves against such a possibility.

But there are difficulties in providing insurance against falling incomes by way of private-market mechanisms. A major difficulty is what is called "adverse selection." Assume that some insurance company offered actuarily fair insurance against this risk and charged all persons the same premium. (That is, the amount of the premium equals the expected cost of having a low income.) Since most persons are averse to risk, they might buy this insurance even though the premium would be somewhat greater than the expected cost because of the expense of writing the insurance. Some persons would be better risks than average, and new insurance companies would compete with the first company for these better risks. This would leave the original company insuring only the bad risks, which the company would then find financially intolerable. Ultimately, one class of persons would be unable to obtain any insurance.

This would be an example of market failure and an argument for government provision of insurance, since the government can force everyone to join the same insurance pool. The appropriate form of insurance to those who experience a temporary loss of income is a cash grant. Welfare payments and unemployment compensation may be viewed as just this sort of insurance.

The second argument for government transfers to the poor is an argument based on benevolence. Many people prefer not to live in a society where there is poverty and thus have an incentive to transfer some of their resources to the poor voluntarily. When one individual performs such a transfer, all individuals who dislike poverty benefit. Thus, most people will have an incentive to reduce their contributions to the poor and rely on the contributions of others. In all likelihood, such voluntary transfers would be too low to keep people out of poverty; it may become necessary for the government to do it.

In cases where transfers of income are desirable, economic theory can indicate the most efficient form of transfer. One goal should be to minimize interference in private markets. Price controls on gasoline and laws decreeing minimum wages, for example, are considered by many economists to be inefficient ways of helping the poor.

The way in which resources should be transferred to the poor depends on the goal of the donors. If the goal is simply to improve the welfare of the poor, the most efficient solution probably would be a system of cash transfers, since it can be assumed that recipients are best able to determine the pattern of spending that maximizes their welfare. But if the donor is more concerned with the specific goods which the recipient consumes, a direct transfer of goods may be preferable. In this case the argument can be made for using some form of voucher. A voucher is essentially a coupon usable only for the purchase of a specific type of good. Food stamps are one example. Use of vouchers instead of a direct transfer of goods allows recipients to determine their own consumption but restricts the type of goods which the recipient may purchase.

Regardless of the form of transfer, there is still an efficiency cost. Transfers reduce the incentive of recipients to work, and the taxes imposed on the rest of society to finance these transfers also cause losses in efficiency. There are also costs of administering the program. Economists are able to give advice on ways of transferring income which may serve to minimize these effects, but the decision as to the amount of the transfers is a political decision, not an economic one.

MACROECONOMIC STABILITY

A market system may sometimes be subject to unacceptably large fluctuations in income. When this occurs, it has implications for the general welfare. First, average income levels may be smaller with fluctuations than if the level of activity is more stable. Second, even if the average level of incomes is unaffected by such fluctuations, people are generally risk-averse. That is, most people prefer a steady stream of income to a fluctuating stream, even if their total income is the same over a period of time. For these reasons, government may have a role in helping to provide stability.

An alternative view is that a market economy is inherently quite stable. According to this view, government actions are the primary destabilizing factors in the economy. That is, many fluctuations in income which seem to be caused by private sector actions are actually caused by attempts to outguess the government. (This issue is discussed in more detail in Chapter 3.)

Macroeconomic stability also involves the question of what to do about money. Money performs several functions in an economy. Its use economizes on transaction costs and on information costs, since all persons accept the same money and are aware of its value. However, the government must be careful in its money creating function not to exacerbate cyclical fluctuations. Excess creation of money leads to inflation, which reduces money's value.

Although the Federal Government is the appropriate agent for stabilizing the economy, the limits of such action must be understood. This Administration believes that "fine tuning" of the economy—attempting to offset every fluctuation—is not possible. The information needed to do so is often simply not available, and when it becomes available it is quite likely that underlying conditions will already have changed. As a result, a policy of fine tuning the economy is as likely to be counterproductive as it is to be helpful. Though it is necessary for the government to have macroeconomic policies, including both monetary and fiscal policies designed to achieve some desired growth of income, such policies are not suitable for correcting small fluctuations in economic activity.

THE DIVISION OF ROLES IN A FEDERAL SYSTEM

The preceding sections have discussed situations where government intervention in private economic activities may be appropriate. An equally important concern is determining the level of government at which intervention, when desirable, should take place.

Our system of government is a Federal system, one in which certain powers have been granted to the Federal Government while other powers have been granted to the States. In recent decades, however, there has been a substantial centralization of power at the national level.

One constraint on the power of any government to impose costs on its citizens is the ability of those citizens to move elsewhere. Thus, one argument for reliance on State government is essentially the argument that it restricts the power of government, since any State which passed laws which were sufficiently inefficient would probably find itself losing residents. The long-term increase in the power of the Federal Government at the expense of the State governments has probably weakened this constraint on governmental power.

Another argument for federalism is that State and local governments are more likely to choose the amount and quality of governmental services preferred by their voters, whose preferences and resources vary greatly. This argument has important implications for both the types of services that should be provided at the different levels of government and the structure of the tax system. Decisions on government services that benefit people throughout the Nation, such as national defense and the protection of basic constitutional rights, are appropriately made by the Federal Government, and such services should be financed by Federal taxes. But, government services that provide benefits only or predominantly to residents of a specific region, such as urban transit and sewer systems, can probably be provided more efficiently by State or local governments and financed by State and local taxes or user charges on those persons directly benefited.

In this view, Federal grants-in-aid to State and local governments should be restricted to services provided by these governments that have significant benefits for residents in other regions of the country. Over the last several decades, however, Federal grants-in-aid have not been directed at assisting such services. Instead, these grants have in many cases reduced the State or local "tax price" of a wide range of other services and therefore have increased their utilization beyond that which most local residents would prefer. Consequently, the relative growth of Federal financing of State and local services has probably increased the total size of government in the United States while reducing its efficiency and responsiveness. The case for a return to a more balanced federalism is a case for both efficiency in the provision of public services and for greater individual freedom and choice in the Federal system.

LIMITS ON THE EXERCISE OF THE FEDERAL ROLE

So far, this chapter has summarized the theoretical reasons for a limited role of the Federal Government in the economy. Even when the government justifiably undertakes certain activities, however, there are reasons for believing that it is unlikely to do a perfect job. Just as there sometimes are reasons for expecting "market failure," sometimes there also are reasons for expecting "government failure." In this section we discuss some of these reasons.

THE POLITICAL PROCESS

For several reasons the political process is overly responsive to special interest groups. One cause of this is the high cost of information. Consider, for example, an import quota program that will give rather large benefits to firms and workers in the industry to be protected by the quota. Although such a program will impose only small costs on everyone else in the economy, it will be inefficient because the sum of the losses will be greater than the sum of the gains. However, each of the losers will lose so little that it will often not pay to spend the resources necessary to learn about the losses. The average voter would have to make a detailed study of law and economics, for example, to determine how much government-induced cartelization of the trucking industry costs him. It is quite rational for the average voter not to bother to learn about this cost, for the resources spent in doing so would probably be greater than the per capita cost of the government activity that led to cartelization. (Economists refer to this as "rational ignorance.") On the other hand, the beneficiaries of government policies gain substantial amounts, and it pays for them to spend resources in learning about government activities. Thus, trade associations hire lobbyists whose job includes informing members of an industry about political decisions which may affect their operations.

Moreover, even if the average voter had the information required to make a rational decision on how to vote in the next election, it is not clear what effect this would have. Assume that a citizen knows that his or her legislative representative voted for an import quota that will cost the voter $50 but also voted for some other bill which will benefit the voter's own special interest group and give him or her a benefit worth $500. The rational behavior of the voter will therefore be to vote for the reelection of the representative. That is, there are good reasons for expecting the political process to be responsive to special interests. It is possible for a representative to be elected by favoring a set of special interest policies, each of which appeals only to a minority of the electorate. Moreover, achieving a victory with such a "coalition of minorities" would be possible even if all the voters had all the information they needed to make a reasoned choice. That is because the gains from such special interest policies will be concentrated among the majority, while the costs will be borne by members of both the majority and the minority. Therefore, it is possible for a majority coalition made up of several special interest groups to gain benefits for themselves, even if the sum of the costs to all affected parties is greater than the sum of the benefits.

The same arguments also apply to other political activities. It will pay for concentrated special interests (including both business and unions) to make campaign contributions to those who vote for benefits for people in the industry, but it will not, in general, pay for citizens to make contributions to representatives who vote against such bills. This is because the losses suffered by each voter are small and because overturning inefficient legislation is a public good. It does not generally pay to contribute voluntarily to the provision of a public good that affects a large number of people.

The fact that the political process is likely to be overly responsive to interest groups constitutes an argument for limiting the power of government to intervene in the economy. Each citizen would like to use government to transfer resources to himself but is often skeptical or hostile when the government transfers resources to others. Moreover, the net result of all such transfers is an efficiency loss. One of the ways by which particular special interest programs can be constrained is to limit the power of government to provide any such programs.

For a long period the Federal Government behaved as if constraints on such legislation were binding. More recently, its power to intervene in many areas has been greatly expanded, and the amount of transfers, and of resources spent on obtaining transfers, has increased to a marked degree.

The essence of the problem is that each individual has an incentive to take actions which, considered in their entirety, have a net negative impact on society, even though they are generally rationalized as being in the public interest. Intervention begets intervention. Only by changing the general principles which encourage intervention in many areas can we resist the multiple appeals for special interest laws which, taken as a whole, reduce the general welfare.

SUPPLY BY GOVERNMENT AGENCIES

When government directly provides some service, the service is ordinarily performed by government employees. Government employees are sometimes criticized for being inefficient and sometimes praised for being dedicated to the public interest. Most theories of bureaucratic behavior make neither of these assumptions. Rather, it is assumed that government employees behave like everyone else and are concerned primarily with promoting their own interests. Thus, to study the effects of government provision of goods and services, it is important to study the incentives that motivate government employees.

There are several incentives for government managers to increase the size and power of their agency. First, the salary and promotion prospects of a manager depend in good measure on the size and influence of the agency, as does the manager's power. Second, even when government employees are motivated by their perceptions of the public interest, this often leads to the same desire to enlarge their agency's size and influence. Once a person goes to work for an agency which fulfills his vision of the public interest, he will then be likely to want to expand the power of the agency, independent of his own self-interest, because he believes such expansion will benefit the public. This is a partial explanation of the relatively long life of agencies and the difficulty in terminating them—those who work for the agency become a special interest group. It is also a partial explanation for overspending by government.

It can be argued that the risk structure arising from government regulation also creates perverse incentives for agency managers. Two errors can occur, for example, when a government official must decide whether to approve a new drug. If the official approves a drug which is unsafe, some persons who use it will suffer harmful side effects. Alternatively, the official may fail to approve some safe drug, in which case some persons will suffer needlessly from a disease.

These types of errors will always be possible, no matter what decisionmaking process is used. Nonetheless, the official faces an asymmetric situation. If the drug is approved and someone dies from having used it, the official will be blamed for approving an unsafe drug. Conversely, if the drug is not approved, those who would benefit from using it are not likely to know that the drug has been disapproved. Thus, in circumstances like these, agency managers can be expected to be overly risk-averse—not because of the nature of the manager but because of the incentive structure in which the official must operate.

Since these types of responses by agency managers are predictable, they must be considered in designing programs. We must begin with the realization that government will not function perfectly and then attempt to determine if a predictably imperfect government program will achieve better results than those of an unregulated market.

DIVERSITY OF CONDITIONS AND PREFERENCES

One advantage of a market economy, mentioned earlier, is that such an economy is responsive to varying consumer demands. Individuals have different preferences and desire different goods and services. Tastes differ. If these desires are matched by a willingness to pay for them, then firms will find satisfying them worthwhile. The market will produce diverse products in response to diverse demands.

If a good is a public good, however, this diversity will probably not be found. We are all provided the same amount of national defense, whether we are pacifists or hawks. That is the nature of public goods, and for true public goods there is no alternative. However, government sometimes treats goods which could be private as if they were public goods only. Thus, students from families that are not willing to pay the full cost of private school tuition have no choice but to attend the same public school system. Voucher plans are attempts to get around this problem, as are proposals for refundable tuition tax credits.

Detailed government regulation of technology also works to reduce the responsiveness of the economy to changed conditions. Such regulation, by not allowing entrepreneurs to take advantage of new technologies, retards economic progress.

LIMITS ON INFORMATION

If government policies are to achieve their goals, they must be based on correct information, a condition which is not always satisfied. Examples of problems in obtaining the information needed to formulate and implement macroeconomic policy were discussed above.

Sometimes the problem is that policymakers cannot predict the extent to which individuals will respond to changes in policy. The imposition of credit controls in 1980 had surprisingly rapid and perverse effects on the economy. Policymakers also underestimated the extent to which the cost of medical care would rise as a result of the medicare and medicaid programs. As a result, there were substantial unanticipated budgetary consequences.

In general, it can be predicted that people will respond to new rules or regulations by trying to minimize the adverse impact of such regulations on themselves. However, it is generally difficult or impossible to predict the exact nature of this response, since there may be millions of individuals affected by a given regulation and some of them will think of alternatives which did not occur to the policymakers. The myriad of ways in which individuals subvert price controls is illustrative. One solution is to attempt to devise policies which make use of incentives. Too often, regulation takes the form of specific rules which ignore the possibility of unexpected responses.

One critical advantage of a market economy is that it is "informationally efficient." That is, a market will function well even if each individual knows only his own preferences and opportunities. When government controls an activity, on the other hand, much more information must be collected. This is an expensive process, and sometimes the necessary information is simply not available. This places another restriction on the ability of the government to achieve its goals.

TIME HORIZON

Elected officials are generally interested in reelection. Thus, it is often argued that a program which imposes costs today in return for future benefits will be overly discounted by elected representatives, even if the program has a positive net present value. ("Net present value" refers to the sum of benefits less costs, adjusted for the time value of money.) Conversely, elected officials are likely to prefer programs with near-term benefits and deferred costs. In such cases, costs may not be appropriately discounted and net benefits may be overstated. In the private market, on the other hand, projects with a positive value over an extended time period are more likely to be undertaken because the benefits of such projects can be capitalized and the property rights sold. Although government does undertake some such projects, it is more often preoccupied with short-term effects.

Recently, for example, some analysts have detected a "political business cycle" in which government spending projects or programs initiated just before an election lead to higher taxes or inflation which do not occur until after the election. This is a predictable result of the political process. Wage and price controls, which produce short-run moderation in the rate of inflation, lead to longer term losses because they reduce the responsiveness and flexibility of the economy. Since some of these ill effects occur long after controls are imposed, there sometimes are incentives to impose such controls just before an election. The short time horizon inherent in a political process with nontransferable property rights is another obstacle to the development of truly effective programs.

PRINCIPLES GUIDING THE PRESIDENT'S ECONOMIC PROGRAM

The problems discussed in this chapter have prompted the new economic policies of the Administration. In this section the Administration's Program for Economic Recovery is related to general principles concerning the proper role of government in the economy and to the necessary constaints on government action discussed above.

EMPHASIS ON PERSONAL RESPONSIBILITY

Many government programs, such as detailed safety regulations or the provision of specific goods (rather than money) to the poor, are best described as paternalistic. Paternalism occurs when the government is reluctant to let individuals make decisions for themselves and seeks to protect them from the possible bad effects of their own decisions by outlawing certain actions. Paternalism has the effect of disallowing certain preferences or actions. This Administration rejects paternalism as a basis for policy. There is no reason to think that commands from government can do a better job of increasing an individual's economic welfare than the individual can by making choices himself. Moreover, the long-term cost of paternalism may be to destroy an individual's ability to make decisions for himself.

42

As discussed above, there are economic arguments for transferring resources to the poor. However, if the primary concern is the welfare of the poor, the most efficient form of transfer is probably cash rather than benefits in kind. (Examples of benefits in kind are public housing, food stamps, and medical care.) Poor people given money can best determine for themselves what goods to buy. If they are given goods or services instead, their ability to learn to make their own choices is limited.

REFORM OF REGULATION

As discussed above, many current regulations cannot be based on allegations of market failure, and many regulations which do have such justification are administered inefficiently. Efforts are being made by the Administration to cut back the scope of the first kind of regulation and to improve the workings of the second. One area where there has been a major effort at reducing the scale of government intervention is energy, which is discussed in Chapter 6.

The Administration is also involved in a careful review of Federal enforcement of the antitrust laws. The purpose of these laws is to maximize consumer satisfaction by reducing monopoly power. In the past, however, the laws often have served both to protect smaller businesses and to penalize larger ones, even when greater size was due to increased efficiency. Efforts are being made at both the Federal Trade Commission and the Department of Justice to reform the enforcement of the antitrust laws to make them more consistent with the promotion of economic efficiency.

Because property rights in air and water have not been sufficiently extensive there are grounds for government intervention to alleviate pollution. However, the form of much prior intervention was inefficient. Most of this regulation has been carried out by specifying the allowable pollution control technology rather than by defining property rights or by charging fees for polluting.

This Administration is also making a major effort to emphasize the use of benefit-cost analysis in regulation. Regulation which imposes more costs than benefits is inefficient. For example, regulations that limit entry to a potentially competitive industry, such as interstate trucking, generate high transportation costs which are ultimately borne by consumers. The most elementary benefit-cost analysis would demonstrate the inefficiency of such regulation.

Even if used as well as possible, however, benefit-cost analysis is only the second best solution. The best solution is to respect the judgment of the private market whenever it is available. In many areas of safety regulation, for example, the best solution would probably be to rely on market judgments about the value of safety. Where this may not be possible, benefit-cost analysis can improve the information on which regulation is based.

In areas such as environmental regulation, where the market will not work unaided, benefit-cost analysis may be necessary to identify the optimal degree and form of pollution control. Even if a system of effluent charges were used, for example, an analysis of costs and benefits would be necessary to determine the optimal charge. If a system of pollution rights were used, the amount of rights to be created would have to be determined in some similar way.

FEDERALISM

One important principle of this Administration is an increased reliance on State and local governments to carry out necessary governmental activities. The replacement of many categorical grant programs by large block grants is one example of this policy change. A longer term policy of the Administration is to shift a substantial number of programs—and a portion of the Federal tax base—to the States.

As indicated earlier, there are economic reasons for this increased reliance on State governments. States are generally more responsive to voters in their jurisdiction than is the Federal Government and can make better judgments about local conditions.

LONG-RUN FOCUS

As discussed above, the political process has placed its major emphasis on the achievement of short-term goals. This Administration intends to place emphasis on long-run policies. For example, the Economic Recovery Tax Act of 1981 cuts tax rates over a 3-year period, after which the personal income tax structure will be indexed so that inflation will not increase marginal tax rates on real income. The Administration is also seeking a long-term solution to the financial problems facing the social security system.

However, there is a more fundamental sense in which emphasis is being placed on long-term goals. Many of the Administration's policies have reduced government expenditures for various groups or provided less of an increase in such outlays than has been expected. The fundamental premise behind these reductions is that they ultimately will lead to substantial and sustainable economic growth. This has particular relevance for the poor, most of whom probably have historically benefited more from sustained economic growth than from government transfer programs.

INCREASED RELIANCE ON THE MARKET

Another principle mentioned several times in this chapter is an increased reliance on market-like devices when appropriate government interventions are undertaken. Since this is an important principle, an indication of how such a principle will be translated into action will demonstrate some relationships between seemingly disparate changes in the forms of intervention.

First, consider the reason for reliance on devices which simulate market operations where intervention is the desired policy. The only alternative is direct regulation, which puts the government in an adversarial position to the party being regulated. Such adversary relationships create ill will between the government and business or other regulated parties. Ill will is also created when, for example, government employees monitor and control the spending of welfare recipients. Besides creating ill will, monitoring of behavior is expensive. Yet monitoring allows regulators to achieve their goals only imperfectly, since there are millions of regulated individuals, businesses, and other private institutions, and regulators will be able to monitor only a small fraction of these agents.

The advantage of market-like devices is that they can create incentives to behave in the desired way. That is, if we can simulate an effective market, we can rely on self-interest to achieve the desired goals. This will reduce the cost of achieving the regulatory goal and also increase the extent to which the goal will be achieved.

A good example is provided by comparing government safety regulation of firms with private market insurance against risks. In the case of government regulations, violators are punished, commonly with a fine, which may create incentives for the regulated firms to conceal possible violations and to avoid cooperation with safety inspectors. If, on the other hand, a firm which is insured can make its operations safer, it will usually benefit by having its insurance premium reduced. Thus, such firms have an incentive to cooperate with insurance company inspectors and adopt any recommendations which are made. This is but one example of how a market device, by eliciting cooperation, is more efficient in achieving desired goals than is regulation, which elicits conflict.

EMPHASIS ON THE GENERAL WELFARE

As stressed throughout this chapter, many current programs provide benefits to special interest groups. These programs are inefficient in that the gains to the beneficiaries are generally less than the cost to the public as a whole. Nonetheless, the political process, if unconstrained, would continue to establish such programs. In recent years effective constraints have been reduced. But if these special interest programs could be eliminated, almost everyone would benefit because of the losses in economic efficiency caused by these programs. However, it is extremely difficult politically to reduce such programs one at a time, since the beneficiaries would then perceive their losses clearly and seek to regain them.

The alternative, which this Administration adopted in both its spending and tax cuts, is to reduce a large number of programs simultaneously. If enough cuts in both spending and tax rates can be made simultaneously, most individuals may recognize that, while they may lose from cuts in a specific program, they gain enough from cuts in other programs and in lower taxes to compensate for their losses. Thus, the principles of optimal government intervention explain why the Administration insisted on very broad cuts in spending. Congressional approval of much of this plan indicates that this strategy was appropriate. A general reduction in special interest programs is a necessary step to meet the constitutional charge to "promote the general Welfare. . . ."

CHAPTER 3

Monetary Policy, Inflation, and Employment

THE ECONOMIC STORY of the late 1960s and the 1970s was a story of rising inflation, slackening growth, and rising unemployment. The challenge of the 1980s is to eliminate inflation, restore growth, and reduce unemployment. Despite differences over the precise combination of policies that will do the job, there is widespread agreement that inflation can and must be reduced if the economy is to operate successfully. The obstacles to successful implementation of an anti-inflation policy have been largely political, although public understanding of this has been complicated by the economic consequences of the oil price shocks of 1974–75 and 1979–80. The proper policy would be one based on a careful weighing of the long-term benefits of ending inflation against the costs which are essentially short run. It is the nature of the political process, however, to focus primarily on the short-run costs of dealing with inflation, as these appear to be more easily quantifiable, and to ignore the more distant but equally important benefits of price stability.

As the acute costs of rising inflation have become more widely recognized, the public has demanded action. That has made possible the implementation of the current set of fiscal and monetary policies aimed at reducing inflation. The decision to end inflation over a period of several years will be sustained by this Administration, even though short-run costs will be suffered before long-term benefits begin to accrue. A broad public understanding of the nature of the immediate but transitory costs and the longer run benefits of reducing inflation can contribute to the overall success of the current policies. On the other hand, any perception that the policies may soon be reversed would cause transitional costs to rise, since upward adjustments in inflation expectations—and, subsequently, prices and wages—would then be realized. In short, any lack of credibility would greatly extend the period of adjustment, thereby increasing the size and duration of short-term costs.

Chapters 1 and 2 reviewed the economic policies and problems inherited by this Administration and the challenges that its economic recovery program poses. This chapter focuses first on the legacies resulting from macroeconomic policymaking over the past two decades before turning to a discussion of monetary policy issues whose successful resolution is central to the Administration's economic recovery program. The concluding section of the chapter outlines the challenge to policymakers to improve upon the past.

THE LEGACIES

THE LEGACY OF ECONOMIC STABILIZATION POLICY

To policymakers in the early 1960s, the main solutions to future economic problems seemed to be in hand. The Federal Government was thought to have all of the tools needed for economic stabilization, along with the skills to use them. Recessions might still occur because investment shifted erratically or because the response to government action was variable, but it was believed that a discretionary stablization policy could successfully limit the frequency and magnitude of recessions. Inflation might result from decisions to reduce unemployment and increase output beyond the point consistent with price stability, but for the most part inflation seemed manageable. Essentially, it was thought that the economy could be kept on a steadily rising trend by "fine tuning" government actions.

Three key elements characterized policy prescriptions. Greater use was made of models and forecasts of short-term economic activity, prices, and interest rates. Policy decisions were based on a perceived short-run tradeoff between inflation and unemployment, and there was some belief that a long-run tradeoff between inflation and unemployment could also be exploited. Greater emphasis was given to planned changes in budget deficits or surpluses as a means of achieving annual (and sometimes quarterly) targeted rates of inflation and unemployment.

To avoid a potentially painful reliance on fiscal and monetary discipline, budget policy was supplemented by other programs. One approach, the creation of guideposts, was designed to influence changes in individual prices and wages. The belief was that guideposts announced by the government could improve the tradeoff between inflation and unemployment. Proponents of guideposts regarded them as efficient devices for slowing inflation during periods of rising employment and expanding output, and controlling, in the language of the time, "cost-push" inflation. Another program, aimed at reducing the U.S. balance of payments deficit and sustaining an international monetary system based on fixed-exchange rates, involved levying taxes on interest payments from foreign sources to Americans and restricting the amount of U.S. Government and private spending abroad.

Both policy and theory have undergone substantial change since then. A major reason for the change is that additional research revealed the errors and limitations of earlier policy recommendations. Although there was some research that supported the activist policies implemented in the past two decades, many subsequent studies have cast doubt on those findings.

The major failure of the late 1960s and 1970s was to give insufficient weight to the long-term effects of economic policies. For example, the so-called Phillips curve—the observed inverse relationship between wage inflation and unemployment—and its implication that a tradeoff is possible was one of the key notions relied on by economic advisers. But nothing in Phillips' work or in subsequent studies showed that higher inflation was associated with sustainable lower unemployment, and nothing in economic theory gave reason to believe that the relationship uncovered by Phillips was a dependable basis for policies designed to accept more inflation or less unemployment. Nevertheless, Phillips curves jumped quickly from scholarly journals to the policy arena. The speed with which the case made for this tradeoff was accepted as a cornerstone of economic policy contrasts with the slow acceptance of both neoclassical economic theory and the substantial body of evidence which suggests that there is no lasting tradeoff between inflation and unemployment. The economic policies which are now being implemented by the Administration are grounded in this tradition.

Another example of policy failure was the imposition of direct controls on prices, which were defended on grounds that they would bring about lower unemployment in an economy subject to "cost-push" inflation without imposing uneven burdens on the various sectors of the economy. The decision to impose these controls was based on the presumably favorable effects they would have on the expectations of consumers, unions, and businessmen.

Neither guideposts nor price controls, however, have succeeded in stopping inflation. The failures of these approaches have not been failures of economic theory. Instead, they have shown that political expediency or guesses about expectations of inflation are a less reliable guide to successful policy than sound economic analysis.

While economic analysis provides a framework for policy recommendations designed to reduce inflation, increase efficiency, and expand long-run growth of output and employment, policy recommendations based on the notion that it is possible to "fine tune" the economy from quarter to quarter or year to year promise more than economics can deliver. The events of the past 15 years are a good illustration of the dangers of pursuing economic policies based on short-run analysis and focused on immediate problems. Sound policy requires emphasis on a time horizon during which the sometimes lengthy, and usually unpredictable, lags in economic processes can work. Good economic policy means long-run economic policy. In light of the political incentives that place a premium on quick results, good economic policy also means resisting the previous tendency in our system to change the course of policies prematurely.

THE LEGACY OF STAGFLATION

The irony of the 1970s was that the attempt to trade inflation for employment resulted in more inflation and rising unemployment. This period was characterized by relatively high unemployment rates and high rates of inflation, a phenomenon often called "stagflation." The growth of real output in the United States was slower than during the preceding two decades, even though the growth rate of the labor force increased. The rate of increase in the productivity of labor declined, in part because of the effects of externally imposed oil price shocks. The combination of inflation with progressive income tax rates led to steady increases in actual and prospective taxes on real income in the latter part of the 1970s. Government appeared unable to reduce inflation without increasing unemployment or to reduce unemployment without, sooner or later, increasing inflation. The actual result was that rates of inflation and unemployment rose with each succeeding round of expansion and recession, and measured productivity growth was disappointing at best (Chapter 5).

There are those who argue that a permanent reduction in the rate of inflation brings about a permanent rise in the unemployment rate. But the lesson to be learned from the experience of the United States since World War II is that high rates of unemployment can co-exist with either high or low inflation. There is no reason to expect a systematic association between the average unemployment rate and the average rate of price-level change, and none is found in the data when one considers periods of several years or longer (Chart 3-1).

Many factors influence the average rate of unemployment over an extended period of time. Demographic factors—age, work experience, marital status, and other characteristics of the population—affect the supply of labor and entry into and exit from the active work force. Economic policies can either reinforce or offset these demographic factors by influencing the real wage at which workers choose between labor and leisure and the price at which potential investors choose between consumption and capital accumulation. As is discussed in Chapters 4 and 5, government taxes and expenditures have increased relative to national output during the past quarter century, reducing on the margin the incentive to work and the "cost" of leisure.

Chart 3-1

Inflation and Unemployment Rate

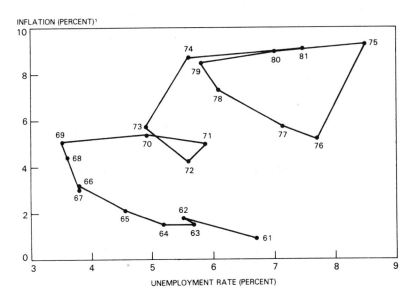

INFLATION (PERCENT)¹

UNEMPLOYMENT RATE (PERCENT)

¹ PERCENT CHANGE IN GNP IMPLICIT PRICE DEFLATOR.

SOURCES: DEPARTMENT OF COMMERCE AND DEPARTMENT OF LABOR.

During 1977 and 1978 there was emphasis on idle resources and an output gap that was to be closed by expansive economic policies. The belief was that stimulative policies would be less inflationary as long as excess capacity existed. The amount of idle capacity was probably overestimated for a variety of reasons—errors in assessing the effects of the 1974 oil price shock, failure to account for the effects of regulation, and the effects of tax and income transfer policies on unemployment and potential output. The presumed gap, however, was not a reliable buffer that would permit additional output without provoking an increase in the rate of inflation. The effort to reduce the unemployment rate by stimulating aggregate demand led to a much higher inflation rate, higher interest rates, and a sharp depreciation of the dollar, but it had no lasting effect on the unemployment rate.

The primary reason for the increase in the underlying rate of inflation in 1979–81 was the excessive fiscal and monetary expansion of 1977–78. Moderate policies probably would have left us with an average rate of unemployment no higher, and possibly lower, coupled with lower inflation. The average rate of unemployment and the average rate of inflation are best regarded as unrelated in the long term. The failure of previous policymakers to accept this conclusion is one of the principal reasons we have had a decade of stagflation.

THE BUSINESS CYCLE AND RISING INFLATION LEGACY

A shift toward less inflationary economic policies usually affects output and employment first. Inflation, and people's expectations about future inflation, only start to fall after restraint has been maintained for some time.

The more persistent and variable past rates of inflation have been, the less credible the new noninflationary policies will be and, hence, the longer it will take for those policies to achieve the intended results. Conversely, an abrupt policy shift toward greater stimulus first affects output, then employment, and later prices. The lag in the response of prices to stimulative policy also varies; a history of high inflation and frequent policy reversals will tend to shorten these lags.

Cyclical fluctuations in business activity occur primarily because prices and wage rates (that is, nominal magnitudes) do not adjust immediately to change, whether it is change in government policy or change in economic factors, such as the price of raw materials. In the past, this pattern of delayed response was used to justify aggregate-demand management. Most cyclical changes in employment were regarded as "involuntary," the result of insufficient spending by the private sector. The loss to society was deemed equal to what the unemployed would have produced if they had continued to work. Hence, government policies to reduce unemployment were regarded as having low costs and large social benefits. Because the rate of inflation was slow to adjust, policymakers acted as if there was no reason to expect inflation to increase significantly until after a high level of employment had been reached.

Repeated attempts to use fiscal and monetary policy to stimulate output, all the while assuring the public that inflation would be slowed later, left a residue of higher inflation. These attempts, in turn, generated expectations about future trends. The entrenchment of expectations of further inflation induced policymakers to respond with another episode of restraint, thereby creating another recession, followed by another attempt at stimulus—in short, repeated rounds of stop-and-go policy and performance. So long as economic policy had a short-run perspective, this alternating cycle of restriction and stimulus persisted. Meanwhile, the trend in the rate of inflation moved steadily upward.

The costs of adjusting to a low-inflation environment are often underestimated. Policymakers are impatient with the transitory costs accompanying such a change. Even when policymakers fully intend to make a permanent change, workers are unable to distinguish immediately between permanent and transitory changes in market conditions affecting their industry. They do not know whether a layoff is temporary or permanent, or whether the real wages prevailing in their industry will be sustainable in the future. Immediate reductions in wages are therefore resisted, and workers are often willing to experience a period of unemployment while waiting to be called back to work in the same industry and at the same wages, rather than change occupation or relocate.

Although changes in labor market conditions do occur, it is not always obvious to those affected whether the changes are permanent. Workers and employers must decide on a course of action while laboring under a high degree of uncertainty. Accepting a lower real wage will entail a reduction in lifetime income if the reduction in demand is temporary. But failing to cut real wages when the reduction in demand proves to be permanent also will mean a reduction in lifetime income as a consequence of lost jobs. The proper choice is usually not obvious at the time. This is a major reason why businesses and workers are slow to adjust prices and wages.

For at least two decades the government has responded to recessions by pushing up Federal spending and monetary growth to stimulate the economy. Each time this has been done, output has recovered and employment has risen. Meanwhile, however, the rate of inflation has been higher in each trough than in the previous trough, and higher at each peak than at the previous peak (Chart 3-2).

The public has apparently drawn two lessons from this experience. First, people have come to expect on average that the rate of price and wage change will rise from cycle to cycle. As a result, resistance to price and wage reduction relative to the increase in the general price level has increased through successive recessions. As anticipated inflation increased, the pressure for higher wages intensified. Second, all recessions are expected to be offset by stimulative government policies, and the costs of unemployment are expected to be reduced by unemployment compensation and related benefits. Thus, there are fewer incentives to look for employment at lower real wages and more reasons to wait for stimulative policies to restore employment in the old jobs at the same real wages.

Discretionary monetary and fiscal policies have added an additional element of uncertainty to economic life. People who want to know whether tax rates will rise or fall must guess whether the bulge in government spending during a recession is a portent of permanently higher spending and tax rates or simply an indication of temporarily higher spending. Past experience gives imperfect guidance. Yet dif-

Chart 3-2

The Inflation Ratchet (CPI)

PERCENT

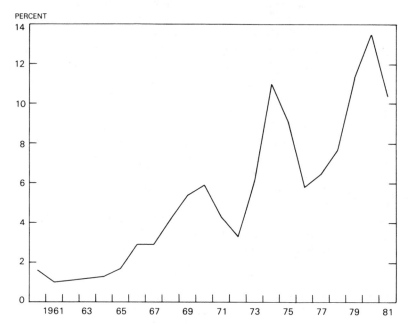

NOTE.—YEAR-TO-YEAR CHANGE IN CONSUMER PRICE INDEX FOR ALL URBAN CONSUMERS.
SOURCE: DEPARTMENT OF LABOR.

ferences in anticipated tax rates often have been a key factor in decisions to invest in durable capital, to invest in land or other tax-sheltered capital, or to consume.

We have been through four cycles in the past 15 years. Each time, government has made a renewed commitment to conquer inflation. But people's decisions concerning consumption, saving, and investment are now conditioned by the expectation that these cycles will continue to occur in the future, just as they have in the past.

THE NATURE OF THE INFLATION PROCESS

Inflation is essentially a monetary phenomenon. This is not to deny the importance of other factors, such as changes in the price of petroleum, in causing increases in the general price level. What the statement does deny, however, is that persistent inflation can be explained by nonmonetary factors.

Monetary policy actions affect primarily nominal quantities—exchange rates, the price level, national income, and the quantity of money—as well as the rate of change in nominal quantities. But central bank actions do not have significant long-run effects in achieving *specific* values of real magnitudes—the real rate of interest, the rate of unemployment, the level of real national income, the real quantity of money—or rates of growth of real magnitudes.

Economists recognized long ago that output and employment may be no higher when prices are high than when they are low. A main point of Adam Smith's *Wealth of Nations* is that a country's wealth and income depend on the country's real resources and the way in which production is organized, and not on the level of prices. It was realized that changes in the price level had some short-term effects on output, but these effects were recognized as the result of transitory changes in demand.

The classical gold-standard mechanism embodied these principles. Unanticipated increases in the flow of gold from abroad stimulated domestic production but gradually raised domestic prices relative to foreign prices. The rise in domestic prices then reduced exports and raised imports, thereby lowering domestic production and employment and eventually lowering prices. The continuous ebb and flow of gold was expected, but the timing of the movements could not be predicted accurately. Inability to predict the movements was recognized as a cause of changes in prices and output.

Once people anticipate that prices will rise, they seek higher wages for their labor and higher prices for their products. The increase in employment produced by stimulative policies vanishes, but the inflation remains. Attempts to reduce unemployment by increasing inflation will work only if people are fooled by the changes in policy. Once people learn to expect inflation, the short-run gains in employment disappear.

It is often stated that inflation is an intractable problem, caused by forces beyond our control. But the monetary nature of inflation suggests that this is not so. More importantly, it suggests that a decrease in money growth is the necessary strategy to end inflation. Frequent use of monetary policy to reduce unemployment at certain times and inflation at others would raise the prospect of generating the same kind of cyclical behavior in economic activity that we have experienced in the past and analyzed in the previous section.

Stop-and-go policies cause uncertainty, hamper the ability of monetary authorities to achieve noninflationary conditions, and ultimately raise the transitional costs of eliminating inflation. The next section discusses in detail the nature of these costs.

THE COSTS OF INFLATION

Over the last decade, as inflation worsened, the attention of the general public focused on the detrimental effects that rapidly rising prices have on economic performance. These effects were felt in many ways, but the mechanisms by which inflation generated them were not well understood.

The effects of inflation fall into two general categories: (1) those that occur because no one is able to predict the precise rate of inflation; and (2) those that occur even when the rate of inflation is fully anticipated.

The concept of a "fully anticipated inflation" implies a rate of inflation that people can predict and hence take action to minimize its effects. But it is doubtful that a high rate of inflation that was also predictable could ever exist because the same lack of monetary discipline which leads to unacceptably high inflation is also likely to lead to more variable inflation. Indeed, periods of high inflation rates generally have been associated with periods of higher variability of inflation rates. It would take at least as much monetary discipline to maintain a constant high inflation rate as it takes to maintain price-level stability. Once a positive rate of inflation is accepted it becomes difficult to argue against a slightly higher rate.

One of the most important costs of unanticipated inflation is its arbitrary redistribution of wealth and income. Economic transactions are often formalized in contracts that require one party to pay a fixed dollar amount to the other party at some point in the future. When both parties anticipate inflation during the life of the contract, these future dollar payments will be adjusted upward to compensate for their expected lower real value. This upward adjustment is the so-called inflation premium. If, however, the actual rate of inflation turns out to be different from the anticipated rate, the real terms of the contract will have been altered arbitrarily. If the actual rate is higher than anticipated, the fixed payments in dollars will have a lower than expected real value, and the debtor will gain at the expense of the creditor. The same kind of arbitrary transfer occurs when workers and firms agree to wage contracts that implicitly or explicitly assume rates of inflation which later turn out to be incorrect.

In a market economy, changes in the price of one good relative to another signal changes in demand and supply conditions among various markets. An uncertain rate of inflation obscures these signals and thereby reduces economic efficiency. Since prices are rising more or less together during a general inflationary period, the fact that a price has risen is no guarantee that it has risen relative to other prices. The difficulty of distinguishing between relative and absolute price changes increases as inflation and its variability increase. This leads people to use more time and resources to attempt to decipher relative price changes, as opposed to engaging in more productive activities. Differently stated, inflation tends to make the economic information that people accumulate through experience more rapidly obsolescent than when prices are stable.

Perhaps more importantly, inability to correctly anticipate inflation creates confusion about relative prices over time and compounds the problem of efficient resource allocation. Economic decisionmaking, especially in the private sector, is inherently forward-looking. Decisions made today determine tomorrow's levels of capital stock, production, and consumption. Decisions based on correct anticipation of future relative prices lead to a more efficient allocation of resources over time. High and variable inflation, on the other hand, leads to divergent inflation expectations, and therefore to a larger proportion of incorrect decisions.

Because inability to anticipate the rate of inflation correctly increases the uncertainty associated with economic decisions, especially those that involve fixed-dollar commitments far into the future, it leads to a shortening of the time horizon over which such commitments are made. In the financial markets, uncertainty about inflation causes a relative decline in the volume of long-term bond financing. Neither borrowers nor lenders are willing to compensate the other adequately for the risk. Consequently, the sales volume of fixed-rate long-term debt instruments shrinks and the volume of real investment normally financed in this way decreases. More generally, productive activities yield a relatively lower real return than activities aimed at "beating" inflation. Hence, as more and more resources are devoted to coping with the uncertainty that accompanies inflation, fewer resources are available for real productive activities.

Two costs of anticipated inflation have been widely recognized. In the economics literature they have been dubbed "menu" and "shoe leather" costs. Because inflation requires frequent changes in published (that is, "menu") prices, these changes absorb resources that could be used in other activities. "Shoe leather" costs are those incurred by people attempting to minimize their money holdings by more frequent trips to the bank. Since a great deal of money is held as a noninterest-bearing asset, its real value declines with inflation. People therefore make more strenuous efforts to realize the highest return on their assets and hence they economize on noninterest-bearing balances.

57

The interaction of a nonindexed tax system with inflation would impose costs even if the rate of inflation were correctly anticipated. Imperfect adjustment for inflation in the taxation of both current labor income and income from capital causes changes in inflation to affect real after-tax levels of income. These, in turn, alter the level and composition of these activities relative to each other and relative to activities on which the return is not distorted. One analyst has estimated the unavoidable costs from this cause alone to be 0.7 percent of gross national product (GNP), and perhaps as high as 2 to 3 percent of GNP. The indexation of tax brackets beginning in 1985, as legislated by the Economic Recovery Tax Act of 1981, will substantially reduce this problem.

The interaction between the tax system and inflation also affects capital formation because of the way in which depreciation allowances are treated. Depreciation allowances for capital assets are based on historical cost rather than current replacement cost. During periods of high inflation the difference between historical cost and replacement cost widens rapidly, leading to allowances smaller than would be considered justifiable. Since deductions for depreciation are determined on the basis of the actual purchase price, smaller real deductions mean higher capital costs. This, in turn, reduces the pace of investment and hence of economic growth. (See Chapter 5 for an extended discussion of these issues.)

THE COSTS OF REDUCING INFLATION

There is, as noted above, a short-lived tradeoff between unemployment and the rate of inflation. This means that policies designed to reduce inflation significantly will temporarily increase unemployment and reduce output growth. The temporary decline in output growth induced by anti-inflation policies forms a rough benchmark against which the subsequent benefits of reduced inflation can be compared. The extent of these costs of reducing inflation depends on four factors: (1) the institutional process of setting wages and prices; (2) the role of expectations in this process; (3) the policy instruments employed to reduce inflation; and (4) the initial rate of inflation.

Flexibility in wages and prices reduces the transitional costs of ending inflation. A policy-induced decline in the growth rate of monetary aggregates will be associated with a decline in the growth of real output, but the more rapidly this decline in output is followed by a moderating of inflation, the more rapidly will output growth return to a rising trend. One important factor affecting the flexibility of wages and prices is the institutional environment in which they are determined. The costs of continuously negotiating and resetting prices and wages, for example, has given rise to the common practice of changing wage and price agreements relatively infrequently. While this practice makes economic sense for individuals and firms, it builds a degree of inertia into the system.

Wage contracts in major industries in the United States typically cover a 2- or 3-year period. Since these contracts specify basic wage increases over the life of the contract, the current rate of wage inflation was determined in part as long as 3 years ago. Because major wage contracts are staggered over approximately 3 years, wage settlements in the first year of each "3-year round" tend to set the pattern for settlements in the following 2 years. This extends the influence of any year's wage settlements beyond the lives of the contracts. In addition, many contracts include automatic cost-of-living adjustments that preclude downward wage flexibility, even when it might be justified by conditions specific to a particular industry or firm.

Government regulations or standards that dictate prices or wages, reduce competition, or otherwise reduce the flexibility of firms and workers in responding to economic conditions also add to the inflexibility of wages and prices. Programs now under way to bring regulatory relief to industries that have been overregulated in the past should diminish this source of rigidity (Chapter 6).

Decisions concerning the determination of prices and wages are dominated by perceptions of future market conditions, such as the expected rate of inflation. Workers will accept nominal wage increases that, given their expectation of inflation, imply an acceptable real wage. If their expectations about inflation are revised downward in light of announced policies to end inflation, wage and price increases will moderate. The pace of this adjustment in expectations is an indication of the degree of public confidence in anti-inflationary policies.

The primary policy tool for ending inflation is a decrease in the rate of growth of money. The question of how rapidly the monetary deceleration should proceed must be answered in the context of public expectations. In view of past experience, when efforts to reduce inflation were abandoned as the short-run costs began to accrue, the public has come to expect that such policies will continue to be short-lived and that inflation will persist. Frequent swings from restrictive to stimulative policy and back have led to a "wait and see" attitude on the part of the public. The mere announcement of new policies is not sufficient to convince people that they will be carried out. Rather, public expectations regarding the future course of policy are adjusted only gradually as policy actions turn out to be consistent with policy pronouncements. The credibility of policy authorities, like the credibility of anyone else, is enhanced when they do what they say they are going to do. For the Federal Reserve, this means setting money growth targets consistent with a sustained decrease in the rate of inflation and then adhering to those targets. The more success the Federal Reserve has in meeting those targets, the less time it will take before the public is convinced of the policy's credibility.

In the current environment, even if a successful effort is made to reduce money growth, past experience with high and variable inflation will affect the speed at which financial markets reflect progress toward a long-run noninflationary policy. Having repeatedly suffered sizable capital losses on their holdings of long-term bonds, investors will be unwilling to commit new funds to these markets unless they are compensated for the risk that the current commitment to overcome inflation might be abandoned. Without adequate compensation for this risk, individuals will continue to prefer to invest in short-lived rather than long-lived financial assets. While this preference may prevent investors from maximizing the expected return on their assets, it allows them to minimize the adverse effects of future increases in inflation and interest rates.

Present concern about future monetary growth, inflation, and interest rates is related to the knowledge that the Federal budget will continue to show large deficits for the next several years. Financial investors fear that these deficits will cause either a sharp increase in interest rates—which would slow the recovery from recession—or an increase in monetary growth if the Federal Reserve attempts to hold interest rates down by adding reserves to the banking system through open market purchases of government securities.

Interest rates that are considerably higher than the current rate of inflation can have an adverse effect on investment and real economic growth. The level of long-term interest rates at the end of 1981 did not reflect investor willingness to believe that inflation will decline over the next several years. The presumably large but unmeasurable premiums being demanded by investors constitute a major obstacle to achieving rising output and employment with falling inflation.

Expectations about future rates of money growth, like expectations of future inflation, are likely to be more divergent the greater the variability of past money growth. These expectations should converge more rapidly as the Federal Reserve improves its ability to control money growth. More precise control of money growth around the target path will reduce the difficulty of inferring from actual growth rates whether or not the announced targets are, in fact, a reliable indicator of future money growth. In such an environment, variations in money growth will reflect only random and short-lived deviations, which would have little effect on either short- or long-run expectations about monetary policy. But failure to achieve more precise monetary control, by impeding a rapid adjustment of expectations, would significantly raise the costs of reducing inflation. Thus, the payoffs of greater precision could be quite large.

In summary, high and varying inflation imposes costs on society by reducing future standards of living. These costs, though presumed to be large and pervasive, are not easily calculated. There is a temporary output loss in the initial stage of a transition to price stability. Such loss, however, must be weighed against the future increases in output that would be achieved by ending inflation. The policies of the Administration are based on the view that the cost of continuing to endure the high rates of inflation of the 1970s would be greater than the costs of implementing a successful noninflationary policy.

MONEY AND MONETARY POLICY

MONEY CREATION AND FEDERAL FINANCE

The deficit of the Federal Government is financed by the issuing of interest-bearing liabilities, such as Treasury bills and long-term bonds, and noninterest-bearing liabilities, which include currency and bank reserves held as deposits with the Federal Reserve System. The noninterest-bearing liabilities constitute the monetary base. When there is unanticipated inflation, holders of the interest-bearing liabilities are implicitly taxed because the nominal interest rates on their holdings no longer fully compensate for inflation. Holders of currency and reserves, however, bear an implicit tax even when inflation is anticipated. Banks usually seek to shift some of the implicit tax on their reserves to depositors. The portion of the tax ultimately absorbed by depositors depends on the administrative limits on interest paid on these deposits, and on the degree of competitiveness in the banking industry.

The purchasing power of the dollar declines over time when the growth of the money stock exceeds the growth of demand for real money balances. As a result, holders of money incur a loss that is related to the rate of inflation. As discussed more fully in Chapter 5, the Federal Government benefits from anticipated inflation because the real value of its noninterest-bearing liabilities falls. It also benefits from unanticipated inflation because the nominal interest on its interest-bearing debt does not fully compensate for the decline in the purchasing power of money. The revenues obtained in this fashion by the Federal Government serve as a substitute for other, more direct taxes. This "inflation tax" may be more or less efficient than other taxes in financing government expenditures, but while all other taxes are legislated by the Congress (or State and local governments), the inflation tax is not.

One troublesome aspect of the inflation tax is not so much its existence as uncertainty about its amount. Historically, high average rates of inflation have been associated with high volatility—that is, large swings in inflation rates from year to year. Financial markets readily incorporate expected rates of inflation into interest rates, but they are unable to price that portion of the inflation rate that is unanticipated.

MONEY VERSUS CREDIT

Discussions of monetary policy frequently fail to take account of the difference between money and credit. Money is an asset that people generally accept as payment for goods and services. It consists of coins, currency, and checkable deposits. Credit, in contrast, is one party's claim against another party, which is to be settled by a future payment of money. Confusion about the difference between money and credit arises because people can increase their spending either by reducing their money balances or by obtaining credit.

The market for money is distinct from the market for credit. The supply of and demand for credit influence primarily the interest rate, which is the price of credit. The supply of and demand for money, on the other hand, determine the purchasing power of money. Additional confusion about the difference between money and credit arises because the monetary authorities create money primarily by purchasing credit market instruments. These actions tend to increase the supply of available bank credit and consequently tend to lower interest rates, at least initially. Over a longer period of time, however, the creation of money has important effects on economic activity that tend to raise interest rates. Monetary expansion leads to an expansion in nominal income and economic activity, which in turn generates an increased demand for credit, thus reversing the initial decline in interest rates. In addition, a sustained higher rate of monetary growth will soon produce higher nominal interest rates to compensate lenders for the expected decline in the real value of their wealth.

When interest rates are high, credit is often said to be "tight," meaning that it is expensive. This does not necessarily mean that money is tight in the sense that its quantity is restricted. Indeed, quite the opposite is likely to be the case. "Easy" money, in the sense of rapid growth in the stock of money, may very well be the underlying reason for a tight credit market. Conversely, tight money in the sense of slow growth in the stock of money is likely to lead eventually to a fall in nominal interest rates as inflation expectations subside. But it is credit, not money, that is easy. Over the long run, the effect of the growth of money on the real volume of credit is essentially neutral. Monetary expansion can succeed in driving up the nominal supply of credit as well as other nominal magnitudes. But it cannot significantly alter the real supply of credit or the real interest rate (the nominal rate adjusted for inflation), except indirectly through the uncertainty associated with inflation and because of the effects of an unindexed tax system. Monetary expansion can permanently reduce the purchasing power of money, but not the real price of credit.

It is often stated that such financial innovations as money-market funds undermine the conduct of monetary policy. Statistical support for this assertion is dubious. What would have to be demonstrated is that financial innovation—which is to a large extent the result of policy-imposed constraints on the financial system in an inflationary environment—has made it more difficult to achieve a given monetary target, and that the link between changes in nominal GNP and changes in the monetary aggregates—that is, changes in velocity—has become less predictable. The evidence does not seem to support either proposition. A study recently published by the Federal Reserve suggests that the monetary authorities have the ability to control the measure of transactions balances known as M1 with a reasonable degree of precision. Furthermore, changes in velocity do not appear to be any more volatile than they have in the past. Indeed, changes in the trend of the growth rate of nominal GNP over the period 1960 to 1981 are almost entirely attributable to changes in the trend of the growth rate of the money stock, (M1), as opposed to changes in the trend of the growth rate of velocity (Chart 3-3).

It is inflation and a highly regulated financial system that have spurred financial innovation. Inflation, and consequent higher interest rates, have also raised the real cost of reserve requirements for financial institutions. At the same time, the public has tended to economize on noninterest-bearing money balances. Thus, incentives were created for the public to demand, and for financial institutions to supply, substitutes for existing transactions accounts that are subject neither to reserve requirements nor interest rate restrictions. But innovations which are attractive only because they provide a means of avoiding existing regulations waste resources. The inefficiencies which such innovations are designed to circumvent could have been minimized by payment of interest on required reserves and on transactions balances. These inefficiencies will be greatly reduced when price level stability is restored.

MONETARY POLICY OBJECTIVES AND STRATEGY

A slow and steady rate of money growth is one of the four basic elements of the Administration's economic recovery program. While the formulation and implementation of monetary policy is the re-

Chart 3–3

Money and GNP Growth

PERCENT CHANGE (ANNUAL RATE)[1]

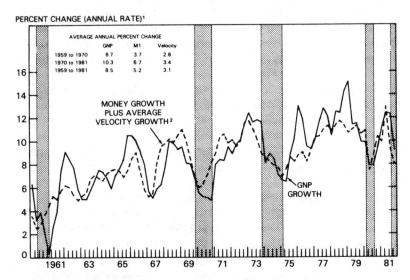

AVERAGE ANNUAL PERCENT CHANGE			
	GNP	M1	Velocity
1959 to 1970	6.7	3.7	2.8
1970 to 1981	10.3	6.7	3.4
1959 to 1981	8.5	5.2	3.1

MONEY GROWTH
PLUS AVERAGE
VELOCITY GROWTH[2]

GNP
GROWTH

1961   63   65   67   69   71   73   75   77   79   81

[1] PERCENT CHANGE IN 4-QUARTER MOVING AVERAGES OF SEASONALLY ADJUSTED MONEY STOCK (M1) AND GNP.

[2] AVERAGE VELOCITY GROWTH IS AVERAGE ANNUAL PERCENT CHANGE OVER THE PERIOD 1959 TO 1981.

NOTE.—SHADED AREAS INDICATE RECESSIONS AS DEFINED BY THE NATIONAL BUREAU OF ECONOMIC RESEARCH.

SOURCES: DEPARTMENT OF COMMERCE AND BOARD OF GOVERNORS OF THE FEDERAL RESERVE SYSTEM.

sponsibility of the Federal Reserve, the Administration believes the announced policy of the Federal Reserve is consistent with the economic recovery program. Thus, the Administration expects that the Federal Reserve will achieve an orderly reduction in the trend of money growth to a noninflationary rate. (See Chapter 8 for a discussion of recent monetary developments.)

We have discussed in the previous section how large risk premiums—the inflationary psychology—impose costs on the economy and constitute a major obstacle to achieving a high rate of saving and investment and rapidly rising standards of living. Announced changes in policy cannot lower these risk premiums in the short run. Credibility must be earned by performance. The longer the heritage of inflation, the longer it will take to demonstrate the credibility of current policy.

Controlling Monetary Aggregates

Some basic principles can be used to evaluate monetary policy actions. First, the monetary aggregate that is selected for policy purposes should be chosen with two factors in mind. One is that growth of the aggregate should be closely related to a primary objective of policy, which is to reduce inflation. This means that the aggregate must be closely related to national income in current prices. The second factor is that the Federal Reserve should be able to control the aggregate. Although a broader monetary aggregate may bear a closer relationship to nominal income than a narrower one, it is not appropriate for the Federal Reserve to emphasize the broader aggregate if it cannot be controlled as closely. Such a broader aggregate, however, may be a useful indicator of the effects of policy if timely data are available. As has already been discussed, the Federal Reserve has the ability to control the M1 aggregate with a reasonable degree of precision.

Success in controlling monetary aggregates is in part dependent on prevailing exchange-rate policy. A policy designed to maintain a given value of the dollar on foreign exchanges is inconsistent in the long run with a policy of achieving given monetary targets. As will be discussed in detail in Chapter 7, the policy of the Administration is to permit exchange rates to be determined by market forces. Such a posture relaxes an important constraint on the ability of the monetary authorities to set and achieve monetary targets.

Financial innovations in recent years have complicated the evaluation of the inflationary potential of monetary growth. The development of new financial instruments necessitated a recent redefinition of the monetary aggregates used by the Federal Reserve. The new measure of transactions balances (M1), in addition to including the public's holdings of currency and demand deposits at commercial banks, also includes the new types of checkable deposits offered by financial institutions, such as negotiable order of withdrawal (NOW) accounts. These interest-bearing checkable deposits are clearly used for transaction purposes and thus properly belong in M1.

Under the operating procedures of the Federal Reserve, accuracy in controlling a particular monetary aggregate depends upon the reserve requirement structure. In principle, reserve requirements should be applied uniformly to all deposits included in the monetary aggregate that the Federal Reserve is most committed to controlling and held at zero on deposits the Federal Reserve is less interested in controlling. Since the existing structure of reserve requirements was originally specified for other reasons, such as bank safety and allocation of credit, it does not meet this principle. As a result, the Federal Reserve must continuously monitor and compensate for the shifting relationships between the various monetary aggregates and total bank reserves.

This problem, which has been severe in the past, will be reduced greatly over the next few years. A restructuring of reserve requirements that will allow closer control of M1 is currently being carried out under provisions of the Depository Institutions Deregulation and Monetary Control Act of 1980. After complete implementation of these provisions is achieved by 1988, reserve requirements on transaction accounts will be nearly uniform, and those on most other accounts could be eliminated.

Interest Rates Versus Money Stock Targets

Prior to the 1970s the Federal Reserve (like most central banks) judged the appropriateness of monetary policy primarily by looking at credit conditions and interest rates—specifically, by watching short-term interest rates as an indicator of money-market conditions. However, the problem raised by this procedure was the difficulty in knowing exactly how much to vary interest rates in order to stabilize the economy. In times when credit demand was strong, too small an increase in interest rates generated spending in excess of the economy's capacity to produce, thereby fueling inflation. Similarly, interest rates might be allowed to decline by too little at times of weak credit demand, contributing to a recession.

In practice, monetary policymakers tended to be cautious in attempting to change interest rates, with the result generally being too much expansion of money when credit demand was strong and too little expansion when credit demand was weak. This procyclical money growth has tended to exacerbate, rather than dampen, business cycle fluctuations (Chart 3-3).

The procyclical growth in money was accompanied by a secular growth in money and increases in inflation. As the rate of inflation soared in the 1970s, market interest rates became an even less reliable guide to monetary policy. Market interest rates tend to be high when the inflation rate is high and low when inflation is low, given private and public borrowing demand. Consumption and investment decisions are based on real (inflation–adjusted) interest rates, not nominal interest rates. High nominal interest rates do not necessarily mean that "money is tight." High interest rates, in fact, may go hand-in-hand with "easy money." Since it is difficult to measure inflation expectations, it is difficult to know how much of an adjustment to make in nominal interest rates to determine the real interest rate. For these reasons, monetary policy is more appropriately based on changes in the growth of money than on changes in market interest rates.

When the Federal Reserve first adopted monetary targets in the early 1970s, it attempted to alter interest rates to achieve a desired rate of monetary growth. The growth of money was controlled through the marginal cost to banks of acquiring additional reserves, as indicated by the Federal funds rate, rather than through direct control of the quantity of reserves. (The Federal funds rate is the rate at which banks borrow excess reserves from each other.) In 1975, however, the Congress urged the Federal Reserve to adopt annual targets for monetary growth. With passage of the Full Employment and Balanced Growth Act of 1978 (the Humphrey-Hawkins Act), the requirement for money growth targeting became more specific. Since then, monetary authorities have been modifying their procedures in order to achieve their monetary targets.

On October 6, 1979, the Federal Reserve adopted a new approach which put much less emphasis on fluctuations in short-term interest rates. Instead, the new procedure placed primary emphasis on the amount of bank reserves as an operating target and allowed interest rates to be determined more freely by the market. What the Federal Reserve decided to do at that point was to control the *quantity* of reserves, rather than their price. Under the old procedures the average Federal funds rate typically did not vary by much more than one-half of a percentage point between monthly meetings of the Federal Open Market Committee. But after October 1979 the allowable range of the Federal funds rate was increased.

Enhancing Monetary Control

Stable monetary growth will serve to stabilize prices, act as an automatic stabilizer against temporary output fluctuations, and help to make public expectations about inflation consistent with the underlying rate of monetary growth. Achievement of stable monetary growth will require adequate control over total bank reserves. Two types of reserves are available. Nonborrowed reserves are owned outright by banks and are supplied by the Federal Reserve through open market operations. Borrowed reserves are supplied through temporary loans from the discount window of the Federal Reserve. The monetary authorities can directly control the amount of nonborrowed reserves, but they have only indirect control over the small but potentially volatile amount of reserves which bank borrow at the discount window.

Although borrowed reserves constitute, on average, only 2 to 3 percent of total reserves, fluctuations in borrowing can contribute significantly to short-run changes in total reserves. Reform of the discount window has therefore been proposed to make borrowed reserves more controllable and thus more predictable. Under these conditions, the Federal Reserve would be able to meet its targets for total banks reserves and the monetary base more accurately.

The volatility in borrowed reserves could be reduced by tying the discount rate to market rates so as to reduce variability in the incentive to borrow. To keep such variability to an absolute minimum, the Federal Reserve would also have to set its discount rate somewhat above market interest rates—that is, to act as a penalty. A penalty discount rate would be especially effective when the Depository Institutions Deregulation and Monetary Control Act of 1980, which makes reserve requirements significantly more uniform, is fully implemented.

An even more successful operation of a penalty rate would require a switch from the Federal Reserve's lagged reserve-requirement rule to a system of contemporaneous reserve requirements. The current rule, which became effective in 1968, states that in any given week institutions must hold reserves (as deposits at a Federal Reserve Bank or vault cash) in prescribed percentages of their various types of deposits 2 weeks earlier. The earlier system of contemporaneous reserve accounting required banks to hold reserves based on the current week's deposits.

Under lagged reserve accounting, the amount of borrowed reserves fluctuates considerably over the short run. During any 2-week period the total reserve requirement is predetermined by deposits 2 weeks earlier. This means that reserves must be supplied within the period, either borrowed or nonborrowed. Under current operating procedures, the Federal Reserve controls the growth of total reserves in future periods by varying the mix between borrowed and nonborrowed reserves. If a penalty discount rate tied to market interest rates were introduced, borrowed reserves would probably shrink to a small and relatively constant amount.

The Federal Reserve Board has requested public comment on its proposal to return to a system of contemporaneous reserve accounting. An important reason for going back to contemporaneous accounting would be to permit greater flexibility in the discount rate, at a penalty level or otherwise, which in turn would provide more precise short-run control over total reserves by reducing the volatility of borrowings. Even in the absence of a penalty discount rate, however, contemporaneous reserve accounting would allow open market operations to have a more immediate effect on total bank reserves.

INSTITUTIONALIZATION OF A NONINFLATIONARY MONETARY POLICY

The existence of high and varying rates of inflation, high and varying rates of interest, and volatile exchange rates for more than a decade clearly suggests that monetary management can be improved in the future. The Administration has supported and will continue to support the pursuit of a noninflationary monetary policy. The issue discussed in this section is: Once inflation has been eliminated, how can price-level stability be maintained?

Price stability is an objective that is arrived at through the political process, but it often conflicts with other political and economic objectives in the short run. It has therefore been difficult to establish institutional arrangements that will ensure price-level stability. The traditional argument for an independent monetary authority is that insulation from politics enables the central bank to resist pressures for inflating, even when the government would find an inflationary policy politically appealing.

Existing institutional arrangements have not ensured price stability. In the past 17 years, gold reserve clauses related to demand deposits at commercial banks, and then to currency held by the public, have been terminated. The Bretton Woods fixed exchange-rate system began to break down in the late 1960s, and the last link between the U.S. dollar and gold was formally severed in 1971. Since then, the monetary authorities have had considerable discretion in determining the rate at which new money is created.

As a result of the rising and volatile inflation of the past, economists have been evaluating alternative approaches to achieving and maintaining a noninflationary monetary policy. The congressional mandate to create a Gold Commission is symptomatic of a desire to find institutional arrangements that will ensure price-level stability. The remainder of this section discusses two approaches to the problem. One would involve some linkage of our monetary system to the official U.S. gold stock. The other would involve statutory or constitutional rules limiting monetary growth or requiring a stable price level.

It is important to keep in mind that alternatives to the present arrangement should be evaluated in terms of the answers they provide to these two questions: Is the rule or norm perceived to be credible by the public? Will departures from the stated norm impel policy-making institutions to correct them? If the answer to either question is "no," institutional change would not have served its purpose.

GOLD STANDARD

Some economists and elected officials have recently been advocating a return to a gold standard as a lasting way to restore confidence in the U.S. monetary system. The basic idea is that excessive money creation could be prevented by anchoring money to a scarce resource. In addition, it is argued that the establishment of a gold standard would induce savers to accept lower nominal rates of return on their assets. This would occur because fiat money would be convertible into gold at a fixed price, and thus an effective constraint would be placed on growth of the money stock and the rate of inflation. Lower rates of interest, in turn, would result in a rapid resump-

tion of economic growth. So, in essence, the contention is that restoration of a gold standard would not only stabilize prices but also
raise and stabilize output growth.

It is useful to review at this point how gold standards actually performed in the past. The evidence does not suggest that it achieved
greater stability in price levels or growth. Much of the claimed price-
level stability achieved under previous gold standards is based on
Gustav Cassel's observation that "the general level of prices in 1910
was practically the same as in 1850." [1] Professor Phinney of Harvard
was one of the first to point out that "unfortunately, when Cassel
came to choose base years, he completely forgot the distinction between the secular and the cyclical to which he had called attention." [2]

Chart 3-4

Jevons-Sauerbeck Index
of Wholesale Commodity Prices

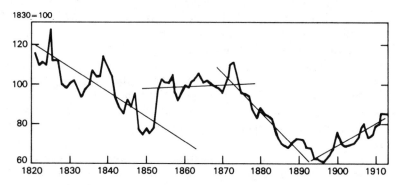

1830=100

NOTE.—INDEX OF PRICES IN BRITISH POUNDS OF A SELECTED GROUP OF INTERNATIONALLY
TRADED COMMODITIES.

SOURCE: REPRODUCED FROM J. T. PHINNEY, "GOLD PRODUCTION AND THE PRICE LEVEL: THE
CASSEL THREE PERCENT ESTIMATE," *QUARTERLY JOURNAL OF ECONOMICS*, VOL. 47,
1932-33, pp. 647-679.

Chart 3-4 reproduces the Jevons-Sauerbeck index which appeared in
the Phinney article. The index shows large and extremely long
swings in prices lasting up to 30 years. Increases and decreases were
on the order of 30 to 50 percent. The chart reveals very little evidence of long-run price-level stability. More information can be
gleaned by considering the wholesale price indexes of four countries
for the period 1814–1913 (Table 3–1). Perusal of the table leads to two
conclusions. First, the gold-standard period was very deflationary on

---

[1] "The Supply of Gold," in *Interim Report of the Gold Delegation* of the Financial Committee,
Geneva, 1930, p. 72. See also his *Theory of Social Economy*, p. 441.
[2] J. T. Phinney, "Gold Production and the Price Level: The Cassel Three Percent Estimate,"
Quarterly Journal of Economics, Vol. 47, 1932–33, p. 650.

the whole, with the price levels in the United States and the United Kingdom dropping by 44 percent. Second, price-level cycles were deep and protracted.

TABLE 3-1.—*Wholesale price indexes, 1814-1913*

Item	United States	United Kingdom	Germany	France	Italy
Indexes (1913 = 100):					
1814	178	178	129	[1] 132	
1849	80	90	71	96	
1872	133	125	111	124	
1896	67	76	71	71	74
1913	100	100	100	100	100
Percent change:					
1814 to 1849	−55	−49	−45	[2] −27	
1849 to 1872	66	39	56	29	
1872 to 1896	−50	−39	−36	−43	
1896 to 1913	49	32	41	41	35
1814 to 1913	−44	−44	−22	−24	

[1] Data are for 1820.
[2] Change from 1820.
Source: Robert Triffin, "The Evolution of the International Monetary System: Historical Reappraisal and Future Perspective," *Princeton Studies in International Finance* No. 12, 1964, p. 13.

Table 3-2 compares the sample mean and coefficient of variation [standard deviation divided by sample mean] of the rate of change of the wholesale price level for the United States and the United Kingdom for three different periods.

TABLE 3-2.—*Comparison of the behavior of price level, real output, and money growth in the United Kingdom and the United States, selected periods, 1821-1979*

Item	The Gold Standard [1]		The Interwar Period		Post-World War II	
	United Kingdom	United States	United Kingdom	United States	United Kingdom	United States
	1870–1913 (1821–1913)	1879–1913 (1834–1913)	1919–38	1919–40	1946–79	1946–79
(1) Average annual percent change in the price level	−0.7 (−.4)	0.1 (−.1)	−4.6	−2.5	5.6	2.8
(2) Coefficient of variation of annual percent changes in the price level (ratio)	−14.9 (−16.3)	17.0 (6.5)	−3.8	−5.2	1.2	1.3
(3) Coefficient of variation of annual percent changes in real per capita income (ratio)	2.5	3.5	4.9	5.5	1.4	1.6
(4) Average level of the unemployment rate (percent)	[2] 4.3	[3] 6.8	13.3	11.3	2.5	5.0
(5) Average annual percent change in the money supply	1.5	6.1	.9	1.5	5.9	5.7
(6) Coefficient of variation of annual percent changes in the money supply (ratio)	1.6	.8	3.6	2.4	1.0	.5

[1] Data for the longer periods (in parentheses) were available only for the price level. Years 1838–43 and 1861–78 were excluded for the United States.
[2] 1888–1913.
[3] 1890–1913.
Note.—Lines 1 and 5 calculated as the time coefficient from a regression of the logarithm of the variable on a time trend. Lines 2, 3, and 6 calculated as the ratio of the standard deviation of annual percent changes to their mean.
Source: Michael David Bordo "The Classical Gold Standard: Some Lessons for Today", Federal Reserve Bank of St. Louis *Review,* May 1981, Vol. 63, No. 5.

Again, the evidence is clear that the achievement of low (and often negative) rates of inflation over the long run during previous gold-standard periods came at the cost of a high variability in inflation rates.

To the extent that deviations of the price level from its long-run equilibrium were unanticipated, growth would be expected to be more variable than in periods when inflation rates were more stable. The third line of Table 3–2 bears on this question. The coefficient of variation of the growth rate of real per capita income was about twice as high in the pre-World War I gold-standard period as in the post-World War II period.

In addition, recessions in the United States lasted twice as long, on average, from 1879 to 1913 than from 1945 to 1980, while periods of expansion and recovery were about one-third shorter. Finally, the measured unemployment rate during the pre-World War I gold-standard period was on the average two-thirds higher than during the post-World War II period in the United Kingdom and was one-third higher in the United States.

Under a gold standard, the rate of growth in the supply of monetary gold depends on the rate of gold production and the rate at which demand for gold for nonmonetary uses increases. Gold production depends in part on the purchasing power of gold (the ratio of the gold price in dollars to the average price level). Table 3–3 contains data on the yearly production of gold from 1800 to 1980. The numbers encompass a wide range, from a maximum average annual growth rate of 7.1 percent for the period 1834–1848 to a minimum of −1.6 percent for the most recent period 1969–1980.

TABLE 3–3.—*Changes in gold output, 1800–1980*

[Percent change per year]

Period	Gold output
1800–33	0.4
1834–48	7.1
1849–70	6.2
1871–89	−.3
1890–1913	6.0
1920–33	3.4
1934–40	7.0
1950–68	2.7
1969–80	−1.6

Source: Anna J. Schwartz, National Bureau of Economic Research, Inc., Memorandum of September 10, 1981 to Members of the Gold Commission.

Even during the pre-World War I gold standard period, monetary gold was only a fraction of the total money stock, the bulk of which consisted of paper currency and bank deposits. The last two lines of Table 3–2 show the sample mean and coefficient of variation of the annual growth rate of M1. The average growth rate of M1 for the United Kingdom during the pre-World War I gold standard period was one-fourth of the average during the post-World War II period. For the United States the two sample means are approximately the same. However, the variability of M1 growth was over 50 percent higher in the gold-standard period than in the post-war period.

In sum, the evidence presented indicates that previous gold-standard periods were characterized by: (1) lower *average* inflation and money supply growth; (2) greater *fluctuations* in inflation, money supply growth, and output growth; and (3) higher unemployment rates than in the period 1946 to 1979. Although comparisons across time periods are difficult to make because of the difficulty of controlling for differences, including the effects of wars, droughts, and other shocks to the economy, it is far from clear that gold standards produced better overall results than those produced during the post-World War II period.

Could the United States forge a better gold standard now? There are two options: restore some form of gold cover requirement without convertibility or restore a gold cover requirement with convertibility; either with partial or full gold backing. The first option prevailed from 1934 until 1968, a period during which Federal Reserve Banks were required to keep a minimum of legal value gold certificates (valued at $35 an ounce) behind each $1 of their note liabilities. A more structured variant would be to restrain money creation by linking the central bank's ability to create liabilities to a legislated schedule of changes in the official price of gold and changes in the amount of gold reserves required for each dollar of central bank liabilities. Central to such a proposal would be a requirement that the actual gold stock remain fixed in size and that changes in its value occur only through variations in the official or bookkeeping price of gold. Not only would there be no requirement to buy and sell gold at the official price, the Treasury would be prohibited from doing so. In other words, there would be a gold reserve requirement for the money supply, but no convertibility regardless of whether the official price of gold was below, at, or above the market price. In sum, this option would essentially constrain the annual growth of the monetary base.

Under the second option the United States would fix permanently the dollar price of gold—that is, make the dollar convertible into gold—without concern for whether or not other countries would follow our example. The difference between a partial and a full backing would be that, whereas full backing would establish a one-to-one link between the gold stock and the money stock, partial backing would not. But in both cases, random shocks in the gold markets would create serious problems in controlling monetary aggregates and hence the general price level.

A MONETARY RULE

Enactment of a statute or constitutional amendment requiring the monetary authorities to abide by a rule regarding monetary growth or inflation is another method that has been suggested for dealing with the problem of maintaining long-run price stability. Such a rule would free the Federal Reserve from having to interpret either the "social welfare function" of the country or, more practically, the objectives of current elected officials. The rule could be stated either in terms of an ultimate objective for inflation, as it is in some industrial countries, or in terms of a monetary growth target that would be consistent with the maintenance of price-level stability.

A rule fixing a final outcome for inflation would oblige the monetary authorities to maintain monetary conditions consistent with the stability of a broad index of commodity and service prices (for example, the consumer price index). One might argue that the Humphrey-Hawkins Act implicitly incorporates such a rule. This legislation has as goals the reduction of "the rate of inflation to no more than 3 per centum" in the interim and ultimately to zero. The act, however, does not make the Federal Reserve responsible for the achievement of price-level stability. Furthermore, it mandates that "policies and programs for reducing the rate of inflation shall be designed so as not to impede achievement of goals and timetables" for reducing unemployment. In sum, there is no recognition in the act of a division of responsibilities that would include assigning responsibility for price-level stability exclusively to the Federal Reserve.

The advantage of formulating a rule on the final outcome for inflation is that the monetary authorities would be free to devise the best monetary strategy to achieve the mandated outcome. The disadvantage would be the rule's potential inflexibility. Temporary changes in the price level can be caused by a variety of shocks for which the monetary authorities cannot be held accountable. One approach would be to state the final outcome in terms of the average rate of growth of the consumer price index or nominal GNP over a period of several years.

The alternative of a target rule for monetary growth would have to be specified in such a way as to be consistent with price-level stability, again, over a period of several years. The rule could be revised from time to time in light of any changes in the relation of money growth to inflation. Such calibration would be the job of the central bank. Of course, the mere enactment of a rule would not ensure its successful implementation. Suitable institutional constraints would have to be present to correct for possible deviations from desired outcomes.

At this time it is not clear which rule, if any, would be optimal and likely to prove preferable over a long period. Hence, the Federal Reserve's current policy of gradually reducing the target growth rate of money over several years is providing a transition to a less inflationary environment.

One of the Administration's long-run objectives is the elimination of inflation. The implementation of a monetary policy that is consistent with this objective can be viewed in the following way. Each year, the monetary authorities would announce the rate of growth of the money supply that is consistent with achieving their medium-term objectives for nominal income and inflation. Over the longer run the rate of growth of the money supply must be consistent with the achievement of the rate of nominal income implied by the inflation objective. To implement this procedure, the Federal Reserve would determine the rate of growth of total bank reserves that was consistent with the targeted growth of the deposit component of M1. Open market operations by the Federal Reserve would expand the monetary base by a sufficient amount to provide total bank reserves and the currency component of targeted M1 growth.

Ultimately, the Federal Reserve would set a reserve growth path consistent with the desired price level performance on the basis of estimates of several parameters. These would include the trend path of real output, the trend of M1 velocity, and the trend of the ratio of M1 to the monetary base. As these changed, the targets for nominal income, M1 growth, and growth of the monetary base would be altered to maintain a stable price level. Unexpected changes in any of these parameters could be offset to maintain long-run price stability.

THE FUTURE CHALLENGE

A few basic propositions about inflation can summarize the role of monetary policy in the future. First, there is more agreement now than there was a decade ago that inflation is essentially a monetary phenomenon. In addition, events that occurred during the 1970s showed the importance of distinguishing between a transitory change in the rate of inflation occasioned by a "real shock" and the underlying rate of inflation. Second, an assumption of a positive but predictable rate of inflation is not very realistic. For the past 20 years the United States has experienced several cycles around a rising trend of inflation. We are now experiencing a cyclical decline in inflation. A major objective of the Administration's economic recovery program is to achieve the elimination of inflation in the long run. The ultimate costs of adjusting to a significantly less inflationary environment will be influenced by how rapidly expectations about future inflation are revised downward.

Finally, in a world where the U.S. dollar is the dominant international currency, many other countries' policy options are influenced by the success of U.S. anti-inflation policies. Most other countries find it difficult to maintain an inflation rate that is significantly below that of the United States, although Germany, Japan, and Switzerland have done so in recent years. Realization of that fact has increased the sense of urgency felt in the United States about achieving and maintaining a low rate of inflation.

The appropriate policy for reducing the inflation rate is a decrease in the rate of money growth. Unfortunately, a slowing of money growth in the past has tended to reduce output and employment within roughly two quarters, while as many as eight quarters typically have had to pass before monetary restraint produced a significant reduction in the inflation rate. However, the whole process of renewed economic growth without inflation can be speeded up if the policy of monetary restraint is believed by the public, since it is an unanticipated decrease in the rate of money growth that significantly affects output and employment in the short run.

If the decrease is generally anticipated, wages and prices will begin to rise more slowly and the adverse short-run effects on output and employment will be minimized. That is why it is so important for the public to be convinced that an anti-inflationary monetary policy has finally been adopted. The Federal Reserve can maximize the credibility of its monetary policy, and hence reduce the transition costs of eliminating inflation, by announcing a specific target for the rate of money growth and by minimizing short-run deviations from that target.

Theoretically, restrictive monetary policy could achieve price-level stability regardless of fiscal policy. As a practical matter, however, reducing the growth of government spending and reducing deficits in the Federal budget will help to strengthen the belief that anti-inflationary policies will be maintained. That, in turn, will help lower the costs of adjusting to lower rates of inflation. In short, the credibility of monetary policy is influenced by the fiscal policy that accompanies it.

The monetary system is evolving toward one in which the Federal Reserve will have very close control over M1, suitably redefined from time to time, through control of reserves. With uniform reserve requirements on transaction accounts, there will be relatively little variability in the ratio of M1 to the monetary base. Longer term movements in this ratio can be offset by open market operations. Monetary aggregates other than M1 may serve as useful indicators of the effects of policy actions, but they will not be directly controllable by the Federal Reserve and therefore will not be useful as short-run targets.

A policy of providing slow and steady growth of money will not permit the central bank to attempt to offset the effects of transitory shocks to aggregate demand or productivity. In other words, short-run fluctuations in inflation and output growth will occur: economic expansion and contraction induced by changes in productivity or price shocks cannot be completely avoided. What can be avoided are the procyclical changes in the growth of the money supply that have occurred in the past.

CHAPTER 4

Federal Budget Issues

THE FEDERAL BUDGET presents economic policymakers with three fundamental questions. First, how much should the Federal Government spend? Second, how should that spending be allocated? Third, how should the spending be financed—by current taxes only, by borrowing to cover a deficit in tax revenues, or by adding to the monetary base. Without spending there would be no need to impose taxes or to borrow to cover deficits. The composition of a given level of spending has implications for how it should be financed. And the choice of the level of spending is influenced by the recognition that government spending cannot indefinitely grow faster than the economy and that the financing mechanisms available to the government impose costs on the economy.

This chapter examines issues related to the size and allocation of the Federal budget and explores the implications for the economy of financing a part of Federal spending through budgetary deficits. Financing Federal spending through various forms of taxation, together with related issues, are the subject of Chapter 5.

The Administration's spending policies rest on both philosophical beliefs and economic judgments. As discussed in Chapter 2, the view that the size and scope of the Federal Government are too large reflects the belief that most individuals know best what they want and how best to attain it. In the aggregate their actions will generally result in the most appropriate distribution of our economic resources. This belief is accompanied by the judgment that resources left in the private sector generally are more effective in generating growth and productive employment than resources moved to the public sector.

Because of these philosophical beliefs and economic judgments, the Administration has initiated a major transformation of the role of the Federal Government in the U.S. economy. The Administration's economic recovery program will change both the size and the nature of government involvement, reversing the trend of recent decades when the Federal budget usually grew faster than the rest of the economy as the Federal Government took upon itself responsibilities that had previously been left to the private sector or to State and local governments.

Federal spending is a highly visible form of government involvement in the economy, and the Administration's economic program calls for a slowdown in the growth of Federal spending. Federal spending rose from 20.2 percent of the gross national product (GNP) in 1970 to 23.0 percent in 1981. By fiscal 1987, Federal spending is projected to fall to 19.7 percent of GNP. Federal tax rates on individuals and businesses will also fall, as will the share of gross national product used to pay Federal taxes. By 1987, Federal tax revenues will represent 2.3 percentage points less of the gross national product than they did in 1981. At the same time the Federal budget deficit also will shrink relative to the size of the economy, dropping from 2.0 percent of GNP in 1981 and 3.2 percent in 1982 to 1.1 percent by 1987.

In 1981 the Congress and the Administration took important steps toward achieving this shift in emphasis from the public to the private sector. The enactment of the Economic Recovery Tax Act of 1981 will reduce income tax rates over the next few years, and the Omnibus Budget Reconciliation Act of 1981 will restrain the growth of many open-ended entitlement programs. This shift will be incomplete, however, without further Federal spending restraint in the years ahead.

The shift in the role of the Federal Government is more than a reduction in size. It also encompasses a restructuring of priorities at the Federal level and a reallocation of responsibilities and resources between the Federal and the State and local levels of government. Within the Federal budget, spending will shift toward those activities that, in this Administration's view, reflect truly national needs, such as strengthening the Nation's defenses and maintaining the integrity of the social insurance programs.

Economic criteria will be applied to various spending programs to help ensure that the resulting benefits offset the costs to the taxpayers who ultimately must bear them. These criteria should apply not only to direct Federal spending, but also to on- and off-budget credit activities. Such Federal credit programs reallocate national resources by financing activities that might not be attractive to investors in the private market.

The first step in the realignment of responsibilities among Federal, State, and local jurisdictions was the consolidation of a number of categorical grant programs into block grants in fiscal 1982. The second step, proposed in the budget for fiscal 1983, is to shift responsibility for some programs now jointly operated by the States and the Federal Government either to the States or to the national government, and to turn some other programs that are now wholly federally funded back to the States. The proposed restructuring of functions would be accompanied by a phased withdrawal of the Federal Government from the excise tax base. These proposals are intended to strengthen the Federal system by improving the operation of government at all levels, making it more responsive to the people.

THE OVERALL LEVEL OF FEDERAL SPENDING

The benefits of many types of Federal spending are easily seen. Parks are built, research is conducted, and the sick and the elderly are supported with Federal dollars. Yet Federal spending in the aggregate also imposes many costs on the economy. First, costs arise through the mechanisms used to pay for what the government spends. The government can raise taxes now or in the future to obtain the funds it needs, or it can obtain those funds indirectly through monetary expansion. As discussed in Chapter 5, taxes tend to reduce growth in the private sector by transferring productive resources from private to public hands, using tax methods that generally distort the decisions of households and firms to supply labor and capital to the economy. Deficits also impose real costs on the economy (as explored later in this chapter), whether financed by lower future spending, higher future taxes, or by expanding the money supply. For government spending to be economically justified, therefore, the benefits resulting from that spending—whether in terms of more economic growth or the enhanced well-being of the society— must exceed the costs.

Discretionary changes in the level of government spending made in the attempt to offset cyclical fluctuations in the economy can impose additional costs. Such changes, which increase the uncertainty faced by households and firms in making their economic decisions, can discourage the supply of productive factors to the economy. Furthermore, attempts to implement discretionary countercyclical policy can in fact prove to be procyclical.

A third way in which Federal spending can impose costs on the economy is by altering the allocation of resources, both currently and over time. For a given level of spending and method of financing, the allocation of federal resources between current consumption and investment can affect economic growth.

Government spending can be divided into four categories: consumption, transfers, investment (both defense and nondefense investment), and other (which mainly includes interest payments and grants to State and local governments). Government spending may absorb private sector resources for use by the public sector or reallocate resources within the private sector, or both; the predominant effects differ by category.

Transfer payments do not absorb resources aside from administrative costs, but they may have strong allocative effects within the economy. Transfer payments may lead recipients to change their work or saving behavior, and they may change the composition of the demand for goods and services. (Examples of the factor supply response are discussed in Chapter 5.) Federal grants to State and local governments affect the use of resources in the economy through their effect on the behavior of those jurisdictions. State and local governments may respond to the Federal grants by changing the level of spending and taxing, as well as the composition of the outlays.

The direct effect of government purchases of goods and services for either consumption or investment is to absorb resources from the private sector. To the extent that such spending substitutes for private purchases public sector purchases may also redirect the use of resources within the private sector. For example, public provision of education or police services reduces the private demand for such activities. The dominant effect that government purchases have on the economy, however, is likely to be through absorption rather than reallocation of private sector resources. Since a dollar of government consumption spending is unlikely to substitute fully for a dollar of private consumption, an increase in government consumption spending would tend to increase the share of total consumption in GNP (apart from any effects of the financing arrangements). Similarly, government investment tends to increase the share of total investment in the economy. Furthermore, government consumption and investment spending is likely to alter the composition of both consumption and investment in the economy from what would have prevailed if the resources had stayed in private hands.

In practice, the distinction between government consumption and investment is difficult to make. The government consumption figures shown in Table 4-1 include various expenditures to promote education, training, and research and development. Like physical capital, these activities contribute to economic growth. Published measures of government investment expenditures encounter similar problems. For example, current Federal investment expenditures mainly comprise purchases of military hardware and structures, whose acquisition will provide future benefits in terms of stronger national security that cannot be captured in GNP. Although services of government capital are not counted in GNP, the future services resulting from the construction of airports, highways, and other civilian investment outlays are reflected in part in the recorded output of private sector

users. In practice, therefore, statistics that allocate government purchases between consumption and investment must be viewed with
caution.

TABLE 4-1.—*Structure of Federal Government expenditures, NIPA, calendar years 1951–83*

[Percent of GNP]

Period	Total Federal Government expenditures	Federal Government consumption [1]	Federal Government transfer payments [2]	Federal Government investment [3]		Other Federal expenditures [4]
				Defense	Non-defense	
1951–60	18.7	7.5	3.8	4.6	0.2	2.6
1961–70	19.5	7.6	5.2	2.7	.3	3.7
1971–80	21.5	6.2	8.4	1.3	.3	5.3
1981 [5]	23.4	6.1	9.8	1.3	.3	5.9
1982 [6]	24.0	6.4	10.1	1.4	.3	5.8
1983 [6]	22.9	5.9	9.6	1.7	.2	5.5

[1] Purchases of goods and services except durables and structures.
[2] Includes transfers to foreigners.
[3] Purchases of durables and structures. The allocation between defense and nondefense was estimated for years before 1972 by Council of Economic Advisers.
[4] Primarily interest payments and grants to State and local governments.
[5] Preliminary.
[6] Estimated by Council of Economic Advisers.

Note.—Based on data from the national income and product accounts (NIPA). Expenditures by the Federal Government include off-budget items such as the Postal Service and the Federal Financing Bank as well as regularly budgeted expenditures.

Sources: Department of Commerce (Bureau of Economic Analysis), Office of Management and Budget, and Council of Economic Advisers.

Despite these limitations, the statistics in Table 4–1 are a useful
summary of changes in Federal spending in these categories in recent
years and how these categories are likely to change under the Administration's current budget plans. Total Federal spending (on a national income accounts basis) as a percent of GNP rose nearly 3 percentage points between the 1950s and the 1970s. The category with the
largest growth was Federal transfer payments. Most of the increase
there—77 percent—represented expansion of the social security
system (discussed later in this chapter). This increase in transfers was
partially offset by a drop in Federal consumption as a share of GNP.
Measured Federal expenditures on investment goods have fallen substantially, largely because less of the Nation's output in the 1970s
was spent on defense hardware than in the earlier postwar decades.
The Administration's budget plans for fiscal 1983 envision a reversal
in the trend of transfer payments rising as a share of GNP. Federal
consumption expenditures should resume their decline as a share of
GNP. Government spending classified here as investment will increase in relative importance primarily because of rising defense outlays.

REALLOCATION OF BUDGET PRIORITIES

A substantial shift in the composition of the budget has accompanied the expansion of the Federal role in the economy since 1960. Table 4-2 shows how the priorities of the Federal Government have evolved over the last 20 years and how this Administration intends to restructure them.

TABLE 4-2.—*Composition of Federal unified budget outlays, selected fiscal years, 1960–87*

[Percent]

Item	Fiscal years								
	1960	1965	1970	1975	1980	1981[1]	1982[2]	1983[2]	1987[2]
Defense[3]	48.2	38.9	38.7	24.5	21.5	22.2	23.8	27.0	35.4
Payments for individuals[4]	26.4	28.4	33.7	48.3	49.1	50.2	50.5	50.5	49.0
Retirement[4]	17.0	19.6	20.4	26.7	27.1	28.1	28.4	29.2	29.7
Unemployment	3.0	2.4	1.7	4.2	3.1	3.3	4.0	3.7	2.0
Medical care	1.2	1.5	6.3	8.3	10.1	10.5	10.7	11.0	12.0
Food, nutrition, and public assistance	3.9	4.2	3.8	5.9	5.9	5.4	4.9	4.1	3.4
Other	1.5	.8	1.5	3.2	2.8	3.0	2.5	2.5	1.9
Interest	9.0	8.7	9.4	9.5	11.2	12.6	13.7	14.9	11.9
Other[5]	16.2	23.9	19.9	17.7	18.2	15.0	12.0	7.6	3.7
International, justice, general government	4.7	6.0	3.6	4.0	3.4	3.1	2.9	2.9	2.2
Energy, natural resources, environment	2.2	2.7	2.1	2.9	3.5	3.6	2.6	1.9	1.1
Agriculture	2.8	3.3	2.6	.5	.8	.8	1.2	.6	.3
Commerce and community development	2.0	1.9	2.3	2.9	3.1	2.7	2.2	1.5	.9
Transportation	4.4	4.9	3.6	3.2	3.6	3.5	2.9	2.5	2.0
Education and training	1.0	1.8	4.2	4.4	4.5	3.8	3.0	1.8	1.4
General fiscal assistance	.2	.2	.3	2.2	1.5	1.0	.9	1.0	.8
Other, net of offsetting receipts	−1.1	3.1	1.2	−2.4	−2.2	−3.7	−3.6	−4.6	−4.8
Addendum:									
Grants to State and local governments: Total	7.6	9.2	12.3	15.4	15.9	14.4	12.6	10.7	8.9
Not for individuals	4.9	5.9	7.7	10.1	10.0	8.3	6.8	5.8	4.1

[1] Preliminary.
[2] Estimated by Council of Economic Advisers.
[3] Excludes military retirement.
[4] Includes military retirement.
[5] Includes grants to State and local governments other than payments for individuals.
Note.—Detail may not add to 100 percent due to rounding.
Sources: Office of Management and Budget and Council of Economic Advisers.

The most notable change over this period was the substantial reduction in the share of the budget going to national defense, from nearly one-half to less than one-quarter. While the defense share was falling, transfer payments to individuals were growing. In 1960 transfer payments absorbed about one-quarter of the budget, whereas by 1981 they accounted for one-half. Most of this growth came in two types of programs: (1) retirement programs, principally social security, but also outlays for military and civil service pensions, and (2) the medical assistance programs of medicare for the elderly and medicaid for the poor. (A section of Chapter 6 examines factors contributing to medical cost increases.) The third notable shift in the composition of the budget was the greater fraction of Federal revenues transferred to State and local governments through such programs as

general revenue sharing. (In Table 4–2, grants to State and local governments are included with direct Federal spending in each of the
functional categories.)

This Administration has a different set of spending priorities than
those reflected in the budgets of the recent past. This difference is
expressed in the following guidelines used in developing the Administration's plans for restraining the growth of Federal spending:

- Strengthen the national defense.
- Maintain the integrity of social insurance programs while reform-
  ing entitlement programs to ensure that they serve those in
  greatest need.
- Reduce subsidies to middle- and upper-income groups.
- Apply sound economic criteria to programs where subsidies are
  justified.
- Recover costs that can clearly be allocated to users of services
  provided by Federal programs.
- Strengthen the Federal structure of government.
- Reduce the Federal role in allocating credit by restraining on-
  and off-budget credit activities.

The Administration's estimate of 1987 budget outlays reflects
these guidelines, which are consistent with the role for the Federal
Government described in Chapter 2. Despite the substantial changes
accomplished in the budget for fiscal 1982, reforming the budget
cannot be achieved in a year or two. The difference in priorities can
best be seen by comparing the Administration's projections for fiscal
1987 with the budget that ended September 30, 1981.

As Table 4–2 indicates, the Administration intends to raise significantly the share of the budget spent on defense, from 22.2 percent of
total outlays in 1981 to 35.4 percent in 1987. Funding for retirement
programs will increase as a share of the budget while other payments to
individuals are being reduced. An example of a program in this latter
category is trade adjustment assistance, which has provided more generous unemployment benefits to workers who may have been displaced
by foreign competition than to other unemployed workers. Increases
in the share of the budget going to retirement programs and decreases
in the share of other transfer programs will mean that total payments
for individuals will account for approximately the same fraction of
Federal spending in 1987 as in 1981.

The reordering of Federal priorities raises a number of issues that
warrant special attention. First, what will be the economic effects of
the large increase in defense spending? Second, what caused the substantial expansion in retirement programs, and what issues should be
addressed for the future? Third, what advantages can be expected

from reallocating responsibilities between the Federal Government and the State and local governments? Finally, how will changes in Federal credit activity affect the economy?

DEFENSE

Real military spending is expected to grow 9 percent annually between 1981 and 1987. Over that period, military spending (including military retirement) will rise from 5.6 percent to 7.8 percent of GNP, and from 25 percent to 37 percent of total Federal spending. As is clear from Chart 4–1, such an increase would not even restore defense spending to its pre-Vietnam share of GNP. Although the military's shares of national output and Federal spending will not be as high as in the early 1960s, the buildup will be a sharp reversal of the trend of the last decade. As a result, some concern has been expressed about whether this increase could adversely affect the economy. Any economic effects, however, must be assessed in the context of the overriding need for maintaining the level of defense spending necessary for national security.

Chart 4–1

Defense Outlays as Percent of GNP

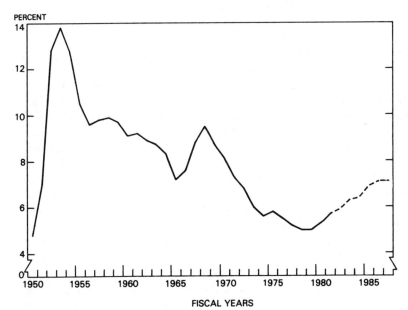

FISCAL YEARS

SOURCES: DEPARTMENT OF COMMERCE, OFFICE OF MANAGEMENT AND BUDGET, AND COUNCIL OF ECONOMIC ADVISERS

The concern over the economic impact of defense spending has probably been overstated. The U.S. economy as a whole should be able to accommodate the projected expansion in defense spending without experiencing an increase in the general inflation rate. Monetary and budget policies can offset the impact of a large increase in government spending for national security, although unusual growth in any spending category, military or civilian, makes the goal of overall restraint that much more difficult to achieve. Moreover, the economy currently has ample slack to accommodate the beginning of a major expansion in defense work.

As the economy emerges from the current recession, however, growth in the defense program will compete with expanding demands in the private sector. As the Administration's economic recovery program begins to take full effect, private demand for producer durables should rise significantly. Expenditures for defense also will be concentrated in the durables sector. Real purchases of defense durables (research and development and procurement of major weapon systems) will grow at an estimated rate of 16 percent annually between 1981 and 1987. This exceeds the 14 percent annual rate of increase that occurred during the 3 peak years of the Vietnam buildup. The current defense buildup thus will add to pressures on the durable manufacturing sector in these years.

Although it is difficult to predict which industrial markets will be especially affected, three results of the defense buildup can be anticipated. First, the substantial transfer of resources in the durables sector to defense production may increase relative prices in at least some of the affected industries. Both the Department of Defense (DOD) and private purchasers may have to pay more for goods from these industries. Second, increased demand may produce delays in the delivery of military goods. Delivery timetables that seem realistic today may in some cases become obsolete as producers try to accommodate the defense buildup and vigorous expansion in civilian investment at the same time. A third effect may be some temporary crowding out of private investment. Defense procurement and associated production equipment use many of the same physical resources needed for private investment in civilian producer durables. Some private firms may turn to foreign sources for materials while others may cancel or postpone plans for expansion.

The Department of Defense is attempting to minimize the potentially adverse economic effects of the defense buildup through long-term planning, better management of defense contracts, and the development of more comprehensive cost estimates. This long-term planning will help defense industries increase their capacity in anticipation of new orders. The department's plans to place greater reliance on multiyear contracts will also help defense contractors operate more efficiently, especially by providing incentives to increase capacity and to plan optimal production rates.

In the private sector, competition tends to prevent inefficient producers from passing their higher costs on to consumers. In the defense sector the function of encouraging efficiency is largely performed by DOD analysts of contract negotiations and administration. Their jobs are always difficult because of unanticipated problems in developing high technology equipment, lack of competition among suppliers, and a history of erratic fluctuations in defense procurement levels. The defense buildup will therefore increase the challenge to DOD administrators. Careful planning, tight management, and accurate cost estimates can reduce the adverse consequences of the buildup, but some problems may arise.

Economic Impact of Increased Military Manpower

Over the next 5 years the armed services plan to increase their active duty forces by 9 to 10 percent. Quality standards for recruits are also scheduled to rise. Declining unemployment rates and a reduction in the available manpower pool because of the decline in the recruiting-age population will make these goals difficult to achieve and will increase pressure to shift the costs of achieving them from taxpayers onto the young—that is, by reinstituting the draft.

As the Administration's economic recovery program begins to take effect, increases in the number of civilian jobs will make it harder for the military to attract personnel. The problem of attracting first-time recruits is likely to be especially serious. Between 1980 and the end of the decade the number of 18-year-old males will fall by 19 percent, from 2.1 million to 1.7 million, with the bulk of that decline occurring before 1985. Thus, the armed services will need to attract a considerably higher percentage of high school graduates than it does today. Although a considerably smaller U.S. population supported a somewhat larger military throughout the 1950s, the United States had a draft in those years.

Just as the potential supply of recruits will be diminishing, the demand—especially for high-quality recruits—will be rising. Without the right combination of incentives, the costs of military compensation may rise sharply while a shortage of recruits may create pressures for a return to a peacetime draft. To prevent such problems, bonuses for recruits in certain areas and for experienced military personnel with special skills may have to be raised.

Resumption of the draft would bring about an increase in force levels at substantially lower budget outlays. However, the real costs to the economy would not disappear; they would simply be moved out of DOD's budget and onto the draftees, and the costs would probably rise in the process. The output that the draftees would have produced as members of the civilian work force would be lost in any case.

SOCIAL SECURITY

Over the past 20 years, 29 percent of the growth in Federal spending has been due to increases in retirement programs, with most of the growth occurring in the social security program. Over the next 5 years the retirement portion of social security will rise nearly 50 percent faster than the total Federal budget. Because of the large fraction of Federal resources devoted to the social security program, its rapid growth, and the program's importance to so many Americans, it is useful to understand the causes of its growth and the problems that may occur in the future.

Three major factors apart from inflation have contributed to the growth in social security retirement expenditures over the past two decades. First, there are 9 million more people 65 or over today than there were 20 years ago, an increase of 54 percent. Second, social security eligibility has been broadened steadily since the system began in the 1930s. In 1960, 66 percent of the elderly received social security benefits, compared to 93 percent in 1980. Furthermore, the number of people between 62 and 65 who received retirement benefits more than tripled between 1960 and 1980.

Third, the level of social security benefits, after adjusting for inflation, has also risen substantially. The average real benefit paid to a retired worker was $191 a month in 1960 (in 1980 dollars) and $341 in 1980. In part, this increase reflects growth in the real wages that the average worker earns over a lifetime and therefore in the retirement benefit for which the worker is eligible. The growth in eligibility for survivor and dependent benefits, and their levels, has also been substantial. Much of this liberalization in benefits came in the late 1960s and early 1970s when the Congress, faced with projected and growing surpluses in the social security trust funds, chose to raise benefits. In 1972 the Congress sought to index benefits to inflation, in part to discourage discretionary increases that had been raising benefits faster than inflation. However, the Congress effectively "double-indexed" them through a technical flaw in the indexing procedure. As a result, nominal social security benefits continued to rise faster than consumer prices. Congressional action in 1977 corrected the technical problem but did not return real individual benefits to their 1972 level.

Expansion of the social security system has substantially improved the lot of the elderly poor. The system has been a major factor in reducing both the percentage and the absolute number among the elderly with incomes below the official poverty line. In 1959, 35.2 percent of individuals age 65 and over were classified as poor, compared to 22.4 percent of the total population. There was a substantial decline in poverty during the 1960s, so that by 1970, 24.5 percent of the elderly and 12.6 percent of the rest of the population had measured incomes below the poverty line. During the 1970s the percentage of those classified as poor among the general population stopped declining but continued to decline for the elderly. Thus, by 1980 only 15.7 percent of those 65 and over were formally considered to be living in poverty, compared to 13.0 percent of the rest of the population. In addition to reducing poverty among the elderly, the indexing of social security benefits in 1972 assured them that inflation would not erode at least that part of their incomes.

The social security system now faces serious problems, however, both in the short run and in the long run. The short-run problem is that the Old-Age and Survivors Insurance Trust Fund is in danger of running out of money. Because of high unemployment and slow growth in earnings, relative to the consumer price index by which benefits are automatically adjusted, trust fund receipts have not kept pace with the rise in outlays required by indexing. In 1981 the Congress authorized borrowing among the Old-Age Survivors Insurance, Disability Insurance and Hospital Insurance Trust Funds. This action will ease the short-run problem, which is expected to disappear as economic growth resumes and inflation subsides.

The long-term problem in the social security system arises from the fact that the baby-boom generation will begin to reach retirement age around the year 2010. The ratio of the working-age population (20 to 64) to the elderly (65 and over) will fall from 5.1 today to 4.7 in 2005, and to 3.0 in 2030. After the turn of the century, contributors will not be able to support beneficiaries at today's retirement age, replacement rates, and payroll tax rates. Because of this shift in age distribution, today's young workers are unlikely to receive the same rate of return on their contributions to social security that their parents received. Thus, some combination of an increase in the retirement age, a decrease in benefits relative to prior earnings, and an increase in contribution rates will almost certainly be necessary in the long run. The President has established a National Commission on Social Security Reform to examine the problems and propose solutions to both the short-run and long-run problems by January 1983.

Indexing in General

The practice of adjusting benefits automatically for inflation raises a set of issues that applies to all indexed Federal programs. Currently, 30 percent of Federal outlays rise automatically with inflation. Indexing benefit payments to inflation has been intended to preserve the real purchasing power of benefits—to serve as a kind of insurance against inflation. Experience with indexing has revealed problems, however.

One problem is the accuracy of the consumer price index (CPI) as a measure of inflation. In recent years at least, the method of computing the CPI has caused it to overstate increases in the cost of living. In October 1981 the Bureau of Labor Statistics announced its intention to correct these technical deficiencies. The correction will first affect Federal outlays in fiscal 1985. The cumulative effect of mismeasurement may have increased the real level of benefits paid by as much as $10 billion in 1981 alone. These same measurement problems should have the opposite effect over the next few years, however, as interest rates come down.

There are more fundamental problems with indexing. Since a continuous inflation is caused by excessive money growth, all incomes tend to rise proportionally, so that increases in other incomes tend to keep pace with indexed benefits. However, when supply shocks, such as the Organization of Petroleum Exporting Countries (OPEC) oil price increases of the 1970s, cause changes in the price level, wage incomes typically do not keep pace with inflation. In such circumstances, recipients of indexed benefits have an advantage, since most taxpayers who pay for the benefits have no such protection for their incomes. Several proposals have suggested that, when real wages fall, it would be more equitable to adjust benefit payments only by the amount of increases in wages. Automatic increases in benefit payments also give recipients an advantage in times of budget stringency, when the real levels of other programs are being reduced.

STRENGTHENING THE FEDERAL SYSTEM

A central feature of the Administration's budget policies is a commitment to strengthening the concept and the practical application of federalism. The goal is a system that includes an effective central government interacting with effective and responsive State governments. As the Federal Government has extended its involvement in the economy in recent years, it has tended to reduce the autonomy of State governments and to centralize the responsibility for a number of social, economic, and regulatory programs. In the Administration's view, the result has made the entire public sector less effective and less efficient.

There are four major reasons for seeking to create a stronger and more balanced Federal system. First, such a system would encourage diversity among State and local governments. The diversity that exists among communities and regions requires a structure of government that recognizes the differences in circumstances, preferences, and demands for public services. Many services that are appropriately provided by the public sector generate benefits sufficiently limited geographically that they are properly the responsibility of State or local governments. This permits the individuals who will benefit from and pay for a given service to decide whether it should be provided and if so, in what quantity.

That diversity also permits a "portfolio" approach to solving problems that are common to many communities, in that a single approach—the Federal Government's approach—is not the only method that can be tried. As different jurisdictions choose different strategies for handling similar problems, the chances of finding superior solutions increases. This portfolio approach means that some methods will fail, possibly more severely than the single method that the national government would have chosen. But each jurisdiction can learn from the experience of others, and the portfolio approach should help the public sector function more effectively.

A second reason for strengthening the Federal system is to make the public sector more accountable for its actions. Accountability comes from matching the responsibility for providing services with the resources for financing them. It can be argued that voters can see more clearly at the State and local levels of government the connection between their tax bills and the use to which government funds are put. Greater accountability would make for a more informed balancing of the costs and benefits of public spending and, again, a more efficient allocation of resources.

The current array of Federal programs reflects some desire for both greater accountability and diversity. Revenue sharing is an example of a Federal attempt to promote diversity with Federal tax dollars by distributing Federal funds to local governments (and formerly to State governments too) to use essentially as they wish. Although such a strategy may achieve substantial diversity, it lacks accountability. Local officials who run revenue sharing programs do not have to answer at the next election to the taxpayers who pay for the programs. Block grants suffer from some of the same failings.

The usual Federal solution to accountability has been through regulation that by its nature effectively limits diversity. Even where several levels of government are involved in operating a program—such as medicaid—diversity is often hindered by the need for accountability. This need has been used to justify the imposition of many complex and burdensome regulations, and thereby administrative costs, on lower levels of government. Thus a third reason for the Administration's commitment to federalism is to reduce some of the administrative burdens that Washington now places on State and local governments participating in Federal programs.

Finally, a heightened role for State and local governments is consistent with the Administration's shift in Federal budget priorities toward clearly national needs, such as defense. In a time of budget restraint at the Federal level, State and local government may well want to assume responsibility for some of the activities that can no longer be financed by the Federal budget.

The consolidation of a number of categorical grant programs into block grant programs in the fiscal 1982 budget was the first in a series of steps toward revising the role of the central government in the Federal system. The Administration is proposing further consolidations of categorical programs in the 1983 budget. A more historic step toward strengthening the Federal system is the Administration's proposal to turn back the excise tax base to the States and to produce a clearer division of labor between the States and Washington. Beginning in 1984, for example, the States would become responsible for the major income-based transfer programs for able-bodied residents, while the Federal Government would assume full responsibility for medicaid, the major program of medical assistance to the poor.

One reason for this revised division of labor is a basic tenet of the Administration that income redistribution is not a compelling justification in the 1980s for Federal taxing and spending programs. It is the Administration's view that the Federal Government can do more to provide lasting assistance to the disadvantaged by assuring strong and less inflationary economic growth than through income transfer programs.

FEDERAL CREDIT ACTIVITY

Although Federal credit programs, unlike direct Federal purchases of goods and services, do not take resources out of the private sector of the economy, they do redirect the allocation of resources within the private sector. In some instances this redirection can improve the efficiency of the economy if the private market fails to realize the full range of benefits that would result from extending particular types of credit. Otherwise, however, Federal credit programs provide funds for projects that bring a lower rate of return than if those funds had been lent by the private sector, thereby reducing the overall efficiency of the economy. In addition, many Federal credit activities add to the Treasury's borrowing requirements.

Three types of Federal and federally assisted loan programs have proliferated in recent years. First, there are direct loans by both on-budget and off-budget agencies, which amounted to an estimated $26.1 billion in net lending in 1981. Direct lending activity includes credit extensions by such agencies as the Export-Import Bank and the Small Business Administration. These loans must be financed by Treasury borrowing from the public if tax receipts are not sufficient to cover them. At one time the unified budget deficit reflected the outlays of most of these direct Federal lending programs, but in recent years borrowing to supply the loan programs of off-budget Federal entities has increased dramatically. Most of this borrowing has been undertaken through the Federal Financing Bank which in turn receives its funds from Treasury borrowing. The Farmers Home Administration and the Rural Electrification Administration originate the bulk of the off-budget direct loans.

The effects of direct Federal loan programs on the national allocation of credit depend upon the degree of subsidy involved. When a loan is subsidized, it is equivalent to providing the loan at market rates and giving borrowers a cash grant equal to the present value of the subsidy. The Office of Management and Budget estimates a $14.5 billion present value of subsidy on $57.2 billion in new obligations for direct Federal loans in 1981.

The second major type of federally related lending activity consists of loans for which the Federal Government (wholly or partly) guarantees or insures the payment of loan principal or interest. The interest rate on guaranteed loans is below market rates because Federal participation removes any default risk and because the government promises to pay a share of the interest in some cases. The oldest and best known examples are FHA-insured and VA-guaranteed mortgages. However, in recent years Federal guarantees and insurance have increasingly been used outside the housing sector. Net guaranteed and insured loans amounted to $28.0 billion in 1981. The Office of Management and Budget has estimated a $4.3 billion present value of subsidy on $7.8 billion of the most heavily subsidized new guaranteed and insured loan obligations.

The third major type of loan activity is the lending generated by government-sponsored but privately owned enterprises, including the farm credit system, the Federal Home Loan Bank system, the Federal National Mortgage Association, and the Federal Home Loan Mortgage Corporation. Like federally owned corporations, these sponsored enterprises channel credit to certain sectors of the economy, primarily through purchases of loans in the private sector. In 1981, borrowing by federally sponsored agencies amounted to $34.8 billion.

Loans by government-sponsored institutions typically provide a smaller subsidy to borrowers than either direct Federal loans or guaranteed loans. The subsidy in the former type of loan is created by the ability to sell the obligations of sponsored agencies at interest rates only slightly above the rates on comparable U.S. Treasury issues. In the area of housing it has been estimated that for every $1 billion infusion of mortgage credit by sponsored agencies, the stock of home mortgages has increased by only $150 million, indicating a relatively smaller subsidy. The addition to the stock of home mortgages is much smaller than the amount of debt issued by the sponsored agencies largely because their debt issues draw funds away from thrift institutions.

As shown in Table 4–3, the importance of Federal credit programs has greatly increased in recent years. Government redirection of part of the Nation's credit resources has added to the financing costs borne by private borrowers who do not receive Federal credit assistance.

TABLE. 4.3—*Federal and federally assisted credit programs, fiscal years 1970–81*

[Billions of dollars, except as noted]

Item	Fiscal years			
	1970–74 [1]	1975–79 [1]	1980	1981
Total funds raised in U.S. credit markets	156.9	309.4	344.7	361.0
Total Federal credit activity	22.0	42.6	79.9	86.5
Direct loans	2.6	14.9	24.2	26.1
Guaranteed loans	14.4	14.8	31.6	28.0
Government-sponsored loans	5.0	12.9	24.1	32.4
Total Federal credit activity as percent of total funds raised (percent)	14.0	13.8	23.2	24.0

Sources: Board of Governors of the Federal Reserve System and Office of Management and Budget (OMB).

This, in turn, leads to reduced demand for credit by unassisted borrowers. Increasingly, therefore, political judgments, rather than marketplace judgments, have been responsible for allocating the supply of credit. As the discipline of the marketplace is replaced by the political process, less efficient economic activities are financed, and productivity in the economy declines.

The Administration is committed to reducing Federal credit programs. A plan for reducing new Federal loan guarantee commitments by $20.3 billion for the 1982 fiscal year is already in place. Further actions are being proposed to reduce Federal and federally assisted credit commitments in fiscal 1983 and 1984. In addition, the Administration strongly supports efforts to formalize a Federal credit budget and to incorporate it into the budget process.

FEDERAL DEFICITS IN PERSPECTIVE

The President and the Congress together determine the annual level of government spending and tax rates. These decisions, when carried out in the context of prevailing economic conditions, determine the size of the Federal budget deficit. The deficit cannot be known in advance; it can only be projected using assumptions about the future course of the economy. During the last year, better-than-expected progress on inflation has reduced taxable income, slowing the growth of revenues below earlier projections. The recession has temporarily slowed the growth of the tax base while increasing outlays for employment-related programs. In addition, the projected decline in inflation increases the projected deficit because the associated reduction in revenue growth precedes the later reduction in spending growth, largely as a result of the indexing of government programs.

All these factors together have contributed to projected deficits. Thus, the fiscal 1983 Budget projects the unified Federal deficit at $98.6 billion in fiscal 1982, $91.5 billion in 1983, and $82.9 billion in 1984.

WHY DEFICITS MATTER

The Administration is strongly committed to reducing the projected deficits in the years ahead. A variety of economic reasons, as well as considerations of practical policymaking, make deficits a cause for continuing concern. In particular, the magnitude of the projected deficits demands attention to their current and prospective economic impacts.

Financing a budget deficit may draw on private saving and foreign capital inflows that otherwise would be available to the private sector. The Federal Government's demand for funds is insensitive to changes in interest rates—that is, the Treasury will raise the funds that it requires regardless of interest rates. Weak and marginal borrowers may be "rationed" out of the market by higher interest rates unless saving flows are adequate.

The impact of a specific deficit will vary, however, depending on the conditions that lead to it. For example, during a recession—as now exists—the borrowing requirements of business and consumers tend to be relatively small. At such a time a given deficit can be financed with less pressure on interest rates than during a period of growth, when business and consumer demands for credit are increasing. This is why it is important for the government to reduce the budget deficit in fiscal 1983 and beyond, a period of anticipated rapid economic growth when private investment demands are expected to rise substantially.

The impact of a deficit of a given size will also depend on the extent of private saving in the economy. An economy with a higher saving rate can absorb the demands of public sector borrowing more easily than one with lower saving and still accommodate the needs of private borrowers. Much of the Administration's tax program is designed to increase the private saving of the Nation. As a consequence, both public and private borrowing will be accommodated more easily.

A higher volume of Federal borrowing to finance deficits makes the task of the Federal Reserve System more difficult when it is following a policy of monetary restraint. However, maintenance of monetary restraint is a key part of the Administration's program and hence the potentially inflationary effects of monetizing the Federal deficit will not be realized.

Continued budget deficits may generate uncertainty about the ability of government to control spending. Any increases in interest rates which reflect this uncertainty, in turn, will tend to increase further the size of the deficit. In contrast, the maintenance of a long-term policy to reduce the size of budget deficits—the policy of the Administration—will tend to counterbalance the pressures for further increases in government spending.

MEASURING THE DEFICIT

It is important to recognize that there are several measures of the deficit. The unified deficit, the figure generally cited as "the deficit," includes only the deficit arising from on-budget expenditures. But the Federal Government borrows to finance off-budget activities as well. Including off-budget activities, the Federal deficit for fiscal 1983 is projected to be $107 billion.

Of course, the Federal Government constitutes only one part of the public sector; State and local budgets affect the economy in a fashion similar to the Federal budget. Given the large transfers of federally raised funds to State and local budgets, Federal, State, and local deficits should be considered jointly. Because the other levels of government have been accumulating funds to meet employee pension obligations, their budgets tend to be in current surplus (although some States and localities are generating unfunded liabilities for future retirement payments). In calendar year 1981, when the Federal Government reported a total deficit of $62 billion (on the national income and product accounts basis), the State and local sector showed a surplus of $37 billion. A broader perspective on the Federal debt is contained in the appendix to this chapter.

Regardless of how inclusive the definition of the deficit, it is not only the annual deficit that affects the economy but also the trend in deficits over the business cycle and beyond. Because of the structure of certain spending and tax programs, deficits tend to vary inversely with the economy. To some extent, deficits that are generated when the economy is weak can be made up when the economy is strong. It is the trend of deficits that serves as an indicator of fiscal discipline.

The relative size of the deficit is far more important than the dollar magnitude. To the extent that deficits affect the economy, the effects of a given deficit will be relatively small in a large economy and large in a small economy. From an historical perspective, the projected budget deficits for fiscal years 1982–1984 are clearly substantial, yet they are not unprecedented when measured against the size of the economy. In recent years only the fiscal 1976 deficit was larger, as a share of GNP, than the projected deficit for fiscal 1982, as Table 4-4 indicates. However, the ratio is projected to decline fairly rapidly so that by 1985 the deficit, relative to GNP, will be below the average for the decade of the 1970s.

In view of concern over the current projections of a large deficit during economic recovery in 1982, it is worth noting that the 1976 deficit also occurred during a period of economic recovery. In the four quarters ending in June 1976, nominal GNP rose 12 percent, real output gained 6 percent, and interest rates were essentially unchanged.

AN ANALYSIS OF DEFICITS AND DEBT FINANCING

A given deficit is consistent with different levels of spending and taxes. Even if economic conditions do not change, a deficit may increase because spending is increased and tax rates are not increased to yield the necessary added revenues, or because spending is unchanged but tax rates are reduced, or because spending is reduced but lower tax rates reduce revenues by a greater amount.

These three circumstances may yield the same deficit but have quite different effects. The effects will depend on the timing, level, and composition of government spending as well as the means used to pay for that spending. The spending imposes a cost on the economy by taking resources away from private use. As discussed earlier, government spending may augment or it may substitute for private spending. It will therefore alter decisions about private spending. Each of the methods of financing spending imposes costs in addition to the simple transfer of resources from the private sector to the

TABLE 4-4.—*Total Federal budget and off-budget surplus or deficit and gross national product, fiscal years 1958-87*

[Amounts in billion of dollars]

Fiscal year	Total Federal budget and off-budget surplus or deficit (−)	
	Amount	As percent of GNP
1958	−2.9	−0.7
1959	−12.9	−2.7
1960	.3	.1
1961	−3.4	−.7
1962	−7.1	−1.3
1963	−4.8	−.8
1964	−5.9	−1.0
1965	−1.6	−.2
1966	−3.8	−.5
1967	−8.7	−1.1
1968	−25.2	−3.0
1969	3.2	.4
1970	−2.8	−.3
1971	−23.0	−2.2
1972	−23.4	−2.1
1973	−14.9	−1.2
1974	−6.1	−.4
1975	−53.2	−3.6
1976	−73.7	−4.5
1977	−53.6	−2.9
1978	−59.2	−2.8
1979	−40.2	−1.7
1980	−73.8	−2.9
1981	−78.9	−2.8
1982 [1]	−118.3	−3.8
1983 [1]	−107.2	−3.1
1984 [1]	−97.2	−2.6
1985 [1]	−82.8	−2.0
1986 [1]	−77.0	−1.7
1987 [1]	−62.5	−1.3

[1] Estimates.

Sources: Department of Commerce (Bureau of Economic Analysis), Department of the Treasury, Office of Management and Budget, and Council of Economic Advisers.

public sector. The manner of financing, like the type of government spending, will alter the incentives which determine private resource allocation and hence may reduce economic efficiency.

If the government wants to pay for its spending on a current basis, it can set tax rates so that revenues equal outlays. As discussed in Chapter 5, however, the distorting effects of the tax system will reduce total output, now and in the future. At recent marginal tax rates the associated cost may be quite high.

If the government issues bonds instead of raising taxes, it must pay interest on the added debt. Furthermore, government debt-creation can impose added costs by absorbing private saving and hence reducing growth. Economic growth will not be reduced to the extent that an increase in private saving offsets the decline in government saving measured by growing Federal indebtedness. Private saving may increase, for example, if households anticipate that their future taxes will increase and they respond by setting aside additional saving to pay for the expected increase in tax liabilities. Since individuals' saving also tends to be affected by what services they perceive they are getting from the government, the composition of government spending associated with the deficit will play a key role in determining the response of saving.

Distortions may also occur in the allocation of resources if the government chooses to finance deficits by adding excessively to the monetary base. This burdens the economy with inflation in ways discussed in Chapter 3.

Whichever approach, or combination of approaches, the government chooses to pay for its spending, it cannot avoid the reality that government spending, while it may confer benefits on the economy, also imposes costs. The choice among financing mechanisms depends on which is the least-cost approach, or on which approach imposes the most appropriate patterns of costs on the economy over time.

Evaluating these costs is not a simple matter. Since deficits affect expectations about the future course of economic policies, only part of the effect of a deficit is an immediate consequence of what the increases in debt do to markets. Deficits also work indirectly through the changes they produce in individual expectations and the resultant changes in their behavior. Neither the direct effect nor the effect on expectations is readily observable. In addition, analysts differ in their views about the relative effects of different conditions on inflation, investment, and economic growth. Unless these differences in opinion are recognized, debates that ostensibly focus on the deficit often mask broader, underlying debates on how the economy works.

Deficits and Inflation

As discussed in Chapter 3, it is now generally agreed that continued excessive growth in the money supply will cause sustained inflation. Thus, deficits financed by money creation will have persistent inflationary consequences.

Additional government debt might also raise the price level through its impact on desired money balances. If the increased supply of government bonds raises interest rates, households and firms will respond by reducing their money balances and increasing total nominal spending. This implies an increase in velocity. Unless the monetary authorities offset the higher velocity by reducing the monetary base, both the price level and output will rise in the short run, although the mix of increases in the price level and in output is indeterminate. To the extent workers and firms believe that deficits are inflationary, however, and bargain accordingly, the relative effects on the price level will be correspondingly larger.

The magnitude of the increase in aggregate demand that results from added government debt will depend both on the responsiveness of money demand to interest rates and on the size of the increase in interest rates. For the former, empirical studies consistently show the demand for money to be only weakly responsive to interest rates, so that any given increase in interest rates will result in a relatively small increase in nominal spending.

As to the size of the increase in interest rates resulting from the added debt, the evidence is less clear cut. There are two forces moderating any increase. First, market interest rates equate the demand for financial assets with their supply. In any given year, added debt represents only a small increment to the total stock of government debt, and is also small by comparison with the market value of other assets in the economy. Second, a higher interest rate today means that saving is more attractive and current consumption relatively less attractive. Thus, the effect of additional government debt on interest rates will tend to be moderated by an increase in the flow of private saving attracted by the higher rates.

On the other hand, two factors may add to the increase in interest rates. If participants in financial markets believe that deficits are inflationary, long-term bond rates may include an additional inflation premium in response to larger deficits. The incremental uncertainty caused by deficits may also increase real interest rates. This results in large measure from the past history of discretionary, countercyclical policies. The prospect of large deficits contributed to uncertainty in the financial markets in 1981 and may have raised market interest rates to a higher level than they otherwise would have been.

If added debt does raise the price level through its effect on desired money balances, this is not equivalent to continued inflation. For the price level to increase in a sustained fashion, the annual increments to government debt would have to grow continually at a rate faster than the growth of the economy. Thus, deficits will be inflationary only if the monetary authorities monetize the debt or if the added debt continually grows as a share of GNP. This is precisely why the Administration is determined to reduce the budget deficit in fiscal 1983 and beyond. The maintenance of monetary restraint will ensure that deficits will not be monetized and that the potentially inflationary effects that might otherwise result from government borrowing will not be realized.

Debt Financing, Crowding Out, and Growth

It has been argued that net government borrowing may preempt credit that otherwise would have been used to finance private investment. Unless the supply of private saving expands to provide completely for the increased government borrowing, thereby preventing a rise in real interest rates, the additional government debt will tend to deter some private investment. Some saving could also come from abroad. If international credit flows respond sufficiently to only slightly higher interest rates, significant crowding out of U.S. private investment may be prevented.

When private saving rates are relatively high (perhaps because of a tax system that fosters saving rather than consumption), a larger deficit can be accommodated more easily than if saving rates are low. In recent years, for example, Japan and a number of Western European nations have experienced larger budget deficits (measured as a percent of their Gross Domestic Product) than has the United States. As a result of higher rates of saving, however, their ratios of private investment to GNP have also been higher. As discussed in Chapter 5, a dominant thrust of the Economic Recovery Tax Act of 1981 is to provide increased incentives to household and business saving.

Any current increase in government debt leaves future generations facing either a higher tax bill or lower government services, or a combination of the two, than would otherwise have prevailed. This reduces their economic well-being in two ways. First, if current generations do not provide their successors with the resources to pay for the accumulated debt, current deficits make future generations worse off. But even if later generations inherit the additional resources to meet the tax bill, the tax revenues are likely to be collected in ways that distort their economic choices and impair the efficient operation of their economy. There is, then a tradeoff between these later distortions and the distortions from taxing now. Again, a choice of the less costly alternative must be made. In the case of government spending in war time, for example, it has long been recognized that the cost of taxing all at once may be significantly larger than the cost of issuing debt and paying the debt with taxes spread over many years.

THE DEFICIT AND POLITICS OF THE BUDGET

Perhaps the most damaging effects of deficits are not directly economic but result from the political process. There are many advocates for government spending because the beneficiaries of spending have an interest in promoting it. At the same time, those who pay for additional government spending through taxes have an interest in holding taxes down. But the interests of future taxpayers are not well represented in our political process. Deficit spending allows government to be financed in a way that is almost invisible to the taxpayer, and the pull and tug of the political process may result in more government spending than is generally desired. To counteract this tendency, many have argued that policymakers ought to follow a rule—such as balancing the budget each year (that is, financing it only through taxes) or limiting Federal revenues to a fixed percent of GNP—to restrain the tendency toward excessive government spending.

Perhaps the most useful and practical of these rules is the simplest rule: balance the budget. Even this needs to be seen as a long-run rule, however, since the business cycle does cause variations that are difficult to calculate and offset. Furthermore, a strategy of reducing taxes in advance of spending cuts implies that it will take some time to achieve the desired level of deficits. Enforcing a trend toward a balanced budget would impose the fiscal discipline necessary to restrain the growth of government and send a message of governmental restraint to private individuals who can incorporate this essential information into their planning.

In sum, government spending can never be costless. Although the government can use direct taxes, debt finance, or money creation to pay its bills, each imposes costs on the economy. The goal of fiscal policy is to achieve the mix of financing that minimizes these costs. Given the high cost of further direct taxes on capital and labor income, and the high costs imposed on society by excessive expansion of the monetary base, the Administration has chosen what it views at this time as the least costly means of financing government spending. But its current actions are an essential part of a long-term strategy of reducing the scope of the Federal Government. To achieve this end, the Administration will continue to enforce a trend toward a balanced budget.

APPENDIX TO CHAPTER 4

A BROADER PERSPECTIVE ON THE FEDERAL DEBT

The Federal debt is the sum of past budget deficits—the cumulative excess of past spending over past tax receipts. As discussed in Chapter 4, increases in government debt can alter the Nation's rate of capital formation as well as real interest rates. Deficits can also influence the distribution across generations of the burden of paying for government spending.

This appendix discusses different measures of the Federal Government's debt. The broadest measure first subtracts the government's assets from its liabilities to determine the government's net liabilities. It uses market prices rather than book values of those assets and takes account of the erosion of the real value of the debt through inflation by measuring net liabilities in constant dollars rather than current dollars. This measure of government debt also includes most of the implicit liabilities of the social security system. Table 4–5 presents estimates of these measures over time in constant (1980) dollars.

In 1980 the book value of the financial liabilities of the U.S. Government and its credit agencies equaled $1.046 trillion, of which approximately two-thirds was privately held. Because the book value does not change as interest rates fluctuate, the market value is a better measure of the claim on tax resources that would be needed to pay off the outstanding debt. The market value in 1980 was $981 billion, $65 billion less than the gross book liability.

Although government debt increases when spending exceeds tax revenues, some of that spending purchases assets that should be considered as well. To the extent that the government has marketable assets—financial assets in particular, such as gold, U.S. Government securities, and mortgages—these assets could be sold to finance its expenditures and thus obviate (at least for a while) the need for taxes. In 1980 the market value of the government's financial liabilities less the market value of its financial assets equaled $450 billion.

Valuing tangible assets is particularly difficult. The conventional approach is to value government buildings, highways, dams, etc., on a depreciated cost basis, although this value may differ substantially from the asset's value to the economy. Although certain tangible assets may not be marketable, they provide a stream of services that would otherwise have to be purchased through additional taxes. One private estimate, presented in Table 4–5, values the government's tangible assets—reproducible capital plus land—at $727 billion. This estimate does not include the value of mineral resources on Federal property. Mineral wealth is especially difficult to estimate since it can change both with fluctuations in the prices of minerals and with new information on the size of the mineral reserves. In light of these problems, estimates of the replacement cost of the government's net tangible assets should be viewed with caution.

Government debt issued by the Treasury means delaying taxation to pay for government expenditures. The purchasers of official government debt are not adversely affected by these transactions, but future generations may be if they have to reduce government services or pay higher taxes to meet interest payments on the accumulated debt. If crowding out also occurs future generations will have a smaller capital stock with which to produce goods and services.

A similar delay in taxation occurs in the case of implicit debt associated with the social security system and the civil service and military retirement programs. The social security system is financed on a "pay as you go" basis; the program collects money from younger people to pay retirement and other benefits to older people and other beneficiaries. Unlike other taxes, which reduce lifetime income, some economists view social security "tax" contributions as purchases of implicit government pledges of similar benefits in the future. The contributions do not cover both current outlays and the expected future benefits. In this manner the levying of taxes to cover these future benefits is delayed. Hence, succeeding generations may end up paying for these implicit shortfalls by receiving a lower rate

TABLE 4-5.—*Illustrative measures of Federal Government's net liabilities, 1950–80*

[Billions of 1980 dollars]

Year	Book value of gross financial liabilities [1]	Market value of gross financial liabilities [2]	Market value of net financial liabilities [3]	Replace-ment value of tangible assets [4]	Value of unfunded social security retirement liabilities [5]	Total net liabilities including social security retirement liabilities [6]
1950	792	797	650	372	240	564
1951	750	743	582	370	358	618
1952	758	753	590	414	611	840
1953	769	769	605	474	702	889
1954	767	769	616	523	829	983
1955	752	742	581	549	1,054	1,150
1956	718	696	542	565	1,029	1,069
1957	693	689	535	550	1,055	1,100
1958	710	688	540	549	1,238	1,288
1959	720	686	525	536	1,298	1,340
1960	710	704	536	535	1,310	1,363
1961	728	715	539	537	1,240	1,292
1962	739	733	546	546	1,288	1,334
1963	744	731	535	558	1,326	1,349
1964	752	740	537	567	1,322	1,339
1965	751	730	520	571	1,421	1,414
1966	754	738	516	570	1,492	1,485
1967	768	740	521	579	1,356	1,352
1968	776	744	512	583	1,673	1,658
1969	751	702	464	592	1,576	1,510
1970	760	746	491	584	2,012	1,982
1971	776	773	514	578	2,366	2,364
1972	785	773	506	580	2,504	2,493
1973	792	771	465	600	3,086	3,013
1974	782	763	416	621	3,405	3,258
1975	851	842	511	613	3,629	3,580
1976	921	933	581	622	3,749	3,757
1977	961	949	587	647	4,018	4,000
1978	1,004	963	552	676	(7)	(1)
1979	1,011	962	456	706	(7)	(1)
1980	1,046	981	450	727	(7)	(1)

[1] The sum of total liabilities of the U.S. Government and federally sponsored credit agencies as reported in the flow of funds accounts of the Federal Reserve.

[2] Estimates of the market value of liabilities of the U.S. Government and credit agencies prepared by Eisner and Pieper.

[3] Estimates by Eisner and Pieper of market value of financial liabilities less market value of financial assets held by the U.S. Government and credit agencies.

[4] Estimates of the replacement value of tangible assets owned by the government prepared by Eisner and Pieper. Total includes land as well as depreciable assets.

[5] Estimate of unfunded social security retirement liabilities by Leimer and Lesnoy. This series assumes social security benefits kept pace with income growth and uses the legislated social security taxes of the period. Social security unfunded retirement liabilities equals the estimated present value of future retirement benefits less future taxes for the adult population less the value of the OASI trust fund.

[6] Total net liabilities equals the market value of net financial liabilities plus the Leimer and Lesnoy estimated unfunded social security liabilities less U.S. Government tangible assets plus the OASI trust fund.

[7] Not available.

Note.—Data converted to 1980 dollars using GNP implicit price deflator.

Sources: Department of Commerce (Bureau of Economic Analysis); Board of Governors of the Federal Reserve System; Robert Eisner and Paul Pieper, "Government Net Worth: Assets, Liabilities and Revaluations" (1982); and Dean Leimer and Selig Lesnoy, "Social Security and Private Saving: A Reexamination of the Time Series Evidence Using Alternative Social Security Wealth Variables" (1980).

of return on their contributions to social security than they would, on average, have received on money invested elsewhere.

There are important differences, however, between implicit and explicit debt. These implicit promises to pay social security benefits are not legal commitments; as a consequence, they have a different legal standing from explicit forms of government debt. Social security benefits can be, and have been, changed. Although the social security system has become an enduring feature of U.S. society, and sizable social security benefits will be paid to current generations when they retire, the amount of those benefits cannot be predicted with certainty. In addition, most individuals do not know precisely the retirement benefits to which they would be entitled under existing law. A given amount of implicit liabilities is, therefore, likely to reduce saving by a smaller amount than would the same amount of explicit debt.

Social security and Federal employee retirement programs are not the only implicit future liabilities that the Federal Government is firmly committed to pay. The Department of the Treasury lists three categories of financial commitments that are not fixed, legally binding liabilities: undelivered orders, long-term contracts, and contingencies. These vary in the likelihood that they will become legal obligations and in the time when they are apt to mature into liabilities. The implicit pension liabilities are by far the largest component in any of these categories. Although there is no single correct way to measure total implicit and explicit government liabilities, one reasonable approach would be to separate other nonbinding commitments from the unfunded social security and other pension liabilities because of their size and their possible effects on household saving.

The data presented in Table 4-5 are rough but reasonable illustrations that are useful in examining trends and making general comparisons. Tangible assets are valued at replacement cost, since market values are not available; the replacement costs of the government's tangible assets, however, can vary substantially from their potential market value, which is ultimately the measure of interest in terms of the broader concept of debt described here. Estimates of the unfunded implicit retirement liabilities are extremely sensitive to assumptions concerning real interest rates, future birth, death, and immigration rates, labor force participation rates, and benefit to earnings ratios. The unofficial figures reported in Table 4-5 as estimates of social security's unfunded retirement liabilities include types of benefits that represent about two-thirds of total social security unfunded liabilities.

While actuaries of the social security, civil service, and military retirement systems have made recent estimates of their unfunded liabilities that range from $3.5 to $6.5 trillion, depending on the interest rate assumed in the calculations, they have no historical data that could be included in this table. The estimates in the table refer to unfunded social security retirement liabilities associated with workers and retirees currently in the social security system. These figures do not include either expected future benefit payments to or future tax receipts from generations not yet in the system. Hence, these estimates reflect a snapshot of the system at one point in time in order to evaluate the current net claims against it, that is, the current trust fund that would be necessary to fully fund the system.

The first two columns of Table 4–5 compare the government's gross financial liabilities in 1980 dollars, measured at book and market values, for the years 1950 through 1980. While the columns are generally quite similar in many years, the difference in these values has been growing recently.

Column 3 presents the market value, in constant 1980 dollars, of the Federal Government's net financial liabilities. The government's real financial debt in 1980 equaled $450 billion, having fallen fairly steadily from $650 billion in 1950.

Simultaneous with this decline in real net financial debt has been an increase in the value of the government's tangible assets, measured at replacement cost, from $372 billion in 1950 to $727 billion in 1980.

While these components of the broader concept of government debt suggest an improving fiscal position, the sixth column of Table 4–5 suggests that Federal debt, broadly defined, has increased enormously over the past three decades. While the constant dollar market value of financial liabilities only rose from $797 billion in 1950 to $949 billion in 1977, unfunded social security retirement debt, according to this estimate, rose from $240 billion in 1950 to over $4 trillion by 1977. In 1981, actuaries of the social security system officially estimated the system's total unfunded liabilities to be $5.9 trillion.

Broadly defined, government debt is large relative to total household net worth, even when household net worth is also broadly defined to include expected claims to future retirement benefits net of future contributions to these retirement systems for individuals currently in social security. Table 4–6 presents the ratio of Federal Government total net liabilities to this broad measure of household wealth. The ratio equaled 0.17 in 1950 and rose to 0.35 by 1977. The table also presents the ratio of unfunded social security retirement liabilities to the estimate of total Federal net liabilities. In 1950, this ratio was less than one-half; by 1977 the unfunded social security retirement liabilities represented almost all of total Federal Government net liabilities.

TABLE 4-6.—*Comparisons of total measured Federal Government's indebtedness, unfunded social security retirement liabilities, and household wealth, 1950–77*

[Ratio]

Year	Ratio of Federal Government's total net liabilities (including social security retirement liabilities) to household wealth	Ratio of unfunded social security retirement liabilities to total net liabilities
1950	0.166	0.426
1951	.172	.579
1952	.212	.727
1953	.217	.790
1954	.218	.843
1955	.231	.917
1956	.210	.962
1957	.219	.959
1958	.230	.961
1959	.231	.969
1960	.234	.961
1961	.211	.959
1962	.220	.965
1963	.212	.983
1964	.202	.988
1965	.201	1.005
1966	.210	1.005
1967	.183	1.002
1968	.203	1.009
1969	.193	1.044
1970	.241	1.015
1971	.267	1.001
1972	.265	1.005
1973	.304	1.024
1974	.326	1.045
1975	.344	1.014
1976	.342	.998
1977	.350	1.005

Note.—Federal Government's total net liabilities equals the market value of net financial liabilities plus estimated unfunded social security retirement liabilities less U.S. Government tangible assets plus the OASI trust fund. Tangible assets are valued at replacement cost. Net financial liabilities are valued at market prices. These estimates include liabilities of the U.S. Treasury held by the OASI.

Unfunded social security retirement liabilities equals the present value of projected retirement benefits less the present value of projected tax contributions to social security less the value of the OASI trust fund. Retirement benefits and tax contributions are projected for the adult population separately for each year from 1950 through 1977.

Household net worth as estimated by the Board of Governors of the Federal Reserve System plus unofficial estimates of social security retirement wealth prepared by Leimer and Lesnoy.

Sources: Department of Commerce (Bureau of Economic Analysis); Board of Governors of the Federal Reserve System; Robert Eisner and Paul Pieper, "Government Net Worth: Assets, Liabilities and Revaluations" (1982); and Dean Leimer and Selig Lesnoy, "Social Security and Private Saving: A Reexamination of the Time Series Evidence Using Alternative Social Security Wealth Variables" (1980).

Conclusion

These adjustments to the traditional book value measure of government liabilities put projected official government deficits in some perspective. When government's explicit debt is adjusted to take account of inflation and assets, its real net liabilities show a decline over the last twenty years. Official deficits that merely offset the devaluation of the debt due to inflation or that finance the purchase of assets do not increase the government's claim on private resources.

Since 1960, however, implicit liabilities have grown considerably so that by some estimates they greatly overshadow the explicit liabilities. Under the broader measure that includes implicit debt, total Federal debt tripled between 1967 and 1977. Compared to historical increases in the broad measure of government debt, the unified deficits projected for the 1980s are small. If the effect of implicit liabilities on economic behavior is similar to the effect of explicit liabilities, the effects of the official projected deficits on national investment and real interest rates would be small relative to the impact of the accumulation of total explicit and implicit debt over the last 20 years. Thus, when inflation, government holdings of assets, and implicit debt are taken into account in measuring Federal debt, government deficits in the range of those projected for the 1980s will add only marginally to the burden of the debt.

CHAPTER 5

Tax Policy and Economic Growth

THE ADMINISTRATION, in cooperation with the Congress, brought about a fundamental change in Federal tax policy in 1981. The new policy involves far more than simply reducing tax burdens. The Economic Recovery Tax Act of 1981 has changed the basic character of the tax system by shifting the burden of taxation away from capital income, thereby providing substantially greater incentives for capital investments and personal saving.

This tax policy is a sharp break from the policies of the recent past. It reflects a different understanding of the way tax policy affects the U.S. economy. This chapter provides a framework for analyzing the effects of the Administration's tax policy on the economy. The Administration's fiscal policy has two key characteristics. First, the Administration views the principal fiscal policy instruments—spending, taxing, and deficit—chiefly in terms of their impact on the individual decisions of households and businesses, since it is these decisions that ultimately generate employment and growth.

The second key element that distinguishes current policies from those of the past is that they are fundamentally long term in nature. Economic growth is a long-run process that is determined by technological change and the supply and allocation of such productive factors as raw materials, labor, and capital. Households and businesses look to the future in making current economic decisions. The government has some direct influence on factor inputs, but its main influence is through the indirect and long-term incentives it provides to work and save.

The fact that households and businesses make long-term as well as day-to-day decisions underscores the importance of consistency in government policy. Frequent changes in policy generate uncertainty about the probable duration of current policies and jeopardize the chances that any particular policy will succeed. Since the long run is simply a sequence of short runs, short-run policies that deviate from long-run goals ultimately mean abandoning long-run goals. The current economic policies, more than those of any recent Administration, are policies for the long term.

Fiscal policy involves three interrelated choices. One is choosing an expenditure policy—how much to spend, and what kind of expenditures to make. The second is taxation—how much to collect, and which tax instruments to use, including implicit taxation through the creation of money, to raise revenues. The third, deficit policy, involves deciding on the size and distribution of the deficit over time; that is, the difference in the time pattern of receipts and expenditures.

The government's long-term budget constraint provides a framework for considering the coordination of fiscal and monetary policy, for understanding the impact of deficits on economic growth, and for discussing the allocation across generations of the burden of taxation. The American people must eventually pay for what the government spends. While the government can borrow from the private sector to delay payment for its spending on consumption and transfer payments, such borrowing is subject to a limit. Eventually the government must either reduce spending or raise tax revenues to pay the interest payments on past accumulations of debt. When the government borrows, and thereby delays levying taxes to pay for its current spending, it shifts the burden of paying for its current spending to future generations.

The government uses explicit taxation, such as personal and corporate income taxes, to raise revenue. As will be shown in this chapter, it also raises revenue with implicit taxes. By increasing the supply of money, for example, the Federal Government, in effect, creates some of the dollars needed to pay for current expenditures. But excessive expansion of the money supply results in a rise in prices that reduces the real value of the existing stock of money held by the private sector. This is one way in which the money creation process transfers real resources from the private to the public sector. A second way is that the inflation produced by excessive monetary expansion reduces the real value of the nominal government debt held by the private sector. By creating inflation the government can pay off its obligations in cheaper dollars. The purchasers of government bonds require higher interest rates to compensate for the expected inflation. Consequently, the government collects real resources from devaluing the stock of nominal bonds only when the actual inflation rate exceeds the expected inflation rate. The reduction in the real value of outstanding debt that results from inflation means that the government requires less revenue from explicit taxes. The Administration's program is based on a commitment to reducing both explicit and implicit taxation.

The fact that explicit taxation and money creation are alternative ways to finance government expenditures means that conventional fiscal and monetary policy must be coordinated. If the government does not pay for its expenditures with explicit taxes, now or in the future, it will eventually be forced to resort to the printing press. Hence, the ultimate path to lower explicit and implicit taxation is a reduction in the growth of government spending.

The Administration, with the support of the Congress, has significantly changed national macroeconomic policy. However, the ultimate success of the Administration's policy will depend on the degree to which it is credible in the eyes of the public. Households will increase their long-term saving and labor supply in response to lower taxes on capital and labor income if they believe those taxes will remain low. Workers and employers will agree to moderate nominal wage increases only to the extent that they believe inflation will moderate. Businesses will raise prices at slower rates only if they know that other prices—primarily those of their competitors—are also increasing at slower rates. In short, the problem of coordinating the private sector's response to government policy is a problem of convincing the public that the Federal Government will be steadfast in maintaining its new economic course.

ECONOMIC GROWTH: PAST PERFORMANCE AND FUTURE POTENTIAL

Economic growth in the United States has been unusually low since 1973. Annual growth in real disposable per capita income between 1973 and 1979 slowed to 1.6 percent from an average rate of 3.0 percent in the period 1959 to 1973. The country is now experiencing its third recession since 1973.

Our recent economic performance has been unsatisfactory not only in comparison with our own postwar experience but also in comparison with the economic performance of our principle trading partners. In the 1970s, annual rates of increase in real per capita income among the other developed countries exceeded U.S. rates by nearly one-fourth. Other indications of economic malaise were declines in the measured growth rates of total output, capital input, and total factor productivity. While the period from 1959 to 1973 witnessed average annual growth rates in real gross national product (GNP) of 4.0 percent, the rate from 1973 to 1979 was only 2.8 percent.

MEASURING GROWTH

Economic growth reflects increases in factor inputs and total factor productivity. Each of these concepts, as well as output itself, is difficult to quantify. The growth of productivity is not directly observable. Rather, it is a measure of the real economic growth that is not accounted for by growth of the labor force or growth in the capital stock. Several problems in defining both output and input must therefore be addressed in any attempt to measure economic growth and productivity growth.

The measure of output—real GNP—primarily reflects the value placed on goods and services traded in the marketplace. While pollution control devices and similar capital goods designed to improve the quality of life are counted in the input figures, the output figures exclude such items as cleaner air and water. In addition, there are problems in measuring the true quantities and qualities of some goods and services. One problem, for example, is determining the value of government output. Government services are measured in terms of their labor costs, which may differ substantially from their marginal value; other government outputs, such as the value of the services from tangible assets, are not counted in GNP at all.

Quality changes in tangible commodities also present difficult problems in measuring productivity growth. Today's color television set technologically surpasses the 1960 model, and 1981 computers differ greatly from their 1970 predecessors. These changes in quality are not adequately reflected in government reports of GNP growth. The procedures followed for some products ignore quality changes, in effect, counting a computer as a computer regardless of its year of manufacture.

There are also difficulties in quantifying inputs. Private capital is typically measured as the sum of accumulated investment expenditures, with allowances for depreciation rather than as the amount of capital actually in productive use. In addition, the amount of capital available for use is miscounted when changes in the longevity of investments are not recognized and depreciation allowances are not adjusted accordingly. The statistics on labor input also fail to capture many changes in the quality and quantity of labor services. There is, for example, little available data indicating the intensity with which workers actually work within any given period of time.

ECONOMIC GROWTH—THE HISTORICAL RECORD

Table 5-1 shows the historic growth rates in real gross national product, capital input, labor input, and total factor productivity. Because of the problems of aggregating private and public outputs and inputs, the table also shows growth in the private economy, excluding the farm and housing sectors. These data, based on estimates prepared by the Council of Economic Advisers, are presented for four periods. Each of these periods encompasses a full economic cycle.

TABLE 5-1.—*Average annual growth rates of real GNP, total factor productivity, and factor inputs, 1959-79*

[Percent]

Period	Real GNP	Total factor productivity	Capital	Labor
	Total GNP			
1959 to 1965................	4.3	2.5	3.8	0.9
1965 to 1969................	4.0	1.9	4.1	1.2
1969 to 1973................	3.6	2.3	3.5	.4
1973 to 1979................	2.8	1.2	2.5	1.6
	Private nonfarm nonhousing GNP			
1959 to 1965................	4.4	2.5	4.1	1.0
1965 to 1969................	4.0	1.3	5.8	1.3
1969 to 1973................	4.1	2.4	4.2	.7
1973 to 1979................	2.8	.6	3.2	1.8

Sources: Department of Commerce (Bureau of Economic Analysis); Gollop, Frank and Jorgenson, Dale, "U.S. Productivity Growth By Industry 1947-1973"; and Council of Economic Advisers.

Labor input is measured as total annual hours worked, adjusted by age and sex. In accounting for total GNP growth, labor input includes agricultural workers, government and civilian workers, and military personnel. Capital input includes government capital plus private residential, nonresidential, and agricultural capital. For private GNP, factor inputs are taken to be only those specific to this segment of the economy. The growth rate of total factor productivity is computed for both total GNP and private GNP assuming a simple production relationship between output and the supplies of capital and labor.

Some of the poorer growth performance in recent years reflects a slowdown in capital formation. The Nation's total net capital stock, including both private and government capital, but excluding consumer durables, grew at an average annual rate of 3.8 percent during the period 1965 to 1973, but at only 2.5 percent per year between 1973 and 1979. The slowdown in capital formation was equally pronounced in the private nonfarm nonhousing sector; the 1973 to 1979 growth rate was less than two-thirds of the growth rate from 1965 to 1973. This reduction in the rate of capital formation coincided with a decline of nearly one-fourth in the Nation's saving rate. The Nation's saving rate is defined here as the share of net national product not consumed by either the government or household sectors. Household consumption includes purchases of consumer durables.

Since 1973 the growth of labor input has greatly exceeded that experienced in the previous 25 years. Adjusted for age and sex, labor input grew at only 0.7 percent per year between 1950 and 1973, less than half the rate of growth between 1973 and 1979. The primary causes of the acceleration of labor input are the rapid rise in female employment rates, particularly for women aged 25 to 44, a rise in the population aged 18 to 35, and a leveling off of employment rates for males aged 65 and over.

Table 5–1 indicates a sizable reduction in productivity growth rates during the middle and late 1970s in comparison with prior years. This reduction reflected a combination of a lower growth rate for other, nonmeasured inputs and a less efficient allocation of resources. Measured productivity growth of total GNP declined by 48 percent between these periods; the decline for the private nonfarm nonhousing sector was 73 percent. By itself, the slower productivity growth from 1973 to 1979 can account for a 1.1 percentage point decline in GNP growth from that experienced in the previous 14 years. This method of growth accounting attributes a 1.8 percentage point decline in the growth of private nonfarm nonhousing output to the productivity slowdown between these periods.

EXPLAINING THE PRODUCTIVITY SLOWDOWN

There have been concerted efforts to explain the measured slowdown. These efforts have met with only limited success. While there are a number of possible explanatory variables, available studies suggest that none separately nor in combination is capable of explaining more than half of the decline. Capital expenditures for pollution abatement equipment (which provides no measurable output) appear responsible for a small fraction of the slowdown. Another explanation is the growth of productive factors other than capital and labor that are typically not included as inputs in growth accounting. As a result, changes in the availability or use of such inputs as energy or improved land are measured as a change in productivity. The reductions in the use of energy following the 1974 and 1979 oil price shocks also explain some fraction of the measured productivity slowdown.

Other possible, but less well-documented, explanations include a decline in economic efficiency associated with higher levels of distorting taxes and increased levels of government regulation. Regulation of energy in the 1970s was a prime example of the way in which government intervention in the private economy reduced economic efficiency.

Productive efficiency can also be reduced by tax policies that distort the allocation of inputs. Federal subsidies to particular industries permit them to gain more access to productive inputs than is economically efficient, and differential tax treatment of productive inputs can also result in economic inefficiency. For example, if the return on capital expenditures of a particular type, such as spending for equipment, is taxed at a lower rate than the return on other capital expenditures, such as those for plant, business investment will shift toward the favorably treated input. Hence, the composition of the capital stock will be altered, and national output would be produced less efficiently from what would occur with neutral tax treatment.

One-time changes in regulation or the tax structure that impair the efficient operation of the economy are more likely to produce a one-time decline in output than permanently alter the growth rate. During the period in which output drops, however, measured productivity growth will be smaller. Hence, the drop in measured productivity shown in Table 5-1 may reflect, in part, the progressive increase in regulation and effective marginal tax rates through the 1970s.

PROSPECTS FOR GROWTH IN THE 1980s

The Administration projects a 3.2 percent annual rate of growth in real GNP over the period 1979 through 1987. While higher than the rate from 1974 to 1979, this rate is one-fifth lower than the rate experienced from 1959 to 1973. An increase in the rate of capital formation from the 1973–79 rate of 2.5 percent per year to the 1969–73 rate of 3.5 percent per year would, by itself, raise output growth to 3.1 percent, even if productivity and labor growth rates remained constant. Given the incentives for capital formation provided by the Economic Recovery Tax Act of 1981, a 3.5 percent growth in capital over this period seems attainable. Growth in output will also be stimulated by demographic changes. Between 1979 and the mid-1980s a large segment of the baby-boom generation will become fully integrated into the U.S. labor market. The associated changes in the age and sex composition of the labor force should, by themselves, account for a 0.3 percent annual rate of growth in output between 1979 and 1986. Growth in labor input is expected to exceed this, however, as the Administration's new incentives for additional labor supply lead to long-term increases in employment rates and hours worked.

A growth in total factor productivity greater than the 1.2 percent experienced from 1973 to 1979 is not essential to meet the Administration's 1987 GNP projection, but it is likely to occur as a result of the reduction in the general level of distorting taxation and the new regulatory environment.

INCREASING FACTOR SUPPLY

Current and future supplies of labor and capital to the economy primarily reflect the long-term supply and demand decisions of households and firms. At any point in time the aggregate supplies of labor and capital depend not only on the number and types of workers and the amount of plant and equipment available, but also on the rate of utilization of these productive factors. People can work and machines can be worked more or less within any period of time. In the very short run, changes in the supplies of factor services involve changes in factor utilization rates. In the longer run, the number and quality of workers, and the quantity and quality of structures and equipment, are variable.

Near-term increases in the stock of physical capital require producing or importing more capital goods in the current period. But producing more capital goods means producing fewer goods for consumption. Hence, one way to expand the stock of physical capital is for the household and government sectors to reduce their combined demands for current consumption. Another way to expand capital formation is simply to expand current output faster than current consumption. A third way is to import capital.

The Administration seeks to increase capital formation by both raising the level of output and reducing the fraction of output consumed. A reduction in the Federal Government's own rate of consumption is an important element in this equation, but creating an environment where households choose to save a larger share of their income is of paramount importance. The figures in Table 5–2 illustrate this point.

Table 5–2 presents historical data on household and government consumption rates and the rate of total net national saving. These consumption and saving rates are useful for portraying aggregate saving behavior. The household consumption rate is defined as household (private sector) consumption divided by the difference between net national product and total government consumption. National output less government consumption provides a measure of the private sector's effective disposable income, because the private sector must pay for the government's current consumption, either now or in the future.

TABLE 5–2.—*Average annual consumption and saving rates, 1951–80*

[Percent of net national product (NNP)]

Period	Total Government consumption as percent of NNP	Federal Government consumption as percent of NNP	Household consumption as percent of nongovernmental NNP	Net national saving as percent of NNP
1951–60	14.1	8.2	81.0	16.4
1961–70	16.7	8.3	81.7	15.2
1971–80	18.9	7.0	85.5	11.7

Sources: Department of Commerce (Bureau of Economic Analysis) and Council of Economic Advisers.

Government consumption is defined here as government expenditures on goods and services immediately consumed. Government purchases of capital goods are not included. The table also indicates average rates by decade of net national saving, defined as net national product less household and government consumption, divided by net national product.

From the 1960s to the 1970s the Nation's total net saving rate fell from 15.2 percent to 11.7 percent. Changes in both government and household consumption rates played a role in reducing the saving rate, but the changes in the household consumption rate were far more important. If the rate of household consumption out of total disposable income—output less government consumption—had not changed over this period, the Nation's saving rate would have fallen by only 0.4 percentage point rather than by 3.5 percentage points, despite an increase in government consumption as a share of net national product from 16.7 to 18.9 percent. Thus, to achieve higher national saving rates it is important to lower the household consumption rate.

There are two ways in which the household consumption rate can be reduced and the national saving rate increased. One way is for households to increase total output by supplying more labor without at the same time increasing current consumption proportionately. The other is for households to maintain their current supply of labor (and therefore output) but reduce their levels of consumption. In either case the household consumption rate falls, and the economy saves more.

THE ECONOMIC EFFECTS OF TAX POLICY

In making the decisions that determine national output and capital formation households consider their options. Each household makes decisions on consumption, saving, and work based on the household's current and future resources. These include the household's net worth (the current market value of all financial and real assets minus liabilities), the household's expected inheritances, the household's expected receipt of government transfer payments, and the household's human capital endowment. The endowment of human capital is the present value of after-tax income the household would earn if it was solely interested in maximizing its labor earnings.

Household choices between consumption and saving and between work and leisure are influenced by after-tax wage rates and after-tax rates of return on capital. When the government changes either the level or the structure of taxes, it ultimately alters household decisions about consumption, saving, and work effort. All aspects of the tax system, including both personal and business taxes, influence these decisions. For example, higher after-tax returns on capital income make present consumption more expensive than future consumption;

forgoing a dollar of consumption today and investing that dollar provides more than a dollar of consumption tomorrow, with the additional amount determined by the after-tax return on the investment.

It is customary to associate taxes on wage income with changes in incentives to work and to associate taxes on capital income with changes in incentives to consume or to save. Wage taxes also influence consumption and saving decisions, however, and taxes on capital income influence labor and leisure decisions. Lowering taxes on capital income raises the after-tax return on that income. The larger after-tax return effectively lowers the cost of enjoying leisure as well as consuming in the future relative to the present. Hence, a reduction in taxes on capital income increases the incentive to work now and can thus stimulate the supply of labor.

U.S. households and businesses face, at best, a highly uncertain economic environment resulting from continuing changes in preferences, prices, and productivity. Uncertainty with respect to government fiscal and monetary policy increases the uncertainty under which households make current and future consumption and labor supply decisions. In such an environment, households may choose to postpone supplying labor and businesses may decide to postpone new investment until the economic environment is more settled.

The Administration and the Congress have greatly reduced uncertainty with respect to the tax policy. The Economic Recovery Tax Act of 1981 clearly spells out the major features of the U.S. tax system for the next several years; the indexation of the Federal income tax slated to begin in 1985 will reduce the uncertainty associated with inflation pushing households into higher marginal tax brackets.

THE STRUCTURE OF THE TAX SYSTEM

The United States has a complex tax system that influences the choices households make between current and future consumption and current and future work effort. The tax system also influences the types of investments businesses undertake and the set of commodities households choose to purchase. The Federal personal and corporate income taxes, the social security program, the welfare system, and the money creation process all affect the economic behavior of firms and households. This section describes the changes introduced by the Economic Recovery Tax Act of 1981 to the personal and corporate income tax systems, and discusses the likely effects of these changes on labor supply and saving rates. Tax aspects of the social security system, the welfare system, and monetary policy are also addressed.

THE PERSONAL INCOME TAX

Last year's tax legislation made three important changes in the Federal personal income tax. First, marginal tax rates on given levels of nominal income will be reduced, in three stages, by 23 percent by 1984. Beginning in 1985 the personal income tax structure will be indexed to inflation. In addition, the top rate on income from capital was reduced from 70 percent to 50 percent. Table 5-3 presents marginal tax rates (excluding the social security tax on earnings) at various levels of real income for the next 5 years, based on Administration projections of future inflation. This table also presents the marginal tax rates that would have occurred in the absence of the Economic Recovery Tax Act of 1981.

TABLE 5-3.—*Comparison of marginal personal income tax rates by real income level under the Economic Recovery Tax Act of 1981 and old law, 1979–86* [1]

[Percent]

Real income (1979 dollars)	1979	1980	1981[2]	1982	1983	1984	1985	1986
Single:								
$10,000:								
Old law	21	21	21	24	24	24	24	26
New law			21	22	19	18	18	18
$20,000:								
Old law	30	30	34	34	34	34	39	39
New law			34	31	28	26	26	26
$30,000:								
Old law	39	39	39	44	44	49	49	49
New law			39	40	36	38	38	34
$50,000:								
Old law	49	50	50	50	50	50	50	50
New law			49	50	45	48	48	48
Married, two workers:								
$10,000:								
Old law	16	16	18	18	18	18	18	18
New law			18	16	15	14	14	14
$20,000:								
Old law	21	24	24	24	28	28	28	28
New law			24	22	19	22	18	18
$30,000:								
Old law	28	32	32	32	37	37	37	43
New law			32	29	26	28	28	28
$50,000:								
Old law	43	43	43	49	49	49	49	49
New law			42	44	40	38	38	38

[1] Excludes social security taxes and State and local income taxes.
[2] Tax rates for 1981 under new law rounded to nearest whole percent.
Source: Department of the Treasury, Office of Tax Analysis.

Two points are clear from this table. First, without the tax cut, marginal tax rates for low- and middle-income households would have been 30 percent to 50 percent higher. Second, although the tax cut will significantly lower marginal tax rates at all levels of income, tax rates at given levels of real income will decline by much less. Bracket creep will offset much of the effect of the tax cut between

1981 and 1985. Under the Administration's inflation projections, most households will still face marginal tax rates that are high by historical standards. Table 5-4 presents past and projected marginal tax rates for households at 3 points in the income distribution from 1965 to 1984. For the projected inflation path, marginal tax rates for median income households in 1984 will decline to roughly their 1977-80 levels, but will remain considerably above earlier rates. Thus, despite the substantial reductions introduced by the 1981 tax cut, most rates in 1984 will remain near the historical high rates on real income.

TABLE 5-4.—*Marginal personal income tax rates for four-person families, selected years, 1965-84* [1]

[Percent]

Year	Family income		
	One-half median income	Median income	Twice median income
1965	14	17	22
1970	15	20	26
1975	17	22	32
1980	18	24	43
	Under Economic Recovery Tax Act of 1981		
1981	17.8	27.7	42.5
1982	16	25	39
1983	15	23	40
1984	16	25	38
	Under old law		
1981	18	28	43
1982	18	28	43
1983	18	28	49
1984	21	32	49

[1] Excludes social security taxes and State and local income taxes.
Source: Department of the Treasury, Office of Tax Analysis.

To discuss the effects of the tax cuts on labor supply and saving decisions, it is necessary to understand the various incentives on household behavior created by reductions in marginal tax rates. Cutting tax rates increases an individual's after-tax wage rate. With the Federal Government taking a smaller share of the last dollar of earnings, the return to an individual from an extra hour of work or a more demanding job will increase, strengthening the incentive to work more hours, or accept a more demanding job.

Similarly, cutting tax rates increases after-tax interest rates. The higher the after-tax interest rate, the higher the level of future consumption possible for a given reduction of current consumption. The increase in after-tax interest rates resulting from the tax cuts will thus tend to decrease present consumption, including consumption of leisure as well as goods. In other words, households will tend both to work more and to save more.

Operating in the other direction is the effect of the tax cut on household income. As marginal tax rates fall, the total tax bill paid by a household will fall and its after-tax income will rise. As disposable incomes rise, both in the present and in the future, consumption of both goods and leisure will rise. Thus the effect of increased income will tend to decrease saving and decrease work effort. The net effect of the tax cut on saving and labor supply will vary according to household circumstances. The preponderance of empirical studies suggests that the labor supply effects of a tax cut are small for married men, somewhat larger for unmarried people, and substantial for married women. The most important effect of these changes in personal marginal income tax rates may thus be to increase labor force participation rates and hours of work by married women.

The second important change in the personal income tax introduced by last year's tax legislation was the extension of the opportunity to use Individual Retirement Accounts (IRAs) to all working households. Under the new law, each worker may contribute up to $2,000 to these accounts regardless of whether the worker is already covered under an employer-sponsored pension plan. One-earner couples can contribute up to $2,250. IRAs provide two tax advantages to contributors. First, contributions are deductible from taxable income. Second, returns on IRA investments accumulate tax-free as long as the funds are not withdrawn from the account. Given the sizable tax savings available from IRAs, the total amount of money invested in them can be expected to rise sharply. Some of this money will simply be transferred from other types of savings, including stocks, bonds, and savings accounts. However, for many households without sufficient liquid assets to transfer to IRAs, the last dollar contributed to an IRA will correspond to their marginal saving. That is, the last dollar of current consumption forgone will correspond to the last dollar invested in an IRA. Since the marginal tax rate on capital income obtained from these accounts is quite low, this provision is expected to increase the national saving rate as well as contribute to an increase in the labor supply.

The prospect of moving into higher marginal income tax brackets biases households away from activities that would generate higher future incomes. Hence, income tax progressivity encourages current consumption and leisure and discourages saving for the future. In the presence of inflation and an unindexed tax system, "bracket creep" strengthens this disincentive for generating future income. Indexation of the tax system in 1985 will, therefore, provide further stimulus for saving and economic growth.

Other changes in the tax code will also provide taxpayers with greater incentives to join the work force. The new law provides married couples filing a joint 1982 return with a 5 percent deduction in 1982 and a 10 percent deduction starting in 1983 on the earnings up to $30,000 of the lower earning spouse. If the couple's marginal tax rate would otherwise be 30 percent, the 10 percent deduction after 1982 will reduce the marginal tax rate on earnings of the second spouse to 27 percent. The spousal deduction will also place certain households in lower marginal tax brackets, thus further lowering marginal tax rates. This change should help sustain the growth of female labor force participation.

TAXATION OF INCOME FROM BUSINESS INVESTMENT

The Economic Recovery Tax Act of 1981 also made major changes in the taxation of business income. The most important change is the more generous treatment of the way in which capital can be depreciated for tax purposes, known as the accelerated cost recovery system (ACRS). A second change was the introduction of leasing rules that provide businesses with temporarily low taxable income the same investment incentives as other businesses. A third provision of the act is an increase in the investment tax credit for some types of equipment. Finally, a fourth provision allows small businesses to expense up to $5,000 of new investment in 1982 and 1983. The $5,000 limit will rise to $7,500 in 1984 and 1985, and $10,000 thereafter. These changes should substantially increase business investment by increasing the after-tax return available on new business projects.

TAX TREATMENT OF DEPRECIABLE PROPERTY

The ACRS will encourage business investment by shortening the period over which assets can be fully depreciated and by allowing firms to claim more of the depreciation early in the tax life of the asset. Before the adoption of ACRS, businesses were permitted to write off industrial equipment over an average period of 8.6 years. The ACRS asset life for this equipment is 5 years. For industrial plant, asset lives have been reduced by 37 percent, from an average of 23.8 years to 15 years. The ACRS depreciation schedules represent a combination of the declining balance and straightline method of depreciation through 1984. For 1985 and beyond, declining balance switching to sum of years digits is used. The depreciation schedules for the years after 1984 provide increasingly more acceleration of depreciation. The combined result of the ACRS and the investment tax credit will be a decline in effective tax rates on new investment over the period 1982 to 1987.

Table 5–5 shows historic and projected before-tax real rates of return in new capital investment required to provide a 4 percent after-tax real return. This real return is a commonly used analytical assumption. These numbers reflect the combined effect of the depreciation provisions and the investment tax credit. Historical numbers are based on historical rates of inflation. Rates of return in future years are based on the Administration's inflation projections. A before tax rate of return of 8 percent, for example, implies an effective tax rate of 50 percent on new investments. The calculations assume the new investment is equity financed. Hence, the tax advantages from the deduction of interest expense associated with debt financing are not included.

TABLE 5–5.—*Real before-tax rate of return required to provide a 4 percent real after-tax return, 1955–86*

[Percent]

Period	Construction machinery	General industrial equipment	Trucks, buses, and trailers	Industrial buildings	Commercial buildings
1955–59	8.9	9.5	10.8	8.0	8.0
1960–64	7.4	7.8	8.7	7.9	7.9
1965–69	6.5	6.9	7.5	7.6	7.6
1970–74	6.6	6.7	7.6	8.6	8.4
1975–79	6.1	6.4	7.6	9.0	8.7
1981	3.4	3.5	3.5	6.6	6.2
1982	3.1	3.3	3.1	6.4	6.1
1983	2.9	3.2	3.0	6.4	6.0
1984	2.9	3.1	2.9	6.4	6.0
1985	2.3	2.7	2.6	6.3	6.0
1986	2.2	2.6	2.5	6.3	6.0

Note.—Data for 1955–79 are based on Auerbach and Jorgenson calculations of expected inflation in each year. Data for 1981–86 are based on the Administration's projections of inflation (year-over-year percent change in the GNP implicit price deflator): 1982, 7.9; 1983, 6.0; 1984, 5.0; 1985, 4.7; 1986, 4.6; and 1987 and beyond, 4.5.

Sources: Auerbach, Alan and Jorgenson, Dale, "Inflation Proof Depreciation of Assets," *Harvard Business Review*, Sept.-Oct. 1980 (1955–79), and Council of Economic Advisers (1981–86, based on Economic Recovery Tax Act of 1981).

Under the assumptions made here, in comparison with the years 1975 to 1979, the 1982 real before-tax rate of return required to justify a new investment in general industrial equipment has been reduced from 6.4 to 3.3 percent. For investment in plant the required rate of return estimated here declines from 9.0 to 6.4 percent. The effective tax rates associated with these numbers decline between 1982 and 1986. This reflects both the more favorable depreciation schedules after 1984 and projections of continued declines in inflation.

Since depreciation allowances are not indexed, higher rates of inflation will raise effective tax rates. Table 5–6 presents the before-tax rates of return required in 1986 to provide a 4 percent after-tax return under different assumptions about the rate of inflation prevailing in 1986 and beyond. The table shows that a reduction in inflation from 8 percent to 5 percent will lower the required before-tax rate of return from 3.2 percent to 2.7 percent in general industrial equipment and from 6.9 percent to 6.4 percent on plant. Conversely, a 1986 level of inflation of 12 percent would raise required before-tax rates of return to 3.7 percent for equipment and 7.4 percent for plant.

TABLE 5–6.—*Real before-tax rate of return required to provide a 4 percent after-tax return in 1986 at selected rates of inflation*

[Percent]

Type of capital	Inflation rate (percent)		
	5	8	12
Construction machinery	2.3	2.9	3.7
General industrial equipment	2.7	3.2	3.7
Trucks, buses, and trailers	2.5	3.1	3.7
Industrial buildings	6.4	6.9	7.4
Commercial buildings	6.1	6.5	6.9

Source: Council of Economic Advisers.

Tables 5–5 and 5–6 also indicate that the ACRS does not treat all types of business investment equally. Although favorable to all new investment, ACRS is relatively more favorable to investment in equipment. As a consequence, industries for which short-lived equipment represents a large fraction of their total capital will face lower effective tax rates than industries with a low equipment-intensive capital structure. Table 5–7 presents calculations of industry specific tax rates on new investment for 1982. There are two sets of numbers; the first indicates the tax rates that would have prevailed under the old law, while the second column indicates tax rates in 1982 under the Accelerated Cost Recovery System.

TABLE 5–7.—*Effective tax rates on new depreciable assets, selected industries, 1982* [1]

Industry	Old Law	New law
Agriculture	32.7	16.6
Mining	28.4	−3.4
Primary metals	34.0	7.5
Machinery and instruments	38.2	18.6
Motor vehicles	25.8	−11.3
Food	44.1	20.8
Pulp and paper	28.5	.9
Chemicals	28.8	8.6
Petroleum refining	35.0	1.1
Transportation services	31.0	−2.9
Utilities	43.2	30.6
Communications	39.8	14.1
Services and trade	53.2	37.1

[1] Industries chosen had at least $5 billion in new investment in 1981.
Note.—Assumes a 4 percent real after-tax rate of return and 8 percent inflation.
Source: Department of the Treasury, Office of Tax Analysis.

The table shows substantial reductions in tax rates for all industries, but differences among industries in the rate of tax reduction. The effect on each industry is different because each industry uses a different mix of capital. Tax rates vary across industries, from a high of 37 percent in the services and trade sector to a low of −11 percent in the motor vehicle industry. Effective tax rates on new investment are negative for some industries. The result will be lower total corporate tax liabilities rather than direct payments by the Treasury. These differential rates of taxation at the industry level will probably lead to relatively more investment in industries with lower tax rates.

LEASING PROVISIONS

The ACRS provides the same investment incentives to firms with taxable income and those with nontaxable income. The leasing provision of the Economic Recovery Tax Act of 1981 should enhance efficient allocation of capital across industries and across firms within the same industry. The fundamental principle underlying the leasing provisions is that investment incentives should be equal for all businesses in a given industry and across industries; that is, investment incentives should not favor investment in one firm over another. Prior to the establishment of these leasing provisions, firms with temporary tax losses (a condition especially characteristic of new enterprises) were often unable to take advantage of investment tax incentives. The reason was that temporarily unprofitable companies had no taxable income against which to apply the investment tax deductions. As a result, these companies were placed at a relative disadvantage, although the new investment undertaken by these companies was potentially as profitable as investment undertaken by firms with temporarily positive profits.

The leasing provisions will permit companies with no current taxable income to take advantage of investment incentives by transferring their tax credits and additional deductions associated with investment to firms with taxable income. For example, American automobile manufacturers who are currently reporting losses will now be able to take the same advantage of the incentives as more profitable firms. In the absence of the leasing provisions, investment would probably be too low in the automobile industry relative to the most productive mix of investment.

The leasing provisions will also have the advantage of reducing incentives for mergers. Under the old law, companies with positive taxable income had an incentive to merge with companies with tax losses because these tax losses could be used to offset the parent company's taxable income. The leasing provisions, by permitting companies with positive taxable income to effectively purchase the negative taxable income of other companies, will eliminate this motivation for mergers.

EFFECTS OF TAX ACT ON HOUSING AND CONSUMER DURABLES

The 1981 act will alter the allocation of existing capital and labor among industries. It will also affect the allocation of new business investment, the fraction of investment allocated to business as opposed to residential investment, and the division of consumption between durable commodities—such as residential real estate, automobiles, and furniture—and nondurable commodities.

The Tax Act improves the attractiveness of business investment relative to other forms of investment. As relative returns rise for business investment, financial institutions will tend to increase their business lending and decrease their consumer and mortgage lending. Households themselves will tend to lower their investments in these goods in order to put more of their savings directly into business capital by purchasing corporate stocks and bonds, or indirectly by placing their savings with financial institutions who will make these investments for them. In either case, more money will be channeled to business investment and less to housing and consumer durables than would have occurred without the ACRS.

To understand the effects of the new depreciation system on the consumption of durables versus nondurables, one must first realize that the implicit price of consuming durable goods is the after-tax return the owners of these durables would otherwise receive if they sold these assets and invested the proceeds.

The sizable reductions in tax rates on capital income mean that real after-tax returns on household saving will be substantially higher than they have been in the recent past. As a result, the implicit price of consumer durables has risen, and a long-run shift in demand away from housing, automobiles, and other consumer durables may result. While housing and durables provide important service flows, the tax treatment of service flows from durables may have led to overinvestment in them in the 1970s. Much of the spectacular rise in housing prices during the last decade was associated with the increasingly pro-durables bias imbedded in a very inflation-senstive system of capital income taxation. As inflation rose, so did effective taxes on capital income. This rise lowered the relative price of consuming durables because it lowered the opportunity costs of holding these durables. As a result, the demand for consumer durables in general, and housing in particular, was greatly stimulated. In the short run, housing prices were bid up dramatically, reflecting the tax-induced increased demand for housing services. The higher housing prices, in turn, stimulated construction of new housing, since it increased the price at which newly constructed houses could be sold.

An offsetting consideration with respect to the durables industries is the relatively more favorable treatment of the motor vehicle industry under the 1981 Tax Act (Table 5–7). The effective tax rate on the return to new investment in the motor vehicle industry has been cut from 26 to −11 percent.

Another pertinent point is that the tax structure is simply one of numerous determinants of the demand for different commodities. The surge in new family formation resulting from the baby-boom of the 1950s will lead to a strong demand for housing that could well swamp the effects of the tax change on residential investment. The same is likely to be true of other durables that are in relatively greater demand by young families setting up a household.

IMPLICIT TAXATION OF LABOR SUPPLY BY THE SOCIAL SECURITY AND WELFARE SYSTEMS

It is ironic that the social security and welfare programs may, themselves, contribute to the relatively low income levels of the elderly and the poor. Social security and welfare recipients may well face the highest marginal tax rates of any members of our society. These systems provide very small incentives to work. Not surprisingly, therefore, relatively few beneficiaries of these two programs work, especially at full-time jobs.

There is mounting evidence that the social security earnings test has contributed significantly to the dramatic increase in early retirement. In 1950 the labor force participation rate of males 65 and over was 46 percent; today it is only 20 percent. Not only are there fewer older men working on any given day during the year, but there are fewer older men who work at any time during the year. The fraction of men 65 to 69 who are completely retired has risen from 40 percent to 60 percent since 1960. For males 60 to 64 the retirement rate is now 30 percent, double the 1960 figure of 15 percent. Those older males who do choose to work are working fewer hours. Since 1967 the fraction of working males 65 and over who work part-time has increased from one-third to almost one-half. This reduction in work has occurred despite a substantial increase in the general health of people in this age group.

The social security earnings test currently reduces benefits by 50 cents for every dollar of earnings above $6,000 and represents a 50 percent implicit tax for workers aged 65 to 72. In combination with the Federal and State income taxes and the social security payroll tax, this 50 percent tax on earnings penalizes the work effort of the elderly at rates that can easily exceed 80 percent. These exceedingly large tax rates extend over a wide range of the typical older worker's potential supply of labor hours.

Eliminating the earnings test, as has been proposed by the Administration, would unquestionably increase the incomes of older workers as well as generate tax revenues that would offset a portion of the costs of doing so. Because of impending changes in the demographic structure of the population, it is important to reverse the trend toward early retirement. By the year 2025 the proportion of the population age 62 and over will rise to 24.5 percent, compared to 13.6 percent in 1981. The ratio of workers paying social security taxes to retired beneficiaries will fall from a current level of 3.7 to 2.4. If the work disincentives for older citizens were reduced, U.S. per capita income would rise more rapidly and social security's long-run financial position would be improved.

Current provisions of the social security system also generate work disincentives for a significant fraction of married women. While married women are joining the labor force in increasing numbers, the typical wife's earnings are still one-third to one-half that of husbands. Hence, the marginal tax contributions to social security of many wives will yield them no marginal social security benefits because they will collect benefits based on their husband's earnings record. (This applies only to retirement and medicare benefits. A wife who becomes disabled cannot currently collect disability benefits based on her husband's account.) The combined employer-employee retirement and medicare tax rates total 11.75 percent and represent a pure marginal tax on the work effort of married women. The response to females to the level of net compensation is estimated to be quite high. Hence, the bias in the current structure regarding dependent and survivor benefits may represent a significant disincentive to the participation of married females in the labor force.

Similar work disincentives potentially reduce the labor supply of welfare recipients. Welfare recipients do not face a single and easily understood tax schedule relating their gross earnings to their net disposable income. Instead, they are confronted with eight different and highly complicated implicit and explicit tax schedules. These include the work and income tests of Aid to Families with Dependent Children (AFDC), food stamps, housing assistance, social security insurance and medicaid, the earned income tax credit, the Federal income tax, and State income taxes. Each of the welfare programs has its own eligibility requirements, its own definition of income, its own set of deductions and exclusions, and its own tax rates. These explicit and implicit tax systems differ across States as well. Even within a State, implicit tax schedules vary, depending on both the characteristics of the recipient and the discretion of the social service worker. The result of all this is a complex set of uncoordinated rules and regulations that surely leave welfare recipients confused and dismayed. Past reforms of the system simply added more and more programs, with little emphasis on how the work disincentives of new programs would interact with those of old programs.

The efficacy of any particular income transfer program cannot be determined in isolation from the rest of the system. Analyses of marginal tax rates arising from the combined earnings tests of the various welfare programs and the explicit Federal and State tax systems suggest that typical welfare recipients, namely single mothers with children, face marginal tax rates in excess of 75 percent. Reductions in these very high implicit and explicit tax rates might generate a sufficiently large addition to their labor supply to pay for themselves. As State and local governments assume fuller responsibility for the welfare system, they could effectively offset these high, marginal tax rates by providing additional work incentives.

As this section has shown, many households still face considerable work disincentives, despite the substantial changes enacted in the Economic Recovery Tax Act of 1981. Future reforms of social security and welfare policy should take account of these concerns.

MONETARY POLICY AS A FISCAL INSTRUMENT

The inclusion of monetary policy in a discussion of taxation may seem out of place, but monetary policy is an important instrument of taxation in the U.S. economy. Increases in the supply of money raise revenues for the Federal Government in three ways. First, faster growth of monetary aggregates leads to higher rates of inflation. Since the Federal personal income tax will not be indexed until 1985, inflation will continue to raise real taxes through the process of "bracket creep." Inflation pushes taxpayers into higher marginal tax brackets, although their real incomes may not have changed—i.e., their increase in nominal income may only have kept pace with inflation. Higher inflation rates also raise effective tax rates on capital income earned by corporate and noncorporate business (Table 5-6). This is due to the nonindexation of depreciation allowances, and, in many cases, the reduction in real tax deductions resulting from changes in inventories valued at historic rather than current cost. A reduction in inflation will have the effect of lowering marginal personal income tax rates and effective taxation of capital income.

The second way monetary policy acts as a fiscal instrument involves the interaction between deficit financing by the government and central bank open market operations. In the past the Treasury has paid in part for goods and services, by selling bonds to the public. When the Federal Reserve purchases Treasury bonds, it increases the monetary base. The net effect of these transactions is that the government acquires goods and services while the private sector is left holding a larger stock of money. The larger stock of money for the same amount of goods and services in the economy translates into a higher price level. The increase in prices then lowers the real purchasing power of the money held by the private sector, and the transfer of resources from the private sector to the government is complete.

A third way in which the government "taxes" the private sector through expansion of the monetary base is that the ensuing higher prices devalue nominal outstanding debt. The real capital losses experienced by the private sector on their holdings of outstanding government liabilities correspond to the real capital gains accruing to the government. Private investors are not, however, so foolish as to purchase government bonds in an inflationary environment without requiring higher interest payments to offset expected real capital losses on the nominal value of these bonds. Given this fact, the government collects real revenues from "watering down" the value of nominal debt only if the actual inflation rate exceeds the rate expected by the private sector. Actual rates of inflation in excess of expected rates appear to have been the case for much of the 1970s.

Standard government accounting procedures fail to record either the increase in base money or the real capital gains on outstanding nominal government debt as sources of financing government expenditures. Even when actual inflation equals expected inflation, an alternative method of bookkeeping would suggest entering the government's real capital gain as revenue, since the higher nominal interest payments required because of expected inflation are entered on the government's books as current real expenditures. The failure to use accounting procedures that recognize the impact of inflation disguises the government's actual method of financing its expenditures.

There are a variety of possible ways of analyzing changes in the government's net liabilities. Table 5–8 presents estimates of changes in the real market value of outstanding Federal net financial liabilities from 1966 to 1980. The table relates changes in the Federal Government's real net financial debt (valued at market prices) in 1980 dollars to the differences between its real expenditures and its real taxes, including taxation associated with money creation.

TABLE 5–8.—*Sources of changes in Federal Government's real net financial liabilities, 1966–80*

[Billions of 1980 dollars]

Year	Expenditures [1]	Sources of Government finances				Change in Federal Government's net financial liabilities [6]
		Tax revenues [2]	Change in monetary base [3]	Revaluation of net financial debt [4]	Other revenue sources plus statistical discrepancy [5]	
1966	331.9	327.7	9.2	7.9	−3.2	−9.7
1967	367.4	337.8	8.3	21.9	−.4	−.2
1968	388.0	374.9	10.1	24.0	−7.5	−13.5
1969	385.1	402.4	6.3	27.4	−4.1	−47.0
1970	396.3	372.3	10.1	−10.3	−.2	24.5
1971	407.6	367.0	13.9	12.1	−2.8	17.4
1972	433.5	403.7	6.0	31.7	−.7	−7.2
1973	443.5	434.1	12.6	46.0	−.8	−48.3
1974	461.9	444.2	9.1	55.9	−.5	−46.8
1975	504.0	406.1	10.2	−5.9	−7.8	101.5
1976	516.8	445.6	8.3	.1	−6.2	68.9
1977	534.9	476.0	15.0	57.0	−11.9	−1.1
1978	544.9	510.3	18.0	73.7	−11.1	−46.0
1979	555.0	538.9	10.4	105.2	−11.7	−87.8
1980	602.0	540.9	9.3	57.8	−2.5	−3.4

[1] Total expenditures, national income and product accounts (NIPA) basis.
[2] Total receipts, NIPA basis, deflated by GNP implicit price deflator.
[3] Changes in the monetary base equal the sum of changes in member bank reserves, vault cash of commercial banks, and currency outside banks, flow of funds accounts.
[4] Capital gains accruing to the Federal Government on its net financial liabilities.
[5] Other revenue sources include Federal sales of mineral rights and household insurance credits and the surplus of federally sponsored credit agencies' flow of funds accounts.
[6] The value of the Federal Government's net financial liabilities equals total liabilities minus financial assets valued at market prices. Liabilities of the Treasury held by the Federal Reserve as well as the social security trust funds are excluded from this series.

Sources: Department of Commerce (Bureau of Economic Analysis); Board of Governors of the Federal Reserve System; Eisner, Robert and Pieper, Paul, "Government Net Worth: Assets, Liabilities and Revaluations (1982)"; and Council of Economic Advisers.

In terms of this accounting framework, taxes associated with money creation—changes in the real monetary base and in the real worth of net financial debt—were quite significant in many of the last 30 years. In 1979, for example, these sources are estimated to have yielded $115.6 billion of real revenues to the government, or 18.0 percent of total 1979 revenue. According to these calculations, in 1979 the Federal Government's real net financial liabilities declined by $87.8 billion. In contrast, using the deflated statistics shown in Table 5–8, the difference between explicit expenditures and explicit tax revenues, was a $16.1 billion increase in government debt.

The estimates in Table 5–8 show that the Federal Government's real net financial assets increased in 11 of the 15 years between 1965 and 1980 in part as a result of the use of money creation to finance its expenditures. Official reports indicated a decline in government debt only in 1969. Given the financial markets' interests in increases in government debt, this approach to analyzing the Federal Government's financial status should be of interest.

While this concept of Federal debt suggests an improving fiscal position over the 1970s, a broader concept of Federal debt discussed in the appendix to Chapter 4 indicates that the Federal Government's total explicit and implicit liabilities have risen enormously over the last 20 years. The narrower focus of this section and objective of Table 5-7 is to point out that monetary growth raises sizable real taxes for the Federal Government. Monetary growth is a form of taxation. It is an insidious form of taxation. It is taxation that is not legislated by the Congress, it is taxation that is hard to understand, and it is taxation that inhibits economic growth by raising effective marginal tax rates on wages and on saving.

STRUCTURAL TAX POLICY AND ECONOMIC GROWTH

Structural tax policy probably constitutes the Federal Government's most powerful tool for influencing economic growth. If households anticipate their own and their descendants' future tax liabilities, changes in the tax structure generating the same revenue have only "substitution" effects on their decisions; "income" effects are zero or negligible. If households consider only their own future tax liabilities and not those of their descendants, income effects do arise for different age groups, but they are largely offsetting. Such changes in the tax structure do not change household budgets, in the aggregate, but they do change household incentives to work and save. The rate of savings and capital formation can be increased significantly by switching away from taxes on capital income to some other tax base, such as wages or consumption. As described earlier, reductions in the tax rates on capital income reduce the relative cost of future consumption and leisure and encourage the substitution of future consumption and leisure for current consumption and leisure. Such substitution leads to increases in the current supplies of both capital and labor.

The 1981 Tax Act's reduction in marginal tax rates on capital income under both personal and corporate income taxes, the provision for substantial increases in Individual Retirement Accounts and Keogh accounts, and the recent expansion of pension fund savings all constitute major reductions in taxation of capital income. These historic changes in the structure of taxation, assuming they are maintained for the indefinite future, are expected to lead to a significant long-term rise in the private business capital stock and increases in labor supply over what would otherwise be the case.

While capital formation and economic growth are predicted to be enhanced, it should be emphasized that the choice of a tax base should be determined on grounds of economic welfare and efficiency, rather than simply the effect of structural tax change on factor supplies. Economic research suggests that rather sizable efficiency and welfare gains are available from switching from the taxation of wage and capital income to the taxation of consumption. In contrast, there is evidence that switching from wage and capital income taxation to wage taxation alone can reduce economic welfare and efficiency, even though this structural tax change would lead to more capital formation. In recent years, Federal tax policy has increasingly moved away from marginal taxation of capital income toward an alternative structure that can best be described as a hybrid mixture of wage and consumption taxation.

The change in the structure of taxation will increase labor supply and capital formation over time, provided there is no significant deterioration in the government's real net debt position. While the move away from marginal capital income taxation is necessary to stimulate saving, the Nation still retains a tax system that is overly complex, that is still sensitive to inflation (especially with respect to effective business taxation), that is administratively expensive, and that absorbs too much talent in the fundamentally nonproductive endeavor of what is gently termed "tax planning." In short, there is a need for further simplification and rationalization of the U.S. tax code.

CHAPTER 6

Reforming Government Regulation of Economic Activity

GOVERNMENT REGULATION OF ECONOMIC ACTIVITY expanded rapidly during the 1970s. Although regulation can serve useful purposes, changes in the world and national economies have aroused increasing concern that regulation is imposing excessive burdens on individuals and businesses. This chapter focuses on the Administration's efforts to reform the regulatory process. The present scope of Federal regulation is reviewed, and a framework is presented for judging the desirability of specific regulations. This framework is then used in reviewing the status of regulation in a number of important industries and sectors of the economy. The chapter concludes with a set of guidelines for regulatory reform.

THE GROWTH OF FEDERAL REGULATION

The number and size of the agencies devoted to carrying out Federal regulation have expanded rapidly during the past 15 years. Since the mid-1960s we have seen the formation of the Consumer Product Safety Commission, the Environmental Protection Agency, the Department of Energy, and the Occupational Safety and Health Administration, to cite just the better known ones. The recent growth in the number and size of regulatory agencies has been greater than that which took place during the New Deal period (Chart 6–1).

The direct costs of Federal regulatory activities to the taxpayers are large. As shown in Table 6–1, the regulatory expenses of Federal agencies were $2.8 billion in fiscal 1974 and increased to $5.5 billion in fiscal 1979. A further increase to $7.1 billion was budgeted for 1981, an amount 50 percent higher in constant dollars than the 1974 total.

It is apparent that the biggest budgets are not those for the independent regulatory commissions, such as the Interstate Commerce Commission or the Federal Communications Commission. The largest proportion of funds in recent years has been devoted to broader regulatory activities, such as those conducted by the Environmental Protection Agency, and the Department of Agriculture (mainly food inspection).

Chart 6-1

Growth of Federal Regulatory Agencies

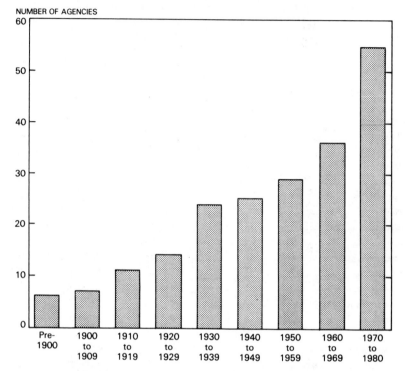

SOURCE: CENTER FOR THE STUDY OF AMERICAN BUSINESS.

REASONS FOR REGULATION

Why do governments become involved in regulating private economic activity? The question is not, of course, a simple one to answer, and numerous justifications for public intervention in the private sector have been offered. The basic reason advanced by economists is the occurrence of "market failure"—that is, the failure of competitive market forces to function efficiently in the allocation of goods and services. When there is no market failure, most economists would conclude that decentralized market decisions are superior to centralized government regulation.

Although regulation is often used by the government as a means of correcting market failure, regulatory action is not necessarily the only means available. For instance, consumers can be provided with information about goods or services offered for sale. Special taxes can be levied on polluters, or property rights could be extended to include the resources subject to pollution as discussed in Chapter 2.

TABLE 6-1.—*Regulatory outlays of Federal agencies, fiscal years 1974-81*

[Fiscal years; millions of dollars]

Agency	1974	1975	1976	1977	1978	1979	1980	1981 [1]
TOTAL	2,834	3,268	3,598	4,062	4,916	5,518	6,526	7,088
Agriculture	410	447	475	590	921	979	1,258	1,213
Commerce	76	75	86	94	99	115	129	147
Defense	10	16	22	32	38	43	41	45
Energy	33	6	40	49	79	82	132	144
Health and Human Services	165	201	218	245	276	300	326	347
Interior	5	6	9	13	22	55	105	184
Justice	22	30	31	35	45	66	62	60
Labor	208	257	314	332	373	446	486	539
Transportation	466	460	506	603	679	767	865	971
Treasury	161	166	185	246	267	288	317	335
Civil Aeronautics Board	89	81	91	103	101	99	117	147
Commodity Futures Trading Commission		1	11	13	14	15	16	19
Comptroller of the Currency	50	65	77	83	91	97	113	127
Consumer Product Safety Commission	19	34	38	40	40	39	44	42
Environmental Protection Agency	629	850	772	718	885	1,024	1,259	1,321
Equal Employment Opportunity Commission	42	56	59	72	74	92	131	140
Federal Communications Commission	38	48	52	56	64	70	76	80
Federal Deposit Insurance Corporation	58	66	74	88	105	115	116	130
Federal Energy Regulatory Commission	27	34	36	41	38	50	67	79
Federal Maritime Commission	6	7	8	8	9	10	11	12
Federal Trade Commission	32	39	44	52	59	63	68	69
International Trade Commission	7	8	10	11	12	12	14	18
Interstate Commerce Commission	38	44	47	59	65	67	77	77
National Labor Relations Board	55	61	68	81	90	97	109	119
National Transportation Safety Board	8	9	11	13	16	15	18	18
Nuclear Regulatory Commission	80	86	180	231	271	309	378	435
Securities and Exchange Commission	35	44	51	54	61	66	74	78
All other	65	71	83	100	122	137	117	192

[1] Data for 1981 are estimated using the budget revisions made in March 1981.

Source: "Directory of Federal Regulatory Agencies," Center for the Study of American Business, 3rd Edition, 1981.

Outside the realm of market failure, it is often claimed that "distributive justice," a concern about political or social equity, is a reason for governmental intervention. In other words, the government's involvement is seen primarily as a way of bringing about a transfer of wealth to a worthy segment of society. But in practice a small group (that is, a "special interest") usually benefits at the expense of the mass of consumers. This type of regulation is different from that designed to correct market failure, although the stated rationale may be similar. Although economics cannot provide sufficient guidance to resolve equity issues, it can assist by identifying the costs and benefits of alternative policies addressed to these issues.

AN OVERVIEW OF REGULATION

Many Federal rules have yielded benefits to the public. The automobile emission standards, for example, have substantially reduced emissions from this source.

Regulations, however, can also impose substantial costs on society. Regulations themselves can create problems which call for additional regulations. Furthermore, the resources used to comply with regulations are diverted from other activities, with a resultant loss in productivity and economic growth. Restrictions on the development of nuclear energy, for example, have resulted in expanding coal mining, which increases the probability that coal miners will be injured. Nor is it likely that the costs and benefits of regulations will be evenly shared. One group in society may receive the bulk of the benefits from a Federal regulation, while the costs are borne primarily by some other group. For example, regulations making it uneconomical to use low sulfur (low-polluting) coal have been supported by people in areas producing high sulfur coal. To the extent that these regulations have been successful in making low sulfur coal uneconomical, the producers in the low sulfur coal areas and consumers generally are losers as a result.

BENEFIT-COST ANALYSIS OF GOVERNMENT REGULATION

Interest has risen in efforts to determine more precisely the benefits and the costs of regulation. The motive for incorporating benefit-cost analysis into the regulatory decisionmaking process is to achieve a more efficient allocation of government resources by subjecting the public sector to the same type of efficiency tests used in the private sector. In making an investment decision, for example, business executives compare the costs to be incurred with the expected revenues. The investment is likely to be pursued only if the expected costs are less than the expected revenues.

The government agency decisionmaker does not face the same array of economic incentives and constraints. If the costs of an agency action exceed the benefits, the result may not have an immediate adverse impact on the agency. Analytical information on economic costs has in the past rarely existed in the public sector, so that, more often than not, the governmental decisionmaker has not been aware of approving a regulation that is economically inefficient. The aim of requiring agencies to perform benefit-cost analysis is to make the regulatory process more efficient and to eliminate regulatory actions that, on balance, generate more costs than benefits. This result is not assured by benefit-cost analysis, since political and other important considerations may dominate the decisionmaking. Even in those cases, however, benefit-cost analysis may provide valuable guidance.

The review of a proposed Federal regulatory activity should involve analysis of three types of questions. The first is whether some form of market failure has occurred that warrants the imposition of regulation. The second is whether Federal regulation, in contrast to State and local regulation, is appropriate. The last question, assuming the response to the first two is positive, is whether a specific regulation will increase net benefits to society. Traditionally, much of the responsibility for answering the first two questions has fallen on the Congress, while the last question has been addressed by the regulatory agencies.

Careful analysis of the first two questions, unfortunately, has often been neglected. Such analysis should address itself to whether there is any significant market imperfection in the absence of regulation. Observed differences in safety conditions among workplaces, for example, are not sufficient evidence of a market imperfection, because employer and employee knowledge of these conditions may lead to compensating differences in wages and employment conditions. Observed differences in economic outcomes among demographic groups are not sufficient evidence of discrimination because these differences may be the result of nondiscriminatory processes. More careful analysis of these types of issues is necessary to determine the existence and nature of any market imperfection.

For Federal regulations, in addition, it is important to determine whether the nature of the imperfection is such that Federal regulation, rather than State or local regulation, is appropriate. Federal regulation is most likely to be appropriate where the externalities of an activity in one State have substantial effects in other States or countries, the activity affects basic constitutional rights, or interstate commerce would be significantly disrupted by varying local regulations. In the absence of these conditions, State and local regulation is likely to be more efficient by more accurately reflecting local preferences and conditions.

When some Federal regulation is clearly appropriate, an analysis of its benefits and costs can provide valuable information to help select the form and extent of the regulation. In practice, a benefit-cost analysis will not always be a sufficient basis for resolving all controversy about the regulation. Given the increasing concern about the efficiency of Federal regulations, however, a more general use of benefit-cost analysis can contribute to a broader consensus on appropriate changes in the nature and degree of Federal regulations.

QUANTIFICATION

The benefits and costs attributable to regulation are the difference between the benefits and costs that would occur because of regulation and those that would prevail in its absence. Although this idea may seem straightforward, its application can be complex. Determining what would occur in the absence of regulation may involve a considerable amount of judgment.

Sometimes the indirect effects of regulation may be as important as the direct ones. Consider, for example, the question of tighter standards on emissions from new automobiles. Higher new car prices, attributable in part to these tighter standards, have reduced the rate at which older cars with higher emissions are being scrapped. A recent study indicates that the tighter emission standards implemented in the 1981 model year may increase total emissions for several years as a result of this process.

Even when it is not possible to put a dollar sign on benefits, a cost-effectiveness analysis still can be helpful by ranking the relative economic efficiency of alternatives. By using this method, originally developed for military programs, estimates can be made of the costs of different ways to accomplish an objective. Cost-effectiveness analyses permit policymakers to identify least-cost solutions. In this more limited approach, the analyst begins with the assumption that the regulatory objective is worth achieving. This approach may be particularly useful in dealing with programs to reduce personal hazards. Instead of dealing with such a difficult conceptual question as the economic value of human life, the emphasis shifts to identifying regulatory approaches that would maximize the number of lives saved for a given amount of resources.

Reliable measures of costs and benefits are not easily achieved or always possible. Should the loss of a forest, for example, be measured only by the value of the timber cut? What of the beauty destroyed? What of the area's value as a wildlife habitat? Such unquantifiable questions usually arise in the course of making a decision about any Federal regulation.

However, the difficulties involved in estimating benefits or costs need not serve as a deterrent to analysis. Merely identifying important but often overlooked impacts may be useful to the decisionmaking process. An example on the cost side is the beneficial drugs that are not available because of regulatory obstacles. An example on the benefit side is the more productive work force that results from a lower rate of accidents on the job.

THE EVOLUTION OF REGULATORY REVIEW

The last decade has been marked by a shift in emphasis from industry-specific regulations to rules affecting specific aspects of the operation of virtually all industries, such as occupational safety and environmental protection.

The recent expansion of Federal regulatory activity has occurred despite the fact that the Federal Government has no explicit power to regulate intrastate economic activity. The 10th amendment, which reserves to the States and the people all powers not delegated to the United States, confirms the States' powers to enact laws to protect public health, safety, morals, and general welfare. The Federal Government was not given comparable power, except as such activity affects interstate commerce.

The recent growth of Federal regulation of economic activities has been based largely on broadened judicial interpretation of the scope of the "commerce clause," which gives the Congress the power "to regulate Commerce with foreign Nations, and among the several States, and with the Indian Tribes." Until the Great Depression, Federal regulation of the economy was small in comparison to control exercised by the States. Since that time, however, Federal regulation has expanded and numerous Federal regulatory agencies have been created and given broad discretion by the Congress to regulate the economic activity of private institutions. But the Congress and the executive branch have been limited in their ability to control the specific decisions of regulatory agencies, although both can exert some control through the appointments process, the budget, and changes in enabling statutes.

Concern has grown that many of the decisions of regulatory agencies are economically inefficient. Explicit guidance to an agency to weigh the costs and benefits of its decisions has been Federal law since it was included in the Rivers and Harbors Act of 1902. The benefit-cost procedure was explicitly required for the first time under the Flood Control Act of 1936. Until the 1970s, however, the benefit-cost technique was used with regularity only in reviewing expenditure programs.

In 1975 a major expansion in the use of benefit-cost analysis occurred when the President directed regulatory agencies to prepare "inflation impact statements" to accompany proposed rules. Under the next Administration this approach was modified to require "regulatory analyses." However, it was stressed that its requirements for regulatory analysis should not be interpreted as subjecting proposed rules to a benefit-cost test.

Regulatory relief is a key element of the President's economic recovery plan, along with expenditure restraint, tax cuts, and monetary stability. Executive Order 12291, issued on February 17, 1981, directs agencies, to the extent permitted by law, to use benefit-cost analysis when promulgating new regulations, reviewing existing regulations, or developing legislative proposals concerning regulation. Administrative decisions on regulations are to be based on adequate information concerning the need for the regulations and their economic consequences. Not only must the benefits from the regulation exceed the costs, but the Executive order requires that the approach selected (where alternative approaches exist) should be chosen to maximize net benefits.

In the case of major rules, agencies must publish preliminary and final regulatory impact analyses (RIAs) that set forth conclusions regarding the benefit-cost balance and feasible alternatives. Major rules consist of those that will have any of the following three effects: (1) an annual effect of $100 million or more; (2) a major increase in costs or prices; or (3) a significant adverse effect on a specific industry or on the economy in general. Regulatory impact analyses are to include: (1) a description of the potential costs and benefits of the proposed rule; (2) a determination of its potential net benefits; and (3) a description of feasible cheaper alternatives with an explanation of the legal reasons why such alternatives, if proposed, could not be adopted. The analyses and rules must be submitted to the Office of Management and Budget before publication in the *Federal Register*.

In addition, regulatory agencies must review rules currently in effect and prepare regulatory impact analyses for those which are classified as major. The Executive order also requires agencies to publish semiannual calendars of proposed regulations and current regulations that are under review.

To spearhead the Administration's regulatory relief efforts, the President created the Task Force on Regulatory Relief, which is chaired by the Vice President. The task force reviews proposed regulations, using the guidelines established by Executive Order 12291, and is assessing existing regulations with an eye toward their revision. During 1981 the task force earmarked 100 existing rules and paperwork requirements for review, and more than a third of those reviews have already resulted in formal proposals or final action to eliminate or revise the rules and programs involved. The task force will designate other existing programs for review, and it will continue to press for formal action to implement the conclusions of the reviews.

Through December 31, 1981, the Office of Management and Budget (OMB) had reviewed 2,715 proposed regulations and had approved 2,546 as being consistent with the Executive order. These numbers do not reflect the number of regulations that were evaluated within the agencies and found to be inconsistent with the Executive order and therefore not submitted to OMB. Agencies have issued 40 major regulations. Nineteen were supported by regulatory impact analyses, while analyses of the 21 others were waived for such reasons as emergency conditions.

Although the Executive order is an important procedural reform, some important regulatory areas are still immune from OMB review. These are areas under the regulatory authority of independent agencies, such as the Federal Trade Commission, and programs under the authority of executive branch agencies which are guided by other standards based on their enabling legislation. In these areas it will take legislative changes to open up regulatory activities to OMB review.

Recent court decisions have demonstrated the importance of including specific economic efficiency criteria in the enabling legislation of agencies. In its June 1981 decision on standards established for acceptable levels of cotton dust in textile plants, the Supreme Court held that an agency must meet the standard of "feasibility" if that is the standard established by its enabling legislation, whether or not the regulation is reasonable on the basis of other criteria, such as economic efficiency.

Just as a standard of feasibility can cause agencies to make inefficient regulatory decisions, so can a standard of reasonableness. For example, the Fifth Circuit Court held that Interstate Commerce Commission (ICC) guidelines that allowed motor carriers to seek the removal of restrictions on which commodities they might carry, but only by choosing to carry commodities in one of three categories, exceeded ICC's authority under the Motor Carrier Act of 1980 to "reasonably broaden" existing carrier certificates. Although the guidelines could be supported on economic grounds as increasing competition, they were rejected by the court because they failed to meet the legal definition of "reasonable." Although the agency can still exercise some discretion in broadening categories, substantial further deregulation of the for-hire trucking industry may be dependent on a change in the law that would eliminate limitations on the commodities that a certificated carrier can transport.

The Administration has also been working with the Congress on legislation that would require economic analysis of proposed regulations. The Congress has held extensive hearings on several bills that would require all Federal regulatory agencies to analyze the costs and benefits of their major regulations. The Administration is supporting S. 1080, which would codify the requirements of Executive Order 12291 so that it would apply to all agencies. In addition, the bill would require that each major rule be reviewed every 10 years.

THE CLEAN AIR ACT AND ECONOMIC ANALYSIS

The most important regulatory enabling legislation now being reviewed by the Congress is the Clean Air Act. Many of the questions that permeate social regulation arise in the case of this landmark law. The Council of Economic Advisers has developed three general principles which illustrate the role of economic analysis in designing a regulatory program such as the Clean Air Act.

First, Federal regulation should focus on situations where there is a clear national problem. An example of this approach would be strengthening Federal responsibility for dealing with air pollution transported across State and national boundaries while leaving air pollution problems that are local in nature to State or local governments whenever practical.

Second, the benefits and costs of regulation should be considered in designing a new regulatory program. For example, various emission standards could be set at levels at which the incremental benefits are equal to the incremental costs, and benefits and costs could be considered when determining State implementation strategies.

Third, consumers, businesses, and State and local governments should be granted flexibility in the way they meet Federal standards. Thus, those subject to regulation would be encouraged to use the lowest cost means for achieving standards.

The following discussion shows how these three principles relate to several important provisions of the Clean Air Act.

LONG-RANGE TRANSPORT

The pollution control programs established under the current Clean Air Act focus on improving ground-level air quality relatively near the sources of pollution. Although the act contains provisions for States to notify the Environmental Protection Agency (EPA) if a neighboring State is "exporting" its pollution, EPA's authority to order remedies is limited. Moreover, the States typically have been unable to arrive independently at appropriate and inexpensive solutions to such problems through negotiation or litigation. Therefore, a case can be made for strengthening Federal involvement in air pollution problems which transcend State or national boundaries.

AMBIENT AIR STANDARDS

The Clean Air Act requires EPA to set uniform primary and secondary National Ambient Air Quality Standards (NAAQS) for several pollutants that are considered to endanger public health and welfare. The primary NAAQS are to be set at levels adequate to "protect the public health," with an "adequate margin of safety" to account for scientific uncertainties. However, a Federal court has ruled that the consideration of costs in setting the primary standards is prohibited.

The secondary standards are to be set at levels that protect the public welfare, which covers such things as property damage. The consideraton of costs is also constrained in setting secondary standards.

If the Federal Government were given effective authority to regulate pollution that crosses State and national boundaries, then the States could play a major role in establishing the primary air quality standards and an exclusive role in establishing secondary standards. The Federal Government could set a presumptive primary ambient air standard, but the States would be free to modify the national primary standard applicable to them in light of local conditions. The setting of secondary standards could be left entirely to the States. The desirability of such changes, of course, depends on a variety of factors in addition to economic impact.

TECHNOLOGY-BASED STATIONARY SOURCE STANDARDS

The Clean Air Act requires EPA and the States to establish emissions standards for stationary sources. EPA must set new source performance standards primarily on the basis of the cost and availability of control technologies and the financial strength of the individual industries.

The current system of technology-based emissions standards, however, creates numerous difficulties. EPA does not consider benefits when setting stationary source standards. The standards are set primarily on the basis of the feasibility of the control technology, subject to an industry's ability to pay for the controls. The benefits and costs of air pollution control are, therefore, only considered indirectly.

Second, under these standards the marginal cost of emission controls may vary widely among different sources within a given region, thereby unnecessarily increasing the total costs of abatement. For example, more stringent controls on new sources than on existing sources often lead to a much higher marginal cost per ton of pollutant removed in new plants than in old, even though a ton of pollutant causes comparable health damage, regardless of its source. The requirement for more stringent standards on new sources may inhibit plant modernization and, by delaying the replacement of older plants, may even increase near-term pollution.

Many students of the subject have urged that the current system be changed to a system in which marketable permits would be used as the principal means of achieving control over stationary source emissions. Under a marketable permit system, the State or local pollution control authority would issue a number of emissions permits consistent with ambient air quality goals. In areas currently within the standards but experiencing economic growth, the operators of existing sources of pollution would have an incentive to sell their permits to new polluters when the market value of the permits exceeded the costs of controlling existing sources of pollution. This would ensure that ambient standards were achieved at lowest total cost. In areas not yet meeting the standard, some of the emissions permits would expire on a predetermined schedule to bring the area into compliance. In this view, the trading of permits among sources would help to assure that the standard was reached using the most efficient controls.

EPA has been moving toward a transferable permit system with its "bubble," "emission banking," and "offset" policies. However, EPA's efforts are seriously constrained by statutory directives that require the establishment of various technology-based standards for different types of sources of air pollution.

In addition, the 1977 amendments to the act require new source performance standards for fossil-fuel-fired stationary sources to be set in terms of a percentage reduction from uncontrolled emissions rates rather than as a maximum allowable emissions rate. Hence, the percentage reduction in emissions must be the same for both low and high sulfur coal. Since low sulfur coal is generally more expensive than high sulfur coal and the legislation requires that the percentage reduction in emission rates be the same for sources using either type of coal, the legislation creates an incentive to burn high sulfur coal even though low sulfur coal might be the most cost-effective method of meeting the goals of the legislation.

MOBILE SOURCE STANDARDS

The Clean Air Act directs EPA to enforce uniform national standards for motor vehicle emissions. California has been allowed to maintain a more stringent set of standards for vehicles sold in that

State. In the view of some analysts, the uniform Federal standards result in overcontrolling motor vehicle emissions in some relatively clean areas and perhaps undercontrolling emissions in some relatively polluted areas.

An alternative approach would be to allow EPA to issue two sets of standards: a stringent set for autos registered in areas with severe air pollution problems, and a less stringent set for autos registered in relatively clean areas. Each State would decide which of the two sets of standards its cars would be required to meet, which would depend on the State's ambient air standards.

According to its proponents, such a strategy would not cause significant environmental or health damage, since the less stringently controlled vehicles would be registered in areas where additional automotive emissions would not violate the standards. Moreover, studies show that such a strategy might substantially reduce the national costs of controlling automotive emissions.

The Clean Air Act has been interpreted to mean that every automobile line must meet applicable national emissions standards. This prevents EPA from allowing the manufacturers to meet the standards by averaging the results of different model lines. An alternative approach, allowing EPA to use an averaging procedure in determining compliance, might save consumers millions of dollars. Such a change would not increase overall emissions and thus presumably would leave average public health conditions unaffected.

The Clean Air Act requires that, starting in the 1984 model year, all cars and light trucks must meet the act's high altitude standards, regardless of the area in which the vehicles are sold. This requirement will have the effect of significantly increasing the amount of emissions control required of all cars. Since only 3.5 percent of the country's cars are sold at the specified high altitudes (principally in and around Denver), this uniform national requirement may require a large amount of unnecessary expenditures.

HAZARDOUS EMISSIONS STANDARDS

The Clean Air Act instructs EPA to prepare a list of air pollutants that may cause serious damage to human health and to set emissions (but not ambient) standards for them. The emissions standards are to be set at levels which provide "an ample margin of safety to protect the public health."

Consideration of benefits and costs is not prohibited in listing the pollutants or setting emissions standards, but it is not required either. In its rulemakings to date and in its proposed "Airborne Carcinogens Policy," EPA has not always balanced the benefits of air pollution control against its costs.

THE CONTROL OF HEALTH CARE COSTS: A CONTRAST OF APPROACHES

The policies of this Administration toward the health care industry offer an interesting contrast to the policies of earlier Administrations. Few analysts doubt that there are serious economic problems in this industry. The previous Administration attempted to solve these problems by proposing a Hospital Cost Containment Act, but the Congress did not pass the proposed bill, which would have imposed a detailed regulatory scheme on hospital managements. This Administration has examined the basic causes of inefficiencies in medical care and is attempting to change the factors which lead to them. These inefficiencies are due to inappropriate tax policy and to inadequate incentives for both consumers of medical services and providers of health care to reduce costs. In this section the structure of the industry will be examined to show the nature of the problems, and the changes proposed by the Administration to resolve these problems are discussed.

THE INDUSTRY

The health care industry is large, and it is growing rapidly. In 1980 the Nation spent nearly $250 billion on health, representing 9.4 percent of the total gross national product (GNP), substantially more than the $42 billion and 6.0 percent of GNP in 1965. Prices for health care have risen more rapidly than prices as a whole throughout the postwar period. From 1975 to 1980 prices in the health sector rose at an annual rate of 9.1 percent, compared to a rise of 7.4 percent for all personal consumption.

Rising expenditures resulted in a larger quantity and a higher quality of health care, as well as better access for the poor and elderly to medical services. But because of the structure of the health care industry, this expansion caused a substantial amount of waste. Were the rising expenditures simply due to changing consumer preferences, rising incomes, or improved technology, there would be no policy problem. The manner in which people choose to make unsubsidized purchases is generally not a policy matter. Much of the increase, however, has been due to perverse incentives that are built into the medical system. A set of arrangements for buying and selling health services has developed which insulates the participants from the economic consequences of their actions and raises serious questions about the effectiveness of these increased expenditures in buying more "health." The major problems are the prevalence of third-party payments and the exclusion of employer contributions for health insurance from the taxable income of employees.

147

A major defect of the system is a lack of competitive forces among those who supply health care. Providers of care who are paid according to the costs they incur—cost-based reimbursement—have little incentive to provide care in a cost-effective manner. Retrospective payments, where payments are based on expenses previously incurred, require large administrative bureaucracies in the private as well as the public sectors, and provide little reward for attempts to improve efficiency.

Health maintenance organizations (HMOs), which provide virtually complete coverage for a flat premium, have introduced an element of competition into the supply side of the industry. The incentives for efficient use of health resources rest with the HMOs, not the patients, and health maintenance organizations appear to have succeeded in reducing hospitalization use among their members.

Third-Party Payments

Meanwhile, third-party payments by private insurance companies or through government programs lower the prices of medical services to people covered by the programs, thus increasing the quantity of medical services which they seek and bidding up total medical costs. The larger the fraction of costs borne by third parties, the larger the effect of third-party payments on the price and quantity of services consumed.

Two-thirds of the personal health care expenditures of $218 billion in 1980 were paid by third parties. One hundred and seventy million people have private insurance for hospital care, 18 million of the nonelderly poor are covered under medicaid, and 24 million elderly receive medical care under the medicare program. (There is some overlap among people in these categories, particularly private plans and medicare.) About 23 million people in the country do not have public or private insurance coverage.

The particular provisions of insurance plans determine the prices that individual patients face and the effect of third-party payments on demand. For example, a system of deductibles and copayments makes the individual share in the costs. It leads to a more efficient use of resources than a plan that covers all medical expenses, beginning with the first dollar of expense. With "first-dollar" coverage, the individual has no financial incentive not to seek treatment if it has any chance of being beneficial, regardless of its cost. First-dollar coverage is necessarily more "shallow" than cost-sharing plans with the same premium and provides less insurance against unexpected serious illnesses.

The extent of first-dollar coverage and its costs to the individual vary greatly, but it is prevalent in the private sector. In the public sector one finds medicare, which, like first-dollar coverage, is not designed to encourage efficient use of health care resources. The medicare program only imposes cost sharing late in the hospital stay, when the patient can least afford it and when it is least likely to influence doctor or patient behavior, and it puts no limit on the out-of-pocket costs people can incur. States are required to provide basic services to medicaid recipients but are unable to require even minimal copayments. Instead, nonmarket mechanisms, such as regulation and rationing of services, are used to restrain utilization and costs.

Since most people are risk-averse they seek to avoid large and uncertain costs, such as those which may be imposed by a serious illness. This is why individuals buy insurance, even though the cost of insurance is greater than the expected value of the benefits. Expenses which are relatively small and predictable, on the other hand, are generally not covered by insurance. It is not rational for medical insurance to provide first-dollar coverage, since much of this insurance would be for predictable routine expenses. Rational medical insurance would contain coverage against catastrophic occurrences where medical expenses might bankrupt an individual. The reality is quite different from the logical arrangement just outlined. Some private plans provide first-dollar coverage but no catastrophic coverage. This is also true of medicare.

The inefficient use of resources that results from third-party payments leads to higher insurance premiums, even though the insurance is sold in the private market, where competitive forces presumably would lead to a lower premium. One reason why this does not happen is that employer contributions for health insurance premiums are not subject to payroll or income taxes.

Tax Exclusion

This tax exclusion lowers the price of health insurance to employers and employees, thereby leading to greater spending on insurance than if employer contributions for health care were included in taxable income or if individuals bought insurance with their own money. For the employee in the 30 percent income tax bracket paying social security tax of 6.65 percent, a $100 contribution by the employer to health insurance costs the worker in effect only $63.35 compared to receiving the $100 as taxable income and buying the insurance directly. Even though the worker may not want to spend another $100 of his own money on health insurance, if he values the additional insurance at more than $63.35, he will prefer that his employer put the $100 into health insurance rather than into his taxable earnings. For workers in higher tax brackets the amount of inefficiency is even greater. Employers also prefer to put the $100 into insurance premiums rather than into wages, since they do not pay social security and unemployment insurance taxes on the premiums.

149

The dilution of competition in the health care industry and the resultant inefficiencies have frequently led consumers to purchase more health care than they would have purchased if compelled to pay true costs. The lack of competition means that people receive less "health" for their expenditures, and by spending so much on health they have less to spend on other goods and services. It is difficult to quantify this loss in efficiency, but recent estimates place it in the range of $25 billion a year.

PROPOSALS FOR REFORM

Policymakers have recognized these inefficiencies and have attempted to devise solutions, but the standard solution chosen has been detailed regulation of the behavior of participants in the system. The alternative to that kind of regulation, as discussed in Chapter 2, is to give participants in the medical care system more incentive to use resources efficiently. This Administration is adopting this approach.

A proposal is under consideration which would require medicare beneficiaries to pay a part of the costs for each day they are in the hospital. In addition, a catastrophic health insurance plan which would guarantee that annual costs to the patient would not exceed a certain amount is also being considered. These proposals would reduce many inefficiencies in the system. Other proposals aimed at increasing competition in the medical care system are currently under development.

Some analysts have suggested replacing medicare with a voucher scheme. Recipients would be given a voucher nearly equal to the current cost of medicare and would be able to use this voucher to buy whatever form of medical insurance they desired, subject to certain constraints. This would give beneficiaries an incentive to purchase more efficient forms of medical insurance, since they would reap the savings.

REGULATORY REFORM IN THE AGENCIES

The current status of Federal regulation can be illustrated by a review of the situations in five key areas: financial institutions, agriculture, energy, transportation, and telecommunications.

FINANCIAL INSTITUTIONS

Federal regulation of financial institutions was initially designed to assure that savings channeled into investments were protected and that investors had enough information to make rational decisions on investments. The early regulatory statutes, however, reflected an ambivalent attitude toward competition in the financial industry. Restrictions on bank mergers and interstate branch banking were imposed to prevent banking monopoly, but at the same time restrictions on types of assets, entry, and rates of interest paid to depositors were imposed to limit competition and dissuade managers from risky ventures. A legal separation of depository institutions and securities firms was written into law in response to concern about conflicts of interest.

Over the last decade, however, technological innovation, high inflation, and the slowness of some regulatory bodies to adjust their regulations to conditions in the financial markets have made traditional depository institutions less attractive to depositors. They have found it more advantageous to shift their funds among institutions or, in many cases, to move them outside the banking system itself.

Thrift Institutions

The principal cause of the thrift industry's current problems is the imbalance between increasingly rate-sensitive liabilities and long-term fixed-rate assets. Time and savings deposits, the major sources of funds for thrift institutions, have traditionally been subject to Federal interest rate ceilings. These funds enabled the thrifts to make long-term loans, for such things as residential mortgages, at fixed rates of interest during times of steady and low interest rates. As interest rates began to rise in the 1970s, however, regulation prevented the thrift institutions from increasing the interest they paid on deposits to compete with other institutions, which had begun to offer a higher return on alternative instruments. Some regulatory changes then were made to allow thrifts to pay market rates of interest on certain types of deposits as well. These changes, however, did not eliminate the long-term problem faced by many thrifts. The need to finance large numbers of fixed-rate long-term loans at low interest rates with deposits on which they paid higher interest rates severely strained many thrift institutions.

The removal of two restrictions provided some relief for thrifts. In 1979 they were given limited authority to make loans at variable rates of interest, and in 1981 most restrictions on variable-rate loans were lifted. Meanwhile, they have also obtained permission to invest in the futures markets as a way of hedging their risks.

The Administration supports proposed legislation that would give thrift institutions greater flexibility in carrying out their operations. Various proposals would give thrift institutions many of the same powers to vary their assets and liabilities that commercial banks now have. Thrift institutions would be permitted to make additional short-term consumer and commercial loans in addition to residential mortgage loans, and alternative mortgage instruments would be established to make real estate lending more attractive. Other provisions of proposed legislation would clarify the authority to utilize interstate and interindustry mergers to rescue troubled thrifts and commercial banks, thereby leading to stronger financial institutions.

Commercial Banks

Under the Glass-Steagall Act of 1933, depository institutions and securities firms became legally separate entities offering quite different types of services. In recent years, however, high interest rates have led securities firms to offer investors the opportunity to invest in money-market mutual funds, a change that has, in effect, circumvented the 1933 act. The funds invested in money-market funds, unlike those deposited in commercial bank and thrift institution savings accounts, are not subject to interest rate ceilings, and investors are generally allowed limited checkwriting privileges. As a result, depositors over the last several years have withdrawn substantial amounts of funds from low interest accounts at banks and thrifts to place their money in high yielding money-market instruments, including money-market funds and government securities.

Within the bounds of their statutory constraints, banks have been trying to meet this new form of competition. They have, for example, been offering their customers access to market-level rates of interest through repurchase agreements against their portfolios of government securities. In many respects, however, the regulations that apply to banks remain more restrictive than those that apply to securities firms.

The Administration has proposed that commercial banks be permitted to engage in some activities previously reserved for securities firms through the establishment of bank holding company subsidiaries. Commercial banks would be authorized to set up these subsidiaries to underwrite and deal in municipal revenue bonds and to sponsor and underwrite shares in mutual funds. Such a change would help to equalize competition for funds between commercial banks and securities firms. The use of the holding company subsidiary would help separate the riskier securities activities of a bank from its federally insured depository activities.

Regulatory Relief

Thrift institutions, commercial banks, and securities firms should be allowed to compete on an equal basis, without the restrictions that prevent them from offering similar services and paying competitive rates. The Congress has recently passed laws that should go further toward achieving a competitive environment, and the regulatory agencies themselves have taken decisions to bring about more competition.

Under the Depository Institutions Deregulation and Monetary Control Act of 1980, interest rate ceilings on time and savings deposits are to be raised over a period of 6 years, after which the ceilings will be abolished. The same law permitted depository institutions to offer negotiable order of withdrawal (NOW) accounts, and certain State usury ceilings were preempted. Uniform reserve requirements on transactions liabilities at all depository institutions are being phased in, and the Federal Reserve System has begun charging banks for certain services previously provided without charge.

The Depository Institutions Deregulation Committee, created under authority of the 1980 act, adopted two significant deregulatory actions in 1981. It removed the ceiling on interest rates paid on 2½ to 4-year small saver certificates, resulting in a 50 percent increase in purchases of such certificates between August and the end of 1981, and it authorized a 1½-year account that would not be subject to interest rate ceilings for Individual Retirement Accounts (IRAs) and Keogh deposits.

During the last decade, the financial regulatory system has not adapted quickly to a changing economic environment. To ensure the future adaptability of financial institutions to evolving technology and competitive forces, regulation of the financial industry needs to be reviewed and reformed.

AGRICULTURE

Three important regulatory programs relating to agriculture present important issues: food safety, Federal marketing orders, and meat inspection.

Food Safety

Certain food safety laws and regulations are outdated and fail to show adequate recognition of the fact that there is a degree of risk inherent in providing an economical and sufficient food supply. These points can be illustrated by a discussion of the problems that have arisen in connection with the Delaney anticancer clauses of the 1958 Food Additives amendment to the Federal Food, Drug, and Cosmetic Act. The Delaney clauses prohibit the use of any chemical substance in any amount as a food additive if the substance has been found, by appropriate tests, to induce cancer in people or laboratory animals.

Scientific progress since the Delaney clauses were enacted in 1958 has brought about a quantum improvement in the ability of scientists to measure chemical substances. It is now possible to detect parts per trillion of a chemical substance in food. This is significant, since uncertainty exists regarding the degree of risk to human beings from exposure to extremely low levels of carcinogens, and strict enforcement can result in ignoring severe impacts on food availability and preservation.

It seems clear that the zero-risk approach embodied in the Delaney clauses has become untenable. Policymakers and scientists need to establish procedures for defining levels of food contaminants that represent acceptable levels of risk for consumers, develop ways to help consumers protect themselves against significant risks when such risks are found to exist for particular foods, and give firms incentives to develop safe food additives and to reduce contaminants.

Marketing Orders

Legislative authority for Federal marketing orders is contained in the Agricultural Marketing Agreement Act of 1937. The orders originally were designed partly to reflate farm prices and thus increase farmer income during the 1930s. Federal marketing orders for fruits, vegetables, and specialty crops establish restrictions on the quality and quantity of products that can be marketed. Those restrictions vary, but they may include minimum grade and size requirements, limits on product shipments during all or part of the marketing season, limits on quantities entering the fresh market, restrictions on total marketings (in a few cases), and rules on packaging standards. During 1980 commodities marketed under the orders had a farm value of $5.2 billion.

As a part of the Department of Agriculture's regulatory reform effort, a team comprised of Department of Agriculture and university economists was appointed during 1981 to examine the economic effects of marketing orders for fruits, vegetables, and specialty crops. The study revealed that Federal orders for hops, spearmint oil, California-Arizona navel oranges, valencia oranges, and lemons (and perhaps those for walnuts and filberts) had been used in ways that resulted in significant resource misallocation. Marketing allotments, market allocation provisions, and season-long prorates were the provisions identified as having the greatest capacity for causing misallocation. It was also reported that marketing orders can increase economic efficiency by stabilizing returns to growers, providing quality assurance for buyers, and facilitating research and container standardization.

Early in 1982, Department of Agriculture officials issued policy guidelines on marketing orders calling for changing the procedures to curb the supply restrictions resulting from the use of producer allotments, to lessen restrictions on handler shipments caused by prorate provisions, to reduce supply restrictions caused by stockpiling of reserves, and to limit the incentives for chronic overproduction. If carried out, these changes will produce substantial efficiencies.

Federal milk orders establish the minimum prices that milk processors pay farmers for Grade A milk. Basically, these orders are price discrimination (classified pricing) devices. Approximately two-thirds of the milk marketed in the United States (valued at $12.2 billion at the plant level) was priced under Federal milk orders in 1981.

Without this kind of regulation, some milk processors would have an incentive to purchase concentrated milk products (e.g., unsalted butter and nonfat dry milk) from lower cost sources and add water to produce a reconstituted fluid milk product. Little reconstituted milk is now sold in the United States, partly because Federal milk order regulations strongly encourage processors to buy fresh milk.

During 1979 the Department of Agriculture was asked to hold a hearing on the question of whether to make reconstituted milk less expensive for use by processors. This also would have reduced retail milk prices, since market forces would tend to force processors to pass along a portion of their savings to consumers. After extensive study, the Department denied the request for a hearing in April 1981, chiefly because the proposal would have undermined the classified pricing system, caused losses to dairy farmers that would have exceeded the gains to consumers and the Federal Government, and ignored the fact that consumers presently have a lower cost alternative to fresh milk priced under the orders—that is, to buy dry milk and add the water themselves. These are important considerations. However, if new technologies for handling concentrated milk products are to be accommodated under the Federal orders, this issue will deserve reexamination in the future.

Meat Inspection

The Department of Agriculture has developed draft legislation to increase the flexibility and reduce the costs of its meat and poultry inspection programs. Present meat and poultry inspection laws—some of which date back to the early 1900s—emphasize continuous, on-site inspection of slaughtering and processing plants. The proposed change would permit periodic inspection—for example, once a week or once a month—of meat and poultry processing plants which have good quality control systems, while retaining continuous inspection of slaughtering plants. The proposed change would reduce the Department of Agriculture's costs as well as those of plants with effective quality control systems.

While this proposed legislation would produce savings in the Federal meat inspection program, where costs now run to $300 million a year, other methods might permit still larger savings and produce other efficiencies. Such alternative programs would include user fees to cover certain meat and poultry inspection costs, licensed and bonded private inspectors rather than government inspectors, inspection and insurance arrangements that would give meat processors incentives to maintain effective quality control systems to qualify for low-cost product liability insurance, and periodic rather than continuous inspection of poultry slaughtering plants.

ENERGY

Many of the past energy policies of the government have not been consistent with the general principles presented in Chapter 2 for government intervention. The actual effects of such policies have been highly adverse to the interests of the Nation. The policy of this Administration is to remove the inconsistency, inefficiencies, and uncertainty caused by inherited policy, and thereafter to facilitate the operation of market forces as the guiding and disciplining constraints shaping investment, production, and consumption decisions in the energy sector.

Decontrol of the Petroleum Markets

Beginning with the Economic Stabilization Program of 1971, the petroleum sector has been subject to continuous price and allocation controls. Because price controls increase quantities demanded and reduce quantities supplied, they must be accompanied by nonprice rationing mechanisms. The complex system of controls included entitlements regulations, the "buy-sell" program, and other rules serving that purpose. These made the task of efficiently allocating available supplies of crude oil and refined products much more difficult. Other rules gave special consideration to small refiners and other interests, thus introducing additional distortions into the system. In particular, the rules provided strong disincentives to prepare for possible future supply interruptions.

As the inefficiencies and other adverse effects of the controls became increasingly manifest, the Congress enacted a law to phase out all petroleum controls by September 30, 1981. Using the legal discretion available to him, the President moved the date of full decontrol forward by about 8 months. It is instructive to review the data on some of the more salient effects of full decontrol.

The steady decline in domestic production (excluding oil from Prudhoe Bay) during the price control period has been reversed (Tables 6-2 and 6-3). November 1981 marked the fourth consecutive month of production increases over year-earlier levels, a feat not observed in the United States for 10 years. Furthermore, oil-drilling activity in 1981 was almost 40 percent greater than in 1980 (Table 6-2). There has also been a reduction in petroleum imports, part of which is probably due to other factors (Table 6-4). The entitlements regulations provided artificial incentives to import crude oil and residual fuel oil; the abolition of the regulatory framework has removed that incentive. The end of artificially high oil import levels has had a favorable effect upon exchange rates, and thus upon the prices of foreign goods in the United States. This reduced price of the foreign goods basket is a major benefit of oil decontrol to the domestic economy. One study has estimated the value of this wealth gain at almost $6 billion a year.

TABLE 6-2.—*Domestic crude oil production and drilling activity, 1973–81*

Period	Production (thousands of barrels per day)	Oil wells drilled (excludes dry holes)
1973	9,208	9,902
1974	8,774	12,784
1975	8,375	16,408
1976	8,132	17,059
1977	7,937	18,912
1978	7,618	17,775
1979	7,269	19,383
1980	7,076	27,026
1981	[1] 7,050	[1] 37,645
1981:		
January	7,020	[1] 1,789
February	7,068	[1] 2,462
March	7,069	[1] 3,102
April	7,020	[1] 2,905
May	7,001	[1] 2,604
June	7,072	[1] 3,497
July	6,902	[1] 2,790
August	7,054	[1] 3,137
September	7,117	[1] 3,416
October	[1] 7,107	[1] 3,775
November	[1] 7,082	[1] 3,587
December	[1] 7,095	[1] 4,581

[1] Preliminary.

Note.—Production data exclude Prudhoe Bay.

Sources: Department of Energy and American Petroleum Institute.

TABLE 6-3.—*Domestic crude oil production, 1980–81*

[Thousands of barrels per day]

Month	1980	1981	Change
January	7,121	7,020	−101
February	7,168	7,068	−100
March	7,155	7,069	−86
April	7,130	7,020	−110
May	7,103	7,001	−102
June	7,012	7,072	60
July	7,041	6,902	−139
August	6,906	7,054	148
September	7,102	7,117	15
October [1]	7,045	7,107	62
November [1]	7,033	7,082	49
December [1]	7,102	7,095	−7

[1] Preliminary.

Note.—Data exclude Prudhoe Bay.

Sources: Department of Energy and American Petroleum Institute.

TABLE 6-4.—*Imports of crude oil and refined products, 1980–81*

[Thousands of barrels per day]

Month	Total	Crude oil	Refined products
1980:			
January	8,342	6,359	1,983
February	7,847	5,936	1,911
March	7,509	5,785	1,724
April	6,985	5,555	1,430
May	6,549	5,071	1,478
June	6,893	5,480	1,413
July	6,046	4,645	1,401
August	6,102	4,723	1,379
September	6,128	4,653	1,475
October	6,173	4,570	1,603
November	6,253	4,524	1,729
December	6,660	4,848	1,812
1981:			
January	6,709	4,817	1,892
February	6,697	4,793	1,904
March	5,887	4,382	1,505
April	5,370	4,060	1,310
May	5,317	3,881	1,436
June	5,104	3,766	1,338
July	5,634	4,161	1,473
August	5,480	3,908	1,572
September	5,891	4,279	1,612
October [1]	5,027	3,957	1,070
November [1]	5,436	3,972	1,464
December [1]	5,532	3,844	1,688

[1] Preliminary.

Note.—Data exclude Strategic Petroleum Reserve.

Source: American Petroleum Institute.

Natural Gas Policy

Wellhead prices of natural gas sold in interstate commerce have been regulated by the Federal Government since 1954. Because intrastate gas prices were not subject to control, a two-market system resulted. This led to shortages in the interstate market because interstate pipeline companies were hampered in competing for gas supplies, while the artificially low prices encouraged consumers to demand more natural gas than otherwise would have been the case.

Rising oil prices in the 1970s exacerbated the shortage of gas in the interstate market, leading to nonprice rationing. Existing industrial users of gas were curtailed during periods of particularly intense shortages, and many potential new users, both at the industrial and residential level, were proscribed from using gas. The cold winter of 1977 produced a severe shortage of interstate gas, thus illustrating vividly the adverse effects of the regulations. In short, the wellhead price controls produced serious inefficiencies: (1) underproduction of gas for the interstate market, and (2) inefficient allocation of gas, both between the interstate and intrastate markets and between different users within the interstate market.

Natural gas regulation was changed substantially with passage of the 1978 Natural Gas Policy Act (NGPA). A small amount of (high cost) new gas was deregulated under the NGPA almost immediately, and the price of between 40 and 60 percent of all gas is scheduled to be deregulated on January 1, 1985. The price of a smaller volume of gas will be deregulated on July 1, 1987. Under the NGPA, price controls were extended to gas sold in intrastate markets. About 20 categories of gas were created, each with its own ceiling price and inflation adjustment or other escalation factor.

Because of the various price categories of gas under the NGPA, producers receive distorted signals and incentives affecting development and production decisions. Instead of producing the lowest cost gas first and moving successively to higher cost sources, producers have been induced by the different price categories to produce high-cost sources first in many cases, and otherwise to shift their production efforts away from those most efficient. This means that total gas production will consume more resources than necessary. The current boom in drilling for high-cost (deep) gas is illustrative of this process.

Another problem is likely to arise because the prices for new gas that are scheduled to be decontrolled in 1985 and 1987 are tied until then by the NGPA to 1978 oil prices. Since oil prices have roughly doubled since then, and are not likely to fall substantially, partial decontrol will generate a sharp increase in delivered gas prices, as consumers bid up gas prices to levels equivalent to those of close substitutes, such as oil. The Department of Energy estimates that average domestic wellhead prices in 1980 dollars per thousand cubic feet will rise under the NGPA from $2.27 in 1982 to $4.45 in 1985. Because the prices of decontrolled gas can be averaged (rolled in) with those of controlled gas, and because consumer demands are determined in substantial part by the prices of substitute fuels, average 1985 prices under the NGPA are not likely to differ greatly from those that would evolve under full decontrol. This implies that the prices of decontrolled gas will be bid up well above the levels that would be observed in a fully decontrolled market. Indeed, decontrolled high-cost gas is now being sold at the wellhead for over $9, while the Department of Energy estimates that the average 1985 price under full decontrol would be $4.65.

The high prices that will be paid for decontrolled gas in 1985 and thereafter imply that gas consumers in general will not be the beneficiaries of the remaining controls. Instead, the beneficiaries will be the producers of decontrolled gas. However, under the NGPA different groups of consumers will fare differently. Pipeline companies with access to substantial quantities of price-controlled gas will be able to bid deregulated gas away from other pipelines because the higher prices on decontrolled gas can be averaged with the lower prices paid for gas still subject to controls. This means that different consumers may well pay substantially different average prices, and that large quantities of gas will be reallocated artificially because of differential access to controlled gas. In particular, the intrastate pipelines will have relatively little access to controlled gas, and so a very substantial amount of gas will shift out of the intrastate market into the interstate market. Interstate pipelines also will vary in their ability to bid for decontrolled gas. In short, in addition to the resource waste involved in gas production under the NGPA, both controlled and decontrolled gas will be allocated inefficiently. The Department of Energy estimates that the efficiency gain to the economy from full gas decontrol in 1982 would be about $10 billion.

The prospect of a sharp price increase in 1985, along with the other problems inherent in the NGPA, may provide an impetus toward extension of price controls on all gas beyond 1985. This would resurrect all of the additional consumption and production inefficiencies experienced before passage of the NGPA. If price controls were extended, gas production would be reduced and oil consumption and imports would be stimulated. Furthermore, the total net decrease in proved domestic gas reserves from 1971 through 1979 was almost 96 trillion cubic feet. Extension of controls therefore would have very serious effects upon future domestic gas reserves.

Some observers have argued that decontrol would make producers better off at the expense of consumers, and that decontrol would hurt the poor. Both of these assertions are subject to serious question. Compared to conditions under the NGPA, decontrol would make some producers and consumers better off and some worse off. The averaging of controlled and uncontrolled prices under the NGPA results in high prices for some producers and lower ones for others. Decontrol would move all prices toward the common market-clearing level. Similarly, the NGPA forces some consumers implicitly to subsidize others, so that consumers as a group would be no better off under the NGPA than under full decontrol. Moreover, decontrol would benefit a wide class of individuals and groups, including the poor, by improving the productive efficiency of the economy as a whole. Hence, decontrol would make some poor individuals worse off, but others better off. Price controls are a costly and inefficient method of avoiding the adverse effects of rising fuel prices.

Some commentators have argued that gas decontrol ought to be accompanied by a "windfall profits" tax, perhaps patterned after the crude oil "windfall profits" tax. It should be noted that the latter tax is not based on profits, windfall or otherwise. It is actually an excise tax on domestic crude oil production. A "windfall profits" tax on gas would be likely to generate the same sort of inefficiencies: reduced domestic production, increased imports, and consumption of more resources in domestic production than otherwise would be the case. Other taxes, such as severance taxes on old gas, may be less harmful if they generate only small distortions in incremental production incentives.

TRANSPORTATION

The reduction in Federal economic regulation of the transportation industry is promoting a more efficient transportation system. The airline, motor carrier, railroad, and intercity bus industries are not now characterized by any of the market failures discussed in Chapter 2. There are many competitors in each industry. Transportation is not a public good, since individuals pay for each trip or shipment. There are no external costs or benefits that would warrant the regulation of prices or the number of competitors.

Since 1978 the Congress has passed three major pieces of legislation to reduce the regulation of these industries. A phased deregulation of the airlines is now being carried out and will be completed with the elimination of the Civil Aeronautics Board (CAB) on January 1, 1985. The Motor Carrier Act of 1980 and the Staggers Rail Act of 1980 provide the authority to eliminate significant portions of the economic regulation of trucks and railroads, but they do not prescribe an end to regulation. Both require definite action by the Interstate Commerce Commission to eliminate as much regulation as the law permits. A bill to reform regulation of the intercity bus industry passed the House of Representatives in November 1981.

Airlines

Deregulation of domestic airlines continued in 1981 according to the schedule of the Airline Deregulation Act of 1978. On December 31, 1981, the Civil Aeronautics Board lost the power to determine the routes of individual airlines. Earlier in the year CAB approved a proposal to allow the airlines to file only maximum fares. In the past they have been required to include in their tariff filings every price that they offered to the public.

A pending prohibition on U.S. airline participation in the International Air Transport Association conference, which determines air fares between the United States and Europe, became a bargaining point in multilateral meetings with European governments. A tentative interim agreement was reached in December 1981. If implemented, greater price flexibility could allow airlines to offer new discount fares for flights to and from Europe. In exchange, U.S. airlines will be able to participate in the conferences to set prices.

Intercity Trucking

The regulatory framework for the motor carrier industry was changed by the Motor Carrier Act of 1980. The act's provisions were rapidly implemented initially by ICC. A large number of applications for authority to provide service were granted, the geographic and commodity authority in new certificates was broadened, and price reductions occurred in both the truckload and less-than-truckload sectors. The industry, although not fully deregulated, appears to be much more competitive than in the past.

More recently, however, the pace of regulatory reform has slowed. Restrictions on the scope of new certificates have increased, and some applications for rate reductions have been rejected by the ICC. Discounts offered to shippers have been called "blatantly illegal."

Railroads

The deregulatory provisions of the Staggers Rail Act of 1980 have helped to increase the efficiency of the railroads and to improve their performance. A new standard of revenue adequacy, based on the current cost of capital, gives greater rate flexibility to railroads with inadequate revenues. Despite an improved financial position during the last year, almost all railroads are currently considered as having inadequate revenues.

Significant changes in ICC regulation of the rail industry have been implemented as a result of the Staggers Rail Act of 1980. Contracts between railroads and individual shippers are now legal and are virtually free of any ICC regulation. Approximately 550 such contracts were filed at the ICC during the first year of the new law. Rates that are less than 165 percent of variable cost are not regulated. Rates and practices for shipping trailers or containers on flatcars are now exempt from regulation. Rates and practices for shipping fresh fruits and vegetables have been exempt since 1979. In addition, four railroad mergers have been submitted and two have received ICC approval without the attachment of the traditional restrictive conditions to protect affected railroads.

Intercity Buses

Federal regulation of the intercity bus industry began almost accidently in 1935, when motor carriers of passengers (buses) were included under ICC regulation of intercity trucks. In November 1981 the House of Representatives passed a bill that would provide for some regulatory reform of the bus industry. The bill would eliminate one of the many criteria that the ICC uses to determine whether a bus company can begin new service. It would also allow more price flexibility by establishing a zone in which the ICC cannot reject fare changes, but the rate bureau, which sets collective rates for the industry, would continue. The Administration will work with the Senate during 1982 to strengthen the deregulatory initiatives in the House-passed legislation.

TELECOMMUNICATIONS

Government regulation of telecommunications affects both broadcasters, including owners of cable television systems, and common carriers.

Broadcasting

The Federal Communications Commission (FCC) exercises control over broadcasting through the issuance of radio and television broadcasting licenses. There were 4,575 commercial AM, 3,272 commercial FM, and 751 commercial TV stations (518 VHF and 233 UHF) on the air on November 30, 1980. Because no party can own more than 7 AM, 7 FM, and 7 TV licenses, ownership is fairly unconcentrated. Cable television (CATV) had approximately 17 million subscribers in 1980, with the five largest firms having about 30 percent of the subscribers.

The economic justification for government regulation of this industry has been based on perceived rather than actual conditions. The usual justification has been scarcity of available broadcasting frequencies. Closer examination, however, reveals that the scarcity was a product of government action as much as it was a product of natural causes. This was apparent in the manner in which the FCC allocated channels for TV stations in 1952 to protect existing VHF licensees. Whatever the justification for regulation in the past, the growth of CATV, pay TV, and the possibility of direct satellite transmissions are reducing the importance of the frequency spectrum.

The FCC has made several moves toward deregulation. In February 1981 the Commission deregulated most commercial radio broadcasting, while in May it introduced a simplified renewal application which has only five questions. On the other hand, the FCC withdrew its proposal to allow AM radio stations to broadcast at intervals of 9 kilohertz rather than the present 10 kilohertz. This change would have increased the number of AM stations, although at some cost to existing AM stations. The standard in most of the world has become 9 kilohertz.

The Congress also contributed to the deregulation of broadcasting by including some important provisions in the Omnibus Budget Reconciliation Act of 1981. This act extended the length of TV licenses from 3 to 5 years and radio licenses from 3 to 7 years, while establishing a lottery to determine who will get new licenses.

In September 1981 the Commission transmitted legislative proposals to the Congress designed to streamline FCC operations and allow it to rely on market forces as the primary factor in telecommunications policymaking. These proposals would be an important step forward in the deregulation of broadcasting.

Common Carrier

At the present time there is no competition in the provision of local telephone service. Such service is provided on a franchised monopoly basis by American Telephone and Telegraph (AT&T) (80 percent) and independent telephone companies (20 percent). AT&T handles 95 percent of long-distance telephone calls, but it now faces competition in this area from other suppliers, such as MCI and Southern Pacific.

The growth of effective competitors for AT&T, especially in customer equipment and long-distance service, has eroded some of AT&T's ability to cross-subsidize from high-profit to low-profit activities. Since regulation has been based on the assumption that the cross-subsidy would be maintained, the market's new conditions have made the existing regulatory framework inappropriate.

A restructuring of the industry has come from three directions. In 1980 the FCC permitted AT&T to start selling customer equipment and enhanced services through a fully separate subsidiary to be established by March 1, 1982. That date has been shifted to January 1, 1983. Meanwhile, the Congress has been considering legislation that would alter the structure of AT&T by separating it into regulated and unregulated components under the same corporate framework. More recently, the Justice Department's antitrust suit against AT&T, which had sought full divestiture of the company's potentially monopolistic services, was resolved by a tentative agreement that AT&T would divest itself of all of its local operating companies in exchange for an end to the court suit. Since the local operating companies are regulated monopolies, their divestiture is an essential development for the remainder of AT&T to be a truly competitive force.

ANTITRUST

There has been a dramatic shift in antitrust policy under this Administration. Enforcement will focus on the critical areas implied by the analysis in Chapter 2: horizontal mergers among dominant firms in an industry, and price-fixing agreements among competing firms.

Meanwhile, antitrust enforcement actions whose benefits are questionable are under continuous review. The Robinson-Patman Act, which prohibits price discrimination, can restrict the ability of wholesale producers to give quantity discounts to retail sellers. Because sellers find it hard to erect long-term barriers to competition from other sellers, it is illogical for them to try to carry on the predatory practices which the law seeks to prohibit. Vertical mergers and agreements, which can be illegal under the Clayton Act, generally are motivated more by a desire for greater economic efficiency than a wish to eliminate competition. For example, it is a common practice for a dealer to sell the product of one firm after obtaining the contractual protection of having an exclusive right to make sales in a given territory. Without territorial protection, a dealer would have only a limited incentive to advertise the qualities of the product, since much of the benefit of advertising would be captured by competitors. Since advertising is an important source of information for buyers, territorial restrictions can promote its dissemination.

Enforcement of the antitrust laws has now taken a clearly economic orientation in both the Antitrust Division of the Department of Justice and the Federal Trade Commission. In the Antitrust Division, decisions on which companies to investigate and what cases to pursue are carefully scrutinized to determine whether the cases are economically sound. The department has also been developing a new set of merger guidelines that would follow broader economic criteria than the present set, which focuses almost exclusively on concentration ratios and market shares within an industry.

In addition to the tentative agreement in the AT&T case mentioned above, the Department of Justice settled its longstanding case against International Business Machines (IBM) in early 1982. The IBM case was dismissed because the Department of Justice decided that the government's case was without merit. The restructured AT&T will be an important new competitive element in the markets that have been served by IBM.

GUIDELINES FOR REGULATORY REFORM

During its first year in office the Administration has attempted to establish a new regulatory environment. The Administration's goal is to eliminate wasteful or outdated regulation and to make necessary regulation more efficient and more flexible. This effort includes three tasks: (1) review of the basic statutes authorizing regulation; (2) review of existing regulations; and (3) review of proposed regulations. The Administration's program has not yet focused on the first of these tasks (except for the Clean Water Act construction grants program and the Clean Air Act), but it will do so next year after it has completed its review of the major existing regulatory programs.

In pursuit of the goal of better Federal regulation, several guidelines may be useful.

1. *Individuals should have maximum opportunity for personal choice.* Regulation is not a substitute for efficient markets but an alternative to

unregulated markets which have failed to allocate resources efficiently. Therefore, regulation should be limited to cases where market failure has been demonstrated and the cost of government intervention is less than the benefits of improved resource allocation. Even though there is a need for government regulation of some markets, the means used should maintain consumer sovereignty to the maximum extent possible.

2. *Regulation should take place at the appropriate level of government.* The primary economic reason for most regulation is the existence of external effects. The costs or tolerance of these external effects may vary among locations. Economic efficiency, therefore, calls for the degree and type of regulation to vary also. National standards tend to be too severe in some regions, while being too lax in others. Federal regulation should be limited to situations where the actions in one State have substantial external effects in other States, constitutional rights are involved, or interstate commerce would be significantly disrupted by differences in local regulations.

3. *Wherever possible, the government should provide incentives rather than directives.* Regulation occurs within a dynamic environment. The lowest cost technology for pollution abatement at the present time, for example, will certainly be obsolete at some time in the future. Directives do not create incentives for commercial firms to search for lower cost technologies, unlike such approaches as the establishment of marketable rights in pollution emissions, which would create a continuing incentive for firms to search for methods to achieve lower levels of pollution. Benefit-cost analysis can be a valuable tool in evaluating alternative regulatory schemes.

CHAPTER 7

The United States in the International Economic System

THE SUCCESSFUL IMPLEMENTATION OF POLICIES to control inflation and restore vigorous real growth in the United States will have a profound and favorable impact on the rest of the world. As the President told delegates at the 1981 Annual Meetings of the World Bank and International Monetary Fund, ". . . the most important contribution any country can make to world development is to pursue sound economic policies at home." More generally, the Administration's approach to international economic issues is based on the same principles which underlie its domestic programs: a belief in the superiority of market solutions to economic problems and an emphasis on private economic activity as the engine of noninflationary growth.

This chapter reviews three areas important to U.S. international economic policy: the role of the dollar in the international monetary system, the increased importance of international trade and finance for the U.S. economy, and the evolving role of international institutions in promoting a more open international economic environment.

During much of the postwar period, under what was known as the Bretton Woods system, most governments held their exchange rates fixed against the dollar by intervening in the exchange markets whenever supply of and demand for their currencies were not in balance at the prevailing exchange rate. The U.S. Government usually did not intervene in the exchange markets, but stood ready to buy and sell gold against dollars at a fixed price with foreign official agencies. In 1973 the Bretton Woods system of fixed but periodically adjustable exchange rates collapsed. An increasingly expansionary U.S. monetary policy and a decline in U.S. economic performance accelerated that collapse, but the end of the fixed-rate system probably would have occurred in any case.

Although the role of the dollar in international markets has declined somewhat over the past three decades, it remains the central currency of the international monetary system. Consequently, both the United States and the rest of the world benefit from having a strong and stable dollar, that is, one with stable purchasing power.

This cannot be met through government intervention in exchange markets. Rather, it requires that the United States pursue noninflationary economic policies designed to strengthen its economic performance.

A strong economy requires the maintenance of open markets both at home and abroad. Open trade based on mutually agreed upon rules is consistent with, indeed integral to, the Administration's commitment to strenthening the domestic economy. The maintenance of open markets has become increasingly important in recent years as the shares of foreign trade and investment have grown relative to the size of the U.S. economy.

International institutions have contributed greatly to the economic prosperity the world has enjoyed since World War II by helping to promote increased international trade and investment and to strengthen individual economies. In his World Bank–International Monetary Fund speech President Reagan also remarked that, "The Bretton Woods institutions and the General Agreement on Trade and Tariffs (GATT) established generalized rules and procedures to facilitate individual enterprise and an open international trading and financial system. They recognized that economic incentives and increased commercial opportunities would be essential to economic recovery and growth." As the economic environment in which these institutions operate continues to change, we must assure that these institutions continue to evolve in a manner suitable to maintaining and strengthening the open international economic system from which we all benefit.

INTERNATIONAL FINANCIAL MARKETS

THE DOLLAR IN THE INTERNATIONAL SETTING

The availability of a stable and convertible dollar for use as a store of value and a medium of international exchange contributed significantly to the sustained world economic recovery following World War II. The U.S. dollar still holds a major position in world financial markets. However, this position was weakened by high and varying inflation in the United States relative to that abroad during the 1970s. Poor U.S. economic performance and stronger records in such countries as Japan and West Germany led to a depreciation of the dollar in foreign exchange markets and to the diversification of private and official asset holdings in international financial markets into other currencies. When the purchasing power of the dollar became less stable than the purchasing power of other major currencies, foreigners did not want to continue to hold as large a share of their wealth in dollar-denominated assets or rely as much on the dollar as the standard currency in international transactions.

The dollar remains the principal currency for international commercial and financial transactions. Because of this, both the United States and the rest of the world would benefit from a stronger and more stable U.S. dollar. The strength and stability of the dollar depend directly on the ability of the United States to pursue noninflationary economic policies. In the late 1960s and the 1970s the United States failed to meet this objective. A continuing high and varying rate of inflation led to a sharp decline in the dollar's foreign exchange value during the late 1970s and to the dollar crisis of 1978, which threatened the stability of international financial markets.

It would be desirable to lessen the differences in economic policies and performance at home and abroad which have caused much of the exchange-rate volatility in the recent past. Formal arrangements which peg exchange rates, however, cannot guarantee lasting coordination, as was demonstrated by the history of the Bretton Woods system. As a general proposition, one way to achieve compatibility of policies is for countries *voluntarily* to adopt the monetary rule of a large country whose avowed goal is to stabilize prices. Such a commitment becomes a *de facto* affiliation which will last as long as that larger country performs its task reliably and the smaller countries determine the arrangements to be beneficial. The larger country must be aware that a systematic oversupply of its money will erode confidence and hence reduce the foreign exchange value of its currency. In international markets, where there is competition among monies, high confidence monies eventually replace low confidence monies.

EXCHANGE-RATE MOVEMENTS

Changes in exchange rates, like changes in stock market prices, are largely unpredictable in the short run. New infomation continuously leads exchange-market participants to revise their forecasts of the state of the economy and the stance of economic policies. Exchange rates can exhibit large short-run fluctuations in response to such changes in economic outlook.

Over a longer period, exchange-rate changes reflect differences in inflation rates between countries; that is, purchasing power parity should hold in the long run. In Chart 7–1, measures of the nominal and the real effective exchange rates are shown for the United States from 1973 to 1981. The real effective exchange rate is here defined as the nominal effective foreign exchange value of the dollar (a trade-weighted exchange rate) multiplied by the ratio of the U.S. consumer price index (CPI) to the foreign consumer price index (March 1973 = 100). Purchasing power parity holds when the real effective exchange rate is 100; below 100 the dollar depreciates in real terms; above 100 the dollar appreciates in real terms. Two observations about the graph are in order. First, there were substantial and persistent deviations from purchasing power parity but a tendency for the real effective exchange rate to gravitate around the 100 line. Second, nominal and real effective exchange rates generally moved in the same direction.

Chart 7-1

Nominal and Real Effective Foreign Exchange Value of the Dollar

MARCH 1973 = 100

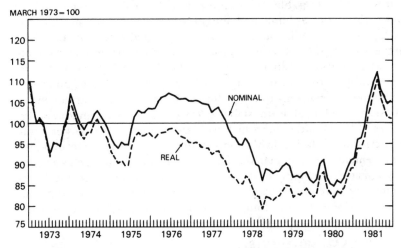

NOTE.—THE EFFECTIVE EXCHANGE RATE IS COMPUTED USING MULTILATERAL TRADE SHARES OF THE G-10 COUNTRIES PLUS SWITZERLAND. THE REAL EXCHANGE RATE IS CALCULATED BY ADJUSTING THE NOMINAL INDEX FOR RELATIVE MOVEMENTS IN CONSUMER PRICES (THIS IS ONE AMONG VARIOUS WAYS TO MEASURE REAL EXCHANGE RATES).

SOURCES: DEPARTMENT OF LABOR AND BOARD OF GOVERNORS OF THE FEDERAL RESERVE SYSTEM.

The substantial movement in this measure of real exchange rates, however, does not invalidate the long-term purchasing power parity relationship. There are three main reasons why short-run deviations from long-run purchasing power parity occur. First, changes in the general price level, accompanied by changes in the ratio of traded to nontraded commodities prices (the internal terms of trade), affect real exchange rates. This is so because the net export surplus (deficit) of the country experiencing an improvement in the relative price of traded goods rises (falls). For a given price level, the exchange rate must adjust to restore long-run equilibrium in the current account.

Movements in real exchange rates also can take place because the "terms of finance" change. That is, there may be shifts in the currency preferences and risks faced by participants in international financial markets which in turn affect expected yields on assets denominated in various currencies.

Finally, real exchange rates tend to move in the same direction as nominal exchange rates because prices change more slowly than nominal exchange rates. As a consequence, changes in monetary policy quickly affect nominal interest rates in financial markets, and more gradually, the price level. Thus, changes in monetary growth affect both real and nominal exchange rates in the short run. Over the longer term, however, monetary growth does not influence real exchange rates.

All of these forces have been present during the last decade. Over this period the U.S. economy has been subjected to significant changes in the prices of internationally traded goods, especially oil. For instance, the external terms of trade, measured by the ratio of the price deflator for exports of goods and services to the price deflator for imports of goods and services, fell sharply in 1973 and in 1979 as the two oil price shocks of the 1970s left their marks on the U.S. economy (Chart 7-2). In addition, the U.S. economy became

Chart 7-2

U.S. External Terms of Trade

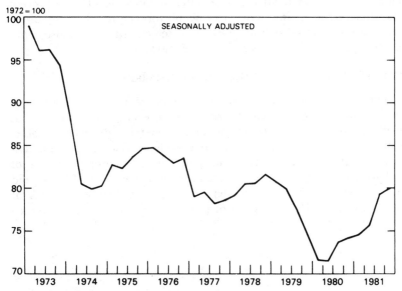

1972 = 100

NOTE.—DATA ARE RATIO OF IMPLICIT PRICE DEFLATOR FOR EXPORTS OF GOODS AND SERVICES TO IMPLICIT PRICE DEFLATOR FOR IMPORTS OF GOODS AND SERVICES.

SOURCE: DEPARTMENT OF COMMERCE.

much more open in the 1970s than it used to be. As an example, exports as a proportion of gross national product (GNP) nearly doubled during the 1970s.

Historically, real exchange rates generally have moved in the direction of restoring long-term equilibrium in external accounts. In the 1977–78 period the United States had a cumulative current account deficit of $28.2 billion. The United States and foreign central banks then intervened massively in an effort to contain the depreciation of the dollar. Foreign net purchases of dollars were more than double the amount of the cumulative current account deficit. Yet the dollar continued to depreciate, both in nominal and real terms. Market participants judged the intervention to be ineffective and viewed the deterioration in the U.S. current account as an accurate reflection of underlying U.S. economic policies and performance. The depreciation was pronounced and persistent, but achieved the expected result of redressing the current account imbalance during 1979 and 1980.

In 1981 the dollar appreciated sharply, both in nominal and real terms. The nominal appreciation of the dollar on a trade-weighted basis relative to other major currencies was 15.6 percent. This movement is explained only in part by the current account surplus of the United States relative to that of its trading partners. Another factor was a shift toward dollar-denominated assets, which may have been a consequence of the President's economic recovery program. Large sales of dollar assets by foreign central banks and an increase in foreign interest rates relative to U.S. interest rates did little to prevent the dollar from rising. The growing preference for dollar-denominated assets relative to other assets reflected a positive response to underlying economic policies of the Administration.

OFFICIAL INTERVENTION IN THE EXCHANGE MARKETS

There is a long tradition among monetary authorities of intervening in the foreign exchange markets to prevent what is known as overshooting, undershooting, or, more generally, disorderly market conditions. But there is no conclusive evidence that official intervention in the past has achieved its purpose. The large purchases of dollar-denominated assets by foreign central banks in 1977–78 did not prevent the dollar from depreciating, and their large sales of dollar assets in 1980–81 did not prevent the dollar from appreciating. Moreover, intervention may have been counterproductive. Market participants did not know whether it signaled a change in monetary policy, thereby leading to increased uncertainty on their part.

When the previous Administration left office, intervention by the United States was being conducted at a relatively high volume, virtually on a day-to-day basis, with the objective of using the periods of dollar strength first to cover outstanding foreign currency liabilities and later to build foreign currency reserves. This was the first time, at least in recent history, that the United States had embarked on a deliberate policy of acquiring substantial foreign currency reserves. (For a brief history of U.S. Government intervention in the exchange markets, see the appendix to this chapter.)

Early in 1981 the new Administration scaled back U.S. intervention in foreign exchange markets. In conjunction with a strong emphasis on economic fundamentals, this Administration has returned to the policy of intervening only when necessary to counter conditions of severe disorder in the market.

As in the past, no attempt has been made to define disorderly market conditions in advance. When making a decision on whether exchange-market conditions justify intervention, the U.S. Government will consult closely with the governments of other major industrial countries. Also as in the past, the Department of the Treasury and the Federal Reserve will keep the public informed regarding U.S. exchange-market intervention policy. Although the Administration does not expect intervention in the exchange markets to occur on a regular basis, it will continue to monitor closely developments in those markets.

With the President's economic program firmly in place, and with the Federal Reserve following a policy of gradually reducing the rate of monetary growth to a noninflationary level, the occurrence of disorderly conditions is likely to be significantly less in the future than in the past. But unforeseen circumstances at home or abroad could cause disorderly conditions, and intervention may at times be necessary.

IMPLICATIONS FOR U.S. MONETARY POLICY

In Chapter 3 it was argued that monetary authorities have the ability to achieve given values and growth rates of nominal magnitudes and that price stability is the principal objective of monetary policy. Under such a policy, interest rates cannot be fixed. But market interest rates and exchange rates are related by what is known as interest rate parity: the premium in the forward exchange markets approximates the difference between comparable domestic and foreign interest rates. It follows that as interest rates change over time, nominal exchange rates will vary as well. A stable price level, therefore, may not necessarily imply constant nominal interest rates or constant exchange rates.

Price stability in the United States might lessen considerably the dispersion of inflation rates now prevailing in the world, but cannot eliminate them altogether. Economic policies and performance will continue to differ from country to country. Hence, exchange rates will adjust to reflect such differences. But even if differences in inflation were to disappear, exchange rates would have to accommodate changes in relative prices. Real exchange rates cannot be held constant in dynamic economies. The greatest contribution that U.S. price stability will make to the exchange market is that it will act to reduce exchange rate volatility.

Current U.S. monetary and intervention policies are not expressions of "benign neglect." That notion was based on the premise that the foreign trade sector of the United States was so small relative to the rest of the economy that it could be ignored. By contrast, the Administration stresses the pivotal role of the United States in the world.

TRADE ISSUES AND POLICIES

TRADE IN THE U.S. ECONOMY

Foreign trade has become a vital factor in U.S. business activity and employment. In 1980 exports and imports of goods and services each represented over 12 percent of the gross national product. Twenty years ago exports were less than 6 percent of GNP; imports, less than 5 percent. Much of this shift has occurred in the last decade, during which exports and imports as shares of GNP have about doubled. In real terms, however, the rate of growth in U.S. imports of goods and services was stronger in the 1960s than in 1970s, while U.S. export growth was stronger in the 1970s than in the 1960s. The improved export performance reflects two key factors apart from the evolving ramifications of the trade liberalization of the postwar period and the real depreciation of the dollar in the 1970s: our increased trade with developing countries, whose real GNP growth slowed less in the 1970s than that of the developed countries,

174

and our specialization in exports of high technology products, agricultural products, and services.

Recent movements in merchandise trade are shown in Table 7-1; they reflect in part cyclical factors. The sharp decline in real GNP during the second quarter of 1980 was accompanied by a substantial drop in U.S. merchandise imports. From a seasonally adjusted total of $65 billion in the first quarter of 1980, merchandise imports fell to $59 billion in the third quarter. At the same time, demand for U.S. exports remained buoyant, yielding in the third quarter of 1980 the smallest merchandise trade deficit since 1976—$11.6 billion at an annual rate. Thereafter, the rebound in U.S. economic activity from the extremely weak level in the second quarter of 1980, coupled with a slowing of growth abroad and the lagged impact of dollar appreciation on U.S. international competitiveness, acted to widen the deficit. By the the last quarter of 1981, it had risen to $37.0 billion at an annual rate.

TABLE 7-1.—*U.S. merchandise exports, imports, and balance, 1977-81*

[Billions of dollars; f.a.s.]

Period	Exports		Imports		Balance
	Agricul-tural	Nonagri-cultural	Petro-leum and products	Non-petro-leum	
1977	24.3	96.5	45.0	106.7	−30.9
1978	29.9	112.2	42.3	133.5	−33.8
1979	35.6	148.9	60.5	151.3	−27.3
1980	42.2	181.7	78.9	170.4	−25.3
1981 [1]	44.2	192.0	77.6	186.4	−27.8
1980:					
I	10.3	44.6	21.2	43.9	−10.1
II	10.1	45.6	21.0	41.4	−6.7
III	10.8	45.4	17.4	41.8	−2.9
IV	11.1	46.1	19.3	43.4	−5.6
1981:					
I	12.7	48.3	20.8	44.9	−4.7
II	11.0	49.3	21.2	46.1	−6.9
III	10.0	47.9	17.9	47.0	−7.0
IV [1]	10.4	46.4	17.7	48.4	−9.3

[1] Preliminary.
Note.—Data are on a balance of payments basis and exclude military.
Quarterly data are seasonally adjusted.
Data contain revisions for the first three quarters of 1981.
Detail may not add to balance due to rounding.

Source: Department of Commerce, Bureau of Economic Analysis.

A very broad breakdown of trade by major commodity groups is also shown in Table 7-1. Until recently, agricultural goods accounted for about 20 percent of total U.S. exports. Quarterly changes in the value of U.S. imports during 1980 and 1981 were determined largely by movements in the value of petroleum imports. Petroleum import volume in 1981 declined 13 percent compared to 1980, in the face of an increase in price of 12 percent. The value of petroleum imports fell dramatically in the last half of 1981, with both volume and price declining. The latter reflected reduced worldwide demand for oil due to the continued appreciation of the U.S. dollar and the down-turns in economic activity in the United States and Europe, all in tandem with adjustments to oil inventories.

While the dollar price of oil has fallen, the appreciation of the dollar has caused the price of oil in European and Japanese curren-cies to rise. For Europe and Japan, therefore, oil import values rose more rapidly than in the United States during 1981 and a parallel in-crease in their concern with their own trade balances has added to protectionist pressures in some of those countries.

Although cyclical factors have played and will continue to play an important role in movements of the trade account, the strong appre-ciation of the dollar through much of 1981 has already begun to be reflected in trade flows. While changes in economic activity are quickly translated into movements of exports and imports, changes in relative prices generally take more time to alter trade flows. Hence, trade flows in early 1982 will continue to be influenced by the earlier sharp real appreciation of the dollar.

In some instances the impact of exchange-rate changes in 1981 was stronger than cyclical effects. U.S. imports of nonpetroleum products grew steadily throughout 1981, despite the weakening of U.S. eco-nomic activity. The volume of nonpetroleum imports grew very strongly, while their price fell during the year, both reflecting the ap-preciation of the dollar.

THE STANCE OF U.S. TRADE POLICY

The Administration spelled out in its July 1981 "Statement on U.S. Trade Policy" its commitment to pursue, at home and abroad, poli-cies aimed at achieving open trade and reducing trade distortions. There are five central components to that policy.

- *Restoring strong noninflationary growth at home.* Fundamental to any effective trade policy is carrying out domestic programs that in-crease the incentives to invest, to raise productivity, and to reduce costs, thus helping to lower inflationary pressures. These policies will strengthen the ability of American firms to respond to changes in domestic and international markets.
- *Reducing self-imposed trade disincentives.* Confusing and needlessly complex laws and regulations that inhibit exports and imports will be reformed.
- *Effective and strict enforcement of U.S. trade laws and international agree-ments.* Our policy toward other nations' barriers to trade and to investment or export subsidies is one of strong opposition. Our trading partners must recognize that it is in their own interest, as well as ours, to assure that international trade and investment remain a two-way street.

- *A more effective approach to industrial adjustment problems.* In a healthy economy some industries and regions will grow more rapidly than others, and some sectors will experience more difficulty. If unhindered, the market will signal these changes and provide incentives for adjustments. Market forces, rather than government bail-outs, will be relied upon to make appropriate adjustments.
- *Reducing government barriers to the flow of trade and investment among nations.* To this end it is necessary to continue efforts to improve and expand existing international trade rules, particularly into the areas of services and investment.

At home, as well as in other nations, public policy discussions about international trade often lead to disagreement. The direct beneficiaries of import relief or export subsidy are usually few in number, but each has a large individual stake in the outcome. Thus, their incentive for vigorous political activity is strong.

But the costs of such policies may far exceed the benefits. It may cost the public $40,000–$50,000 a year to protect a domestic job that might otherwise pay an employee only half that amount in wages and benefits. Furthermore, the costs of protection are widely diffused—in the United States, among 50 States and some 230 million citizens. Since the cost borne by any one citizen is likely to be quite small, and may even go unnoticed, resistance at the grass-roots level to protectionist measures often is considerably less than pressures for their adoption.

The decisions taken in trade cases inevitably reflect political and social forces as well as basic economic considerations. The record of decisions, not surprisingly, continues to be mixed. For example, the extension of the Multifiber Arrangement, agreed upon in December 1981, is more restrictive than open-trade advocates might have preferred, but the principle of openness was adhered to closely in the decision concerning the nonrubber footwear industry. A similar contrast can be found in the automobile and industrial fastener cases.

CHANGING ATTITUDES TOWARD INTERNATIONAL TRADE

The gradual opening of the world economy to trade in the postwar period has brought major benefits both to the United States and to our trading partners. Long experience has shown that the benefits of trade tend to be mutual. Competition, whether domestic or international, fosters the allocation of resources to relatively more productive activities. Better products, at lower prices, appear in the marketplace. Consumer choice is expanded. Technologies are more readily diffused. Inflationary pressures are reduced. With time, productivity, and hence income, rise.

The benefits from open trade are derived as much from reductions in barriers to imports as from expansion of exports. American exporters seek foreign buyers who have access to the U.S. dollars necessary to buy U.S. goods and services. While the U.S. dollar is a convertible currency that is widely used in a variety of international transactions, significant amounts of dollars are made available when Americans import foreign goods and services, paying in U.S. dollars. Put simply, our imports put U.S. dollars into the hands of foreigners who then use those dollars—be it to buy U.S. goods, services, or assets, or to exchange currencies with others who want dollars. In the short run, we can, and in many cases do, lend foreigners the dollars to finance their purchases of our exports. When such loans are made at market rates of interest, trade is advanced. But when government-subsidized credit is provided, instead, such funds are denied to other, more productive uses.

Restricting U.S. imports would reduce the amount of dollars available to those in other countries who would buy our wheat, aircraft, chemicals, or machinery unless we made up the difference by loans to foreigners. In some cases, the connection between imports and exports is even more direct. Import restraints can reduce employment and profits in our more productive export industries. The nonrubber footwear industry offers one such example. U.S. exporters of hides to foreign shoe producers suffered as a result of our restraints on imports of foreign shoes. More generally, import restriction by one country may invite others to retaliate.

Pressures for retaliation, which tend to strengthen when, as now, output growth rates are declining and unemployment is rising, are one of a number of forces threatening to stem the growth of world trade. In the last year or so, the U.S. automobile, footwear, steel, and textile industries have been among those actively seeking relief from import competition. There are similarly strong pressures for government subsidy of export expansion—for example, in agriculture and in high technology industries.

Such pressures for further government intervention reflect a potentially troublesome "neomercantilist" view which stresses export expansion to the near exclusion of all other factors in a healthy international trading climate. If the U.S. Government, the reasoning runs, were to take steps to favor sectors with export potential, the domestic economy would benefit. In this view, a large surplus in the merchandise trade account is deemed an unmitigated "good," a deficit "bad."

There is a fundamental inconsistency between such neomercantilism and the overall economic philosophy of the Administration, which is committed to the goal of less, not more, government interference in the marketplace. It is just as easy to waste taxpayer dollars and scarce economic resources on subsidizing exports as it is to waste them on better-known examples of Federal profligacy. What is desirable, indeed necessary, is that, consistent with the Administration's "Statement on U.S. Trade Policy," the U.S. Government assure the proper enforcement of trade laws, remove any unnecessary domestic impediments to trade, and likewise seek elimination of foreign trade barriers which effectively limit our exports.

Competitiveness that is impaired by market forces should not be restored by raising tariffs or subsidizing export industries. Such actions simply protect the trade-dependent industries, inviting them to postpone the steps necessary to meet world competition while raising costs to consumers and reducing the choices available in the marketplace. Policymakers can design and implement policies that invite improvements in investment, productivity, and employment, but the decision on whether to make such improvements is best left to the private sector.

THE SIGNIFICANCE OF EXTERNAL IMBALANCES

In most circumstances a trade deficit by itself should not cause concern. A trade deficit is a narrow concept. Goods are only part of what the world trades; another major part of trade is composed of services. Hence, the current account, which includes both, better indicates the country's international payments position. But the current account balance is not a complete measure of international competitiveness either. What also matters is how current account deficits are financed.

Table 7-2 sets out the major components of the current account of the U.S. balance of payments: exports and imports (from Table 7-1), services, and unilateral transfers. The growing importance of trade in services is evident. The major contributor, by far, to the surplus on services is investment income. Net investment income rose from less than $18 billion in 1977 to almost $33 billion in 1980. As has been the case in the recent past, large surpluses in the services account offset large deficits in the merchandise account, yielding a small surplus in the current account for the first three quarters of 1981.

Concern with the country's international payments position is appropriate when the basis of that concern is that the country is simultaneously experiencing a sustained deficit in its current account and a persistent depreciation of its currency in the exchange markets. The joint occurrence of these two events should alert economic policymakers to the possibility that the country may be losing competitiveness.

TABLE 7-2.—*U.S. international transactions, 1977-81*

[Billions of dollars]

Period	Merchandise [1]			Services			Unilateral transfers, net	Current account balance
	Exports	Imports	Balance	Exports	Imports	Balance		
1977	120.8	151.7	−30.9	63.5	42.1	21.4	−4.6	−14.1
1978	142.1	175.8	−33.8	79.0	54.2	24.8	−5.1	−14.1
1979	184.5	211.8	−27.3	104.5	70.1	34.4	−5.6	1.4
1980	224.0	249.3	−25.3	120.7	84.6	36.1	−7.1	3.7
1981 [2]	236.1	264.0	−27.8					
1980:								
I	55.0	65.0	−10.1	30.9	21.0	9.9	−1.9	−2.1
II	55.7	62.4	−6.7	28.0	20.4	7.5	−1.3	−0.5
III	56.3	59.2	−2.9	30.4	21.0	9.4	−1.5	5.0
IV	57.1	62.7	−5.6	31.5	22.2	9.3	−2.3	1.4
1981:								
I	61.0	65.7	−4.7	33.3	23.9	9.5	−1.5	3.3
II	60.4	67.3	−6.9	34.6	25.0	9.6	−1.5	1.1
III [2]	57.9	65.0	−7.0	36.2	25.2	11.0	−1.9	2.1
IV [2]	56.8	66.1	−9.3					

[1] Excludes military.
[2] Preliminary.
Note.—Data are on a balance of payments basis.
Quarterly data are seasonally adjusted.
Merchandise trade data contain revisions for the first three quarters of 1981.
Detail may not add to balances due to rounding.
Source: Department of Commerce, Bureau of Economic Analysis.

It is particularly important not to become unduly preoccupied with the trade or current account balances with a single foreign country. Any policy to reduce a bilateral imbalance by restricting imports is likely to reduce the absolute volume of trade, and in consequence, the level of economic well-being of both countries, and could have wider repercussions. A far more constructive approach would be for the nations with restrictive trade practices and institutional barriers to imports to reduce systematically those obstacles to the freer flow of trade and investment. Actions like those recently taken by Japan, for example, should prove far more beneficial than measures by the United States to restrict imports.

More broadly, and setting aside the sometimes significant statistical discrepancies, global current account imbalances must add up to zero. All countries cannot possibly run surpluses simultaneously. If each nation tried to achieve such a goal, strong deflationary forces would be set in motion. Today, for example, the Organization of Petroleum Exporting Countries (OPEC) continues to report large current account surpluses; these have to be matched by current account deficits in other countries. Given the important role of the United States in world financial markets, one need not be concerned if the U.S. current account moves into deficit as domestic economic policies begin to revitalize the economy. With strong domestic performance, U.S. import demand will also strengthen; the effects of this revitalization on U.S. exports will take more time. Thus, a deficit on current account will simply reflect the adjustment process at work.

Nor should a current account deficit that is comfortably financed by net inflows of capital evoke concern. The relationship is straightforward: goods and services comprise one aspect of international commerce, financial and real assets another. If foreigners purchase more U.S. real and financial assets in the United States—land, buildings, equities, and bonds—then the United States can afford to import more goods and services from abroad. To look at one aspect without considering the others is misleading.

In sum, the macroeconomic significance of a current account deficit depends on what gave rise to it and how it is financed. It is in itself neither good nor bad. Nor should exchange-rate changes required by long-term current account considerations be viewed as, in themselves, good or bad; the costs to society of suppressing exchange-rate movements must be compared to the costs of allowing those movements. It is for these reasons that interference with market mechanisms—whether in markets for goods or markets for foreign exchange—is not part of the Administration's policy.

DEVELOPMENT, ADJUSTMENT, AND INTERNATIONAL INSTITUTIONS

THE HERITAGE AND THE CHALLENGES

In his speech to the World Affairs Council of Philadelphia on October 15, 1981, President Reagan said:

"The postwar international economic system was created on the belief that the key to national development and human progress is individual freedom—both political and economic. This system provided only generalized rules in order to maintain maximum flexibility and opportunity for individual enterprise and an open international trading and financial system."

The record of this economic system is a record of more achievements than failures. As Table 7-3 shows, the industrialized world has not been the only beneficiary of an open international trading and financial system. A number of developing countries have done well too. The real per capita GNP of 60 middle-income countries rose about as fast as that of the industrial countries over the period 1950 to 1980, while GNP in those middle-income countries grew over 30 percent faster than in the industrial countries. On the other hand, there are many low-income countries whose economic progress has been disappointing.

As a result of faster economic growth abroad than in the United States, the U.S. share of world output declined substantially over the same period. Immediately after World War II this share was estimated to be approximately 40 percent. By 1950, with Europe and Japan back on their feet, it had declined to one-third. It dropped to 25 percent by 1970 and further declined to 23 percent by 1980.

TABLE 7–3.—*Real GNP growth rates, 1950 to 1980*

[Average annual percent change]

Country grouping	GNP	GNP per capita
Industrial countries	4.2	3.2
Market	4.2	3.1
Nonmarket	4.5	3.4
Developing countries	5.5	3.2
Middle-income countries	5.6	3.1
Low-income countries	5.1	2.9
Capital-surplus oil exporters	11.2	7.9

Note.— Country groupings are classified according to *World Development Report,* 1981, World Bank.
Source: National Foreign Assessment Center.

Despite this favorable record for much of the rest of the world and the United States, the open international system today faces three major challenges. The first challenge arises from the conflict between each country's short-term internal domestic objectives and mutual longer term external interests. In the past, leadership in meeting such a challenge was provided by large countries. The United Kingdom fulfilled this role for much of the 19th century up to World War I, while the United States played a larger role after World War II. Under U.S. leadership the Western alliance developed a nuclear "umbrella," achieved massive reductions of tariffs and other impediments thus giving major impetus to world trade, and created an international monetary system which provided rules of conduct for adjusting balance of payments imbalances. In today's environment, addressing issues such as defense and the evolution of international economic arrangements are part of this challenge. The nature and mutual importance of these issues implies that solutions to these problems must be arrived at through consultation.

The second challenge is to maintain an open international economic system. A new wave of protectionism has taken the form of quotas, subsidies, international cartels, administrative delays, and burdensome enforcement of product standards. Imposition of such measures has increased dramatically since the international negotiations in the Kennedy Round (completed in 1967) sharply reduced both tariffs and the scope for their future use. The gains made in opening markets for international trade, investment, and finance are now threatened.

The third challenge is to respond to the aspirations of the developing countries for greater growth and development. Work under the rubric of the New International Economic Order, as well as the

Brandt Commission report and the Tinbergen report, have focused global attention on important development and resource issues before the world community. While these reports make an effective case for aid to the least developed countries, they in general place too much emphasis on resource transfer and not enough emphasis on resource development through private market mechanisms. Indeed, these reports tend to downplay the role of the private sector in the development process and instead rely on governments and international organizations as the best vehicles to promote development.

As already noted, a sizable number of developing countries have done well in the post-World War II era. On the other hand, developing countries continue to be justified in claiming that the world trading system discriminates against them. Some industrial countries have restricted trade in sensitive sectors of particular export interest to developing countries, such as textiles.

MEETING THE CHALLENGES

The U.S. response to these challenges is based on an explicit shift toward market-oriented solutions to economic problems. Solutions to common problems in the world economy should be found through continued efforts at cooperation and consultation among nations. These efforts should aim at a renewed resolve to fight inflation and secure higher investment with sustainable growth. At the Ottawa Summit in July 1981 the President, along with other Western leaders, reaffirmed "our common objectives and our recognition of the need to take into account the effects on others of policies we pursue. We are confident in our joint determination and ability to tackle our problems in a spirit of shared responsibility . . ."

International cooperation is particularly vital in stemming the drive for greater protectionism both at home and abroad. The response of many countries during the recent period of sluggish worldwide growth has been to call for or impose new barriers to investment and trade flows. The United States will continue to resist these tactics and work for reductions in trade barriers through the General Agreement on Tariffs and Trade (GATT) and through bilateral relationships.

In approaching the challenge to contribute to the needs of the developing world, the Administration seeks to emphasize the important and historically dominant roles of trade and investment in economic development. Although economic assistance on concessionary terms continues to be a vital part of U.S. policy, establishment of a vibrant private sector through trade and investment offers the best hope for sustained noninflationary growth. The program for action that the

President put forth at the Cancun Summit in October 1981 contains five guiding principles for development policy:

- stimulating international trade by opening up markets;
- tailoring particular development strategies to specific needs and regions;
- guiding assistance toward the development of self-sustaining productive capacities;
- improving the climate in many developing countries for private investment and technology transfer; and
- creating a political climate in which practical solutions can move forward rather than founder on the reef of government policies that interfere unnecessarily with the marketplace.

In line with these principles, the major goal of concessional foreign aid programs should be to help those poorer countries which, for reasons beyond their control, have not been able to improve their standards of living. The rationale for aid to countries whose low economic performance results more from inappropriate domestic policies than from external factors needs to be reexamined.

EVOLVING ROLE OF INTERNATIONAL INSTITUTIONS

The United States recognizes the important roles and specialized functions of the international financial institutions and believes these institutions must continue to evolve. It is important to review the roles of these institutions to ensure that they remain effective in the years ahead. Most importantly, these institutions should be directed toward promoting market-oriented rather than government-administered solutions to international and domestic economic problems.

General Agreement on Tariffs and Trade

The General Agreement on Tariffs and Trade has served the world well in promoting and monitoring progress toward a liberalized trading system. Originally written in the immediate post-World War II era with a small number of Western industrial countries as Contracting Parties, the GATT system has had to adapt to the changing world economy. During the 1960s a Part V was added to the General Agreement to take into account the special problems of developing countries and to allow many of them to be brought within the GATT system. Special Protocols of Accession were drafted to bring Eastern European nonmarket economies under the GATT umbrella as well.

Over the years, the emphasis of GATT has been altered to cope with the ingenuity of governments and interest groups in devising new forms of economic protectionism. The first several rounds of negotiations under GATT were concerned mainly with reducing high tariff levels. The Kennedy Round, in addition to achieving sizable tariff reductions, made a modest attempt to negotiate other commitments—including one on antidumping—while the principal focus of the Tokyo Round (completed in 1979) was on extending GATT discipline to areas other than tariffs. These agreements proved decisively that the GATT system is flexible and can be improved over time.

However, GATT now faces a challenge because of increasing protectionist pressures worldwide and because the effectiveness of GATT rules, which formally include all goods, has tended in practice to be limited to trade in manufactures. GATT must now address areas of international commerce where existing norms are inadequate, such as agriculture, and must define its role in establishing norms in areas which traditionally have not been dealt with in GATT, such as trade in services. Another area where distortions exist and where greater international efforts are needed is in international investment. Finally, steps to integrate developing countries more completely into the GATT framework should be made, along with efforts to encourage nonmembers to join agreements under GATT.

A new political impetus among developed and developing countries is required to revitalize GATT. The GATT Ministerial meeting set for November 1982 will offer the international community an opportunity to maintain momentum toward a more open trading system.

The World Bank

The International Bank for Reconstruction and Development (IBRD) was created to lend funds for reconstruction of the war-ravaged economies and for economic development. Having accomplished the first task admirably, it has, over the last quarter century, come to focus heavily on the second. With the creation in 1956 of the International Finance Corporation—mandated to promote private sector enterprise in developing countries—and in 1960 by the establishment of the International Development Association (IDA) to lend on highly concessional terms to the poorest countries, the World Bank group was formed.

During the 1970s these three institutions underwent rapid growth and innovation, some of which has been controversial. President Reagan indicated at the 1981 World Bank-International Monetary Fund Annual Meetings that because the United States strongly supports the World Bank, the Administration also feels "a special responsibility to provide constructive suggestions to make it more effective." A major U.S. policy reassessment of the World Bank and the regional development banks was thus carried out during 1981 and the final report was recently released.

That study strongly endorses the overall performance of the multi-lateral development banks, but also identifies key aspects which require improvement. Loan quality, not quantity, should have highest priority. In addition, renewed attention should be focused on the criteria under which countries "mature" from soft loan window to hard loan window, and "graduate" to unsubsidized participation in international capital markets. The study recommends that the United States should begin to reduce its contributions to the soft loan facilities, noting that such reductions would not adversely affect users of these facilities as long as strengthened "maturation" and "graduation" policies are followed.

In further assessing how the World Bank can be most effective, it is useful to distinguish between its soft loan window (IDA) and its hard loan window (IBRD), since these give it the capacity to tailor its financing to a broad range of developing countries. There is no dispute that a good many countries need development assistance. But views do vary on how best to give assistance—that is, through loans or grants—and whether assistance should be on a multilateral or bilateral basis. A multilateral approach to official aid has the presumed advantages of being cost-effective (that is, greater volumes of resources can be obtained for a given budget dollar), of allowing politics to be bypassed to some extent, and of facilitating policy reform by conditioning loans and grants on certain changes. An arguable disadvantage is that taxpayers in donor countries lose some control both over where aid goes (since decisions are made collectively) and how it is used. Verification of the effectiveness of aid is an issue which was emphasized at times during the 1970s when the Bank itself was among the chief spokesmen for larger aid programs. In light of these considerations, the Council takes the view that official aid would be more effective on a bilateral basis, and the Administration has repeatedly stressed its intention to pursue a larger bilateral aid program.

In any case, soft loan resources disbursed by the World Bank should be directed to countries which are making serious attempts to develop their economies on a rational basis but have inadequate debt-servicing capacity and hence have little or no access to credit markets. Part of the inability of some countries to achieve greater development can be traced to their domestic policies, and aid from both the soft and hard loan windows should be more explicitly conditioned on improvements in those policies. In practice, there has been resistance in some recipient countries to adopting policies which reduce government intervention and allow a fuller play of market forces. The chances that more efficient development will take place are improved to the extent that the lending activities of the Bank are designed so as to generate an increase in privately produced output.

Finally, there remain unresolved questions about the future size and emphasis of World Bank activities. The success of the Bank should not be measured by its ability to obtain funds from donor countries, but rather by its performance in fostering economic growth in developing countries.

The International Monetary Fund

The International Monetary Fund (IMF) currently provides a framework in which governments can consult and cooperate in determining the structure and functioning of the international monetary system. In particular, the Fund extends technical assistance and temporary balance of payments financing to members, in part conditioned on the implementation of economic policy measures designed to correct the factors underlying their balance of payments imbalances. In addition, it serves as a means for monitoring the exchange rate arrangements and policies of member governments. Finally, the IMF is also charged with reviewing the adequacy of international liquidity and with supplementing reserves, when necessary, through the allocation of Special Drawing Rights.

The Administration's approach to the IMF reflects a basic view of the world economy which focuses on economic fundamentals, support for timely adjustment, and recognition of the pervasiveness and benefits of market forces. The IMF Articles of Agreement recognize that exchange-rate stability requires stability in the underlying economic and financial determinants of exchange rates.

Although nations may differ on the appropriate degree of exchange-market intervention, there is consensus that exchange-rate developments are influenced fundamentally by domestic economic conditions within member countries. The Administration strongly supports further development under the IMF surveillance procedures of what has become known as the Article IV consultation process.

Under the second amendment to the Articles of Agreement, the Fund set forth a set of principles to govern developments and policy actions that are consistent with an open international economic system. In cases where the Fund believes that these principles may not have been honored, it may send a staff mission to a member's capital to discuss the member's economic policies with government officials.

IMF Article IV consultations contribute to international stability in a number of ways. First, such consultations provide information to member governments regarding the national economic policies of other member governments. Such information may be helpful in shaping each member's domestic policies as well as useful in avoiding conflicts because of misundertandings. Second, Article IV consultations provide a valuable base of information for Fund staff assessments of global economic and exchange-rate developments which in turn provide useful information for national economic authorities. Third, Article IV consultations provide a framework for frank critiques among the representatives of member governments. Fourth, Article IV consultations provide a base from which all nations can develop a better understanding of the economic linkages among nations. And finally, these consultations can help a country to identify and address emerging payments problems at an early stage.

The Administration, however, has encouraged the Fund to give renewed attention to the kinds of financial programs that it supports in member countries. The U.S. Government has stressed the importance of effective IMF conditionality in promoting balance of payments adjustments. The justification for IMF financing is to encourage appropriate payments adjustment.

With the emergence of very large imbalances in world payments since 1974, a major effort was made to expand access to IMF resources and to enhance the Fund's ability to support its members' adjustment efforts. The access of individual countries to IMF financing has been increased significantly. In addition, IMF resources have been expanded through the implementation of a 50 percent quota increase at the end of 1980 and through the establishment of IMF borrowing arrangements with Saudi Arabia and a few other countries. The duration of IMF adjustment programs has been lengthened in many cases because of the structural nature and depth of countries' adjustment problems. Also, greater emphasis is being placed on structural change—the reduction of economic distortions and disincentives, and enhancement of factors that will lead to greater saving, innovation, investment, and growth.

The IMF must ensure that its increased resources are used in a manner that is consistent with its Articles of Agreement. Traditionally, this has meant that access to IMF resources is available on a temporary basis to countries confronted with an external imbalance and willing to undertake economic policy adjustments to eliminate these imbalances and repay the Fund. Effective balance of payments adjustment frequently requires wider acceptance of market-oriented solutions. Import and export restrictions, price controls, rigid exchange rates, and excessive government regulation often prevent a country from achieving a sustainable balance of payments over time as well as higher domestic growth rates.

Finally, the Administration has looked closely at the justifications for a new proposed allocation of Special Drawing Rights. This issue is controversial, given some countries' financing problems and differences of opinion about the meaning and role of international liquidity. Although many countries have advocated an increase in holdings of this international reserve asset, the United States has opposed such an allocation at this time, given world inflation and the current level of world liquidity. Even a modest new allocation of Special Drawing Rights in present circumstances would appear to conflict with the policies of monetary restraint being pursued in many countries.

Most international institutions were created after World War II, each with clear objectives to satisfy. Over the last three and a half decades the economic environment has changed dramatically, and the member governments of these institutions have had to reach agreement on how to reorganize the priorities and functions of the institutions. These institutions continue to play vital roles in the world economy. But to guarantee their ongoing viability, member governments must continue to review the approaches and goals of these institutions in light of the changing economic environment.

APPENDIX TO CHAPTER 7

U.S. POLICIES ON EXCHANGE-RATE INTERVENTION SINCE 1973

The current era of floating exchange rates formally began in March 1973, when most major industrial countries abandoned their efforts to maintain fixed-exchange rates against the dollar. Although rates were no longer held fixed, many governments outside the United States continued to intervene in exchange markets from time to time to influence their exchange rates. Initially the United States adopted a policy of nonintervention, but substantial changes in dollar exchange rates led the United States to intervene during the summer of 1973 and from late 1974 to early 1975.

In July 1973 the U.S. Government adopted a policy of active intervention at whatever times and in whatever amounts were appropriate for maintaining orderly market conditions. In November 1975, as part of the "Declaration of Rambouillet" following an economic summit meeting, the heads of the industrial countries announced that they had agreed to act to counter disorderly market conditions or erratic fluctuations in exchange rates. Although the difference between the statements may appear to be only one of nuance, the latter statement more accurately reflected what in effect was a limited intervention policy on the part of the United States.

The previous Administration also began its term of office supporting limited intervention in exchange markets. Official U.S. statements, however, were interpreted as favoring a decline in the dollar to reduce the U.S. current account deficit (that is, "benign neglect" of the dollar). Using Federal Reserve swap arrangements, the United States intervened in support of the dollar, beginning in September 1977.* In total, the United States sold (net) $2.6 billion in foreign currencies in support of the dollar between September 1977 and March 1978, financed by Federal Reserve and Department of the Treasury drawings under swap agreements. When the dollar recovered in the second and third quarters of 1978, the United States was able to acquire $2.1 billion in foreign currencies, permitting repayment of a substantial portion of the earlier swap drawings.

In April 1978, pursuant to the notification provisions of the amended IMF Articles of Agreement, the United States notified the IMF that, ". . . exchange rates are determined on the basis of demand and supply conditions in the exchange markets. However, the [U.S.] authorities will intervene when necessary to counter disorderly conditions in the exchange markets."

The definition of disorderly markets was left open and of necessity subject to interpretation by officials. Although at times intervention was heavy, it is fair to characterize U.S. policy until late 1978 as one in which intervention was the exception, and not the rule.

In late 1978, however, the character of U.S. intervention changed. In August 1978 pressure on the dollar renewed amid spreading recognition of serious U.S. economic problems—including inflation and inadequate energy adjustments—and growing skepticism over the effectiveness of the previous Administration's plans to deal with them. President Carter announced a dollar support package on November 1, 1978. A major element of this program was a commitment to a more active intervention policy, to be funded by mobilizing large foreign currency resources, including the issuance of foreign currency securities (which became known as "Carter bonds"). From November 1, 1978, until shortly after the Administration took office in January 1981, U.S. intervention in exchange markets often reached massive proportions by historical U.S. standards (although not by the more activist standards of many foreign governments). As of March 1981, the U.S. Government had acquired $11.9 billion worth of foreign currencies. Since the values of these currencies dropped dra-

*Under a swap agreement, the Federal Reserve and Department of the Treasury borrow foreign currencies from foreign central banks and then use the currencies to intervene in foreign exchange markets. The United States has used swap agreements with Belgium, France, Germany, Japan, the Netherlands, and Switzerland since July 1973, all but Belgium and the Netherlands since November 1978.

matically relative to the U.S. dollar in 1981, as of October 31, 1981, the government (Federal Reserve System plus Treasury) sustained a bookkeeping loss on these holdings of $661 million. This loss would have been realized had the United States sold these currency holdings and repaid its liabilities.

CHAPTER 8

Review and Outlook

ECONOMIC DEVELOPMENTS IN 1981 reflected the inflationary economic policies of more than a decade and the transitory effects of reversing those policies. Past policies alternated periodically between short-run efforts to reduce unemployment and short-lived attempts to fight inflation. Economic forecasting, however, was not sufficiently accurate to produce finely tuned countercyclical policies that made proper allowance for the lag between policy actions and their effects. Stimulative policies had relatively immediate effects on employment, followed by delayed effects in the form of higher inflation. Restrictive policies for fighting the inflation were not seen by the public as part of a credible long-term commitment and therefore were not expected to be sustained. Consequently, they tended to have a more severe impact on output and employment than on inflation. The result has been a ratcheting-up in the trend rate of inflation from one cycle to the next.

This legacy of stop-and-go policies prevented a direct move to lower inflation and higher real growth in 1981. During the first half of 1980, restrictive policies—in the form of credit controls and a sharp reduction in monetary growth—had produced a brief, sharp recession. The subsequent removal of these controls and a postwar record high rate of monetary growth then led to an unsustainable rate of economic expansion through early 1981.

OVERVIEW OF 1981

The historical patterns of monetary growth, inflation, and real output are shown in Chart 8-1. The average growth of money over 5-year periods (solid line) has trended upward since the 1960s; this is reflected in the rising rate of inflation. The two-quarter growth rate of money (dashed line) has fluctuated sharply, compared to the underlying growth trend, and has contributed to rapid expansions and contractions of real economic growth, after a one- or two-quarter lag. Variations in money growth result in changes in spending and nominal income growth. During short periods, such changes show up as changes in real income growth since inflation responds to money growth only after a considerable lag.

Chart 8–1

Growth Rates of Money Stock, Real GNP, and GNP Deflator

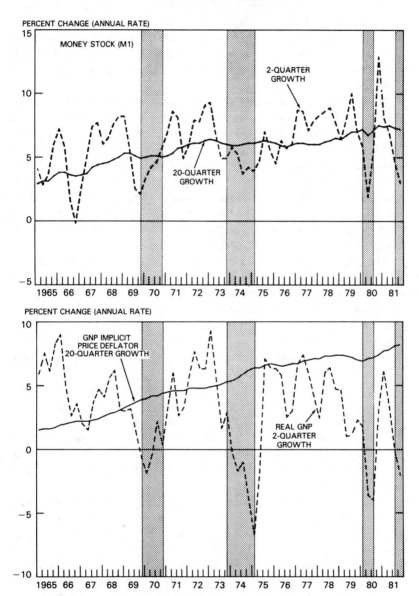

NOTE.—BASED ON SEASONALLY ADJUSTED DATA. SHADED AREAS INDICATE RECESSIONS
AS DEFINED BY THE NATIONAL BUREAU OF ECONOMIC RESEARCH.

SOURCES: DEPARTMENT OF COMMERCE AND BOARD OF GOVERNORS OF THE FEDERAL
RESERVE SYSTEM.

193

This pattern held true in 1981 as well. In the last half of 1980 the money stock, as measured by M1, rose at a 12.9 percent annual rate, a postwar record. Then, in the first quarter of 1981, the rate of growth in nominal gross national product (GNP) leaped by 19.2 percent, with growth in real output rising 8.6 percent. Money growth in the first two quarters of 1981 receded to a 6.9 percent rate, followed by a further reduction to 3 percent in the final two quarters. These decelerations in monetary growth led to a sharp decline in real output in the final quarter of the year.

Continued business investment demand and high inflation in early 1981 sustained a rise in short-term interest rates, which peaked during the spring. Long-term interest rates peaked in early fall. These increases had their most adverse effects on the most credit-sensitive industries—housing, consumer durables, and, to a lesser extent, business investment. The sharp reduction in money growth in the summer and fall led to a sharp decline in total output and interest rates. By December 1981, short-term interest rates were about 5 to 6 percentage points lower than in December 1980, while long-term interest rates were about one point higher.

The average level of real GNP in 1981 was 1.9 percent higher than in 1980, but this increase for the year as a whole masked a pattern of declining output for two of the final three quarters. After growing at an unsustainable rate in the first quarter, the economy remained on a plateau for a time: a modest annual rate of decline of 1.6 percent in the second quarter and an increase of 1.4 percent in the third. In the final quarter the economy dropped sharply, with real GNP declining at an annual rate of 5.2 percent.

The unemployment rate at the close of 1980 had been 7.3 percent, and it averaged around 7.4 percent through the first 9 months of 1981. But the weakening of the economy in the last quarter brought with it a rapid increase in the unemployment rate to 8.8 percent in December. Civilian employment grew slowly, from 99.6 million at year-end 1980 to over 101 million by May 1981, before dipping to 99.6 million at year-end 1981.

Meanwhile, however, the deceleration in monetary growth began to produce declining inflation in 1981. The growth of M1 slowed to 4.9 percent during 1981, compared to an average growth rate of 7.8 percent over the previous 4 years. The GNP deflator advanced 8.6 percent through 1981, down from 9.8 percent during the four quarters of 1980, while the consumer and producer price indexes slowed more sharply. The producer price index for finished goods, which had risen 12.4 percent during 1980, rose at a 10.1 percent annual rate in the first two quarters of 1981 and at only a 4.4 percent rate in the last two quarters.

TABLE 8-1.—*Performance in 1981 compared to January 15 projections*

Item	Projected	Actual	Projected	Actual
	Year to year		Fourth quarter to fourth quarter	
Percent change:				
Real GNP	0.9	1.9	1.7	0.7
Consumer price index [1]	12.5	10.2	12.6	9.4
	Year		Fourth quarter	
Level:				
Unemployment rate (percent)	7.8	7.6	7.7	8.3

[1] Consumer price index for urban wage earners and clerical workers.

Sources: Actual data: Department of Commerce (Bureau of Economic Analysis) and Department of Labor (Bureau of Labor Statistics); projected data: Office of Management and Budget (January 15, 1981).

As shown in Table 8-1, the average performance of the economy in 1981 was better than had been predicted by the prior Administration. Actual real GNP in 1981 was 1.9 percent higher than in 1980, compared with a 0.9 percent growth rate forecast by the prior Administration. Consumer prices in 1981 exceeded their 1980 level by 10.2 percent, but this was significantly less than the 12.5 percent rate of inflation that had been forecast. In addition, the average rate of unemployment for 1981 turned out to be 0.2 percentage point less than had been forecast. However, real growth from the fourth quarter of 1980 to the fourth quarter of 1981 was lower than forecast, and unemployment in the fourth quarter of 1981 was greater than forecast as a result of the decline in output and employment late in the year.

Although the Administration was able to effect some reductions in the growth of Federal spending in fiscal 1981, such spending as a share of GNP continued to rise. In nominal terms, Federal spending growth (including off-budget outlays) in 1981 slowed to 14.8 percent, from 17.4 percent in fiscal 1980, one of the largest peacetime increases in history.

The real Federal tax burden was increased by the scheduled payroll tax increase on January 1, 1981, and the tax burden drifted upward during most of the year as inflation contributed to higher nominal incomes and rising marginal tax rates. The Economic Recovery Tax Act of 1981, however, provided an initial 5 percent cut in marginal tax rates for individuals, effective October 1. This had the effect of reducing marginal tax rates by only 1¼ percent over the full 1981 tax year, not large enough to prevent a substantial increase in the total tax burden. For business, however, many of the changes in the tax code were retroactive to the beginning of the year.

Since tax revenues as a share of GNP will decline by about 2 percentage points over the next few years and budget outlays will not yet have been reduced as much, large Federal budget deficits can be expected unless the growth of Federal spending is reined in even more. The possibility of large deficits received much attention in the financial markets during 1981. The concern was that these deficits might engender an acceleration of inflation and higher interest rates. Fear of inflation kept long-term interest rates at high levels, although some decline did occur in the final months of the year.

In the climate of high interest rates, investments in money-market funds provided savers with some of the highest yields in history. Many thrift institutions were not able to compete successfully for deposits, and the resulting outflow of funds contributed to a reduction in the availability of mortgages and construction financing. Mortgage rates on new homes remained above 15 percent throughout 1981. In consequence, home sales and housing starts were among their postwar lows. The motor vehicle industry also suffered from the high cost of credit.

MAJOR SECTORS OF AGGREGATE DEMAND

Mirroring the small expansion in real output during 1981 was the slow expansion in the real growth of consumer expenditures (1.2 percent), business fixed investment (1.4 percent), and total government purchases (1.2 percent). Purchases of consumer durables declined 4.4 percent, partially offsetting modest gains in purchases of other consumer items. As shown in Table 8-2, residential construction decreased by a dramatic 21.9 percent. Net exports also declined last year, as real exports declined 1.0 percent while imports increased 9.5 percent.

TABLE 8-2.—*Growth in major components of real gross national product, 1977-81*

[Change, fourth quarter to fourth quarter]

Component	1977	1978	1979	1980	1981[1]
Percent change:					
Real gross national product	5.8	5.3	1.7	−0.3	0.7
Personal consumption expenditures	5.0	4.8	2.0	.6	1.2
Business fixed investment	13.5	9.0	2.9	−4.3	1.4
Residential fixed investment	12.5	−.0	−6.1	−12.9	−21.9
Government purchases of goods and services	3.6	1.6	1.9	1.6	1.2
Federal	5.0	−1.3	2.1	4.1	6.6
State and local	2.7	3.3	1.7	.1	−2.0
Real domestic final sales [2]	5.9	4.4	1.7	−.3	.4
Change in billions of dollars:					
Inventory investment	5.9	2.3	−11.3	−6.5	15.7
Net exports of goods and services	−5.5	12.6	11.7	6.3	−11.8

[1] Preliminary.
[2] GNP excluding change in business inventories and net exports of goods and services.

Source: Department of Commerce, Bureau of Economic Analysis.

PERSONAL CONSUMPTION EXPENDITURES

Although the rising costs of borrowing discouraged purchases of consumer durables, growth in personal income was sufficient to sustain purchases of nondurables and services. The latter categories managed to show a modest increase for the year. But durables purchases (approximately 20 percent of which are expenditures on new autos) exhibited sharp swings from quarter to quarter, with the fourth quarter level 4.4 percent below the same quarter in 1980. The slow pace of durables purchases ensured a modest improvement in the consumer debt burden, as the ratio of consumer installment credit to personal income declined from its recent peak in May 1979 of 14.9 percent to 13.2 percent in November. The personal saving rate, after dropping one-half of a percentage point to 4.6 percent in the first quarter, recovered somewhat in the next two quarters and rose sharply to 6 percent in the final quarter of the year.

Real expenditures on consumer durables declined for the third consecutive year. The pace of durables purchases had been stalled by the imposition of credit controls in the first half of 1980, but rebounded sharply in the last two quarters of 1980 and the first quarter of 1981. Then came the termination of rebates on auto sales and rapidly rising interest rates, resulting in a sharp 23.3 percent reduction in durables purchases at an annual rate in the second quarter. A moderation in interest rates in the third quarter, in conjunction with factory subsidized financing and further rebates, then helped to stimulate auto sales, allowing outlays for consumer durables to rise moderately. Although the fourth quarter saw a significant drop in interest rates, it was not enough to boost total durables purchases. The result was another steep decline in such purchases, this time at a 19.2 percent annual rate.

At the beginning of 1981 new cars were being sold at an annual rate of about 10 million units, some of this relatively high volume being attributable to manufacturers' rebates. In the second quarter sales dropped to an annual rate of 7.8 million units; they then rose to 9.1 million units in the third quarter, before falling to 7.4 million units in the final quarter. Sales of American cars accounted for about 73 percent of all U.S. car sales for the year. In order to defuse protectionist pressures in the United States, the Japanese government instituted an export restraint program, which limited Japanese car exports to the United States to 1.68 million units during its first year. Because of the weak U.S. market, however, the limit probably has not been binding.

RESIDENTIAL INVESTMENT

Investment in residential structures during 1981 continued a decline that started in 1979. The decline was evident in the construction of both single-family homes and multiple units. By the fourth quarter of 1981, starts of new single-unit structures had declined 44.8 percent below their year-earlier level, and multiple-unit construction declined 34.5 percent. In the last quarter of 1981 the inventory of new private homes waiting to be sold was about eight times the monthly sales pace. During the latter half of the 1970s the inventory-sales ratio typically was less than that, approximately six times sales.

The continued slow pace of residential construction was primarily due to tightness in the financial markets in which the housing industry competes for funds. Mortgage rates on new homes rose to over 18 percent in October, up from 15 percent at the beginning of the year. By year-end, however, the rate had fallen to 17 percent.

Home purchase prices were essentially unchanged during 1981. Thus, there was a significant decrease in the real price of housing—that is, housing prices in relation to the general price level. In contrast the rapid increase in house prices from 1977 to 1980 had reflected rising expectations about inflation and a growing tendency to view real estate as a good hedge against inflation.

BUSINESS FIXED INVESTMENT

Real business fixed investment finished the year above the previous year's fourth quarter level. This fact, however, masks the underlying variations that occurred during the year. Business investment varied from quarter to quarter in the same direction as real GNP, but the percentage deviations were much larger. Real business investment rose at a 13.3 percent annual rate in the first quarter of 1981, remained relatively flat in the second and third quarters, and then fell 10.9 percent in the fourth quarter.

Producers' durable equipment was responsible for most of the variation in business fixed investment, with fleet sales of cars and trucks accounting for a large part of this instability. The structures component of investment maintained a steady increase that began in the fourth quarter of 1980. Though investment in structures is less than half as large as investment in producer's durable equipment, its increase of 7.5 percent from the fourth quarter of 1980 to the fourth quarter of 1981 more than offset the decline in the latter, allowing a modest increase in total real business investment.

INVENTORY ACCUMULATION

Inventory levels at the start of 1981 were lean. Real business inventory levels in the fourth quarter of 1980, after declining for four of the five previous quarters, were equivalent to 2.7 months of output. In the first quarter of 1981, real output rose to nearly match final sales so that the real level of inventories declined only $1.4 billion at an annual rate. In the second quarter inventory accumulation was led by a rise in new car inventories, and there was also some buildup in other stocks in the third quarter. The speed with which output declined in the fourth quarter prevented an excessive accumulation of stocks at year-end.

NET EXPORTS

Economic growth abroad was subdued during 1981, contributing to a small decline in real exports from the United States. In contrast to 1980, the volume of non-oil imports grew briskly during the year due in part to the steady appreciation of the dollar from the latter part of 1980 through August 1981. For the year as a whole, net exports (measured in 1972 dollars) slipped $7.7 billion below the level of 1980.

Measured in current dollars, the merchandise trade deficit (NIPA basis) increased $4.2 billion from the $27.7 billion registered for 1980. Merchandise exports increased moderately in the first quarter and then declined to post a small gain for the year, while merchandise imports rose during most of the year. Growth in the value of agricultural exports was weak, as a strong U.S. dollar and better harvests abroad dampened foreign demand. The strong growth in the value of imports of nonpetroleum products was only partly offset by a drop in imports of petroleum and related products. Average net oil imports in the first three quarters of 1981 fell to their lowest level since 1972, partly as a result of reduced domestic consumption. That, in turn, was due primarily to higher oil prices.

Net service inflows for 1981 increased $4.8 billion over 1980 to $55.8 billion. Almost all of this increase was due to a rise in net receipts of factor income. This continued strong performance on the service account produced an overall net export surplus for 1981 of $23.8 billion in current dollars.

THE FARM ECONOMY

Record large crops, sluggish demand for farm products, high interest rates, and a nearly constant tonnage of agricultural exports limited the recovery of farm incomes and created cash flow problems for some farmers during 1981. In nominal terms, farm exports totaled a record $43 billion in 1981; however, the tonnage of farm exports for the year was about the same as in 1980.

According to Department of Agriculture forecasts, net farm income for 1981 in current dollars will be approximately $23 billion. This figure is about $3 billion higher than the comparable income figure for 1980, but approximately $10 billion lower than the total for 1979, which was a prosperous year for U.S. farmers. For 1981, real net farm income is forecast to exceed the 1980 total by about 4 percent. The value of large crop inventories, which is reflected in the 1981 income figures, accounts for part of the increase.

Large grain stocks and weakness in the demand for certain livestock and crop products are expected to exert downward pressure on farm prices and net farm incomes during much of the first half of 1982, but the expected recovery of the economy should expand the demand for farm products during the final two quarters of 1982. Also, farm price support payments provided under the Agriculture and Food Act of 1981 will supplement the incomes of farmers during 1982.

The statistics on aggregate farm income mask how different groups of farmers fared during 1981. Farmers carrying small amounts of debt experienced a less severe cash flow squeeze than highly leveraged operators. Many in the latter group had cash flow problems because of high interest rates and lower commodity prices. However, some farmers who experienced cash flow problems used equity accumulated from rapid appreciation of their farmland to refinance their operations. As usual, income earned by farmers from off-farm sources, which recently has comprised over 60 percent of the average farmer's income and a substantially larger share of the income of small farmers, supplemented farm incomes.

Food prices generally exerted a moderating influence on the consumer price index during 1981, although two minor supply shocks produced temporary increases in food prices. The first was a mid-January freeze in Florida, which pushed up prices for citrus products and tomatoes last winter and spring. The second was a reduction in meat supplies during the summer. Food prices for the fourth quarter of 1981 were 5.0 percent higher than in the fourth quarter of 1980. This increase was 5.2 percentage points less than the comparable year earlier figure.

The moderate increases in food prices largely reflected supply phenomena. Supplies of many raw food products, including poultry, dairy products, sugar, and grain were abundant during 1981, as were beef supplies during the first half of the year. Data available so far suggest that marketing costs, which account for about two-thirds of every dollar spent for food, were about 9 percent higher for the fourth quarter of 1981 than a year earlier.

LABOR MARKET DEVELOPMENTS

Changes in employment during 1981 lagged slightly behind changes in real output. Total civilian employment during the year reached a peak of 101 million workers in May before declining to 99.6 million at year-end. The ratio of civilian employment to the total noninstitutional working-age population also declined in the last half of the year. Declines in employment during the year were initially limited to interest-sensitive sectors, such as motor vehicles and residential construction and their suppliers. By the end of 1981, however, the decline had spread to other manufacturing industries as well. The overall unemployment rate, which was 7.4 percent at the beginning of last year, fluctuated between 7.2 and 7.6 through September, then rose sharply to 8.8 percent in December.

TABLE 8-3.—*Labor market developments, 1977–81*

Component	1977 IV	1978 IV	1979 IV	1980 IV	1981 IV
	Percent change from year earlier [1]				
Increase in civilian employment (16 years and over)	4.5	3.8	2.3	−0.2	0.6
Males 20 years and over	3.5	2.7	1.5	−.6	.2
Females 20 years and over	5.4	5.6	4.0	1.6	2.8
Both sexes 16–19 years	8.0	2.7	−.8	−6.6	−8.9
White	4.4	3.3	2.2	−.1	.6
Black and other	5.2	7.3	3.3	−.6	.1
	Percent [2]				
Unemployment rate (16 years and over) [3]	6.6	5.9	6.0	7.5	8.3
Males 20 years and over	4.8	4.1	4.4	6.3	7.2
Females 20 years and over	6.7	5.8	5.7	6.7	7.2
Both sexes 16–19 years	16.6	16.3	16.2	18.2	21.1
White	5.7	5.1	5.2	6.6	7.3
Black and other	13.2	11.5	11.2	13.8	15.4
Participation rate (16 years and over) [4]	62.6	63.5	63.8	63.7	63.8
Males 20 years and over	79.9	79.9	79.6	79.3	78.9
Females 20 years and over	48.6	50.1	51.0	51.5	52.3
Both sexes 16–19 years	56.7	58.2	57.9	56.3	54.6
White	62.8	63.6	64.0	64.0	64.2
Black and other	61.2	62.4	62.3	61.9	61.5

[1] Changes for 1978 IV adjusted for the increase of about 250,000 in employment and labor force in January 1978 resulting from changes in the sample and estimation procedures introduced into the household survey.
[2] Seasonally adjusted.
[3] Unemployment as percent of civilian labor force.
[4] Civilian labor force as percent of civilian noninstitutional population.

Source: Department of Labor, Bureau of Labor Statistics.

As Table 8-3 indicates, employment growth during 1981 varied considerably by demographic group. Adult female employment rose by 2.8 percent, while adult male employment rose by 0.2 percent; teenage employment fell by a dramatic 8.9 percent. The unemployment rate for adult men, who tend to work in disproportionate numbers in cyclically sensitive industries, rose from 6.1 percent in December 1980 to 7.9 percent in December 1981. The unemployment rate for adult women, who work in industries that exhibit more cyclical stability, rose 0.7 of a point, from 6.7 percent to 7.4 percent, during the same period. The teenage unemployment rate increased, from 17.8 percent to 21.5 percent, over the year.

The age-sex composition of the unemployed depends on the unemployment rates of different demographic groups and on their share of the total labor force. Teenagers, for instance, have relatively high unemployment rates, but in December 1981 they comprised only 7.9 percent of the labor force. Adult men have relatively low unemployment rates, but in 1981 they constituted 52.8 percent of the labor force. Thus, 19.4 percent of the unemployed in December 1981 were teenagers, 47.5 percent were adult men, and 33.2 percent were adult women.

The unemployment insurance system is designed to moderate the financial burden placed on experienced workers who lose their jobs by providing income until they can find employment. However, the system does not cover recent entrants to the labor market or workers who quit their jobs voluntarily. In December 1981 the number of individuals receiving unemployment compensation was 41 percent of the total unemployed. This was partly because 44.2 percent of the unemployed had left their jobs voluntarily or had no recent work experience. Over two-thirds of the people who had lost their jobs involuntarily were receiving unemployment benefits.

The percentage of take-home pay replaced by unemployment benefits varies widely according to an individual's weekly earnings, marginal tax rate, and State of residence. Replacement rates are generally higher for lower paid workers than for higher paid workers. However, several studies suggest that the average replacement rate is about one-half of take-home pay.

A combination of cyclical and secular trends produced disparate changes in labor force participation rates during 1981. Labor force participation rates continued to increase for adult women, and by the fourth quarter 52.3 percent of all women 20 or older were in the civilian labor market, an increase of 0.8 of a percentage point over 1980. Meanwhile, the labor force participation rates of adult men continued their long-term downward trend.

The ratio of civilian employment to the total working-age population varied inversely with the unemployment rate. The number of employed rose from 58.3 percent of the noninstitutional population in December 1980 to 58.8 percent in May 1981, but fell to 57.5 percent in December. Although this percentage was less than the last peak of 59.3 percent, reached in the fourth quarter of 1979, it exceeded the previous 1973 peak (Chart 8-2).

Chart 8-2
Employment Ratio and Unemployment Rate

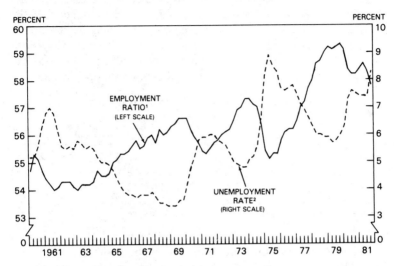

PERCENT   PERCENT

¹ EMPLOYMENT AS PERCENT OF NONINSTITUTIONAL POPULATION.
² UNEMPLOYMENT AS PERCENT OF CIVILIAN LABOR FORCE.

NOTE.—DATA RELATE TO PERSONS 16 YEARS OF AGE AND OVER; SEASONALLY ADJUSTED
QUARTERLY AVERAGES.

SOURCE: DEPARTMENT OF LABOR.

WAGES, PRICES, AND PRODUCTIVITY

Wage increases showed moderation in 1981. As indicated in Table 8-4, the average hourly earnings index, compensation per hour, and wages set in larger collective bargains slowed significantly, while the employment cost index increased at about the same rate as in 1980.

TABLE 8-4.—*Measures of compensation, 1978–81*

[Percent change, fourth quarter to fourth quarter, except as noted]

Measure	1978	1979	1980	1981 [1]
Employment cost index [2]	7.7	8.7	9.0	[3] 9.1
Union	8.0	9.0	10.9	[3] 9.9
Nonunion	7.6	8.5	8.0	[3] 8.8
Average hourly earnings index [4]	8.4	8.0	9.6	8.3
Compensation per hour [5]	9.0	9.9	10.2	9.3
Wage changes in large collective bargaining agreements (total effective adjustment)	8.2	9.1	9.9	9.1

[1] Preliminary.
[2] Data are for wages and salaries of all private nonfarm workers.
[3] Changes are from third quarter to third quarter.
[4] Data are not seasonally adjusted.
[5] Data are for private business sector, all employees.

Source: Department of Commerce (Bureau of Economic Analysis), Department of Labor (Bureau of Labor Statistics), and Council of Economic Advisers.

Labor productivity declined by 0.5 percent during 1981 (Table 8–5). This was the fourth successive year of little change in productivity. Chapter 5 has discussed various reasons for the disappointing trends in productivity over the last decade. In addition, during the last 3 years, total output growth has been low, which has also tended to depress productivity performance. The near-zero productivity result meant that unit labor costs, the largest single cost in production, had to increase roughly one-for-one with total compensation last year.

TABLE 8–5.—*Changes in productivity and unit labor costs, 1977–81*

[Percent change, fourth quarter to fourth quarter]

Item	1977	1978	1979	1980	1981[1]
Output per hour	2.1	−0.5	−0.6	0.2	−0.5
Unit labor costs	5.2	9.5	10.5	9.9	9.8

[1] Preliminary.
Note.—Data relate to private business sector, all employees.
Sources: Department of Labor (Bureau of Labor Statistics) and Council of Economic Advisers.

During a year in which unit labor costs rose by 9.8 percent, prices could not rise at a substantially lower rate without sharply squeezing profits. The GNP deflator rose by 8.6 percent during 1981, somewhat lower than the 9.8 percent increase experienced during 1980 (Table 8–6).

TABLE 8–6.—*Measures of price change, 1977–81*

[Percent change, fourth quarter to fourth quarter]

Item	1977	1978	1979	1980	1981[1]
Implicit price deflators:[2]					
Gross national product	6.1	8.5	8.1	9.8	8.6
Personal consumption expenditures	5.9	7.8	9.5	10.1	7.8
Private nonfarm business output	5.7	8.3	8.3	10.0	9.3
Consumer prices:					
CPI–U, X–1	6.2	7.8	10.6	10.8	8.8
CPI–U	6.6	9.0	12.7	12.6	9.6
Farm value of food	6.4	17.5	7.3	13.5	−5.2
Energy[3]	8.2	7.5	36.5	18.9	12.6
Home purchase and finance[4]	8.9	13.4	19.8	17.8	11.9
All other	6.1	7.5	8.0	9.8	9.2
Producer prices of finished goods	7.1	8.8	12.8	12.4	7.2
Food	7.7	11.1	7.6	8.3	1.8
Energy	11.0	7.4	56.9	29.2	15.2
All other	6.4	8.0	9.4	11.1	7.6

[1] Preliminary.
[2] Seasonally adjusted data.
[3] Includes only prices for direct consumer purchases of energy for the home and for motor vehicles.
[4] Consists of home purchase and financing, taxes, and insurance on owner-occupied homes.

Sources: Department of Agriculture, Department of Commerce (Bureau of Economic Analysis), and Department of Labor (Bureau of Labor Statistics).

The deflator for personal consumption expenditures rose only 7.8 percent last year, down significantly from the year before. Inflation, as measured by the consumer price index for urban workers (CPI-U), declined even more, from 12.6 percent during 1980 to 9.6 percent during 1981. The CPI-U is widely recognized as having an upward bias in a period of rising mortgage interest rates, due to its treatment of owner-occupied housing. Some of the components that are used to measure the cost of homeownership—finance, insurance, and taxes—jumped quite sharply during much of 1981. An alternative measure of consumer prices known as "CPI-U, X-1" more appropriately measures the consumer cost of owner-occupied homes. It advanced only 8.8 percent. In late 1981 the Bureau of Labor Statistics announced plans to incorporate this alternative method of measuring the rise or fall in homeowner costs into the index. As shown in Table 8-7, real compensation per hour, computed on the basis of either the deflator for personal consumption expenditures or the alternative CPI measure, rose in 1981 after declining for 2 straight years.

TABLE 8-7.—*Alternative measures of changes in real earnings per hour, 1979-81*

[Percent change, fourth quarter to fourth quarter]

Item	1979	1980	1981[1]
Average hourly earnings index:			
Deflated by:			
CPI-U	−4.2	−2.6	−1.1
CPI-U, X-1	−2.4	−1.1	−.5
Fixed-weight price index for personal consumption expenditures (PCE)	−2.1	−.9	.2
Compensation per hour: [2]			
Deflated by:			
CPI-U	−2.5	−2.1	−.2
CPI-U, X-1	−.7	−.6	.4
Fixed-weight price index for PCE	−.4	−.4	1.1

[1] Preliminary.
[2] Data are for the private nonfarm business sector, all employees.
Sources: Department of Commerce (Bureau of Economic Analysis) and Department of Labor (Bureau of Labor Statistics).

CREDIT MARKETS

During the first three quarters of 1981, total funds raised in U.S. credit markets rebounded from the depressed levels of a year earlier, when credit controls and the recession restrained borrowing. Nevertheless, borrowing by all private domestic nonfinancial sectors remained well below the pace reached in 1979. High interest rates discouraged borrowing for purchases of consumer durables and housing and resulted in a rate of household debt accumulation, although up from 1980, only about three quarters of that experienced in 1979. Borrowing by the nonfinancial business sector grew only modestly during the first three quarters of 1981. This sector relied heavily on short-term financing, as extremely high and rising long-term bond rates restrained net bond issues to only half the total of the previous year. As a result, bank loans to businesses and the volume of outstanding commercial paper surged.

Borrowing by State and local governments declined modestly in 1981, as growth of expenditures slowed relative to tax receipts. However, Federal Government borrowing was up from 1980, and at more than double the rate of 1979. Federal borrowing totaled $79.3 billion, of which approximately $55.6 billion was used to finance expenditures on goods and services or transfer payments, while the rest was used for relending. Federally guaranteed loans declined in 1981, but borrowing by federally sponsored enterprises grew by almost two-thirds. Overall Federal participation in the credit markets rose to approximately the level of the previous peak in 1976.

INTEREST RATES AND MONETARY DEVELOPMENTS

One of the four key elements of the Administration's program is support for a policy of continued gradual reductions in the rate of monetary growth to bring down inflation. This restraint was more important to the 1981 economy than other features of the Administration's program, which are aimed at encouraging long-term growth. From the fourth quarter of 1979 to the fourth quarter of 1980, M1 (currency plus checkable deposits) grew at a 7.3 percent annual rate. The Administration assumes a gradual but steady reduction in the growth of money to one-half that rate by 1986. After a period of adjustment, sustained declines in inflation and nominal interest rates are expected.

Federal Reserve policy in 1981 did produce a substantial reduction in monetary growth (as measured by M1) on a fourth-quarter to fourth-quarter basis—from 7.3 percent during 1980 to 4.9 percent in 1981. Nonetheless, interest rates remained high on average. The yield on 3-month Treasury bills, which had averaged 15.5 percent in December 1980, fell in early 1981, then rose again and peaked at 16.3 percent in May 1981. The prime rate charged by commercial banks declined from a peak of 21.5 percent in January 1981 to 17 percent in April 1981 before rising again to 20.5 percent by the end of May. By year-end, the prime rate had declined to 15.75 percent. Given that prices were advancing at somewhat less than double-digit rates, real short-term interest rates (that is, adjusted for inflation) were unusually high during most of 1981 (Chart 8-3).

Chart 8-3

Interest Rates in 1981

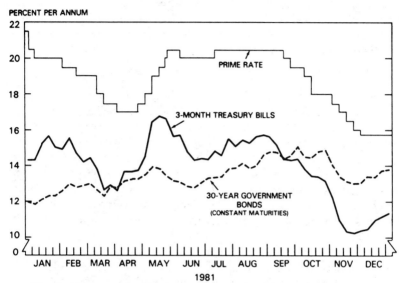

SOURCES: DEPARTMENT OF THE TREASURY AND BOARD OF GOVERNORS OF THE FEDERAL
RESERVE SYSTEM.

When allowance is made for the effects of taxes on interest rates, the high average level of short-term rates becomes more understandable. In an environment of high expected inflation, interest rates tend to rise sufficiently to compensate lenders for the anticipated loss in purchasing power of their money. Under the U.S. tax system, interest payments are deductible, and interest receipts are taxed as ordinary income. We would expect market interest rates to exceed a given real after-tax interest rate by more than the expected inflation. For example, if the real after-tax interest rate is 3 percent and the applicable income tax rate is 30 percent, an expected inflation rate of 10 percent would tend to produce a nominal interest rate of 19 percent—not very different from the peaks in short-term rates actually experienced in 1981. Viewed in this light, the question is not why short-term interest rates were so high in 1981, but why they were so low in the 1970s.

At least a partial answer to this question is that in the 1970s low State usury and Regulation Q ceilings prevented the effects of expected inflation from being fully reflected in interest rates, while the inflation that actually occurred was probably more than had been anticipated. Also, the oil price shocks of the 1970s, coupled with increasing regulatory and tax burdens, may have reduced the expected real return on capital. With the change in the investment outlook brought about by the Administration's program, this negative influence on real interest rates began to disappear. However, as the Federal Reserve's program of bringing down the rate of monetary growth succeeds in reducing current and expected rates of inflation, nominal interest rates will fall somewhat more than the expected rate of inflation, even as real after-tax interest rates rise somewhat.

INTERNATIONAL CAPITAL FLOWS

High real returns on U.S. securities helped to attract foreign investment to the United States during 1981. The dollar's foreign exchange value rose 23 percent on a trade-weighted average basis from January through August before falling back slightly through December. Net foreign private purchases of U.S. securities during the first three quarters of 1981 totaled $8.3 billion, an increase of 68 percent over the same period a year earlier. A large part of this increase was in purchases of U.S. stocks, possibly suggesting confidence abroad in the medium-term potential of U.S. industry and the Administration's program.

Direct U.S. investment abroad in the first three quarters of 1981 slowed somewhat from its 1980 rate, making 1981 the second year of decline. The drop was due in part to sluggish foreign economic activity. In contrast, foreign direct investment in the United States remained strong during 1981 and may have approached the record levels of 1979.

Monetary flows associated with official transactions between the United States and other industrialized countries swung from a moderate net inflow in late 1980 to a substantial net outflow in the first three quarters of 1981. These net outflows primarily reflected sales of dollar-denominated assets by foreign central banks (mainly U.S. Treasury securities) related to intervention in foreign exchange markets. Changes in official U.S. reserve assets moved from net acquisitions of foreign currencies in late 1980 and the first quarter of 1981 to negligible acquisitions from the second quarter on. This reflected the decision by this Administration to adopt a policy of nonintervention in foreign exchange markets, except in conditions of severe disorder. (The issues involved in this policy are discussed in Chapter 7.)

Net capital flows between the United States and the Organization of Petroleum Exporting Countries (OPEC) recently have been quite stable relative to flows between the United States and the industrialized countries. The capital movements between the OPEC countries and the United States have been net inflows since early 1979 and generally have taken the form of investments in U.S. Treasury securities, although investments in real estate and energy-related industries have risen during the past year.

THRIFT INSTITUTIONS

High interest rates and regulatory restrictions had an adverse effect on thrift institutions in 1981. From November 1980 to November 1981, the net worth of thrifts dropped over $5.7 billion, or approximately 13 percent. Net new deposits also declined.

In response to the plight of the thrift institutions, the Congress included in the Economic Recovery Tax Act a provision authorizing those institutions, as well as commercial banks, to issue All-Savers Certificates. The certificates were given tax-exempt status so as to provide thrifts and banks with a lower cost of funds. From October to December, the first 3 months of issuance, thrift institutions issued approximately $24 billion in certificates. Their impact on the net deposit inflows of the thrifts is in some doubt, however, since the availability of the certificates caused some savers to transfer funds from other thrift accounts, such as passbook savings, 6-month money-market certificates, and small savers' certificates.

Meanwhile, delinquent loans rose and liquidity ratios for insured savings and loans deteriorated. The delinquent loan ratio—the dollar amount of mortgage loans and contracts delinquent 60 days or more as a percentage of total mortgages and contracts held at the end of each month—increased steadily last year. The ratio rose from just over 1 percent in late 1980 to almost 1½ percent in late 1981. The liquidity ratio—cash and other liquid assets as a percent of savings deposits plus loans payable in a year or less—declined from almost 9 percent to about 8.5 percent in late 1981. The deterioration of these ratios was not surprising in light of historically high inflation and interest rates and the weakness of the economy in the past couple of years. The financial condition of thrift institutions can be expected to improve substantially, however, as inflation expectations and interest rates fall and financial asset prices rise.

PROSPECTS FOR 1982 AND 1983

The current recession is expected to end early in 1982, followed by a resumption of growth by mid-year. The moderating pattern of price increases which began last year should become more generalized and significant this year. With money growth expected to be moderate, the extent of the deceleration of inflation will become the critical factor in sustaining economic recovery beyond 1982. Apart from the very high rate of expected inflation reflected in current interest rates, the economy is generally free of impediments to expansion.

The proportion of employed working-age adults will turn upward by this summer, reversing the general decline that began in 1979. Even at the expected low point of the employment ratio this spring, the proportion of people with jobs will be significantly higher than at the trough of all past recessions, except the very short 1980 contraction. The strong economic recovery this year and next is expected to expand civilian employment to over 103.5 million for 1983, well above the 98.8 million employed in 1979 before output declined.

The key areas of rebound in the economy this year are expected to be consumer goods, housing, autos, and defense (Table 8–8). The principal areas that are anticipated to lead the expansion next year are business investment, inventories (including a rising trend of defense work in progress), and a further acceleration in defense deliveries.

TABLE 8–8.—*Economic outlook for 1982*

Item	1981[1]	Forecast range 1982
Growth, fourth quarter to fourth quarter (percent):		
Real gross national product	0.7	3.0
Personal consumption expenditures	1.2	2½ to 3½
Nonresidential fixed investment	1.4	6½ to 7½
Residential investment	−21.9	24 to 27
Federal purchases	6.6	−2 to −1
State and local purchases	−2.0	−1½ to −½
GNP implicit price deflator	8.6	7 to 7½
Compensation per hour[2]	9.3	8 to 9
Output per hour[2]	−.5	1 to 1½
Level, fourth quarter:[3]		
Unemployment rate (percent)	8.3	8.4
Housing starts (millions of units)[4]	.9	1 to 1½

[1] Preliminary.
[2] Private business, all employees.
[3] Seasonally adjusted.
[4] Annual rates.
Sources: Department of Commerce (Bureau of Economic Analysis), Department of Labor (Bureau of Labor Statistics), and Council of Economic Advisers.

The decline in inflation, which has so far been most evident in the consumer price index and in producer prices, will influence trends in wages as 1982 progresses. But the expected 1 to 1½ percentage point slowdown of inflation in product prices will be only slightly less than the slowdown of labor costs. Therefore, the currently narrow margin of corporate profits is likely to recover only modestly during the year.

The unemployment rate is expected to reach the vicinity of 9 percent this spring until growth strengthens in the summer. Thereafter, the rapid pace of expansion should pull the unemployment rate down between one-quarter and one-half of a percentage point a quarter.

The growth in household consumption was restrained last year by high interest rates as well as by modest income growth. By the last quarter of 1981, consumption was approximately 1 percent higher in real terms than a year earlier, and new auto sales had fallen to an annual rate of 7.4 million. The decline in interest rates that began last fall, and improvements in household financial positions due to the reduced consumer debt burden and the first step of the personal tax cut, should lead to increased consumption early this year. The second step of the tax cut and the scheduled step-up in social security benefits will raise household disposable income roughly 2 percent this summer. It is difficult to predict how much of this increase will be allocated to saving or consumption. If between one-quarter and one-half of it is saved and the remainder is spent, the addition to the growth rate of consumption in the second half of this year would be about 3 percent at an annual rate. A large share of this would be expected to be used for the purchase of durables, whose annual growth rate in the second half is projected to approach 10 percent.

The recent improvement in early indicators of housing activity presages a rapid recovery that should be apparent by spring and proceed through the year. In 1980 the decline in housing early in the year was quickly reversed, and the ensuing recovery was quite rapid. Though the second reversal in the housing industry in as many years has forced some builders out of business, a rapid expansion this year is still possible. The necessary capital equipment remains, and additions to the stock of construction equipment and tools can be made rapidly. Though the supply of unsold homes relative to monthly sales is large, the absolute number of available new homes is not. Hence, rising sales will quickly generate faster building activity. While housing starts for 1982 as a whole may only exceed last year's by 10 percent, the increase during the year could exceed 50 percent. This would raise the pace of new housing starts from about 900,000 at an annual rate for the last quarter of 1981 to the vicinity of 1.5 million by the end of this year.

Business fixed investment has been maintained at a reasonably high level during the past year. The stimulus of the Accelerated Cost Recovery System depreciation package should make itself felt when recovery begins. Since businesses have not allowed inventories to build by large amounts, stepped-up sales this spring and summer will translate quite directly into rising output.

The Administration's program of strengthening U.S. defense capabilities will continue to be reflected in the overall economy as 1982 progresses. Deliveries of defense goods and services in real terms will rise about 8½ percent during this fiscal year, about twice the increase in 1981. The rise in procurement of military hardware will be steeper. It will also generate stepped-up economic activity prior to deliveries. Defense industries are beginning to build up inventories of work in progress as components and materials move through the stages of fabrication toward delivery to the Department of Defense. Though this step-up has not yet become particularly evident in statistics of work in progress, this type of inventory accumulation will be strengthened in coming quarters.

Nondefense Federal purchases increased 10.7 percent in real terms during 1981 but may shrink as much as 9 percent during 1982 as the Administration's fiscal 1982 budget cuts take effect. The much larger volume of purchases by State and local governments is also expected to decline slightly in real terms. Taken in aggregate, the budgets of State and local units of government have shown small operating surpluses in the past 2 years. Increased revenue from economic growth is expected to more than offset declines in Federal grants, permitting a modest increase in nominal spending by State and local units.

Earlier parts of this *Report* have emphasized the relative size of the prospective Federal deficits in comparison to GNP. While it is helpful to standardize deficits against the size of the economy, this relation gives little feel for the distribution through the economy of the flow of government securities. These are purchased by banking, other corporate, household, and foreign savers, who are also filling their portfolios with privately issued notes for everything from consumer loans to mortgages to loans for business capital projects.

It is anticipated that each of these groups will not be called upon to raise their holdings of U.S. Government securities disproportionately. Thus, household purchases of U.S. securities should be about one-quarter of the volume of personal saving, which is near historic rates, and domestic financial institution purchases should be near 1.5 percent of GNP, also close to historic experience. While foreign investors also can be expected to take some of the securities issued, these two domestic sectors likely will account for most U.S. security purchases.

The net export balance of the United States is expected to be boosted by rising exports of goods and services as the economic recovery abroad strengthens but depressed by a large expansion of imports as growth picks up here later this year. Continued market adjustments to last year's appreciation of the dollar may also depress net exports. Depending on the timing of these effects, net exports of the United States may decline from a surplus of $23.8 billion last year to an approximate balance this year. Because the United States earns much more abroad through the export of services than it spends on services imports, our net export position is stronger than the frequently cited trade balance on merchandise alone would suggest. That balance will move to a sizable negative position by year-end.

With a continuation of monetary restraint and further significant downward adjustments in inflationary expectations, 1982 and 1983 should become the first of several years of prosperous growth and declining inflation occurring simultaneously. While business investment and defense will continue to expand more rapidly than other sectors, the total growth in the economy should be sufficient to accommodate further sizable increases in the output of consumer durables, motor vehicles, and housing.

PROSPECTS BEYOND 1983

Continuing deceleration in money growth, fairly rapid adaptation of expectations to lower inflation, and growth aided by tax policies that are weighted toward investment are expected to be characteristic of the mid-1980s. The combination of growth-oriented fiscal policy and anti-inflationary monetary policy should mean substantial progress toward the economic goals embodied in the Full Employment and Balanced Growth Act of 1978.

The general objectives of this act—and those of the Administration—are to achieve full employment, growth in productivity, price stability, and a reduced share of governmental spending in the Nation's output. The act states clearly that ultimate price stability means eliminating inflation altogether. Although it does not define full employment as any specific unemployment rate, the act establishes as a national goal "the fulfillment of the right to full opportunities for useful paid employment at fair rates of compensation of all individuals able, willing, and seeking to work." It places emphasis on encouraging capital formation and relying on the private sector to meet the act's objectives of full employment, growth in productivity, and price stability. It requires an annual Investment Policy Report, which is provided in Chapters 4 and 5 of this volume. In addition, the act responds to the widespread desire for reduced governmental intervention by calling for steady reductions in the share of the Nation's output accounted for by governmental spending, and for the ultimate reduction of Federal outlays to 20 percent of GNP.

To provide a focus for the government in its effort to achieve these general objectives, the Full Employment and Balanced Growth Act requires that the Administration set annual numerical goals for key indicators over a 5-year horizon leading toward a group of interim goals set forth by the Congress. Table 8–9 responds to this requirement, based on the economic outlook for 1982 and 1983, and the longer term economic projections included in the fiscal 1983 budget. The act sets an interim goal for Federal outlays equal to 21 percent of GNP for 1981, and interim goals of a 4 percent unemployment rate and a 3 percent inflation rate for 1983. However, according to the act, the President may, if he deems it necessary, recommend modification of the timetable for achievement of the interim and final goals for unemployment, inflation, and Federal outlays as a share of GNP. The prior Administration extended the timetable for achieving all three goals beyond its 5-year planning horizon.

TABLE 8-9.—*Economic Projections, 1982–1987*

Item	1982	1983	1984	1985	1986	1987
	Level					
Employment (millions) [1]	100.9	103.8	106.2	108.6	110.9	113.0
Unemployment rate (percent)	8.9	7.9	7.1	6.4	5.8	5.3
Federal outlays as percent of GNP (fiscal year basis)	23.5	22.1	21.3	21.0	20.4	19.7
	Percent change, fourth quarter to fourth quarter					
Consumer prices	6.6	5.1	4.7	4.6	4.6	4.4
Real GNP	3.0	5.2	4.9	4.6	4.3	4.3
Real disposable income	4.3	4.1	2.7	4.6	4.0	4.0
Productivity [2]	.6	2.3	2.7	2.6	2.6	2.6

[1] Includes 1980 census benchmark.
[2] Real GNP per hour worked.

Source: Council of Economic Advisers.

Economic projections consistent with this Administration's policies indicate attainment of the interim and final goals for Federal outlays as a share of GNP within a 5-year horizon. The interim goal for Federal outlays as a share of GNP is expected to be met by 1985. The act's final goal of a 20 percent share of Federal outlays in GNP is anticipated to be achieved by 1987. Significant progress toward the interim goals for unemployment and inflation is also anticipated within this period. The economic expansion will reduce unemployment rates for significant subgroups of the labor force as well, including youth, women, minorities, handicapped persons, veterans, and middle-aged and older persons.

The Council emphasizes two points about the setting of a timetable for reaching these goals and about targeting economic performance in general. First, as has been emphasized elsewhere in this *Report*, the speedy adaptation of inflationary expectations to the antiinflationary monetary regime set for the 1980s is of central importance in turning away from the rising inflation and unemployment of the last decade to an extended period of declining inflation with prosperous growth. However, as this *Report* points out—particularly in Chapter 3—government efforts to intervene directly in wage and price setting in the private sector are essentially destabilizing and do not alter the longer term path of the economy. Second, the Federal Government cannot fully anticipate the course of the economy; neither can it direct economic outcomes precisely. In view of these limits, the annual goals should best be viewed as benchmarks of economic progress.